Preface

These are exciting times for writers and teachers of writing. New genres are emerging almost daily, online and off. Vocabulary is changing and growing before our very eyes, spelling and capitalization along with it. Stylistic choices long unavailable to ordinary writers — varied fonts, color, boxes, charts, tables, icons, sidebars, graphics, even sound and video — now seem practically second nature. Audiences for writing also continue to expand on the Web, calling for new thinking about how to craft messages for such worldwide audiences and how to work with others across long distances. In a time of such challenging possibilities, taking a rhetorical perspective is particularly important. Why? Because a rhetorical perspective rejects either/or, right/wrong, black/white approaches to writing in favor of asking what choices will be most appropriate, effective, and ethical in a given writing situation.

The St. Martin's Handbook has always taken such a perspective, and the numerous changes to the fifth edition reflect this tradition. Throughout, this text invites student writers to take each choice as an opportunity for critical engagement with ideas, audiences, and texts. In pursuit of this overarching goal, the design has been improved to make this book even easier to navigate and use. To help students find answers to the many new questions they face — in class and out — the *Handbook* provides crucial new material about writing, reading, and conducting research online; about argument; about collaboration; about plagiarism and intellectual integrity; and about writing in specific disciplinary settings. As I've incorporated this new material, I've been careful not to lose sight of the mission of any handbook: to be an accessible reference to students and instructors alike.

Crucial new advice about writing online

New chapters on working with media. Four new chapters (Chapters 7-10) bring issues of design to bear on the processes of research, writing, and speaking. New content includes treatment of writing effective email and working with word-processing programs, using and understanding visual images, creating Web pages, and making oral and multimedia presentations.

Integrated advice on computers and writing. Discussion of computers and writing —

from sharing files to creating Web texts — is highlighted throughout the book by means of a computer icon in the margins. Practical tips help students incorporate computers into their writing in every way, every day.

Links to the new Web site throughout the book. Links to *The St. Martin's Handbook* companion Web site supplement and expand the *Handbook*'s coverage. The Web links in the margins take students to practical online resources — from tutorials on avoiding plagiarism to additional grammar exercises, model papers, a writer's almanac, and links to additional resources on the Web.

Expanded coverage of academic writing

The most up-to-date advice on research and documentation. New technologies have forever changed the face of research, and much student research now takes place online. In fact, my own recent research has shown that students confess to beginning *all* their research online. Because of this shift, advice about library and Internet research is now integrated. Coverage includes three new chapters on working with sources online and off — including one complete chapter on integrating sources — and full coverage of MLA, APA, CBE, and Chicago documentation.

A unique chapter on intellectual property and plagiarism. Chapter 18 offers not only a candid discussion of the larger issues surrounding intellectual property but also advice for students about avoiding the potential plagiarism that they now face on a daily basis.

Three new chapters on argument and critical thinking. My work on *Everything's an Argument* has strengthened my belief that argument is integral to many kinds of writing, and I wanted to carry over what I have learned to the *Handbook*. These new chapters (Chapters 11–13) offer greater depth of coverage than any other handbook, including attention to cultural contexts for arguments, a complete student essay, and a unique chapter on visual argument.

A comprehensive new section on writing across the curriculum. Written with Lisa Ede of Oregon State University, a new section on writing across the curriculum features chapters on writing and researching in the humanities, social sciences, natural and applied sciences, and business, and chapters on essay exams and portfolios. The many student writings in this section include a literary analysis and a history essay, as well as excerpts from student writing projects in the social sciences and natural and applied sciences and both print and online résumés.

More attention to language and style

A new chapter on writing "U.S.A. style." Chapter 58, "Learning U.S. Academic Conventions," demystifies and articulates for multilingual students what is expected from writers, texts, and readers in the United States.

A unique new chapter on writing to the world. Chapter 24 offers advice about communicating effectively with readers across a range of cultures.

The ST. MARTIN'S Handbook 5
EDITION

Andrea A. Lunsford
STANFORD UNIVERSITY

A section on academic and professional writing
with **Lisa Ede**
OREGON STATE UNIVERSITY

A section for multilingual writers
with **Franklin E. Horowitz**
TEACHERS COLLEGE, COLUMBIA UNIVERSITY

BEDFORD / ST. MARTIN'S
Boston ◆ New York

*In memory of Robert J. Connors,
and for Colleen and Aillinn Connors*

For Bedford/St. Martin's

Developmental Editors: Stephanie Carpenter, Kristin Bowen, John Elliott
Senior Production Editor: Shuli Traub
Senior Production Supervisor: Dennis J. Conroy
Marketing Manager: Richard Cadman
Art Director: Lucy Krikorian
Text and Cover Design: Anna George
Copy Editor: Judith Green Voss
Composition: Monotype Composition Company, Inc.
Printing and Binding: R. R. Donnelley & Sons Company

President: Joan E. Feinberg
Editorial Director: Denise B. Wydra
Editor in Chief: Nancy Perry
Director of Marketing: Karen R. Melton Soeltz
Director of Editing, Design, and Production: Marcia Cohen
Managing Editor: Erica T. Appel

Library of Congress Control Number: 2002107346

Manufactured in the United States of America.

8   7   6   5
f

For information, write: Bedford/St. Martin's,
75 Arlington Street, Boston, MA 02116   (617-399-4000)

ISBN: 0-312-41314-9   (hardcover)
        0-312-41313-0   (paperback)

Acknowledgments

Sharon Begley. "Science Failing to Share." From *Newsweek*, February 4, 2002. Copyright © 2002 Newsweek, Inc. All rights reserved. Reprinted by permission.
Acknowledgments and copyrights are continued at the back of the book on pp. 991–992, which constitute an extension of the copyright page.

Unique tips on considering disabilities. These boxes, which appear throughout the book, help students make their work accessible to readers with disabilities, especially when writing online. They also point writers with disabilities to resources and strategies they may want to use.

Stronger focus on collaboration

New chapter on collaboration. Tips and activities throughout the book, along with a new chapter (Chapter 6, "Collaborating—Online and Off"), prepare students for meaningful collaboration in their writing courses and beyond. Chapter 6 offers advice and guidelines for collaborative writing, from peer response to sharing files electronically to preparing complete group projects.

Easy to use, easy to understand

Clear, colorful design and appealing format. The design of the fifth edition is brighter, with a new, larger typeface to make the *Handbook* even easier to navigate than before. A shorter, wider page size allows room for key reference information — correction codes, most cross-references, Web links — to appear in the margins where it's easy to find.

Boxed editing tips. All handbooks provide rules, but *The St. Martin's Handbook* goes the extra step by providing tips that help students apply those rules to their own writing. Printed on green boxes for easy reference, these editing tips appear on the second page of most chapters and elsewhere in the book as well.

Attention to everyday language. Most chapters open with brief vignettes of language in everyday use, linking the material in the handbook (and the classroom) to students' lives beyond the classroom. And everyday language pervades the book, giving students clear, straightforward answers they can easily understand.

A guide to editing the most common errors. The Introduction serves as a "crisis control center" for writers, providing guidelines for recognizing, understanding, and editing the most common errors. With cross-references to the rest of the book, this section works nicely as a brief handbook within the larger handbook.

Hand-edited examples. Most examples are shown hand-edited in blue, allowing students to see the error and its revision at a glance. Blue pointers and boldface type make these examples easy to spot on the page.

A user-friendly index. Even the index is especially easy to use, listing everyday words (such as *that* or *which*) as well as grammatical terms (such as *relative pronoun*), so that students can find information even if they don't know grammatical terminology.

Other highlights

For all the dramatic changes resulting from electronic forms of communication, student writers still work to understand and to enter academic discourse — and to think about the audiences, purposes, and rhetorical situations their writing addresses. Online or off, students carry out research and work to draft, design, edit, and proof-read their work. *The St. Martin's Handbook* continues to provide helpful, up-to-date advice in all these areas.

Attention to writing, not just to correctness. My ongoing research and experience convince me that students need extensive practice in writing, and in writing that is compelling and powerful. Like all composition handbooks, this book provides guidance in checking and revising for correctness. Unlike most others, however, it also pays attention to rhetorically effective writing throughout the book, including the chapters dealing with grammar and mechanics. The chapter on adjectives and adverbs (Chapter 36), for instance, asks students to focus not only on how to use adjectives and adverbs correctly but also on the more compelling question of why and in what circumstances to use them at all. The end punctuation chapter (Chapter 50) provides rules for using periods, question marks, and exclamation points, and, in addition, asks students to try revising a piece of their own writing for sentence variety using declarative, interrogatory, and exclamatory structures. In other words, I present grammar and mechanics as tools to use for a writing purpose, not simply to use "correctly."

Attention to rhetorical situations. Since writing always responds in some ways to its context — including audiences, purposes, and other texts — I put special emphasis on the importance of understanding rhetorical situations that student writers encounter. Chapter 2, for example, urges students to think critically and imaginatively about what they want to do in writing, whom they want to reach, and how they want to do so. This emphasis on rhetorical choice is present throughout the text, which shows students over and over again how to go about making particular choices (which word to use, what example to choose for particular situations, what medium to use to present a project).

Three other chapters put special focus on rhetorical situations. Chapter 24, "Writing to the World," asks students to examine their own assumptions — about what "good writing" is, about what counts as effective evidence, style, and so on. Such an examination leads students to consider various cultural values and thus to engage in more open and effective cross-cultural communication. Chapter 25, "Considering Others: Building Common Ground," rests on two major assumptions: that writers will wish to address readers whose backgrounds, values, and perspectives will vary widely and will also be different from their own; and that language offers a primary means of both respecting and bridging such differences. This chapter asks students to take a close look at how the words they use can help them include — or exclude — their readers. Chapter 26, "Considering Varieties of Language," discusses standard, regional, ethnic, and occupational varieties of English, showing students how different varieties of English (and of other languages as well) can be used appropriately and effectively, not only outside of school but also in their academic writing. This chapter helps students "shift language gears" as needed among the contexts of community, workplace, and school.

Systematic attention to reading. Because writing and reading are inextricably linked (and particularly so in online environments), reading instruction occurs throughout *The St. Martin's Handbook*. Not only does this text offer extensive guidance to help students read observantly and critically — whether evaluating a draft, an argument, a paragraph, or an online source — but it also presents reading as one more tool that can help improve writing and research skills. Chapter 1 offers explicit guidelines for reading, as do the chapters on argument, on research, on the disciplines, on literature, and on using and evaluating sources.

Attention to critical thinking throughout. Beginning with the Introduction, this handbook focuses on critical thinking in almost every chapter. The Introduction provides a framework to help students approach writing with a critical eye, including guidelines to help them check for the most common errors. This framework continues through subsequent chapters, with editing guidelines to help students think about and revise their drafts, along with end-of-chapter activities that ask them to think critically about issues in the chapter and to apply what they learn to their own writing.

Attention to the needs of multilingual writers. For this edition of *The St. Martin's Handbook,* I have added a new chapter (Chapter 58, "Learning U.S. Academic Conventions") aimed at making explicit some common U.S. expectations regarding such conventions as the writer's stance, the writer's relationship to audience and sub-ject, and organizational patterns. As in earlier editions, this new chapter benefits from the astute and careful attention of Franklin Horowitz of Teachers College, Columbia University, who in Part 11 provides coverage of grammatical issues of concern to multicultural writers. In addition, blue boxes throughout the book offer advice on topics that are helpful to multilingual writers, in language-specific terms whenever possible. A separate index at the end of the book (p. I-42) provides a convenient guide to this advice.

Attention to the needs of basic writers. Several features of this text are especially appropriate for basic writers. The focus on reading not only provides instruction and practice in critical reading but also offers practice drawing conclusions and inferences from reading — practice that is valuable for basic writers. In addition, the focus on their own writing helps basic writers to make crucial links between their first-year writing courses and other academic and professional writing they might do. Finally, the use of actual student sentences and essays throughout the book and the emphasis on everyday uses of language invite students — and especially basic writing students — to link the language of this handbook and the classrooms it is used in with their lives beyond the classroom.

A wide array of ancillaries

Several useful resources accompany *The St. Martin's Handbook*. All are available free of charge to instructors. The software, *Source-*

book for *Writing Tutors, Workbook,* and *Pocket Guide to Research and Documentation* are available for students to purchase.

TEACHING RESOURCES

Instructor's Notes, Fifth Edition
by Andrea A. Lunsford, Cheryl Glenn, and Alyssa O'Brien

The St. Martin's Guide to Teaching Writing, Fifth Edition
by Cheryl Glenn, Melissa Goldthwaite, and Robert Connors

Answer Key to The St. Martin's Handbook, Fifth Edition

The St. Martin's Sourcebook for Writing Tutors, Second Edition
by Christina Murphy and Steve Sherwood

Bedford Bibliography for Teachers of Writing, Fifth Edition
by Nedra Reynolds, Patricia Bizzell, and Bruce Herzberg

Assigning, Responding, Evaluating, Third Edition
by Edward M. White

The St. Martin's Manual for Writing in the Disciplines
by Richard Bullock

STUDENT RESOURCES

The St. Martin's Pocket Guide to Research and Documentation, Third Edition
by Andrea A. Lunsford and Marcia Muth

The St. Martin's Workbook, Fifth Edition
by Lex Runciman

ELECTRONIC RESOURCES

The Electronic St. Martin's Handbook 5.0

The St. Martin's Handbook book companion site (including additional grammar exercises, and help preparing for the CLAST and TASP), www.bedfordstmartins.com/smhandbook

The St. Martin's Handbook Electronic Exercises
e-Content for Online Learning
www.bfwpub.com/mediaroom
Comment for *The St. Martin's Handbook*

Research for *The St. Martin's Handbook*

From the beginning, *The St. Martin's Handbook* has been informed by research into student writing. In fact, Bob Connors and I first began work on *The St. Martin's Handbook* in 1983, when we realized that most college handbooks were based on research into student writing conducted almost fifty years earlier. Our own historical studies had convinced us that student writing and what teachers think of as "good" writing change over time, so we began by gathering a nationwide sample of over 21,000 marked student essays and carefully analyzing a scientifically stratified sample of those to identify the twenty surface errors most characteristic of contemporary student writing. One of the most intriguing discoveries was how many of these errors related in some way to visual memory—wrong words; wrong or missing verb endings; missing or misplaced possessive apostrophes, even the *its/it's* confusion—which suggests that students today are less familiar with visual aspects of print-based writing than students once were. One effect of an oral, electronic culture seems to be that students do not automatically bring with them the visual knowledge of writing conventions that textwise writers possess and use effortlessly.

This problem of visualization was most pronounced in terms of spelling errors, which occurred—by a factor of 300 percent—

more frequently than any other error, so we next undertook a second research study examining all the spelling errors in our sample of student essays. Out of this study came our own list of the words student writers misspell most frequently, as well as the discovery that most of these words are homonyms. These findings further suggest that the visual aspect of spelling is particularly important. In a world of secondary orality, we need to find ways to help students visualize their language.

Since our original research revealed that many errors are governed not so much by hard-and-fast rules as by large-scale rhetorical decisions, we turned back to the 21,000 essays in a third study, looking this time at content and organization. Again, we got some provocative results. We found, for instance, that these aspects of the composing process are as important to readers today as they were over two thousand years ago: the use of good reasons, proof, evidence, and examples — the rhetorical tools of invention — elicited the most consistent commentary from teachers, followed by commentary on the ways in which such materials were arranged and organized. These findings strongly suggest that readers are interested in the *what* as well as the *how* of student writing. More specifically, they suggest that student writers need to become conversant with traditional methods of analysis and patterns of development not simply to demonstrate that they can recognize the difference between classification and division, for example, but rather to gain the understanding and assent of their readers.

Good research, of course, always generates new research questions that beg to be pursued. As we approached the third edition, we found ourselves wondering, "How are we doing here?" Were we providing the guidance that student writers need? Next, then, we turned to the students using *The St. Martin's Handbook,* aiming to find out how students actually use our book and what we could do to make it more useful. Their astute judgments and suggestions and their complex realization that good writing means more than just following rules led us, in the third edition, to add a chapter on oral presentations (95 percent of our student respondents asked for help here); to develop a special section providing help for multilingual writers; to provide guidelines for using varieties of English (and other languages) in academic writing; and to offer more help with using and documenting electronic sources.

However, even as the third edition went to press reflecting all we had learned from over a decade of ongoing research, we already had our sights set on what we needed to do next. Our student respondents had convinced us that the increased availability of home computers, access to the Internet, and the advent of something called the World Wide Web (which was a very new electronic space back in 1992) would have a swift and major impact on student writing. Thus for the fourth edition of *The St. Martin's Handbook,* we again conducted a nationwide survey, this time of 2,500 students and 53 teachers, about their computer-based and online work.

This study confirmed our intuitions that almost all students are doing most of their work on a computer, with all the challenges that entails. In addition, we found that most students have experimented with using the Web — and that those who have not want to do so. Most important, students voiced a number of concerns and questions about how to get online and how to work effectively once there. In their questions, they often seemed to be straining for language to describe writing situations that were new and unfamiliar.

In 1999, Bob Connors decided to focus his attention more completely on his historical research, and I assumed sole responsibility for this text. When an accident took Bob's life in June 2000, I faced the much more serious loss — this time not of a collaborator who was turning to new tasks but of a close and long-time friend. This book is dedicated to Bob's family, and throughout I attempt to carry on the tradition of research that has informed every earlier edition.

More specifically, this edition is informed by a series of intensive interviews with first-year student writers, interviews that reveal a great deal about the kinds of writing students are doing today. While I am still involved in this research, I can report intriguing findings: students are being asked to engage a wide range of writing tasks early in their college careers (interviewees identified nineteen different kinds of writing). Ninety-eight percent of them report communicating with others online on a daily basis, and indeed about 18 percent report that they do their "best writing" on email or instant messaging. Certainly, they are making more oral and multimedia presentations than ever before, and they are often asked to do so in collaborative groups, though the pace of change on this front is slower than I had earlier imagined. Most of the students with whom I spoke marked a distinct difference between high school and college writing, describing high school tasks as concentrating on personal essays or journals and on traditional readings of literary texts, most often in the form of a three- to four-page essay that follows the format of a five-paragraph theme. In college, they are faced with a much wider range of texts to write and with increased demands in terms of critical reading, of argument, and of research-based writing. In terms of research, most students have heard that they should not rely solely on Google or Yahoo! Web searches, but all of them say, somewhat sheepishly, that this is inevitably where they start, leaving the library's much more reliable and complete databases for later. Finally, the students I interviewed make complex distinctions related to fair use and intellectual property, embracing peer-to-peer music file sharing, for example, as fair use if there is no commercial intent but condemning those who download essays from term-paper mills. At every turn, I have tried to incorporate these findings into practical guidance for student writers.

Looking back over twenty years of research gives me a renewed sense of the dramatic changes that have taken place in the writing that students do. I began this research with a historical understanding that writing conventions and notions of correctness change over time. Ongoing investigations have only emphasized this linguistic fact of life: in 1985, I was counting conventional "errors" in student essays that were largely typewritten (some were even handwritten); today, students work in virtual or paperless environments where what counts as error is daily called into question. Formerly simple choices — about what words to capitalize, for example — are now much more complex, as some new words include internal capitalization (*eBay,* for example) and some online writers eschew capitalization altogether.

This complexity makes even more important the clear message I have always tried to send about the role of correctness in standard academic English. Without oversimplification, my goal now as always is to help student writers make effective choices.

Throughout, *The St. Martin's Handbook* seeks to serve students as a ready reference that will help them make appropriate grammatical and rhetorical choices. Beyond this immediate goal, I hope to guide students in understanding and experiencing for themselves the multiple ways in which truly good writing always means more than just following the rules. Truly good writing, I believe, means applying those rules in specific rhetorical situations for specific purposes and with specific audiences in ways that will bring readers and writers, teachers and students, to spirited conversation as well as to mutual understanding and respect.

Acknowledgments

The St. Martin's Handbook remains a collaborative effort in the best and richest sense of the word. For this edition, I am enormously indebted to Stephanie Carpenter, whose insights and sheer hard work are everywhere apparent. Also invaluable have been the contributions of Kristin Bowen and John Elliott, friends, colleagues, and terrific editors. I am also deeply indebted to friend and colleague Nick Carbone, whose extensive and detailed review of all material relating to online writing and research have been, simply, the *sine qua non.* As always, Nancy Perry, Denise Wydra, and Joan Feinberg have provided support, encouragement, and good advice, and my former editor Marilyn Moller continues to provide support and friendship. Shuli Traub has managed the entire handbook from manuscript to bound book with skill and grace — and together with Dennis Conroy has made an enormously complex project run smoothly. Judy Voss, the *Handbook*'s multitalented copy editor, edited and reorganized the text with great skill and good humor. In many matters large and small, Nick Wolven has provided valuable assistance. For the wonderful cover and interior design, I am indebted to Anna George, Lucy Krikorian, and Donna Dennison. I am fortunate indeed to have had Karen Melton and Richard Cadman as my marketing team; in my experience, they set the standard. And, as always, I am grateful to the entire Bedford/St. Martin's sales force; they are the *best.*

The St. Martin's Handbook is available in an imaginative and highly interactive CD-ROM version. For her extraordinary work in creating this electronic version, I thank Kristin Bowen.

From its inception, this text has had the benefit of meticulous reviews by Franklin Horowitz, Teachers College of Columbia

University—and, starting with the third edition, Frank has contributed a superb section for multilingual writers to which I have now added a new chapter. For this edition, my friend and constant collaborator Lisa Ede has brought her special brand of wit and wisdom to a new section on academic and professional writing, for which I am particularly grateful. Special thanks also go to colleagues Richard Bullock, Lex Runciman, and Ed White, who contributed uncommonly innovative books to accompany the handbook; to Christina Murphy and Steve Sherwood for their excellent new edition of the *Sourcebook for Writing Tutors*; to Alyssa O'Brien for her brilliant work on the *Instructor's Notes;* to Mike Hennessy for his thoughtful and practical introduction to the *Instructor's Notes;* and to Cheryl Glenn and Melissa Goldthwaite for a thoroughgoing and theoretically smart revision of *The St. Martin's Guide to Teaching Writing.* Brenda Brueggemann contributed her wealth of knowledge of disabilities studies to revisions of the new Considering Disabilities boxes throughout the book. I am grateful for her generosity and friendship.

As always, I am extremely fortunate to have had the contributions of very fine student writers, whose work appears throughout this text or on its companion Web site: Michelle Abbott, Carina Abernathy, Milena Ateyea, Julie Baird, Kelly Darr, Tara Gupta, Bory Kea, James Kung, Merlla McLaughlin, Laura Montgomery, Sheba Najmi, Shannan Palma, Heather Ricker, Melissa Schraeder, and Dennis Tyler. For this edition, I am especially grateful to Emily Lesk, whose imaginative and carefully researched essay appears in Chapter 4.

In addition, I am grateful to the many instructors who generously shared their assignments and guidelines: Marvin Diogenes, Claude Reichard, Corrine Arraèz, and Alyssa O'Brien of Stanford University; Genevieve Coogan of Houston Community College; Beverly Moss of Ohio State University; Cheryl Glenn of Penn State University; Jaime Mejia of Southwest Texas State University; and Gerald Lucas of the University of South Florida. For their help in providing useful guides to writing in various disciplines, Lisa Ede and I would also like to thank the departments of Chemistry, Microbiology, Nuclear Engineering, Philosophy, Political Science, and Sociology at Oregon State University.

For *The St. Martin's Handbook,* we have been blessed with a group of very special reviewers. Their incisive comments, queries, criticisms, and suggestions have improved this book immeasurably: Alan Ainsworth, Houston Community College; Julia Allen, Sonoma State University; J. Robert Baker, Fairmont State College; Susan J. Beebe, Southwest Texas State University; Diane Belcher, Ohio State University; Glenn Blalock, Texas A&M University–Corpus Christi; Kimberly D. Braddock, Blinn College; Vicki Tolar Burton, Oregon State University; Duncan A. Carter, Portland State University; Patrice J. Coleman, Scott Community College; Genevieve Coogan, Houston Community College; Linda Daigle, Houston Community College; Michael J. Day, Northern Illinois University; C. Bradley Dilger, University of Florida; Marvin Diogenes, Stanford University; Janet Carey Eldred, University of Kentucky; Joel A. English, Old Dominion University; Frank

Farmer, University of Kansas; Robert Ford, Houston Community College; Philip Gaines, Montana State University; Edwin Gallaher, Houston Community College; Catherine Gillis, University of California, Riverside; Margaret Graham, Iowa State University; Loretta S. Gray, Central Washington University; William Gary Griswold, California State University, Long Beach; Carolyn Handa, Southern Illinois University, Edwardsville; Gary Hatch, Brigham Young University; James C. McDonald, University of Louisiana at Lafayette; Cindy Moore, Indiana University; Daryl Ogden, Georgia Institute of Technology; Cathy Palmer, University of California, Irvine; Joe Pellegrino, Eastern Kentucky University; Debora Person, University of Wyoming; Rossana Pronesti, Arizona Western College; Kelly Ritter, Southern Connecticut State University; David Roger Russell, Iowa State University; Carol Rutz, Carleton College; Michael J. Salvo, Northeastern University; Wendy B. Sharer, East Carolina University; Allison Smith, Louisiana Technical University; Cheryl Smith, California State University, Bakersfield; Margaret Sokolik, University of California, Berkeley; Joshua Stein, University of California, Riverside; Linda Strahan, University of California, Riverside; Todd Taylor, University of North Carolina, Chapel Hill; Deborah Coxwell Teague, Florida State University; Bill Toth, Western New Mexico University; Martha A. Townsend, University of Missouri; Kim van Alkemade, Shippensburg University; Peter J. Vandenberg, DePaul University; Kay J. Walter, Blinn College; Margaret E. Weaver, Southwest Missouri State University; Eve Wiederhold, East Carolina University; Donna Winchell, Clemson University; and Meg Worley, Stanford University.

I am grateful to the thousands of students who responded so thoughtfully to the survey about online writing. Their names are far too numerous to list here, but I would like to thank the instructors who distributed surveys to their students and offered their own thoughtful and helpful advice: Julia Allen, Sonoma State University; Kimberly D. Braddock, Blinn College; Patrice J. Coleman, Scott Community College; Janet Carey Eldred, University of Kentucky; Loretta S. Gray, Central Washington University; Carolyn Handa, Southern Illinois University; Gary Hatch, Brigham Young University; Rossana Pronesti, Arizona Western College; Allison Smith, Louisiana Technical University; Deborah Coxwell Teague, Florida State University; Bill Toth, Western New Mexico University; Kim van Alkemade, Shippensburg University; Kay J. Walter, Blinn College; and Donna Winchell, Clemson University.

Finally, I wish to offer very special thanks to the extraordinary community of teacher-researchers at the Bread Loaf School of English, whose responses to this text have helped to shape and refine its goals.

I could go on and on in praise of the support and help I have received, for I am fortunate to be part of a unique scholarly community, one characterized by compassion as well as passionate commitment to students and to learning. I remain grateful to be among you.

Andrea A. Lunsford

▼ A Note to Students

The main goal of *The St. Martin's Handbook* is to help you become a competent and compelling writer—both throughout and beyond your college years.

The introductory chapter of this book, "Learning from Your Errors," will help you analyze the writing patterns and strategies most college students need to practice. The introduction—and indeed, the entire book—offers a critical-thinking program for building on strengths and eliminating weaknesses in your own writing.

This text encourages you to carefully analyze your own prose. Most chapters not only provide explanations and opportunities for practice but also ask you to apply the principles presented directly to your own writing. If you follow these directions, they will guide you in becoming a systematic self-critic—and a more effective writer. And since writing and reading in many ways go hand in hand, many chapters also offer you a chance to read with an eye for various logical or stylistic or conventional aspects of writing, often in the work of some of the finest writers in English. Sometimes you will be asked to try to imitate their sentences, or to work collaboratively with a classmate to edit or create prose. As your writing improves, so will your reading, your thinking, and your research.

Chapters 1-5 guide you through the process of crafting an effective college project, from your first choice of a topic to your final product—an essay or some other kind of text. Chapter 6 offers advice on working collaboratively and on producing texts with others. Chapters 7-10 focus on media and writing—from learning the basics of file sharing and word processing to creating oral and multimedia presentations—while Chapters 11-13 help you analyze and construct arguments and consider their visual design.

Next come Chapters 14-23, which show you how to carry out and use research in your own writing. Chapters 24-30 are devoted to improving your ability to communicate with style, empathy, and clarity, while Chapters 31-57 provide thorough discussion of writing conventions—grammar, word choice, punctuation, and mechanics. These chapters provide examples and practice to help you master such conventions.

Chapters 58-62 offer special advice to multilingual writers. Finally, Chapters 63-69 guide you in examining writing in various disciplines, in writing effective essay exams, and in assembling a writing portfolio.

How to use *The St. Martin's Handbook*

This book has been designed to be as easy as possible to use. Depending on what information or advice you're looking for, you may want to consult any or all of the following:

- **Tables of Contents.** If you know what general topic you're looking for (such as using commas), the **Brief Contents** on the inside front cover will lead you to the chapter where you'll find that topic. If you're looking for a specific kind of information within a general topic (such as using commas in a series), the detailed **Contents** on the inside back cover or the even more detailed **Contents** following this introduction can lead you to this information.

- **Index.** The index lists everything covered in the book. It's especially useful for finding specific words you need help with (such as *that* or *which*) but don't know the exact technical term for (*relative pronouns*).

- **Information about Online Writing.** If you have questions specific to working online, from how to indicate italics to how to design Web sites, you'll find answers in Part 2. Additional information about writing with computers and working online is highlighted throughout the book with a computer icon in the margins. A directory to all this advice appears on p. I-40.

- **Common Errors.** On pp. 14–27 you will find an explanation and examples of twenty of the most common surface errors in the writing of U.S. college students, with references to pages in the book where you can find additional help in revising those errors.

- **Revising and Editing Guidelines.** On the second page of most chapters, and elsewhere as well in some chapters, are brief guidelines — set off in green boxes — for revising and editing your writing that focus on the issues covered in that chapter (such as paragraphs or sentence fragments).

- **Documentation Guidelines.** For information on documenting sources, see the directories for MLA (p. 416), APA (p. 466), CBE (p. 482), and Chicago (p. 489) styles.

- **Glossaries.** The **Glossary of Usage** (p. 982) gives help with troublesome words (such as *accept* and *except*); the **Glossary of Grammatical and Computer Terms** (p. 969) gives definitions of these kinds of terms (such as *clause* and *listserv*).

- **Web Links.** In the margins of the text are links to the book's companion Web site. These links offer more information or interesting insights about issues under discussion in the text. Web resources, organized by academic discipline, are also listed in Chapters 64–67.

- **Multilingual Issues.** Chapters 58–62 cover some of the most common and most important problems that speakers of other languages face in understanding and using English. In addition, throughout the book advice on specific issues appears in blue boxes; a list of these boxes is on p. I-42.

- **Considering Disabilities.** Brown shaded boxes throughout the book offer advice on making writing and presentations more accessible to people with disabilities; these boxes also point writers with disabilities to resources and strategies that may be helpful. A list of these boxes appears on p. I-41.

A tutorial on using *The St. Martin's Handbook*

For this book to serve you well, you need to get to know it — to know what's inside and how to find it. The following tutorial is designed to help you familiarize yourself with *The St. Martin's Handbook;* the answers, given by chapter number and section letter, are on pp. xviii–xix.

Starting with the table of contents

1. Where will you find advice on revising a draft?
2. Where will you find quick information on checking verbs for *-s* and *-es* endings? On checking subject-verb agreement in general?
3. Where will you find guidelines on documenting Internet sources?
4. Does the handbook offer any help for multilingual students, including those who speak English as a second language?
5. Where will you find information on preparing a résumé?

For planning and drafting

6. It's the first week of class, and you are at work on your first assignment. Where in the handbook can you find general guidelines on planning and drafting?
7. Assigned to write an essay that argues a claim, you've been warned to be very careful about using any personal narratives as support for your argument. Does the handbook offer any advice about how to use narrative appropriately in college writing?
8. In an essay arguing for "equal pay for equal work" addressed to members of your writing class, you want to avoid any language that stereotypes members of any group. Where in the handbook can you find advice about using considerate rather than hurtful language?
9. You've been assigned to give a multimedia presentation. Where does the handbook offer advice on writing and giving such presentations? How did you find this information?
10. You are using some visuals in the writing assignment you are working on. Where will you find advice about integrating visuals into your text and labeling them appropriately?

For editing

11. As you edit a final draft, you stop at the following sentence: *Winning may be the name of the game but it isn't a name I care for very much.* You can't decide whether to put a comma before *but.* What does the handbook recommend that you do? How and where do you find this answer?
12. You speak several languages, and you still confuse the English prepositions *in* and *on.* Where in the handbook can you find help?
13. Does the word *none* take a singular or plural verb form? You can't decide. Where in the handbook can you find a quick answer to this question? How did you find the answer?
14. Your instructor has written *ref* next to this sentence: *Transmitting video signals by satellite is a way of overcoming the problem of scarce airwaves and limiting how they are used.* Where do you look in the handbook for help responding to your instructor's comment?

For doing research

15. You've found some Web sites related to your topic, but you aren't sure how reliable they are. Where can you find help in evaluating them?
16. Should you quote, paraphrase, or summarize? Are there any guidelines in the handbook to help you decide? How do you find these guidelines?

17. You're required to use something called *APA* style in a psychology paper. Where in the handbook can you find this information?
18. Using *MLA* style, how do you document information obtained from a DVD source?
19. You are keeping all your research notes online, and they are beginning to get out of control. Where can you find help in organizing them?

For all your college courses

20. A take-home exam in political science asks you to compare Marx's and Lenin's theories of revolution. You've never before written a political science paper, so you're not sure how to proceed. Do you need to cite sources — and if so, do they need to be primary? Do political science papers follow any set format? Where in the handbook can you look for help?
21. You need to write a proposal as part of a biology project. Is there a model in the handbook?
22. For a literature course, you're writing an essay interpreting a poem by Emily Dickinson. Where can you find help in the handbook?
23. A report you're working on must include both tables and figures. You aren't sure of the difference, nor do you know how to set them up. Where in the handbook can you get help?

I hope that this book will prove to be a useful reference. But in the long run, a book can be only a guide. You are the one who will put such guidance into practice, as you work to become a precise, powerful, and persuasive writer. Why not get started on achieving that goal right now?

Andrea A. Lunsford

1. Chapter 4.
2. Chapter 33, on using verbs, includes quick-reference guidelines on editing -*s* and -*es* verb endings. Chapter 34 covers subject-verb agreement.
3. Chapter 20 is on documenting sources, including Internet sources, in MLA style; Chapters 21–23 are on documenting sources in APA, CBE, and Chicago styles, respectively.
4. Part 11 includes five chapters (Chapters 58–62) that cover language issues of special interest to students who speak languages in addition to English. Page I-42 has a quick reference chart that refers you to all the materials in the handbook for multilingual writers.
5. Chapter 67, on writing for business, includes guidelines for creating both print and electronic résumés.
6. Chapter 3 offers guidelines on exploring, planning, and drafting.
7. Looking up *narrative* in the index leads you to a discussion of using narrative to support an argument in 13f, with guidelines on checking your own use of narrative on p. 275.
8. Looking up *stereotypes* in the index leads you to Chapter 25, on considering others and building common ground.
9. A look at the table of contents leads you to Chapter 10, on making oral and multimedia presentations.
10. Looking up *visuals* in the index leads to 8d, which provides instructions for incorporating and labeling visuals, along with examples.
11. Looking up *but* in the index leads to 48b, which explains that a comma usually precedes a coordinating conjunction such as *but* when it joins two independent clauses in a compound sentence. You could also get to this section by turning directly to Chapter 48, on using commas, and looking for examples of how to use commas in similar sentences.

12. The table of contents tells you that Chapter 61 covers prepositions; 61a includes a set of strategies for using prepositions idiomatically, including several examples of sentences using *in* and *on*.

13. Looking up *none* in the index leads to 34e, where you learn that *none* can be singular or plural, depending on the noun it refers to: *none of the cake was eaten; none of the cakes were eaten.*

14. *Ref* is a revision symbol commonly used by instructors. A list of revision symbols appears on p. I-43 of the handbook. Consulting this list tells you that *ref* refers to unclear pronoun reference and that this subject is discussed in Chapter 37.

15. Skimming the table of contents leads you to Chapter 16, on evaluating sources, and in particular to 16b, on evaluating potential sources, and to 16c, on reading sources with a critical eye.

16. Consulting the index under *quotations, paraphrases,* or *summaries* leads you to guidelines in 17b on deciding whether to quote, paraphrase, or summarize.

17. The table of contents tells you that Chapter 21 covers APA documentation, and that a student essay using APA style appears in Chapter 65.

18. The table of contents leads you to Chapter 20, which provides a full discussion of MLA documentation conventions. It also lists a directory to MLA style, which leads you to section 20c3, on documenting electronic sources.

19. Scanning the table of contents leads you to Chapter 14, on preparing for a research project; section 14g, on taking notes and beginning a research log, offers advice on organizing your notes.

20. Scanning the table of contents leads you to Part 12, which covers academic and professional writing in general, and to Chapter 65, which covers social science subjects, and Chapter 63, which includes sections on understanding the vocabulary, style, use of evidence, and conventional formats in different disciplines.

21. Consulting the index under *biology,* you see that Chapter 66, on writing for the natural and applied sciences, contains a research proposal in biology.

22. A glance at the table of contents leads you to Chapter 64, on writing about literature for the humanities. Section 64c provides guidelines for reading a literary work and an example of a student's annotations of a poem. Section 64c also includes a glossary of literary terms, and section 64d includes a student's essay interpreting a novel.

23. Looking up *tables* or *figures* in the index leads you to 8d, on using visuals, with examples and guidelines on constructing tables and figures.

◼️ Contents

PART 10 MECHANICAL CONVENTIONS 793

Introduction: Learning from Your Errors

What do Mia Hamm, Martha Stewart, and Denzel Washington all have in common? Because one is an expert soccer player, one a famous cook and designer, and another a popular actor, they are all engaged in activities that call for constant practice—and for learning from their errors. Many well-known people speak convincingly of how mistakes—missing the goal, messing up the recipe, or flubbing their lines—were important to their eventual success. One philosopher even defines error not as a mistake or action that calls for some kind of punishment but as an "exercise in competence." To become really skilled at almost anything, and certainly at writing, you need to give yourself permission to experiment, to try out different styles and arrangements of words, to *not* get it right every time. In this way, with practice, you can eventually not just get it right but get it brilliantly right.

As a college student, you share with Hamm, Stewart, and Washington the need for intensive practice and for learning from your errors. In science classes, you may conduct an experiment over and over again, learning from each attempt how to come closer to success. Before your math midterms, you can study every error you usually make in order to ensure not only that you understand the mathematical concepts involved but also that you can solve the problems while making fewer and fewer errors. In a writing class, you can study your writing and the responses you get to it, looking for ways to become a better writer by learning from your mistakes. In each case, you will need to ask yourself, "What counts as an error in this particular writing situation?" since what seems appropriate and correct in an email chat, a love letter, a college essay, or a job application will probably vary significantly. In short, errors are always part of a rhetorical situation: in effective writing, one size definitely does not fit all. Thus this textbook stresses the importance of understanding your rhetorical situation and the purposes of your writing before you decide what is—and what is not—a weakness or an error.

Using *The St. Martin's Handbook* to practice critical thinking

The kind of error-and-response analysis this book asks you to undertake is known as **critical thinking**, which calls for stepping back from your own work and taking a good, hard, close-up look at it—examining the big picture as well as the fine details to see how well your writing works to achieve your purposes. This close-up examination provides the data from which you can draw conclusions about how to improve and strengthen your writing. Almost every chapter in *The St. Martin's Handbook* has a section that invites you to reflect on what you have learned from that chapter and to apply those lessons to your own writing. These "thinking critically about your own writing" sections (which appear at the ends of chapters) all aim to engage you in close analysis of your writing and thus provide opportunities for you to learn from your errors. Eventually, this kind of thinking can become habitual. In the meantime, you can speed the process along by beginning an analysis of your own writing through a writing inventory.

■ *Taking a writing inventory*

What is a writing inventory? How can taking one help you develop critical-thinking abilities? The word *inventory* comes from a Latin word meaning "find," and in reference to writing, taking inventory carries the familiar meaning of taking stock—finding items in your stock of writing and cataloging those items—much as you might take inventory of your CDs or as a store manager might take inventory of items on hand. But taking inventory also carries another sense of "find," one we more often associate with the words *invent* and *invention*. In this sense, taking inventory means to discover new things about your writing and to use your discoveries to articulate its strengths and weaknesses as well as to build a plan for improvement.

This dual sense of taking inventory runs throughout the fifth edition of *The St. Martin's Handbook,* asking you to think critically and analytically about your own writing as a means of learning from your errors. How might you identify those features of your writing most important for such an inventory? Analyzing a representative sample of over twenty thousand essays from first- and second-year writing courses in U.S. colleges revealed that the features instructors most often comment on fall into three categories:

1. broad content issues
2. organization and presentation
3. surface errors

These research findings suggest that you can benefit from organizing an inventory of your own writing according to these three major categories. Following are some guidelines for doing so:

TAKING A WRITING INVENTORY

1. If you are using this introductory chapter in a writing course, assemble copies of the first two or three pieces of writing you do, making sure to select pieces to which either your instructor or other students have responded.

2. Read through this writing, adding your own comments about its strengths and weaknesses.

3. Examine the instructor and peer comments very carefully, and compare them with your own comments.

4. Group all the comments into the categories discussed in this chapter—broad content issues, organization and presentation, and surface errors.

5. Make an inventory of your own strengths in each category.

6. Study your errors, marking every instructor and peer comment that suggests or calls for an improvement and putting them all in a list.

7. Identify the appropriate sections of this book for more detailed help in areas where you need it.

8. Make up a priority list of three or four particular writing problems you have identified, and write out a plan for improvement.

9. Note at least two strengths you want to build on in your writing.

10. Record your findings in a writing log (see following section), which you can add to as the class proceeds.

One very good way to keep track of your writing strengths and weaknesses is by establishing a **writing log**, a notebook or computer file in which you can record observations and comments about your writing — from instructors, other students, or yourself. This book will offer you frequent opportunities to make entries in a writing log, beginning with this introduction. As you take inventory of some of your writing, you will be gathering information about how readers respond to various features of it — broad content issues, organization and presentation, and surface errors. This information can serve as the data for an opening entry in your writing log. Here is an example of one such entry, made by Tamara Washington, an undergraduate at Ohio State University:

ENTRY 1 WRITING INVENTORY

I've taken a first look at the essay I wrote on the second day of class, one my response group and the instructor read. Here's what I've found by studying their comments and looking for ways to improve:

	Strengths	Weaknesses
Broad content issues	lots of good examples	some examples unclear to some readers
Organization, presentation	great title! (Everyone loved it.) thesis is clear	paragraphs too short to make my points (Two are only one sentence long.)
Surface errors	semicolons used correctly — I was worried about this!	one unintentional sentence fragment, an *its/it's* mistake (!) (See p. 767, and *never* make this mistake again!!)

ASSESSING BROAD CONTENT ISSUES

As a writer, you are in some ways like the conductor of an orchestra or the supervisor of a large construction job: you must orchestrate all the elements of your writing into a persuasive performance, assemble all the ideas, words, evidence, and so on into one coherent structure. Doing so calls on you to attend carefully to several big questions: What is the purpose of your writing? To whom is it addressed? What points does it make? Does it fully develop, support, or prove those points?

The research conducted for this textbook indicates that instructors comment most often on the following broad content issues in student writing:

1. use of supporting evidence
2. use of sources
3. achievement of purpose
4. attention to audience
5. overall impression

Use of supporting evidence

Readers expect that a piece of writing will make one or more points clearly and illustrate or support those points with ample evidence — good reasons, examples, or other details. Effective use of such evidence helps readers understand a point, makes abstract concepts concrete, and offers proof that what you are saying is sensible and worthy of attention. In fact, this element is the one instructors in research conducted for this book commented on *most often,* accounting for 56 percent of all comments analyzed. These instructors tended to make statements like these:

This point is underdeveloped.

I like the way you back this claim up.

The details here don't really help me see your point.

I'm not convinced — what's your authority?

The three reasons you offer are very persuasive.

Good examples.

For a brief discussion of the use of good reasons, see 13d; of examples and details, see 13f–g. For more on providing such support in paragraphs, see 5e.

Use of sources

One special kind of supporting evidence for your points comes from source materials. Choosing possible sources, evaluating them, and using the results of your research effectively in your writing not only support your claim but also build your credibility as a writer, demonstrating that you understand what others have to say about a topic and that you are fully informed about varying perspectives on the topic. But finding enough sources, judging their usefulness, and deciding when to quote, when to summarize, and when to paraphrase — and then doing so accurately and effectively—are skills that take considerable practice, ones you should develop throughout your college writing career. You can begin sharpening those skills now by taking a close look at how well you use sources in your writing. The instructors whose responses were studied commented regularly on use of sources. Here are some of their remarks:

Your list of sources is extraordinarily thorough—impressive reading!

Only two sources? You need at least several more.

Who said this? Identify your source.

Excellent integration of visual sources into your essay.

One of the clearest paraphrases I've seen of this crucial passage.

Your summary leaves out three of the writer's main points.

Your summary is just repetition—it doesn't add anything new.

This quotation beautifully sums up your argument.

Why do you quote at such length here? Why not paraphrase?

You cite only sources that support your claim—citing one or two with differing views would help show me you've considered other opinions.

You are too dependent on Web resources. How reliable are they?

For more discussion of choosing, reading, and evaluating sources, see Chapters 15 and 16; of quoting, paraphrasing, and summarizing, see 16e; and of incorporating source materials in your text, see Chapter 17.

Achievement of purpose

Purposes for writing vary widely—from asking for an appointment for a job interview to sending greetings or condolences to summarizing information for a test to tracing the causes of World War II for an essay. In college writing, your primary purpose will often be directly related to the assignment you receive. As a result, you need to pay careful attention to what an assignment asks you to do, noting particularly any key term in the assignment such as *analyze* or *argue* or *define* or *summarize*. Such words are important in meeting the requirements of the assignment, staying on the subject, and thus achieving your purpose.

Instructors' responses often reveal how well you have achieved your primary purpose. Here are some comments concerning purpose:

Why are you telling us all this?

What is the issue here, and what is your stand on it?

What is your purpose here? What do you want to happen as a result of your argument?

You simply give a plot summary here, one that does little to analyze character development.

Your writing will profit from some time spent identifying the purposes of several pieces of writing you have done and thinking about how well you achieved those purposes.

●— For guidelines on
considering pur-
poses, see p. 47.

Attention to audience

Most college writing is addressed to instructors and other students, though you may sometimes write to another audience—a political figure, a prospective employer, a campus administrator. The most effective writing reflects a sensitivity to readers' backgrounds, values, and needs. Such writing, for example, includes definitions of terms readers may not know, provides necessary background information, and takes into account readers' perspectives on and feelings about a topic. Here are some instructor comments on audience:

This doesn't sound like something written for middle school students.

Careful you don't talk down to your readers.

You've left me behind here. I can't follow.

Your level of diction is perfect for relating to the Board of Trustees.

I'm really enjoying reading this!

Don't assume everyone shares your opinion about this issue.

Who are you excluding from your audience? Are these exclusions intentional?

●— For guidelines on
considering your
audience, see
p. 51 and 25b.

Overall impression

When friends or instructors read your writing, they may often give you information about the overall impression it makes, perhaps noting how it seems to be improving or how you may be lapsing into bad habits. As the writer, you need to make such comments as concrete as you can by trying to determine, for instance, exactly what has caused some improvement or weakness in your writing. Setting up a conference with the instructor is one way to explore these general responses. Before doing so, however, carry out your own analysis of what the comments mean, and then find out what your instructor thinks.

In the sample of twenty thousand essays, instructors tended to give their overall impression most often in a note at the very beginning or the very end of an essay, saying things like the following:

I was looking for more critical analysis from you, and I've found it!

Much improved over your last essay; this is a very convincing argument.

Your grasp of the material here is truly impressive.

What happened here? I can't understand your point in this essay.

I know you can do a much better job of summarizing than this shows.

You have a strong thesis, but you don't support it fully.

For more specific ⸱⸱⸱⸱⸱● ways of assessing the overall impression your writing creates, see the Thinking Critically exercises in most chapters of this book. Each of these exercises is set up to help you take inventory of your use of the topics in the chapter.

● **EXERCISE 1.1**

Begin your writing inventory by recording the results of a careful look at broad content issues in at least one piece of your own writing. (1) First, list all comments your instructors and classmates have made about your use of supporting evidence, use of sources, achievement of purpose, attention to audience, and overall impression. If you find other large-scale issues referred to, include them in your list. (2) Then look over your writing with your own critical eye, using the advice in this introduction to evaluate your handling of broad content elements. (3) After examining the lists, summarize your major areas of strength and those areas in which you need to improve. (4) If you are keeping a writing log, enter this inventory there.

ASSESSING ORGANIZATION AND PRESENTATION

The most important or brilliant points in the world may have little effect on readers if they are presented in a way that makes them hard to recognize, read, or follow. Indeed, research for this book confirms that readers depend on writers to organize and present their material — sections, paragraphs, sentences, arguments, details, source citations — in ways that aid understanding. After use of supporting evidence, the features of student writing most often commented on had to do with organizational issues. In addition to clear and logical organization of information, readers appreciate careful formatting and documentation of sources. Although you can't always "tell a book by its cover," our research suggests that the "cover" of your writing — its physical format — can offer an important aid to readers and help establish your credibility as a conscientious writer. Careful attention to the conventions of source documentation can produce the same result. Here are those organizational and presentational features most often commented on in the student writing examined:

1. overall organization
2. sentence structure and style
3. paragraph structure
4. format
5. documentation

Overall organization

Readers expect a writer to provide organizational patterns and signals that will help them follow the thread of what the writer is trying to say. Sometimes such cues are simple. If you are giving directions, for example, you might give chronological cues (*first you do A, then B,* and so on), and if you are describing a place, you might give spatial cues (*at the north end is A, in the center is B,* and so on). But complex issues often call for complex organizational patterns, so you might need to signal readers that you are moving from one problem to several possible solutions, for example, or that you are moving through a series of comparisons and contrasts. Instructors responded in the following ways to organizational features:

> I'm confused here — what does this point have to do with the one before it?
>
> Your most important point is buried here in the middle. Why not move it up front?
>
> Organization here is chronological rather than topical; as a result, you write synopsis, not analysis.
>
> How did we get here? You need a transition.
>
> Very clear, logical essay. A joy to read.
>
> I'm lost: this sentence seems totally out of place.
>
> You need to reorganize the three details: son, friend, then *you.*

●— For more discussion of overall organization, see 4e and 13j. For more on organizational methods of development, see 3d; on transitional signals that aid organization, see 5d and f; and on ways of linking paragraphs, see 5h.

Sentence structure and style

Effective sentences form the links in a chain of writing, guiding readers and aiding their understanding. If you have never taken a close look at how your sentences work (or don't work) to help organize your writing and guide readers, a little time and effort now will provide an overview.

How long do your sentences tend to be? Do you use strings of short sentences that make the reader work to fill in the connections between them? Do any long sentences confuse the reader or wander off the topic? How do your sentences open? How do you link them logically? Here are some comments instructors made about sentences:

> The pacing of your sentences here really keeps me reading — excellent variation of length and type.

> Combine sentences to make the logical connection explicit here.

> Your use of questions helps clarify this complex issue.

> This is not effective word order for a closing sentence — I've forgotten your main point.

> These sentences all begin with nouns — the result is a kind of dull clip-clop, clip-clop, clip-clop.

> Too many short, simple sentences here. This reads like a grocery list rather than an explanation of a complex issue.

> This sentence goes on forever — how about dividing it up?

For guidelines ⋯⋯● on editing sentences, see p. 581. For detailed discussion of sentence types, see 31d; of sentence effectiveness, see Chapter 43; and of sentence variation, see Chapter 46.

Paragraph structure

Just as overall organization can help readers follow the thread of thought in a piece of writing, so, too, can paragraph structure. You may tend to paragraph by feel, so to speak, without spending much time thinking about structure. In fact, the time to examine your paragraphs should generally be *after* you have completed a draft. Begin by studying any readers' comments that refer to your paragraphs. Here are some of the kinds of comments you might find:

> The sentences in this paragraph don't follow in a logical order.

> Why the one- and two-sentence paragraphs? Elaborate!

> Your introductory paragraph immediately gets my attention and gives an overview of the essay — good!

> I can't follow the information in this paragraph.

> This paragraph is not unified around one main idea.

> Very effective ordering of details in this paragraph.

> This paragraph skips around two or three points. It has enough ideas for three paragraphs.

For guidelines on ⋯● editing paragraphs, see p. 114. For detailed information on paragraph development in general, see Chapter 5.

Readers depend on the format of a piece of writing to make their job as pleasant and efficient as possible. Therefore, you need to pay very close attention to how your materials are physically presented and to the visual effect they create. Because format guidelines vary widely, part of your job as a writer is always to make certain you know what format is most appropriate for a particular course or assignment.

Learning from Your Errors

In the research conducted for this book, instructors made the following kinds of comments about format:

> You need a title, one that really works to get across your meaning.

> This tiny single-spaced type is almost impossible to read.

> The table of contents here is very clear and helpful.

> Number pages — these were not in the right order!

> Your headings and subheadings helped me follow this report.

> You need a new printer cartridge — I can barely read this!

> The design of your Web document is readable and engaging.

● For a more thorough discussion of format, see Chapters 7 and 8.

Documentation

Any writing that uses source materials requires careful documentation — parenthetical references, endnotes, footnotes, lists of works cited, bibliographies — to guide readers to your sources and let them know you have carried out accurate research. A close look at your writing may reveal that you have learned certain documentation rules — listing an author's last name first, for instance — but that you don't understand others at all. Here are some instructors' comments that focus on documentation:

> I checked my copy of *Emma,* and this quotation's not on the page you list.

> Footnote numbers should come at the *end* of quotations.

> What are you paraphrasing here? Your introduction merely drops readers into the middle of things. *Introduce the material paraphrased.*

> What are you summarizing here? Where do these ideas come from?

> I can't tell where this quotation ends.

> Keep your parenthetical references as simple as possible. (See 17b.)

> Why aren't works listed in alphabetical order?

> This is *not correct* MLA citation style. Check your book!

What is the date of this publication?

What or who sponsors this Web site? Did you check credentials?

For more infor-
mation on docu-
menting sources
in MLA style, see
Chapter 20; in
APA style, see
Chapter 21; in
CBE style, see
Chapter 22; in
Chicago style,
see Chapter 23.

EXERCISE 1.2

Continue your writing inventory by analyzing at least one piece of your writing in regard to the five features of organization and presentation just described. (1) Chart your instructor's comments, and consider asking a classmate whose opinions you value to comment on your use of these features. (2) Then add your own observations about your use of these features. (3) On the basis of these analyses, summarize what you take to be your major areas of strength as well as those areas in which you need to improve. (4) If you are keeping a writing log (see p. 4), enter the results of your analysis there.

LEARNING FROM YOUR SURFACE ERRORS

Readers may notice your handling of broad content issues and your organization and presentation either because these provide stepping stones for following your meaning or because they create stumbling blocks to such understanding. Surface errors, however — such as errors in spelling, grammar, punctuation, word choice, and other small-scale matters — will seldom draw attention unless they look wrong. Because such surface errors disrupt communication between writers and readers, they are an important source of information about your writing.

What can be said about the kinds of surface errors you are likely to find in your writing and the responses they elicit from readers? Research of student writing reveals, first of all, that — even with spell checkers — spelling errors are *by far the most common,* by a factor of more than three to one. Second, readers are not disturbed by all surface errors, nor do instructors always mark all of them. In fact, whether your instructor comments on an error in any particular assignment will depend on his or her judgment about how serious and distracting it is and what you should be dealing with at the time. Finally, not all surface errors are even consistently viewed as errors. In fact, some of the patterns identified in the research for this book are considered errors by some instructors but stylistic options by others.

For a list of the
words most
often misspelled,
see Chapter 30.

Although many people may tend to think of "correctness" as absolute, based on hard and fast, unchanging "rules," instructors and students know better. We know that there are "rules," all right, but that the rules change all the time. "Is it okay to use *I* in essays for this class?" asks one student. "My high school teacher wouldn't let us." "Will more than one comma error flunk an essay?" asks another. These questions show that rules clearly exist, but they also suggest that these rules are always shifting and thus deserve reconsideration.

Research for this textbook shows some of the shifts that have occurred in the last century alone. Mechanical and grammatical questions that no longer concern most people used to be perceived as extremely important. In the late nineteenth century, for instance, instructors at Harvard said that the most serious writing problem their students had was an inability to distinguish between the proper uses of *shall* and *will*. Similarly, split infinitives seemed to many instructors of the 1950s a very serious problem, but at least since the starship *Enterprise* set out "to boldly go" where no one has gone before, split infinitives have wrinkled fewer brows.

These examples of shifting standards do not mean that there is no such thing as "correctness" in writing—only that *correctness always depends on some context*. Correctness is not so much a question of absolute right or wrong as it is a question of the way the choices a writer makes are perceived by readers. The world judges us by our control of the conventions we have agreed to use, and we all know it. As Robert Frost once said of poetry, trying to write without honoring the conventions and agreed-upon rules is like playing tennis without a net.

A major assumption this book makes is that you want to understand and control not only the broad content issues and organizational features of writing but the surface conventions of academic writing as well. Since you already know the vast majority of these conventions, the most efficient way to proceed is to focus on those that are still unfamiliar or puzzling. Achieving this practical focus means identifying, analyzing, and overcoming patterns of surface error in your writing.

Why not decide right now to take charge of your own writing by charting and learning from your errors? This effort should not mean becoming obsessed with errors to the exclusion of everything else in your writing. Perfectly correct writing is, after all, a limited and limiting goal. You want to aim for a perfectly persuasive and enlightening piece of writing—that also happens to be "correct" for the audience and situation it addresses.

To aid you in producing writing that is conventionally correct, look at the twenty most common error patterns (other than misspelling) among U.S. college students. Here they are, listed in the order of occurrence:

Learning from
Your Errors

**www • bedford
stmartins.com/
smhandbook**

For an online
version of the 20
Most Common
Errors with links to
exercises, click on

▶ **20 Common
Errors**

1. missing comma after an introductory element

2. vague pronoun reference

3. missing comma in a compound sentence

4. wrong word

5. missing comma(s) with a nonrestrictive element

6. wrong or missing verb ending

7. wrong or missing preposition

8. comma splice

9. missing or misplaced possessive apostrophe

10. unnecessary shift in tense

11. unnecessary shift in pronoun

12. sentence fragment

13. wrong tense or verb form

14. lack of agreement between subject and verb

15. missing comma in a series

16. lack of agreement between pronoun and antecedent

17. unnecessary comma(s) with a restrictive element

18. fused sentence

19. misplaced or dangling modifier

20. *its/it's* confusion

Statistically, these twenty errors are the ones most likely to result in negative responses from your instructor and other readers. In fact, one instructor begins every new class by telling students that correcting these twenty errors will take care of about 95 percent of the issues that are most bothersome to readers. A brief explanation and examples of each error are given in the following sections, and each error pattern is cross-referenced to at least one place elsewhere in this book where you can find more detail or additional examples.

1   Missing comma after an introductory element

When a sentence opens with an introductory word, phrase, or clause, readers usually need a small pause between the introductory element and the main part of the sentence. Such a pause is most often signaled by a comma.

▶ Frankly, we were baffled by the committee's decision.

▶ In fact, the Philippines consists of more than eight thousand islands.

▶ To tell the truth, I never have liked the Lakers.

▶ Because of its isolation in a rural area surrounded by mountains, Crawford Notch doesn't get many visitors.

▶ Though I gave detailed advice for revising, his draft became only worse.

Short introductory elements do not always need a comma. The test is whether the element seems to need a pause after it. The following sentence, for example, would at first be misunderstood if it did not have a comma—readers would think the introductory phrase was *In German nouns,* rather than *In German.* The best advice is that you will rarely be wrong to add a comma after an introductory element.

●— For more on
commas and
introductory ele-
ments, see 31c,
46b, and 48a.

▶ In German, nouns are always capitalized.

2   Vague pronoun reference

A pronoun like *he, she, it, they, this, that,* or *which* should usually refer clearly to a specific word (or words) elsewhere in the sentence or in a previous sentence. When readers cannot tell for sure whom or what the pronoun refers to, the reference is said to be vague. There are two common kinds of vague pronoun reference. The first occurs when there is more than one word that the pronoun might refer to; the second, when the reference is to a word that is implied but not explicitly stated.

POSSIBLE REFERENCE TO MORE THAN ONE WORD

the latter
▶ Before Mary Grace physically and verbally assaulted Mrs. Turpin, she was
                                                                    ^
a judgmental woman who created her own ranking system of people.

REFERENCE IMPLIED BUT NOT STATED

▶ The troopers burned an Indian camp as a result of the earlier attack.
    destruction of the camp
This was the cause of the war.
    ^

▶ They believe that a zygote, an egg at the moment of fertilization, is as
                                                    such an assertion
deserving of protection as the born human being, but it cannot be
                                                              ^
proven scientifically.

For guidelines on
editing for clear
pronoun refer-
ence, see p. 661.
For more on pro-
noun reference,
see Chapter 37.

3   Missing comma in a compound sentence

A compound sentence is made up of two (or more) parts that could each function as an independent sentence. If there are only two parts, they may be linked by either a semicolon or a coordinating conjunction (*and, but, so, yet, nor, or, for*). When a conjunction is used, a comma should usually be placed before it to indicate a pause between the two thoughts.

▶ The words "I do" may sound simple, but they mean a complex
                                            ^
commitment for life.

▶ We wish dreamily upon a star, and then we look down to see that we have
                                    ^
stepped in the mud.

For further dis-
cussion and
examples of
commas in
compound sen-
tences, see 31d1
and 48b.

In *very* short sentences, this use of the comma is optional if the sentence can be easily understood without it. The following short sentence, however, could be misunderstood if it did not have a comma — readers would think at first that Meredith was wearing her feet. The best advice is to use the comma before the coordinating conjunction because it will always be correct.

▶ Meredith wore jeans, and her feet were bare.

4   Wrong word

Wrong-word errors range from simple lack of proofreading, like using *should* for *would,* to mistakes in basic word meaning, like using *prevaricate* when you mean *procrastinate,* to mistakes in shades of meaning, like using *sedate* when you mean *sedentary.* Many errors marked "wrong word" are *homonyms,* words that are pronounced alike but spelled differently, like *their* and *there.*

●— For guidelines on checking a draft for wrong words, see p. 539. For additional, more detailed information about choosing the right word for your meaning, see Chapter 27.

                    assumed
▶ A knowledge of computers is inherent in his office.
                               ^

                fragrance
▶ Mark noticed the stench of roses as he entered the room.
                     ^

                    allusions
▶ *Paradise Lost* contains many illusions to classical mythology.
                             ^

5   Missing comma(s) with a nonrestrictive element

A nonrestrictive element is a word, phrase, or clause that gives additional information about the preceding part of the sentence but does not restrict or limit the meaning of that part. A nonrestrictive element is not essential to the sentence; it can be deleted without changing the sentence's basic meaning. As an indication that it is not essential, it is always set off from the rest of the sentence with a comma before it and, if it is in the middle of the sentence, after it as well.

●— For additional explanation and examples of commas with nonrestrictive elements, see 48c.

▶ Shahid, who was the president of the club, was first to speak.
        ^   ^

▶ Louis was forced to call a session of the Estates General, which had not
                                                          ^
met for 175 years.

▶ The bottom of the pond was covered with soft brown clay, a natural base
                                                        ^
for a good swimming hole.

The verb endings -s (or -es) and -ed (or -d) are important markers in standard academic English. It is easy to forget these endings in writing because they are not always pronounced clearly when spoken. In addition, some varieties of English do not use these endings in the same way as standard academic English.

▶ *uses*
   Eliot use feline imagery throughout the poem.
        ^

▶ I runs a mile every morning before breakfast.

▶ *dropped*
   The United States drop two atomic bombs on Japan in 1945.
                    ^

▶ *imagined*
   Nobody imagine he would actually become president.
        ^

An -s (or -es) ending must be added to present-tense indicative verbs whose subjects are singular nouns; *he, she,* and *it;* and most indefinite pronouns (such as *anyone, each, everybody, nobody, nothing, someone*). The ending is not added to verbs whose subjects are plural nouns; *I, you, we,* and *they;* and indefinite pronouns that have a plural meaning (such as *both* and *few*). The past-tense and past-participle forms of most verbs must end in -ed (or -d).

For guidelines on ──●
editing for verb
endings, see pp.
618 and 620. For
more on verb
endings, see
Chapter 33 and
34a.

7   Wrong or missing preposition

Many words in English are regularly used with a particular preposition to express a particular meaning; for example, throwing a ball *to* someone is different from throwing a ball *at* someone. The first ball is thrown to be caught; the second, to hurt someone. Using the wrong preposition in such expressions is a common error. Because most prepositions are so short and are not stressed or pronounced clearly in speech, they are also often accidentally left out of writing or mixed up.

▶ The bus committee is trying to set a schedule that will meet the needs of
                                                    on
   most people who rely in public transportation.
                      ^

▶ Anna compared the loss ~~with~~ *to* a kick in the head.

▶ Finally, she refused to comply ~~to~~ *with* army regulations.

▶ In his moral blindness, Gloucester is similar ~~with~~ *to* Lear.

▶ Jo is absolutely enamored ~~with~~ *of* Barbie.

● For guidelines on using prepositions, see p. 847. For additional information about choosing the correct preposition, see 30b6.

8 Comma splice

A comma splice occurs when two (or sometimes more) clauses that could each stand alone as a sentence are written with only a comma between them. Such clauses must be either clearly separated by a punctuation mark stronger than a comma—a period or semicolon—or clearly connected with a word such as *and* or *although,* or else the ideas they state should be combined into one clause.

● For guidelines on editing for comma splices, see p. 672. For additional information about ways to avoid or revise comma splices, see Chapter 39.

▶ Westward migration had passed Wyoming by, even the discovery of gold in nearby Montana failed to attract settlers.

▶ I was strongly attracted to her, *for* she had special qualities.

▶ *Having* ~~They always had~~ roast beef for Thanksgiving, ~~this~~ was a family tradition.

9 Missing or misplaced possessive apostrophe

To show that one thing belongs to another, either an apostrophe and an *-s* or an apostrophe alone is added to the word representing the thing that possesses the other. An apostrophe and *-s* are used for singular nouns (words that refer to one thing, such as *leader* or *Chicago*); for indefinite pronouns (words like *anybody, everyone, nobody, somebody*); and for plural nouns (words referring to more than one thing) that do not end in -*s*, such as *men* and *women*. For plural nouns ending in -*s*, such as *creatures* or *Green Bay Packers*, only the apostrophe is used.

For guidelines
on editing for
possessive apostrophes, see
p. 766. For more
detailed information on possessive apostrophes, see 51a.

▶ Overambitious parents can be very harmful to a childs well-being.
                                                  child's

▶ Randy Johnson is one of the Diamondback's most electrifying pitchers.
                                    Diamondbacks'

10   Unnecessary shift in tense

An unnecessary shift in tense occurs when the verbs in a sentence or passage shift for no reason from one time period to another, such as from past to present or from present to future. Such tense shifts confuse the reader, who must guess which tense is the right one.

For guidelines on
editing for confusing shifts in
tense, see p. 667.
For more on
using verb tenses
in sequence,
see 33g.

▶ Venceslav was watching the great blue heron take off when he
   slipped   fell
   slips and falls into the swamp.

▶ Each team of detectives works on three or four cases at a time. They will
   investigate only those leads that seem most promising.

11   Unnecessary shift in pronoun

An unnecessary pronoun shift occurs when a writer who has been using one kind of pronoun to refer to someone or something shifts to another for no reason. The most common shift in pronoun is from *one* to *you* or *I*. This shift often results from an attempt at a more formal level of diction, which is hard to maintain when it is not completely natural.

For more discussion of unnecessary pronoun
shifts, see 38d.

▶ When one first sees a painting by Georgia O'Keeffe, you sense power
                                           one senses
   and stillness.

▶ If we had known about the ozone layer, you could have banned aerosol
                                     we
   sprays years ago.

12   Sentence fragment

A sentence fragment is a part of a sentence that is written as if it were a whole sentence, with a capital letter at the beginning and a period, question mark, or exclamation point at the end. A fragment lacks one or both of the two essential parts of a sentence, a subject and a complete verb; or else it begins with a subordinating word, which means that it depends for its meaning on another sentence.

LACKING SUBJECT

▶ Marie Antoinette spent huge sums of money on herself and her
        Her extravagance helped
favorites. Helped bring on the French Revolution.
    ^

LACKING COMPLETE VERB

                  was
▶ The old aluminum boat sitting on its trailer.
              ^

BEGINNING WITH SUBORDINATING WORD

                       where
▶ We returned to the drugstore. Where we waited for the rest of the gang.
                   ^

● For guidelines on editing for sentence fragments, see p. 679. For more detailed information on sentence fragments, see Chapter 40.

13   Wrong tense or verb form

One error in tense or verb form is not indicating clearly that the action or condition it expresses is (or was or will be) completed — for example, using *walked* instead of *had walked* or *will go* instead of *will have gone*. In some dialects of English, the verbs *be* and *have* are used in ways that differ significantly from their use by most native speakers; these uses may also be labeled as the wrong verb form. Finally, many errors of this kind occur with verbs whose basic forms for showing past time or a completed action or condition do not follow the regular pattern, like *begin, began, begun* and *break, broke, broken*. Errors may occur when a writer confuses the second and third forms or treats these verbs as if they followed the regular pattern — for example, using *beginned* instead of *began* or *have broke* instead of *have broken*.

> *had*
> Ian was shocked to learn that Joe died only the day before.
> ^

> *is*   *has*
> The poet be looking at a tree when she have a sudden inspiration.
> ^   ^

> *broken*
> Venus Williams has broke many records in tennis.
> ^

> *built*   *brought*
> The Greeks builded a wooden horse that the Trojans bringed into the city.
> ^   ^

For guidelines
on editing verb
tenses, see
p. 629. For more
detailed infor-
mation about
verb tenses and
forms, see 31b1
and Chapters 33
and 34.

14   Lack of agreement between subject and verb

A subject and verb must agree, or match. In many cases, the verb must take a different form depending on whether the subject is singular (one) or plural (more than one): *The old man is angry and stamps into the house* but *The old men are angry and stamp into the house.* Lack of agreement between a subject and verb is often just a matter of leaving the *-s* ending off the verb out of carelessness and failure to proofread, or of using a dialect form that does not have this ending (see errors 6 and 13). Sometimes, however, it results from particular kinds of subjects or sentence constructions.

When other words come between a subject and verb, a writer may mistake the noun nearest to the verb for the verb's real subject. In the following sentence, for example, the subject is the singular *part,* not the plural *goals.*

> *has*
> A central part of my life goals have been to go to law school.
> ^

Other problems can arise from subjects made up of two or more parts joined by *and* or *or;* subjects like *committee* or *jury,* which can take either singular or plural verb forms depending on whether they are treated as a single unit or as multiple individuals; and subjects like *mathematics* and *measles,* which look plural but are singular in meaning.

> My brother and his friend Angel commutes every day from Louisville.

were
▶ The committee ~~was~~ unable to agree among themselves.

has
▶ Measles ~~have~~ become much less common in the United States.

Pronoun subjects cause problems for many writers. Most indefinite pronouns, such as *each, either, neither,* or *one,* take a singular verb. The relative pronouns *who, which,* or *that* take verbs that agree with the word the pronoun refers to.

coordinates
▶ Each of the items in these designs ~~coordinate~~ with the others.

were
▶ Johnson was one of the athletes who ~~was~~ disqualified.

Finally, some problems occur when writers make a verb agree with the word that follows or precedes it rather than with the grammatical subject. In the following sentences, for example, the subjects are *source* and *man,* not *parents* and *curtains.*

was
▶ His only source of income ~~were~~ his parents.

stands
▶ Behind the curtains ~~stand~~ an elderly man producing the wizard's effects.

●── For guidelines on editing for subject-verb agreement, see p. 637. For additional information about subject-verb agreement, see Chapter 34.

15   Missing comma in a series

A series consists of three or more parallel words, phrases, or clauses that appear consecutively in a sentence. Traditionally, all the items in a series are separated by commas. Many newspapers and magazines do not use a comma before the *and* or *or* between the last two items, and some instructors do not require it. Check your instructor's preference, and be consistent in either using or omitting this comma.

▶ Sharks eat mostly squid, shrimp, crabs, and other fish.

▶ You must learn to talk to the earth, smell it, squeeze it in your hands.

●── For more on parallel structures in a series, see 45a. For more on using commas in a series, see 48d.

Learning from
Your Errors

Most pronouns (words like *I, it, you, him, her, this, themselves, someone, who, which*) are used to replace another word (or words) so that it does not have to be repeated. The word that the pronoun replaces or stands for is called its antecedent. Pronouns must agree with, or match, their antecedents in gender—for example, using *he* and *him* to replace *Abraham Lincoln* and *she* and *her* to replace *Queen Elizabeth*. They must also agree with their antecedents in referring to either one person or thing (singular) or more than one (plural)—for example, using *it* to replace *a book* and *they* and *them* to replace *fifteen books*.

Most people have few problems with pronoun-antecedent agreement except with certain kinds of antecedents. These include words like *each, either, neither,* and *one,* which are singular and take singular pronouns; antecedents made up of two or more parts joined by *or* or *nor;* and antecedents like *audience* or *team,* which can be either singular or plural depending on whether they are considered a single unit or multiple individuals.

▶ Every one of the puppies thrived in ~~their~~ *its* new home.

▶ Neither Haivan nor Selena brought ~~their~~ *her* partner to the party.

▶ The team frequently changed ~~its~~ *their* positions to get varied experience.

The other main kind of antecedent that causes problems is a singular antecedent (such as *each* or *an employee*) that could be either male or female. Rather than use masculine pronouns (*he, him,* and so on) with such an antecedent, a traditional rule that excludes or ignores females, a writer should use *he or she, him or her,* and so on, or else rewrite the sentence to make the antecedent and pronoun plural or to eliminate the pronoun.

For guidelines
on editing for
pronoun-
antecedent
agreement, see
p. 646. For addi-
tional informa-
tion about
pronoun-
antecedent
agreement, see
Chapter 35.

▶ Every student must provide his *or her* own uniform.

▶ ~~Every student~~ *All students* must provide his own uniform*s*. *their*

▶ Every student must provide ~~his own~~ *a* uniform.

Learning from Your Errors

A restrictive element is a word, phrase, or clause that restricts or limits the meaning of the preceding part of the sentence; it is essential to the meaning of what precedes it and cannot be left out without changing the sentence's basic meaning. Because of this close relationship, it is *not* set off from the rest of the sentence with a comma or commas.

► An arrangement, for orchestra, was made by Ravel.

► Several groups, opposed to the use of animals for cosmetics testing, picketed the laboratory.

► People, who wanted to preserve wilderness areas, opposed the plan to privatize national parks.

► The vice president succeeds, if and when the president dies or becomes incapacitated.

► Shakespeare's tragedy, *Othello*, deals with the dangers of jealousy.

In the last example above, the appositive is essential to the meaning of the sentence because Shakespeare wrote more than one tragedy.

●— For additional information about restrictive phrases and clauses, see 48c and j.

18 Fused sentence

Fused sentences (sometimes called run-on sentences) are created when two or more groups of words that could each be written as an independent sentence are written without any punctuation between them. Such groups of words must be either divided into separate sentences, by using periods and capital letters, or joined in a way that shows their relationship—by either adding words and punctuation or by rewriting completely.

●— For guidelines on editing for fused sentences, see p. 672. For more information about ways to revise fused sentences, see Chapter 39.

         He
► The current was swift.he could not swim to shore.

         but
► Klee's paintings seem simple,they are also very sophisticated.

         nevertheless,
► She doubted the value of meditation;she decided to try it once.

19 Misplaced or dangling modifier

A misplaced modifier is a word, phrase, or clause that is not placed close enough to the word it describes or is related to. As a result, it seems to modify some other word, phrase, or clause, which may confuse or puzzle readers.

▶ *With binoculars, they*
They could see the eagles swooping and diving~~with binoculars.~~

▶ *When he was ten years old, he*
He had decided he wanted to be a doctor~~when he was ten years old.~~

▶ ~~Slowly and precisely~~ I watched the teller count out the money, *slowly and precisely.*

▶ The architect ~~only~~ wanted to use *only* pine paneling for decoration.

▶ *T*
~~Rising over the trees,~~ the campers saw a bright red sun, *rising over the trees.*

A dangling modifier is a word, phrase, or elliptical clause (a clause from which words have been left out) that is not clearly related to any other word in the sentence. The word that it modifies exists in the writer's mind, but not on paper in the sentence. Such a modifier is called "dangling" because it hangs precariously from the beginning or end of the sentence, attached to nothing very solid.

▶ A doctor should check your eyes for glaucoma every year if *you are* over fifty.

▶ Looking down the stretch of sandy beach, *one sees* people ~~are~~ lying face down trying to get a tan.

▶ *M* *that I, a white male college student,*
~~As a white male college student,~~ many people seem surprised at ~~my~~ support ~~for~~ feminism.

For guidelines
on editing mis-
placed and dan-
gling modifiers,
see p. 684. For
additional infor-
mation on mis-
placed and dan-
gling modifiers,
see 41a and c.

20 Its/It's confusion

The word *its*, spelled without an apostrophe, is the possessive form of *it*, meaning "of it" or "belonging to it." The word *it's*, spelled with an apostrophe, is a shortened form of *it is* or *it has*. Even though with nouns an apostrophe often indicates a possessive form, the possessive form of a pronoun in this case is the one *without* the apostrophe.

▶ **The car is lying on it's side in the ditch.**

▶ **It's a white 2003 BMW.**

For guidelines on
editing for mis-
use of *its* and *it's*,
see 51b.

▶ **It's been lying there for two days.**

**THINKING CRITICALLY ABOUT STRENGTHS AND WEAKNESSES
IN YOUR WRITING**

Continue your writing inventory by analyzing the surface errors (and strengths) in one piece of your writing. (1) Go through your writing, noting all comments, positive or critical, in such areas as spelling, grammar, punctuation, capitalization, and other issues like those discussed in the preceding section. (2) Then go through once more, using the guidelines on the twenty most common errors in this introduction, to add your own observations about strengths and areas that need improvement. (3) Finally, compile a list of both strengths and weaknesses, and decide which areas you plan to work on first. (4) If you are keeping a writing log, enter the results of your writing inventory there.

PART 1

THE ART AND CRAFT OF WRITING

"Writers (our memories and experiences) and the world around us are sources, and it's likely that most anything we write will involve some form of reading and research: for inspiration, for details, for enriching memories, for learning."
— MELISSA GOLDTHWAITE

1

◥ Reading, Writing, and Research

More than two thousand years ago, a Roman writer named Quintilian set out a plan for education, beginning with birth and ending only with old age and death. Surprisingly enough, Quintilian's recipe for a lifelong education has never been more relevant than it is in the twenty-first century. Today some of your biggest challenges as a student will be learning how to learn; how to communicate what you have learned across vast distances, to larger and increasingly diverse sets of audiences; and how to do so while using a wide range of media and genres. Along the way, you will probably be doing more — and more different kinds of — writing than you may have been accustomed to. This chapter will alert you to some of the new opportunities open to college students today and will provide an overview of the ways in which you will be using the communicative arts: writing, reading, speaking, listening, and research. ■

1a Discovering new opportunities for writing

How do you define *writing?* Chances are, you think of writing as putting words on paper or onscreen, and until recently such a definition would have served fairly well. But not today. In fact, it's quite possible that some of the words we use to describe literate practices—*reading, writing, speaking,* and *listening*—are no longer adequate. When you watch and listen to the nightly news, you are in one sense reading the meanings of the events described, and the announcer speaking is likely reading a text that has already been written. Without new words for these complicated and shifting acts, we need to expand our understandings of the old terms. Writing, for example, now includes much more than words, as images and graphics often convey an important part of the meaning. In addition, writing can now include such elements as sound and video streaming. Perhaps more important, writing now often contains many voices, as information from the Web is brought into the texts we write with increasing ease.

Writing in a new century is also often collaborative: you work with a team to produce an illustrated report, on the basis of which the members of the team make a key presentation to management; you and a colleague carry out an experiment, argue over and write up the results together, and present your findings to a class or other gathering; a class project for a business course calls on you and others in your group to divide up the work along lines of expertise and then to pool your efforts in meeting the assignment.

Perhaps most notably, this expanded sense of writing challenges us to think very carefully about what the writing is for and whom it can and will reach. Email provides a good case in point. In the aftermath of the September 11, 2001, attacks on the World Trade Center and the Pentagon, Tamim Ansary, who was born in Afghanistan and now lives in San Francisco, where he writes children's books, found himself stunned by the number of people attacking Arabs or those of Muslim faith, and he sat down to send to friends an email letter expressing his horror at the events, his condemnation of Osama bin Laden and the Taliban, and his hope that people in the United States would not act on the basis of gross stereotyping. The few dozen friends to whom Ansary wrote hit their FORWARD buttons. Within days, the letter had circled the globe more than once, and Ansary's words were published by the Africa News Service, the *Philippine Daily Inquirer*, the *Evening Standard* in London, the *San Francisco Chronicle* and many other papers in the United States — as well as on Internet bulletin boards and Web sites.

As the example of Ansary shows, writers can no longer assume that they write only to a specified audience or that they can easily control the dissemination of their messages. We now live not only in a city, a state, and a country but also in the world — and we write to speakers of many languages, to members of many cultures, to believers of many creeds.

If it is true that "no man [or woman!] is an island," then it is equally true that no piece of writing is an island, isolated and alone. Instead, all writing is connected to a web of other writings and words that it may be extending, responding to, or challenging. Today, when an email message can literally circle the world in seconds, it's important to remember this principle about writing: all writing exists within a broad and rich context in which any writer says or writes something to others for a purpose. The chapters in Part 1 will show you how closely related writing is to reading, speaking, listening, and researching. All of these arts of communication interweave in the act of writing.

FOR COLLABORATION

Working with two other classmates, spend fifteen to twenty minutes writing in response to these questions: How do you define *writing*? List all the ways that you use writing. In what ways has writing changed in, say, the last ten years? What forms of writing seem to be most like talking? Do you ever think visually about a piece of writing — how it will be laid out, designed, formatted, and illustrated? What would you most like to learn to improve your writing? After each of you has written responses to these questions, read them aloud to one another, and spend some time comparing your responses, noting both similarities and differences. Bring your notes and writing to class for discussion.

1b   Considering the processes of writing

You may be familiar with the phrase *writing process* from courses you have taken or textbooks you have used. Indeed, this process may have been presented to you as a linear march from plan to outline to draft to final copy. But most writers will confirm that writing rarely, if ever, proceeds in such a neat, orderly way. Rather, the writing process is a collection of activities that often overlap and sometimes even occur simultaneously. As a result, the process of writing is often described not as linear but as **recursive,** meaning that its goals or stages are constantly flowing into and influencing one another, without any clear break between them. At a given moment, for example, a writer may be deciding how to organize a paragraph. A moment later, that same writer may be using the knowledge gained from that decision to help her revise the wording of a sentence. And while working on the sentence, she might think of a new point to add to the paragraph, which then might encourage her to rethink the paragraph's overall organization.

In many ways, it is inaccurate to envision a single writing process. There are, in fact, as many different writing processes as there are writers — more if you consider that individual writers vary their writing processes each time they sit down to write! Even though the various parts of the writing process overlap, recur, and result in different processes altogether, it can still be useful to look at the parts one by one.

1. *Planning.* During this stage, you consider the **rhetorical situation** (the full context in which a piece of writing occurs); the **purpose** of the writing (Is it to learn material for a take-home exam? to demonstrate your knowledge to an instructor? to connect to an audience in order to offer an explanation or an argument?); and the **audience,** or particular readers, you are addressing. Planning also calls for a preliminary investigation of your topic: brainstorming, reading, browsing online resources, or talking to friends and classmates about your ideas. (See Chapter 2.)

2. *Exploring and researching.* Writing worth reading often starts with a nagging question or puzzle or idea that calls for some **exploration** — thinking about what you already know, coming up with a working thesis (see 3b), gathering information. Depending on the writing task at hand, exploration may last an hour or a month. If you have to write a

one-page essay in class about your family, you will probably jot down a few notes and start writing fairly quickly. If, on the other hand, you have six weeks to prepare a fifteen-page paper on current U.S.–Japanese trade relations, you will need to do some research and explore the topic thoroughly. (See Chapter 3.)

r/w/r

1b 33

3. *Organizing and designing.* Sometimes an **organizational plan** will occur to you at an early stage, helping to shape your thesis and direct any more research you need to do. More often, though, a plan will grow out of the thesis or your search for information. Part of a writer's job today includes thinking carefully about how to design as well as organize a piece of writing: What visuals will be included? Will color be used? What role will white space play in the design? Answering these and other questions (see Chapter 8) helps you think effectively about the presentation or delivery of your writing. However your plan for organization and design develops and however tentative it is, it should act as a guide as you produce a first draft.

●— For advice on composing a Web-based document, see Chapter 9.

4. *Drafting.* No matter how thoroughly you have explored your topic, you will almost certainly discover more about it while drafting. Sometimes these new insights will cause you to turn back — to change your organizational plan, to find new information, to approach the subject from a new angle, to rethink the way you appeal to your audience, even to reconsider your purpose. **Drafting,** then, is *not* just putting ideas down on paper. More often than not, it involves coming up with new ideas. Because writing a draft is just one part of this overall recursive process, experienced writers rarely try to make their writing come out perfectly the first time. The goal of drafting is not a final copy or even a version good enough to show someone else. Smooth sentences and ideal wording can come later; in your first draft, just write until you run out of ideas to explore. (See 3f.)

5. *Reviewing.* **Reviewing** calls for you to look at your draft with a very critical eye, seeing it anew and deciding if it accomplishes your original goals. Unlike editing or correcting, reviewing means examining the draft to reassess the main ideas, the organization, the structure of paragraphs, the variety of sentences, the choice of words, the attitudes toward topic and audience, the thoroughness with which the topic is developed. In addition to analyzing the draft yourself, you should get responses from other people — friends, classmates, your instructor, a tutor in the writing center, or members of online communities you belong to.

6. *Revising.* **Revising** involves reworking your draft on the basis of the review. It also means polishing to achieve memorable prose. It may mean writing new sentences, moving paragraphs, eliminating sections, doing additional research, or even choosing a new topic and starting over. (See 4g.)

7. *Editing, formatting, and proofreading.* **Editing** involves making what you have written ready for the world, which means making it meet those conventions of written form usually referred to as "correctness."

Sentence structure, spelling, mechanics, punctuation—all should ordinarily meet conventional standards. Editing may sometimes lead you to reconsider an idea, a paragraph, a transition, or an organizational pattern—and you could wind up planning or drafting once again. While you edit, you also need to make final decisions about document **format** and design: What font will you use? Will you use color or other visual devices? When all editing and formatting are done and you have a final text, you then must spell-check and **proofread** it to catch and correct any typographical errors. (See 4i and j.)

You probably already have a characteristic writing process, and one of the best ways to improve this process is to analyze it from time to time in a **writing log**—a computer file or notebook in which you jot down your thoughts about a writing project while you are working on it, after you have feedback from your peers, after you have completed it, and after you have gotten it back from your instructor. Studying your notes on your writing process will help you identify patterns of strength and weakness in your writing. Answering the following questions can help get you started on this task. Try to revisit these questions periodically to see how your writing process changes over time and depending on the type of writing situation or assignment.

- How do you typically go about preparing for a writing assignment?
- When and where do your best ideas often come to you?
- Where do you usually write? Are you usually alone and in a quiet place, or is there music, conversation, or other sound in the background?
- What materials do you use—a computer? pen or pencil? notepad? What do you find most and least helpful about your materials?
- What audience do most assignments ask you to address? the instructor? classmates? a wider audience? How much thought do you typically give to your audience?
- What strategies do you typically use to explore a topic?
- How do you usually go about writing a first draft? Do you finish in one sitting, or do you prefer to work in sections?
- How do you typically go about revising, and what do you pay most attention to as you revise?
- If you get stuck while writing, what do you usually do to get moving again?
- What would you say is most effective about your writing and your writing process?
- What about your writing and your writing process worries you? What specific steps can you take to address these worries?
- What is your favorite part of your writing process—and why?

● **EXERCISE 1.1**

Take a few moments to remember all the writing you did when you were applying
to college: the letters you wrote, the forms you completed, and so on. In a brief
paragraph, describe this writing, and speculate on how it may have helped you
gain admission to the college(s) that accepted you.

1c Considering the processes of reading

If you have ever read a book or seen a movie about Helen Keller, you will
remember the electrifying moment when she first learns to read, when
she first realizes that the symbols traced in her palm contain meanings.
So it is with all readers, for all of us build imagined worlds—virtual
realities—from words and images. Think of a time when you were reading alone and suddenly realized that you were not understanding what
you were reading but just looking at marks on a page or a screen. Only
when you went back and concentrated on the meanings of those words
(and images) were you really reading.

■ *Reading as a writer*

Since reading is closely related to writing, one good way to improve your
writing is by paying close attention to what you read, taking tips from
writers you especially admire. Throughout, this handbook will be examining the work of well-known writers to see how they accomplish what they
set out to do, to see what they do with the strategies you yourself will be
practicing. In addition, many chapters include exercises asking you to read
a passage with a writer's eye for some element—use of adjectives, dashes,
repetition, and so on. These exercises are designed to help you learn to use
these elements in your own writing to make it more accurate and effective.

■ *Reading online*

Writers today do a great deal of their reading online—using a library's
online holdings, browsing the Web, and so on. And while some reading
processes online are similar to reading print text, there are some important differences. Most notable, perhaps, is the need to read in a kind of
layered way, scrolling through long texts while following a complex set
of hyperlinks, which may use sound, video, and other images. Reading
on a computer screen requires close concentration and a different way of
proceeding because an online text has no clear beginning, middle, and
ending. Research shows that online readers are very picky about what

**www • bedford
stmartins.com/
smhandbook**

For more
information on
reading online,
click on

▶ Links
   ▶ Working Online

they actually read and that skimming is very common. They are also likely to want to control the text rather than be guided by it, choosing to leap back and forth or to find their own paths. Finally, while it seems that online readers do pay attention to the visual elements of a text, recent research conducted by the Poynter Institute, an organization devoted to journalism, raises some questions about just how this relationship works. In its eye-tracking studies, Poynter found that print news readers' eyes go first to photos and graphics. But when researchers studied readers of online news, they found something different: in this medium, readers turned to news briefs and captions first. In short, online readers of the news are gathering information, and they are doing so through words first, pictures second.

When you read online, keep notes on where your eyes go first and what you focus on, sketching a portrait of your online reading self. Do your eye movements vary depending on the type of site (news reading versus browsing an online catalog, for example) and the kind of information you hope or expect to find? Paying attention to your own eye movements can sharpen your critical-reading abilities by helping you identify what the Web site designer thinks is most important and is thus trying to draw to your attention quickly. Taking note of how you read online can also help you consider your own online readers when you create Web text. (See Chapter 9.)

Many Web sites—and especially news sites—offer you the opportunity to click on a button for a print-friendly, or text-only, version of the story. Use this option if your interest in reading the article is primarily with the text rather than the visuals. This option also makes it easier to save a copy of what you are reading in one easy step by selecting from your browser's FILE menu the SAVE AS command.

CONSIDERING DISABILITIES: Screen Readers

Keep in mind that many people who are blind or vision-impaired use screen readers, software programs that scan text and read it aloud, and thus can't access "styled" texts well. These texts include those saved as HTML and those with fancy fonts, colored fonts, and overly large fonts.

When forwarding emails it is best to remove any beginning-of-line carets (">") since these are often read—each and every one—as "greater than" by a screen-reading program. Always give a brief and descriptive subject line in an email; blind and vision-impaired users who might be reading your mail with a screen-reading program benefit greatly from such pointed information.

Writer Anatole Broyard once cautioned readers about the perils of "just walking through" a text. A good reader, he suggested, "stomps around" in a book or onscreen — highlighting passages, scribbling in the margins, jotting questions and comments. The following guidelines can help you do more than "just walk through" your reading.

WRITING

Considering the Processes of Reading

●── For more information on reading and evaluating online sources, see 16b; for more on thinking critically, see Chapter 11.

SOME GUIDELINES FOR CRITICAL READING

PREVIEWING

→ Determine your purpose for reading. Is it to gather information for an assignment? to determine whether a source will be useful for a research project? to study for a test? to prepare for class discussion?

→ Consider the title. What does it tell you about what is to come?

→ Think about what you already know about the subject. What opinions do you hold on this subject? What do you hope to learn?

→ What do you know about the author? What is the author's purpose? What expertise does he or she have on this subject? What biases might he or she have?

→ Look at how the text is structured. Are there subdivisions? Where are visuals placed, and what effect might they have? Read over any headings. Skim the opening sentences of each paragraph.

→ Decide what you think the main point or theme of the text will be.

READING AND ANNOTATING

→ Identify key points, important terms, recurring images, and interesting ideas, either by underlining them or by making notes in the margin. If you are reading online, you can often annotate Web pages or bookmarks you have created (see 16e6). You can also use word-processing programs to annotate texts you have downloaded. In all cases, be careful not to blur the lines between the original text and your comments.

→ Mark places that are confusing or that you want to reread.

→ Note any statements that you disagree with or question and any counterevidence or counterarguments that occur to you.

→ Note any sources used in the text.

SUMMARIZING

→ Summarize the main points. Do they match your expectations? (16e4)

→ Jot down any ideas you want to remember, questions you want to raise, and ideas for how you may use this material.

(Continued on p. 38)

(Continued from p. 37)

ANALYZING

→ Identify evidence that supports or illustrates the main point or theme, as well as any that seems to contradict it.

→ Consider the relationship between the words and visuals in the text. Are they well integrated, or are they sometimes at odds with one another? What function(s) do the visuals serve — to capture attention? to provide more detailed information or illustrations? to appeal to readers' emotions?

→ Decide whether the sources used are trustworthy.

→ Identify the writer's underlying assumptions about the subject, as well as any biases revealed in the text. (See Chapter 11.)

TALKING WITH OTHERS

→ Compare your understanding of the text with that of some classmates.

→ Pinpoint any differences between your interpretation of main points and that of your classmates.

→ Take turns saying what is most memorable about the reading, what is most confusing or unclear, and what you would like to know more about.

REREADING

→ Reread quickly to be sure you have understood the reading, keeping in mind any alternative views offered by your classmates.

→ Identify the author's purpose. Was that purpose accomplished?

→ Determine whether all the questions you had during the first reading have been answered.

RESPONDING

→ Think about the reading as a whole. What did you like best about it? What puzzled or irritated you? Were your expectations met? If not, why not? What more would you like to know about the subject?

→ Note what you have learned about effective writing from this reading. If you keep a writing log, record your notes there.

● **EXERCISE 1.2**

Following the preceding guidelines, read one of the assigned essays from your course text or the student essay in Chapter 4 or Chapter 13 of this book. Summarize the reading briefly, and note any thoughts you have about your critical reading process (in your writing log, if you keep one).

The reading and writing you do in college are part of what we broadly think of as research: your own *re*curring search — that is, your own on-going search for knowledge. In fact, much of the work you do in college turns this sometimes informal search into various kinds of more formal research. An idea that comes to you over pizza, for example, may lead you to conduct a survey that in turn becomes an important piece of evidence in a research project for your sociology class.

Many of your writing assignments will require extensive or formal research. Even if you know the topic very well, your research will be an important tool for establishing credibility with your audience and thus gaining their confidence in you as a writer.

WRITING

Remembering the Importance of Talking and Listening

●— For a complete discussion of research, see Chapters 14 – 19.

1e Remembering the importance of talking and listening

For a number of reasons, the arts of language — reading, writing, speaking, and listening — are often treated separately in school. As printed or electronic text has taken on more and more importance in our society, reading and writing have come to take precedence over talking and listening in most formal education.

Recent developments in media and technology, however, have made it seem both impractical and unwise to draw strict boundaries among these arts. After all, writers are always readers of their own texts; they may also hear their texts read aloud, and they may read or speak them aloud themselves. To take a familiar example, when we watch a presidential State of the Union Address, we appear to be listening. But we are also "reading" the president's presentation — his facial expressions, gestures, and other body language. And if we go on to think about or otherwise interpret the address, then in some sense we may be said to be "writing" as well. Moreover, the president is almost always reading a carefully crafted written text and listening to the responses of the live audience and perhaps even to electronic cues from his advisors in order to make minute changes in his delivery.

1 Talking to learn

In your college work, you will do plenty of talking and listening, and those activities will add immeasurably to the quality of your thinking and learning. Throughout, this text encourages you to talk over your work with others, to engage in collaborative learning, and to speak purposefully in all your classes. Talking in this way can help you in all of the following areas:

- making points you can use later
- explaining your ideas to others and getting immediate feedback
- testing out ideas to see how others, including your instructor, will respond
- working out problems with writing and other assignments
- putting what you learn into your own words
- warming up for writing or reading assignments

2 Listening to learn

The flip side of talking is listening, an art that is of tremendous importance to success in personal relationships as well as in college. You can maximize the value of listening if you use these tips:

- *Really* listen—consistently and attentively. Practicing this kind of concentration will yield surprisingly quick results.
- Try to listen purposefully. Concentrate on the big points and on what you most need to know.
- Ask questions that will yield answers worth listening to, that will help you get the information you need.
- Take notes. Try to repeat information in your own words.

3 Using spoken and written language appropriately

Writing is linked to talking in important ways, particularly if the speaker is a political leader or a talk-show host working on television or radio—or anyone using technologies that tend to blur distinctions between speech and writing (such as email). In spite of their close connection, however, spoken and written forms don't always mix well. In most college writing, stick primarily to written forms of standard academic English (see p. 48), inserting spoken forms only to quote others, to capture the sounds and rhythms of speech, or to create other special effects. Even in making oral presentations, you will probably want to write out your presentation to make sure it is clear and accessible.

For a discussion
of oral presentations, see Chapter 10.

In much college work, good note-taking is a kind of survival skill; and learning how to take notes most effectively will add to your success as a critical reader, writer, and listener. Here are some guidelines to help you review your own note-taking processes.

WRITING
Taking Notes

• For guidelines on taking notes while doing research, see 14g and Chapter 16.

• *Consider your purpose.* Are you taking down a quotation that you intend to use in an essay? recording key words and phrases in outline form during a lecture to use when you study for an exam? recording the major points in a reading assignment, using your own words, paraphrases, or summaries in preparation for a class discussion? noting your personal responses and reactions to something you are reading, looking for an idea you may turn into the beginning of an essay? Knowing your purpose in note-taking can help you decide exactly what you should write down.

• *Consider your own style.* Do you think best with pencil in hand or a keyboard, stopping often as you read to jot down an idea or writing notes almost continuously as you listen to a lesson or lecture? Or does the act of writing distract you so you lose track of what you are reading or hearing? Thinking about these questions can help you decide whether you should take notes while reading and listening—or whether it is more effective for you to listen or read first and then take notes soon thereafter.

• If you are taking notes while reading or attending a lecture, *look for the major points, and note their relationships to one another.* When you want to recall information from a reading or a lecture, a series of random jottings is usually less helpful than a series of clearly related points.

• *Label your notes* so that you can remember where they came from. If you are taking notes in class, simply head the sheet of paper with the course title and date. If you are taking notes from a printed source, note the book's or the article's author, title, and place and date of publication. If you are taking notes from an online document, write down the precise electronic address as well as the date and time of your access. If you are taking personal notes, consider heading the page with a label reminding you of the purpose for the notes.

CONSIDERING DISABILITIES: Note-Taking

Remember that we learn in a very wide range of ways and that note-taking may be more difficult for some students than for others. Especially for dense or hard-to-understand material, consider working with classmates to share and compare notes. Doing so will give all of you new perspectives on the material covered in class.

One good way to recognize differences in degree between spoken and written language is to record yourself and a friend in casual conversation for half an hour or so. Listen to the tape, choose a five-minute segment, and transcribe it word for word, trying to get down exactly what you said. You may have to invent some spellings to capture your speech accurately. Then choose a two-page example of your writing that you think represents some of your best work. Compare the two samples, noting differences in the occasion or purpose for speaking or writing, in content, in sentence types, and in word choice. What differences can you note between your own speaking and writing?

■ Considering Rhetorical Situations

2a Deciding to write

Because elements like purpose and audience are such important considerations in effective writing, you should start thinking about them at an early stage, as soon as you make the decision to write. In a general sense, of course, this decision is often made for you. Your editor sets a deadline for your newspaper story; a professor announces that a research project is due next month; your employer asks for a full report on a complex issue before the next management meeting. But even in such situations, consciously *deciding to write* is important. Experienced writers report that making up their minds to begin a writing task represents a big step toward getting the job done.

2b Identifying a problem

When a topic is left open, many writers put off getting started because they can't think of or decide on the topic. Experienced writers say that the best way to choose a topic is literally to let the topic choose you. That is, the subjects that compel you — that puzzle, confuse, irritate, or in some way pose a problem for you — are likely to engage your interests and hence evoke your best writing. You can begin to identify a problem by thinking through the following questions:

W hat do an engaging magazine article, a letter that leads to a correction in your Visa bill, and a successful proposal for a scientific research grant all have in common? Most likely, the writers of all three have analyzed their rhetorical situations astutely and then responded to them in appropriate ways. The **rhetorical situation** is made up of a number of important elements: the writing assignment (if any), the writer's purpose(s) and stance toward the topic, the audience for which the writing is intended, and the genre of writing and kind of language these elements seem to call for. And now electronic contexts bring many new rhetorical questions to consider. This chapter will get you started in thinking about these crucial elements of any writing situation. ■

- What topics do you wish you knew more about?
- What topics are most likely to get you fired up?
- What about one of these topics is most confusing to you? most exciting? most irritating? most tantalizing?
- What person or group might this topic raise problems for?

Remember that regardless of the topic you choose, it must be manageable. To limit your topic to a manageable size, make the topic as explicit as possible (rather than "The war in Afghanistan," for example, narrow it to "The use of special forces in the Kabul area").

For help with
limiting a topic,
see Chapter 14.

EXERCISE 2.1

Think back to a recent writing assignment. What helped you finally decide to write? Once you had decided to write, what exactly did you do to get going? In a paragraph or two, describe your situation, and answer these questions. Then compare your description with those of two or three classmates.

2c Understanding writing assignments

Most on-the-job writing addresses specific purposes, audiences, and topics: a group of scientists produces a report on food additives for the federal government; an editorial assistant composes a memo summarizing the problems in a new manuscript for an editor; a team of psychologists prepares video scripts intended to help companies deal with alcoholism among their employees. These writers all have one thing in common: specific goals. They know why, for whom, and about what they are writing.

College writing assignments, in contrast, may seem to appear out of the blue, with no specific purpose, audience, or topic. In extreme cases, they may be only one word long, as in a theater examination that consisted of the single word *Tragedy!* At the opposite extreme come assignments in the form of fully developed, very specific cases, often favored in business and engineering courses.

In between the one-word exam and the fully developed case, you may get assignments that specify purpose but not audience — to write an essay arguing for or against censorship on the Internet, for example. Or you may be given an organizational pattern to use — to compare and contrast two of the novels you have read in a course — but no specific topic. Because comprehending an assignment accurately and fully is cru-

→ *What exactly does the assignment ask you to do?* Look for words like *analyze, classify, compare, contrast, describe, discuss, define, explain,* and *survey.* Remember that these words may differ in meaning among disciplines — *analyze* might mean one thing in literature, another in biology.

→ *What knowledge or information do you need?* Do you need to do any research? (3a and c)

→ *Do you need to gather illustrations or other visuals?* What purpose will they serve? (3d)

→ *How can you limit — or broaden — the topic or assignment to make it more interesting?* Do you have interest in or knowledge about any particular aspect of the topic? Be sure to check with your instructor if you wish to redefine the assignment in any way.

→ *What problem(s) does the topic suggest to you?* How might the problem(s) give you an interesting angle on the topic? (2b)

→ *What are the assignment's specific requirements?* Consider genre, length, format, organization, and deadline. Being sure of such things will help you know the scope expected. Your instructor is not likely to expect extensive library research for a paper due in twenty-four hours, for example. If no length is designated, ask for some guidelines. (2c and e)

→ *What is your purpose as a writer?* Do you need to demonstrate knowledge of certain material? Do you mainly need to show your ability to express certain ideas clearly? (2d)

→ *Who is the audience for this writing?* Does the task imply that you will *assume* a particular readership besides your instructor? (2h)

cial to your success in responding to it, you should always make every effort to do so.

In this and the next two chapters, we will follow the work of Emily Lesk on an essay for her first-year English course at Stanford University. Her class was given the assignment "Explore the ways in which one or more media (television, print advertising, and so on) have affected an aspect of American identity, and discuss the implications of your findings for you and your readers."

Emily saw that the assignment was broad enough to allow her to focus on something that interested her, and she knew that the key word *explore* invited her to examine — and analyze — an aspect of American identity that was of special interest to her. Her instructor said to assume

rhet

46 **2d**

WRITING

Considering
Rhetorical
Situations

that she and members of the class would be the primary audience for this essay.

● **EXERCISE 2.2**

The following assignment was given to an introductory business class: "Discuss in an essay the contributions of the Apple and Microsoft companies to the personal computing industry." What would you need to know about the assignment in order to respond successfully? Using the questions in 2c, analyze this assignment.

2d Deciding on your purposes

The writing of college essays, reports, and other assignments almost always involves multiple purposes. On one level, you are writing to establish your credibility with your instructor, to demonstrate that you are a careful thinker and an effective writer. On another level, though, you are writing to achieve goals of your own, to say as clearly and forcefully as possible what you think about a topic.

For example, if you are writing an essay about free speech on campus, your purposes might be to inform your readers, to persuade them to support or oppose speech codes, or even to clarify in your own mind the issues related to free speech on college campuses and the moral debate over them. If you are writing a profile of your eccentric grandfather, you might be trying to amuse your readers and to pay tribute to someone who has been important to you.

In ancient Rome, the great orator Cicero noted that a good speech generally fulfills one of three major purposes: to delight, to teach, or to move. Today, our purposes when we communicate with one another remain pretty much the same: we seek to *entertain* (delight), to *inform and explain* (teach), and to *persuade or convince* (move).

Most of the writing you do in college will address one or some of these purposes, and it is thus important for you to be able to recognize the overriding purpose of any piece of writing. If, for example, a history professor asks you to explain the events that led up to the 1964 Civil Rights Act (primary purpose: to explain) and you write an impassioned argument on the need for the act (primary purpose: to persuade), you have misunderstood the purpose of the assignment.

For most college writing, you should consider purpose in terms of the *assignment,* the *instructor's expectations,* and *your own goals.*

→ *What is the primary purpose of the assignment* — to entertain? to explain? to persuade? or some other purpose? What does this purpose suggest about the best ways to achieve it? If you are unclear about the primary purpose, have you talked with your instructor about it? Are there any secondary purposes to keep in mind?

→ *What are the instructor's purposes in giving this assignment* — to make sure you have read certain materials? to determine whether you understand certain materials? to evaluate your thinking and writing abilities? to determine whether you can evaluate certain materials critically? How can you fulfill these expectations?

→ *What are your goals in carrying out this assignment* — to meet the instructor's expectations? to learn as much as possible about a new topic? to communicate your ideas as clearly and forcefully as possible? How can you achieve these goals?

As she considered the assignment (on p. 45), Emily Lesk saw that her primary purpose was to explain the significance and implications of her topic to herself and to her readers, but she recognized some other purposes as well. Because this essay was assigned early in the term, she wanted to get off to a good start; thus one of her purposes was to write as well as she could to demonstrate her ability to her classmates and her instructor. In addition, she decided that she wanted to find out something new about herself and to use this knowledge to get her readers to think about themselves.

FOR COLLABORATION

Working with two other members of your class, choose one of the following assignments, and describe its various purposes. Take notes during your collaborative work, and bring them to class for discussion.

1. Compare two book-length studies of Malcolm X.

2. Discuss the controversies surrounding the use of genetic engineering to change characteristics of unborn children.

3. Analyze the use of headlines in a group of twenty advertisements.

4. Describe a favorite spot in your hometown.

5. Explain the concept of virtual reality.

For more infor-
mation on devel-
oping a claim,
see 11f.

2e Considering genre and academic discourse

Most of the writing you do in college will fall into the broad genre of academic discourse. Thus you can benefit from considering what distinguishes academic discourse from other **genres,** or kinds, of writing, such as poetry, drama, fiction, business correspondence, or advertising copy, to name but a few examples. The **academic writing** you do most often will have the following characteristics:

- *standard academic English,* characterized by the conventional use of grammar, spelling, punctuation, and mechanics
- *reader-friendly organization,* which introduces and links ideas clearly so that readers can easily follow the text — or hypertext
- *a clearly stated claim, or debatable statement, supported by various kinds of information,* including examples, statistics, personal experiences, anecdotes, and authority
- *conventional academic formats,* among them lab reports, literature reviews, research essays, and, increasingly, Web-based projects
- *a conventional and easy-to-read type size and typeface*

2f Considering language

Although most of your college writing will be done in standard academic English, some of it may demand that you use specialized occupational or professional varieties of English — those characteristic of med-

FOR MULTILINGUAL WRITERS: Bringing in Other Languages

Even when you write in English, you may want or need to include words, phrases, or whole passages in another language. If so, consider whether your readers will understand that language and whether you need to provide a translation, as in this example from John (Fire) Lame Deer's "Talking to the Owls and Butterflies":

> Listen to the air. You can hear it, feel it, smell it, taste it. *Woniya waken* — the holy air — which renews all by its breath. *Woniya, woniya waken* — spirit, life, breath, renewal — it means all that.

In this instance, translation is necessary because the phrase Lame Deer is discussing has multiple meanings in English. (See 26f for details about how to provide translations in your text.)

icine, say, or computer science or law or music. Similarly, you may wish to use regional or ethnic varieties of English to catch the sound of someone's spoken words. You may even need to use words from a language other than English—in quoting someone, perhaps, or in using certain technical terms. In considering your use of language, think about what languages and varieties of English will be most appropriate for reaching your audience and accomplishing your purposes.

WRITING
Focusing on Your
Audience

For a discussion
of using different
varieties of En-
glish and other
languages, see
Chapter 26.

● **EXERCISE 2.3**

Consider a writing assignment you are currently working on. What are its purposes in terms of the assignment, the instructor, and you, the writer? What genre, or kind, of writing does it call for?

2g   Considering your rhetorical stance

"Where do you stand on that?" is a question often asked, particularly of those running for office or occupying positions of authority. But as writers, we must ask the question of ourselves as well. Understanding where you stand on your topic, your **rhetorical stance,** has several advantages: it will help you examine where your opinions come from and thus help you address the topic fully; it will help you see how it might differ from the stances held by members of your audience; and it will help you establish your credibility with that audience. This part of your rhetorical stance—your **ethos** or credibility—helps determine how well your message will be received. To be credible, you will need to do your homework on your subject, present your information fairly and honestly, and be respectful of your audience.

A student writing a proposal for increased services for people with disabilities, for instance, knew that having a brother with Down syndrome gave her an intense interest that her audience might not have in this topic. She would need to work hard, then, to get her audience to understand—and share—her stance.

2h   Focusing on your audience

We know that skilled writers consider their audiences carefully. In fact, one of the characteristic traits of a mature writer is the ability to write for a variety of audiences, using language, style, and evidence appropriate to

→ What is your overall attitude toward the topic? approval? dislike? curiosity? indifference? How strong are your opinions?

→ What social, political, religious, personal, or other influences have contributed to your attitude?

→ How much do you know about the topic? What questions do you have about it?

→ What interests you *most* about the topic? Why?

→ What interests you *least* about it? Why?

→ What seems important — or unimportant — about the topic?

→ What preconceptions, if any, do you have about it?

→ What do you expect to conclude about the topic?

particular readers. The key word here is *appropriate:* just as a funeral director would hardly greet a bereaved family with "Hi, there! What can I do for you?" neither would you be likely to sprinkle jokes through an analysis of child abuse written for a PTA. Such behavior would be wildly inappropriate given the nature of your audience.

Although an instructor may serve as the primary audience for much of your college writing, you may sometimes find yourself writing for others: lab reports addressed to your class, business proposals addressed to a hypothetical manager, or information searches posted to an online audience that is potentially so vast that making any hard and fast assumptions about its members is impossible. Nevertheless, every writer can benefit from thinking carefully about who the audience is, what the audience already knows or thinks, and what the audience needs and expects to find out.

In addition to her instructor, Emily Lesk's audience included the members of her writing class. Thinking about her classmates, Emily saw that they were mostly her age; that they included African American, Latino/Latina, American Indian, and Caucasian students; and that they came from many areas of the country. She was sure that they had many differences, which she would learn about as they all worked together.

1 Addressing specific audiences

Thinking systematically about your audience can help you make decisions about a writing assignment. For example, it can help you decide

→ What person or group do you most want to reach? your boss? other students? scientists? people already sympathetic to your views? people unsympathetic to your views? potential voters? an online group you belong to — or don't belong to?

→ How much do you know about your audience? In what ways may its members differ from you? from one another? Think in terms of education, geographical region, age, gender, occupation, social class, ethnic and cultural heritage, politics, religion, marital status, sexual orientation, disabilities, and so on. (See Chapter 25.)

→ What assumptions can you make about your audience members? What might they value? Think about qualities such as brevity, originality, conformity, honesty, security, adventure, wit, seriousness, thrift, generosity, and so on. What goals and aspirations do they have? Remember that the Internet now allows you to reach countless readers, so you need to take special care to examine how — and if — such distant readers will understand references, allusions, and so on.

→ What languages and varieties of English do your audience members know and use? What special language, if any, will they expect you to use? (See Chapter 26.)

→ What stance do your audience members have toward your topic? What are they likely to know about it? What preconceived views might they have?

→ What is your relationship to the audience? Is it student to instructor? friend to friend? employee to employer? citizen to community? something else?

→ What is your attitude toward the audience? Do you feel friendly? hostile? neutral? admiring? impatient?

→ What attitudes will audience members expect you to hold? What attitudes might disturb or offend them?

→ What kind(s) of response(s) do you want to evoke?

what sort of organizational plan to follow (you might choose one that would be easiest for a particular audience to understand), what information to include or exclude, and even what specific words to use. If you are writing an article for a journal for nurses about a drug that prevents patients from developing infections from intravenous feeding tubes, you will not need to give much information about how such tubes work or to define many terms. But if you are writing about the same topic in a pamphlet for patients, you will have to give a great deal of background information and define (or avoid) technical terms.

● **EXERCISE 2.4**

To experiment with how considerations of appropriateness for a particular audience affect what you write, describe one of your courses to three audiences: your best friend, your parents, and a group of high school students attending an open house at your college. Then describe the differences in content, organization, and wording that the differences in audience led you to make.

2 Appealing to your whole audience

All writers need to pay very careful attention to the ways in which their writing can either invite readers to participate as part of the audience or leave them out. Look at the following sentence:

> As every schoolchild knows, the world is losing its rain forests at the rate of one acre per second.

The writer here gives a clear message about who is—and who is not—part of the audience: if you don't know this fact or have reason to suspect it is not true, you are not invited to participate.

There are various ways you, as a writer, can help make readers feel they are part of your audience. Be especially careful with the pronouns you use, the assumptions you make, and the kinds of support you offer for your ideas.

CONSIDERING DISABILITIES: Your Whole Audience

Remember that considering your whole audience means thinking about members with varying abilities and special needs. If you are writing to veterans in a VA hospital or to a senior citizens group, for example, you can be sure that most will be living with some form of disability. But it's very likely that *any* audience will include those with disabilities, from anorexia to dyslexia, multiple sclerosis, or attention deficit disorder. Current figures indicate there were approximately 54 million Americans living with a disability in the year 2000; this averages one in five Americans! All writers need to think carefully about how their words reach out and connect with such very diverse audiences.

■ Using appropriate pronouns

The pronouns you use can include or exclude readers. Study the following example:

As U.S. citizens, we have an absolute constitutional right to bear arms.

The sentence implies that all of "us" Americans agree that "we" have the right to carry guns. But what if you are not in favor of this proposition? Then this language is likely to make you feel even more antagonistic, because the writer is speaking for you in ways you don't like. This statement also excludes those who are not U.S. citizens. As a writer, use *we* to include your readers only when those you are addressing really fall into the group you are implying.

■ Making no unfounded assumptions

Be careful about any assumptions you make about your readers and their views, especially in the use of language that may unintentionally exclude readers you want to include. Use words like *naturally* and *of course* carefully, for what seems natural to you — that English should be the official U.S. language, for instance, or that smoking should be outlawed — may not seem at all natural to some members of your audience. The best advice about any audience you wish to address is to take nothing about them for granted.

■ Offering appropriate evidence

The examples and other evidence you offer in support of your arguments can help draw in your readers. The student mentioned in 2g, for example, who was writing about services for people with disabilities, might ask readers who have no personal experience with the topic to imagine themselves in a wheelchair, trying to enter a building with steps but no ramp. She would be clearly inviting them to be part of her audience and would be helping them accept her ideas. On the other hand, inappropriate evidence can leave readers out. Complex statistical evidence might well appeal to public-policy planners but may bore or even irritate ordinary citizens.

●⸺ For more about building common ground with an audience, see Chapter 25.

WRITING

Considering
Rhetorical
Situations

Before the advent of writing systems, the contexts for communication were always oral, what many now call *f2f,* or face-to-face. Contexts for oral exchanges still vary widely (from an intimate dinner conversation, say, to a formal lecture), but written scripts have made these contexts ever more varied. Today, with the wide availability of personal computers, the possibilities for written communication can seem almost endless, as children in Alaskan villages exchange email with counterparts in Samoa or as teams of investigators around the world converse simultaneously online to solve a mutual problem.

Although the contexts for online communication are changing and multiplying daily, what can we say about them as they currently exist?

First, *online contexts offer many new ways to get information and join conversations.* As a result, you will need to learn to manage large amounts of information and to sharpen your critical-thinking skills so that you are able to distinguish what is reliable, accurate, and useful to you.

Second, *online contexts are primarily public.* List managers, institutional officers, often anyone with technical know how or even just access to your name can retrieve past email you have sent. What may seem like a private email conversation is routinely archived and accessible, as was the case with messages sent between Microsoft employees, which were later used in the Justice Department's suit against the company. Therefore you will need to consider whether you are willing to have what you are putting online become public knowledge.

www • bedford stmartins.com/ smhandbook

To read about how going online affected one person's writing, click on

► Links
  ► Working Online

Third, *online messages travel.* Just as you may clip a paragraph out of a message and send it on to a friend, so your online messages may be forwarded to others, downloaded, and disseminated (see the example of Tamim Ansary in Chapter 1). As a result, you have to consider how such traveling may affect the messages you send—and keep careful track of what you may be moving from one context to another. In the same way, you have to think carefully before you forward someone else's messages: do you think you have the writer's permission to do so?

Finally, *online writing is faster than other forms of written communication.* The flashing indicator onscreen, the ability of Instant Messenger participants to converse back and forth or of Web browsers to call up whole texts and images with the click of a mouse—all create sensations of speed and urgency in readers' minds, making people expect to be able to process and respond to messages quickly. Thus even lengthy messages may need to be clearer and more concise online than offline.

For further help with writing online, see Chapters 7 and 9 and 53g and 54f.

→ What is your purpose for writing? If it is to gather information, what is the best way to phrase questions you might send out to an email discussion list or an expert on your topic? If it's to create a Web page on an issue you care about, what will readers need to know, and what else do you want to tell them?

→ Have you considered your audience carefully? Remember that an email to your best friend differs from an email to a professor or prospective employer. Are your tone and level of formality appropriate? Does your audience know you, or are you introducing yourself for the first time?

→ If you are writing for a Web site, what design elements should you use? a template? frames for featuring content? simple navigation buttons or links?

→ What visual elements should you use? color to signal response to email? colors and graphics that can be quickly downloaded in a Web document?

→ If you are writing to a listserv or a chatroom, are you following expected conventions? Have you checked for a welcome page or an FAQ section for a discussion of these conventions?

→ If you are relying on information you found online, are you sure of its accuracy and validity?

→ Have you revised online writing carefully unless the situation (a fast-moving chat, for example) is very informal?

→ Have you observed the rules of online etiquette? (7a)

THINKING CRITICALLY ABOUT RHETORICAL SITUATIONS

Reading with an Eye for Purpose and Audience

Advertisements provide good examples of writing that is tailored carefully for specific audiences. Find two ads for the same product that appeal to different audiences. You might compare ads in a men's magazine to those in a women's magazine to see what differences there are in the messages and photography. Or you could look at products that seem to appeal to men (Marlboro cigarettes, perhaps) next to those that are marketed to women (such as Virginia Slims). What conclusions can you draw about ways of appealing to specific audiences?

rhet

2i

Thinking about Your Own Attention to Purpose and Audience

Consider something you have written or are working on right now.

1. Can you state its purpose(s) clearly and succinctly? If not, what can you do to clarify its purpose(s)?

2. What other purposes for this piece of writing can you imagine? How would fulfilling some other purpose change the writing?

3. Can you tell from reading the piece who the intended audience is? If so, what in your text clearly relates to that audience? If not, what can you add that will strengthen your appeal to this audience?

4. What other audiences can you imagine? How would the writing change if you were to address a different audience?

5. Does your writing follow the conventions of standard academic discourse — and if not, how should you revise so that it will?

If you are keeping a writing log, enter any conclusions you can make about purpose and audience in your own writing.

◤ Exploring, Planning, and Drafting

3a Exploring a topic

The point is so simple that we often forget it: we write best about topics we know well. One of the most important parts of the entire writing process, therefore, is exploring your topic, surveying what you know about it and then determining what you need to find out about it. If you do not already have a system for exploring topics you wish to write about, this chapter's brief description of strategies may be very useful. The strategies include brainstorming, freewriting, looping, clustering, and questioning.

1 Brainstorming: talking with others

The most immediate way to begin exploring a topic is also the easiest and most familiar: *talk it over* with others. As you talk about your topic, you can hear your mind at work, articulating what you think about the topic and what you most need to know about it. You can also seek out those who know about your topic and talk with them, listening carefully and taking notes. An email message asking an expert if he or she would respond to two or three questions could yield a gold mine of information.

One excellent way to talk with others about your topic is in a brainstorming session. Used widely in business and industry, **brainstorming** means tossing out ideas — either in person or via computer — to discover new ways to approach a topic. If you don't have others to talk with,

The late Lewis Thomas, one of America's most celebrated essayists, began writing essays when he was invited to contribute a monthly column to the *New England Journal of Medicine*. A scientist and medical doctor, Thomas at first tried various methods of planning and organizing, including making meticulous outlines. Nothing seemed to work. After producing several "dreadful" essays, he shook off all attempts at detailed planning and just plunged right in, thinking about and developing his ideas by simply writing as fast as he could.

Like Thomas, you may do your best by diving right into your writing projects, exploring your topics as you draft. Or you may work more effectively by producing detailed blueprints before you ever begin drafting. There are many productive ways to go about exploring, planning, and drafting. This chapter takes a close look at some of the ways these activities work in practice. ■

plan

58 **3a**

WRITING

Exploring,
Planning, and
Drafting

however, you can still easily brainstorm. All you need is a pen or pencil and some blank paper or a computer keyboard, and you are ready to carry out the following steps:

1. Set a time limit of five or ten minutes to list *every* word or phrase that comes to mind about your topic. Just put down key words and phrases, not sentences. No one has to understand the list but you. Don't worry about whether something will be useful or not. Just get it *all* down.

2. If nothing much seems to occur to you, try thinking the opposite. If you are trying, for instance, to think of reasons to reduce tuition at your college and are coming up blank, try concentrating on reasons to *increase* tuition. Once you start generating ideas in one direction, you can move back to exploring the other side of the topic.

3. When the time is up, stop and read over your list. If anything else comes to mind, add it to the list. Then reread the list, looking for patterns, clusters of interesting ideas, or one central idea.

2 Freewriting

Freewriting is a method of exploring a topic by writing about it—or whatever else it brings to mind—for a period of time *without stopping*. Here is the way to do it:

1. Set a time limit of no more than ten minutes. Begin by thinking about your topic, and then simply let your mind wander, writing down everything that occurs to you, in complete sentences as much as possible. Don't stop for anything; if necessary, write "I can't think of what to write next" over and over until something else occurs to you.

2. When the time is up, look at what you have written. You are sure to find much that is unusable, irrelevant, or nonsensical. But you may also find important insights and ideas.

3. If you are using a computer for freewriting, remember to save everything to a special file. You can then go back and reread, easily cutting and pasting sentences or even parts of paragraphs into a draft.

CONSIDERING DISABILITIES: Try Freespeaking

If you are better at talking out than writing out your ideas, try *freespeaking*, which is basically the talking version of freewriting. Begin by speaking into a tape recorder or into a computer with voice recognition software, and just keep talking about your topic for at least seven to ten minutes. Say whatever comes to your mind, and don't stop talking. You can then listen to or read the results of your freespeaking and look for an idea to pursue at greater length.

3 Looping

Looping is a form of directed freewriting that narrows or limits a topic in five-minute stages, or loops. Here is how to do looping:

1. With your topic in mind, spend five minutes freewriting *without stopping*. This is your first loop.
2. Look back at what you have written. Find the strongest or most intriguing thought. This is your "center of gravity," which you should summarize in a single sentence; it will become the starting point of your next loop. If you are using a computer, simply cut and paste, or copy, the sentence you have chosen to a new page—and continue with your looping.
3. Starting with the summary sentence from your first loop, spend another five minutes freewriting. Look for a center of gravity within this second piece of freewriting, which will form the basis of a third loop. Keep this process going until you discover a clear angle on your topic.

4 Clustering

Clustering is a way to generate ideas using a visual scheme or chart. It is especially useful for understanding the relationships among the parts of a broad topic and for developing subtopics. To begin clustering, follow these steps:

1. Write down your topic in the middle of a blank piece of paper, and circle it.
2. In a ring around the topic circle, write down what you see as the main parts of the topic. Circle each part, and draw a line from it to the topic.
3. Think of any ideas, examples, facts, or other details relating to each main part. Write each of these down near the appropriate part, circle it, and draw a line from it to the part.
4. Repeat this process with each new circle until you can't think of any more details. Some trails may dead-end, but you will still have various trains of thought to follow and many useful connections among ideas.

● For an example of one student's clustering, see 3a7.

5 Questioning

The strategies presented thus far for exploring topics are all informal and based on the freewheeling association of ideas. There are also more formal, structured strategies, which involve asking—and answering—questions. Following are several widely used sets of questions designed

plan

60   **3a**

WRITING

Exploring,
Planning, and
Drafting

to help you explore your topic, either on your own or with one or two others.

■ *Questions to describe a topic*

Originally developed by Aristotle, the following questions can help you explore any topic by carefully and systematically describing it:

1. *What is it?* What are its characteristics, dimensions, features, and parts? What does it look like?
2. *What caused it?* What changes occurred to create your topic? How is it changing? How will it change? What part of the changing process is your topic involved with? What may your topic lead to in the future?
3. *What is it like or unlike?* What features differentiate your topic from others? What analogies can you make about your topic?
4. *What larger system is your topic a part of?* How does your topic relate to this system?
5. *What do people say about it?* What reactions does your topic arouse? What about the topic causes those reactions?

■ *Questions to explain a topic*

This is the well-known question set of *who, what, when, where, why,* and *how.* Widely used in news reporting, these questions are especially useful when you are explaining a topic:

1. *Who* is doing it?
2. *What* is at issue?
3. *When* does it take place?
4. *Where* is it taking place?
5. *Why* does it occur?
6. *How* is it done?

■ *Questions to persuade*

For more about Toulmin's system, see 11f and 13c.

When your purpose is to persuade or convince, the following questions, developed by philosopher Stephen Toulmin, can help you think analytically about your topic:

1. What *claim* are you making about your topic?
2. What *good reasons* support your claim?
3. What valid *underlying assumptions* support the reasons for your claim?
4. What *backup evidence* can you find for your claim?
5. What *refutations* of your claim should you anticipate?
6. In what ways should you *qualify* your claim?

For generating and exploring ideas — the work of much brainstorming, freewriting, looping, clustering, and questioning — you may be most successful at coming up with good ideas quickly and spontaneously if you work in your native language. Later in the process of writing, you can choose the best of these ideas and begin working with them in English.

6 Trying other genres

One good way to get yourself thinking in a fresh, new way about a topic, to get a new angle or a different take on it, is to try translating your subject into a different genre, or kind, of writing. If, for example, you have been assigned to write an essay on the Wife of Bath in *The Canterbury Tales,* why not try writing some rap lyrics that she might have come up with — or country blues? If you are a visual thinker, try drawing a picture of your subject(s). The idea is to jog your customary thinking patterns, to try seeing your subject from a new perspective and thus to find something new and compelling to say about it.

7 Looking at one student's exploratory work

Emily Lesk, the student whose work we began following in Chapter 2, tried two strategies to explore her topic: brainstorming and clustering. Since she was already part of a peer group, she turned to members of the group to discuss the general topic the class was working on: an aspect of national identity affected by one or more media. After the group brainstormed for half an hour, the members made separate notes. Here are some of Emily's notes, which focus on her narrowed topic, American advertising.

American advertising and national identity

1. portrayal of women in advertising — does it affect U.S. identity?
2. portrayal of children/families in advertising — affect identity?
3. wartime advertising and how it relates to national identity?
4. advertising of a specific company? Would have to be large, visible, well known, and very familiar to the average American. How does such a company's advertising link to American identity?
   - McDonald's?
   - Mattel?
   - Coca-Cola?
   - Weight Watchers?

In investigating what she came up with during her brainstorming session, Emily Lesk found a large Coca-Cola advertising archive and decided to see if she could establish a link between Coca-Cola and American identity. Later in her planning and exploring, Emily produced the following clustering map of her emerging ideas:

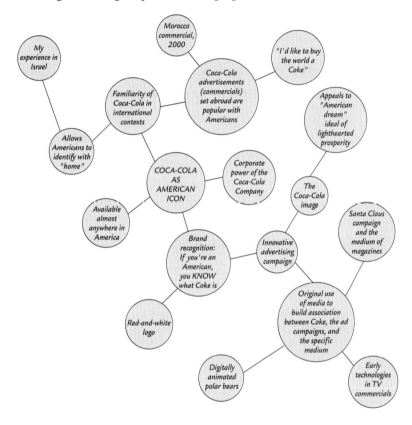

CONSIDERING DISABILITIES: Word Processing All Your Work

If handwriting poses problems for you, either because you have difficulty writing or others have difficulty reading your handwriting, consider word processing *all* your work for assignments, including notes and other exploratory work. Doing so can save you time and effort in the long run.

Choose a topic that interests you, and explore it by using two of the strategies described in 3a. When you have generated some material, you might try comparing your results with those of other members of the class to see how effective or helpful each strategy was. If you have trouble choosing a topic, use one of the preliminary working theses in Exercise 3.2.

3b Developing a working thesis

A **thesis** states the main idea of a piece of writing. Most kinds of college writing contain a thesis statement, often near the beginning, which functions as a promise to the readers, letting them know what will be discussed. You should establish a tentative **working thesis** early on in your writing process. Even though it will probably change as you write, a working thesis is important for two reasons: (1) it focuses your thinking, research, and investigation on a particular point about the topic and thus keeps you on track; and (2) it provides concrete questions to ask about purpose, audience, and your rhetorical stance (helping you see, for example, what you must do to design a thesis for a particular audience).

A working thesis should have two parts: a **topic** part, which states the topic, and a **comment** part, which makes an important point or expresses an opinion about the topic. Here is an example:

┌──────── TOPIC ────────┐ ┌──────────── COMMENT ────────────
Recent studies of depression suggest that it is much more closely related
to physiology than scientists had previously thought.

A successful working thesis has three characteristics:

1. It is potentially *interesting* to your intended audience.
2. It is as *specific* as possible.
3. It limits the topic enough to make it *manageable*.

You can assess a working thesis by checking it against each of these criteria. The following example is for a working thesis on global warming:

PRELIMINARY WORKING THESIS

┌──────── TOPIC ────────┐ ┌──────── COMMENT ────────┐
Theories about global warming are being debated around the world.

INTEREST The topic itself holds interest, but the comment makes no important point about the topic. The thesis merely states a bare fact, and the only place to go from here is to more bare facts.

SPECIFICITY The thesis is fairly clear but not specific. Who is debating these theories? What is at issue in this debate?

MANAGEABILITY The thesis is not manageable: it would require research on many countries and in many languages.

ASSESSMENT

This thesis needs to be narrowed with the addition of a workable comment before it can be useful. Also, the field for investigation is too large and vague. This preliminary thesis can be narrowed into the following working thesis:

WORKING THESIS

————————————————— TOPIC —————————————————
Scientists from several countries have challenged global-warming theories
————————————— COMMENT ————————————
by claiming that they are more propaganda than science.

Emily Lesk produced this preliminary working thesis: "Advertising icons shape American identity." Subjecting this thesis to the criteria of interest, specificity, and manageability, she decided that it was interesting but not very specific or manageable. After further discussion with her peer group and her instructor, she decided to focus more specifically on one particular advertising icon, the world-famous Coca-Cola logo. Her revised working thesis then became "Coca-Cola is a cultural icon that shapes American identity."

FOR MULTILINGUAL WRITERS: Stating a Thesis Explicitly

In some cultures, it is considered rude to state an opinion outright. In the United States, however, academic and business practices require writers to make key points and positions explicitly clear.

● **EXERCISE 3.2**

Choose one of the following preliminary working theses, and after specifying an audience, evaluate the thesis in terms of interest, specificity, and manageability. Revise it as necessary to meet these criteria.

1. Homeland security presents the United States with an ongoing problem.

2. Abortion is a right.

3. Othello is a complex character whose greatest strength is, ironically, also his greatest weakness.

4. White-collar crime poses greater danger to the economy than street crime, even though the latter is more obvious.

5. An educated public is the key to a successful democracy.

● **EXERCISE 3.3**

Using the topic you chose in Exercise 3.1, write a preliminary working thesis. Evaluate it in terms of interest, specificity, and manageability. Revise it as necessary to create a satisfactory working thesis.

3c   Gathering information

Many of your writing assignments will call for some research at various stages of the writing process — early on, to help you understand or define your topic, or later on, to find additional examples in support of your thesis. But once you have developed a working thesis, consider what additional information you might need.

If you find it necessary to do research, you should probably begin with those resources closest at hand: your instructor, who can help you decide what kind of research to do, and your textbooks, which may include a bibliography or list of references. Basically, you can do three kinds of research: traditional **library research,** which includes books, periodicals, and databases — all of which you can access from your college library or through interlibrary loan; **online research,** which gives you access to texts, visuals, and people on the Internet and World Wide Web; and **field research,** which includes personal observation, interviews, surveys, and other means of gathering information directly.

● For a detailed discussion of how to conduct all three kinds of research, see Chapter 15.

For her essay, Emily Lesk consulted documents on the official Coca-Cola Web site as well as several books and a study of magazine advertisements. She also looked for illustrations to include in her essay.

3d   Organizing verbal and visual information

While you are finding information on your topic, you should be thinking about how you will group or organize that information so that it will be accessible and persuasive to your readers. At the simplest level, writers most often group information according to four principles:

1. **space** — *where* bits of information occur within a setting
2. **time** — *when* bits of information occur, usually chronologically
3. **logic** — *how* bits of information are related logically
4. **association** — *how* bits of information are related in terms of images, motifs, personal memories, and so on

For more infor-•
mation on using
visuals in an
essay, see 8d.

Whichever of these principles you use to begin organizing an essay or project, take special care in planning for the inclusion of images and other visuals.

- Choose visuals that are closely related to your topic and that add to the points you are making. Visuals shouldn't just be window dressing.
- Plan to place each visual as near as possible to the text it illustrates.
- Remember that, for your final draft, you need to introduce each visual clearly: *As the map to the right depicts . . . .*
- In addition, comment on the significance or effect of the visual: *Figure 1 corroborates the claim made by geneticists: while the human genome may be mapped, it is far from understood.*
- Finally, plan to label each visual appropriately, providing a label and citing the source.

1 Organizing information spatially

For questions •
that help you
describe a topic,
see 3a5.

For examples of •
information
organized spa-
tially, see 5d1.

If the information you have gathered is *descriptive,* you may choose to organize it spatially. Using **spatial organization** allows the reader to "see" your information, to fix it in space. A report on a college library's accessibility to students in wheelchairs, for example, might describe the spaces in the library that are most often used and then evaluate their accessibility to a student in a wheelchair — one room or space or area at a time. In this case, the description might be accompanied by a map or by another graphic that would help readers visualize the literary space.

2 Organizing information chronologically

You are probably already very familiar with **chronological organization,** since it is the basic method used in stories, cookbooks, and instruction manuals. All of these kinds of writing group information according to when it occurs in some process or sequence of events. Reports of laboratory studies and certain kinds of experiments also use chronological order.

A student studying the availability of motorcycle parking in a campus lot ordered his information chronologically to show the times when motorcycles entered and exited the lot and thus identified peak periods of demand for parking spaces. If you choose to present information in a narrative, or story form, you will probably use chronological order. But changing that order—starting in the middle or at the end and then using a flashback to the beginning—can also be effective.

Chronological order is especially useful in *explaining a process,* step by step by step. A biology report might require describing the process of circulation in a frog. An anthropology essay might include an explanation of the initiation rituals in Navajo culture. In either case, visuals would probably be useful: a diagram in the biology essay, photographs in the anthropology essay.

3 Organizing information logically

In much of the writing you do in college, you will find it appropriate to organize information according to some set of logical relationships. The most commonly used **logical patterns** include *illustration, definition, division and classification, comparison and contrast, cause and effect, problem and solution, use of analogies,* and *narration.*

• For examples of paragraphs organized according to these logical patterns, see 5e1.

▥ *Illustrating a point*

Often much of the information you gather will serve as examples to **illustrate a point.** An essay discussing how one novelist influenced another might cite a number of examples from the second writer's books that echo themes, characters, or plots from the first writer's works. An appeal for donating money to the Red Cross might be organized in a series of examples of how donations are used, along with a variety of illustrations. For maximum effect, arrange your examples and accompanying visuals in order of increasing importance.

▥ *Defining terms*

Often a topic can be developed by **definition:** by saying what something is—or is not—and perhaps by identifying the characteristics that distinguish it from things that are similar or in the same general category. A magazine article about poverty in the United States, for example, would have to define very carefully what level of income, assets, or other measure defines a person, family, or household as "poor." An essay about Pentecostalism for a religion class might develop the topic by explaining what characteristics separate Pentecostalism from related religious movements.

■ *Dividing and classifying*

Division means breaking a single topic into separate parts; **classification** means grouping many separate items of information about a topic according to their similarities. An essay about the recruiting policies of the U.S. military, for instance, might be organized by dividing the military into its different branches — army, air force, and so on — and then discussing how each branch recruits volunteers. If you were reading histories of the eighteenth century in preparation for writing an essay on women's roles in that time, you could begin to organize your notes by classifying them into categories: information related to women's education, women's occupations, women's legal status, and so on.

■ *Comparing and contrasting*

Comparison focuses on the similarities between two things, whereas **contrast** highlights their differences, but the two are often used together. Asked to read two case studies in an advertising text (one on Budweiser ads and the other on ads by Ralph Lauren), to analyze the information, and to write a brief response, you might well organize the response by presenting all the information on Budweiser advertising in one section and all on Ralph Lauren ads in another (*block comparison*) or by alternating between Budweiser and Ralph Lauren ads as you look at particular characteristics of each (*alternating comparison*).

■ *Analyzing causes and effects*

Cause-effect analysis either examines why something happens or happened by looking at its causes, or it looks at a set of conditions and explains what effects result or are likely to result from them. An environmental-impact study of the probable consequences of building a proposed dam, for instance, might move from causes to effects. On the other hand, a newspaper article on the breakdown of authority in inner-city schools might be organized by tracing the effects of the breakdown back to their causes.

■ *Considering problems and solutions*

Moving from a **problem** to a **solution** is a natural and straightforward way of organizing certain kinds of information. The student studying motorcycle parking decided to organize his paper in just this way: he

plan

3d   69

WRITING
Organizing Verbal
and Visual
Information

identified a problem (the need for more parking) and then offered two possible solutions, along with visuals to help readers imagine the solutions. Many assignments in engineering, business, and economics call for a similar organizational strategy.

Using analogies

An **analogy** establishes connections between two things or ideas. Analogies are particularly helpful in explaining something new in terms of something very familiar. Likening the Internet, for example, to an information *superhighway* helped those unfamiliar with the Internet understand something about how it worked. In the same way, scientists make an analogy between the human genome and a map.

Narrating

Narration involves telling a story of some kind. You might, for example, choose to tell the story of your first day on campus as a way of illustrating some of the challenges new students face. Or you might tell the story of the conflict between President Bush and Congress over the 2002 budget bill in order to explore the causes and effects of the final bill's enactment. Narrating calls on the writer to set the story in a context readers can understand, providing any necessary background and descriptive details as well as chronological markers and transitions (*later that day, following,* and so on) to guide readers through the story.

4 Organizing information associationally

Many contemporary essays are organized through a series of **associations** that grow directly out of the writer's memory or experience. Henry Louis Gates Jr. uses such a method in an essay about his mother's kitchen beauty parlor. He opens with an evocation of vividly remembered smells, and that leads to a series of images related to washing, cutting, treating, and, especially, straightening hair, made even more vivid by a series of original sketches. These sensory memories call up other associations for Gates: his own hair type, style, and process—and those of people he is interested in, such as Malcolm X, Sammy Davis Jr., and Nat King Cole. All of these associations come together for Gates, he says in his concluding paragraph, one day in "an Arab restaurant on the island of Zanzibar" as he suddenly catches the strains of a Nat King Cole song. As this example suggests, associational organization is most often used in personal narrative, where writers can use a chain of associations to render an experience vividly for readers.

5 Combining organizational patterns

In much of your writing, you will want to combine two or more organizational patterns. You might, for example, combine several passages of narration with vivid descriptive illustrations so as to make a striking comparison, as one student recently did in an essay about the dramatic differences between her life in her Zuñi community and her life as a teacher in a predominantly Anglo school. The possibilities for combining patterns have increased considerably with the advent of electronic forms of text production; such combinations may now include not only pictures but sound and other multimedia effects as well.

Emily Lesk begins her essay (p. 75) with what she calls a "confession": *I don't drink Coke.* She follows this opening with an anecdote about a trip to Israel during which she nevertheless bought a T-shirt sporting the Coca-Cola logo. She goes on to explore what lies behind this purchase, relating it to the masterful advertising campaigns of the Coca-Cola Company and illustrating the way that the company's advertising "sells" a certain kind of American identity along with its products. She closes her draft (p. 80) by reflecting on the implications of this relationship between corporate advertising and national identity. Thus her essay, which begins with a personal experience, combines the patterns of narrative with cause-effect and comparison.

FOR MULTILINGUAL WRITERS: Organizing Information

You may know ways of organizing information that differ markedly from those discussed in 3d. A Navajo teacher notes, for example, that explicit linear organization, through chronology or other strictly logical patterns, doesn't ever sound quite right to her. As she puts it, "In traditional Navajo, it's considered rude to get right to the point. Polite conversation or writing between two engaged people always takes a while to get to the point." If your language or culture uses or values other kinds of organizational patterns, you may want to share them with your instructor and your classmates.

● **EXERCISE 3.4**

Using the topic you chose in Exercise 3.1, identify the most effective means of organizing your information. Write a brief paragraph explaining why you chose this particular method (or these methods) of organization.

FOR COLLABORATION

Working with another member of your class, decide which method or methods of organization you would recommend for students who are writing on the following topics, and explain why. Bring the results of your work to class for comparison with others' recommendations.

1. the need for a new undergraduate library
2. the autobiographical elements in Virginia Woolf's *To the Lighthouse*
3. why voting rates in U.S. elections are low
4. education to prevent the spread of AIDS
5. the best contemporary rap artist or group

3e   Writing out a plan

A writer who has organized information carefully is one who already has a plan for a draft, a plan that he or she should then write down. The student who wrote about the motorcycle-parking shortage (see 3d2) organized all his data and developed the following plan. Notice that his plan calls for several organizational strategies within an overall problem-solution framework.

INTRODUCTION

give background on the problem (use *chronological order*)
give overview of the problem in detail (use *division*), and use a photograph of overcrowding in the lot
state purpose — to offer solutions

BODY

describe the current situation (use *narration*)
present proof of the problem in detail (use *illustration*), including a graph representing findings
present two possible solutions (use *comparison*)

CONCLUSION

recommend against first solution because of cost and space
recommend second solution, and summarize benefits of doing so

■ *Preparing a formal outline*

You may wish — or be required — to prepare a more formal outline, which allows you to see before drafting exactly how the parts of your essay will fit together. It is likely that your word-processing program has an outline feature. (In Microsoft Word, it appears when you click on FORMAT, then BULLETS AND NUMBERING, and then OUTLINE NUMBERED.) This feature can help you organize — and reorganize — your essay. Most formal outlines follow a conventional format of numbered and lettered headings and subheadings, using Roman numerals, capital letters, Arabic numerals, and lowercase letters to show the levels of importance of the various ideas and their relationships. Each new level is indented to show its subordination to the preceding level. The following example shows the structure:

Thesis statement
I. First main topic
  A. First subordinate idea
    1. First supporting idea
    2. Second supporting idea
      a. First supporting detail
      b. Second supporting detail
    3. Third supporting idea
  B. Second subordinate idea
    1. First supporting idea
    2. Second supporting idea
II. Second main topic
  A. (continues as above)

Each level contains at least two parts, so there is no A without a B, no 1 without a 2. Comparable items are placed on the same level — the level marked by capital letters, for instance, or by Arabic numerals. Each level develops the idea before it — 1 and 2 under A, for example, include the points that develop, explain, or demonstrate A. Headings are stated in parallel form — either all sentences or all grammatically parallel topics.

Formal outlining requires logical thought and careful evaluation of your ideas, and this is precisely why it is valuable. (A full-sentence outline will reveal the relationships between ideas — or the lack of relationships — most clearly; so if you want to give your organization the most rigorous test, try working it into a full-sentence outline.) Remember, however, that an outline is at best a means to an end, not an end in itself. Indeed, whatever form your plan takes, you may want or need to change it as you begin drafting.

For an example —— ●
of a formal out-
line, see Shannan
Palma's essay in
20d.

● **EXERCISE 3.5**

Write out a plan for an essay supporting the working thesis you developed for Exercise 3.3.

CONSIDERING DISABILITIES: Speak Your Draft

Using a word processor with voice-recognition capability will allow you to speak your ideas, which will then appear onscreen. A "talking" draft of this kind can be a very good way to get your initial draft done, especially if you have difficulty with the physical act of writing. If voice-recognition software isn't available, try to find another student who will work with you to produce talking drafts: as one of you talks, the other types in what is being said.

3f   Producing a draft

Most of us are in some sense "producing a draft" the moment we begin thinking about a topic. At some point, however, we sit down, usually at the computer, to attempt an actual version of a draft.

1 Remaining flexible

No matter how good your planning, investigating, and organizing have been, chances are you will need to return to these activities as you draft. This fact of life leads to the first principle of successful drafting: be flexible. If you see that your organizational plan is not working, do not hesitate to alter it. If some information now seems irrelevant, leave it out, even if you went to great lengths to obtain it. You may learn that your whole thesis must be reshaped or that your topic is still too broad and should be narrowed further.

2 Knowing your best writing situation

There may be almost as many ways to produce a successful draft as there are people to do it. Nevertheless, you can profit by learning as much as possible about what kind of situation is likely to help you produce your best writing. *Where* and *when* are you most comfortable and productive writing? *What conditions* do you prefer—complete quiet? music? Do you have any *rituals* that help—exercising beforehand? making a pot of coffee?

Since it's likely that you will do some or all of your drafting on a computer, take advantage of working with a word processor and using online writing environments, such as email, Web discussion boards, or MOOs. Here are three ways to manage your drafting:

- *Copy and paste writing from other places.* Remember that the writing you do online can serve as content for a draft. If your class uses a discussion list to share responses to readings, for example, or if you belong to an email discussion group that includes messages on your topic, take a look at the messages you have written in these settings. You may find useful information that you can cut and paste into your word-processor document. Remember, however, that any material you want to quote from other people's writing on such lists must appear in quotation marks and that you will need the appropriate information to cite the source fully. (See Chapter 18.)

- *Save and name your files to distinguish among drafts.* Most writers make changes to a file document they are working on over time. To capture all versions of your draft, you will need to save a copy of each version. If you are sending a copy to classmates for review, attach a copy of your draft to an email message, or upload a copy to the class Web site. To do so, use SAVE AS and give the file a new but related name. For example, for a draft saved as *religion essay 1,* use the SAVE AS to save a copy as *religion essay 2.* When you receive responses from your classmates, you can leave the copy of your own first draft (*religion essay 1*) as is and open *religion essay 2* and make your revisions there.

- *Track changes within a file.* Some word processors allow you to track changes you make within a draft. In Word, for example, this function is called TRACK CHANGES. Choose TOOLS, then TRACK CHANGES, then HIGHLIGHT CHANGES, and then click on TRACK CHANGES WHILE EDITING. With this function on, text you delete will appear with a line through it, and text you add will appear in a color font, letting you compare one version to the other. The TRACK CHANGES function is especially useful when you are working on a piece with another writer. You can suggest changes using this feature, and your cowriter can select TOOLS, then TRACK CHANGES, then ACCEPT OR REJECT CHANGES. Even when you're working on your own, TRACK CHANGES can be helpful, especially when you're not sure which version of a draft you like best. You can take a break from the essay and then come back to it, accepting or rejecting the changes you made earlier. Here is an example of how Emily Lesk used this function to capture variations so that she could compare them later on. In this passage, her computer's TRACK CHANGES function crossed out parts of her first version, which is from her first draft (p. 75), and underlined additions to the second version, which she ultimately incorporated into her final essay.

But while countless campaigns with this general
strategy have together shaped the Coca-Cola image,
presenting a product as key to a happy life ~~represents~~
is a fairly typical approach to advertising everything
from ~~Fords~~ Allstate insurance to ~~Tylenol~~ Ziploc bags.
Coca-Cola's advertising strategy is ~~truly~~ unique,
however, for the original way the beverage giant has
~~utilized~~ used the specific advertising media ~~--namely~~ of
magazines and television ---to drive home this message.
As a result, Coca-Cola has become associated not only
with the images of Americana portrayed in specific
advertisements but also with the general forms of
advertising media that dominate American culture.

You may feel safer experimenting with different versions if you can still
see what you originally wrote.

SOME GUIDELINES FOR DRAFTING

→ *Set up a computer folder or file for your essay.* Give the file a clear and relevant name, and save to it often.
→ *Have all your information close at hand and arranged according to your organizational plan.* Stopping to search for a piece of information can break
your concentration or distract you.
→ *Try to write in stretches of at least thirty minutes.* Writing can provide
momentum, and once you get going, the task becomes easier.
→ *Don't let small questions bog you down.* Just make a note of them in
brackets — or in all caps — or make a tentative decision and move on.
→ *Remember that first drafts aren't perfect.* Concentrate on getting all your
ideas onscreen, and don't worry about anything else.
→ *Stop writing at a place where you know exactly what will come next.* Doing so
will help you start easily when you return to the draft.

4 Looking at one student's draft

Here is Emily Lesk's first draft. She uses brackets to identify questions
and comments she has for herself and others.

www • bedford
stmartins.com/
smhandbook

To see another
student's draft,
click on

▶ **Student Samples**
   ▶ **Essays**

All-Powerful Coke

    I don't drink Coke. Call me picky for disliking the
soda's saccharine aftertaste. Call me cheap for choosing

a water fountain over a twelve-ounce aluminum can that costs a dollar from a vending machine but only pennies to produce. Even call me unpatriotic for rejecting the potable god that over the last century has come to represent all the enjoyment and ease to be found in our American way of life. But don't call me a hypocrite when I admit that I still identify with Coke and the Coca-Cola culture.

I have a favorite T-shirt that says "Drink Coca-Cola Classic" in Hebrew. It's Israel's standard tourist fare, like little nested dolls in Russia or painted horses in Scandinavia, and before setting foot in the Promised Land three years ago, I knew where I could find one. The T-shirt shop in the central block of a Jerusalem shopping center did offer other shirt designs ("Macabee Beer" was a favorite), but that Coca-Cola shirt was what drew in most of the dollar-carrying tourists. I waited almost twenty minutes for mine, and I watched nearly everyone ahead of me say "the Coke shirt" (and "thanks" in Hebrew).

At the time, I never asked why I wanted the shirt. I do know, though, that the reason I wear it often, despite a hole in the right sleeve, has to do with its power as a conversation piece. Few people notice it without asking something like, "Does that say Coke?" I usually smile and nod. They mumble a compliment and we go our separate ways. But rarely does anyone want to know what language the world's most famous logo is written in. And why should they? Perhaps because Coca-Cola is a cultural icon that shapes American identity.

Throughout the Company's history, marketing strategies have centered on putting Coca-Cola in scenes of the happy, carefree American life we never stop striving for. What 1950's teenage girl wouldn't long to see herself in the soda shop pictured in a Coca-Cola ad appearing in the 1957 issue of <u>Seventeen</u> magazine? A clean-cut, handsome man flirts with a pair of smiling girls as they laugh and drink Coca-Colas. And any girls who couldn't put themselves in that perfect, happy scene, could at least buy a Coke for consolation. The malt shop--complete with a soda jerk in a white jacket and paper hat--is a theme that, even today, remains a symbol of Americana.

But while countless campaigns with this general strategy have together shaped the Coca-Cola image, presenting a product as key to a happy life represents a fairly typical approach to advertising everything from Fords to Tylenol. Coca-Cola's advertising is truly unique, however, for the original way the beverage giant has utilized specific advertising media--namely magazines and television--to drive home this message.   5

One of the earliest and best known examples of this strategy is artist Haddon Sundblom's masterpiece of Santa Claus. Prior to Coca-Cola's Santa campaign of 1931, Saint Nicholas took many different forms, although he was usually quite slim and came in a wide variety of colors. [LOOK FOR A PICTURE OF THIS ORIGINAL COKE SANTA.] The round, jolly, Coca-Cola red-and-white American icon who today receives the authority of any biblical hero was born when Sundblom (ironically, a Swede) decided to use himself as a model. But the success of Santa Claus goes far beyond Sundblom's magazine advertisements depicting a warm, happy grandfather figure delighting in an ice cold Coke after a tiring night of delivering presents. The way in which Coca-Cola advertisers presented that inviting image represents Coca-Cola's brilliant manipulation of the medium itself.   6

In today's world of CNN, e-journals, and newsweek.com, it is often easy to forget how pervasive a medium the magazine was prior to the advent of television. Until the late 1950s, American households of diverse backgrounds and geographic locations subscribed loyally to general subject weeklies and   7

monthlies such as <u>Life</u> and the <u>Saturday Evening Post</u>.
These publications provided the primary source of news,
entertainment, and other cultural information to
families nationwide. This large and constant group of
subscribers enabled Coca-Cola to build a perennial
Christmastime advertising campaign that used an
extremely limited number of ads ["DESIGNS" BETTER WORD?]
[ADD SOURCE], which Americans soon came to look forward
to and seek out each holiday season. The marketing
strategy was not to capture consumers with a few color
drawings, but rather to make them wait eagerly by the
mailbox each December so that they could flip through
the <u>Saturday Evening Post</u> to find the latest scene
featuring Santa gulping a Coke. For this strategy to be
successful, the advertisements had to be seen by many,
but also be just hard enough to come by to be exciting.
What better location for this than the December issue of
an immensely popular magazine?

There is no denying that this strategy worked
brilliantly, as this inviting image of Santa Claus
graduated from the pages of <u>Saturday Evening Post</u> to
become the central figure of the most celebrated and
beloved season of the year. Travel to any strip mall in
the United States during December (or even November--
that's how much we love Christmas!) and you will no
doubt run into Santa clones left and right, punched out
of cardboard and sculpted in tinsel hung atop lampposts,
all in Coca-Cola red and white. And while, in today's
nonmagazine world, Coca-Cola must celebrate Christmas
with specially designed diet Coke cans and television
commercials, the Coca-Cola Santa Claus will forever
epitomize the former power of the magazine advertising
in America. [AM I GETTING OFF TRACK HERE?]

In other words, Coca-Cola has hammered itself into
our perceptions--both conscious and subconscious--of an
American cultural identity by equating itself with media
that define American culture. When the omnipresent

general magazine that marked the earlier part of the century fell by the wayside under television's power, Coke was there from the beginning. In its 1996 recap of the previous fifty years in industry history, the publication <u>Beverage Industry</u> cites Coca-Cola as a frontrunner in the very first form of television advertising: sponsorship of entire programs such as, in the case of Coke, <u>The Bob Dixon Show</u> and <u>The Adventures of Kit Carson</u>. Just as today, we associate national patriotic events such as the 2002 Olympics with their list of corporate sponsors (which in this case, includes the Coca-Cola company), viewers of early television programs will forever equate them with Coke.

When networks switched from offering sponsorships   10
to selling exclusive commercial time in short increments (a format modeled after magazine advertisements), Coca-Cola strove to distinguish itself once again, this time by producing new formats and technologies for these commercials. [THIS SENTENCE IS WAY TOO LONG!] Early attempts at this--such as choppy "stop motion" animation, where photographs of objects such as Coke bottles move without the intervention of actors-- attracted much attention, according to the Library of Congress Motion Picture Archives. Coca-Cola also experimented with color advertisements early enough that the excitement of color advertising technology drew additional attention to these commercials.

But the Coke advertising campaign, that perhaps   11
best illustrates the ability of Coca-Cola advertisers to equate their product with a medium/technology [REWORD!], did not appear until 1993. Who can forget the completely digitally animated polar bears, that roll, swim, snuggle, slide, and gurgle about, in a computerized South [?] Pole and finish off the playful experience with a swig of Coke? This campaign captured America's attention and held it for six separate commercials, and not because the bears are cute and cuddly. Their main

draw--and the reason they remain in our minds--was the groundbreaking technology used to create them. In 1993, two years before the release of Toy Story, these were some of the very first widely viewed digital films. With these bears, as with other campaigns, Coke didn't just utilize the latest technology--Coke introduced the latest technology.

As a result of this brilliant advertising, a   12
beverage which I do not even let enter my mouth [REWORD!] is a significant part of my American cultural identity. That's why I spent thirty Israeli shekels and twenty minutes in a tourist trap I would ordinarily avoid buying my Hebrew Coca-Cola shirt. That shirt-- along with the rest of the Coca-Cola collectibles industry--demonstrates the power of [SOMETHING ABOUT COKE CONNECTING ITSELF WITH THE AMERICAN IDEAL OF A LIFE OF DIVERSION AND LIGHTHEARTEDNESS.] Seeing the logo that embodies all of this halfway around the world gave me an opportunity to affirm a part of my American identity.

The red-and-white logo's ability to appeal to   13
Americans even in such a foreign context speaks to Coke advertisers' success at creating this association. A 1999 American television commercial described by the Library of Congress archive as highly successful is set in Kenya, with dialogue in a local dialect and English subtitles. In it, two Kenyan boys taste their first Cokes and comment that the experience is much like the way they imagine kissing a girl will be. This image appeals to Americans because it enables us to use the symbol of Coca-Cola to make ourselves comfortable even in the most unfamiliar situations. And if that can't sell your product, nothing can.

● **EXERCISE 3.6**

Write a draft of an essay from the plan you produced for Exercise 3.5.

Once you finish a draft, make a point of reflecting a bit on your own exploring, planning, and drafting so that you can note your thoughts in your writing log if you are keeping one. Jot down what went well, what gave you problems and why, what you would like to change or improve. You might also use the COMMENT function of your computer to add comments about your draft while it is fresh in your mind. In Microsoft Word, for example, click on INSERT and then COMMENT; then type your thoughts in the comment box that will open at the bottom of the screen.

When Emily Lesk reflected in this way, she discovered that brainstorming with her classmates and clustering had been the most fruitful methods for generating ideas and examples and that answering questions to explain the topic hadn't added much. She also recognized that she felt very comfortable with her classmates and her professor (her audience), so writing a first draft was relatively easy. In addition, she saw that she'd worked extra hard to make her essay interesting, wanting to impress an audience she liked and respected so much. The main weaknesses, she decided, were in tone, punctuation, and diction, and in including some information that got away from her main point.

WRITING

Reflecting on Your Own Writing Process

● For an example of the COMMENT function, see p. 311.

● For a checklist of questions to use in reviewing your writing process, see 1b.

THINKING CRITICALLY ABOUT YOUR WRITING PROCESS

Using the following guidelines, reflect on the process you went through as you prepared for and wrote the draft of your essay for Exercise 3.6. Make your answers an entry in your writing log if you are keeping one.

1. How did you arrive at your specific topic?

2. When did you first begin to think about the assignment?

3. What kinds of exploring or planning did you do? What kinds of research did you need to do?

4. How long did it take to complete your draft (including the time spent gathering information)?

5. Where did you write your draft? Briefly describe the setting.

6. How did awareness of your audience help shape your draft?

7. What have you learned from your draft about your own rhetorical stance on your topic?

8. What did you learn about your ideas for this topic by exploring, planning, and talking to others about it?

9. What do you see as the major strengths of your draft? What is your favorite sentence(s), and why?

10. What do you see as the major weaknesses of your draft? What are you most worried about, and why?

11. What would you like to change about your process of exploring, planning, and drafting?

⯆ Reviewing, Revising, and Editing

4

4a Getting distance from your writing

The ancient Roman poet Horace advised aspiring writers to get distance from their work by putting it away for nine years. However impractical it sounds, Horace's advice holds a germ of truth: the more time you give yourself between the writing of a draft and its final revision, the more objectivity you will gain and the more options you will have as a writer. Even putting the draft away for a day or two will help clear your mind and give you some distance from your writing.

4b Rereading your draft

After giving yourself—and your draft—a rest, review the draft by rereading it carefully for meaning, by recalling your purpose, by reconsidering your rhetorical stance, and by considering your audience.

1 Rereading for meaning

Effective writers are almost always effective readers, particularly of their own writing. You can best begin reviewing, then, by rereading your draft carefully. For this reading, concentrate on your meaning and how clearly you have expressed it. If you see places where the meaning seems unclear, note them in the margin.

Whether you are writing a wedding invitation or a history essay, make time to get reviews of your work and to revise and edit. Although reviewing, revising, and editing all involve making changes, noting the distinctions among them can help you become a more powerful and more efficient writer.

Reviewing calls for reading your own writing with a critical eye and asking others to look over your work. When reviewing, you and others take a fresh look at how clearly your thesis is stated and developed, how effective your organization is, how varied your sentences are, and how appropriate your choice of words and visuals is. **Revising** involves reworking your draft on the basis of the review you and others have performed. Revision and review are in this way closely related.

Editing involves fine-tuning your prose, attending to details of grammar, usage, punctuation, and spelling. Of course, you also need to format and proofread your writing carefully to make it completely ready for public presentation. ∎

2 Remembering your purpose

After rereading, quickly note the main purpose of the piece of writing, and decide whether it matches your original purpose. You may want to go back to your original assignment to see exactly what it asks you to do. If the assignment asks you to propose a solution to a problem, make sure you have indeed set forth a well-supported solution rather than, for instance, an analysis of the problem.

3 Reconsidering your rhetorical stance

For more about
considering
your rhetorical
stance, see 2g.

Before or during the reviewing process, you can profit by taking time to look at your draft with one central question in mind: where are you coming from in this draft? That is, you should articulate the rhetorical stance you take in the draft and ask yourself what factors or influences have led you to that position. Early on in her reviewing process, Emily Lesk noted that she sounded a bit like a know-it-all, especially in the opening of her essay. After brainstorming with her group and talking with her instructor, she decided that some of what she sensed about the stance and tone of the introduction was related to trying, perhaps too hard, to get her audience's attention. She decided to work on this problem in her revision.

4 Considering your audience

For more about
considering your
audience, see 2h.

How appropriate is the essay for your audience? Think carefully about how your audience's experiences and expectations may be different from yours. Will they be interested in and able to follow your discussion? Is the language formal or informal enough for these readers? Have you defined any terms they may not know? What objections might they raise?

EXERCISE 4.1

Take twenty to thirty minutes to look critically at the draft you prepared for Exercise 3.6. Reread it carefully, check to see how well the purpose is accomplished, and consider how appropriate the draft is for the audience. Then write a paragraph about how you would go about revising it.

● **EXERCISE 4.2**

To prepare for a peer review, write a description of your purpose, rhetorical stance, and audience for your reviewer(s) to consider. For example, Emily Lesk might write, "I wanted to figure out why Coca-Cola seems so American and how the company achieves this effect. My audience is primarily college students like me, learning to analyze their own cultures. I wanted to sound knowledgeable, and I want this essay to be fun and interesting to read." This type of summary statement can help your readers keep your goals in mind as they give you feedback.

4c   Collaborating with others: responding to drafts

In addition to your own critical appraisal, you should get responses from friends, classmates, or colleagues you have met in classes — or online. Indeed, you may be part of a peer-review group in your class, and, if so, you want to use these reviewers to greatest advantage.

● — For more
detailed infor-
mation on col-
laborating with
others, see
Chapter 6.

1 Getting the most from reviewers' comments

Remember that your reviewers are ideally acting as coaches, not judges, and that their job is to help you improve your essay as much as possible. Listen to and read their comments carefully, and if you don't understand a particular suggestion, ask for clarification, examples, and so on. Remember, too, that reviewers are commenting on your writing, not on *you,* so be open and responsive to what they recommend. In the end, you are the foremost authority on your essay; you will decide what suggestions are most useful.

FOR MULTILINGUAL WRITERS: Understanding Peer Reviews

If your language or culture discourages direct criticism of others or considers it rude, you may find it disturbing if some or most of your classmates take a questioning or even challenging stance toward your work. As long as the questions and suggestions are constructive, however, they are appropriate to peer-review collaboration. Your peers will expect you to join in the critical collaboration, too, so be sure to offer your questions, suggestions, and insights.

The most helpful reviewers are interested in the topic and the writer's approach to it. They ask questions, make concrete suggestions, report on what is confusing and why, and offer encouragement.

To begin your review, *read straight through the essay or project* to make sure that you get the big picture and could summarize the main idea(s) of the piece of writing. Be sure to take any requests of the writer seriously. If, for example, the writer has asked you to look at specific aspects of his or her writing and to ignore others, be sure to respond to that request. If you have trouble understanding or following the writer's ideas, jot down what you think may be causing problems.

Next, *reread the essay* using requests from the writer or the guidelines on p. 87 to analyze the essay's effectiveness. As you respond to the review questions, insert into the draft marginal comments that fully describe your response, and make any suggestions you think might help: *I think a logical connection may be missing here, because when I went from the first sentence to the second, it seemed like you had left something out. Would your conclusions be stronger if you ended with the quotation in line 6? I don't quite understand this point: can you provide an example?* Since such descriptive comments may not always fit within the margins of a printed essay, you may want to write your comments with a word processor, keying each comment to a specific part of text (for example, *Page 2, par. 2, third sentence*).

Finally, *compose a final response to the essay* in a paragraph after the end of the essay. Address your comments directly to your classmate (*Dear Javier:*); then point out what you see as the major thesis, idea, or claim of the essay, and summarize how the essay gets its various points across. You can then comment on how effectively the essay makes its points and suggest revisions. Close by signing your name.

When you respond to writing, think of the response you are giving—whether orally or in writing—as a mini-essay. Like any writing, peer response works best with a little planning and some revision. So read over your comments, and check for tone and clarity.

FOR MULTILINGUAL WRITERS: Asking a Native Speaker to Review Your Draft

One good way to make sure that your writing is easy to follow is to have someone else read it. You might find it especially helpful to ask a native speaker to read over your draft and to point out any words or patterns that are unclear or not idiomatic.

1. *Overall thoughts.* What are the main strengths and weaknesses of the draft? What surprised you, and why? What was the single most important thing said? What do you want to know more about?

2. *The assignment.* Does the draft carry out the assignment? What could the writer do to better fulfill the assignment? Is the topic specific enough? (4b2)

3. *The title and introduction.* Does the title tell the reader what the draft is about? Does it catch the reader's interest? How? What does the opening accomplish? How else might the writer begin? (4f1 and f2)

4. *The thesis and purpose.* Paraphrase the thesis as a promise: *In this paper the writer will. . . .* Does the draft fulfill that promise? Why, or why not? Does it fulfill the writer's major purposes? (4b2 and 4d)

5. *The audience.* How does the draft capture the interest of and appeal to the intended audience? (4b4)

6. *The rhetorical stance.* Where does the writer stand on the issues involved in the topic? Is the writer an advocate or a critic? What words or phrases in the draft indicate the stance? Where does the writer's stance come from — that is, what influences have likely contributed to that stance? (4b3)

7. *The major points.* List the main points in order of presentation. Then number them in order of interest to you. Review them one by one. Do any need to be explained more or less fully? Should any be eliminated? Do any seem confusing or boring? Do any make you want to know more? How well are the major points supported by evidence, examples, or details? (4d)

8. *The visuals.* How are visuals — photographs, charts, graphs, maps, screenshots, and so on — used to support the major ideas in the essay? How well are visuals integrated into the text? Are the visuals introduced, commented upon, and labeled? (4e)

9. *The organization.* What kind of overall organizational plan is used — spatial, chronological, logical, or some other plan? Are the points presented in the most useful order? What, if anything, might be moved? Can you suggest ways to make connections between paragraphs clearer and easier to follow? (4e)

(Continued on p. 88)

(Continued from p. 87)

10. *The paragraphs.* Which paragraphs are clearest and most interesting to read, and why? Which ones are well developed? How are they developed? Which paragraphs need further development? What kind of information seems to be missing? (4g1)

11. *The sentences.* Choose the three sentences you consider the most interesting or the best written—particularly effective, entertaining, or otherwise memorable. Then choose three sentences you see as weak—confusing, awkward, or uninspired. Are the sentences varied in length, structure, and openings? (4g2)

12. *The words.* Mark words that are particularly effective, that draw vivid pictures or provoke strong responses. Then mark words that are weak, vague, or unclear. Do any words need to be defined? Are the verbs active and vivid? Are any words potentially offensive to the intended audience or to anyone else? (4g3)

13. *The tone.* What dominant impression does the draft create—serious, humorous, satiric, persuasive, passionately committed, highly objective? Mark specific places where the writer's attitude comes through most clearly. Is the tone appropriate to the topic and the audience? Is it consistent throughout? If not, is there a reason for its being varied? (4g4)

14. *The conclusion.* Does the draft conclude in a memorable way, or does it seem to end abruptly or trail off into vagueness? If you like the conclusion, tell why. How else might it end? (4f3)

FOR MULTILINGUAL WRITERS: Reviewing a Draft

Your knowledge of languages other than English or cultures other than the United States may give you special insights into an essay and help you point out unclear or confusing ideas in your peers' work. Even if you are not used to speaking up in class, remember that you have much to offer!

3 Reviewing a draft online

If you are doing your peer review online in the body of an email message, you can copy the message into an email of your own and then insert your comments directly into the writer's text by putting them in brackets. Use a subject line that alerts your classmate that you are sending back a review of a draft.

If the draft comes as an attachment, save the document in a peer-review folder under a name you will recognize (for example, *Jabari's draft*). Then use the COMMENT function (if you have one, it will usually be found under the INSERT menu) to insert your comments into the text. If you don't have access to this feature, you can insert a footnote into the text, usually through the INSERT menu. Finally, you can always simply insert your comments in brackets, boldface, all caps, color, or italics. You can then save the reviewed text and email it as an attachment back to your classmate. Below are comments on Emily Lesk's paper, inserted using the FOOTNOTE function.

WRITING

Collaborating
with Others:
Responding to
Drafts

**www • bedford
stmartins.com/
smhandbook**

To explore the
COMMENT and
FOOTNOTE functions
yourself, click on

▶ **Working Online**
  ▶ **Word Processors**

FOOTNOTE FUNCTION USED IN PEER REVIEW

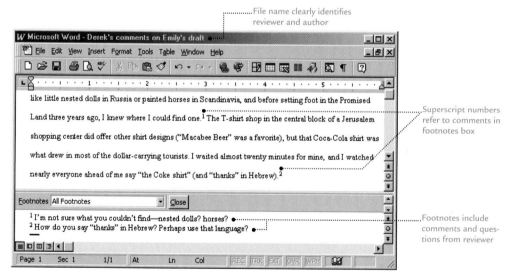

............File name clearly identifies
reviewer and author

Superscript numbers
refer to comments in
footnotes box

Footnotes include
comments and ques-
tions from reviewer

If your instructor has set up a Web site for your class to post drafts to, you can simply go to the site and add your responses there. Unless you can insert comments directly into a text, be sure to let the writer whose work you are reviewing know what line, passage, or paragraph you are commenting on (for example, *par. 1, line 4*).

●— For more infor-
mation on class
Web sites, see
6c.

Here are the first three paragraphs of Emily Lesk's draft, as reviewed by two students, Beatrice Kim and Nastassia Lopez:

I'm not sure your title really says
what your paper will argue.
—NL → All-Powerful Coke

You surel
my atten
here, and
wonder w
this essay
going.
—BK

The very beginning → I don't drink Coke. Call me picky for disliking
seems kind of abrupt.
—NL

the soda's saccharine aftertaste. Call me cheap for

choosing a water fountain over a twelve-ounce aluminum

can that costs a dollar from a vending machine but

only pennies to produce. Even call me unpatriotic for

rejecting the potable god that over the last century

has come to represent all the enjoyment and ease to be

found in our American way of life. But don't call me a

hypocrite when I admit that I still identify with Coke

and the Coca-Cola culture. ←

What's
connecti
between
and seco
paragra
—Bk

I have a favorite T-shirt that says "Drink Coca-

Cola Classic" in Hebrew. It's Israel's standard

tourist fare, like little nested dolls in Russia or

painted horses in Scandinavia, and before setting foot

I'm not sure what   in the Promised Land three years ago, I knew where I
you couldn't find—
nested dolls? horses? could find one. The T-shirt shop in the central block
—NL

of a Jerusalem shopping center did offer other shirt

designs ("Macabee Beer" was a favorite), but that

Coca-Cola shirt was what drew in most of the dollar-carrying tourists. I waited almost twenty minutes for

mine, and I watched nearly everyone ahead of me say

s a great "the Coke shirt" (and "thanks" in Hebrew). *How do you say "thanks" in Hebrew? Perhaps use*
—many *that language?* —BK
have   At the time, I never asked why I wanted the
ial
ersation shirt. I do know, though, that the reason I wear it
' shirt.
NL often, despite a hole in the right sleeve, has to do

with its power as a conversation piece. Few people

notice it without asking something like, "Does that

say Coke?" I usually smile and nod. They mumble a

compliment and we go our separate ways. But rarely

does anyone want to know what language the world's

most famous logo is written in. And why should they?

Is this your thesis?

Perhaps because Coca-Cola is a cultural icon that *I was kind of*
surprised—it
shapes American identity. *← Isn't this a sentence* *seems to come*
fragment? *out of the blue.*
—BK *—BK*

WRITING

Collaborating
with Others:
Responding to
Drafts

As this review shows, Nastassia and Bea agree on some of the major problems—and good points—in Emily's first draft. The marginal notes on the draft itself, however, reveal their different responses. You, too, will find that different readers do not always agree on what is effective or ineffective. In addition, you may find that you simply do not agree with their advice. In examining responses to your writing, you can often proceed efficiently by looking first for areas of agreement (*everyone was confused by this sentence—I'd better revise it*) or strong disagreement (*one person said my conclusion was "perfect," and someone else said it "didn't conclude"—better look carefully at that paragraph again*).

Here is the email message Emily's two peer-review partners wrote to her, giving her some overall comments to accompany those they had written in the margins of her draft:

r/r/e

92   **4c**

WRITING

Reviewing,
Revising, and
Editing

To: elesk@stanford.edu
From: "Beatrice Kim" <bkim@stanford.edu>
Subject: your draft
Cc:
Bcc:
Attached: c:\WPDATA\Comments for Emily

Hi Emily:

We're pasting in our overall response to your draft and also attaching it as a Word document. Good luck on revising!

First, we think this is a great draft. You got us interested right away with the story about your T-shirt and we just wanted to keep on reading. So the introduction seems really good. But the introduction goes on for a while--several paragraphs, we think, and we were beginning to wonder what the point was. And when you get to your thesis, could you make it a little more specific or say a little more about what it means that Coca-Cola is an icon that shapes identity??

Your stance is very clear to us, and we liked that you talked about how you were pulled into the whole Coke thing even though you don't particularly like the soda. Sometimes we got bogged down in a ton of details, though, and felt like maybe you were telling us too much.

We were impressed with some of the words you use--we had to look up what a "potable" god is! But sometimes we weren't sure a word was the very best one--we marked some of these words on your draft for you.

See you in class.

Nastassia and Bea

P.S. Could you add a picture of your T-shirt?? It would be cool to see what it looks like.

r/r/e

4d

93

WRITING

Revising the Thesis
and Its Support

**www • bedford
stmartins.com/
smhandbook**

To see another
instructor's
response to
another student's
draft, click on

▶ **Student Samples**
  ▶ **Essays**

Emily also got advice from her instructor, Professor Corinne Arraéz, who suggested that Emily do a careful outline of this draft to check for how one point led to another and to see if the draft stayed on track. Based on all of the responses she received, Emily decided to (1) make her thesis more explicit, (2) delete some extraneous information and examples, (3) integrate at least one more visual into her text, and (4) work especially hard on the tone and length of her introduction and on word choice.

● **EXERCISE 4.3**

Using the questions listed in 4c as a guide, analyze the draft you wrote for Exercise 3.6.

4d Revising the thesis and its support

Once you have received advice on your draft from all available sources and have studied the responses, you should reread the draft once more, paying special attention to your thesis and its support. Make sure your thesis sentence contains a clear statement of the *topic* that you will discuss and a *comment* explaining what is particularly significant or noteworthy about the topic. As you continue to read, ask yourself how each paragraph relates to or supports the thesis and how each sentence develops the paragraph topic. Such careful rereading can help you to eliminate irrelevant sections or details or identify sections needing further details or examples.

Be particularly careful to note what kinds of evidence, examples, or good reasons you offer in support of your major points. If some points are off topic, look back at your exploratory work. Emily Lesk found, for example, that an entire paragraph in her draft (par. 8) did nothing to support her thesis and that, in fact, she had wondered at the time of drafting if she was on track. Thus she deleted the entire paragraph.

●···· For more about
exploring a topic
and gathering
information, see
3a and c.

● **EXERCISE 4.4**

After rereading the draft you wrote for Exercise 3.6, evaluate the revised working thesis you produced for Exercise 3.3, and then evaluate its support in the draft. Identify points that need further support, and list those things you must do to provide that support.

One good way to check the organization of a draft is by outlining it. After numbering the paragraphs in the draft, read through each one, jotting down its main idea or topic. When you come across a visual in your paper, note this in your outline by inserting the caption. Then examine your outline, and ask yourself the following questions:

What organizational strategies did you use? spatial? chronological? logical? associational? Are they used effectively? Why, or why not?

Do the main points clearly relate to the thesis and to one another? Are any of them irrelevant?

Can you identify any confusing leaps from point to point? Do you need to provide additional or stronger transitions?

Have you integrated visuals into your text by introducing them carefully and commenting on their significance? Have you integrated them appropriately?

Can you identify clear links between paragraphs and ideas? Do other links need to be added?

Have any important points been left out?

When Emily looked at her draft, she saw that she had made a note to herself in paragraph 6 saying, *Look for a picture of this original Coke Santa.* Emily remembered that her mother had a button depicting one of Sundblom's Santas, so she took a photograph of the button to use in her paper. She also noted that peer reviewers suggested that she include a photo of her Coca-Cola T-shirt, so she began thinking about where that photo should go and about how she would integrate both of these illustrations into her text.

● **EXERCISE 4.5**

Draw up a brief outline of Emily Lesk's first draft (in 3f), and evaluate its organization. Begin by answering the questions in 4e.

● **EXERCISE 4.6**

Check the paragraph transitions in Emily Lesk's first draft (in 3f). Did you find any that were weak or missing? If so, suggest at least two ways to strengthen them or add others.

FOR COLLABORATION

Ask a classmate to read and outline your paper, and offer to do the same for him or her. This will give you an idea of how well your organization comes across. If possible, exchange papers with more than one reviewer. You can then compare their outlines of your paper, which will help you pinpoint possible areas of confusion.

4f Reconsidering the title, introduction, and conclusion

First and last impressions count. In fact, readers remember the first and last parts of a piece of writing better than anything else. For this reason, it is wise to pay careful attention to three important elements — the title, the introduction, and the conclusion.

1 The title

A good title gives readers information, draws them into the piece of writing, and may even indicate the writer's view of the topic. The title of Emily Lesk's draft, "All-Powerful Coke," did not imply the link Emily wanted to establish between Coca-Cola and national identity. Following a discussion of this draft, she produced a new draft and titled it "Red, White, and Everywhere." This title piques readers' curiosity and suggests that the familiar "red, white, and blue" is going to be linked to something that is everywhere.

2 The introduction

A good introduction accomplishes two important tasks: first, it draws readers into the piece of writing, and second, it presents the topic and makes some comment on it. It contains, in other words, a strong lead, or hook, to attract readers' interest and often an explicit thesis as well. One common kind of introduction opens with a general statement about the topic and then goes into more detail, leading up to a statement of the specific thesis at the end. A writer can also begin an introduction effectively with a *vivid statement* of the problem that led to the thesis or with an *intriguing quotation,* an *anecdote,* a *question,* or a *strong opinion.* The rest of the introduction then develops this beginning item into a more general or detailed presentation of the topic and the thesis.

● For more discussion and examples of introductory paragraphs, see 5f1.

In many cases, especially when a writer begins with a quotation or an anecdote, the introduction consists of two or three paragraphs: the first provides the hook, while the second paragraph and perhaps the third explain the significance of the hook. Emily Lesk used this pattern in her introduction. Her first paragraph contains such a hook, which is followed by a two-paragraph narrative anecdote about a trip to Israel that makes a link between Coca-Cola advertising and Americans' sense of identifying with the product. After considering the responses of her peers and analyzing her opening, Emily decided that the introduction took too long to get to the point and that it didn't lead up to a clearly articulated thesis. She decided to tighten up and shorten the introduction and to make her thesis more explicit and detailed.

3 The conclusion

A good conclusion leaves readers satisfied that a full discussion has taken place. Often a conclusion will begin with a restatement of the thesis and end with more general statements that grow out of it: this pattern reverses the common general-to-specific pattern of the introduction. Writers can also draw on a number of other ways to conclude effectively, including a *provocative question,* a *quotation,* a *vivid image,* a *call for action,* a *warning.*

Emily Lesk's two-paragraph conclusion emphasizes the main point of her essay, that the Coke logo now represents America, but it then goes on to discuss the impact of such advertising in other countries, such as Kenya. On reflection, Emily decided that the final paragraph on Coke in Kenya didn't really draw her essay to a close but rather went off in a slightly different direction. As a result, she cut this paragraph from her revised essay.

For more discussion and examples of concluding paragraphs, see 5f2.

● EXERCISE 4.7

Review Emily Lesk's draft in 3f, and compose an alternative conclusion. Then write a paragraph commenting on the strengths and weaknesses of the two conclusions.

4g   Revising paragraphs, sentences, words, and tone

In addition to the large-scale task of examining the logic, organization, and development of their writing, effective writers look closely at the smaller elements: paragraphs, sentences, and words. Many writers, in fact, look forward to this part of revising because its results are often dramatic. Turning a bland sentence into a memorable one — or finding exactly the right word to express a thought — can yield great satisfaction and self-confidence.

Many students with dyslexia and other language-processing disabilities can benefit from the use of assistive technologies such as real-time spell checkers or programs to check mechanics and punctuation. You may want to make these technologies a regular part of your revising process.

WRITING

Revising
Paragraphs,
Sentences, Words,
and Tone

1 Examining paragraphs

Paragraphing serves the reader by visually breaking up long expanses of writing and signaling a shift in focus. Readers expect a paragraph to develop an idea or a topic, a process that almost always demands several sentences or more. The following guidelines can help you evaluate your paragraphs as you revise:

● For guidelines on paragraphing for readers, see 5a.

1. Look for the topic or main point of each paragraph, whether it is stated or implied. Then check to see that every sentence expands, supports, or otherwise relates to the topic.
2. Check to see how each paragraph is organized — spatially, chronologically, associationally, or by some logical relationship. Then determine whether the organization is appropriate to the topic of the paragraph and whether it is used fully to develop the paragraph. (See 5c and d.)
3. Count the number of sentences in each paragraph, noting paragraphs that have only a few. Do these paragraphs sufficiently develop the topic of the paragraph?

Paragraph 5 in Emily Lesk's draft contains only two sentences, and these sentences don't lead directly into the next paragraph. In her revision, Emily lengthened (and strengthened) paragraph 5 by adding a sentence that points out the *result* of Coca-Cola's advertising campaign. (For information on how Emily made her language more lively in this paragraph, see p. 102.)

● See also the guidelines for editing paragraphs at the beginning of Chapter 5.

```
        But while countless campaigns with this general

    strategy have together shaped the Coca-Cola image,

    presenting a product as key to a happy life represents

    a fairly typical approach to advertising everything

    from Fords to Tylenol. Coca-Cola's advertising is
```

truly unique, however, for the original way the

beverage giant has utilized specific advertising

media--namely magazines and television--to drive home

this message.

> *As a result, Coca-Cola has come to be associated not only with the images of Americana portrayed in specific advertisements, but also with the general forms of advertising media that dominate American culture.*

EXERCISE 4.8

Choose two other paragraphs in Emily Lesk's draft in 3f, and evaluate them using the guidelines on pp. 87–88. Write a brief paragraph in which you suggest ways to improve the development or organization of these paragraphs.

FOR COLLABORATION

Working with two other classmates, find a popular newsmagazine (such as *Time* or *Newsweek*), and compare its paragraph structure to that of an academic journal (such as *Critical Inquiry* or the *Journal of Modern History*). Note that paragraph length, organization, layout, and use of visuals vary from newsmagazine to academic journal. How do the paragraphs you looked at compare with those you and your classmates typically write?

2 Examining sentences

See the guide-
lines for editing
sentences at the
beginning of
Chapter 43.

As with life, variety is the spice of sentences. You can add variety to your sentences by looking closely at their length, structure, and opening patterns.

■ *Varying sentence length*

Too many short sentences, especially one after another, can sound like a series of blasts on a car horn — or like an elementary school textbook — whereas a steady stream of long sentences may tire or confuse readers. Most writers, then, aim for some variety of length.

For more about
varying sentence
length, see 46a.

In looking at paragraph 9, Emily Lesk found that the sentences were all fairly long: twenty-eight, twenty-six, fifty, and forty words. In revising, she decided to cut the second sentence to fourteen words, thereby insert-

r/r/e

4g   99

WRITING

Revising
Paragraphs,
Sentences, Words,
and Tone

ing a short, easy-to-read sentence between two long sentences. She also decided that her first sentence wasn't very clear, so she rewrote it.

This is just one example of the media strategies Coca-Cola has used to
~~In other words, Coca-Cola has hammered itself~~ ^
encourage us to equate Coke with the "happy life" element of American identity.
~~into our perceptions--both conscious and subconscious--~~

~~of an American cultural identity by equating itself~~
                                              As
~~with media that define American culture.~~ ^When the

omnipresent ~~general~~ magazine ~~that marked the earlier~~
                              gave way to
~~part of the century fell by the wayside under~~
                      ^
television~~'s power,~~ Coke was there from the beginning.

In its 1996 recap of the previous fifty years in

industry history, the publication <u>Beverage Industry</u>

cites Coca-Cola as a frontrunner in the very first

form of television advertising: sponsorship of entire

programs such as, in the case of Coke, <u>The Bob Dixon</u>

<u>Show</u> and <u>The Adventures of Kit Carson</u>. Just as today,

we associate national patriotic events such as the

2002 Olympics with their list of corporate sponsors

(which in this case includes the Coca-Cola Company),

viewers of early television programs will forever

equate them with Coke.

◾ *Varying sentence structure*

The simple sentence is the most common kind of sentence in modern English, but using only simple sentences can be very dull. On the other hand, overusing compound sentences may result in a singsong or repetitive rhythm, and strings of complex sentences may sound, well, overly complex. It is best to vary your sentence structure.

● — For more about varying sentence structures, see Chapter 46.

For more about ──●
varying sentence
openings, see
46b.

■ *Varying sentence openings*

Most sentences in English follow subject-predicate order and hence open with the subject of an independent clause, as does the sentence you are now reading. But opening too many sentences in a row this way results in a jerky, abrupt, or choppy rhythm. You can vary sentence openings by beginning with a dependent clause, a phrase, an adverb, a conjunctive adverb, or a coordinating conjunction.

Emily Lesk's second paragraph tells the story of getting her Coke T-shirt in Israel, but every sentence in the paragraph opens with the subject. In revising, Emily decided to take out some of the examples and to vary her sentence openings. The result is a dramatic and easy-to-read paragraph.

~~I have a favorite T-shirt that says "Drink Coca-Cola Classic" in Hebrew. It's Israel's standard tourist fare, like little nested dolls in Russia or painted horses in Scandinavia, and~~ *Even* before setting foot in the Promised Land three years ago, I knew *exactly* where I could find one. The T-shirt shop in the central block of ~~a~~ Jerusalem *'s Ben Yehuda Street* ~~shopping center~~ did offer other shirt designs, ~~("Macabee Beer" was a favorite),~~ but ~~that Coca-Cola shirt~~ was what drew in most of the dollar-carrying tourists. *While waiting* ~~I waited~~ almost twenty minutes for ~~mine,~~ *my shirt* ~~and~~ I watched nearly everyone ahead of me say "the Coke shirt *, todah rabah [thank you very much]."* ~~(and "thanks" in Hebrew).~~

the one with the bright white "Drink Coca-Cola Classic" written in Hebrew cursive across the chest

■ *Checking for sentences opening with* **it** *and* **there**

As you go over the sentences of your draft, look especially carefully at those beginning with *it* or *there* followed by a form of *be*. Sometimes such a construction can create a special emphasis, as in "It was a dark and stormy night." But such structures can also easily cause problems. A reader doesn't know what *it* means, for instance, unless the writer has already pointed out exactly what the word stands for. A more subtle problem with these openings, however, is that they allow a writer to avoid taking responsibility for a statement. Look at the following two sentences:

WRITING
Revising
Paragraphs,
Sentences, Words,
and Tone

●— For more about
sentences open-
ing with *it* and
there, see 37c
and 47a1.

> It is necessary to raise student fees.

> The university must raise student fees.

The first sentence avoids responsibility by failing to tell us *who says* it is necessary.

Remember that writing is recursive. So sometimes when you revise and combine sentences, you change the content and shape of the paragraph in which they appear. As a result, you might need to revise the paragraph again.

FOR COLLABORATION

Here are two sentences from Emily Lesk's draft that feature *it is* or *there is.* Working with a classmate, make at least two revisions that eliminate these constructions. Bring your revisions to class, and be prepared to explain the process you went through in your revisions and why the revisions are effective.

1. In today's world of CNN, e-journals, and newsweek.com, it is often easy to forget how pervasive a medium the magazine was prior to the advent of television.

2. There is no denying that this strategy worked brilliantly, as this inviting image of Santa Claus graduated from the pages of *Saturday Evening Post* to become the central figure of the most celebrated and beloved season of the year.

● **EXERCISE 4.9**

Find a paragraph in your own writing that lacks variety in sentence length, sentence structure, or sentence openings. Then write a revised version.

---

3 Examining words

Even more than paragraphs and sentences, **word choice**, or diction, offers writers an opportunity to put their personal stamp on a piece of writing. The following questions should help you become aware of the kinds of words you most typically use:

r/r/e

4g

102

WRITING

Reviewing,
Revising, and
Editing

1. Are the nouns primarily abstract and general or concrete and specific? Too many abstract and general nouns can create boring prose. To say that you bought a new car is much less memorable and interesting than to say you bought a new convertible or a new Volkswagen Bug. (See 27c.)

2. Are there too many nouns in relation to the number of verbs? The *effect* of the *overuse* of *nouns* in *writing* is the *placing* of too much *strain* on the inadequate *number* of *verbs* and the resultant *prevention* of *movement* of the *thought*. In the preceding sentence, one tiny form of the verb *be* (*is*) has to drag along the entire weight of all those nouns. The result is a heavy, boring sentence. Why not say instead, *Overusing nouns places a big strain on the verbs and consequently slows down the prose?*

3. How many verbs are forms of *be*? If *be* verbs account for more than about a third of your total verbs, you are probably overusing them. (See Chapter 33.)

4. Are verbs *active* wherever possible? Passive verbs are harder to read and remember than active ones. Although the passive voice has many uses (see Chapter 33), often your writing will be stronger and more energetic if you use active verbs.

5. Are your words *appropriate*? Check to be sure they are not too fancy — or too casual. (See Chapter 27.)

Emily Lesk made a number of changes in diction on the basis of the responses she received and her own critical analysis. In the second paragraph, she decided to change *Promised Land* to *Israel* since some of her readers might not regard these two as being synonymous. She paid special attention to the verbs she was using, deciding, in paragraph 6, for example, that saying Santa was *dressed in a wide variety of colors* was more accurate and descriptive than saying he *came in* these colors. She also looked for ways to make her diction more lively, changing *from Fords to Tylenol* in paragraph 5 to *from Allstate insurance to Ziploc bags* to take advantage of the A-to-Z reference.

4 Examining tone

Word choice is closely related to **tone,** the attitude toward the topic and the audience that the writer's language conveys. In examining the tone of your draft, you need to consider the nature of the topic, your own attitude toward it, and that of your intended audience. Check for connotations of words as well as for slang, jargon, emotional language, and the level of formality to see whether they create the tone you want to achieve (humorous, serious, impassioned, and so on) and whether that tone is an appropriate one, given your audience and topic.

For more about
creating an
appropriate tone,
see Chaper 27.

Although Emily Lesk's classmates seemed to like the overall tone of her essay, she decided to make some changes in tone, especially in her introduction. Since her peer reviewers had found her opening sentence abrupt, she decided to preface *I don't drink Coke* with another clause, resulting in *America, I have a confession to make: I don't drink Coke.* Emily also shortened her first paragraph considerably, in part to eliminate the know-it-all attitude she had detected in her own review of the draft.

EXERCISE 4.10

Turn to 3f, and read Emily Lesk's last two paragraphs. Describe the tone you think she achieves. Does it seem appropriate to the audience she is writing to — her professor and classmates in a first-year college writing course — and to her topic? Assume these paragraphs are intended instead for a group of third-graders. What would you do to alter the tone for this audience?

4h   Reconsidering format

Before you produce a copy for final editing and proofreading, take the time to consider issues of format. Your word-processing program will allow you to insert headings in a larger size type or in bold type, for instance. You can consider using a different font for examples. If you have a graphics program, you can include charts or other illustrations. You may also have the option of presenting your work as a Web text. Whatever your final decisions, now is the time to think carefully about the overall visual appearance of your final draft.

For more about designing documents, see Chapters 8 and 9.

4i   Editing

Because readers expect, even demand, a final copy that is clean and correct in every way, you need to make time for thorough and careful editing. This work should begin with your spell checker: if you have not run it yet, do so now, and check every word the spell checker flags. You can make editing work for you in future assignments by keeping a personal checklist of the *patterns* of editing problems you find in your writing. Here again, your computer can help: if you notice that you are likely to misuse a certain word, you can use the FIND function to find any instances of that word and then check the usage carefully.

r/r/e

104   4i

WRITING

Reviewing,
Revising, and
Editing

■ *An editing inventory*

To begin, list all the errors or corrections marked on the last piece of writing you did. Then note the context of the sentence in which each error appeared. Finally, try to derive a guideline to spot future errors of the same kind. You can broaden these guidelines as you begin to find patterns of errors, and you can then add to your inventory every time you write and edit a draft. Here is an example of such a checklist:

MARKED ERRORS	IN CONTEXT	LOOK FOR
spelling	*to* for *too*	*to* before adjectives and adverbs
fragment	starts with *when*	sentences beginning with *when*
missing comma	after *however*	sentences opening with *however*
missing apostrophe	*Michael's*	all names
missing apostrophe	*company's*	all possessive nouns
tense shift	*go* for *went*	use of present tense
spelling	*sacrifice*	*sacrafice*
missing comma	after *for example*	use of introductory elements

This writer has begun to isolate patterns, like her tendency to leave out apostrophes in possessives and commas after introductory elements.

Some errors, such as the use of wrong words and misspellings, may seem so random that you are unable to identify patterns in them. In this case, the best you can do is note these errors to see if they fall into patterns you can later identify.

USING FIND AND REPLACE

To help find the words in your editing inventory, use your word processor's FIND AND REPLACE function. Click on FIND under the EDIT menu. In the search box, type a space, the word, and then another space. Otherwise, if you're looking for the word *to*, for example, your word processor will flag all the words that contain the combination *to*, such as to*gether*, to*ward*, and in*to*. To replace all instances of a particular error, click on the REPLACE tab, and enter the correct word in the REPLACE WITH search box. Then click on REPLACE ALL.

● **EXERCISE 4.11**

Using several essays you have written, establish your own editing checklist based on
the one shown in 4i.

● **EXERCISE 4.12**

Using the guidelines in 4c, read the draft you wrote in Exercise 3.6 with an eye for
revising. Try to do this at least a day after you finished the draft. List the things you
need or want to address in your revision. At this point, you may want to exchange
drafts with some classmates and share responses.

4j   Proofreading the final draft

As a writer, you need to make your final draft as free from error as possible. You can do so by taking time for one last, careful proofreading,
which means reading to correct any typographical errors or other slips,
such as inconsistencies in spelling and punctuation. Remember that
running the spell checker, while necessary, is *not* the equivalent of thorough proofreading. To proofread most effectively, read through the copy
aloud, making sure that punctuation marks are used correctly and consistently, that all sentences are complete, and that no words are left out.
Then go through it again, this time reading backward so that you can
focus on each word and its spelling.

You have already seen and read about a number of the revisions Emily
Lesk made in her first draft. On pp. 106–111 is the edited and proofread
version she turned in to her instructor. If you compare her final draft
with her first draft, you will notice a number of additional changes made
in editing and proofreading. For example, she added hyphens to several
compound adjectives, corrected some capitalization errors, and deleted
a number of unnecessary commas. What other improvements can you
spot?

www ● bedford
stmartins.com/
smhandbook

To see another
student's final
draft, click on

▶ **Student Samples**
   ▶ **Essays**

STUDENT WRITER

Emily Lesk

● **EXERCISE 4.13**

Revise, edit, and proofread the draft you wrote for Exercise 3.6.

r/r/e

4i

106

WRITING

Reviewing,
Revising, and
Editing

Emily Lesk
Professor Arraéz
Electric Rhetoric
November 15, 2002

Red, White, and Everywhere

America, I have a confession to make: I don't drink   1
Coke. But don't call me a hypocrite just because I am
still the proud owner of a bright red shirt that
advertises it. Just call me an American.

Even before setting foot in Israel three years ago,   2
I knew exactly where I could find one. The tiny T-shirt
shop in the central block of Jerusalem's Ben Yehuda
Street did offer other designs, but the one with a
bright white "Drink Coca-Cola Classic" written in Hebrew
cursive across the chest was what drew in most of the
dollar-carrying tourists. While waiting almost twenty
minutes for my shirt (depicted in Fig. 1), I watched

nearly every customer ahead
of me ask for "the Coke
shirt, todah rabah [thank
you very much]."

At the time, I never   3
thought it strange that I
wanted one, too. After having
absorbed sixteen years of
Coca-Cola propaganda through
everything from NBC's
Saturday morning cartoon
lineup to the concession
stand at Camden Yards (the
Baltimore Orioles' ballpark),
I associated the shirt with
singing along to the "Just

Fig. 1. Hebrew Coca-Cola
T-shirt. Personal photo-
graph. Despite my dis-
like for the beverage,
I bought this Coca-Cola
T-shirt in Israel.

for the Taste of It" jingle and with America's favorite
pastime, not with a brown fizzy beverage I refused to
consume. When I later realized the immensity of Coke's

corporate power, I felt somewhat duped and manipulated, but that didn't stop me from wearing the shirt. I still don it often, despite the growing hole in the right sleeve, because of its power as a conversation piece. Few Americans notice it without asking something like "Does that say Coke?" I usually smile and nod. Then they mumble a one-word compliment and we go our separate ways. But rarely do they want to know what language the internationally recognized logo is written in. And why should they? They are interested in what they can relate to as Americans: a familiar red-and-white logo, not a foreign language. Through nearly a century of brilliant advertising strategies, the Coca-Cola Company has given Americans not only a thirst-quenching beverage but a cultural icon that we have come to claim as our own.

Throughout the company's history, its marketing   4
strategies have centered on putting Coca-Cola in scenes of the happy, carefree existence Americans are supposedly striving for. What 1950's teenage girl, for example, wouldn't long to see herself in the Coca-Cola ad that appeared in a 1958 issue of Seventeen magazine? A clean-cut, handsome man flirts with a pair of smiling girls as they laugh and drink Cokes at a soda-shop counter. Even a girl who couldn't picture herself in that idealized role could at least buy a Coke for consolation. The malt shop, complete with a soda jerk in a white jacket and paper hat and a Coca-Cola fountain, is a theme that, even today, remains a piece of Americana (Ikuta 74).

But while countless campaigns with this general   5
strategy have together shaped the Coca-Cola image, presenting a product as key to a happy life is a fairly typical approach to advertising everything from Allstate insurance to Ziploc bags. Coca-Cola's advertising strategy is unique, however, for the original way the beverage giant has used the specific advertising media of magazines and television to drive home this message.

As a result, Coca-Cola has become associated not only with the images of Americana portrayed in specific advertisements but also with the general forms of advertising media that dominate American culture.

One of the earliest and best-known examples of this strategy is artist Haddon Sundblom's rendering of Santa Claus. Prior to Coca-Cola's Santa campaign of 1931, depictions of Saint Nick took many different forms, although he was usually slim and dressed in a wide variety of colors. Ironically, it was a Swede who created the round, jolly, red-and-white American icon (see Fig. 2), who just so happens to delight in an ice-cold Coke after a tiring night of delivering presents. The way in which Coca-Cola advertisers utilized the concept of the magazine to present this inviting image represents Coca-Cola's brilliant manipulation of the medium itself (Pendergrast 181).

Fig. 2. <u>Coca-Cola Santa pin</u>. Personal photograph. This pin is an example of Coca-Cola's Santa campaign.

In today's world of CNN, e-journals, and newsweek.com, we often forget how pervasive a medium the magazine was before television became easily and cheaply available to all. Well into the 1960s, American households of diverse backgrounds and geographic locations subscribed loyally to general-subject weeklies and monthlies such as <u>Life</u> and the <u>Saturday Evening Post</u>, which provided a primary source of news, entertainment, and other cultural information to families nationwide. This large and constant group of subscribers enabled Coca-Cola to build an annual

Christmastime campaign that used an extremely limited
number of advertisements. According to the Coca-Cola
Company Web site, Sundblom created only around forty
images of Santa Claus during the campaign's duration
from 1931 to 1964 ("Haddon Sundblom"). As a result,
Americans soon began to look forward to and seek out the
ads each holiday season. The marketing strategy was not
to capture consumers with the attractive color drawings
but rather to make them wait eagerly by the mailbox each
December so that they could flip through the Saturday
Evening Post to find the latest scene featuring Santa
gulping a Coke. For this strategy to be successful, the
advertisements had to be seen by many, but they also had
to be just hard enough to come by to seem special and
exclusive. What better way to achieve these dual goals
than to place an advertisement in the December issue of
an immensely popular magazine?

This is just one example of the media strategies   8
Coca-Cola has used to encourage us to equate Coke with
the "happy life" element of American identity. As the
omnipresent magazine gave way to television, Coke was
there from the beginning. In a 1996 recap of the
previous fifty years in industry history, Beverage
Industry cites Coca-Cola as a frontrunner in the very
first form of television advertising: sponsorship of
entire programs such as The Bob Dixon Show and The
Adventures of Kit Carson ("Fabulous Fifties" 16). Just
as today we associate national and patriotic events such
as the 2002 Winter Olympics with their list of corporate
sponsors (which in this case includes the Coca-Cola
Company), viewers of early television programs will
forever equate them with Coke.

When networks switched from offering sponsorships   9
to selling exclusive commercial time in short
increments, Coca-Cola strove to distinguish itself once
again, this time by experimenting with new formats and
technologies for those commercials. Early attempts--such

as choppy "stop motion" animation, where photographs of objects such as Coke bottles move without the intervention of actors--attracted much attention, according to the Library of Congress Motion Picture Archives Web site. Coca-Cola was also a pioneer in color television; after a series of experimental reels, the company produced its first color commercial in 1964 (Library of Congress). While the subject matter of these original commercials was not particularly memorable (Coca-Cola cans and bottles inside a refrigerator), the hype surrounding the use of new technologies helped draw attention to the product.

But the advertising campaign that perhaps best 10 illustrates the ability of Coca-Cola advertisers to tie their product to a groundbreaking technology did not appear until 1993, just in time for Coke's sponsorship of the 1994 Winter Olympics. Who can forget the six television commercials featuring digitally animated polar bears that roll, swim, snuggle, slide, and gurgle about in a computerized North Pole--and finish off the playful experience with a swig of Coke? In 1993, two years before the release of Toy Story, these commercials were some of the very first widely viewed digital films (Library of Congress). As with Sundblom's Santa Clauses, television viewers looked forward to their next sighting of the cute, cuddly, cutting-edge bears, who created a natural association between Coca-Cola and digital animation and, to a certain extent, Olympic spirit. Once again, Coke didn't just use the latest technology--Coke defined it.

As a result of this brilliant advertising, a 11 beverage I never even drink is a significant part of my American cultural identity--because I connect it with watching the Olympics on TV and my first encounter with digital animation. That's why I spent thirty Israeli shekels and twenty minutes in a tourist trap I would ordinarily avoid buying my Hebrew Coca-Cola shirt.

That shirt, along with the rest of the enormous Coca-
Cola collectibles industry, demonstrates Coke's power
to identify itself with the American ideal of a
lighthearted life of diversion and pleasure. Standing
in line halfway around the world for the logo that
embodies these values gave me an opportunity to affirm
a part of my American identity.

Here is Emily Lesk's list of works cited in her essay.

Works Cited

Coca-Cola Santa pin. Personal photograph by author.
  9 Nov. 2002.

"The Fabulous Fifties." Beverage Industry 87.6 (1996):
  16. 2 Nov. 2002 <http://memory.loc/gov.ammem/
  ccmphtml/indshst.html>.

"Haddon Sundblom." Coca-Cola and Christmas 1999. 2 Nov.
  2002 <http://www.coca-cola.com.ar/Coca-colaweb/
  paginas_ingles/christmas.html>.

Hebrew Coca-Cola T-shirt. Personal photograph by author.
  8 Nov. 2002.

Ikuta, Yasutoshi, ed. '50s American Magazine Ads. Tokyo:
  Graphic-Sha, 1987.

Library of Congress. Motion Picture, Broadcasting and
  Recorded Sound Division. 5 Nov. 2002 <http://
  memory.loc.gov/ammem/ccmphtml/index.html>.

Pendergrast, Mark. For God, Country, and Coca-Cola: The
  Unauthorized History of the Great American Soft
  Drink and the Company That Makes It. New York:
  Macmillan, 1993.

THINKING CRITICALLY ABOUT YOUR REVIEWING AND REVISING PROCESS

1. How did you begin reviewing your draft?
2. What kinds of comments on or responses to your draft did you have? How helpful were they, and why?
3. How long did revising take? How many drafts did you produce?

4. Were most of your revisions additions? deletions? replacements of one word, one example, and so on by another? transfers of material from one place to another?

5. What kinds of changes did you tend to make? in organization, paragraphs, sentence structure, wording, adding or deleting information? in the use of visuals?

6. What gave you the most trouble as you were revising?

7. What pleased you most? What would you most like to change about your process of revising, and how do you plan to go about doing so?

⬛ Developing Paragraphs

5

The hero of the Rex Stout mysteries, Nero Wolfe, once solved a case by identifying the paragraph structure of a particular writer-murderer. A person's style of paragraphing, Wolfe claimed, serves even more reliably than fingerprints as a stamp of identity. Like Stout's character, you probably already have a characteristic way of paragraphing, one you can learn to understand and use to advantage.

In most academic writing, the sentences in a paragraph all revolve around one main idea. When a new idea comes up, a new paragraph begins. Within this broad general guideline, however, paragraph structure is highly flexible, allowing writers to create many different individual effects for various writing purposes. Especially in workplace and online writing, flexibility is paramount as writers create paragraphs for particular purposes and settings. ■

5a   Paragraphing for readers

Numerous studies indicate that most readers of English come to any piece of writing with certain expectations about conventional paragraphs:

- Paragraphs will begin and end with important information.
- The opening sentence will often let readers know what a paragraph is about.
- The middle of a paragraph will develop what the paragraph is about.
- The end of a paragraph may sum up the paragraph's contents, bringing the discussion of an idea to a close in anticipation of the paragraph that follows.
- A paragraph will make sense as a whole; its words and sentences will be clearly related.
- A paragraph will relate or "talk" to the paragraphs around it.

5b   Constructing conventional paragraphs

Let us look now at the elements in a well-written paragraph — one that is easy for readers to understand and follow.

I never knew anyone who'd grown up in Jackson without being afraid of Mrs. Calloway, our librarian. She ran the Library absolutely by herself, from the desk where she sat with her back to the books and facing the stairs, her dragon eye on the front door, where who knew what kind of person might come in from the public? SILENCE in big black letters was on signs tacked up everywhere. She herself spoke in her normally commanding voice; every word could be heard all over the Library above a steady seething sound coming from her electric fan; it was the only fan in the Library and stood on her desk, turned directly onto her streaming face.   – EUDORA WELTY, *One Writer's Beginnings*

This paragraph begins with a general statement of the main idea: that everyone who grew up in Jackson feared Mrs. Calloway. All the other sentences then give specific details about why she inspired such fear. This example demonstrates the three qualities essential to most academic paragraphs: *unity, coherence,* and *development.* It focuses on one main idea (**unity**); its parts are clearly related (**coherence**); and its main idea is supported with specifics (**development**).

EDITING THE PARAGRAPHS IN YOUR WRITING

1. What is the topic sentence of each paragraph? Is it stated or implied? If stated, where in the paragraph does it fall? Should it come at some other point? Would any paragraph be improved by deleting or adding a topic sentence? (5c1)

2. Which sentences, if any, do not relate in some way to the topic sentence? Is there any way to justify their inclusion? (5c2)

3. What is the most general sentence in each paragraph? If it is not the topic sentence, should it remain or be omitted? (5c2)

4. Is each paragraph organized in a way that is easy for readers to follow? By what means are sentences linked? Do any more links need to be added? Do any of the transitional expressions try to create links between ideas that do not really exist? (5d)

5. How completely does each paragraph develop its topic sentence? What methods of development are used? Are they effective? What other methods might be used? Does the paragraph need more material? (5e)

(Continued on p. 115)

6. Does the first sentence in each paragraph let readers know what the paragraph is about? Does the last sentence in some way conclude that paragraph's discussion? If not, does it need to? (5c)

7. Are paragraphs varied in length? Does any paragraph seem too long or too short? Is there any point that might be given strong emphasis by a one-sentence paragraph? (5e2 and 5f3)

8. By what means are the paragraphs linked? Do more links need to be added? Do any of the transitional expressions try to create links between ideas that do not really exist? (5h)

9. How does the introductory paragraph catch readers' interest? How exactly does it open — with a quotation? an anecdote? a question? a strong statement? How else might it open? (5f1)

10. How does the last paragraph draw the essay to a conclusion? What lasting impression will it leave with readers? How exactly does it close — with a question? a quotation? a vivid image? a warning or a call for action? How else might it conclude? (5f2)

11. If you are writing email or creating a Web text, are your paragraphs effective and visually clear to the reader? (5g)

5c   Making paragraphs unified: focusing on a main idea

Highly readable conventional paragraphs generally focus on one main idea. One good way to achieve such paragraph unity is to state the main idea clearly in one sentence and relate all the other sentences in the paragraph to that idea. The sentence that presents the main idea is called the **topic sentence**. Like the thesis for an essay, the topic sentence includes a topic and some comment on that topic. In the earlier paragraph by Eudora Welty, the topic sentence opens the paragraph. Its topic is Mrs. Calloway; its comment, that those who grew up in Jackson were afraid of her.

● For a discussion
 of the thesis of
 an essay, see 3b.

FOR MULTILINGUAL WRITERS: Being Explicit

Native readers of English generally expect that paragraphs will have an explicitly stated main idea and that the connections between points in a paragraph will also be stated explicitly. Such step-by-step explicitness may strike you as unnecessary or ineffective, but it follows the traditional paragraph conventions of English. The examples throughout this chapter can help you adopt these conventions for your own purposes.

1 Positioning a topic sentence

Although a topic sentence often appears at the beginning of a paragraph, it may appear anywhere in the paragraph—or it may not appear at all but, rather, be implied.

■ *Topic sentence at the beginning*

For an example of a letter of application, see Chapter 67; for a discussion of argumentative writing, see Chapter 13.

If you want readers to see your point immediately, open with the topic sentence. Such a strategy can be particularly useful in letters of application or in argumentative writing. The following paragraph opens with a clear topic sentence (shown in italics), on which subsequent sentences build:

> *Our friendship was the source of much happiness and many memories.* We danced and snapped our fingers simultaneously to the tunes of Lenny Kravitz and Sheryl Crow. We sweated together in the sweltering summer sun, trying to win the championship for our softball team. I recall the taste of pepperoni and sausage pizza as we discussed the highlights of our team's victory. Once we even became attracted to the same young man, but luckily we were able to share his friendship.

■ *Topic sentence at the end*

When specific details lead up to a generalization, putting the topic sentence at the end of the paragraph makes sense. In the following paragraph from Alice Walker's "Everyday Use," the topic sentence at the end (shown in italics) is a general statement that sums up and accounts for the specifics that have preceded it:

> During the visit, Dee takes the pictures, every one of them, including the one of the house that she used to live in and hate. She takes the churn top and dasher, both whittled out of a tree by one of Mama's

uncles. She tries to take Grandma Dee's quilts. Mama and Maggie use these inherited items every day, not only appreciating their heritage but living it too. *Dee, on the other hand, wants these items only for decorative use, thus forsaking and ignoring their real heritage.*

■ Topic sentence at the beginning and end

Sometimes you will want to state a topic sentence at the beginning of a paragraph and then refer to it in a slightly different form at the end. Such an echo of the topic sentence adds emphasis, pointing up the importance you attach to the idea. In the following paragraph, the writer begins with a topic sentence announcing a problem:

> *Many of the difficulties we experience in relationships are caused by the unrealistic expectations we have of each other.* Think about it. Women are expected to feel comfortable doing most of the sacrificing. They are supposed to stay fine, firm, and forever twenty-two while doing double duty, in the home and in the workplace. The burden on men is no easier. They should be tall, handsome, and able to wine and dine the women. Many women go for the glitter and then expect these men to calm down once in a relationship and become faithful, sensitive, supportive, and loving. Let's face it. Both women and men have been unrealistic. *It's time we develop a new sensitivity toward each other and ask ourselves what it is we need from each other that is realistic and fair.*

The last sentence restates the topic sentence as a proposal for solving the problem. This approach is especially appropriate, for the essay goes on to specify how the problem might be solved.

■ Topic sentence implied but not stated

Occasionally a topic will be so obvious that no topic sentence is necessary at all. Here is an example of such a paragraph, from an essay about working as an airport cargo handler:

> In winter the warehouse is cold and damp. There is no heat. The large steel doors that line the warehouse walls stay open most of the day. In the cold months, wind, rain, and snow blow across the floor. In the summer the warehouse becomes an oven. Dust and sand from the runways mix with the toxic fumes of fork lifts, leaving a dry, stale taste in your mouth. The high windows above the doors are covered with a thick, black dirt that kills the sun. The men work in shadows with the constant roar of jet engines blowing dangerously in their ears.
> – PATRICK FENTON, "Confessions of a Working Stiff"

Here the implied topic sentence might be stated as *Working conditions in the warehouse are uncomfortable, dreary, and hazardous to one's health.* But the writer does not have to state this information explicitly because we can infer it easily from the examples and specific details he provides.

Though implied topic sentences are common, especially in descriptions, in some college writing they may be viewed as weaknesses.

● EXERCISE 5.1

Choose an essay you have written, and identify the topic sentence of each paragraph, noting where in the paragraph the topic sentence appears and whether any topic sentence is implied rather than stated. Experiment with one paragraph, positioning its topic sentence in at least two different places. What difference does the change make? If you have any implied topic sentences, try stating them explicitly. Does the paragraph become easier to read?

2 Relating each sentence to the main idea

Whether the main idea of a paragraph is stated in a topic sentence or is implied, each sentence in the paragraph should contribute to the main idea. Look, for example, at the following paragraph, which opens an essay about African American music:

> When I was a teenager, there were two distinct streams of popular music: one was black, and the other was white. The former could only be heard way at the end of the radio dial, while white music dominated everywhere else. This separation was a fact of life, the equivalent of blacks sitting in the back of the bus and "whites only" signs below the Mason-Dixon line. Satchmo might grin for days on "The Ed Sullivan Show" and certain historians hold forth *ad nauseam* on the black contribution to American music, but the truth was that our worlds rarely twined.
>   – MARCIA GILLESPIE
>   "They're Playing My Music, but Burying My Dreams"

The first sentence announces the topic (there were two streams of popular music: black and white). The second sentence relates the topic to the positions of black and white music on the radio dial, and the third sentence expands on this notion of musical separation by comparing it to the separate seats for blacks on buses and their exclusion from certain public places. The last sentence rephrases the topic sentence much more pointedly: though black music was heard regularly on television and people have written extensively on the black contribution to American music, the worlds of black and white music were separate. Each sentence clearly relates to the topic, and the paragraph as a whole is unified.

● **EXERCISE 5.2**

Choose one of the following topic sentences, and spend some time exploring the topic (see 3a). Then write a paragraph that includes the topic sentence. Make sure that each of the other sentences relates to it. Assume that the paragraph will be part of a letter you are writing to an acquaintance.

1. I found out quickly that college life was not quite what I had expected.
2. Being part of the "in crowd" used to be of utmost importance to me.
3. My work experience has taught me several important lessons.
4. Until recently, I never appreciated my parents fully.
5. I expect my college education to do more than assure me of a job.

● **EXERCISE 5.3**

Choose an essay you have written recently, and examine the second, third, and fourth paragraphs. Does each have a topic sentence or strongly imply one? Do all the other sentences in the paragraph focus on its main idea? Would you now revise any of these paragraphs—and, if so, how?

5d   Making paragraphs coherent: fitting details together

A paragraph has coherence if its details fit together clearly in a way that readers can easily follow. You can achieve paragraph coherence by organizing ideas, by repeating key terms or phrases, and by using parallel structures and transitional devices.

1 Organizing ideas

If you take a five- or six-sentence paragraph and rearrange the sentences in random order, you will probably *not* create a new paragraph. Why not? Though the sentences will be connected to the same topic, the lack of any organizational relationship will result in incoherence. Clear organization of ideas goes a long way toward creating coherence. The following discussion will review some common means of organizing a paragraph—spatial order, chronological order, logical order, and associational order.

¶

5d

■ *Using spatial order*

Paragraphs organized in **spatial order** take a "tour," beginning at one point and moving, say, from near to far, left to right, top to bottom. Especially useful in **descriptive paragraphs**, spatial order allows a writer to direct readers' attention in an orderly way to various elements of something in physical space. A topic sentence may be unnecessary in such a paragraph because the paragraph's organization will be obvious to the reader. Sometimes, however, a topic sentence at the beginning helps set the scene. Note how the topic sentence (shown in italics) does so in the following paragraph. Note, too, the movement from top to bottom — from ceiling to walls to floor.

> *The professor's voice began to fade into the background as my eyes wandered around the classroom in the old administration building.* The water-stained ceiling was cracked and peeling, and the splitting wooden beams played host to a variety of lead pipes and coils. My eyes followed these pipes down the walls and around corners until eventually I saw the electric outlets. I thought it strange that they were exposed, and not built in, until I realized that there probably had been no electricity when the building was built. Below the outlets the sunshine was falling in bright rays across the hardwood floor, and I noticed how smoothly the floor was worn. Time had taken its toll on this building.

■ *Using chronological order*

Paragraphs organized in **chronological order** arrange a series of events according to time, putting earliest events first, followed in sequence by later events, one at a time. Chronological order is used frequently in **narrative paragraphs**, which tell a story. They may not require a topic sentence if the main idea is obvious in the action. The following paragraph does begin with a topic sentence (shown in italics) and then uses careful chronology to tell a story and build suspense so that we want to know what the last event will be. Putting all of the details in the order in which they occurred helps build this suspense, as do the phrases expressing time: *all of a sudden, three months, a year later,* and so on.

> *The experience of Lloyd S., an Oregon businessperson, is one of the most convincing cases for taking vitamins.* For his first forty years, Lloyd was healthy and robust. He owned a thriving nursery and loved to hike, fish, and camp. All of a sudden, he started feeling fatigued. A loss of appetite and weight soon followed, and in three months he was transformed from a

ruddy, muscular man into a pallid, emaciated one. Lloyd had cancer of the pancreas. After he was given a prognosis of six months to live, his family and friends were devastated, but Lloyd was a fighter. When the conventional treatments of drugs and chemotherapy did not help, he turned to a holistic approach, which emphasized a change in diet and lifestyle — and large doses of vitamins. After a series of blood tests to discover every possible nutritional deficiency, Lloyd was given concentrated vitamin and mineral supplements to ensure maximum cell efficiency and growth so that his body could attempt to heal itself. At the end of six months, Lloyd not only was alive but also showed improvement. A year later he was free of cancer and began the long battle to regain his original vitality.

Chronological order is also commonly used in **explaining a process** — that is, in describing how something happens or how something is done: first one step, then the next, and then the next. You are already familiar with process as a means of organizing information. After all, every set of directions, every recipe, every user's manual presents a series of steps that makes up a process to be learned or followed. In college writing, you will probably use process paragraphs most often to tell readers how a process occurs in general — for example, how a bill becomes law or how aerosol sprays destroy the ozone layer of the atmosphere. Here is an example of such a paragraph, with its topic sentence shown in italics:

> *By the late 20s, most people notice the first signs of aging in their physical appearance.* Slight losses of elasticity in facial skin produce the first wrinkles, usually in those areas most involved in their characteristic facial expressions. As the skin continues to lose elasticity and fat deposits build up, the face sags a bit with age. Indeed, some people have drooping eyelids, sagging cheeks, and the hint of a double chin by age 40 (Whitbourne, 1985). Other parts of the body sag a bit as well, so as the years pass, adults need to exercise regularly if they want to maintain their muscle tone and body shape. Another harbinger of aging, the first gray hairs, is usually noticed in the 20s and can be explained by a reduction in the number of pigment-producing cells. Hair may become a bit less plentiful, too, because of hormonal changes and reduced blood supply to the skin.
>
> – KATHLEEN STASSEN BERGER
> *The Developing Person through the Life Span*

■ *Using logical order*

Paragraphs organized in **logical order** arrange details to reflect certain logical relationships. Explanations and examples of some of these relationships—illustration, definition, division and classification, comparison and contrast, cause and effect, problems and solutions, analogies, narration, and reiteration—appear in 5e. Two other logical patterns commonly used in paragraphs are *general to specific* and *specific to general*.

Paragraphs organized in a **general-to-specific pattern** usually open with a topic sentence presenting a general or abstract idea and are followed by a number of more specific points designed to substantiate or prove or elaborate on the generalization. This pattern is used in the following paragraph: the topic sentence (shown in italics) presents a general idea about racism, which is then supported by specific examples.

GENERAL TO SPECIFIC

One of the most tragic manifestations of the pressure black people feel to assimilate is expressed in the internalization of racist perspectives. I was shocked and saddened when I first heard black professors at Stanford downgrade and express contempt for black students, expecting us to do poorly, refusing to establish nurturing bonds. At every university I have attended as a student or worked at as a teacher, I have heard similar attitudes expressed with little or no understanding of factors that might prevent brilliant black students from performing to their full capability. Within universities, there are few educational and social spaces where students who wish to affirm positive ties to ethnicity—to blackness, to working-class backgrounds—can receive affirmation and support. Ideologically, the message is clear—assimilation is the way to gain acceptance and approval from those in power. – BELL HOOKS, *Talking Back*

Paragraphs can also follow a **specific-to-general organization**, first providing a series of specific examples or details and then tying them together with a topic sentence that provides a conclusion. The following paragraph begins with specific details about Saturday morning television and ends with a topic sentence (shown in italics):

SPECIFIC TO GENERAL

At 8:01 A.M. on Saturday morning, the bright images hawk cereal: Fruit Loops, Frosted Flakes, Captain Crunch. At 8:11, it's toy time, as squads of delighted children demonstrate the pleasures of owning [Barbie, Ken, or GI Joe]. By 8:22, Coca-Cola is quenching thirsts everywhere, and at 8:31, kids declare devotion to their Nikes, ensuring that every child tuned in will want a pair. And so goes Saturday morning children's programming: one part "program" (and that exclusively cartoons) to three parts advertising. *"Children's television" today is simply a euphemism for one long, hard sell, an initiation rite designed to create more and more American consumers.*

Paragraphs that organize information associationally do so by means of a series of associations directly related to the writer's own experiences and memories. This chain of association often relies on a central image or sensory memory—a particular aroma, for instance, or visual pattern. In the following paragraph, Victor Villanueva uses a series of memories that are linked associationally to a central image of differences among children alone. Note how one memory triggers others.

> Walking from Bartlett to John Lee's hand laundry, alone. Maybe aged four. From Bartlett to somewhere. Near the Myrtle Avenue el. Shortest person on street corners. The only one waiting for lights to turn green. No memory of anyone asking where his Mommy is. Just last week, 1992, Flagstaff, Arizona. A little three- or four-year-old child is wandering around a supermarket. A concerned woman bends over: "Did you lose your Mommy?" The same week, the same store, a little three- or four-year-old American Indian child is wandering, bawling loudly. People stop and stare. No one asks.
>
> – Victor Villanueva, *Bootstraps*

Note, too, that the writer uses a series of sentence fragments to suggest the fragmented nature of his memories and their association with more recent experiences.

2 Repeating key words and phrases

A major means of building coherence in paragraphs is through **repetition.** Weaving in repeated references to key words and phrases not only links sentences but also alerts readers to the importance of those words or phrases in the larger piece of writing. Notice in the following example how the repetition of the key words *shop* (*shopping, shoppers, shops*), *market(s), bargain(ing), customers, buy, price, store,* and *item* helps hold the paragraph together:

> Over the centuries, *shopping* has changed in function as well as in style. Before the Industrial Revolution, most consumer goods were sold in open-air *markets, customers* who went into an actual *shop* were expected to *buy* something, and *shoppers* were always expected to *bargain* for the best possible *price*. In the nineteenth century, however, the development of the department *store* changed the relationship between buyers and sellers. Instead of visiting several *market* stalls or small *shops, customers* could now *buy* a variety of merchandise under the same roof; instead of feeling expected to *buy*, they were welcome just to look; and instead of *bargaining* with several merchants, they paid a fixed *price* for each *item*. In addition,

they could return an *item* to the *store* and exchange it for a different one or get their money back. All of these changes helped transform *shopping* from serious requirement to psychological recreation.

● **EXERCISE 5.4**

Read the following paragraph. Then identify the places where the author uses repetition of key words and phrases, and explain how they bring coherence to the paragraph.

This is not to say that technology was an unadulterated plus in the '90s. The Information Superhighway was pretty much of a dud. Remember that? By the mid-'90s, just about everybody was hooked up to the vast international computer network, exchanging vast quantities of information at high speeds via modems and fiber-optic cable with everybody else. The problem, of course, was that even though the information was coming a lot faster, the vast majority of it, having originated with human beings, was still wrong. Eventually people realized that the Information Superhighway was essentially CB radio, but with more typing. By late in the decade millions of Americans had abandoned their computers and turned to the immensely popular new VirtuLib 2000, a $14,000 device that enables the user to experience, with uncanny realism, the sensation of reading a book.

– DAVE BARRY, "The '90s

3 Using parallel structures

Parallel structures—structures that are grammatically similar—are another effective way to bring coherence to a paragraph. They emphasize the connection between related ideas or events in different sentences.

William Faulkner's "Barn Burning" tells the story of a young boy trapped in a no-win situation. If he betrays his father, he loses his family. If he betrays justice, he becomes a fugitive. In trying to free himself from his trap, he does both.

In this paragraph, the writer skillfully uses the parallel structure *if he does x, he does y* in order to give the effect of a no-win situation. At the end of the paragraph, we are prepared for the last sentence in the parallel sequence: *In doing x, he does y.* As readers, we feel pulled along by the force of the parallel structures.

For more on
using parallel
structures, see
Chapter 45.

4 Using transitional devices

Transitions are words and phrases that help bring coherence to a paragraph by signaling relationships between and among sentences. In acting as signposts, transitions such as *after all, for example, indeed, so,* and *thus* help readers follow the progression of one idea to the next within a paragraph. *Finally* indicates that a last point is at hand; *likewise,* that a similar point is about to be made; and so on. To get an idea of how important transitions can be for readers, try reading the following paragraph, from which all transitional devices have been removed:

A PARAGRAPH WITH NO TRANSITIONS

In "The Fly," Katherine Mansfield tries to show us the "real" personality of "the boss" beneath his exterior. The fly helps her to portray this real self. The boss goes through a range of emotions and feelings. He expresses these feelings to a small but determined fly, whom the reader realizes he unconsciously relates to his son. The author basically splits up the story into three parts, with the boss's emotions and actions changing quite measurably. With old Woodifield, with himself, and with the fly, we see the boss's manipulativeness. Our understanding of him as a hard and cruel man grows.

We can, if we work at it, figure out the relationship of these ideas to one another, for this paragraph is essentially unified by one major idea. But the lack of transitions results in an abrupt, choppy rhythm that lurches from one idea to the next, dragging the confused reader behind. See how much easier the passage is to read and understand with transitions added.

THE SAME PARAGRAPH, WITH TRANSITIONS

In "The Fly," Katherine Mansfield tries to show us the "real" personality of "the boss" beneath his exterior. The fly *in the story's title* helps her to portray this real self. *In the course of the story,* the boss goes through a range of emotions and feelings. *At the end,* he *finally* expresses these feelings to a small but determined fly, whom the reader realizes he unconsciously relates to his son. *To accomplish her goal,* the author basically splits up the story into three parts, with the boss's emotions and actions changing quite measurably *throughout. First* with old Woodifield, *then* with himself, and *last* with the fly, we see the boss's manipulativeness. *With each part,* our understanding of him as a hard and cruel man grows.

● For a discussion of using transitional devices to link paragraphs to one another, see 5h.

Most of the transitional devices here point to movement in time, helping us follow the chronology of the story being discussed: *in the course of the story, at the end, finally, throughout, first, then, last.*

It is important to note that transitions can only clarify connections between thoughts; they cannot create connections. As a writer, you must choose transitions that fit your meaning—you should not expect a transition to provide meaning.

Distinguishing among very similar transitions can be difficult for multilingual writers. The difference between *however* and *nevertheless*, for example, is a subtle one: although each introduces a statement that contrasts with what comes before it, *nevertheless* emphasizes the contrast whereas *however* tones it down. To help make such fine distinctions, check the usage of transitions in English dictionaries such as *The American Heritage Dictionary of the English Language* or *The Oxford Advanced Learner's Dictionary*, which provide usage notes for easily confused words.

COMMONLY USED TRANSITIONS

TO SIGNAL SEQUENCE

again, also, and, and then, besides, finally, first . . . second . . . third, furthermore, last, moreover, next, still, too

TO SIGNAL TIME

after a few days, after a while, afterward, as long as, as soon as, at last, at that time, before, earlier, immediately, in the meantime, in the past, lately, later, meanwhile, now, presently, simultaneously, since, so far, soon, then, thereafter, until, when

TO SIGNAL COMPARISON

again, also, in the same way, likewise, once more, similarly

TO SIGNAL CONTRAST

although, but, despite, even though, however, in contrast, in spite of, instead, nevertheless, nonetheless, on the contrary, on the one hand . . . on the other hand, regardless, still, though, yet

(Continued on p. 127)

TO SIGNAL EXAMPLES

after all, even, for example, for instance, indeed, in fact, of course, specifically, such as, the following example, to illustrate

TO SIGNAL CAUSE AND EFFECT

accordingly, as a result, because, consequently, for this purpose, hence, so, then, therefore, thus, to this end

TO SIGNAL PLACE

above, adjacent to, below, beyond, closer to, elsewhere, far, farther on, here, near, nearby, opposite to, there, to the left, to the right

TO SIGNAL CONCESSION

although it is true that, granted that, I admit that, it may appear that, naturally, of course

TO SIGNAL SUMMARY, REPETITION, OR CONCLUSION

as a result, as has been noted, as I have said, as mentioned earlier, as we have seen, in any event, in conclusion, in other words, in short, on the whole, therefore, to summarize

● **EXERCISE 5.5**

Identify the devices — repetition of key words or phrases, parallel structures, transitional expressions — that make the following paragraph coherent.

I must make two honest confessions to you, my Christian and Jewish brothers. First, I must confess that over the past few years I have been gravely disappointed with the white moderate. I have almost reached the regrettable conclusion that the Negro's great stumbling block on his stride toward freedom is not the White Citizen's Counciler or the Ku Klux Klanner, but the white moderate, who is more devoted to "order" than to justice; who prefers a negative peace which is the absence of tension to a positive peace which is the presence of justice; who constantly says, "I agree with you in the goal you seek, but I cannot agree with your methods of direct action"; who paternalistically believes he can set the timetable for another man's freedom; who lives by a mythical concept of time and who constantly advises the Negro to wait for a "more convenient season." Shallow understanding from people of good will is more frustrating than absolute misunderstanding from people of ill will. Lukewarm acceptance is much more bewildering than outright rejection.   – MARTIN LUTHER KING JR., "Letter from Birmingham Jail"

In addition to being unified and coherent, a conventional paragraph should hold readers' interest and explore its topic fully, using whatever details, evidence, and examples are necessary. Without such **development,** a paragraph may seem lifeless and abstract.

Most good academic writing does two things: it presents generalized ideas and explanations, and it backs up these generalities with specifics. This balance, the shifting between general and specific, is especially important at the paragraph level. If a paragraph contains nothing but specific details, with no explanation of how they should be viewed as a whole, readers may have trouble following the writer's meaning. If, on the other hand, a paragraph contains only abstract ideas and general statements, readers may become bored or may fail to be convinced. Consider the following undeveloped paragraph:

AN UNDEVELOPED PARAGRAPH

No such thing as "human nature" compels people to behave, think, or react in certain ways. Rather, from the time of our infancy to our death, we are constantly being taught, by the society that surrounds us, the customs, norms, and mores of our distinct culture. Everything in culture is learned, not genetically transmitted.

This paragraph is boring. Although its main idea is clear and its sentences hold together, it fails to gain our interest, hold our attention, or convince us because it lacks any concrete illustrations. Now look at the paragraph revised to include needed specifics.

THE SAME PARAGRAPH, REVISED

Imagine a child in Ecuador dancing to salsa music at a warm family gathering, while a child in the United States is decorating a Christmas tree with bright, shiny red ornaments. Both of these children are taking part in their country's cultures. It is not by instinct that one child knows how to dance to salsa music, nor is it by instinct that the other child knows how to decorate the tree. No such thing as "human nature" compels people to behave, think, or react in certain ways. Rather, from the time of our infancy to our death, we are constantly being taught by the society that surrounds us, the customs, norms, and mores of our distinct culture. A majority of people feel that the evil in human beings is "human nature." However, the Tasaday, a "Stone Age" tribe discovered not long ago in the Philippines, do not even have equivalents in their language for the words *hatred, competition, acquisitiveness, aggression,* and *greed.* Such examples suggest that everything in culture is learned, not genetically transmitted.

Though both paragraphs argue the same point, only the second one comes to life. It does so by bringing in specific details *from* life. We want to read this paragraph, for it appeals to our senses (a child dancing; bright, shiny red ornaments) and our curiosity (who are the Tasaday?).

Almost every paragraph can be improved by making sure that its general ideas rest on enough specific detail. You can, of course, add too many details, pushing examples at the reader when no more are needed. For every writer who has to chop back jungles of detail, however, there are five whose greatest task is to irrigate deserts of generality.

FOR COLLABORATION

Working with a classmate, rewrite the following undeveloped paragraphs by adding concrete supporting details, examples, and reasons. Bring your collaboratively revised paragraphs to class for discussion.

1. *The introduction to an essay tentatively titled "A Week on $12.80"*

    Nothing is more frustrating to a college student than being dead broke. Not having money for enough food or for the rent, much less for entertainment, is not much fun. And of course debts for tuition and books keep piling up. No, being broke is not to be recommended.

2. *The introduction to a humorous essay contrasting cats and dogs*

    Have you threatened your cat lately? If not, why not? Why not get a *real* pet—a dog? Dogs, after all, are better pets. Cats, on the other hand, are a menace to the environment.

1 Using logical patterns of development

The patterns shown in 3d for organizing essays can also serve as a means of developing paragraphs. These logical **patterns** include illustrating, defining, dividing and classifying, comparing and contrasting, exploring causes and effects, considering problems and solutions or questions and answers, exploring analogies, narrating, and reiterating.

■ *Illustrating*

One of the most common ways of developing a paragraph is by **illustrating a point** with concrete examples or with good reasons. To support her topic sentence (shown in italics), Mari Sandoz uses in the following paragraph one long example about her short hair and short stature.

A SINGLE EXAMPLE

The Indians made names for us children in their teasing way. Because our very busy mother kept my hair cut short, like my brothers', they called me Short Furred One, pointing to their hair and making the sign for short, the right hand with fingers pressed close together, held upward, back out, at the height intended. With me this was about two feet tall, the Indians laughing gently at my abashed face. I am told that I was given a pair of small moccasins that first time, to clear up my unhappiness at being picked out from the dusk behind the fire and my two unhappy shortcomings made conspicuous.   – MARI SANDOZ, "The Go-Along Ones"

In the following excerpt, George Orwell's topic sentence (shown in italics) begins the paragraph and encourages the reader to ask *why?* Orwell then provides several reasons (also in italics) for and against shooting the elephant.

SEVERAL REASONS

But I did not want to shoot the elephant. I watched him beating his bunch of grass against his knees, with the preoccupied grandmotherly air that elephants have. *It seemed to me that it would be murder to shoot him.* At that age I was not squeamish about killing animals, but I had never shot an elephant and never wanted to. (Somehow it always seems worse to kill a large animal.) *Besides, there was the beast's owner to be considered.* Alive, the elephant was worth at least a hundred pounds; dead, he would only be worth the value of his tusks, five pounds, possibly. But I had got to act quickly. I turned to some experienced-looking Burmans who had been there when we arrived, and asked them how the elephant had been behaving. *They all said the same thing: he took no notice of you if you left him alone, but he might charge if you went too close to him.*

– GEORGE ORWELL, "Shooting an Elephant"

■ *Defining*

You will often have occasion to develop an entire paragraph by **defining** a word or concept. Some college courses, particularly ones that deal with difficult abstractions, require writing that calls for this strategy. A philosophy exam, for instance, might require you to define concepts such as *truth* or *validity.* Often, however, you will find it necessary to combine definition with other patterns of development. You may need to show examples or draw comparisons or divide a term you are defining into two parts. In the following paragraph, Timothy Tregarthen starts with a definition of *economics* (shown in italics) and then uses examples to support it:

> *Economics is the study of how people choose among the alternatives available to them.* It's the study of little choices ("Should I take the chocolate or the strawberry?") and big choices ("Should we require a reduction in energy consumption in order to protect the environment?"). It's the study of individual choices, choices by firms, and choices by governments. Life presents each of us with a wide range of alternative uses of our time and other resources; economists examine how we choose among those alternatives.
> — TIMOTHY TREGARTHEN, *Economics*

■ Dividing and classifying

Dividing breaks a single item into parts. **Classifying,** which is actually a form of dividing, groups many separate items according to their similarities. You could, for instance, develop a paragraph evaluating a history course by dividing the course into several segments—textbooks, lectures, assignments—and examining each one in turn. Or you could develop a paragraph giving an overview of history courses at your college by classifying, or grouping, the courses in a number of ways—by the time periods or geographic areas covered, by the kinds of assignments demanded, by the number of students enrolled, or by some other criterion. In the following paragraph, note how Aaron Copland *divides* the listening process into three parts:

DIVIDING

> We all listen to music according to our separate capacities. But, for the sake of analysis, the whole listening process may become clearer if we break it up into its component parts, so to speak. In a certain sense we all listen to music on three separate planes. For lack of a better terminology, one might name these: (1) the sensuous plane, (2) the expressive plane, (3) the sheerly musical plane. The only advantage to be gained from mechanically splitting up the listening process into these hypothetical planes is the clearer view to be had of the way in which we listen.
> — AARON COPLAND, *What to Listen for in Music*

In this paragraph, the writer *classifies,* or separates, fad dieters into two groups.

CLASSIFYING

> Two types of people are seduced by fad diets. Those who have always been overweight turn to them out of despair; they have tried everything,

and yet nothing seems to work. The second group to succumb appear perfectly healthy but are baited by slogans such as "look good, feel good." These slogans prompt self-questioning and insecurity—do I really look good and feel good?—and, as a direct result, many healthy people fall prey to fad diets. With both types of people, however, the problems surrounding such diets are numerous and dangerous. In fact, these diets provide neither intelligent nor effective answers to weight control.

■ *Comparing and contrasting*

You can develop some paragraphs easily and effectively by comparing and contrasting various aspects of the topic or by comparing and contrasting the topic with something else. **Comparing** things highlights their similarities; **contrasting** points to their differences. Whether used alone or together, comparing and contrasting both act to focus the topic at hand more clearly—we can better understand an unknown by comparing it to something we know well.

You can structure comparison-contrast paragraphs in two basic ways. One way is to present all the information about one item and then all the information about the other item (the **block method**). The other possibility is to switch back and forth between the two items, focusing on particular characteristics of each in turn (**alternating method**).

BLOCK METHOD

You could tell the veterans from the rookies by the way they were dressed. The knowledgeable ones had their heads covered by kerchiefs, so that if they were hired, tobacco dust wouldn't get in their hair; they had on clean dresses that by now were faded and shapeless, so that if they were hired they wouldn't get tobacco dust and grime on their best clothes. Those who were trying for the first time had their hair freshly done and wore attractive dresses; they wanted to make a good impression. But the dresses couldn't be seen at the distance that many were standing from the employment office, and they were crumpled in the crush. — MARY MEBANE, "Summer Job"

ALTERNATING METHOD

Malcolm X emphasized the use of violence in his movement and employed the biblical principle of "an eye for an eye and a tooth for a tooth." King, on the other hand, felt that blacks should use nonviolent civil disobedience and employed the theme "turning the other cheek," which Malcolm X rejected as "beggarly" and "feeble." The philosophy of

Malcolm X was one of revenge, and often it broke the unity of black Americans. More radical blacks supported him, while more conservative ones supported King. King thought that blacks should transcend their humanity. In contrast, Malcolm X thought they should embrace it and reserve their love for one another, regarding whites as "devils" and the "enemy." King's politics were those of a rainbow, but Malcolm X's rainbow was insistently one color — black. The distance between Martin Luther King Jr.'s thinking and Malcolm X's was the distance between growing up in the seminary and growing up on the streets, between the American dream and the American reality.

● **EXERCISE 5.6**

Outline the preceding paragraph on Martin Luther King Jr. and Malcolm X, noting its alternating pattern. Then rewrite the paragraph using block organization: the first part of the paragraph devoted to King, the second to Malcolm X. Finally, write a brief paragraph analyzing the two paragraphs, explaining which seems more coherent and easier to follow and why.

■ *Exploring causes and effects*

Certain topics will require you to consider the process of **cause and effect,** and you can often develop paragraphs by detailing the causes of something or the effects that something brings about. A question on geology, for instance, may lead you to write a paragraph describing the major causes of soil erosion in the Midwest — or the effects of such erosion. The following paragraph discusses how a lack of understanding of how age affects fertility (the cause) influences the actions of infertility groups (the effects):

Alarmed by what they view as a widespread lack of understanding about aging as a risk factor for infertility — and a false sense of security about what science can do — infertility groups have decided to turn up the heat on public awareness. This fall [2001] the American Infertility Association, a patient-advocacy group, will pepper doctors' offices with pamphlets educating women about how age can affect fertility — and what can go wrong. And . . . the American Society for Reproductive Medicine, the nation's largest professional organization of fertility specialists, will launch a bold ad campaign that will debut on buses in New York, suburban Chicago and Seattle. The headline: ADVANCING AGE DECREASES YOUR ABILITY TO HAVE CHILDREN. The message: women "in their twenties and early thirties are most likely to conceive." The image: an upside-down baby bottle in the shape of an hourglass. "It's kind of like issuing a warning," says ASRM president Dr. Michael Soules, who spearheaded the campaign. "It's our duty to let people know."

– CLAUDIA KALB, "Should You Have Your Baby Now?"

■ *Considering problems and solutions or questions and answers*

Paragraphs developed in the **problem-solution pattern** open with a statement of a problem, usually the topic sentence, and then offer a solution in the sentences that follow. Similar to the problem-solution pattern is the **question-and-answer pattern** of development, which does just what its name suggests: the first sentence poses a question, and the rest of the paragraph provides the answer. Beginning with a question provides a means of getting — and focusing — readers' attention.

What happened to America's confidence [in matters of foreign policy]? The first answer, of course, is Vietnam. Second, American policy is now conducted largely by a meritocratic elite, which was not bred, as the best members of the old WASP elite were, to seize the responsibilities of leadership. Third, our triumph in the Cold War has had a perversely gloomy effect. That was a great moral and ideological victory, the argument goes, but now we live in a messier and grimmer world, one better suited to the sort of coldhearted caution espoused by so-called realists than to the warmhearted idealism of those who would champion democracy.

– DAVID BROOKS, "A Modest Little War"

■ *Exploring analogies*

Analogies (comparisons that explain an unfamiliar thing in terms of a familiar one) can also help develop paragraphs. In the following paragraph, the writer draws an unlikely analogy — between the human genome and a Thanksgiving dinner. The analogy is introduced in the first sentence and detailed throughout the paragraph.

Think of the human genome as the ingredients list for a massive Thanksgiving dinner. Scientists long have had a general understanding of how the feast is cooked. They knew where the ovens were. Now, they also have a list of every ingredient. Yet much remains to be discovered. In most cases, no one knows exactly which ingredients are necessary for making, for example, the pumpkin pie as opposed to the cornbread. Indeed, many, if not most, of the recipes that use the genomic ingredients are missing, and there's little understanding why small variations in the quality of the ingredients can "cook up" diseases in one person but not in another.

– USA TODAY
"Cracking of Life's Genetic Code Carries Weighty Potential"

Narrating allows writers to provide personal or historical accounts in order to develop ideas. Narrative paragraphs are often arranged chronologically, sometimes with such variations on chronological order as flashbacks and flash-forwards. They sometimes include dialogue and may lead to a **climax**, which provides the point of the story being told. Here is one student's narrative paragraph that tells a personal story in order to support a point about the dangers of racing bicycles with flimsy alloy frames. Starting with a topic sentence (shown in italics), the paragraph then proceeds chronologically. It also uses **description**, adding specific, concrete details to help the reader "see" the story: *catapulted onto Vermont pavement at fifty miles per hour,* for instance, or *My Italian racing bike was pretzeled.* This paragraph builds to a climax, saving the most extreme point (*He couldn't even walk*) for last.

> *People who have been exposed to the risk of dangerously designed bicycle frames have paid too high a price.* I saw this danger myself in the 1984 Putney Race. A Stowe-Shimano graphite frame failed, and the rider was catapulted onto Vermont pavement at fifty miles per hour. The pack of riders behind him was so dense that most other racers crashed into a tangled, sliding heap. The aftermath: four hospitalizations. I got off with some stitches, a bad road rash, and severely pulled tendons. My Italian racing bike was pretzeled, and my racing was over for that summer. Others were not so lucky. An Olympic hopeful, Brian Stone of the Northstar team, woke up in a hospital bed to find that his cycling was over — and not just for that summer. His kneecap had been surgically removed. He couldn't even walk.

One form of narration **embeds a narrative**, often in the middle of a paragraph, to elaborate on a point or relate a personal experience that supports the point. In the following example, the writer embeds a narrative to explain how he got the idea for the essay. Starting with *These are the words that popped into my head,* he tells a story in the middle of the paragraph.

> For the term essay in Ethnic Art, we were free to write on any relevant subject. Openness, however, can bring its own headaches. With so much to choose from, a guy can feel overwhelmed. Or so I thought — until I suddenly said, "Braids and dreads: that's it!" These are the words that popped into my head as I was driving to school recently, just when I was worrying about a subject for my art paper. I was inspired, I suppose, by friends, people around me, and perhaps the rap group Kriss Kross — all people who wear braided hair. My first thought was to write only about braids, but then I thought about people who wear their hair in a

particular style of braids known as dreadlocks, like Bob Marley. As my brain kept churning, I asked myself, "What are the differences between the two hairstyles? What do these styles mean? Why are they 'in' right now?" In short, I was on my way to an exploration of what I claim is one form of ethnic art.

■ *Reiterating*

Reiterating, often used in oral as well as written discourse, is an organizational pattern you may recognize from political discourse or some styles of preaching. In this pattern, the writer states the main point of a paragraph and then reiterates it in a number of different ways, hammering home the point and often building in intensity as well. This strategy found particular power in a number of works by Martin Luther King Jr. In the following example, King reiterates the topic of the paragraph (we are on the move) six different ways, repeating the idea like a drumbeat throughout the paragraph, building to the climactic move *to the land of freedom*:

> *We are on the move now.* The burning of our churches will not deter us. *We are on the move now.* The bombing of our homes will not dissuade us. *We are on the move now.* The beating and killing of our clergymen and young people will not divert us. *We are on the move now.* The arrest and release of known murderers will not discourage us. *We are on the move now.* Like an idea whose time has come, not even the marching of mighty armies can halt us. *We are moving* to the land of freedom.
>
> – MARTIN LUTHER KING JR., "Our God Is Marching On"

■ *Combining patterns*

Most paragraphs combine patterns of development. In the following paragraph, the writer begins with a topic sentence (shown in italics) and then divides his topic (the accounting systems used by American companies) into two subtopics (the system used to summarize a company's overall financial state and the one used to measure internal transactions). Next he develops the second subtopic through illustration (the assessment of costs for a delivery truck shared by two departments) and cause and effect (the system produces some disadvantages).

> *Most American companies have basically two accounting systems.* One system summarizes the overall financial state to inform stockholders,

bankers, and other outsiders. That system is not of interest here. The other system, called the managerial or cost accounting system, exists for an entirely different reason. It measures in detail all of the particulars of transactions between departments, divisions, and key individuals in the organization, for the purpose of untangling the interdependencies between people. When, for example, two departments share one truck for deliveries, the cost accounting system charges each department for part of the cost of maintaining the truck and driver, so that at the end of the year, the performance of each department can be individually assessed, and the better department's manager can receive a larger raise. Of course, all of this information processing costs money, and furthermore may lead to arguments between the departments over whether the costs charged to each are fair.

– WILLIAM OUCHI
"Japanese and American Workers: Two Casts of Mind"

EXERCISE 5.7

Choose two of the following topics or two others that interest you, and brainstorm or freewrite about each one for ten minutes (see 3a1 and 3a2). Then use the information you have produced to determine what method(s) of development would be most appropriate for each topic.

1. the pleasure a hobby has given you
2. Allen Iverson's image and Kobe Bryant's image
3. an average Saturday morning
4. why the game Monopoly is an appropriate metaphor for U.S. society
5. the best course you've ever taken

EXERCISE 5.8

Take an assignment you have written recently, and study the ways you developed each paragraph. For one of the paragraphs, write a brief evaluation of its development. How would you expand or otherwise improve the development?

2 Determining paragraph length

Though writers must keep their readers' expectations in mind, paragraph length must be determined primarily by content and purpose. Paragraphs should develop an idea, create any desired effects (such as suspense or humor), and advance the piece of writing. Fulfilling these aims will sometimes call for short paragraphs, sometimes for long ones. For example, in an argumentative essay, you may put all your lines of argument or all your evidence into one long paragraph to create the impression of a solid, overwhelmingly convincing thesis. In a narrative about an exciting event, on the other hand, you may use a series of short paragraphs to create suspense, to keep the reader rushing to each new paragraph to find out what happens next.

Remember that a new paragraph often signals a pause in thought. Just as timing can make a crucial difference in telling a joke, so the pause signaled by a paragraph can lead readers to anticipate what is to follow or give them a moment to digest mentally the material presented in the previous paragraph.

■ *Reasons to start a new paragraph*

- to turn to a new idea
- to emphasize something (such as a point or an example)
- to change speakers (in dialogue)
- to lead readers to pause
- to break up lengthy text (often to take up a subtopic)
- to start the conclusion

◉ EXERCISE 5.9

Examine the paragraph breaks in something you have written recently. Explain briefly in writing why you decided on each of the breaks. Would you change any of them now? If so, how and why?

5f   Composing special-purpose paragraphs

Paragraphs serving specialized functions include opening paragraphs, concluding paragraphs, transitional paragraphs, and dialogue paragraphs.

1 Opening paragraphs

Even a good piece of writing may remain unread if it has a weak opening paragraph. In addition to announcing your topic (usually in a thesis statement), therefore, an introductory paragraph must engage readers' interest and focus their attention on what is to follow. At their best, introductory paragraphs serve as hors d'oeuvres, whetting the appetite for the following courses, or, as the title sequences in a film, carefully setting the scene. Writers often leave the final drafting of the introduction until last because the focus of the piece may change during the process of writing.

One common kind of opening paragraph follows a general-to-specific pattern, ending with the thesis. Such an introduction is illustrated by the following paragraph. The writer opens with a general statement and then gets more and more specific, concluding with the most specific sentence in the paragraph — the thesis — which is shown here in italics.

> Throughout Western civilization, places such as the ancient Greek agora, the New England town hall, the local church, the coffeehouse, the village square, and even the street corner have been arenas for debate on public affairs and society. Out of thousands of such encounters, "public opinion" slowly formed and became the context in which politics was framed. Although the public sphere never included everyone, and by itself did not determine the outcome of all parliamentary actions, it contributed to the spirit of dissent found in a healthy representative democracy. Many of these public spaces remain, but they are no longer centers for political discussion and action. *They have largely been replaced by television and other forms of media — forms that arguably isolate citizens from one another rather than bringing them together.*
> — MARK POSTER, "The Net as a Public Sphere"

In this paragraph, the opening sentence introduces a general subject, places for public debate; subsequent sentences focus more specifically on political discussion; and the last sentence presents the thesis, which the rest of the essay will develop. Other ways of opening an essay include quotations, anecdotes, questions, and opinions.

■ *Opening with a quotation*

> *There is a bumper sticker that reads, "Too bad ignorance isn't painful."* I like that. But ignorance is. We just seldom attribute the pain to it or even recognize it when we see it. Take the postcard on my corkboard. It shows a young man in a very hip jacket smoking a cigarette. In the background is a high school with the American flag waving. The caption says, "Too cool for school. Yet too stupid for the real world." Out of the mouth of the young man is a bubble enclosing the words "Maybe I'll start a band." There could be a postcard showing a jock in a uniform saying, "I don't need school. I'm going to the NFL or NBA." Or one showing a young man or woman studying and a group of young people saying, "So you want to be white." Or something equally demeaning. We need to quit it.
> — NIKKI GIOVANNI, "Racism 101"

■ *Opening with an anecdote*

> *I first met Angela Carter at a dinner in honor of the Chilean writer José Donoso at the home of Liz Calder, who then published all of us.* My first novel was soon to be published; it was the time of Angela's darkest novel, "The Passion of New Eve." And I was a great fan. Mr. Donoso arrived looking like a Hispanic Buffalo Bill, complete with silver goatee, fringed jacket and cowboy boots, and proceeded, as I saw it, to patronize Angela terribly. His apparent ignorance of her work provoked me into a long expostulation in which I informed him that the woman he was talking to was the most brilliant writer in England. Angela liked that. By the end of the evening, we liked each other, too. That was almost 18 years ago. She was the first great writer I ever met, and she was one of the best, most loyal, most truth-telling, most inspiring friends anyone could ever have. I cannot bear it that she is dead. –SALMAN RUSHDIE, "Angela Carter"

■ *Opening with a question*

> *Why are Americans terrified of using nuclear power as a source of energy?* People are misinformed, or not informed at all, about its benefits and safety. If Americans would take the time to learn about what nuclear power offers, their apprehension and fear might be transformed into hope.

■ *Opening with a strong opinion*

> *Men need a men's movement about as much as women need chest hair.* A brotherhood organized to counter feminists could be timely because — let's be honest — women are no more naturally inclined to equality and fairness than men are. They want power and dominion just as much as any group looking out for its own interests. Organizing to protect the welfare of males might make sense. Unfortunately, the current men's movement does not. –JOHN RUSZKIEWICZ, *The Presence of Others*

2 Concluding paragraphs

A good conclusion wraps up a piece of writing in a meaningful and memorable way. If a strong opening paragraph whets the appetite of readers or arouses their curiosity, a strong concluding paragraph satisfies them, allowing them to feel that their expectations have been met. A strong conclusion reminds readers of the thesis of the essay and leaves them feeling that they know a good deal more than they did when they began. The concluding paragraph provides the last opportunity for you to impress your message on your readers' minds and create desired effects. As such, it is well worth your time and effort.

One of the most common strategies for concluding uses the specific-to-general pattern, often beginning with a restatement of the thesis (but not a word-for-word repetition of it) and moving to several more general statements. The following paragraph moves in such a way, opening with a final point of comparison (shown in italics), specifying it in several sentences, and then ending with a much more general statement (also in italics):

> *Lastly, and perhaps greatest of all, there was the ability, at the end, to turn quickly from war to peace once the fighting was over.* Out of the way these two men behaved at Appomattox came the possibility of a peace of reconciliation. It was a possibility not wholly realized, in the years to come, but which did, in the end, help the two sections to become one nation again . . . after a war whose bitterness might have seemed to make such a reunion wholly impossible. No part of either man's life became him more than the part he played in this brief meeting in the McLean house at Appomattox. Their behavior there put all succeeding generations of Americans in their debt. Two great Americans, Grant and Lee—very different, yet under everything very much alike. *Their encounter at Appomattox was one of the great moments of American history.*
>
> – BRUCE CATTON, "Grant and Lee: A Study in Contrasts"

Other effective strategies for concluding include questions, quotations, vivid images, calls for action, and warnings.

■ *Concluding with a question*

> All so-called "permanent" antifreeze is basically the same. It is made from a liquid known as ethylene glycol, which has two amazing properties: It has a lower freezing point than water, and a higher boiling point than water. It does not break down (lose its properties), nor will it boil away. And every permanent antifreeze starts with it as a base. Also, just about every antifreeze has now got antileak ingredients, as well as antirust and anticorrosion ingredients. Now, let's suppose that, in formulating the product, one of the companies comes up with a solution that is pink in color, as opposed to all the others, which are blue. Presto—an exclusivity claim. "Nothing else looks like it, nothing else performs like it." Or how about, "Look at ours, and look at anyone else's. You can see the difference our exclusive formula makes." Granted, I'm exaggerating. *But did I prove a point?*
>
> – PAUL STEVENS
> "Weasel Words: God's Little Helpers"

■ *Concluding with a quotation*

Despite the celebrity that accrued to her and the air of awesomeness with which she was surrounded in her later years, Miss Keller retained an unaffected personality, certain that her optimistic attitude toward life was justified. "I believe that all through these dark and silent years God has been using my life for a purpose I do not know," she said. *"But one day I shall understand and then I will be satisfied."*

– ALDEN WHITMAN
"Helen Keller: June 27, 1880 – June 1, 1968"

■ *Concluding with a vivid image*

It is, in any case, finally you that I end up having to trust not to laugh, not to snicker. Even as you regard me in these lines, I try to imagine your face as you read. You who read "Aria," especially those of you with your theme-divining yellow felt pen poised in your hand, you for whom this essay is yet another "assignment," please do not forget that it is my life I am handing you in these pages — *memories that are as personal for me as family photographs in an old cigar box.*

– RICHARD RODRIGUEZ, from a postscript to "Aria"

■ *Concluding with a call for action*

It is now almost 40 years since the invention of nuclear weapons. We have not yet experienced a global thermonuclear war — although on more than one occasion we have come tremulously close. I do not think our luck can hold forever. Men and machines are fallible, as recent events remind us. Fools and madmen do exist, and sometimes rise to power. Concentrating always on the near future, we have ignored the long-term consequences of our actions. We have placed our civilization and our species in jeopardy.

Fortunately, it is not yet too late. *We can safeguard the planetary civilization and the human family if we so choose. There is no more important or more urgent issue.* – CARL SAGAN, "The Nuclear Winter"

■ *Concluding with a warning*

Because propaganda is so effective, it is important to track it down and understand how it is used. We may eventually agree with what the propagandist says because all propaganda isn't necessarily bad; some advertising, for instance, urges us not to drive drunk, to have regular dental checkups, to contribute to the United Way. Even so, we must be aware that propaganda is being used. *Otherwise, we will have consented to handing over our independence, our decision-making ability, and our brains.*

– ANN McCLINTOCK

"Propaganda Techniques in Today's Advertising"

3 Transitional paragraphs

On some occasions, you may need to call your readers' attention very powerfully to a major transition between ideas. To do so, consider using an entire short paragraph to signal that transition, as in the following example from an essay on television addiction. The opening paragraphs of the essay characterize addiction in general, concluding with the paragraph about its destructive elements. The one-sentence paragraph that follows arrests our attention, announcing that these general characteristics will now be related to television viewing.

Finally a serious addiction is distinguished from a harmless pursuit of pleasure by its distinctly destructive elements. A heroin addict, for instance, leads a damaged life: his increasing need for heroin in increasing doses prevents him from working, from maintaining relationships, from developing in human ways. Similarly an alcoholic's life is narrowed and dehumanized by his dependence on alcohol.

Let us consider television viewing in the light of the conditions that define serious addictions.

– MARIE WINN

The Plug-In Drug: Television, Children, and the Family

4 Paragraphs to signal dialogue

Paragraphs of dialogue can add life to almost any sort of writing. The traditional way to set up dialogue in written form is simple: start a new paragraph each time the speaker changes, no matter how short each bit of conversation is. Here is an example:

Whenever I brought a book to the job, I wrapped it in newspaper — a habit that was to persist for years in other cities and under other circumstances. But some of the white men pried into my packages when I was absent and they questioned me.

"Boy, what are you reading those books for?"

"Oh, I don't know, sir."

"That's deep stuff you're reading, boy."

"I'm just killing time, sir."

"You'll addle your brains if you don't watch out."

– RICHARD WRIGHT, *Black Boy*

Email, online discussion lists, hypertext — all pose particular challenges for writers trying to create effective paragraphs. Both the limitations of electronic communication (such as lack of indentation in some email software) and the dizzying possibilities (such as ways to arrange hypertext) call for special creativity in writing paragraphs.

■ *Paragraphing in messages and postings*

Even without indentations, you can create paragraphs in online writing by skipping lines every time you shift topics or introduce a new idea. As with any text, remember that long, dense paragraphs — especially in the small fonts characteristic of email — make for hard reading. Here is an example of a student message that uses paragraphing to separate topics:

```
To: lunsford.2@stanford.edu
From: "Shannan Palma" <palma.7@stanford.edu>
Subject: heroes essay

Dear Professor Lunsford,

I've been working on my essay about heroes and film this
past week, and I've found a few new sources on the WWW
that sound interesting. I've printed out hard copies and
will show them to you at our next meeting.

In the meanwhile, I've rewritten my conclusion (again)
and would appreciate it if you could read the new
version and let me know what you think.

Thanks,
Shannan
```

Because online readers expect to be able to understand messages quickly, you may also want to make a point of stating the main idea of a paragraph right at the beginning. Consider, also, whether some information would be faster and easier to read in list rather than paragraph form. But keep your purpose and audience in mind: if you have a reason for leading up to the main idea gradually, or if a list seems too informal for your intended reader, those considerations should determine your choices.

▪ *Paragraphing for Web pages and hypertext essays*

Whereas email offers somewhat limited options for highlighting texts, on the Web there are no holds barred: color, boldfacing, fonts of all kinds, and even pictures and sound are available to writers. In designing effective paragraphs for the Web, then, you will need to think very carefully about your purpose(s) for the page and the readers you expect to visit it.

As with any graphic design, you should design your Web paragraphs to guide the reader's eye easily around the page. For an introductory page, this principle may mean that you will use very few (perhaps no) paragraphs, opting for a strong title and an arresting image, followed by a simple list of links — perhaps with its own set of icons — that readers can click on to visit further pages. In these later pages, you are more likely to use traditional paragraphs, set up as blocks of text (perhaps in columns or other kinds of configurations on the page, such as surrounding three sides of an illustration). Remember that readers will be working with one screen at a time and that your paragraphs should be designed to break up long blocks of text and to ease readability.

● For detailed information on designing Web pages (plus examples), see Chapter 9.

5h   Linking paragraphs

The same methods that you use to link sentences and create coherent paragraphs can be used to link paragraphs themselves so that a whole piece of writing flows smoothly and coherently. Some reference to the previous paragraph, either explicitly stated or merely implied, should occur in each paragraph after the introduction. As in linking sentences, you can create this reference by repeating or paraphrasing key words and terms and by using parallel structures and transitional expressions.

▪ *Repeating key words*

In fact, human offspring remain *dependent on their parents* longer than the young of any other species.
 Children are *dependent on their parents* or other adults not only for their physical survival but also for their initiation into the uniquely human knowledge that is collectively called culture. . . .

■ *Using parallel structure*

Kennedy made an effort to assure non-Catholics that he would respect the separation of church and state, and most of them did not seem to hold his religion against him in deciding how to vote. Since his election, *the church to which a candidate belongs* has become less important in presidential politics.

The region from which a candidate comes remains an important factor....

■ *Using transitional expressions*

While the Indian, in the character of Tonto, was more positively portrayed in *The Lone Ranger,* such a portrayal was more the exception than the norm.

Moreover, despite this brief glimpse of an Indian as an ever loyal sidekick, Tonto was never accorded the same stature as the man with the white horse and silver bullets....

◀ **EXERCISE 5.10**

Look at the essay you drafted for Exercise 3.6, and identify the ways your paragraphs are linked together. Identify each use of repetition, parallel structures, and transitional expressions, and then evaluate how effectively you have joined the paragraphs.

THINKING CRITICALLY ABOUT PARAGRAPHS

Reading with an Eye for Paragraphs

Read something by a writer you admire. Find one or two paragraphs that impress you in some way, and analyze them, using the guidelines at the beginning of this chapter. Try to decide what makes them effective paragraphs.

Thinking about Your Own Use of Paragraphs

Examine two or three paragraphs you have written, using the guidelines at the beginning of this chapter, to evaluate the unity, coherence, and development of each one. Identify the topic of each paragraph, the topic sentence (if one is explicitly stated), any patterns of development, and any means used to create coherence. Decide whether or not each paragraph successfully guides your readers, and explain your reasons. Then choose one paragraph, and revise it.

6 Collaborating— Online and Off

6a Collaborating in college

In college, you find yourself in conversation with many others—in the texts you read; in the writing you produce; in the talks you have with teachers, friends, classmates, and others (whether face-to-face or online); in all the discussions and lectures you listen to; and in all the observations and interviews you may conduct. The variety of these conversations points up the importance of collaboration in many college endeavors.

Although you will find yourself working together with many people on campus, some of your most immediate collaborators will be the members of the class in which you are using this book. You can learn a great deal by talking over issues and comparing ideas with classmates and by using them as a first audience for your writing (see 4c). As you talk and write, you will find the ideas they contribute making their way into your writing, and your ideas into theirs. This exchange is one reason citing sources and help from others is so important (see Chapter 18). In short, the texts you write are shaped in part by all the conversations you have; and the same is true for other writers.

In online communication especially, the roles of "writer" and "reader" and "text" become interchangeable, as almost instantaneously readers can become writers and

The CEO of a very successful software business tells an interesting story: several times a year, the company holds a staff retreat to devise a plan for working toward an important new goal or responding to a major problem. Here's what surprised the leader of this company: effective collaboration was the key to all their improvements. In fact, this CEO noted, it was *impossible* at the end of the day to say that any one person was the key to what the group had accomplished together.

In a memorable statement, philosopher Hannah Arendt confirms what this CEO discovered: "For excellence, the presence of others is always required." Collaboration, then, is essential not only in business and community work but also in college. This chapter will give you advice for participating in the many ways collaboration is done today. ■

147

then readers again, and texts constantly change as you and others add to them, often in unusual and intriguing ways. Because of these possibilities, online communication is often full of multiple voices and texts. Consider, for example, that an email message can carry with it a string of related messages that have accumulated as people have replied to one another. This extended message acts as a portrait of written conversation as well as a record of how meaning is made collaboratively. Whether you are working online or off, however, collaboration always demands special care and attention. This chapter provides advice on how to make your collaborations most effective.

While you will find many and varied reasons for working with others, the two major purposes for collaborating during college are to improve your individual work and to produce successful group projects.

6b   Collaborating on group projects

You may often be asked to work as part of a team in producing a group project, which might ultimately be a print report, an oral presentation, or a Web document or site. Unlike writing assignments that you start on your own—and then obtain feedback on from collaborators—group projects require additional planning and coordination.

1 Considering three models for group collaboration

Experienced collaborative writers often use one of three models for setting up the project: an expertise model, a division-of-labor model, or a process model. Each model allows you to establish clear duties for each participant.

> *Expertise model.* This kind of collaboration plays to the strengths of each member of the team. The person who knows the most about graphics and design, for example, takes on all jobs that require those skills, while the person who knows most about the topic takes the lead in drafting the text.

> *Division-of-labor model.* This model essentially asks each member of the group to become an "expert" on one aspect of the project. For example, one person might agree to be in charge of print-based research, while another searches the library's online databases, and still another

When you are working with other members of your class to share files for peer review or other group activities, remember to consider differences group members may have. Think of such differences not only in terms of computer compatibility but also in terms of the sensory, physical, or learning abilities of yourself and your classmates. You may have colleagues who wish to receive files in a very large type size, for example, in order to read them with ease. Similarly, you may have a peer who uses a voice-screen-reader program (such as JAWS), and these programs do not read charts, tables, and graphs very well since they are typically designed to read only from left to right. You can help your group get off to a good start by making a plan for accommodating everyone's needs.

conducts interviews. This model is particularly helpful if a project is large and time is short.

Process model. You can also consider dividing up the project in terms of its chronology: one person agrees to get the project going, presenting an outline for the group to consider and carrying out any initial research; then a second person takes over and begins a draft to present for discussion, criticism, and review; a third person takes on the task of designing and illustrating the project; and another person takes the job of revising and editing. This model can work well if time constraints prevent members from participating equally throughout the entire project. Once the project is completely drafted, however, the whole group needs to work together to create a final version.

FOR MULTILINGUAL WRITERS: *Giving Constructive Criticism*

In some cultures, writers submitting their work for scrutiny do not expect to give or receive the kind of criticism common in the United States, where writers expect constructive and sometimes aggressive criticism and debate. If such criticism is unusual in your culture (or is considered rude), discuss this expectation with members of your collaborative group, and ask for tips on how you can contribute constructively to the discussion.

Planning goes a long way toward making group collaboration work well. One way to start is to determine how you will communicate within the group. Setting up or subscribing to an email discussion list or joining an online class forum allows you to work with your group at all times of the day or night, though you will need to have some face-to-face meetings as well. Here are some additional ideas for getting off to a good start and completing a successful group project:

SOME GROUND RULES FOR GROUP PROJECTS

1. Set a time for a first meeting, during which group members can discuss the overall project, get to know one another, and establish ground rules for your group work. Ground rules are especially helpful in assuring that the group functions smoothly.
   → Every member has an equal opportunity to contribute to the group.
   → All members agree to be respectful and courteous and to listen actively to all others.
   → All members agree to contribute to the best of their ability to the project.
   → All members agree to recognize and value individual as well as cultural, linguistic, and other differences.
   → Each meeting—whether online or off—will have a set agenda.
   → The group will decide how to resolve disagreements and conflicts and will honor that decision.
   → Each person will meet deadlines and due dates. Those who find they must miss a deadline will let other members of the team know as far in advance as possible.

2. Consider logistics carefully, and establish clear duties for each participant. To take advantage of everything available to you, share information on all electronic resources: what kinds of computers, printing capabilities, and Internet access do all participants have? It's also a good idea to choose an archivist who will be responsible for making frequent backup copies of all material generated in online communication, for archiving all materials, and for providing summaries of conversational strands to help keep everyone on track.

3. Set up an overall agenda to organize the project and each meeting associated with it. If you are working online, take the time to spell

(Continued on p. 151)

out the agenda in writing, and send it to your email group or Web forum for everyone to see. If you are meeting face-to-face, take turns writing up notes of the discussion, and review these notes at the end to make sure everyone is on the same page.

4. Remember that group dynamics can make or break a project and that trust is essential to successful collaboration. As a result, pay very careful attention to other members of your group, to whether some may perceive you or others to have a hidden agenda, and to how the group is working together.

5. Establish periodic times at which to assess the group's effectiveness, with all group members addressing these questions. What has the group accomplished thus far? What has it been most successful in doing? What has it been least successful in doing? What has each member contributed? What about the group is not working well? How can members make the collaboration more effective?

6. Try to foresee unproductive conflicts, and work to resolve them. Will the group work by majority rule? If so, all members must have an opportunity to state their positions fully before a decision is made. When problems do arise, avoid associating them with one particular person or making accusations. It can also help to speak from the "I" rather than the "you" position, saying, for instance, *I don't quite understand this point* rather than *Your point is confusing (or wrong).* Another strategy is to look for some common ground that can serve to get the discussion going again.

7. Remember that creative and constructive conflict is desirable and, in fact, necessary to strong collaborative projects: if everyone just agrees to go along, the result is usually a watered-down effort. What you want instead is a really spirited debate during which members listen to all perspectives and argue out all possibilities — with the goal of producing the best possible project.

6c Using email and Web sites for collaboration

Many college instructors now routinely integrate email or Web sites into classes, providing a means for students to continue discussions out of class and to work together on assignments, readings, and so on.

Your instructor may create a class email discussion list so that you can send and receive messages from the entire class. If not, you may well want to set up a group email for yourself and your collaborators. Here are guidelines for using email for effective collaboration.

USING EMAIL FOR COLLABORATION

→ *Contacting members of your group.* To communicate with a group of classmates easily and efficiently, consider saving individuals' addresses as part of a larger group to whom you send messages. Most email programs let you create such a group in your address book—your list of email addresses. For some collaborations, you may also want to use your email program to create nicknames for all the members of your team.

→ *Considering online issues of tone.* Be aware that online tone can be hard to read: what you intend as a lighthearted joke may strike others as an insult or even an attack. So talk to your collaborators about how to respond to one another.

For more information on the ethics of online discourse, see Chapter 7.

→ *Archiving messages.* Make sure your email program will archive copies of your messages so that you can easily refer to earlier messages. As a backup, send a copy of each message to yourself. Save all group-work messages in folders for easy reference; do not keep them in your inbox, where they might be deleted accidentally.

→ *Attaching or cutting and pasting.* To send a text to your collaborators for response, either cut and paste it into an email message or send it as an attachment. Cutting and pasting works well for short texts that don't have a complicated format. If you want your peers to mark your text using the COMMENT or FOOTNOTE function of a word processor or if you want the text's format to come through, send the document as an attachment. Since group members may have different word-processing programs, you'll always be safe if you save files in Rich Text Format (RTF) before attaching them to messages. Doing so lets other programs read what you write with most formatting (**boldfacing**, *italics*, tables, and so on) intact.

For examples of the COMMENT and FOOTNOTE functions, see pp. 89 and 311.

→ *Making your expectations clear.* Be explicit in telling your collaborators what you expect them to do in response to your email message. For example, you might write *Please take a hard look at my introduction: is it clear? Does it attract and hold your interest?*

(Continued on p. 153)

(Continued from p. 152)

→ *Being consistent.* Be consistent in how you respond to the writing of others: will you insert comments in their text in all caps or boldface, for example, set comments off in brackets, or use the COMMENT or FOOTNOTE function to write longer comments (see 4c3)? If you are using Microsoft Word, experiment with its TRACK CHANGES feature. Whichever method you choose, stick with that choice throughout the paper you are commenting on.

Your instructor may construct a class Web site on which to post the syllabus, assignments, and readings; send reminders and messages; and share files. Or you may find that your instructor is using a commercial package of some kind (such as FirstClass, BlackBoard, or WebCT) or a program developed at your college. Whatever program you use, Web sites offer a space for extending the collaborative work of the classroom. (Indeed, in some distance-learning courses, all collaboration occurs via the class site.)

As always in collaboration, your class should establish ground rules to govern participation: When and how often is each member expected to post messages to class discussions? What code of conduct will everyone agree to follow? If you want your text to be read on a Web site, save the files as HTML.

● For more information on HTML, see 9d and h.

The screen shot on p. 154 comes from a course using a locally designed Web forum for discussion. You can see here the text of one message as well as the most recently posted messages to the discussion.

6d   Presenting a group project

Many of your collaborative projects may end up as print or online documents, but others will call for oral and/or multimedia presentations. If your group is to make such a presentation, follow these guidelines:

● For more on oral and multimedia presentations, see Chapter 10.

- Make sure you know exactly how much time you will have for the presentation, and stick to that time limit.

- Divide the preparatory work fairly. For example, who will revise the written text for oral presentation? Who will prepare the slides or other visuals?

- Decide how each group member will contribute to the presentation. Make sure that everyone has an obvious role, especially if individual grades are being assigned.

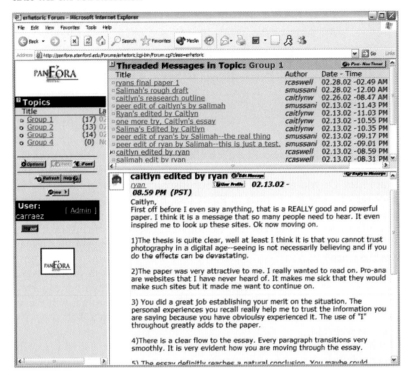

- Leave time for at least two practice sessions. During the first session, time yourselves carefully, and make either a sound or video recording of the performance. Then view or listen to the recording carefully, and make adjustments to the presentation where necessary.

- Make sure that any accompanying handouts, slides, or posters will be readable by your audience, and revise any that fail this test. Use your visuals as you rehearse, and try to do so in a room similar in size and lighting to the room in which you will be making the presentation.

- After your presentation, take time for a debriefing with your instructor, if possible, so that you can make notes for ways to improve future presentations.

FOR COLLABORATION

Working with one or two other members of your class, draw up your own criteria for evaluating group or collaborative presentations. Then use these guidelines to evaluate a presentation you have made—or one you are assigned to make. Finally, compare sets of guidelines with other groups in your class, and come up with a set of guidelines for the entire class to use.

THINKING CRITICALLY ABOUT YOUR COLLABORATIVE WORK

Begin by making a list of all the ways in which you collaborate with others. Then reflect on what kinds of collaboration you find most effective. Finally, take an example of one recent collaboration you have been part of, and examine how well it worked by answering the following questions: What did I contribute to the collaboration? What worked well and did not work well about the collaboration? What could I have done to improve this particular collaboration?

PART 2

CONSIDERING MEDIA

"I have written so many words that
the act of writing and the act of word
processing have become the same thing.
I realized that the computer keyboard is
now an extension of my mind."
— ROGER EBERT

7

Writing with Computers: The Basics

How often do you find yourself at a computer? Many writers today use a word-processing program to draft and revise essays from start to finish; use the **World Wide Web** and online library databases for research; read and write email and instant messages; and visit chat rooms to keep in touch with colleagues, family, and friends. For such writers, the computer becomes an extension of themselves—it is the tool they turn to first to present their ideas in writing. This chapter provides you with some advice, based on what writers across the country have reported, about the two most common ways of writing with computers: email and word processing. ■

7a Email

One writer describes email's powerful presence in her life by saying, "I have been courted by email, been hired by email, learned of friends' deaths by email." So prevalent is this form of communication in our daily lives that you may have stopped thinking about email consciously: it is just there, waiting to be answered or offering a way to reach others. Because email is constant, many writers fall into habits based on the type of email they write most often—usually very informal—and by failing to adjust style and voice for different occasions and audiences, they sometimes undermine their own intentions. As with any kind of writing, therefore, email calls on you to consider your purpose and audience when you write—and respond to—messages. The following advice will help ensure that your email is effective:

- Use a subject line that states your purpose accurately and clearly—whether you are writing an email message or responding to one. (Some email programs automatically delete messages without subject lines.) Some readers prioritize their responses to messages based on the information in the subject line: being accurate may help you get a speedy reply.

- Avoid **flaming**—intentionally rude, insulting, or dismissive language—and remember that tone is very hard to convey in online postings: what you intend as a joke may come across as an insult. In addition, remember that many readers find messages in ALL CAPS irritating and hard to read, as if someone were shouting at them. For an example of a readable email, see p. 161.

CONSIDERING MEDIA
Email

- Be pertinent. Consider your readers, giving them the information they need. Being pertinent means that the length and style of your messages will vary, depending on the subject at hand and your recipients' expectations. For example, friends might expect chatty and informal messages, a teacher might expect short and to-the-point messages, and readers of a scholarly discussion list might expect long, analytical messages.

- Break your long paragraphs into shorter paragraphs, and when a message has several points, create sections with headings. For a long message (more than two screens), it's worth writing an introduction that lists the points your message will address. Within your message, then, you can create corresponding headings — section titles — using those same points. Consider using bulleted lists and indented text as well to give your readers a sense of the framework of your message and to make use of white space to relieve the stream of words.

- Use a more formal tone along with a formal greeting and closing when writing to someone you don't know or to an authority, such as a supervisor or instructor (*Dear Ms. Aulie* rather than *Hello*). In this regard, treat email like a letter.

- Except in very informal situations, use the conventions of academic English. If you want your message to be taken seriously, be sure it is clearly written and as error-free as you can make it. Proofread email messages just as you would other writing. For very important emails — job inquiries, research interview requests, letters to a legislator on an issue, to name a few examples — use your email program's spell checker, if available. Otherwise, compose the message in your word processor, spell- and grammar-check it, and then print a hard copy to proofread yourself. After you make final corrections, copy the message into your email program, check to be sure formatting (italics, spacing, dashes) is intact, and send it.

- Avoid using color fonts or other special formatting unless you know the formatting will appear as you intend on your reader's screen.

- Remember that the Internet is public and that online readers can easily print or forward your messages. When privacy is important, think twice before communicating by email. In addition, always ask permission before forwarding a sensitive message from someone else.

- Before attaching text or graphics files, check with your recipients to make sure they will be able to download them. If you are sending a document as an attachment, save it in **Rich Text Format** (RTF), or copy and paste your text into your email message.

www • bedford stmartins.com/ smhandbook

To see an example of a readable long email, click on

▶ **Working Online**
  ▶ **Email**

●┈ For more on composing paragraphs online, see 5g.

comp

160 **7a**

CONSIDERING MEDIA

Writing with
Computers:
The Basics

- Conclude your message with your name and email address; don't assume this information will appear in a recipient's header. For more formal email, you may want to include your phone number(s) and postal-mail address. Your email program likely includes a command that lets you place this information in a signature file (or **.sig file** for short) that you attach or that the program then automatically appends to every email message you write.

FOR MULTILINGUAL WRITERS: Following Email Conventions

Email conventions are still evolving, and they differ from one cultural context to another. Especially if you do not know the recipients of your email, stick to a more formal tone (*Dear Ms. Ditembe* and *Sincerely yours*, for example) and follow the conventions of print letter writing—complete sentences, regular capitalization, and so on. If you have special knowledge about conventions of email use in a particular culture, draw on that knowledge, and share it with others in your class.

■ *Email lists and discussion forums*

The previous advice in this section applies to writing *all* email, whether to one person, a few people, or a large email discussion list. The advice that follows, however, is especially significant when participating in an email discussion list or other online discussion forum. People who sign up with discussion lists (or **listservs**) receive a copy of every message sent to that list by other members and can send messages to the list themselves. As members respond to one another, the email accumulates, creating a chain effect that forms an online discussion. When taking part in a discussion-list conversation, keep the following tips in mind:

- Avoid unnecessary criticism of spelling or other obvious language errors. These kinds of comments are often taken as flames, especially if the mistake is obvious. If a typo makes a message unclear, ask politely for a clarification. If you disagree with an assertion of fact (if someone gives the wrong date for an event or misquotes someone else, for example), offer what you believe to be the correct information, but don't insult the writer for making the mistake.

- If you think you've been flamed, give the writer the benefit of the doubt. Even if you are sure you've been flamed, resist flaming in return, especially in public spaces like discussion lists. Replying with patience establishes your credibility and helps you come across as mature and fair.

```
To: techsoup@indirect.com
From: Andrea Lunsford <lunsford@stanford.edu>
Subject: help finding a correct address
Cc:
Bcc:


Dear Techsoup:


I am trying to send a message to Irene Whitney at Pacific
Synergies, which is headquartered in Whistler, B.C.    The
email address she gave me is pacsyn@direct.net -- which
is obviously not right since you returned it as undeliv-
erable.    Perhaps I should have tried adding "com" at the
end?    If you have an address for Pacific Synergies, I
would be very grateful to receive it.


Andrea Lunsford, Department of English
<lunsford@stanford.edu>
Stanford University
450 Serra Mall
Stanford, CA 94305-2087
(650) 723-0682 (o)
(650) 723-0631 (f)
```

Precise email address of recipient

Sender's name and email address

Subject line provides accurate and specific information

Salutation

Double spacing between salutation and message

Message kept as succinct and direct as possible

Double spacing between end of message and signature line

Signature line gives name of sender and .sig file

- In general, follow the conventions of a particular discussion forum regarding the use of a growing number of **acronyms**. These letter strings can work like an efficient shorthand for those who understand them. If you have doubts about whether readers will be able to interpret an acronym, write it out. Some of the more commonly used acronyms include FYI (for your information), FWIW (for what it's worth), IMHO (in my humble opinion), IOW (in other words), and BRB (be right back).

- Keep in mind that many email discussion lists are archived. Further, they are often read by subscribers who may not ever write but who will come to know you if you post a message to a list. Writing messages carefully matters because—and this is no exaggeration—you never know when you might meet your readers in other settings, whether professional or personal, and your email messages will already have created a first impression.

CONSIDERING MEDIA

Writing with
Computers:
The Basics

Subject line provides
specific information

Writer has included
the part of an
earlier posting she
is responding to,
which helps other
list members follow
the conversation

Double space
indicates a new
paragraph

Three-paragraph body
of posting responds
to query raised by
another member and
then calls for further
comments. Tone is
engaged, friendly,
and polite

Writer gives only first
name and initial
because this is a
closed listserv for
class members

To: alenglh167@lists.acs.ohio-state.edu
From: Kristen Convery <convery.8@osu.edu>
Subject: Re: class discussion of "self"
Cc:
Bcc:

At 03:48 PM 11/17/02 -0500, Kate wrote:

>Has anyone had any interesting or pertinent discussions
>of the "self" in other classes this term?

I'm taking psychology this quarter and have found some
information that pertains to our discussion on the self.

Carl Rogers studied the self and self-concept, theorizing
that people do things in line with their concept of themselves in order to avoid having to rework that self-
concept. For instance, if I think of myself as an artist
and not as a musician and I want to go to a concert, I
will go to the art museum just so that I do not have to
rethink and maybe change the way I view myself.

Comments from other class members? It strikes me as
interesting that we seem to feel as if we must fit one
mold, and that that mold nullifies all other concepts of
the self. Why can't we be both artists and musicians?
But it's true--especially when I look at families. How
many families do you guys know where the parents proudly
introduce members as "the scientist (writer/artist/
musician/thinker) of the family"? And how does this
inhibit other siblings who might also want to be scientists, writers, artists, musicians, thinkers, but fear
taking over someone else's place?

Just a few thoughts . . .

Kristen C.

For responding to a particular message, keep these guidelines in mind:

- Change the subject line if you are writing about something different from the original subject.

- Check to make sure you are responding to the appropriate person or persons. If, for instance, you receive a message that is copied to several others, decide whether you want to reply to the person who sent the message or to the whole group. Most email systems allow you to click on REPLY to reply to the person who sent you the message or to click on REPLY TO ALL to reach the whole group. People often send very personal messages meant for one person to whole groups or to an entire discussion list because they forget to check where the reply is going. This can be extremely embarrassing, especially if the matter should have been kept private.

- Include only those parts of the original message that you will be addressing, and delete the rest. If you need to, quote from the original message, but only quote as needed, and make sure to set off the quotations from your writing.

- If you're replying to several points in a longer message, begin by summarizing the points you will be addressing. You might write, for example, *James made four points in his post yesterday. They were:* and then go on to list the points. Use the point summaries as section headings for your message.

● **EXERCISE 7.1**

Choose several email messages you have sent recently—at least one of which is more formal than the others. Using the advice in this section, take a critical look at the emails you have chosen, noting differences and similarities and thinking about how easily readers could follow the messages, and bring your findings to class for discussion.

7b   Word processing

The metaphor of word *processing* deserves attention: we use computers literally to process our words, organizing and formatting them in various ways, playing around with organization and stylistic choices. This active role we ascribe to computers is one reason many writers think of their word-processing programs as good friends that help them organize all their work. But getting these programs to work efficiently and

comp

164   **7b**

CONSIDERING MEDIA

Writing with
Computers:
The Basics

effectively for you calls for some care. It requires understanding the various tools that word-processing programs provide, especially those that involve saving and sharing files, formatting, improving your writing, and cutting and pasting.

■ *Saving and sharing files*

In most word processors, you can choose NEW from the FILE menu to create a new document and then save it as a file. You will save yourself time and effort later on, when you're looking for a particular document, if you give each file a clear name (*Rhetorical Analysis draft 1,* for example, instead of *Paper 1*). Save related files in the same folder. In Windows, you can create a new folder by clicking on the "C" drive of your computer and then clicking on FILE and then NEW. File management tools such as Windows Explorer help you move existing files from one folder to another.

If you are handing in your draft electronically to an instructor or giving a copy to someone else, include your name in the file name, along with other pertinent information (Mamta Ahluwalia's essay might be saved as *Mamta Ahluwalia rhet analysis draft 1,* for example). The use of your full name in the file makes it easier for an instructor to see if you've handed in the work and to distinguish it from that of other students.

Always check on the file type another person can receive before sending a draft electronically, since not all users will have the same edition or type of software you have. Someone using Word 97, for example, will not be able to open a file saved in Word 2000 unless you use SAVE AS and select WORD 97. For sharing one file with a group of people, you can choose SAVE AS and select RICH TEXT FORMAT (as long as you are not using graphics or complicated tables in the file).

Make sure that your word processor's auto save function is set; if it's not, remember to save your files every five minutes or right after you've made an important change, since few things are more frustrating to writers than losing part of their work. Also, take the extra precaution of saving a second copy of every file and giving it a slightly different name (*Rhetorical Analysis draft 1 dup*). Put this copy on a floppy disc or somewhere else other than where your original file is located—on another computer account, for example, or emailed to yourself for downloading at home. If both copies are in the same location and you lose access to that location, the backup won't do you any good.

CONSIDERING MEDIA
Word Processing

When you are working with other members of your class to share files for peer review or other group activities, remember to consider differences group members may have, not only in terms of computer compatibility but in terms of varying abilities as well. You may have classmates who wish to receive files in a very large type size, for example, in order to read them with ease. You can help your group get off to a good start by making a plan for accommodating everyone's needs.

■ *Formatting*

When formatting a document, make use of the tools your word-processing program provides rather than trying to format by using hard returns and the space bar. The advantage of using specific formatting tools is that your formatting choices will remain intact even if you change the content. For each format recommendation, consult your word processor's HELP menu to find out how to use the specific feature (see p. 166). The bulleted list below includes some keywords you can search for in your HELP menu index; these have been set in italics.

- Most word processors set the default *margins* at 1 inch for top and bottom and 1.25 inches for left and right sides. Although most instructors will accept those settings, you may need to adjust margins for some documents. If so, you'll need to change the default settings.

● For more information on margins, see 8a and b.

- For text needing *indentation,* type the text first and then highlight it; then use the FORMAT menu or ruler bar to align or format the text as needed. Do not use hard returns when indenting text. This will make the formatting easier to preserve when you go back and edit the text, saving you time as your drafts progress.

- Rather than typing and positioning them yourself, use the word processor to insert *page numbers* automatically and to adjust them if you add or delete pages. If you want to include additional information with the page number—such as your name or the paper's title—you can do so efficiently by adding *headers and footers.* To automatically add *footnote and endnote* numbers to your document, click on FOOTNOTE AND ENDNOTE, then NUMBERING.

● For examples of headers in MLA and APA styles, see 64d and 65d.

- Try using *bullets and numbering* to format your lists by highlighting the text you want to be bulleted or numbered, then clicking on the BULLETS AND NUMBERING command. If you want your list to be formatted in *columns,* click on COLUMNS.

comp

7b

For more infor-
mation on how
to integrate such
illustrations
effectively, see 8d.

- Your word processor will likely include graphics tools for creating charts, graphs, tables, and other illustrations. Your word processor may also have features to help you easily insert a *picture, symbol,* or *hyperlink* into your document (choose INSERT in Microsoft Word).

For more infor-
mation on these
programs,
see 14i.

- Documentation programs such as Research Assistant and EndNote can be very helpful in styling footnotes and works-cited lists.

- Check out the PRINT PREVIEW function in your FILE menu to see what your document looks like and whether you want to change its format. Using *print preview* will save you paper and printer cartridges because it shows you how your document will look when it is printed.

FOR COLLABORATION

Working with one or two classmates, check out the HELP index in your word-processing program. Choose four or five items in the index that address formatting issues (margins, page numbers, bulleted or numbered lists, footnotes or endnotes, and so on). Then, using the advice offered by the HELP index, try using these particular features. Take notes on how clear the HELP index advice was and how well you were able to use it, and bring the results of your investigation to class for discussion.

▓ *Improving your writing — some basic tools*

Several word-processing tools may help you improve the quality of your writing. For starters, your campus writing center or computer lab may have a software program that helps you begin a piece of writing by asking you a series of questions or giving a set of prompts. Many students find that brainstorming and talking with others (online or off) is more effective than such programs, but if one is available to you, try it out and use it if it seems helpful.

Before you start composing, decide whether you want your spelling and grammar checked automatically as you write. (Some writers are annoyed by these prompts while they draft.) If your word processor is set to perform an automatic spell check or grammar check, you can turn the feature off (under TOOLS in Microsoft Word) and then run the spell- or grammar-check program at your proofreading and editing stages. Your HELP index will tell you how to use these features.

The spell-checking systems that come with all word-processing programs can go a long way toward identifying typos and other misspellings. But research indicates that spell checkers can't replace careful proofreaders: a study found that the number of spelling errors in handwritten essays was almost identical to the number in word-processed essays that had been through a spell checker. Word-processed essays written *without* a spell checker, however, had many, many more errors than either of the other two samples. As this study suggests, a spell checker is helpful, but it won't pick up many kinds of mistakes: wrong words that are nevertheless spelled correctly; misspelled proper names; or confused homonyms (*there, their, they're*). The bottom line is that there is no substitute for careful proofreading.

Grammar and style checkers can be more problematic than spell checkers for one simple reason: they are looking at your text out of context, without knowing your purpose, audience, or rhetorical situation. Furthermore, grammar and style checkers sometimes give the wrong

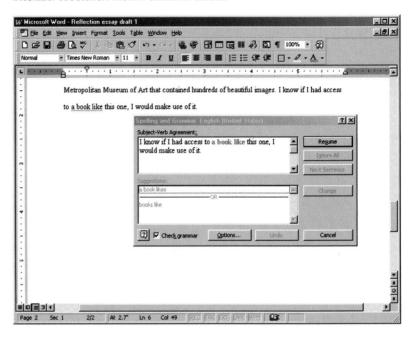

advice, as shown above. Nevertheless, grammar checkers can be useful proofreading and editing aids because they disrupt your reading of the text by literally taking it out of context. Once the text is disrupted in this way, you can often see its surface features, such as typos, much more easily. You can even focus on particular types of surface errors. For example, if you know that you occasionally make mistakes in subject-verb agreement, you can change your grammar-checker settings to look for only that kind of error, as shown on p. 169. In Microsoft Word, from TOOLS select SPELLING AND GRAMMAR, then click on OPTIONS, and then SETTINGS.

In addition to spell and grammar checkers, several other word-processing features can help you improve your writing.

For more about
outlining, see 3e.

- Use the OUTLINE function to check the logical connections in a document you create. An outline can be extremely useful after your entire draft is complete: looking at only the main points of your draft allows you to focus on transitions between points as well as overall logic.

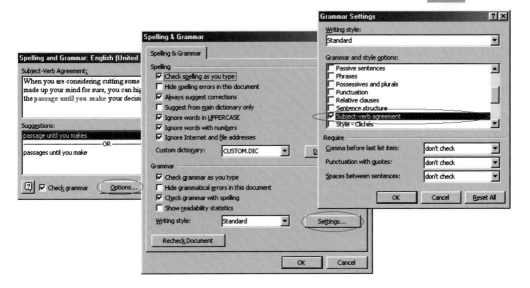

- Use the TRACK CHANGES function (under TOOLS in Microsoft Word) to show cuts and to highlight changes you are making to the text. (Note that some word processors do not offer a tool to mark all your revisions.)

- Use the FIND and REPLACE functions to help you search for certain kinds of errors. For example, if you mistype *it's* for *its,* you can search for all uses of *it's* and replace them with *it is.* Then if you proofread and see a sentence that says something like *The cat chased it is tail,* you'll know that you need *its* instead of *it's* in the sentence.

www • bedford
stmartins.com/
smhandbook

For tips on using
FIND and REPLACE,
click on

► Working Online
  ► Word Processors

● **EXERCISE 7.2**

Take an assignment you are working on, and experiment with the TRACK CHANGES editing function in Microsoft Word (under TOOLS). Practice editing your text, using this function to highlight additions and to cross out material that needs to be changed. Print out a page of your revision, and bring it to class for comparison with other students' work.

■ *Cutting and pasting*

Your word-processing program offers CUT, COPY, and PASTE tools to help you revise. In most word processors, these useful tools are available in

comp

170 **7b**

CONSIDERING MEDIA

Writing with
Computers:
The Basics

several places: from the standard toolbar, under the EDIT menu, and as shortcuts on the keyboard (such as CTRL + X to cut and CTRL + V to paste in Windows). When you highlight and then cut or copy text, the word-processing program saves it in its clipboard memory and lets you paste the cut or copied text in another location, including other files or programs. Note that the clipboard-stored text will be replaced whenever you highlight and cut or copy a new selection of text, so be careful to paste the first bit somewhere before you cut or copy another bit. Otherwise, you will lose that first bit of text. Following are some tips to help you cut, copy, and paste text efficiently:

- You can select text for copying by highlighting a passage and then clicking on COPY in the EDIT menu. The copied text will stay where it was in your document while you experiment with moving it to a more appropriate place. If the passage fits better somewhere else, you can paste it there and then go back and delete it from its original location.

- If you plan to revise the organization of a document extensively (after getting some feedback from a classmate or after using an OUTLINE tool), work from a copy of the file (open the file and use SAVE AS to give the paper a new name) before making additions, cutting, copying, pasting, and so on.

- If you think you'll be cutting text that you like or might want to use in some other essay or for some other purpose, open a new file for these scraps and give it a name associated with the draft you're working on (for example, *cut text from rhetorical analysis draft 2*). You will then be able to retrieve the text if you decide you want to use it later.

- When it comes to cutting and pasting, remember that too much of a good thing is, well, too much of a good thing: indiscriminate cutting and pasting can result in an incoherent text fairly quickly.

THINKING CRITICALLY ABOUT YOUR USE OF COMPUTERS

Take at least one day and note down every time you use a computer—for anything at all. At the end of the day, make an inventory of all your uses, and then stop to think critically about them. Are you using computers as efficiently and effectively as you could? What changes would you like to make in how you use computers? What would you like to learn to do with computers that you can't now do? Bring your inventory to class for discussion and comparison.

Considering Document Design

8

8a   Creating a visual structure

Effective writers think of the documents they are composing as visual structures to which they can apply basic principles of design. When writers consider documents in this way, they use elements such as white space and color and type styles to guide readers, presenting them with documents that are easy on the eye—and easy to understand. The writer's goals are to make each page look inviting and to lead readers smoothly from one page to the next.

When you prepare a print or a Web-based document, remember that there are important differences between these two media. In general, print documents are easily portable, less expensive to read, faster to produce, and more familiar than Web documents. In addition, the tools for producing print texts are highly developed and stable. For the most part, pages you print will look just like they looked in the PRINT PREVIEW function, whereas the look of Web-based pages often varies depending on your browser or your reader's browser. Nevertheless, Web-based documents have significant advantages: publishing on the Web is still fairly cheap; color, sound, and other illustrative materials are often available at no extra cost; updates are very easy to do; distribution is fast and efficient; and you can get feedback on Web documents very swiftly. Whether you are working to produce a print or a Web document, however, you should rely on several important principles of design.

The electronic revolution has dramatically affected the delivery of information. Known in the ancient Greek world as *actio,* delivery was an art every educated person needed to master, for how a speaker delivered a speech— tone and volume of voice, use of gestures, and so on— had a great impact on how it would be received. Today, computers have made it easier for us to present our written texts, allowing us to use headings, lists, graphics, and other visuals. Because these visual elements can be fundamental to readability and to helping us get and keep a reader's attention, they bring a whole new dimension to writing—what some refer to as *visual rhetoric.* This chapter will help you use visual rhetoric effectively in creating various documents, including online documents that can be printed out. (The next two chapters discuss how to design Web texts and oral and multimedia presentations.) ■

Most design experts begin with several very simple principles that guide the design of print and/or Web texts.

→ *Contrast.* The contrast in a design is what attracts your eye to the page and guides you around it. You may achieve contrast through the use of color, icons, boldface or large type size, headings, and so on. If you are trying to capture attention — in a brochure, a report, or some other document — pay very careful attention to contrast. Begin with a focus point — the dominant point, image, or words on the page — and structure the flow of your visual information from this point. Remember that white space also helps guide readers through your document and provides some pauses or breaks.

→ *Proximity.* Parts of a page that are closely related should be together (proximate to one another). Your goal is to position related points, text, and visuals near one another and to use clear headings to identify these clusters.

→ *Repetition.* Readers are guided in large part by the repetition of key words or elements. You can take advantage of this design principle by using a consistent design throughout your document and by repeating elements like color, typeface, and images to help readers follow the document.

→ *Alignment.* This principle refers to how images and text on a page are lined up, both horizontally and vertically. The headline, title, or banner on a document, for example, should be carefully aligned horizontally so that the reader's eye is drawn easily along one line from left to right. Vertical alignment is equally important. In general, you can choose to align things with the left side, the right side, or the center. The overall guideline is not to mix alignments arbitrarily. That is, if you begin with a left alignment, stick with it for the major parts of your page. The result will be a cleaner and more organized look.

→ *Consistent overall impression.* Aim for a design that creates the appropriate overall impression or atmosphere for your document. For an academic essay, you will probably make conservative choices that strike a serious scholarly note. In a newsletter for a campus group, you might choose bright colors and arresting images.

■ *Using white space and margins to frame information*

The white space around text acts as a frame and leads the reader through the text. For most print documents, you will want to frame your page with margins of white space of between one inch and one and one-half inches—depending on the purpose of the document, its content, and its audience. Since the eye takes in only so many chunks of data in one movement, very long lines can be hard to read, especially onscreen. Wider margins help, particularly if the information is difficult or dense. In your college papers, such margins give your instructor room to make comments. Within the page, you can also use white space in other ways—around graphics or lists, for example, to make them stand out. To make Web texts easier to read, set the margins so that the average text line includes about ten words, or no more than seventy-five characters.

■ *Using color*

Many software programs and printers offer the possibility of using color in print documents. As with all decisions, ones about color depend to a large extent not only on the kind of equipment you are using but also on the purpose(s) of your document and its intended audience. As you design your print documents, keep in mind that some colors (red, for example) can evoke powerful responses, so take care that the colors you use match the message you are sending. Here are some tips about the effective use of color:

●— For information
on using color
in designing
Web texts, see
9b and d.

- Use color to draw attention to elements you want to emphasize: headings and subheadings, bullets, text boxes, parts of charts or graphs.

- For most print documents, keep the number of colors to a minimum (one or two, in addition to white and black); too many colors can create a busy or confused look. In addition, avoid putting colors that clash or that are hard on the eyes (like certain shades of yellow or orange) next to one another.

- Be consistent in your use of color; use the same color for all subheads, for example.

- Check to make sure all color visuals or text are legible.

CONSIDERING DISABILITIES: Color for Contrast

Remember when you are using color that not everyone will see it as you do. Some individuals do not perceive color at all; others perceive color in a variety of different ways, especially colors like blue and green, which are close together on the color spectrum. When putting colors next to one another, then, use those that reside on opposite sides of the color spectrum, such as purple and gold, in order to achieve high contrast. Doing so will allow readers to see the contrast, if not the nuances, of color.

■ *Selecting appropriate paper and print*

The quality of the paper and the readability of the print affect the overall look and feel of your document. Although you may well want to use inexpensive paper for your earlier drafts, when your college writing is ready for final presentation use 8½" × 11" good-quality white bond paper. On some occasions, you may wish to use a parchment or cream-colored bond — for a résumé perhaps. For brochures and posters, colored paper may be most appropriate. Make sure that your printer is creating sharp images, and replace the cartridge if it is not. Use a good inkjet or laser printer if at all possible. For color and illustrations, you may need to seek out the best-quality printer available to you for your final product. This may mean using a laser printer in one of the campus computer centers or libraries.

FOR MULTILINGUAL WRITERS: Understanding Reading Patterns

Western readers tend to expect that information will flow from left to right and top to bottom — since that is the way most people from Western cultures read. For a quick example of this principle at work, log on to cnn.com and note that the name of the company appears in the top left corner of the page, where CNN expects readers' eyes to begin reading. Other linguistic cultures, however, may prefer other ways of reading, such as right to left or down columns. Understanding the reading patterns of the language you are working in will help you design your documents most effectively.

8b Using consistency to lead readers through a document

Especially in longer documents, you can help readers a great deal by maintaining consistency of design, including the placement of page numbers, style of the typeface, spacing of lines, and width of margins.

■ *Paginating your document*

Except for a separate title page, which is usually left unnumbered, number every page of your document. Your instructor may ask that you follow a particular format (APA or MLA, for example); if not, number each page consecutively with arabic numerals, beginning with the first page of text. Place your last name and the page number in the upper-right-hand corner of the page, about one-half inch from the top and flush with the right margin. Do not put the number in parentheses or follow it with a period. Most word-processing programs will paginate a document for you.

CONSIDERING MEDIA

Using Consistency to Lead Readers through a Document

For examples of pagination formats in MLA and APA styles, see 64d and 65d.

■ *Selecting type*

Most computers allow writers to choose among a great variety of type sizes and typefaces, or **fonts.** For most college writing, the easy-to-read 11- or 12-point type size is best.

This is 12-point Times New Roman
This is 11-point Times New Roman

Also more readable is a **serif** font (this is serif type; this is sans serif type). Although a smaller or more unusual style — such as *italics* or *cursive* — might seem attractive at first glance, readers may find such styles distracting and/or hard to read. Most important, be consistent in the size and style of typeface you use, especially for the main part of your text. Unless you are striving for some special effect, shifting sizes and fonts within a document can give an appearance of disorderliness.

For information on choosing type size and style in headings, see 8c.

■ *Considering spacing*

Final drafts for most of your college writing should be double-spaced, with the first line of paragraphs indented one-half inch or five spaces. Certain kinds of writing for certain disciplines may call for different spacing. Letters, memorandums, and Web texts, for example, are usually single-spaced, with no paragraph indentation. Lab reports in some disciplines are also single-spaced, and some long reports may be printed with one-and-a-half-line spacing to save paper. Other kinds of documents, such as flyers and newsletters, may call for multiple columns of print. If in doubt, consult your instructor.

For examples of appropriate spacing and margins in MLA, APA, CBE, and Chicago styles, see 64d and e, 65d, and 66c.

You are probably already familiar with the conventions for spacing words. In general, leave one space after all punctuation *except* in the following cases:

For information on spacing with ellipses, see 53f.

• Leave no space before or after a dash (*Please respond—right away—to this message*).

- Leave no space before or after a hyphen (*a red-letter day*).
- Leave no space between punctuation marks (*on my way,"*).

Computers allow you to decide whether or not you want both side margins **justified**, or squared off—as they are on this page. Except in posters and other writing where you are trying to achieve a distinctive visual effect, you should always justify the left margin, though you may decide to indent lists and blocks of text that are off. However, most readers—and many instructors—prefer the right margin to be "ragged," or unjustified.

8c   Using headings

For brief essays and reports, you may need no headings at all. For longer documents, however, these devices serve as friendly signposts for readers, calling attention to the organization of the text and thus aiding comprehension. Some kinds of reports use set headings, which readers expect (and writers therefore must provide); see 8e for an example. If you use headings, you need to decide on type size and style, phrasing, and positioning.

■ *Choosing type size and style*

If you look through this book, which is a long and complex document, you will note the use of various levels of headings. The book uses four levels of headings, distinguished by different type sizes and fonts as well as by color:

1 First-level heading

2 Second-level heading

■ *Third-level heading*

FOURTH-LEVEL HEADING

For your college writing, you might distinguish levels of headings using type—all capitals for the first-level headings, capitals and lowercase underlined for the second level, plain capitals and lowercase for the third level, and so on. You can also use boldface or italics or other options from the font menu in your word-processing program. For example:

ON A TYPEWRITER	ON A COMPUTER
FIRST-LEVEL HEADING	FIRST-LEVEL HEADING
Second-Level Heading	**Second-Level Heading**
Third-Level Heading	*Third-Level Heading*

■ Phrasing headings

Heading styles often follow discipline-specific conventions, but as a general rule look for the most succinct way to word your headings. Most often, this means stating the topic in a *single word,* usually a noun (*Toxicity*); in a *phrase,* usually a noun phrase (*Levels of Toxicity*) or a gerund phrase (*Measuring Toxicity*); in a *question* that will be answered in the text (*How can toxicity be measured?*); or—especially in writing about a process—in an *imperative* that tells readers what steps to take (*Measure the toxicity*). Whichever structure you choose, make sure you use it consistently for all headings of the same level: all questions, for example, or all gerund phrases and *not* a mixture of the two.

●— For more on maintaining parallel structure in headings, see 45a.

■ Positioning headings

Typically, first-level headings are placed at the left margin. The second level of heading may then be indented five spaces from the left, and the third level may be centered.

FIRST-LEVEL HEADING

Second-Level Heading

Third-Level Heading

Other positions are possible; just remember to place each level of head consistently throughout your paper. And remember that you shouldn't put a heading at the very bottom of a page, since readers would have to turn to the next page to find the text the heading is announcing.

8d   Using visuals

Preparing visuals and creating a visual design should be part of your process of generating ideas and planning for a complete document. Visuals can both draw readers into your argument and help persuade them to accept your claim. In some cases, visuals may even be the primary text you present; in other cases, they will be of equal or supplemental importance to your text. In every case, they can help make a point vividly and emphatically by presenting information more succinctly and more clearly than words alone could.

Visuals fall into two categories: **tables,** which present information in columns and rows of numbers or words, and **figures,** which include all other visuals — pie, bar, and line charts; line and bar graphs; photographs; maps; drawings; and other illustrations. Many software packages offer help creating visuals.

In deciding when and where to use visuals, the best rule of thumb is simply to use ones that will make your points most emphatically and will most help your readers understand your document. Researchers who have studied the use of visuals offer some tips about when a particular kind of visual is most appropriate.

- *Use tables* to draw readers' attention to particular numerical information.

- *Use graphs or charts* to draw readers' attention to relationships among data. *Pie charts* compare a part to the whole. *Bar charts and line graphs* compare one element to another, compare elements over time, demonstrate correlations, and/or illustrate frequency.

- *Use drawings or diagrams* to draw readers' attention to dimensions and to specific details.

- *Use maps* to draw readers' attention to location and to spatial relationships.

- *Use cartoons* to illustrate or emphasize a point dramatically or to amuse.

For examples of
the use of photographs in an
essay, see 4j,
13k, and 20d.

- *Use photographs* to draw readers' attention to a graphic scene (such as devastation following an earthquake) or to depict people or objects.

In choosing visuals, you will inevitably be making important rhetorical choices. Tables, for example, express certain kinds of information more precisely than do figures, but if they are long and complex, readers will have difficulty processing the information. Figures, though less precise, can more easily be taken in at a glance. You should make your choices, then, based on your purpose and on the needs of your audience. In any case, remember that your visuals need to be numbered (*Table 1*) and given titles (*Word Choice by Race*) and perhaps captions or subtitles that provide a link to the text (Seesaw *and* Teeter-totter, *Chicago 1986*).

→ Use visuals as a part of your text, not as decoration.

→ Refer to the visual and explain its main point before the visual itself appears. For example: *As Table 1 demonstrates, the cost of a college education has risen dramatically in the last decade.*

→ Tell readers explicitly what the visual demonstrates, especially if it presents complex information. Do not assume readers will "read" the visual the way you do; your commentary on it is important.

→ Number and title all visuals. Number tables and figures separately.

→ Follow established guidelines for documenting visual sources, and ask permission for use, if necessary. (17f)

→ Use clip art sparingly, if at all. Computer clip art is so easy to cut and paste that you may be tempted to fancy up a text, but do so only if the art contributes to the points you are making.

→ Get responses to your visuals in an early draft. If readers can't follow them or are distracted by them, revise accordingly.

→ Do a test-run printout of all visuals just to make sure your printer is adequate for the job.

→ If you are working on a collaborative project, use every team member's talents in creating effective visuals. Two heads will almost certainly be better than one when it comes to this task.

■ *Sample visuals*

Following are examples of several kinds of visuals.

TABLE

Table 1
Word Choice by Race:
Seesaw and *Teeter-totter,* Chicago 1986

	Black	*White*	*Total*
Seesaw	47 (78%)	4 (15%)	51
Teeter-totter	13 (22%)	23 (85%)	36
Total	60	27	87

Michael I. Miller. "How to Study Black Speech in Chicago." *Language Variation in North American English.* Ed. A. Wayne Glowka and Donald M. Lance. New York: MLA, 1993. 166.

PIE CHART

Figure 1
Hispanic Population, by Type of Origin, 1996 (In percent)

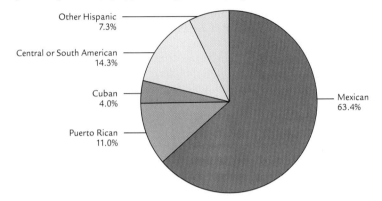

U.S. Census Bureau, Current Population Survey. "The Hispanic Population." *1997 Population Profile of the United States.* Ed. John M. Reed. Washington: U.S. Department of Commerce, September 1998.

LINE GRAPH

Figure 2
Median Household Income by Race and Hispanic Origin, 1967 to 2000
Income increased for Blacks and Hispanics; all groups matched or exceeded highest level recorded

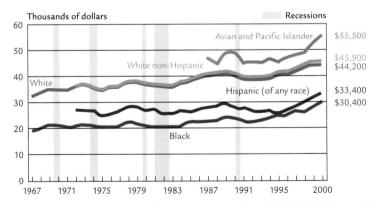

U.S. Census Bureau, Current Population Survey, March 1968–2001. Washington: U.S. Department of Commerce, January 2001.

BAR GRAPH

Figure 3
College Enrollment for Men and Women by Age, 1998 (In millions)

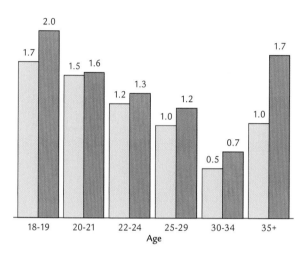

U.S. Census Bureau, Current Population Survey, October 1998. "Scholars of All Ages: School Enrollment, 1998." *Population Profile of the United States.* Washington: U.S. Department of Commerce, March 2001.

DIAGRAM

Figure 4
Spanish-English Bilingualism and the Language Shift Process

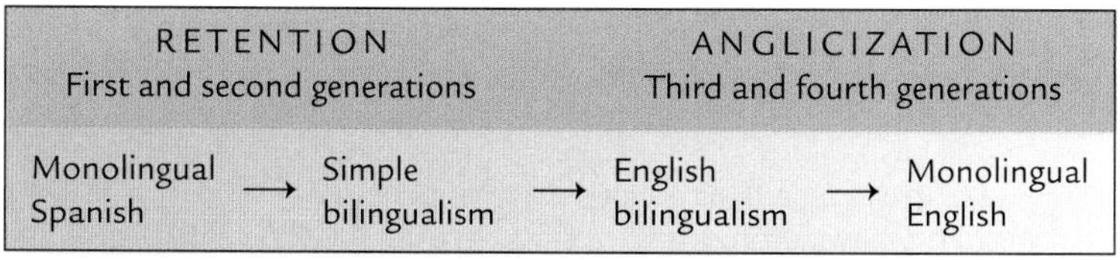

RETENTION	ANGLICIZATION
First and second generations	Third and fourth generations
Monolingual Spanish → Simple bilingualism	English bilingualism → Monolingual English

D. Letticia Galindo. "Bilingualism and Language Variation." *Language Variation in North American English.* Ed. A. Wayne Glowka and Donald M. Lance. New York: MLA, 1993. 202.

MAP

Figure 5
Distribution of the Hispanic Population by State, 1999

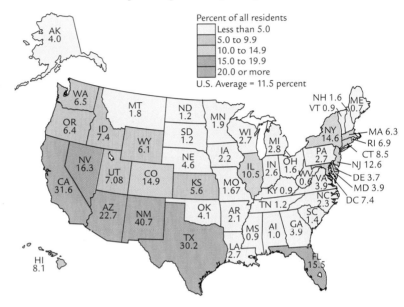

U.S. Census Bureau, Current Population Reports, Series P23–205. *Population Profile of the United States: 1999.* Washington: GPO, 2001. 9.

● **EXERCISE 8.1**

Take an essay or other writing assignment you have done recently, one that makes little use of visuals or the other design elements discussed in this chapter. Reevaluate the effectiveness of your text, and make a note of all the places where visuals and other design elements (color, different type size, and so on) would help you get your ideas across more effectively.

8e   Student documents

Interested in creating a flyer advertising your services as a tutor? Want to put together a newsletter for a campus group you belong to? Need to design a portfolio, including an eye-catching cover, for a course you are taking? Today, thanks to computer technology, such documents are easier to design and create than ever before. As a result, more and more college classes encourage (or require) you to respond to assignments in ways that go beyond the traditional essay or lab report. What follows is a catalog of documents collected from college students and others, along with some tips and annotations that should help you create similar documents for yourself.

CONSIDERING MEDIA
Student Documents

www • bedford stmartins.com/ smhandbook

For more sample documents, click on

▶ **Student Samples**

■ *Tips for formatting an academic essay using MLA style (see p. 184)*

- Use good quality 8½" × 11" white paper, and print on only one side.
- Double-space everything, including quotations.
- Choose a standard serif font such as Times New Roman, and use 11- or 12-point type.
- Put your name, instructor's name, and course and assignment title and the date at the top left margin of the first page.
- Center the title of your essay two lines below the course information. Do not put your title in quotation marks or underline it.
- Set margins of at least one inch on both sides and at the top and bottom.
- Number pages consecutively, beginning with page 1, and put each page number in the upper right-hand corner of the page; put your last name before the page number (*Cousins 1*).
- Use parenthetical references in your text, and add a works-cited list if you have used sources.

●— For more on working with headers, see 7b.

●— For extensive information about preparing citations and works-cited lists in MLA style, see Chapter 20 and the student essay that concludes it.

■ *Tips for preparing a report (see p. 185)*

- Since different disciplines may require different print report formats, check with your instructor for the most appropriate guidelines to follow.
- In general for print reports, center the title and make it as informative as possible (*Not Ready for Roundup: The Dangers of Genetically Engineered Soybeans* rather than *A Major Genetic Danger*).
- Center your name below the title, with the current date below your name.
- Single-space the report, leaving double spaces between paragraphs.
- Use headings and subheadings consistently to guide readers from point to point.
- Use color sparingly, to emphasize certain elements (headings, illustrations).
- Label all figures and tables clearly. (See pp. 179–182 for examples.)
- For some reports, you may choose to begin with an **abstract** or a **summary** that describes your major findings and recommendations.
- Although all original writing is automatically protected by copyright, many writers go to the extra trouble of adding the copyright symbol (©) and their name to their documents. You might choose to do the same at the end of your report.

●— For more on creating reports, see Chapters 65–66.

●— For more on copyrights, see 18d.

Considering
Document Design

Name, name of
instructor, title of
course and assign-
ment, and date are
all at the left margin,
double-spaced

Title centered

Paragraphs indent five
spaces

1"   Shabazz 1

Zakiyyah Shabazz

Professor Melissa Goldthwaite

English 398 Paper 3
                          Double spacing between
September 13, 2002   heading and title

Double spacing
between title and
first line of text

Putting "Me" Back into America

Two hundred years ago, writers like

William Wordsworth thought that language should

be useful, should be able to tell or teach

people something. More than a hundred years

later, along came Langston Hughes, who set out

to do just that. Many of his poems relate to

the loss of dreams--the things that give us

hopes and goals to reach--and to the unfair

treatment of the African American people. In

"Let America Be America Again" and "The Ballad

of the Landlord," Hughes discusses the unfair

conditions and treatment that "ethnic" people

have been subjected to in the United States.

He uses these poems to . . .

For an additional example of an academic essay and MLA format guidelines, see Chapter 20.

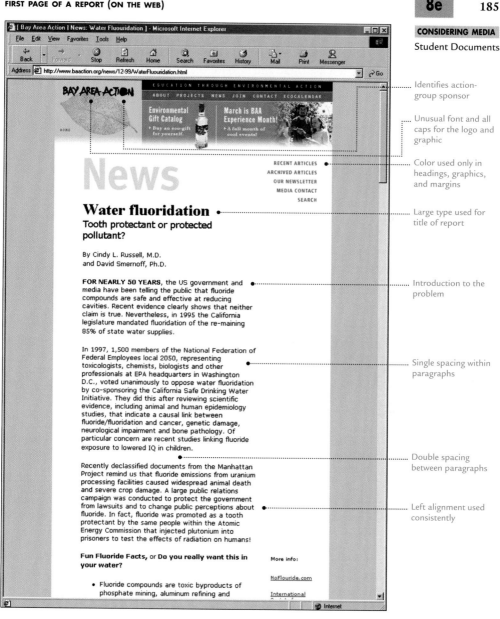

Identifies action-group sponsor

Unusual font and all caps for the logo and graphic

Color used only in headings, graphics, and margins

Large type used for title of report

Introduction to the problem

Single spacing within paragraphs

Double spacing between paragraphs

Left alignment used consistently

■ *Tips for designing a newsletter (see p. 187)*

- Plan your design carefully, deciding how many pages the newsletter will contain, what size paper you will use, and whether the paper will be folded (to produce a smaller newsletter that will be mailed, for example).

- Choose a masthead and logo for the first page to reflect the organization the newsletter represents, and plan for these items to be highlighted with the use of color or bold or large type. Include the date or other publication information as well.

- Remember that the margins must be big enough to allow for binding or stapling or folding.

- Design the layout of the newsletter: will you use columns and, if so, how many? Plot out where any boxed information or visuals will go.

- Plan each page for maximum readability—you don't want readers to have to jump back and forth from page to page to read a story.

- Use a consistent type size and typeface throughout the newsletter, varying it only for titles or major headings. (8b)

- Especially if you're using columns, keep paragraphs short and succinct.

- Get some responses to your design and layout before you have it printed up.

■ *Tips for designing a brochure (see p. 188)*

- Think carefully about who sponsors the brochure and who it is designed to reach. Make sure all design elements are appropriate for your sponsor's purpose and audience.

- Plan your brochure carefully. Many brochures are made by folding one piece of 8½" × 11" paper into thirds, which results in three panels on both the front and back. If the brochure will be mailed out, be sure to use one outside panel for the mailing and return addresses.

- Plan each panel or page of the brochure carefully, sketching out where the text and various illustrations will go. For most brochures, you will want each page or panel to be viewed as a single unit, with its own heading.

- Create a clear and informative title for the brochure, one that will tell readers at a glance what information is included.

- Choose visuals that clearly illustrate material in the brochure, and label them. (8d)

- Keep the design of the brochure simple so that a reader's eye will be drawn to the most important information on each panel or page.

- Be sure to identify the sponsoring organization and include contact information.

NEWS

WEST COAST
environmental law

Volume 26:01 June 12, 2000

FROM WEST COAST ENVIRONMENTAL LAW

Public interest environmental law for British Columbia

Safe to Drink?

The events in Walkerton, Ontario, provide an urgent wake-up call: BC has the highest per capita incidence of water-borne disease of any province in Canada, and the province is not adequately protecting drinking water sources from human related impacts.

The tragic events that have recently unfolded in Walkerton, Ontario, should provide a wake-up call to governments across the country because the agenda of downsizing environment ministries, privatizing government inspection and monitoring services, and abandoning environmental regulation is not unique to the Harris government. We have known for some time that there are very real human costs associated with failing to protect the air we breathe and the water we drink — the horrendous impacts of the E. coli contamination of drinking water in Walkerton remind us of how immediate those consequences can be.

BC's drinking water is at risk
There is certainly no reason for BC residents to be complacent when it comes to water quality. In fact this province has an ignominious record when it comes to safe drinking water. Here are the troubling statistics:
• BC has the highest per capita incidence of water-borne disease of any province in Canada. A 1998 government study reported that there had been 27 outbreaks of toxoplasmosis, cryptosporidium, giardia, and other diseases in the past eighteen years.
• The GVRD's water supply frequently exceeds the minimum federal guidelines for water turbidity. It is the only unfiltered Canadian water

supply which often exceeds the standards on which Canada's safe drinking water guidelines are based.
• Contamination is a serious problem for some provincial groundwater sources. For example, drinking water guidelines for nitrate-nitrogen are not being met in certain aquifers because of contamination from manure and fertilizers.
• The government's first Water Quality Status Report of April 1996 found that of 124 water-bodies surveyed, only 60% had source waters which fell into the "good to excellent" category for drinking water purposes. Even for the 60% in that category, disinfection was still required.
• Over 200 BC communities are on permanent "boil water" advisories, i.e. they cannot safely drink the water from their tap without boiling it first.

Audit brings bad news
A disturbing indictment of the province's efforts to ensure safe drinking water for BC residents was recently offered by the Auditor General (Protecting Drinking Water Sources 1998/99). According to the Auditor: "...the province is not adequately protecting drinking water sources from human

related impacts, and this could have significant cost implications in the future for the province, for municipal governments and for citizens in general."
    The Auditor pointed the finger at the lack of a coherent and integrated approach to land use management. The role of the Ministry of Forests in watershed and agricultural land management is particularly problematic because it bears so little responsibility for the impact or costs associated with poor management decisions. Unfortunately, the Auditor's mandate didn't extend to examining the adequacy of the province's legislative framework for protecting water. Had it, he would have no doubt noted the inadequate patchwork of water quality regulation in BC.
    For instance, BC is the only Canadian province with no groundwater protection legislation. While safe drinking water regulations have been established under the *Health Act*, only one of hundreds of water quality guidelines is actually given the force of regulatory protection. Even where regulatory controls exist, inadequate monitoring and different enforcement policies often render them ineffective.

see *Safe to Drink?*, continued on page 2

2 Emissions Trading: the
   great leap forward?
3 Is Canada Sinking Kyoto?

4 Blowing Cold over Hot Air
5 Chinese brochures
5 Fish habitat workshops

6 Environmental Dispute
   Resolution Fund in Action
7 In Good Company

Considering
Document Design

Cover

Interior Page

Informative title in ....
large, eye-catching
type

Ample space around ....
title and illustration

Appropriate ....
illustration in
central spot

Eating
Vegetarian

Definition used to
organize information

A Vegetarian

IS A PERSON WHO EATS •............
mainly plant foods such as grains,
beans, nuts, fruits and vegetables.

There are several ways of eating vegetarian.

- **Semi-vegetarians** exclude some but not all
  foods of animal origin.* They may not eat
  beef, for example, but will sometimes eat
  poultry or seafood.
- **Lacto-ovovegetarians** include milk or milk
  products and eggs in their diets, but omit
  meat, fish and poultry.
- **Lactovegetarians** include milk products, but
  don't eat eggs, meat, poultry or seafood.
- **Vegans** don't eat any animal products.

*Foods of animal origin = meat, fish, poultry, eggs, milk,
milk products, honey, bouillon

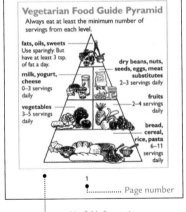

Vegetarian Food Guide Pyramid
Always eat at least the minimum number of
servings from each level.

fats, oils, sweets
Use sparingly. But
have at least 3 tsp.
of fat a day.

**milk, yogurt,
cheese**
0–3 servings
daily

vegetables
3–5 servings
daily

**dry beans, nuts,
seeds, eggs, meat
substitutes**
2–3 servings daily

fruits
2–4 servings
daily

**bread,
cereal,
rice, pasta**
6–11
servings
daily

1

.... Page number

Further explanation
presented in bulleted
list

.... Useful information
presented in a clear
illustration

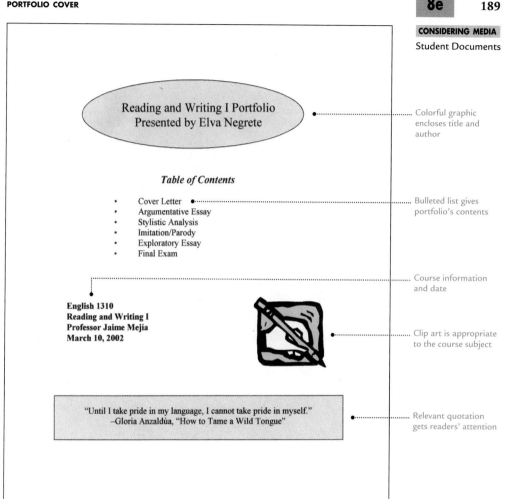

Reading and Writing I Portfolio
Presented by Elva Negrete

.... Colorful graphic
encloses title and
author

Table of Contents

- Cover Letter
- Argumentative Essay
- Stylistic Analysis
- Imitation/Parody
- Exploratory Essay
- Final Exam

.... Bulleted list gives
portfolio's contents

.... Course information
and date

English 1310
Reading and Writing I
Professor Jaime Mejía
March 10, 2002

.... Clip art is appropriate
to the course subject

"Until I take pride in my language, I cannot take pride in myself."
–Gloria Anzaldúa, "How to Tame a Wild Tongue"

.... Relevant quotation
gets readers' attention

For more information on assembling a portfolio, see Chapter 69.

Considering
Document Design

Use of white back-
ground with clearly
contrasting colors
gets attention

Central image draws
attention and makes a
playful allusion to a
popular film, *The
Usual Suspects*

Typefaces and sizes
used consistently to
differentiate sections
of the flyer

Related information
grouped together
makes for easy
reading

Web site address fea-
tured prominently for
further information

five tutors. two dorms. no coincidence

6'6"
6'0"
5'6"
5'0"
4'6"
4'
3'

The Usual Subjects

Katy Barglow	Sheba Najmi	Tania Lombrozo	Manish Patel	Leo Alekseyev
Good with chemicals and biological agents.	Armed with potentially destructive writing skills.	Always right on when it comes to documents and verbal combat.	Implicated in devious econ calculations.	Easily provoked to be physical and mathematical.
Can be found in:	*Can be found in:*	*Can be found in:*	*Can be found in:*	*Can be found in:*
Castano 218 *Mon, Thu* 9 – 11 PM	Lantana 205 *Tue, Thu* 9 – 10:30 PM	Castano 319 *Tue* 8 – 10 PM *Thu* 9 – 10 PM	Castano 205 *Sun* 9 – 11 PM	Lantana 303 *Mon* 7:30 – 9:30 PM

Visit us during our office hours, or make an appointment.
For complete tutoring schedule or more info, see

uac-tutoring.stanford.edu/tutor

■ *Tips for designing a flyer (see p. 190)*

- Create clear contrast between the background, the text, and the visuals. A light background such as cream or pale beige contrasts well, for example, with deep blue or green.

- Build in consistency by keeping major topics the same type size and color; do the same for subsets of information.

- Group related information appropriately. For example, put all contact information together in one place; put an explanatory subtitle right below the main title.

- Use typefaces and sizes consistently within the flyer: a sans serif typeface for blocks of text, for example, and all capitals to emphasize selected features. (8b)

- Make sure that graphics and color contribute to the flyer's message and are not used just for decoration. (8a and d)

- If possible, use white space to balance elements on the flyer and to provide some restful spaces for readers. (8a)

FOR COLLABORATION

Together with two other class members, gather up at least five documents you have received in other classes, through groups you belong to, or through the mail. (These might be reports, newsletters, brochures, flyers, or other kinds of documents.) Then choose two of the documents to analyze according to the advice presented in this chapter. Decide which features make the documents successful or unsuccessful in their delivery of information, and consider how each document's design makes a mediocre point of information stronger or more compelling — or does just the opposite. Bring reports of your analysis to class for discussion.

THINKING CRITICALLY ABOUT THE DESIGN OF YOUR DOCUMENT

Take a look at a piece of writing or a document you have recently finished writing. (If you have created a flyer or one of the other documents shown in this chapter, choose that one.) Using the advice in this chapter, assess your use of visual structure and page design, consistent use of conventions for guiding readers through your document, and the use of headings, color, font size, and visuals for emphasis. Then write a paragraph reflecting on how well your piece of writing or document is designed and how you could improve it.

9 Creating Web Texts

As more and more people go to school, work, play, and shop online, the uses of the World Wide Web are expanding dramatically. In school, you read, analyze, and in many cases create Web pages for your classes. Even if you simply save an essay you've written into HTML using your word processor's SAVE AS function and post that essay to a class Web site for others to read and respond to, you've created a Web text. And if you include any links in your essay, you've made a basic hypertext. In addition to the Web texts created for classwork, you may be among the millions of people who develop Web texts on their jobs or for clubs or other social organizations they belong to.

Because the Web has grown up so quickly, many people have created documents for the Web without thinking very critically about how such documents should be designed and produced. This chapter aims to help you think carefully about how to design and produce effective Web pages. ■

9a Features of Web texts

Writers and readers are quickly growing accustomed to the new opportunities and demands afforded by **Web sites,** a series of electronic "pages" that start with a **homepage.** Unlike print texts — where ideas, paragraphs, visuals, and pages proceed in a linear, sequential way from beginning to end — the **hypertext** that makes up a Web site allows the writer to organize those same elements in a variety of ways by the use of **links,** which can take readers to other parts of the site or to other sites. Whereas a book or essay is arranged as a series of numbered pages, a hypertext can organize information as a cluster of associations.

The underlying assumption most print texts make is that readers will read from start to finish and that the writer will present a coherent argument that unfolds sequentially. But suppose Emily Lesk had decided to write her essay (pp. 106–111) as a hypertext. To begin, she could have designed a homepage represented by the center issue circled on p. 193 and from that page created four major links, each of which would take readers to a set of pages discussing a part of the major issue she was exploring. She might also have chosen to use color coding, perhaps on the menu bar of each page, to let readers know when they've left one section of the Web text and moved to another.

In addition to her text, Emily could have included all the images she used, as long as none had been copyrighted by others (in which case, she would have requested permission; see Chapter 17). She might also have created links to audio clips she taped during her interviews, copies of

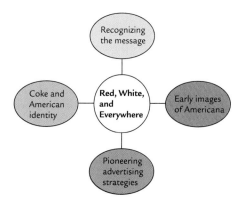

email messages from and to her parents or friends — if they were germane to her essay — and links to a variety of other Web sources on her subject.

**www • bedford
stmartins.com/
smhandbook**

To view a version of
Emily Lesk's essay
as she might have
written it for the
Web, click on

▶ **Working Online**
  ▶ **Web Texts**

9b   Planning Web texts

As with any document, such as a print essay you might post to a class Web site (see 6c and 9i), a Web text must be planned with careful attention to your purpose, audience, topic, and rhetorical stance. In addition, keep a sharp eye on deadlines, and take into consideration your own technical expertise as well as the amount of space available at the site you will post the text to. Let's look at some of these factors, which will help you plan the shape and scope of your Web text.

• For more infor-
  mation on these
  elements, see
  Chapter 2.

Thinking about the purpose of your text should help you determine its overall format and length and the links you need to create. If your purpose is to explain, for example, the methods current cartoonists use to make fun of politicians, you might want to provide links to caricatures of ten contemporary politicians to enhance that explanation.

Closely related to purpose, of course, is the audience for your Web text, which should be identified as clearly as possible. If your intended audience is your instructor, classmates, or others you know, you can make certain assumptions about their background knowledge and likely responses to your text. If your audience is broader than that, however, you may need to provide more explicit information. Remember that once your Web text is posted, it has been "published" and may reach readers you could not predict.

Also consider how clearly and concisely you can state the topic of your Web document. A topic that is vague or overly broad — such as "International Terrorism" — would require far too much text and too many links to make it useful to others. Narrow your topic, and clarify your stance on it until you have something with a more practical scope: "A Proposal to Resist Terrorism: What College Students Can Do."

As you think about your rhetorical stance, consider whether you will present yourself as an expert, as a colleague, or as a novice seeking information and input from others. What information will you need to provide about yourself to seem credible and persuasive to your audience?

Be sure to deal with time-management issues as well. How much technical expertise do you have, and how much will you need to learn in order to create the Web document? It's important to allow enough time for that learning to take place. Also consider how much research you will have to do and how long you will need to scan or resize images and insert them into your Web document. Finally, consider how much time you will need to seek permission to use any images or other texts in your document (see Chapter 17). Then make up a timeline for your Web-document project.

Once you've considered the general factors of purpose, audience, topic, rhetorical stance, and time management, you can look to the specifics of planning a Web text. The following tips should be helpful:

- Think about the overall impression you intend to create. Do you want your design to be bold, soothing, serious — or something else? Articulating this impression clearly can guide your decisions about how much text to include, what kinds of navigation aids to use, and what images, colors, video and sound clips, and so on will help you create that effect.

- Visit some Web sites that you admire or that create effects similar to those you have in mind. Look for effective design ideas and ways of organizing navigation and information (note placement of graphics, how links are named, how color is used, and so on).

- Map your Web document. To do so, draw the array and types of pages you have in mind, and be ready to move the elements around in order to improve the organization. As you work on a map, start planning the underlying page design so that you can create a template for consistent layout of pages or sections. (See 9c.)

- Plan your use of visuals very carefully, making sure that each relates directly to the topic you are addressing in your Web text (see 8d). Make sure your graphics are saved in browser-supported formats such as GIF or JPEG. Check the file size and resolution of photographs and other illustrations to make sure they can be downloaded quickly. (See 9f.)

- Give considerable thought to the use of color, remembering that colors carry strong emotive appeal: reds are attention getters; greens often evoke images of nature or life; blues can seem comforting; yellows evoke sunshine but can be hard to read; grays seem dignified and serious. (See 8a.)

- Try to decide on the menus you will use and how detailed they will need to be.

PROCESS FOR CREATING A WEB TEXT

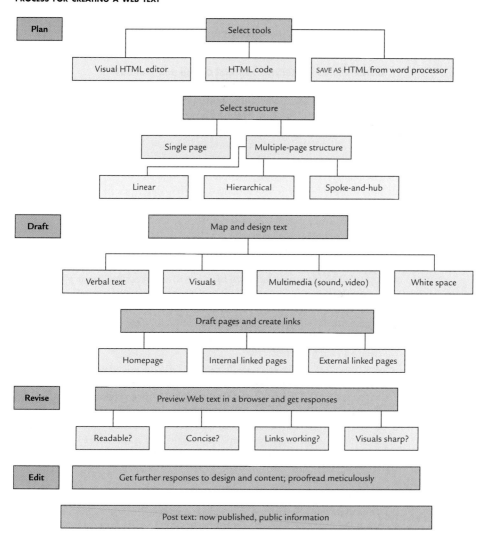

Plan

Select tools
- Visual HTML editor
- HTML code
- SAVE AS HTML from word processor

Select structure
- Single page
- Multiple-page structure
  - Linear
  - Hierarchical
  - Spoke-and-hub

Draft

Map and design text
- Verbal text
- Visuals
- Multimedia (sound, video)
- White space

Draft pages and create links
- Homepage
- Internal linked pages
- External linked pages

Revise

Preview Web text in a browser and get responses
- Readable?
- Concise?
- Links working?
- Visuals sharp?

Edit

Get further responses to design and content; proofread meticulously

Post text: now published, public information

• Consider the technical limitations the readers of your Web document might face. Remember that at home most people still use dial-up modems to access the Web, while at work and school they probably have access to a faster connection. So if you design your Web document on campus or at work, remember to double-check it from a dial-up modem to see how it loads and looks. Then check it in different browsers, remembering that Netscape and Internet Explorer handle coding differently.

• Since Web texts are dynamic rather than static — they are capable of being changed at any point — plan to reassess and maintain your Web text on an ongoing basis.

CONSIDERING DISABILITIES: Special Coding and Features

The Internet offers powerful potential for those with disabilities: access to worlds of information right at home as well as access to computer hardware and software programs that can enhance a computer's usefulness. Nevertheless, much on the Web remains hard to access and read. When planning a Web text, keep these priorities in mind:

→ For readers whose vision is impaired or who are blind, provide a text-only version of your document or verbal descriptions of all visuals. Many visually impaired readers use software that reads onscreen text aloud. You can insert text that will appear as a label that pops up when a reader's mouse goes over the graphic. You can also signal a change in menu buttons by separating them with a vertical line. In addition, do not rely solely on color to carry the meaning of your message: add words as well. And if you use tables to make columns onscreen, be sure to mark them clearly with a textual label rather than an icon or other image. Keep in mind that most screen reader programs only read left to right; such reading will sometimes render tables and charts meaningless.

→ For readers who may be color-blind, make sure to choose colors that create a sharp contrast. (8a)

→ For readers whose hearing is impaired or who are deaf, remember to provide captions for any sound on your Web site. Do not rely on sound (even with captions) to carry the central or singular meaning of your text.

→ For many readers with some physical impairment, using a mouse may be problematic. If you are using forms or other interactive elements, make sure it's possible to move from field to field in the form by using the TAB and ENTER keys so that users won't have to rely on the mouse.

● **EXERCISE 9.1**

The following homepage for the textbook *Everything's an Argument* can be found on the publisher's site <www.bedfordstmartins.com/everythingsanargument>. Using

the preceding advice in this chapter, assess the effectiveness of this page, and prepare a brief critique of it, including tips for improvement.

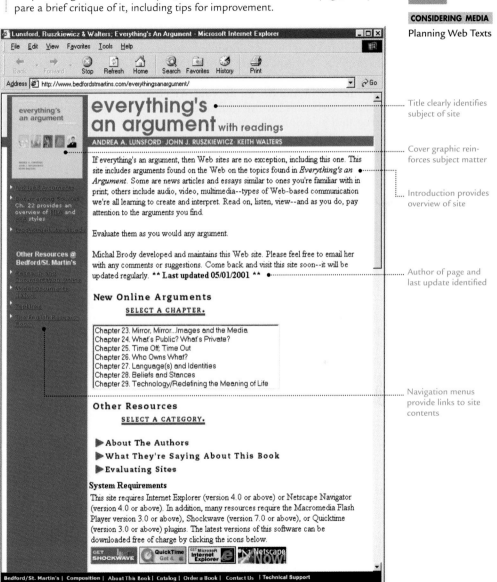

Title clearly identifies subject of site

Cover graphic reinforces subject matter

Introduction provides overview of site

Author of page and last update identified

Navigation menus provide links to site contents

9c Mapping Web texts

Just as you might outline an essay, you should develop a clear structure for your Web texts. You can create a map in several ways: by handwriting and drawing; by using a computer drawing program; by creating a mock-up on 5" × 7" cards arranged on a bulletin board; or by sketching on a large white board with colored dry-erase markers. In any case, your map provides the overall design for your Web text.

Most Web sites involve multiple pages organized according to some structural principle. The most basic organization for a Web site is linear or sequential. In this simple organization, pages are ordered in a straight sequence that leads the reader through the Web site, one page to the next. Since there is only one path, this organization is appropriate for sites where information progresses from the general to the specific.

LINEAR ORGANIZATION

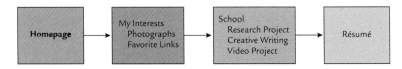

Large Web sites often use a hierarchical structure, which begins with very general information and then takes readers to information that is more and more specific.

HIERARCHICAL ORGANIZATION

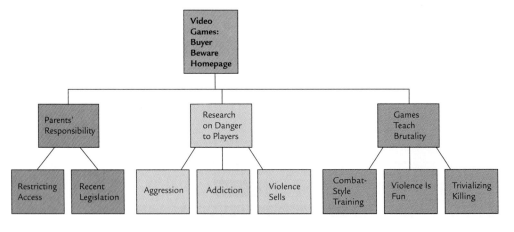

Another common structural pattern looks like a hub with spokes. Rather than guiding readers to more and more specific information, this structure doesn't encourage readers to read in any particular order. The spoke-and-hub organization works well when all the topics of your Web text are of roughly equal weight or importance, and when all the information readers need for understanding the topics can be provided on the homepage. For example, a page for each of your club's activities might follow a hublike structure.

SPOKE-AND-HUB ORGANIZATION

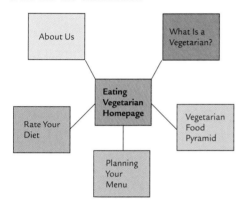

Following are some tips to help you map your Web text:

- Take an inventory of the content material you have, and make a list of what you still need to find or create.

- Sketch the basic text and visuals for each page of your document, beginning with the homepage (see 9d). To do so, use the drawing functions in your word processor, or use index cards or pieces of paper for each page. A simple sketch of one Web homepage is shown on the following page.

- Think of your Web text as a collection of pages that will be mapped and linked in a way that matches your purpose, audience, topic, and rhetorical stance. The home or first page is where your readers will begin, and how that page looks and is organized should depend on the scope of your purpose. If your topic is fairly limited, for example, the homepage will reflect those limitations. In addition, the length of pages, the use and placement of visuals, color, interactive elements (such as forms or search boxes), animation, video, and audio all depend on the type of information you are presenting. If you haven't already done so, study Web sites you admire that seem to have purposes and audiences similar to yours.

Site Title ◄ ►

Page Title

Home

link
link
link

Heading

- ---
- ---
- ---

↑ to top of page

Sam Cohen
Last updated January 1, 2003   email@stanford.edu

- If you are mapping your Web document by hand, arrange the pages on a bulletin board, a large desk, or on the floor, and indicate the links among the pages.

- Check to see if your mapping plan seems sound. Do your pages carry out your purpose thoroughly and effectively? Are they clearly related to one another, and will they be appealing and understandable to your audience?

- Make sure all sections of the Web text link to the homepage.

9d   Designing Web texts

The World Wide Web and hypertext work because of an underlying set of codes called **Hypertext Markup Language** (**HTML**) (see 9h). Essentially, HTML codes tell a Web browser how to interpret the various elements on a page. For example, the use of the codes <B> </B> before and after a letter, word, or phrase (or an entire page) tells the browser to present all that material in **boldface**. Other codes create links to other pages, load images, or call up files or ancillary programs (called *plug-ins*) that work with your browser. These plug-ins create even more options, allowing you, for example, to read documents in Adobe's Portable Document Format (PDF), listen to an audio file with RealTime Player, or view an animation as a QuickTime Movie.

Other programs will help you write and manage the content of your Web document. Current versions of WordPerfect, Microsoft Word, and PowerPoint all allow you to SAVE AS HTML (click on FILE and then SAVE AS). Or you can use simple text editor software (such as NotePad or SimpleText) to write a Web page and enter all the HTML codes manually. You can also use an HTML editor (such as Microsoft FrontPage, Netscape Composer, or Dreamweaver) that lets you see the page and content as it is created. Keep in mind that every commercial program has a less expensive shareware version (such as HomeSite), sometimes even a freeware program, that can be just as useful as the commercial version.

No matter what kind of Web document you are creating, remember to follow these basic principles of good design (see 8a):

- *clear contrast* that differentiates parts of the page and text/visuals from the background
- *proximity* that groups together related items
- *repetition* that creates consistency and guides readers
- *alignment* that arranges elements according to left alignment, right alignment, or centered alignment

www • bedford stmartins.com/ smhandbook

For more resources for designing Web texts, click on

▶ **Working Online**
  ▶ **Web Texts**

●···· For more information on these basic principles, see the guidelines in 8a.

Also remember the importance of the first page or homepage of any Web site: it introduces the topic and sets out the various paths readers can use to explore it. Although the conventions for designing homepages are still evolving, it's pretty clear what *doesn't* work well. The Yale Center for Advanced Instructional Media, for example, uses the term *clown's pants pages* to refer to the kind of haphazard use of color, clip art, and fonts characteristic of many Web texts. Following are some tips on the elements of basic page design that can help you avoid haphazard results:

- Think of each page as containing two main areas: navigation areas (such as menus or links to offsite pages elsewhere on the Web) and content areas (where the words, images, and other elements combine to convey your ideas and information). Your goal is to make these two areas readily distinguishable from each other. In addition, make sure readers can find your content easily and are not overwhelmed by menus or other navigational elements. All of the most important navigation and content information should be viewable from the very first page.

- Use an existing design template, or create one of your own. A template can serve as a model for all the pages of your Web document, helping give consistency to your pages and making them easier to read. Basically, a template sets the background color, heading information, navigation buttons, and contact information — all the elements you want to appear on every page. You can find such templates in some Web writing tools and on Web design sites. Or, you may imitate the design of an existing Web page you find particularly effective. For example, a newspaper's site will have a column, usually aligned left, in which all the sections of the paper are listed. You might use that same navigation concept in your own template. Once this template is saved in your directory or folder, you can resave it by clicking on SAVE AS to create new pages.

- At the top of the homepage, put a *title* (and subtitle, if necessary) along with an eye-catching and easy-to-process *visual* or *statement* that makes clear to readers what the Web text is about. Below this, include an *overview* of what is in the document.

- At the bottom of the homepage, include a logo, if appropriate, along with contact information (such as your email address) and the date you created the page or document. (You can later add the dates on which you revise or update it.)

- Create a navigation area or menu for every main page, listing links to the key sections of the site. For content pages within a major section, you may want to alter your menu so that it leads only to other content within that section. In any case, experiment with navigation. Remember that *every* page within a particular section should offer a link back to that section's main page and to the homepage. Including such links will enable readers who find a page not at the start of your Web site, but by way of an Internet search engine, to get back to the beginning. If a page is long, you may also wish to add a button that users can click on to "return to top of page."

- Use visuals that can be downloaded quickly and easily by your readers. (See 9f.)

- Check out the specific design advice in Chapter 8, such as using easy-to-read fonts; incorporating bullets, numbered lists, and headings; and using color and white space effectively.

- Remember that readers of English are used to reading from left to right and from top to bottom. If you are working in English or another Western language, place your most important text or images at the top left of a page — or at the lower right.

- Maintain consistency among your pages by using the same title or navigation menus on each page.

- Ask some readers to respond to a rough draft of your pages, especially the homepage. How understandable or readable are these pages? How easy are they to navigate? How effective is the use of color, fonts, visuals, sound, and so on?

CONSIDERING DISABILITIES: Vertical Lines to Signal Changes

Remember that some of your readers may not be able to go from one link to another if the links are marked by graphic icons that can't be read by **textreader** software. For this reason, it is better to use a vertical line to signal these changes. In the homepage from the Stanford Writing Center on p. 204, for example, the vertical lines before and after the word *Home* will be read by a textreader, so a reader with impaired vision will find it easier to click on the word between the lines.

Following is the homepage for the Writing Center at Stanford University. Note that its design is simple, that its menu items are listed below the main heading, and that vertical lines separate one menu item from another. This last design feature is intended to aid students with disabilities, such as those who are visually impaired.

CONSIDERING MEDIA

Creating Web Texts

Title and visual make clear what the site is about

Navigation menu at top of page lists links to key sections of the site

Vertical lines clearly separate menu items

Contact information provided at bottom of page

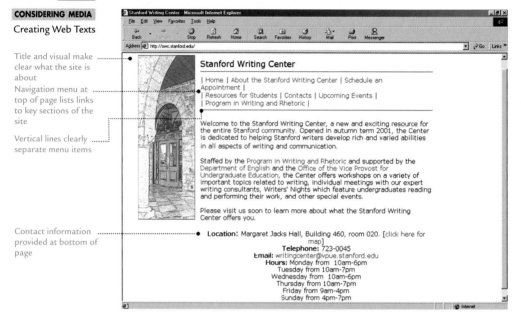

● **EXERCISE 9.2**

You can practice learning to read Web texts critically by comparing several sites.

1. To begin, go to <geocities.com/conalvo/hangook.html> or to <english.ttu .edu/Courses/5360/papers/Richter1.html> to see two sites that are fairly unregulated and unedited. What on these sites indicates credibility? Who is responsible for each site, and how can you tell?

2. Next, compare the preceding sites to <www.loc.gov> (Library of Congress) or to <www.cnn.com>. Knowing who is responsible for a Web site tells you a lot about whether you can trust it. What kinds of connections do you see between the sponsoring organization and the Web site?

3. Finally, working alone or with another member of your class, go online and prepare a comparison of the following sites: <www.ushmm.org> and <www.interlog.com/~mighty/>. Analyze each for trust, credibility, and authority, and bring the results of your analysis to class for discussion.

The success of any Web text is tied to the effectiveness of the links within it, both those to other pages in the same site (internal links) and those to other sites (external links). Think of such links as the elements that add depth and texture to the hypertext: the opening page(s) provide an overview and announce the general purpose of the document, but the links bring this aim to life, providing a level of detail not possible in the homepage, for example. Links are the place for complex explanations, lists of supporting statistics, bibliographies, additional readings, or relevant URLs.

Like all elements of a Web document, links should have clear rhetorical purposes and be in an appropriate location. If, for example, you put a link in the middle of a paragraph on a page, be aware that readers may stop reading where they are and go to another linked page before finishing what's before them — and remember that they may never come back! On the other hand, a link might call up a small pop-up window that provides more information, as a footnote does in an essay or a sidebar does in a magazine article.

Especially as you begin working with Web documents, be conservative in the number of links you plan. Although it can be tempting to add numerous links to a page, too many links can overwhelm both you and readers. And remember that you can put links either in the content portion of a page (that is, embedded in text, visual, or caption) or in the navigation area of a page. Some menus help you navigate long pieces of content information within a page, whereas others help you navigate to other pages.

Make sure that links to visuals or sound and video clips are closely related to your purpose. Readers have quickly tired of clichéd clip art, for example. And if you wish to use images created by others, remember that you may need to ask for permission to download and use these images in your own document. In the long run, it may be best to make your own visuals. (See 9f.)

To signal a link, you may use <u>underlining,</u> color, **boldface,** icons (Δ), or labeling (*for additional readings on taboos, click here*). Regardless of the signal you use, make sure readers will understand the purpose of the link and who created it (if it's an external link). Indeed, you may create much of the text for links, just as you would create the text in footnotes to add information or explain a concept.

CONSIDERING MEDIA
Adding Links

www • bedford stmartins.com/ smhandbook

To see examples of sites using navigation menus and links, click on

▶ **Working Online**
  ▶ **Web Texts**

●⋯ For more on respecting intellectual property, see Chapter 18.

Finally, remember to add clear internal links so readers can return to the homepage, for example, or to a previous page. These internal links may take the form of navigation buttons, pictures, icons such as arrows, or other symbols designed to help readers move quickly through your Web document. Such symbols should be placed at the top, bottom, or side of a page. Remember to add text to the symbol if its meaning will not be instantly clear or if some readers may be unable to see it: an arrow alone, for instance, may not tell readers that clicking it will take them to the next page. In this case, you could label the arrow button *Next*.

9f   Using visuals and multimedia

The Web offers a dizzying array of ways to present your ideas through the use of visuals (borders, icons, graphs and charts, maps, photographs, and illustrations of all kinds) and multimedia, including sound and video files. But the number of possibilities can prove daunting, especially to beginning Web-document designers. The following tips will help you think carefully about how to incorporate visuals and multimedia into your Web document:

- Remember that, except in special circumstances (such as comics or photo essays), visuals add to but do not substitute for text, so integrate the two very carefully, and never use visuals for mere decoration.

- Don't expect readers to instantly see the connection between a visual and text: you need to make the relationship clear in the text or through labels and captions.

- Tables can be created in your word-processing program and then saved as HTML.

- Photographs or other printed graphics can be scanned and saved as files to be inserted into your Web text. A scanner should be available to you in a campus computer lab. If a picture file will not fit into your document, you can use a program such as Adobe Photoshop to change its size and quality.

- To be considerate of readers who may have slower connections and will lack time necessary to download your documents, use graphic formats that are common and work in a variety of browsers and browser plug-ins. Most browsers can view JPEG or GIF images, the most common image file formats. However, remember that the file space an image takes up may make it slow or difficult to download; limit individual images to 30 to 40 kilobytes to be safe, or use a smaller thumbnail image and link users to the original, larger file.

- If you have not taken a photograph or created a graphic yourself, you will need to see if it is copyrighted and, if so, to ask permission to scan or download and use it.

- Free icons, clip art, and other visuals are widely available from sites such as the Clip Art Connection, or you can check most search engines for other free image archives. Also, be aware that clip art can be tiresome; use it only if it contributes something to your text.

- As an alternative to using graphics created by others, if you have access to a scanner, you can create interesting images simply by placing objects on the scanner — a ring, a leaf, a lock of hair, and so on. Experiment with scanning objects, taking pictures with a digital camera and clarifying visuals with photo-editing software. If your computer is linked to a scanner or set up to receive digital photos, the software accompanying the scanner or camera will probably let you manipulate the images you create.

- To download and save an image from the Web when using Windows, position your cursor over the image, right click with your mouse, and select SAVE IMAGE AS. To download an image when using a Mac, hold down the mouse until a menu appears, and select SAVE THIS IMAGE AS.

- Use lines, boxes, and icons carefully and consistently so that they emphasize information rather than detract from it.

- Remember that visuals and audio often will not be accessible to those with disabilities and to those with Web browsers that can't display them. As a result, ask a number of people to try to access your Web site so that you can determine how easy — or difficult — it is to download and read it.

- Remember that most work on the Web is protected by copyright — unless there is an explicit statement that the information is in the public domain and thus available for free use. As a result, you usually need to ask for permission to use a visual, sound clip, and so on. Note that often government documents are in the public domain and are available for free use.

**www • bedford
stmartins.com/
smhandbook**

For advice on using
visuals, audio, and
video, click on

▶ **Working Online**
  ▶ **Web Texts**

• For information
  on how to re-
  quest such per-
  mission, see 17f.

CONSIDERING MEDIA

Creating Web Texts

One good way to prepare for creating your own Web text is, of course, to browse the Web, noting the elements of sites you find particularly effective. Take a look at the first two pages from a Web project created for their first-year writing class by Nkechi Chukwueke, Kelli Copeland, Kyle Duarte, and Andrew Mo.

HOMEPAGE FOR A CLASS PROJECT

Graphic at top of page clearly announces title of site and the course for which it was created

Navigation menus at top and bottom provide multiple links to key sections of site

Introduction provides brief overview of site

Eye-catching graphics reinforce subject matter

Notes alert readers to system requirements and linked footnotes

Icon clearly labeled "Next"

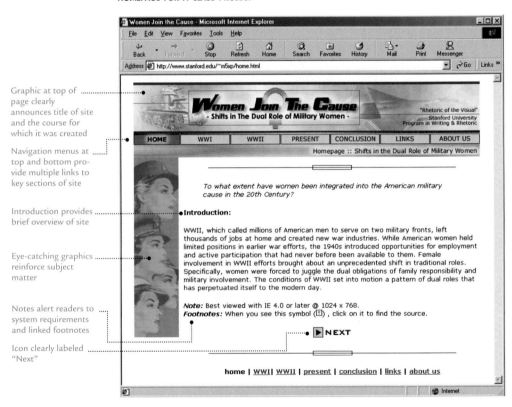

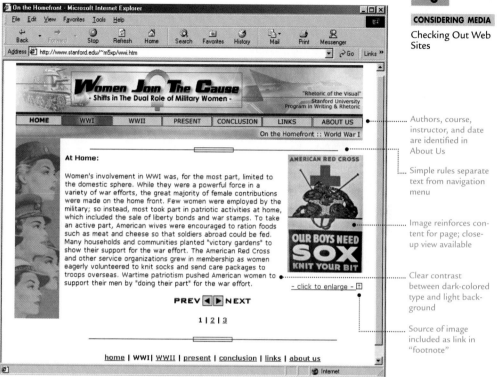

Authors, course, instructor, and date are identified in About Us

Simple rules separate text from navigation menu

Image reinforces content for page; close-up view available

Clear contrast between dark-colored type and light background

Source of image included as link in "footnote"

Here are two pages from a Stanford University site devoted to describing undergraduate life. The pages — including the student journal entry by Dennis Tyler — include helpful headings and navigational menus. The page's photographs include helpful captions and nicely illustrate the journal.

Names and photos—
grouped together—
both link to online
journals of five
students

Introductory para-
graph kept brief

Pleasing balance
between text, images,
and white space

Navigation menu lists
other key sections of
the site as well as
related pages

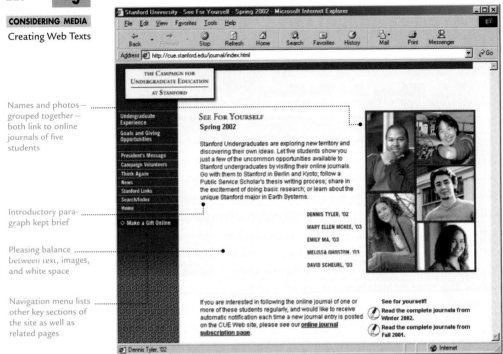

FOR COLLABORATION

Working with a classmate, carry out an analysis of one of the two sets of pages shown on pp. 208–211, using the principles outlined in 9d. Take notes as you analyze the effectiveness of these pages, and prepare a brief report of your findings for your class. Be sure to include tips for how the pages could be improved.

CONSIDERING MEDIA
Writing Web Texts

Continuity with home-page maintained by repetition of title and logo

Page heading clearly identifies the journal entry

Navigation menu at top of page collects links to related pages; vertical bars clearly separate entries

Descriptive photo captions connect images to journal content

Narrow column width makes text easy to read

9h   Writing Web texts

After you plan, map, and design your Web text, you have other important decisions to make. You'll need to have access to the necessary software — a basic text-editing program such as NotePad or SimpleText — as
well as word-processing software. Many writers new to the Web like to
begin by writing a Web document in a word-processing program such as
WordPerfect or Microsoft Word and then saving the material in HTML.
Many writers choose to use an HTML editor, rather than deal with the
code directly. Your computer may have an HTML editor — such as
Netscape's Composer — already installed. Many Windows users will find
FrontPage installed on their PCs, and Mac users may well have PageMill;
both are HTML editors.

www • bedford
stmartins.com/
smhandbook

For more on HTML
editors, click on

▶ Working Online
  ▶ Web Texts

■ *Using HTML codes*

HTML codes (known as *tags*) act like traffic signals, turning on a feature of a text and then turning it off again. One set of codes (usually called document tags) governs the larger aspects of the text (such as the title, body elements, background color, and so on), while another set (usually called appearance tags) governs smaller aspects (italics, boldface, underlining, and so on). Following are the basic tags for an HTML document. Note that tags beginning with a slash mark, like </BODY>, indicate the *end* of a particular element.

<HTML>
<HEAD>
<TITLE>title of your site goes here</TITLE>
</HEAD>
<BODY>
Your text and images go here
</BODY>
</HTML>

The <HEAD> field contains information about your document that Web search tools can use to locate it. Other tags help you create and organize the body of the document.

SECTION HEADING TAGS

Use these tags to create headings and to indicate levels of importance.

<H1>Level one heading text</H1>
<H2>Level two heading text</H2>
<H3>Level three heading text</H3>
<H4>Level four heading text</H4>

DIVISIONAL TAGS

Use these tags to format and to help organize your pages.

<CENTER></CENTER>	centers elements and text
<P></P>	indicates a paragraph
<BLOCKQUOTE></BLOCKQUOTE>	indicates a long quotation
 	indicates a line break (no closing tag)
<HR>	indicates a horizontal rule (no closing tag)

TYPOGRAPHY TAGS

`<B></B>`	**bold text**
`<I></I>`	*italic text*
`<U></U>`	underlined text

LIST TAGS

| `<UL></UL>` | bulleted list |
| `<OL></OL>` | numbered list |

The following sources will help you use HTML and design your site:

A BEGINNER'S GUIDE TO HTML

www.ncsa.uiuc.edu/General/Internet/WWW/HTMLPrimer.html

UNIVERSITY OF VIRGINIA LIBRARY, HTML AND WEB DOCUMENT CREATION

etext.lib.virginia.edu/helpsheets/html/lesshtml.html

FOR COLOR IN YOUR DOCUMENT

home.netscape.com/assist/net_sites/bg/index.html

www.bagism.com/colormaker/

FOR BACKGROUND IMAGES AND COLORS

home.netscape.com/assist/net_sites/bg/backgrounds.html

FOR TABLES

www.bagism.com/tablemaker/

▪ *Incorporating graphics and images*

Graphics are particularly important on Web pages. Make sure, however, that the graphics you use are closely related to your purposes. (See 9f.)

▪ *Creating links*

Providing links that transfer readers effortlessly from place to place calls for a lot of thought on the part of the Web writer. You will probably need to practice creating links or even take a tutorial to learn how to do so. The following steps, however, will get you started:

- Choose a format for your links. Will you use an icon or button to signal them? a change of color? underlining or bold text?

- For basic links, include an anchor tag:

`<A HREF="file name or URL">text or item to be a button</A>`

ANCHOR TAG   REFERENCE TAG   LINK TEXT   ANCHOR TAG

- For internal links to other places on the same Web page, use "jump-to" anchor tags:

`<A HREF="#JUMP-to-Bibliography">bibliography</A>`

ANCHOR TAG   REFERENCE TAG   JUMP-TO TAG   LINK TEXT   ANCHOR TAG

- For internal links to other pages in your Web document, use relative links:

`<A HREF="julio2.html">next page</A>`

ANCHOR TAG   REFERENCE TAG   FILE NAME   LINK TEXT   ANCHOR TAG

- For external links to other sites, use the complete URL:

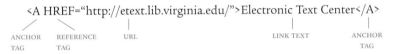

`<A HREF="http://etext.lib.virginia.edu/">Electronic Text Center</A>`

ANCHOR TAG   REFERENCE TAG   URL   LINK TEXT   ANCHOR TAG

■ *Previewing your Web text*

As with any text, asking for responses from readers is crucial to your overall success. Before you make your Web document available on an Internet server, therefore, you should ask others to preview your text.

- Proofread every page, looking for any typos, errors, or confusing passages.
- Check the navigation of the site, verifying that all links work and that readers can find their way around with ease.
- Check the site using several different browsers, if possible, to see that each page displays properly.
- Examine all visuals. Do all graphics and images convey the intended meaning? Is appropriate credit given to sources for any visuals that are not the author's own?

→ Does the Web text accomplish its purpose? Is every page relevant to the topic? (9b)

→ Who is the intended audience? Does the homepage invite those readers in? (9b and d)

→ Does the Web text follow the design principles of clear contrast, proximity, repetition, and alignment? (9d)

→ Does the homepage clearly introduce the topic and give an overview of what is on the site? Is it clear when the site was last updated? Is the author's (or sponsor's) name and contact information on every page? (9d)

→ How easy is it to navigate the Web text? How accessible and quick to download will it be for the readers? (9d and f)

→ How accessible is the document for readers with disabilities? (9b and d)

→ Are all links clear and working? (9e)

→ How are images, graphics, and color used? Do they all help convey the meaning intended? Do the visuals and background contribute to the site's readability? Check to be sure there is an appropriate balance between the visuals and text of the document. If visuals were created by someone else, has proper credit been given to the source? (9d and f)

9i   Posting assignments to the Web

Your instructor may ask that you post an essay or other assignment to an existing Web site. If so, here are some tips you should follow:

• If you composed your essay or assignment in a recent edition of a word processor, save your file as HTML: in Microsoft Word, under the FILE menu, use SAVE AS, and then select HTML. You may want to experiment to see how tables, paragraph returns, and other elements "translate" into HTML format. Many word processors allow you to edit while you are working in HTML, so you can adjust spacing, headings, and other formatting. Many current word processors also allow you to compose in HTML (check the HELP menu to see how), so you may wish to write your essay in HTML from the start. The best advice is to experiment with your word processor and figure out which features work best for you as a writer.

For more about ●
designing read-
able documents,
see 8a–d.

- Keep the design simple: stick to a light background (white or light beige) with clearly contrasting type, and use familiar fonts and readable type sizes (Times New Roman in 12-point type, for example).

- To make your document easy to read, set the margins to allow for about ten words per line, or no more than seventy-five characters.

- Be consistent in your use of headings and subheadings so that your structure will be clear to readers. A second-level heading, for example, should be in the same font style, size, and color throughout your document.

- Position any tables and figures within the text rather than as appendices, and wrap the text around them. Check your program's HELP menu for specific instructions. As always, label each figure and table clearly, and make sure you introduce your visuals as well as comment on their significance.

- Before posting your assignment to the Web site, get some responses to it from your peers: How easily can they navigate your document? How effectively does it make your point(s)?

9i Publishing Web texts

Your final step is to publish your document on the Web, transferring your files to your Internet server. Methods for posting files can vary; check with your Internet service provider or campus computer service for instructions.

As long as your text is saved only to a floppy or hard disc, it is still fairly private: only you and perhaps a small group of reviewers and your instructor have access to that file, and you can change its content any way you like. In short, a private file is still very much in the revision stage. Once you have posted your document to a class Web site, however, the audience for that text is potentially much larger, and the document becomes much more public. Further, if you upload your Web text to other Web-accessible folders or to a server to which the general public has full access, your Web text then becomes a fully public document.

Before you save your document to a publicly accessible folder, consider whether you want the information in the document to reach a wide range of Web surfers. (No doubt you would not want much of your email or other private communication made available on public servers.) And if you are working with peer reviewers on a Web-based forum that is accessible to all members of your class (or beyond), ask whether the

For more on ●
class Web sites
and forums, see
6c.

writer of a text wants you to post your comments to the publicly accessible folder or to send them in private email.

THINKING CRITICALLY ABOUT YOUR WEB TEXTS

Take some time to reflect on a Web text you have produced — it might be an assignment you posted to a course Web site, a single-page site intended for your family and friends, or a major multiple-page Web site. Go back through this chapter, reviewing the advice for designing effective Web texts, and then evaluate your own efforts. Conclude by drawing up a list of tips for future — and better — Web texts.

10

◥ Making Oral and Multimedia Presentations

When the Gallup Poll reports on what U.S. citizens say they fear most, the findings are always the same: public speaking is apparently even scarier than an attack from outer space. Perhaps it is not surprising, then, that students who use this handbook have consistently asked for information on giving oral presentations.

Successful speakers point to four elements crucial to their effectiveness:

- *a thorough knowledge of the subject at hand*
- *careful attention to the interactive nature of speaking and thus to the needs of the audience*
- *careful integration of verbal and visual information*
- *practice, practice, and more practice*

This chapter provides some detailed guidance on how to bring these elements to your own presentations. ■

10a Contributing to class discussions

Some of the most important oral presentations you make during your college career may well be as a participant in classroom discussions. The challenge is to contribute to such discussions without losing track of the overall conversation or aims of the class and without monopolizing the discussion. Especially if you are also taking notes, you may find yourself straining to manage all these tasks at once. Here are a few tips for making good contributions to class discussions:

- Be prepared, so that the comments you make will be directly related to the work of the class.
- Listen purposefully, jotting down related points and following the flow of the conversation.
- If you fear you will lose track of your ideas while speaking, jot down a key word or two that will help keep you on track.
- Make your comments count by asking a key question to clarify a point or to take the conversation in a new or more productive direction. Or offer a brief analysis or summary of the points that have already been made to make sure your understanding of what has been said matches that of your classmates and instructor.
- Respond to questions or comments by others as specifically as possible rather than being vague (*The passage on p. 42 provides evidence to support your point* rather than *I agree* or *Good point*).

- Offer a brief analysis of a problem, issue, or text, one that leaves room for others to build on.

- If you find that you are not participating frequently in class discussions, try making one comment a day. You might also speak with your instructor about ways to contribute to the conversation.

- Remember that there is no direct correlation between talking in class and being intellectually engaged: many students are participating actively, whether or not they are speaking.

CONSIDERING MEDIA

Considering the
Assignment,
Purpose, and
Audience for
Presentations

FOR MULTILINGUAL WRITERS: Speaking Up in Class

Speaking up in class is viewed as inappropriate or even rude in some cultures. In the United States, however, doing so is expected and encouraged. Indeed, some instructors assign credit for such class participation.

10b   Considering the assignment, purpose, and audience for presentations

You will be wise to begin preparing for an oral or multimedia presentation as soon as you get the assignment. Consider the assignment carefully, noting how much time you have to prepare, how long the presentation is to be, and what visual aids, handouts, or other materials might be required to accompany the presentation. Consider whether you are to make the presentation alone or as part of a group so that you can plan and practice accordingly (see 6b2). Finally, make sure that you understand the criteria for evaluation — how will the presentation be graded or assessed?

To understand your assignment fully, you must think about the rhetorical situation. Consider the purpose of your presentation. Are you to lead a discussion? teach a lesson? give a report? engage the class in an activity? Who will be the audience? Since your instructor will almost certainly be an important member of the audience, you will want to think about what he or she expects you to do — and do well. As the other class members will also probably be part of the audience, ask yourself what they know about your topic, what opinions they probably hold about it, and what they need to know and understand to follow your presentation

For more on thinking about audience, see Chapter 2.

→ How does your presentation accomplish the specifications of the assignment? (10b)

→ How does your presentation appeal to your audience's experiences and interests? Does it achieve your purpose? (10b)

→ How does the introduction get the audience's attention? Does it provide any necessary background information? (10c)

→ What organizational structure informs your presentation? (10c)

→ Check for signposts that can guide listeners. Are there explicit transitions? Do you repeat key words or ideas? (10c)

→ Have you used mostly straightforward sentences? Consider revising any long or complicated sentences to make your talk easier to follow. Check your words as well for too much abstraction. Substitute concrete words for abstract ones as often as you can. (10c)

→ Have you marked your text for pauses and emphasis? (10c)

→ Have you prepared all necessary visuals? If so, how do they contribute to your presentation? Are they large enough to be seen? If you have not prepared visuals, can you identify any information that would be enhanced by them? (10c and d)

and perhaps accept your point of view. Finally, consider your own stance toward your topic and audience. Are you an expert? novice? well-informed observer? peer?

10c Making effective oral presentations

More and more students report that formal oral presentations are becoming part of their classwork. As you begin to plan for such a presentation, you will want to consider a number of issues.

- How much time will you have for the presentation, and how much information will you be able to present in that time?

- Will you present most comfortably using a fully written-out text, notes, or notecards?

- What visual aids and handouts will make your presentation most successful? What kind of visuals make the most sense for your presentation? A statistical pie chart may be appropriate in one presentation, whereas photographs might be more appropriate in another.

- Will you need an overhead projector or other equipment? Can you use presentation software and, if so, what equipment will you need?
- Find out where you will make your presentation—in a lecture hall? in an informal sitting area? Will you have a lectern? Will you sit or stand—move around or stay in one place? Will the lighting need to be adjusted?
- How will your presentation be evaluated?

CONSIDERING DISABILITIES: Accessible Presentations

Remember that some members of your audience may not be able to see your presentation or may have trouble hearing it, so do all you can to make your presentation accessible.

→ Do not rely on color or graphics alone to get across information—some may be unable to pick up these visual cues.

→ For presentations you publish on the Web, provide brief textual descriptions in the form of labels or captions of your visuals that can be picked up by a text-to-speech conversion program.

→ If you use video, provide labels for captions to explain any sounds that won't be audible to some audience members. Be sure that the equipment you'll be using is caption-capable.

→ Remember that students have very different learning styles and abilities. You may want to provide a written overview of your presentation or put the text of your presentation on an overhead projector—for those who learn better by reading *and* listening.

1 Writing to be heard—and remembered

Writing to be heard entails several special requirements, among them a memorable introduction and conclusion, explicit structures and helpful signpost language, straightforward syntax and concrete diction, and an effective presentation.

■ Composing a memorable introduction and conclusion

Remember that listeners, like readers, tend to remember beginnings and endings most readily. Work extra hard, therefore, to make these elements memorable. Consider, for example, using a startling statement, opinion, or question; a vivid anecdote; a powerful quotation; or a vivid visual

For examples of
memorable
openings and
conclusions, see
4f and Chapter 5.

image. Shifting language, especially into a variety of language that your audience will identify with, is another effective way to catch their attention. Whenever you can link your subject to the experiences and interests of your audience, do so.

Writer Amy Tan began a 1989 presentation to the Language Symposium in San Francisco with a puzzling statement, especially given that she was addressing a group of language scholars:

> I am not a scholar of English or literature. I cannot give you much more than personal opinions on the English language and its variations in this country or others. —AMY TAN, "Mother Tongue"

Tan's statement not only got the attention of her audience, but she also used the statement as a springboard to address her audience's interests.

■ Using structures and signpost language

Use a clear organizational structure, and give an overview of your main points toward the beginning of your presentation. (You may wish to recall these points again toward the end of the talk.) Throughout, it will be helpful to pause between major points and to use **signpost language** to mark your movement from one topic to the next. Such signposts act as explicit transitions in your talk and thus should be clear and concrete: *The second crisis point in the breakup of the Soviet Union occurred hard on the heels of the first* instead of *The breakup of the Soviet Union came to another crisis point. . . .* In addition to such explicit transitions as *next, on the contrary,* or *finally,* you can offer signposts to your listeners by carefully repeating key words and ideas as well as by sticking to concrete topic sentences to introduce each new idea.

For a list of tran-
sitions, see 5d.

■ Considering syntax and diction

For a discussion
of abstract and
concrete lan-
guage, see 27c.

Avoid long, complicated sentences, and use straightforward syntax (subject-verb-object) as much as possible. Remember also that listeners can hold on to concrete verbs and nouns more easily than they can grasp abstractions. You may need to deal with abstract ideas, but try to provide concrete examples for each.

■ Making your presentation memorable

Memorable presentations call on the power of figures of speech and other devices of language such as careful repetition, parallelism, and climactic order. You can see an example of all these devices in the following text from Martin Luther King Jr.'s speech on the steps of the Lincoln Memorial in Washington, D.C. Speaking on August 28, 1963, with hundreds of thousands of marchers before him, King used memorable language to help call the nation to make good on the promissory note represented by the Emancipation Proclamation.

> It is obvious today that America has defaulted on this promissory note insofar as her citizens of color are concerned. Instead of honoring this sacred obligation, America has given the Negro people a bad check which has come back marked "insufficient funds." But *we refuse* to believe that the bank of justice is bankrupt. *We refuse* to believe that there are insufficient funds in the great vaults of opportunity of this nation. So *we have come* to cash this check — a check that will give us upon demand the riches of freedom and the security of justice. *We have also come* to this hallowed spot to remind America of the fierce urgency of now. This *is no time* to engage in the luxury of cooling off or to take the tranquilizing drug of gradualism. *Now is the time* to rise from the dark and desolate valley of segregation to the sunlit path of racial justice. *Now is the time* to open the doors of opportunity to all of God's children. *Now is the time* to lift our nation from the quicksands of racial injustice to the solid rock of brotherhood. [emphasis added]
>
> – MARTIN LUTHER KING JR., "I Have a Dream"

Marginal notes:
- Metaphor of bad check introduced and then alluded to throughout
- Repetition of "we refuse" and "we have come" creates parallelism
- Repetition of "Now is the time" used to build toward climactic point

▪ *Turning writing into speaking*

You will almost certainly want to rely on some written material. Depending on the assignment, the audience, and your personal preferences, you may even decide to prepare a full text of your presentation. If so, double- or triple-space it, and use fairly large print so that it will be easy to read. Try to end each page with the end of a sentence so that you won't have to pause while you turn a page. In addition, you may decide to mark spots where you want to pause and to highlight words you want to emphasize.

On the other hand, you may prefer to work from a detailed topic or sentence outline, from points listed on an overhead, or from note cards. If so, use the same basic techniques so that you can easily follow the material. Whatever kind of text you decide to prepare (and each kind can be highly successful), you will want to pay special attention to the task of *writing to be heard*.

Look carefully at the following paragraphs. The first is from an essay about the importance of thinking critically before choosing a course of study. The second paragraph presents the same information, this time revised for an oral presentation.

pres

10c

224

CONSIDERING MEDIA

Making Oral and
Multimedia
Presentations

A PARAGRAPH FROM A WRITTEN ESSAY

The decision about a major or other course of study
is crucial because it determines both what we study and
how we come to think about the world. The philosopher
Kenneth Burke explains that we are inevitably affected
not only by our experiences but also by the terminologies
through which our perceptions of those experiences are
filtered. Burke calls these filters "terministic
screens" and says that they affect our perception,
highlighting some aspects of an experience while
obscuring others. Thus the terminologies (or languages)
we use influence how we see the world and how we think
about what we see.

THE PARAGRAPH REVISED FOR AN ORAL PRESENTATION

Why is our decision about a major so crucial? I
can give two important reasons. First, our major
determines what we study. *Pause* ∧ Second, it determines how we
come to think about the world. The philosopher Kenneth
Burke explains these influences this way: our
experience, he says, influences what we think about
ideas and the world. But those experiences are always
filtered through <u>language</u>, through words and terminologies. Burke calls these terminologies "terministic
screens," a complicated-sounding term for a pretty
simple idea. Take, for example, the latest hike in
student fees on our campus. The Board of Trustees and
the administration use one kind of term to describe the
hike: <u>"modest and reasonable</u>," they call it. Students
I know use entirely different terms: "<u>exorbitant and</u>

unjust," they call it. Why the difference? Because

their terministic screens are entirely different. *Pause* ^Burke

says we all have such screens made up of language,

these screens act to screen out some things for us and

to screen in, or highlight, others. Burke's major point

is this: the terms and screens we use have a big

influence on how we see the world and how we think about

what we see.

Note that the revised paragraph presents the same information, but this time it is written to be heard. The revision uses helpful signpost language, some repetition, simple syntax, and the example of student fees to help listeners follow along and keep them interested. Note also how the writer has marked her text, prompting her to pause or to add special emphasis.

2 Using visuals

Visuals may be an integral part of an oral presentation, and they should be prepared with great care. Do not think of them as add-ons but as one of your major means of conveying information. Whatever visuals you decide to use (charts, graphs, photographs, summary statements, or lists), they must be large enough to be easily seen by your audience. Many speakers use presentation software or overhead projections throughout a presentation to help keep themselves on track and to guide their audience. If you use such tools, be sure the information on each frame is simple, clear, and easy to read and understand. If you don't have access to this technology, you might prepare a poster or flip chart, or you could simply use a chalkboard or whiteboard. Regardless of the visuals you use, however, be sure *not* to turn your back on the audience.

Most important, make sure that your visuals engage and help your listeners rather than distract them from your message. One good way to test the effectiveness of the visuals you plan to use is by trying them out on classmates, friends, or roommates. If these colleagues do not clearly grasp the meaning of the visuals, revise them and try again.

●—— For more information on using presentation software or on preparing presentation overhead transparencies or posters, see 10d.

pres

226 **10c**

CONSIDERING MEDIA

Making Oral and
Multimedia
Presentations

You may also want to prepare handouts for your audience: pertinent bibliographies, for example, or text too extensive to be presented otherwise. Unless the handouts include material you want your audience to use while you speak, distribute them at the end of the presentation.

3 Practicing the presentation

In oral presentations, as with many other things in life, practice makes perfect. Prepare a draft of your presentation, including all visuals, far enough in advance to allow for several run-throughs. Some speakers audio- or videotape their rehearsals and then base their revisions on the tape-recorded performance. Others practice in front of a mirror or in front of friends. Do whatever works for you — just as long as you practice!

Make sure you can be heard clearly. If you are soft-spoken, concentrate on projecting your voice. If your voice tends to rise when you are in the spotlight, you may want to practice lowering your pitch. If you speak rapidly, practice slowing down and enunciating words clearly. Remember that tone of voice affects listeners, so it is usually best to avoid sarcasm in favor of a tone that conveys interest in and commitment to your topic and listeners. If you practice with friends or classmates, ask them how well they can hear you and what advice they have for making your voice clearer and easier to listen to.

One student who taped her rehearsal found, to her great surprise, that she had used the word *like* thirty-two times in her eight-minute presentation, even though the word never appeared in her notes. In this case, it took a lot of practice to break the *like* habit.

Once you are comfortable giving the presentation, make sure you will stay within the allotted time. One good rule of thumb is to allow roughly two and a half minutes per double-spaced 8½" × 11" page of text (or one and a half minutes per 5" × 7" card). The only way to be sure about your time, however, is to time yourself as you practice. Knowing that your presentation is neither too short nor too long will help you relax and gain self-confidence; and when the members of your audience sense your self-confidence, they will become increasingly receptive to your message.

4 Making the presentation

Experienced speakers say they always expect to feel some anxiety before an oral presentation — and they develop strategies for dealing with it. In addition, they note that some nervousness can act to a speaker's advantage: adrenaline, after all, can provide a little extra jolt and help you perform well.

The best strategy seems to be to know your material well. Having confidence in your own knowledge will go a long way toward making you a confident presenter. In addition to doing your homework, however, you may be able to use the following strategies to good advantage:

1. Consider how you will dress and how you will move around. In each case, your choices should be appropriate for the situation. Most experienced speakers like to dress simply and comfortably for easy movement. But they are seldom overly casual—dressing up a little signals your pride in your appearance and your respect for your audience.
2. Visualize your presentation with the aim of feeling comfortable during it; go over the scene of your presentation in your mind, and think it through completely.
3. Get some rest before the presentation, and avoid consuming an excessive amount of caffeine.
4. Consider doing some deep-breathing exercises right before the presentation. Concentrate on relaxing.

Most speakers make a stronger impression standing rather than sitting. In addition, you can move around the room if you are comfortable doing so. If you are more comfortable in one spot, at a table or a lectern, then stand with both feet flat on the floor. If you are standing at a lectern, rest your hands lightly on it. Many speakers find that this stance keeps them from fidgeting.

Pause before you begin your presentation, concentrating on your opening lines. During your presentation, interact with your audience as much as possible. You can do so by facing the audience at all times and making eye contact as often as possible. You may want to choose two or three people to look at and "talk to," particularly if you are addressing a large group. Allow time for the audience to respond and ask questions. Try to keep your answers short so that others may participate in the conversation. At the conclusion of your presentation, remember to thank your audience.

● **EXERCISE 10.1**

Take time to attend a lecture or presentation on your campus and analyze its effectiveness. How does the speaker capture and hold your interest? What signpost language and other guides to listening can you detect? How well are visuals integrated

pres

228 **10d**

CONSIDERING MEDIA

Making Oral and
Multimedia
Presentations

into the presentation? How does the speaker's tone of voice, dress, and eye contact affect your understanding and appreciation (or lack of it)? What is most
memorable about the presentation, and why? Bring your analysis to class and
report your findings.

10d Incorporating multimedia into oral presentations

As you learn to create Web pages, you will probably wish to incorporate
some of their qualities into your presentations for college classes as well
as for work or community-related projects. Among the most popular
forms of multimedia presentation are those that use presentation software, those that use overhead transparencies, and those that use posters.

1 Presentation software

You can use presentation software such as **PowerPoint** and similar programs to add images and sound to your own voice (another oral
medium) in order to create a memorable presentation. These programs
allow you to prepare slides you want to display and even to enhance the
images with sound. Before you begin designing your presentation, find
out if the computer equipment and projector you need will be available.
As you design presentation slides, keep some simple principles in mind:

- For captions or any other print text, use fonts for emphasis, and make
  sure your audience can read them: 44- to 50-point type for titles, for
  example, or 30- to 34-point type for subheads.

- For slides that contain print text, use bulleted or numbered points rather
  than running text. Keep these items as concise as possible, and use clear
  language. If you are using the points to guide your own discussion,
  think carefully about the number of points you wish to include on each
  slide. Make sure that these points will actually guide both you and the
  audience.

- Create a clear contrast between any print text or illustration and the
  background. As a general rule, light backgrounds work better in a dark-
  ened room, dark backgrounds in a lighted one.

- Be careful of becoming overly dependent on presentation-software templates such as those provided by PowerPoint's AutoContent Wizard. The
  choices of color, font, and so on offered by such "wizards" may not always
  match your goals or fit with your topic.

- As a general rule, use presentation-software slides for illustrating what you are saying or for talking points; don't read the text of the slides to your audience.
- Choose visuals—photographs, paintings, graphs, and so on—that will reproduce sharply, and make sure they are large enough to be clearly visible to your audience.
- If you are adding sound or video clips, make sure that they are clearly audible and that they relate directly to the topic of your presentation. Especially if sound is to be used as background, make sure it does not in any way distract from what you are trying to say.

The following three slides make effective use of PowerPoint. Prepared by Myles Morrison for his first-year writing class, these slides improve his presentation. The first slide clearly announces the topic, and the second slide provides a graph showing the dramatic rise in divorce rates. The third slide provides an overview of the entire presentation.

CONSIDERING MEDIA

Incorporating Multimedia into Oral Presentations

www • bedford stmartins.com/ smhandbook

For additional examples of effective PowerPoint presentations, click on

▸ **Student Samples**
　▸ **Presentations**

SAMPLE SLIDES FROM A POWERPOINT PRESENTATION

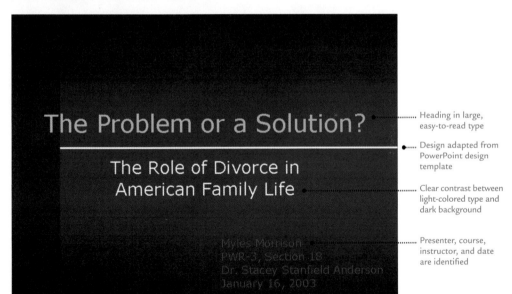

Heading in large, easy-to-read type

Design adapted from PowerPoint design template

Clear contrast between light-colored type and dark background

Presenter, course, instructor, and date are identified

pres

10d

Making Oral and
Multimedia
Presentations

Heading clearly identi-
fies the topic of the
graph

Arrows point out
specific eras for this
presentation

Source of statistics
included at bottom of
graph

Dark background and
light type are easy to
read onscreen in a
well-lit room

Bulleted points
announce presenta-
tion's topics and
subtopics

Bulleted points kept
brief

Overview

• **Many factors contribute to rise in the divorce rate over the last 50 years**
  - Diminished influence of religion
  - Evolution of gender roles within marriages
  - Economically viable alternatives to marriage
  - Changed societal expectations

• **Increased divorce rate the result of changes generally considered constructive**

Your choice of multimedia material may well be guided by the room in which you will be doing your presentation. For most classrooms, over-head projectors are easier to get and to use than the projector necessary for presentation software. As a result, you may decide to prepare slides for an overhead projector — something you have probably already used in making a class- or work-related presentation. Although less techno-logically complex, preparing transparencies for such a presentation involves the same kind of design effort that goes into any other multi-media presentation. Most important, you want the material on the transparencies to augment what you are saying, not to distract from it. In addition, you want your transparencies to help guide you in your speaking and to help guide audience members in following what you say. Overhead transparencies, then, need to be kept sweet and simple: a clear title and a few bulleted items or key phrases, all in easily readable type sizes and fonts. As with PowerPoint, color should be easy on the eyes and should enhance rather than obscure the text. Here is an example of a transparency created for a presentation about the World Wide Web.

SAMPLE TRANSPARENCY FOR A PRESENTATION

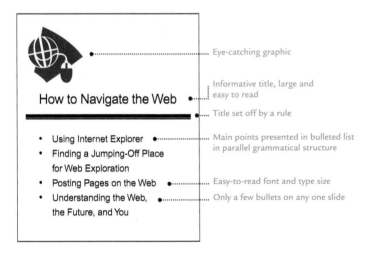

CONSIDERING MEDIA

Making Oral and
Multimedia
Presentations

Many college courses and conferences now call on students to make poster presentations. In general, such presentations use a poster board, usually about 50" × 40", that displays major points or findings, a model or diagram, or a drawing. During the class or conference session, the presenter uses this board as background while he or she talks through the presentation and answers questions. Although guidelines for poster presentations vary, follow these tips if you are preparing one:

- Create a board that can be read from at least three feet away.
- Include a clear title (at least two inches high) at the top of the board.
- Include your name and other appropriate information: course title and number, name of instructor, conference title or session, and so on.
- Use a series of bullets or boxes to identify your major points and to lead the audience through the presentation.
- Include an arresting image or an important table or figure if it illustrates your points in a clear and memorable way.
- Consider using a provocative question toward the bottom of the poster to focus attention and anticipate your conclusion.
- Remember that simple, uncluttered posters are usually easier to follow and therefore more effective than overly complex ones.
- Practice the oral part of the presentation until you are comfortable referring to the poster while keeping your full attention on the audience.

Page 233 shows the poster prepared by Shannan Palma, a student at Ohio State University, for a presentation based on the research essay she had written on movie heroes.

For Shannan
Palma's research
essay, see 20d.

FOR COLLABORATION

Working with two or more classmates, attend a presentation of interest to you, either on campus or in the larger community. Take notes during the presentation on what you find effective and ineffective. Then meet to compare your notes, and using the principles outlined in this chapter, write up a brief review of the presentation and bring it to class for discussion.

.... Title set off by large
font and color back-
ground

.... Photograph draws
attention and adds
emphasis

• **What happened when heroes made the transition from** .... List of bulleted
literature and legend to movie screen? questions provides
talking points to lead
audience through
presentation

• **Why did audiences begin to mistake the movie actor**
for the hero--and with what effects?

.... White space is used
effectively to highlight
• **If the hero is not now dead, what will our future heroes** text and photo
be like?

.... Two hypotheses
elaborated on in
conclusion are high-
lighted as questions
in colored ovals

.... Name of presenter,
conference, place, and
date are identified

CONSIDERING MEDIA

Making Oral and
Multimedia
Presentations

Study the text of an oral or multimedia presentation you've prepared or given. Using the advice in this chapter, see how well your presentation appeals to your audience. Look in particular at how well you catch and hold their attention. How effective is your use of signpost language or other structures that help guide your listeners? How helpful were the visuals you used (PowerPoint slides, overhead projections, posters) in conveying your message? What would you do to improve this presentation?

PART 3

CRITICAL THINKING AND ARGUMENT

"So much of what we receive from others—from family and friends to thirty-second blurbs on TV—is intended to persuade. Recognizing how this is done gives greater power to choose."
—VICTOR VILLANUEVA JR.

11

▼ Analyzing Arguments

How do we come to make up our minds about something? What causes us to give our assent to some ideas but not to others? And how do we seek—and sometimes gain—agreement from others?

These are questions that thinkers have pondered down through the ages, from Plato, Confucius, Mohammed, and the Apostle Paul to Joan of Arc, Mahatma Gandhi, Martin Luther King Jr., and Rigoberta Menchú.

The need to explore such questions has never been more pressing than it is today, as language intended to persuade us—to gain our assent (and often our bank accounts, our votes, and even our souls)—surrounds us more than ever before. In advertisements, news stories, textbooks, reports, and electronic media of all kinds, language competes for our attention and argues for our agreement. Since argument so pervades our lives, we need to be able to recognize and use it effectively—and to question our own arguments as well as those put forth by others. ■

11a Recognizing argument

In one important sense, all language use has an argumentative edge. When you greet friends warmly, you wish to convince them that you are genuinely glad to see them, that you value their presence. Even apparently objective news reporting has strong argumentative overtones. By putting a particular story on the front page, for example, a paper argues that this subject is more important than others; by using emotional language and focusing on certain details in reporting an event, a newscaster tries to persuade us to view the event in a particular way. What one reporter might call a *massive demonstration*, for example, another might call *a noisy protest,* and yet another, *an angry march.*

Emily Lesk's primary purpose in her essay "Red, White, and Everywhere" is to reflect on her own identification with one particular American icon, Coca-Cola (see 4j). But her essay clearly has an argumentative edge: to ask readers to examine their own cultural identifications and to understand the power of advertising in creating and sustaining such identifications.

It's possible, then, to read any message or text, verbal or visual, as an argument, even if argument is not its primary purpose. Poems, for example, can make very powerful arguments, as can movies, novels, or songs. To test this hypothesis, take a look at the lyrics of a song and spend some time identifying the possible arguments it is making.

Here are some questions that can help you judge the effectiveness of an argument:

→ What conclusions about the argument can you reach by playing both the believing and the doubting game? (11b)
→ What cultural contexts inform the argument, and what do they tell you about where the writer is coming from? (11b and c)
→ What is the main issue (or stasis) of the argument, and what does it tell you about what will be the most important means of persuasion? (11d)
→ What emotional, ethical, and logical appeals is the writer making in support of the argument? (11e)
→ How has the writer established credibility to write about the topic? (11e)
→ What is the claim (or argumentative thesis)? Is the claim qualified in any way? (11f)
→ What reasons and warrants support and underlie the claim? (11f)
→ What additional evidence backs up the warrant and claim? (11f)
→ How has the writer used images, graphics, or other visuals to support the argument? (Chapter 12)
→ What fallacies can you identify, and what effect do they have on the argument's persuasiveness? (11g)
→ What is the overall impression you get from analyzing the argument? Are you convinced?

11b Thinking critically about arguments

Although **critical thinking** may be given a number of fancy or complex definitions, it is essentially just the process by which we make sense of all the information around us. As such, critical thinking is a crucial component of argument, for it guides us in recognizing, formulating, and examining the arguments that are important to us.

For the purposes of considering such arguments, we now turn to several elements of critical thinking that are especially important:

Playing the believing—and the doubting—game. Critical readers are able to shift stances as they read, allowing them to gain different perspectives on any argument. One good way to begin is by playing the *believing game:* that is, by putting yourself in the position of the person writing the argument you are reading, seeing the topic from that person's point of

238

arg

11b

ARGUMENT

Analyzing
Arguments

view as much as possible, and thinking carefully about how and why that person arrived at the claim(s) being made. Once you have given the argument a sympathetic reading, you can play the *doubting game*. To do so, revisit the argument, looking skeptically at each claim and examining each piece of evidence to see how well (or if) it supports the claim. Eventually, this process of believing and doubting will become natural.

Asking pertinent questions. Concentrate on asking questions that will get to the heart of the matter. Whether you are thinking about ideas put forth by others or about those you yourself hold, you will want to ask the following kinds of questions:

- What is the writer's agenda—his or her unstated purpose?
- Why does the writer hold these ideas or beliefs? What larger social, economic, political, or other conditions may have influenced him or her?
- What does the writer want readers to do—and why?
- What are the writer's qualifications for making this argument?
- What reasons does the writer offer in support of his or her ideas? Are they *good* reasons?
- What are the writer's underlying values or unstated assumptions? Are they acceptable—and why, or why not?
- What sources does the writer rely on? How current and reliable are they? What agendas do these sources have? Are any perspectives left out?
- What objections might be made to the argument?
- Be especially careful in examining information on the Web. What individual or group is responsible for the site and the argument it makes? (See 16b.)

For more information on using visuals in an argument, see Chapter 12 and 13i.

- Study the visual and audio aspects of arguments, including the use of color, graphics, and all multimedia techniques. How do they appeal to the reader or listener? What do they contribute to the argument?

Getting information. To help you decide whether to accept an argument, often you will need to find *more information* on the topic as well as *other perspectives.*

Interpreting and assessing information. No information that comes to us in language is neutral; all of it has a perspective, a spin, if you will. Your job as a critical thinker is to identify the perspective and to *assess* it, examining its sources and finding out what you can about its context. Asking the kinds of pertinent questions suggested here will help you examine the interpretations and conclusions drawn by others.

Making and assessing your own arguments. The ultimate goal of all critical thinking is to construct your own ideas, reach your own conclusions.

These, too, you must question and assess. The rest of this chapter will guide you in the art of assessing arguments.

ARGUMENT

Getting to the
Main Issue in an
Argument: Stasis
Theory

11c Recognizing cultural contexts for arguments

If you want to understand as fully as possible the arguments of others, you need to remember that writers come from an astonishing variety of cultural and linguistic backgrounds. Perhaps most important for reading critically, pay attention to clues to cultural context, and be open to the many ways of thinking you will encounter. In short, practice the believing game before you play the doubting game — especially when analyzing an argument influenced by a culture different from your own. In addition, remember that within any given culture there are great differences among individuals. So don't expect that every member of a culture will argue in any one way or another.

Above all, watch your own assumptions very closely as you read. Just because you assume that the use of statistics as support for your argument holds more water than, say, precedent drawn from religious belief, you can't assume that all writers agree with you. Take a writer's cultural beliefs into account before you begin to analyze an argument.

●— For more information on understanding cultural contexts, see Chapter 24.

11d Getting to the main issue in an argument: stasis theory

Greek and Roman rhetoricians designed a series of questions aimed at getting to the heart of any argument by identifying its main issue. Referred to as *stasis theory* (in Greek the word *stasis* means "a stand" — literally, where an arguer takes a stand), these four questions can still be very useful in analyzing arguments:

1. The question of conjecture: did an act occur?
2. The question of definition: how is the act defined?
3. The question of quality: how important or serious is the act?
4. The question of procedure: what actions should be taken as a result of this act?

Suppose, for example, that you are reading an article arguing that the attacks on Islamic centers and mosques following September 11, 2001, are acts of patriotism. To begin to analyze this argument, you can use the preceding questions to good effect. *Did an act occur?* Yes, the article

arg

240

11e

ARGUMENT

Analyzing
Arguments

identifies five major attacks on such centers in Ohio alone. *How is the act defined?* In this article, the writer argues that these acts should be defined as patriotic, as part of ongoing homeland security. *How important or serious is the act?* The writer argues that attacking Islamic centers or mosques is defensive, not offensive, thus supporting the definition offered earlier. The writer also suggests that since the act is patriotic it is not such a serious offense. *What actions should be taken?* According to the writer, no punitive action should be taken since no crime has been committed.

By grasping the answers to these four questions, you, as a reader, have now opened the heart of the argument offered and should be ready to play the doubting game well. In other words, you have broken the argument into its key parts, which allows you to examine each element separately to identify the weak points. Although you may accept the response to the first question (an act definitely did occur), you will probably find ample reason to contest the writer's responses to the second, third, and fourth questions. Doing so will sharpen your thinking and lead to a more critical reading of this — or any other — article.

11e Identifying an argument's basic appeals: Aristotle's three types

For information on using appeals in your own arguments, see 13e, f, and g. To use appeals in analyzing visual arguments, see 12b.

Aristotle categorized argumentative appeals into three types: emotional appeals (those that appeal to our hearts and values), ethical appeals (those that appeal to character), and logical appeals (those that involve factual information and evidence). Like the questions in stasis theory, Aristotle's categories can help you open up an argument and thus begin to analyze it.

Emotional appeals stir our emotions and remind us of deeply held values. When President Bush argues that the country needs more tax relief, he almost always uses examples of one or more families he has met, stressing the concrete ways in which a tax cut would improve the quality of their lives. Doing so creates a strong emotional appeal. Some have criticized the use of emotional appeals in argument, claiming that they are a form of manipulation intended to mislead an audience. But emotional appeals are an important part of almost every argument. Critical readers are perfectly capable of "talking back" to such appeals by analyzing them, deciding which are acceptable and which are not. What emotional appeals are at work in the following restaurant advertisement, and how would you analyze their effectiveness?

Carmelo's Italian Restaurant is Houston's answer to an authentic Sicilian kitchen spiced with continental chic. All the ingredients are here — the pungent smells of garlic, the irresistible sounds of an accordion, a wall-to-wall collection of buildings recreating the village of Taormina where Carmelo was born and, of course, a sundry of the best pasta dishes, seafood, poultry, veal and beef specialties, olive oils, coffees, wines and desserts. Private rooms are available to accommodate anywhere from ten to 230 people. Lunch weekdays and dinner nightly. 14795 Memorial Dr., (281) 531-0696. Also located in Austin. http://www.carmelosrestaurant.com

Ethical appeals are those that support the credibility, moral character, and goodwill of the writer. These appeals are especially important for critical readers to recognize and evaluate. We may respect and admire an athlete like Michael Jordan, for example, but should the credibility he has as an athlete necessarily carry over to an argument that we should buy a certain brand of running shoes? To identify ethical appeals in arguments, ask yourself these questions: What is the writer doing to show that he or she is knowledgeable and credible about the subject—has really done the homework on it? What sort of character does the writer build, and how does he or she do so? More important, is that character trustworthy? What does the writer do to show that he or she has the best interests of readers in mind? Do those best interests match your own, and, if not, how does that alter the effectiveness of the argument? Take a look at the following paragraph, which introduces an argument for viewing the Diné, or Navajo, people as a nation within a nation. As you read, try to identify the ethical appeals within the passage, paying special attention to the writer's identification of himself and the Diné people with the land.

One of the most remarkable things about this republic is that there exists within its borders a parallel universe known as Dinetah, a nation of more than 155,000 souls who subscribe to a mind-set completely different from the modern American belief that everything in nature is there for the taking. Dinetah is the ancestral homeland of the Diné, more commonly called the Navajo, a misnomer perpetrated by the Spaniards, as are many of the names for the native tribes of the Southwest. An area larger

arg

242

11e

ARGUMENT

Analyzing
Arguments

than West Virginia that sprawls out of Arizona into New Mexico and Utah, Dinetah is bounded by four sacred mountains—North Mountain (Debe'nitsaa), in the La Plata Mountains of Colorado; South Mountain (Tso Dzil), or Mount Taylor, near Grants, New Mexico; East Mountain (Sis Naajinæ'i), or Sierra Blanca, in Colorado; and West Mountain (Dook Oslid), in the San Francisco Peaks, near Flagstaff, Arizona—and four sacred rivers (the Colorado, the Little Colorado, the San Juan, and the Rio Grande). It is some of the starkest, most magically open-to-the-sky country anywhere—a sagebrush steppe spotted with juniper and ancient, gnarled piñon trees, occasionally gashed by a yawning canyon or thrust up into a craggy, pine-clad mountain range, a magenta mesa, a blood-red cliff, a tiara of lucent, stress-fractured tan sandstone.

"The land is our Bible," a Navajo woman named Sally once explained to me.   – ALEX SHOUMATOFF, "The Navajo Way"

Logical appeals are perhaps the most familiar to us because they are viewed as especially trustworthy: "the facts don't lie," some say. Of course, facts are not the only type of logical appeals, which also include firsthand evidence drawn from observations, interviews, surveys and questionnaires, experiments, and personal experience; and secondhand evidence drawn from authorities, the testimony of others, statistics, and other print and online sources. Critical readers need to examine logical appeals just as carefully as emotional and ethical ones. What is the source of the logical appeal—and is that source trustworthy? Are all terms defined clearly? Has the logical evidence presented been taken out of context, and, if so, does that change the meaning of the data? Look, for example, at the following brief passage:

> [I]t is well for us to remember that, in an age of increasing illiteracy, 60 percent of the world's illiterates are women. Between 1960 and 1970, the number of illiterate men in the world rose by 8 million, while the number of illiterate women rose by 40 million.[1] And the number of illiterate women is increasing.
>
> – ADRIENNE RICH, "What Does a Woman Need to Know?"

As a critical reader, you would question these "facts" and hence check the footnote to discover the source, which in this case is the UN *Compendium of Social Statistics*. At this point, you might decide to accept this document as authoritative—or you might decide to look further into United Nations' publications policy, especially to find out how that body defines *illiteracy*. You would also no doubt wonder why Rich chose the decade from 1960 to 1970 for her example and, as a result, check to see when this essay was written. As it turns out, the essay was written in 1979, so the decade of the sixties would have been the

arg

11f   243

ARGUMENT

Identifying the
Elements of
Arguments: The
Toulmin System

most recent data available on literacy. Nevertheless, you should question the timeliness of these statistics: are they still meaningful thirty years later?

If you attend closely to the emotional, ethical, and logical appeals offered in any argument, you will be well on your way to analyzing—and evaluating—it.

FOR MULTILINGUAL WRITERS: Understanding Appeals in Various Settings

You may be familiar with emotional, ethical, or logical appeals that are not discussed in this chapter. If so, consider describing them—and how they work—to members of your class. Doing so would deepen the entire class's understanding of what appeals carry the most power in particular settings.

11f   Identifying the elements of arguments: the Toulmin system

Philosopher Stephen Toulmin has developed a framework for analyzing arguments; it is sometimes referred to simply as *Toulmin argument* or the *Toulmin system*. According to Toulmin, most arguments contain common features: a *claim* or *claims; reasons* for the claim; *warrants* that provide a link from the claim to the reasons (often found in the form of assumptions, whether stated or not); *evidence* (facts, authoritative opinion, examples, statistics, and so on); and *qualifiers* that limit the claim in some way. In the following discussion, we will examine each of these elements in more detail. The figure that follows shows how these elements might be applied to an argument about sex education.

•— For information on applying the Toulmin system to your own arguments, see 13c and j. To apply the Toulmin system to visual arguments, see 12a.

Claims (also referred to as argumentative theses) are statements of fact, opinion, or belief that form the backbone of arguments. In longer essays, you may detect a series of linked claims or even several separate claims that you need to analyze before you agree to accept them. Claims worthy of arguing are those that are debatable: to say *At 10 degrees Fahrenheit, it's cold today* is a claim, but it is probably not debatable— unless you decide that 10 degrees in northern Alaska might seem balmy. To take another example, if a movie review you are reading has as its claim "Loved this movie!" is that claim debatable? Almost certainly not,

arg

244 **11f**

TOULMIN'S SYSTEM APPLIED TO SEX-EDUCATION ARGUMENT

ARGUMENT
Analyzing
Arguments

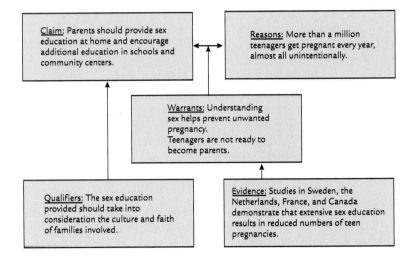

if the reviewer is basing the claim solely on personal taste. But if the reviewer goes on to offer good reasons to accept the claim, along with strong evidence to support it, he or she could present a debatable — and therefore arguable — claim.

In fact, a claim is only as good as the **reasons** attached to it. An essay claiming that grades should be abolished because the writer often earns poor grades is on very thin ice: critical readers will question whether that reason is sufficient to support the claim. As you analyze claims, look for reasons drawn from facts, from authorities, from personal experience, and from examples. Test each reason by asking how directly it supports the claim, how timely it is, and what counter-reasons you could offer to question it.

For an example
of an enthy-
meme, see 13f4.

Putting a claim and reasons together often results in what Aristotle called an **enthymeme,** an argument that rests on an assumption the writer knows the audience to hold. In Toulmin argument, such assumptions are called **warrants.** These assumptions that connect claim and reasons are often the hardest to detect in an argument, partly because they are often unstated, sometimes masking a weak link. As a result, it's especially important to identify the warrants in arguments you are analyzing. Once the warrant is identified, you can test it against evidence and your own experience before accepting it. If a writer argues that grades should be abolished because grading damages both teaching and learning, what is the warrant supporting this claim and reason? It is that *those things that prevent or hinder education should be abolished.* As a critical reader, remember that such assumptions are deeply affected by culture and belief: ask yourself, then, what cultural differences may be at work in your response to any argument.

Evidence, what Toulmin calls "backing," also calls for careful analysis in arguments. In an argument about abolishing grades, the writer may offer as evidence several key examples of the damage grading can cause; a statistical analysis of the correlation between grades and later success in life; a historical precedent from the centuries when grading was not used; or psychological studies of grade-related stress on undergraduate students. As a critical reader, you must evaluate each piece of evidence the writer offers, asking specifically how it relates to the claim, whether it is appropriate and timely, and whether it comes from a credible source.

Qualifiers offer a way of narrowing a claim so that it is as precise as possible. Words or phrases that signal a qualification include *few, often, in these circumstances, rarely, typically,* and so on. Claims having no qualifiers can sometimes lead to overgeneralizations. For example, the statement *Grading damages learning* is less precise than *Grading can damage learning in some circumstances.* Look carefully for qualifiers in the arguments you analyze, since they will affect the strength and reach of the claim.

11g Recognizing fallacies

Fallacies have traditionally been viewed as serious flaws that damage the effectiveness of an argument. But arguments are ordinarily fairly complex in that they always occur in some specific rhetorical situation and in some particular place and time; thus what looks like a fallacy in one situation may appear quite different in another. The best advice may be to learn to identify fallacies but to be cautious in jumping to quick conclusions about them. Rather than thinking of them as errors you can root out and use to discredit an arguer, you might think of them as barriers to common ground and understanding, since they so often shut off rather than engender debate. If a letter to the editor argues *If this newspaper thinks additional tax cuts are going to help the middle-class family, then this newspaper is run by imbeciles,* it clearly indulges in a fallacy—in

arg
11g
246

ARGUMENT

Analyzing
Arguments

this case, an argument *ad hominem* or argument against character. But the more important point is that this kind of argument shuts down debate: few are going to respond reasonably to being called imbeciles.

It may help to identify fallacies by associating them with the major appeals of argument—ethical, emotional, and logical.

1 Ethical fallacies

Some arguments focus not on establishing the credibility of the writer but on destroying the credibility of an opponent. At times, such attacks are justified: if a nominee for the Supreme Court acted in unethical ways in law school, for example, that information is a legitimate argument against the nominee's confirmation. Many times, however, someone attacks a person's character in order to avoid dealing with the issue at hand. Such unjustified attacks are called **ethical fallacies.** They take three main forms: ad hominem charges, guilt by association, and appeals to false authority.

Ad hominem (Latin for "to the man") charges directly attack someone's character rather than focusing on the issue at hand, suggesting that because something is "wrong" with this person, whatever he or she says must also be wrong.

> Patricia Ireland is just a hysterical feminist. We shouldn't listen to her views on abortion.
> [Labeling Ireland *hysterical* and linking that label with *feminist* focuses on Ireland's character rather than on her views on the issue.]

Guilt by association attacks someone's credibility by linking that person with a person or activity the audience considers bad, suspicious, or untrustworthy.

> Senator Fleming does not deserve reelection; one of her assistants turned out to be involved with organized crime.
> [Is there any evidence that the senator knew about the organized-crime involvement?]

You can probably think of advertisers who show famous actors, sports figures, and so on testifying to the greatness of one or another product about which they probably know very little. In doing so, the advertisers are appealing to the fallacy of **false authority.** Some uses of false authority are quite subtle: consider, for example, a politician who argues that her stand on civil rights is based on biblical authority. While the Bible is certainly an authoritative text in many cultures, it is easy to misuse that authority by calling on the Bible *in general* to support a specific claim. Unless the politician refers specifically to biblical chapter and verse, it would be hard to say whether that authority is appropriate in the case at hand; even if it is deemed appropriate, the matter of interpretation would almost certainly come into play. In the same way, a writer might use a study conducted by the National Institutes of Health as an authority even though the study may well have been discredited or the information in it taken out of context.

2 Emotional fallacies

Appeals to the emotions of an audience constitute a valid and necessary part of argument. Unfair or overblown emotional appeals, however, attempt to overcome readers' good judgment. Most common among these **emotional fallacies** are bandwagon appeal, flattery, in-crowd appeal, veiled threats, and false analogies.

Bandwagon appeal suggests that a great movement is under way and the reader will be a fool or a traitor not to join it.

> Voters are flocking to candidate X by the millions, so you'd better cast your vote the right way.
> [Why should you jump on this bandwagon? Where is the evidence to support this claim?]

Flattery tries to persuade readers to do something by suggesting that they are thoughtful, intelligent, or perceptive enough to agree with the writer.

> We know you have the taste to recognize that an investment in an Art-Form ring will pay off in the future.
> [How will it pay off?]

In-crowd appeal, a special kind of flattery, invites readers to identify with an admired and select group.

> Want to know a secret that more and more of Middletown's successful young professionals are finding out about? It's Mountainbrook Manor, the condominiums that combine the best of the old with the best of the new.
> [Who are these "successful young professionals," and will you become one just by moving to Mountainbrook Manor?]

Veiled threats try to frighten readers into agreement by hinting that they will suffer adverse consequences if they don't agree.

arg

248

11g

ARGUMENT

Analyzing
Arguments

If Public Service Electric Company does not get an immediate 15 percent rate increase, its services to you, its customers, may be seriously affected. [How serious is this possible effect? Is it legal or likely?]

False analogies make comparisons between two situations that are *not* alike in most or important respects.

The volleyball team's sudden defeat and descent in the rankings seemed quite reminiscent of the sinking of the *Titanic*.
[What, other than the reference to "descent" and "sinking," do the two events have in common?]

3 Logical fallacies

Although **logical fallacies** are usually defined as errors in formal reasoning, they can often work very effectively to convince audiences. Common logical fallacies include begging the question, *post hoc*, non sequitur, either-or, hasty generalization, and oversimplification.

Begging the question is a kind of circular argument that treats a question as if it has already been answered.

That TV news provides accurate and reliable information was demonstrated conclusively on last week's *60 Minutes*.
[This statement says in effect that television news is accurate and reliable because TV news says so.]

The *post hoc* **fallacy**, from the Latin *post hoc, ergo propter hoc,* which means "after this, therefore caused by this," assumes that just because B happened *after* A, it must have been *caused* by A.

We should not rebuild the town docks because every time we do, a big hurricane comes along and damages them.
[Does the reconstruction cause hurricanes?]

A **non sequitur** (Latin for "it does not follow") attempts to tie together two or more logically unrelated ideas as if they *were* related.

If we can send a spacecraft to Mars, then we can discover a cure for cancer.
[These are both scientific goals, but do they have anything else in common? What does achieving one have to do with achieving the other?]

The **either-or fallacy** asserts that a complex situation can have only two possible outcomes, one of which is necessary or preferable.

If we do not build the new aqueduct, businesses in the tri-cities area will be forced to shut down because of lack of water.
[What is the evidence for this claim? Do no other alternatives exist?]

A **hasty generalization** bases a conclusion on too little evidence or on bad or misunderstood evidence.

I couldn't understand the lecture today, so I'm sure this course will be impossible.
[How can the writer be so sure of this conclusion based on only *one* piece of evidence?]

Oversimplification of the relation between causes and effects is another fallacy based on careless reasoning.

If we prohibit the sale of alcohol, we will get rid of drunkenness.
[This claim oversimplifies the relation between laws and human behavior.]

● **EXERCISE 11.1**

Read the following brief essay by Derek Bok, which argues that college administrators should seek to educate and persuade rather than censor students who use speech or symbols that others find deeply offensive. Then carry out an analysis of the argument, identifying the stasis, or main issue, as well as the claim, reason(s), warrant(s), evidence, and qualifiers (if any). As you work, be sure to identify the emotional, ethical, and logical appeals as well as any fallacies put forward by Bok. You may want to compare your own analysis to the one written by Milena Ateyea in 11h.

For several years, universities have been struggling with the problem of trying to reconcile the rights of free speech with the desire to avoid racial tension. In recent weeks, such a controversy has sprung up at Harvard. Two students hung Confederate flags in public view, upsetting students who equate the Confederacy with slavery. A third student tried to protest the flags by displaying a swastika.

These incidents have provoked much discussion and disagreement. Some students have urged that Harvard require the removal of symbols that offend many members of the community. Others reply that such symbols are a form of free speech and should be protected.

Different universities have resolved similar conflicts in different ways. Some have enacted codes to protect their communities from forms of speech that are deemed to be insensitive to the feelings of other groups. Some have refused to impose such restrictions.

It is important to distinguish between the appropriateness of such communications and their status under the First Amendment. The fact that speech is protected by the First Amendment does not necessarily mean that it is right, proper, or civil. I am sure that the vast majority of Harvard students believe that hanging a Confederate flag in public view — or displaying a swastika in response — is insensitive and unwise because any satisfaction it gives to the students who display these symbols is far outweighed by the discomfort it causes to many others.

I share this view and regret that the students involved saw fit to behave in this fashion. Whether or not they merely wished to manifest their pride in the South — or to demonstrate the insensitivity of hanging Confederate flags, by mounting another offensive symbol in return — they must have known that they would upset many fellow students and ignore the decent regard for the feelings of others so essential to building and preserving a strong and harmonious community.

To disapprove of a particular form of communication, however, is not enough to justify prohibiting it. We are faced with a clear example of the conflict between our commitment to free speech and our desire to foster a community founded on mutual respect. Our society has wrestled with this problem for many years. Interpreting the First Amendment, the Supreme Court has clearly struck the balance in favor of free speech.

While communities do have the right to regulate speech in order to uphold aesthetic standards (avoiding defacement of buildings) or to protect the public from disturbing noise, rules of this kind must be applied across the board and cannot be enforced selectively to prohibit certain kinds of messages but not others.

Under the Supreme Court's rulings, as I read them, the display of swastikas or Confederate flags clearly falls within the protection of the free-speech clause of the First Amendment and cannot be forbidden simply because it offends the feelings of many members of the community. These rulings apply to all agencies of government, including public universities.

Although it is unclear to what extent the First Amendment is enforceable against private institutions, I have difficulty understanding why a university such as Harvard should have less free speech than the surrounding society — or than a public university.

One reason why the power of censorship is so dangerous is that it is extremely difficult to decide when a particular communication is offensive enough to warrant prohibition or to weigh the degree of offensiveness against the potential value of the communication. If we begin to forbid flags, it is only a short step to prohibiting offensive speakers.

I suspect that no community will become humane and caring by restricting what its members can say. The worst offenders will simply find other ways to irritate and insult.

In addition, once we start to declare certain things "offensive," with all the excitement and attention that will follow, I fear that much ingenuity will be exerted trying to test the limits, much time will be expended trying to draw tenuous distinctions, and the resulting publicity will eventually attract more attention to the offensive material than would ever have occurred otherwise.

Rather than prohibit such communications, with all the resulting risks, it would be better to ignore them, since students would then have little reason to create such displays and would soon abandon them. If this response is not possible — and one can understand why—the wisest course is to speak with those who perform insensitive acts and try to help them understand the effects of their actions on others.

Appropriate officials and faculty members should take the lead, as the Harvard House Masters have already done in this case. In talking with students, they should seek to educate and persuade, rather than resort to ridicule or intimidation, recognizing that only persuasion is likely to produce a lasting, beneficial effect. Through such effects, I believe that we act in the manner most consistent with our ideals as an educational institution and most calculated to help us create a truly understanding, supportive community.

—DEREK BOK, "Protecting Freedom of Expression at Harvard"

11h A student's critical analysis of an argument

For a class assignment, Milena Ateyea was asked to analyze Derek Bok's essay by focusing on the author's use of emotional, ethical, and logical appeals. Her critical analysis follows.

STUDENT WRITER

Milena Ateyea

A Curse and a Blessing

In 1991, when Derek Bok's essay "Protecting Freedom of Expression at Harvard" was first published in the Boston Globe, I had just come to America to escape the oppressive Communist regime in Bulgaria. Perhaps my background explains why I support Bok's argument that we should not put arbitrary limits on freedom of expression. Bok wrote the essay in response to a public display of Confederate flags and a swastika at Harvard, a situation that created a heated controversy among the students. As Bok notes, universities have struggled to achieve a balance between maintaining students' right of free speech and avoiding racist attacks. When choices must be made, however, Bok argues for preserving freedom of expression.

In order to support his claim and bridge the controversy, Bok uses a variety

Connects article to personal experience to create ethical appeal

Provides brief overview of Bok's argument

States Bok's central claim

Transition sentence

252

arg

11h

ARGUMENT

Analyzing
Arguments

of rhetorical strategies. The author first
immerses the reader in the controversy by
vividly describing the incident: two
Harvard students had hung Confederate
flags in public view, thereby "upsetting
students who equate the Confederacy with
slavery" (51). Another student, protesting
the flags, decided to display an even more
offensive symbol--the swastika. These
actions provoked heated discussions among
students. Some students believed that
school officials should remove the
offensive symbols, whereas others
suggested that the symbols "are a form of
free speech and should be protected" (51).
Bok establishes common ground between the
factions: he regrets the actions of the
offenders but does not believe we should
prohibit such actions just because we
disagree with them.

The author earns the reader's respect
because of his knowledge and through his
logical presentation of the issue. In
partial support of his position, Bok
refers to U.S. Supreme Court rulings,
which remind us that "the display of
swastikas or Confederate flags clearly
falls within the protection of the free-
speech clause of the First Amendment"
(52). The author also emphasizes the
danger of the slippery slope of censorship
when he warns the reader, "If we begin to
forbid flags, it is only a short step to
prohibiting offensive speakers" (52).
Overall, however, Bok's work lacks the
kinds of evidence that statistics,
interviews with students, and other

Examines the emotional appeal the author establishes through description

Links author's credibility to use of logical appeals

Reference to First Amendment serves as warrant for Bok's claim

Comments critically on author's evidence

representative examples of controversial conduct could provide. Thus, his essay may not be strong enough to persuade all readers to make the leap from this specific situation to his general conclusion.

Throughout, Bok's personal feelings are implied but not stated directly. As a lawyer who was president of Harvard for twenty years, Bok knows how to present his opinions respectfully without offending the feelings of the students. However, qualifying phrases like "I suspect that," and "Under the Supreme Court's rulings, as I read them" could weaken the effectiveness of his position. Furthermore, Bok's attempt to be fair to all seems to dilute the strength of his proposed solution. He suggests that one should either ignore the insensitive deeds in the hope that students might change their behavior, or talk to the offending students to help them comprehend how their behavior is affecting other students.

Nevertheless, although Bok's proposed solution to the controversy does not appear at first reading to be very strong, it may ultimately be effective. There is enough flexibility in his approach to withstand various tests, and Bok's solution is general enough that it can change with the times and adapt to community standards.

In writing this essay, Bok faced a challenging task: to write a short response to a specific situation that represents a very broad and controversial

Examines how Bok establishes ethical appeal

Identifies qualifying phrases that may weaken claim

Analyzes author's solution

Raises points that suggest Bok's solution may work

254

arg

11h

ARGUMENT

Analyzing
Arguments

issue. Some people may find that freedom
of expression is both a curse and a
blessing because of the difficulties it
creates. As one who has lived under a
regime that permitted very limited,
censored expression, I am all too aware
that I could not have written this
response in 1991 in Bulgaria. As a result,
I feel, like Derek Bok, that freedom of
expression is a blessing, in spite of any
temporary problems associated with it.

Returns to personal
experience in conclu-
sion

Work Cited

Bok, Derek. "Protecting Freedom of Expression on the
    Campus." Current Issues and Enduring Questions.
    Ed. Sylvan Barnet and Hugo Bedau. 6th ed. Boston:
    Bedford, 2002. 51-52. Rpt. of "Protecting Freedom
    of Expression at Harvard." Boston Globe 25 May
    1991.

FOR COLLABORATION

Working with a classmate, choose a brief argumentative text — a letter to the editor or editorial, a "My Turn" essay from *Newsweek* or an essay from *Time,* something from your school newspaper, even an advertisement or editorial cartoon. Then work together to analyze this text, playing both the believing *and* the doubting game, and identifying claim(s), reason(s), warrant(s), evidence, and qualifiers, as well as emotional, ethical, and logical appeals. Then, still working together, write a two-page double-spaced critical response to the text you have chosen. Finally, bring your chosen text and your critical response to class, and be prepared to present the results of your analysis.

ARGUMENT

A Student's Critical
Analysis of an
Argument

In this brief review for *USA Today*, music critic Steve Jones takes a look — and a listen — to Lauryn Hill's "MTV2 Presents Unplugged 2.0," a performance the singer later released as a double CD. What central claim(s) does Jones make in this review? What emotional, ethical, and logical appeals does he present in support of his claim (including in the headline and the image of Hill accompanying the review), and how effective are these appeals?

Lauryn Hill just shares the music

Unplugged 2.0: Lauryn Hill
MTV2, Sunday, 8 p.m. ET/PT
★★★½ (out of four)

By Steve Jones
USA TODAY

Watching Alicia Keys collect a record-tying five Grammys last month, you couldn't help but wonder about Lauryn Hill, largely silent since she hit similar heights three years ago.

Judging by her installment of *MTV2 Presents Unplugged 2.0*, the singer/rapper has been on a soul-searching journey aimed at something other than capitalizing on the success of *The Miseducation of Lauryn Hill.*

TV preview

By Scott Gries, ImageDirect/MTV

Return to spotlight: No star trappings for Hill's MTV gig.

The raw, two-hour set of all-new music finds the former Fugees star not only unplugged, but unadorned. Dressed simply in jeans, a denim jacket and New York Yankees cap, it's just Hill with her guitar, singing about the lessons she has learned since she left the spotlight. She reveals an engaging passion and honesty, confessing at one point in the show — taped last July at MTV's intimate Times Square studios — that many of the songs don't even have titles.

"I used to be a performer," says Hill, who will release a double CD of the performance this spring. "Now I'm just sharing the music I've been given. ... Fantasy is what people want. Reality is what they need, and I just retired from the fantasy part."

Like the music from her multiplatinum album, Hill's songs are deeply personal. She sings of stepping away from her public persona to keep from being trapped by the perceptions it brought. She rails against everything from self-delusion to government corruption to religious dogma without being overbearing or pretentious. She refuses to be held down by conceptual chains, traditions or expectations of others.

Hill is brought to tears when singing about the love of her life and father of her children, Rohan Marley, and how their relationship has evolved and grown. She laughingly confesses that she is a handful to put up with, but that he is her "peace of mind."

The show is a courageous re-entry into the public eye. She could have opted for a polished, radio-friendly comeback, but she has chosen to step out with no safety net of dancers or a band. It's not perfection — her voice sometimes cracks — but it gives her an opportunity to truly connect with her audience, experiment with song forms and vocal styles, and, most important, tell the truth as she sees it.

12

▼ Considering Visual Arguments

12a Becoming acquainted with visual arguments

Critical reading and writing involve analyzing visuals and images and the arguments they contain. How do you find out what a visual argument has to "say"? You do so in much the same way that you analyze *any* argument. You begin by looking at content: the elements Stephen Toulmin identifies — claims, reasons, warrants, and so on (see 11f) — as well as Aristotle's emotional, ethical, and logical appeals (see 11e). You also try to determine whether any cultural values, such as love of family or religious freedom, are evident. In addition, you analyze the design of the visual argument, whether it is a photograph, advertisement, diagram, cartoon, or some other visual representation. While doing so, you try to see how color, sound, and the arrangement of images, for example, affect the argument's effectiveness.

The rest of this chapter addresses the content and design of visual arguments in more detail. To help you understand this material, first take a look at the Mike Luckovich cartoon on the following page, which appeared in newspapers across the country during the anthrax attacks of autumn 2001. This cartoon contains very few words, yet it makes a series of subtle arguments. This cartoon will be referred to repeatedly in the discussion that follows.

vis

12b 257

ARGUMENT

Analyzing the
Content of Visual
Arguments

12b Analyzing the content of visual arguments

As you analyze the content of a visual argument, you would probably begin by asking what claim(s) the visual argument makes. Then you would move on to reasons, warrants, and evidence. To analyze the preceding Luckovich cartoon, for example, ask what its claim(s) might be. In a discussion with a group of first-year college students, several possible claims emerged:

POSSIBLE CLAIM The threat of bioterrorism affects people in different ways.

POSSIBLE CLAIM The innocence long associated with Schulz's America is no longer possible.

POSSIBLE CLAIM A symbolic security blanket will no longer offer protection.

POSSIBLE CLAIM In the face of bioterrorism, the best thing to do is continue on as normal.

All of these claims can be supported by the cartoon. If you choose the second one as most likely, what reason do you think would support it? A probable reason might be worded like this: *Because bioterrorism has now occurred on American soil, the kind of innocence associated with Schulz's America*

258

vis

12b

ARGUMENT

Considering Visual
Arguments

is no longer possible. You could go on to identify warrants and evidence in support of this claim — and you would be well on your way to analyzing this visual argument.

When doing this kind of analysis, then, ask yourself the following questions:

- What *claim(s)* does the visual argument make?
- What *reasons* are attached to the claim, and how well are they supported by *evidence?*
- What *warrant(s)* (or assumptions) connect the claim to the reasons?

EXERCISE 12.1

Reproduced below and on p. 259 is the homepage of the Official Peanuts Web site and a page from the Benetton Web site. Choose one, and study it carefully. Then, working alone or with one or two other students, make a list of the possible claims the Web site is making.

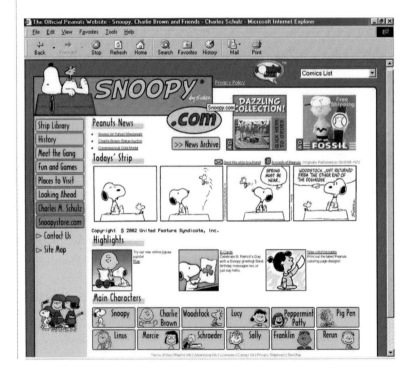

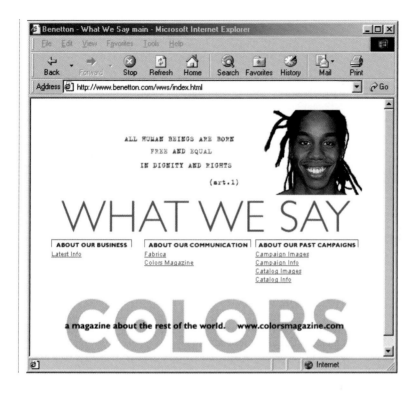

You will also want to analyze a visual argument in terms of the appeals it makes and the cultural values it may advocate or criticize. Consider questions like these as well:

- *Emotional appeals.* What feelings does the visual argument elicit? Does it make you feel guilty, proud, patriotic? What specifically in the visual argument creates these emotions?

- *Ethical appeals.* How would you describe the character — or credibility — of the visual argument, and how is that credibility demonstrated visually? Does the visual argument call on authority of any kind to establish credibility? What symbols, if any, does the visual argument use to establish its credibility?

- *Logical appeals.* Are images arranged in a logical way? Is an important image, for instance, given more space than a less important one? Do words and images work together to create a logical cause-effect relationship? How are any examples used in the visual argument?

• *Cultural values.* Are any particular values reflected in the visual argument? (The flag, for example, often evokes the cultural values of democracy and freedom.) Does the visual argument reinforce and approve of these values — or does it challenge or even satirize them?

Look again at the cartoon by Mike Luckovich on p. 257, and consider its appeals and cultural values. What feelings does the cartoon elicit? nostalgia? anger? fear? sadness? Do the words and images seem to have a logical arrangement? In the lower left-hand corner, Luckovich says "apologies to Schulz." What kinds of appeals does this remark make?

12c Analyzing the design of visual arguments

Creators of visual arguments consider the effects of design very carefully. The relative placement of various elements, and the use of color, sound, or video, are some of the design elements to notice. Here are some questions to ask yourself as you analyze a visual argument's design:

• What detail(s) is your eye first drawn to? Why is your attention drawn to that spot, and what effect does this attention-getting device have on your response to the argument?

• What is in the foreground, and what is in the background? What is placed in the center or high up as opposed to low? What effect do these choices have on the argument itself?

• Are any words or images tucked away in a corner or downplayed? What effect do they have on the argument?

• Do the colors that are used "match" the argument being made, or are they somehow in conflict with it? Does the use of color enhance the argument, and, if so, in what ways? If black and white are used instead of color, are they appropriate for the particular argument?

• If sound or video is used, how effective is it in conveying the argument's message?

• What is the relationship between words and images in the argument? How well do they work together to make the point?

• Are any words or images repeated? If so, does the repetition help to get the point across?

• If you are analyzing a Web page, what overall impression does it create at first glance, and how does closer inspection either change or reaffirm that impression? How are you guided along the Web page; how easy is it to negotiate? Do such considerations affect the argument the page is making?

Return to Mike Luckovich's cartoon, and consider some of its design elements. Is your eye first drawn to the left side of the picture, which features a sickly looking tree and ominous (gas?) clouds as well as Linus wearing the gas mask, or to some other point? The bubble with words partially obscures one of the clouds—what do you think that suggests about the girls' attitude? What is the significance of Linus's standing still while the girls are marching along? Why do you think Luckovich puts his "apologies to Schulz" remark in the lower left-hand corner? How might the effect of the cartoon be different if it appeared in color?

● **EXERCISE 12.2**

Take a close look at the following image, and use the guidelines in this chapter to analyze its content and design. As a result of your analysis, write a brief (one-page) response explaining *how* the Adbusters image achieves its effects and analyzing the values it implicitly holds.

● **EXERCISE 12.3**

Look at the cartoon below, which appeared in the *San Francisco Chronicle* on September 30, 2001. Using the advice in this chapter for analyzing content and design of a visual argument, try your hand at analyzing this cartoon. Then write up the results of your analysis as a set of notes, and bring them to class for discussion.

FOR COLLABORATION

Working with one or two members of your class, get a good, clear copy of your campus map. (Check to see if the campus map might be on your college or university's Web site and whether that electronic map is interactive.) Then take turns answering the following questions: How is your campus laid out — as a circle, a rectangle, a series of concentric circles, or smaller to larger squares? Is the campus divided in any way — by a river, a bridge, a large building? What occupies the central or most premium space on campus — administrative offices, classrooms, dorms, or something else? What occupies the outlying margins of the campus? What do your answers suggest about what is most valued on campus? Try to push your analysis as far as possible, arguing out any points of disagreement. Then prepare a collaboratively written analysis of your campus map, and bring it to class for discussion.

THINKING CRITICALLY ABOUT YOUR USE OF VISUAL ARGUMENTS

Take a look at a piece of your writing (an essay, a Web document, a report, poster, brochure, and so on) that uses visuals to make an argument. Using the guidelines offered in this chapter, evaluate the effectiveness of your own visual argument. If you have not created such a piece of writing, take a project that does not use visuals to advance its argument and reread it, noting ways that visuals could make the argument more effective.

13

Constructing Arguments

Chances are, you've been making convincing arguments since early childhood, and your parents or other providers slowly learned to respond to these arguments. But if parents, other family members, and friends are not always easy to convince, then the job of making effective arguments to those unfamiliar with you presents even more challenges. It is especially difficult to argue with people who are thousands of miles away and are encountering your argument only in cyberspace. This chapter guides you in taking up those challenges as you craft effective arguments of your own. ■

13a Understanding the purposes of argument

Since all language is in some sense argumentative, it goes almost without saying that the purposes of argument will vary widely. For many years, however, traditional notions of argument tended to highlight one purpose — winning. Although winning is still one important purpose of argument, studies of the argument strategies of people from groups historically excluded from public debate — including women and people of color — have demonstrated that it is by no means the only purpose. Nor is winning always going to be *your* purpose. For instance, if you are trying to decide whether to major in business or in chemistry, you may want to consider, or "argue," all sides of the issue. Your purpose is hardly to win out over someone else; instead, it is to understand your choices in order to make a wise decision.

■ *To win*

The most traditional purpose of academic argument, arguing *to win* is used in campus debating societies, in political debates, in trials, and often in business. The writer or speaker aims to control the audience, to present a position that prevails over or defeats the positions of others. Presidential debates and trials, for example, focus most often not on changing the opponent's mind but on

→ What is the purpose of your argument — to convince others? to reach a good decision? to change yourself? (13a)

→ Is the point you want to make arguable? (13b)

→ Have you formulated a clear claim to which you have attached good reasons and a warrant? (13c)

→ Have you formulated a strong argumentative thesis, and have you qualified it sufficiently? (13c)

→ How have you established your own credibility in the argument? (13e)

→ Have you considered, and addressed, counterarguments? (13e3)

→ How have you incorporated logical appeals into your argument? (13f)

→ How have you used emotional appeals in your argument? (13g)

→ How have you used sources in your argument, and how effectively are they integrated into your argument? (13h)

→ How have you used visuals to help make your argument? (13i)

→ How is your argument organized? Do you make use of either the classical Aristotelian or the contemporary Toulmin system to guide organization? (13j)

→ What design elements have you considered in composing your argument? How effective is the design of the essay or piece of writing? (13j)

defeating him or her in order to appeal to another party — the voting public, the judge, or the jury.

■ *To convince*

More often than not, out-and-out defeat of another is not only unrealistic but undesirable. Rather, the goal is *to convince* other persons that they should change their minds about an issue. Doing so calls on a writer to provide reasons so compelling that the audience willingly agrees with the writer's conclusion. Such is the goal of Dr. Jack Kevorkian, who knows he cannot conquer or defeat those who oppose assisted suicide. Rather, Kevorkian realizes he must provide reasons compelling enough to change people's minds. Such would be your purpose if, for example, you were asked to prepare a report on the major causes of the Civil War: your job would be to convince your readers that you have identified the major causes.

cons

13b

266

ARGUMENT

Constructing
Arguments

■ *To reach a decision or explore an issue*

This purpose often calls on the writer to enter into conversation with others, to collaborate in seeking the best possible understanding of a problem, exploring all possible approaches and choosing the best alternative. Argument *to decide or explore* seeks not to conquer or control others or even to convince. Rather, it seeks a sharing of information and perspectives in order to make informed political, professional, and personal choices. This will be your purpose in many situations — from trying to decide which computer to buy to exploring with your family the best health care system for an elderly relative.

■ *To change yourself*

Sometimes you will find yourself arguing primarily with yourself, and those arguments often take the form of intense meditations on a theme, or even of prayer. In such cases, you may be hoping *to transform something in yourself* or to reach peace of mind on a troubling subject. If you know a familiar mantra or prayer, for example, think of what it "argues" for and how it uses quiet meditation to help achieve that goal.

13b Determining whether a statement can be argued

In much of your work in college, you will be asked to take a position and argue for that position — whether to analyze a trend or explain a historical event or prove a mathematical equation. Such work will usually call for you to convince or decide. To do so, you will need to make an arguable statement or claim based on the statement and then to present good reasons and evidence in support of the claim.

An early step in the process of argument to convince or decide is to make a statement about a topic and then check to see that the statement can, in fact, be argued. An arguable statement should have three characteristics:

1. It should attempt to convince readers of something, change their minds about something, or urge them to do something — or explore a topic in order to make a wise decision.
2. It should address a problem for which no easily acceptable solution exists or ask a question to which no absolute answer exists.
3. It should present a position that readers might realistically have varying perspectives on.

ARGUABLE STATEMENT Video games lead to violent behavior.

This statement seeks to convince, addresses a problem — causes of violent behavior — that has no clear-cut solution, and takes a position many disagree with.

UNARGUABLE STATEMENT Video games earn millions of dollars every year for the companies that produce them.

This statement can easily be verified and thus offers a poor basis for argument.

ARGUMENT

Formulating an Argumentative Thesis and Backing It Up

● **EXERCISE 13.1**

Using the three characteristics just mentioned, decide which of the following statements are arguable and which are not.

1. *A Beautiful Mind* was the best movie of the last twenty years.

2. The climate of the earth is gradually getting warmer.

3. The United States must further reduce social spending in order to balance the budget.

4. Shakespeare died in 1616.

5. Marlowe really wrote the plays of Shakespeare.

6. Water boils at 212 degrees Fahrenheit.

7. Van Gogh's paintings are the work of a madman.

8. The incidence of breast cancer has risen in the last ten years.

9. Abortion denies the fetus's inherent right to life.

10. A fifty-five-mile-per-hour speed limit lowers accident rates.

www ● bedford stmartins.com/ smhandbook

For additional exercises on recognizing argument, click on

▶ **Exercise Central**
  ▶ **Argument**

13c Formulating an argumentative thesis and backing it up

Once you have an arguable statement, you need to develop a working thesis. One way to do so is to follow Stephen Toulmin's approach. As you may recall from Chapter 11, this approach begins with the following elements: a **claim** (usually an arguable statement); one or more **reasons** for the claim; and **warrants** (assumptions — sometimes unstated — that link a claim and reasons together). Let's apply these elements to a specific topic — the use of pesticides.

- *Begin with an arguable statement (or initial claim).* The following statement is arguable because it aims to convince, it addresses an issue with no one identifiable answer, and it can realistically be disputed.

●···· For more on developing a working thesis, see 3b.

●···· For a more detailed discussion of Toulmin's approach, see 11f.

ARGUABLE STATEMENT (OR INITIAL CLAIM)	Pesticides should be banned.

- *Attach a good reason.* Although the preceding statement does make a kind of claim — that pesticides should be banned — it offers no reason for doing so. To develop a claim that can become the working thesis for an argument, you need to include at least one good reason to support the arguable statement.

REASON	Because they endanger the lives of farm workers.
WORKING THESIS (CLAIM WITH REASON ATTACHED)	Because they endanger the lives of farm workers, pesticides should be banned.

www • bedford stmartins.com/ smhandbook

For additional help with composing arguments, click on

► Links
  ► Argument

- *Develop or identify the warrant(s).* Once you have your working thesis, it's a good idea to examine your warrant(s). Doing so can help you test your reasoning and strengthen your argument. In this instance, you might identify several warrants (underlying assumptions) that support the working thesis.

WORKING THESIS	Because they endanger the lives of farm workers, pesticides should be banned.
WARRANT 1	Workers have a right to a safe working environment.
WARRANT 2	Substances that endanger the lives of innocent workers deserve to be banned.

Toulmin suggests that once you have an argumentative thesis, you may want to use **qualifiers** to make it more precise and thus less susceptible to criticism. The preceding thesis, for example, might be qualified in this way.

Because they *often* endanger the lives of farm workers, *most* pesticides should be banned.

EXERCISE 13.2

Using two arguable statements from Exercise 13.1 or two that you create, formulate two working argumentative theses, identifying the claim, reason(s), and warrant(s) for each.

EXERCISE 13.3

Formulate an arguable statement, and create a working argumentative thesis, for two of the following general topics.

1. the Palestinian-Israeli conflict

cons

13e 269

ARGUMENT
Establishing
Credibility through
Ethical Appeals

2. mandatory testing of prison inmates for HIV
3. free access to the World Wide Web for all legal residents
4. a new federal student-loan program
5. human cloning

FOR COLLABORATION

Working with two other members of your class, find two current advertisements you consider particularly eye-catching and persuasive. Then work out what central claim each ad is making, and identify reasons and warrant(s) in support of the claim. Finally, prepare a brief collaborative report of your findings for the class.

13d Formulating good reasons

In his *Rhetoric,* Aristotle discusses the various ways one can support a claim. Torture, he notes, makes for a very convincing argument but not one that reasonable people will resort to. In effecting real changes in minds and hearts, we need instead to rely on *good reasons* that establish our credibility, that appeal to logic, and that appeal to emotion. In Chapter 11 (see 11e), you used these appeals to analyze the arguments of others; now these appeals will help you construct an argument of your own.

13e Establishing credibility through ethical appeals

To make your argument convincing, you must first gain the respect and trust of your readers, or establish your credibility with them. The ancient Greeks called this particular kind of character appeal *ethos,* and we refer to it as **ethical appeals**. In general, writers can establish credibility in three ways:

1. by demonstrating knowledge about the topic at hand
2. by establishing common ground with the audience in the form of respect for their points of view and concern for their welfare
3. by demonstrating fairness and evenhandedness

1 Demonstrating knowledge

A writer can establish credibility first by demonstrating his or her knowledge about the topic at hand. You can, for instance, show that you have some personal experience with the subject, such as a background as a Head Start teacher who is arguing for increased funding of this preschool program. In addition, if you show that you have thought about the subject carefully or researched it, you can establish a confident tone.

To determine whether you can effectively present yourself as knowledgeable enough to argue an issue, consider the following questions:

- Can you provide information about your topic from sources other than your own knowledge?
- What are the sources of your information?
- How reliable are your sources?
- Do any sources contradict each other? If so, can you account for or resolve the contradictions?
- If you have personal experience relating to the issue, would telling about this experience help support your claim?

These questions may help you see what other work you need to do to establish credibility. They may well show that you must do more research, check sources, resolve contradictions, refocus your working thesis, or even change your topic.

2 Establishing common ground

Many arguments between people or groups are doomed to end without resolution because the two sides occupy no common ground, no starting point of agreement. They are, to use an informal phrase, coming from completely different places. Such has often been the case, for example, in India-Pakistan talks, in which the beginning positions of each party were so far apart that they could not reach a resolution.

Lack of common ground also dooms many arguments that take place in our everyday lives. If you and your roommate cannot agree on how often to clean your apartment, for instance, the difficulty may well be that your definition of a clean apartment conflicts radically with your roommate's. You may find, in fact, that you will not be able to resolve such issues until you can establish common definitions, ones that can turn futile quarrels into constructive arguments.

For more about establishing common ground, see Chapter 25.

Common ground is just as important in written arguments as it is in diplomatic negotiations or personal disputes. The following questions can help you find common ground in presenting an argument:

- What are the differing perspectives on this issue?
- What aspects of the issue can you find on which all sides agree?
- How can you express such agreement clearly to all sides?
- How can you discover — and consider — opinions on this issue that differ from your own?
- How can you use language — occupational, regional, or ethnic varieties of English, or languages other than English — to establish common ground with those you address?

If you turn to Heather Ricker's essay in 13k, you will see that she attempts to establish common ground by assuming that all her readers are concerned about and feel responsible for their children.

3 Demonstrating fairness and considering counterarguments

In arguing a position, writers must demonstrate fairness toward opposing arguments, sometimes called *counterarguments* (see 13j2). Audiences are more inclined to give credibility to writers who seem to be fairly considering and representing their opponents' views than to those who seem to be ignoring or distorting such views. Part of your job as an effective writer, then, might involve anticipating possible counterarguments to your writing and establishing yourself as open-minded and evenhanded. The following questions can help you discover ways of doing so:

- How can you show that you are taking into account all significant points of view?
- How can you demonstrate that you understand and sympathize with points of view other than your own?
- What can you do to show that you have considered evidence carefully, even that which does not support your position?

Some writers, instead of demonstrating fairness, may make unjustified attacks on an opponent's credibility. Such attacks, which are known as **ethical fallacies,** should be avoided in your writing.

For more information on ethical fallacies, see 11g1.

cons

272

13e

ARGUMENT

Constructing
Arguments

● **EXERCISE 13.4**

Study carefully the following advertisement for a mutual fund, and then list the ways in which the copywriters demonstrate knowledge, establish common ground, and demonstrate fairness. Do you think they succeed or fail in establishing credibility?

Is Your Money Where Your Heart Is?

It is important to invest your money in companies that have proven themselves to be responsible both financially and socially. It is important for you and it is important for the world.

At Working Assets Common Holdings we invest your money in companies that are successful, stable, and have a positive history of caring for people and the planet.

• Working Assets is one of the oldest and largest socially responsible mutual fund families in the US.

• Working Assets has seven mutual fund portfolios to meet a range of investment objectives.
• IRAS, 403B7 Plans, and Automatic Investment programs are available.
• Our minimum investment is $250.

Please call us for a no-obligation prospectus with complete details of fees and expenses. Please read it carefully before you invest or send money.

800-223-7010

Secure the future with socially responsible investing.

WORKING ASSETS®

COMMON HOLDINGS

111 Pine Street • SanFrancisco, CA 94111

©1993. Distributed by Working Assets Capital Management.

● **EXERCISE 13.5**

Using a working argumentative thesis you drafted for Exercise 13.2 or 13.3, write a paragraph or two describing how you would go about establishing your credibility in arguing that thesis.

13f Incorporating logical appeals

While the character we present in writing always exerts a strong appeal (or lack of appeal) in an argument, our credibility alone cannot and should not carry the full burden of convincing readers. Indeed, many are inclined to view the logic of the argument—the reasoning behind it—as equally if not more important. This section will examine the most effective kinds of **logical appeals** for a written argument: examples, precedents, and narratives; authority and testimony; causes and effects; and inductive and deductive reasoning.

1 Providing examples, precedents, and narratives

Just as a picture can sometimes be worth a thousand words, so can a well-conceived **example** be extremely valuable in arguing a point. Examples are used most often to support generalizations or to bring abstractions to life. In an argument about violence and video games, for instance, you might make the general statement that such games send a message that violence is fun; you might then illustrate your generalization with these examples:

> The makers of the game *Quake,* for example, present deadly and deranged acts of violence as entertainment, while the makers of *Postal* imply that preying on the defenseless is acceptable behavior by marketing a game in which players kill innocent, helpless victims.

The generalization would mean little without the examples.

Examples can also help us understand abstractions. *Famine,* for instance, may be difficult for us to think about in the abstract, but a graphic description of a drought-stricken community, its riverbed cracked and dry, its people listless, emaciated, and with stomachs bloated by hunger, speaks directly to our understanding.

Precedents are particular kinds of examples taken from the past. The most common use of precedent occurs in law, where an attorney may ask a judge to rule that a defendant was negligent, for example, because the Supreme Court upheld a ruling of negligence in an almost identical case ten years earlier. Precedent appears in everyday arguments as well. If, as part of a proposal for increasing lighting in the library garage, you point out that the university has increased lighting in four similar garages in the past year, you are arguing on the basis of precedent.

In research writing (see Chapters 14–19), you usually must list your sources for any examples or precedents not based on your own knowledge.

For a discussion of acknowledging sources, see Chapter 18.

The following questions can help you check any use of example or precedent:

- How representative are the examples?
- Are they sufficient in strength or number to lead to a generalization?
- In what ways do they support your point?

cons

274

13f

ARGUMENT

Constructing
Arguments

- How closely does the precedent relate to the point you're trying to make? Are the situations really similar?
- How timely is the precedent? (What would have been applicable in 1520 is not necessarily applicable today.)

Because storytelling is universal, **narratives** can be very persuasive in helping readers understand and accept the logic of an argument. In arguing for increased funding for the homeless, for instance, you might include a brief narrative about a day in the life of a homeless person to dramatize the issue and help readers *see* the need for more funding.

Stories drawn from your own experience can exert particular appeal to readers, for they not only help make your point in true-to-life, human terms but also help readers know you better and therefore identify with you more closely. In arguing for a stronger government campaign against smoking, former President Clinton often drew on personal stories of his own family's experience with lung cancer. In much the same way, the writer bell hooks tells the story of her own experience with elitist educational institutions as a way of arguing for changes in those institutions.

If you include stories in an argument, make sure they are used not merely to add interest but also to support your thesis. In general, do not rely solely on the power of stories to carry your argument, since readers usually expect writers to state and argue their reasons more directly and abstractly as well. An additional danger if you use only your own experiences is that you can seem focused too much on yourself (and perhaps not enough on your readers).

As you develop your own arguments, keep in mind that while narratives can provide effective logical support, they may be used equally effectively for ethical or emotional appeals as well.

FOR MULTILINGUAL WRITERS: Counting Your Own Experience

You may have learned that stories based on your own personal experience don't count in academic arguments. If so, reconsider this advice, for showing an audience that you have personal experience with a topic can carry strong persuasive appeal with many English-speaking audiences. As with all evidence used in an argument, however, narratives based on your own experience must be pertinent to the topic, understandable to the audience, and clearly related to your purpose.

→ Does the narrative support your thesis?
→ Will the story's significance to the argument be clear to your readers?
→ Is the story one of several good reasons or pieces of evidence — or does it have to carry the main burden of the argument?

2 Citing authority and testimony

Another way to support an argument logically is to cite an **authority**. In recent decades, the use of authority has figured prominently in the controversy over smoking. Since the U.S. surgeon general's 1963 announcement that smoking is hazardous to health, many Americans have quit smoking, largely persuaded by the authority of the scientists offering the evidence.

But as with other strategies for building support for an argumentative claim, citing authorities demands careful consideration. Ask yourself the following questions to be sure you are using authorities effectively:

- Is the authority timely? (The argument that the United States should pursue a policy just because it was supported by Thomas Jefferson will probably fail because Jefferson's time was so radically different from ours.)

- Is the authority qualified to judge the topic at hand? (To cite a movie star in an essay on linguistics is not likely to strengthen your argument.)

- Is the authority likely to be known and respected by readers? (To cite an unfamiliar authority without some identification will lessen the impact of the evidence.)

●— For a discussion of the *false authority* fallacy, see 11g1.

Authorities are commonly cited in research writing, which often relies on the findings of other people. In addition, you may cite authorities in an assignment that asks you to review the literature of any field.

Testimony — the evidence an authority presents in support of a claim — is a feature of much contemporary argument. If testimony is timely, accurate, representative, and provided by a respected authority, then it, like authority itself, can add powerful support to an argument. In an essay for a literature class, for example, you might argue that a new edition of a literary work will open up many new areas of interpretation. You could strengthen this argument by adding a quotation from the

●— For a complete discussion of research, see Chapters 14 – 23.

For a discussion
of acknowledg-
ing sources, see
Chapter 18.

author's biographer, noting that the new edition carries out the author's intentions much more closely than the previous edition did.

In research writing, you should acknowledge and list your sources for authority and for testimony not based on your own knowledge.

> **FOR MULTILINGUAL WRITERS: Bringing in Other Voices**
>
> Sometimes quoting authorities will prompt you to use language other than standard academic English. For instance, if you're writing about political relations between Mexico and the United States, you might quote a leader of a Mexican American organization; using that person's *own words* — which may be partly or entirely in Spanish or a regional variety of English — can carry extra power, calling up a voice from a pertinent community. See Chapter 26 for advice about using varieties of English and other languages.

3 Establishing causes and effects

Showing that one event is the cause — or the effect — of another can sometimes help support an argument. To take an everyday example, suppose you are trying to explain, in a petition to change your grade in a course, why you were unable to take the final examination. In such a case, you would probably try to trace the **causes** of your failure to appear — the death of your grandmother followed by the theft of your car, perhaps — so that the committee reading the petition would consider anew the **effect** — your not taking the examination.

Tracing causes often lays the groundwork for an argument, particularly if the effect of the causes is one we would like to change. In an environmental science class, for example, a student may argue that a national law regulating smokestack emissions from utility plants is needed because (1) acid rain on the east coast originates from emissions at utility plants in the Midwest, (2) acid rain kills trees and other vegetation, (3) utility lobbyists have prevented midwestern states from passing strict laws controlling emissions from such plants, and (4) in the absence of such laws, acid rain will destroy most eastern forests by 2020. In this case, the first point is that the emissions cause acid rain; the second, that acid rain causes destruction in eastern forests; and the third, that states have not acted to break the cause-effect relationship established by the first two points. The fourth point ties all of the previous points together to provide an overall argument from effect: unless X, then Y.

In fact, a cause-effect relationship is often extremely difficult to establish. Scientists and politicians continue to disagree, for example, over the extent to which acid rain is responsible for the so-called dieback of many eastern forests. If you can show that X definitely causes Y, though, you will have a powerful argument at your disposal.

4 Using inductive and deductive reasoning

Traditionally, logical arguments are classified as using either inductive or deductive reasoning, both of which almost always work together. **Inductive reasoning,** most simply, is the process of making a generalization based on a number of specific instances. If you find you are ill on ten occasions after eating seafood, for example, you will likely draw the inductive generalization that seafood makes you ill. It may not be an absolute certainty that seafood was the culprit, but the *probability* lies in that direction.

Deductive reasoning, on the other hand, reaches a conclusion by assuming a general principle (known as a **major premise**) and then applying that principle to a specific case (the **minor premise**). In practice, this general principle is usually derived from induction. The inductive generalization *Seafood makes me ill,* for instance, could serve as the major premise for the deductive argument *Since all seafood makes me ill, the plate of it just put before me is certain to make me ill.*

Deductive arguments like these have traditionally been analyzed as **syllogisms,** three-part statements containing a major premise, a minor premise, and a conclusion.

MAJOR PREMISE	All people die.
MINOR PREMISE	I am a person.
CONCLUSION	I will die.

Syllogisms, however, are too rigid and absolute to serve in arguments about questions that have no absolute answers, and they often lack any appeal to an audience. As you may recall from Chapter 11, Aristotle came up with a simpler alternative, the **enthymeme,** which calls on the audience to supply the implied major premise. Consider the following example:

Since violent video games can be addictive and cause psychological harm, players and their parents must carefully evaluate such games and monitor their use.

You can analyze this enthymeme by restating it in the form of two premises and a conclusion.

MAJOR PREMISE Games that cause harm to players should be evaluated and monitored.

MINOR PREMISE Violent video games cause addiction and psychological harm to players.

CONCLUSION Violent video games should be evaluated and monitored.

Note that the major premise is one the writer can count on an audience agreeing with or supplying: concern for children and common sense demand that games that cause harm to players should be evaluated and monitored. As such, this premise is *assumed* rather than stated in the enthymeme. By thus inspiring audience participation, an enthymeme actually gets the audience to contribute to the argument.

Whether it is expressed as a syllogism or an enthymeme, a deductive conclusion is only as strong as the premises on which it is based. The citizen who argues that *Ed is a crook and shouldn't be elected to public office* is arguing deductively, based on an implied major premise: *No crook should be elected to public office.* In this case, most people would agree with this major premise. So the issue in this argument rests on the minor premise—that Ed is a crook. Only if that premise can be proved satisfactorily are we likely to accept the deductive conclusion that Ed shouldn't be elected.

At other times, the unstated premise may be more problematic. The person who says, *Don't bother to ask for Jack's help with physics—he's a jock* is arguing deductively on the basis of an implied major premise: *Jocks don't know anything about physics.* In this case, careful listeners would demand proof of the unstated premise. Because bigoted or prejudiced statements often rest on this kind of reasoning—a type of **logical fallacy**—writers should be particularly alert to it.

For a discussion of logical fallacies, see 11g3.

A helpful variation on Aristotle's deductive argument (the syllogism) is the system developed by Stephen Toulmin, which looks for claims, reasons, and warrants rather than major and minor premises. In Toulmin's terms, the argument about video games looks like this:

For more on the Toulmin system, see 11f, 13c, and 13j2.

CLAIM	Violent video games should be carefully evaluated and their use monitored.
REASON(S)	Violent video games cause addiction and psychological harm to players.
WARRANT	Games that cause harm to players should be evaluated and monitored.

Note that in Toulmin's system the warrant—which is often an unstated assumption—serves the same function as the assumed major premise in the enthymeme shown above.

EXERCISE 13.6

The following sentences contain deductive arguments based on implied major premises. Identify each of the implied premises.

1. Active euthanasia is morally acceptable when it promotes the best interests of everyone concerned and violates no one's rights.

2. Women soldiers should not serve in combat positions because doing so would expose them to a much higher risk of death.

3. Animals can't talk; therefore they can't feel pain as humans do.

EXERCISE 13.7

Analyze the advertisement in Exercise 13.4 for the use of examples, precedents, and narratives; authority and testimony; causes and effects; and induction and deduction.

EXERCISE 13.8

Using a working argumentative thesis you drafted for Exercise 13.2 or 13.3, write a paragraph describing the logical appeals you would use to support the thesis.

13g Considering emotional appeals

Most successful arguments appeal to our hearts as well as to our minds. Thus, good writers supplement appeals to logic and reason with **emotional appeals** to their readers. This principle was vividly demonstrated a number of years ago, when we first began hearing about famine in Africa. Facts and figures (logical appeals) convinced many that the famine was real and serious. What brought an outpouring of aid, however, was the arresting emotional power of photographs of children, at once skeletal and bloated, dying of starvation. As you saw in Chapter 12, visual arguments can be extremely effective. Writers can gain similarly powerful effects with the careful use of stories—and with description, concrete language, and figurative language—as well as by shaping an appeal to their audience.

1 Using description and concrete language

Like photographs, vivid, detailed **description** can bring a moving immediacy to any argument. The student in 3d1 amassed plenty of facts and figures, including diagrams and maps, to illustrate the problem of wheelchair access to the library. But her first draft seemed lifeless in spite of all her information. She decided, therefore, to ask a friend who used a wheelchair to accompany her to the library—and she revised her proposal, opening it with a detailed description of that visit and its many frustrations for her friend.

Concrete language stands at the heart of effective description and hence helps build emotional appeal. Although the student in 3d1, for instance, could have said simply that her friend "had trouble entering the library," such a general statement would not appeal to readers' emotions by helping them imagine themselves in a similar position. Her actual version, full of concrete description, does so: "Maria inched her heavy wheelchair up the narrow, steep entrance ramp, her arms straining to pull up the last twenty feet, her face pinched with the sheer effort."

2 Using figurative language

For more about
figurative lan-
guage, see 27d.

Figurative language, or figures of speech, are crucial elements in painting detailed and vivid pictures and building understanding. They do so by relating something new or unfamiliar to something the audience knows well (saying, for example, that the Internet is like an information *highway*) and by making striking comparisons between something you are writing about and something else that helps a reader visualize, identify with, or understand it.

Figures of speech include metaphors, similes, and analogies. **Metaphors** compare two things directly: *Richard the Lion-Hearted; old age is the evening of life.* **Similes** make comparisons using *like* or *as: Richard is as brave as a lion; old age is like the evening of life.* **Analogies** are extended metaphors or similes that compare an unfamiliar concept or process to a more familiar one to help the reader understand the unfamiliar concept.

I see the Internet as a city struggling to be built, its laws only now being formulated, its notions of social order arising out of the needs of its citizens and the demands of their environment. Like any city, the Net has its charlatans and its thieves as well as its poets, engineers, and philosophers. . . . Our experience of the Internet will be determined by how we master its core competencies. They are the design principles that are shaping the electronic city.   – PAUL GILSTER, *Digital Literacy*

A student arguing for a more streamlined course-registration process may find good use for an analogy, saying that the current process makes students feel like laboratory rats in a maze. This analogy, which suggests manipulation, victims, and a clinical coldness, creates a vivid description and hence adds emotional appeal to the argument. For the analogy to work effectively, however, the student would have to show that the current registration process has a number of similarities to a laboratory maze, such as confused students wandering through complex bureaucratic channels and into dead ends.

As you use analogies or other figurative language to bring emotion into an argument, be careful not to overdo it. Emotional appeals that are unfair or overly dramatic—known as **emotional fallacies**—may serve only to cloud your readers' judgment and ultimately diminish your argument.

For a discussion of emotional fallacies, see 11g2.

3 Shaping your appeal to your audience

As with appeals to credibility and logic, appealing to emotions is effective only insofar as it moves your particular audience. A student arguing for increased lighting in campus parking garages, for instance, might consider the emotions such a discussion might raise (fear of attackers, anger at being subjected to such danger, compassion for victims of such attacks), decide which emotions the intended audience would be most responsive to, and then look for descriptive and figurative language to carry out such an appeal.

In a leaflet to be distributed on campus or in an online notice to a student listserv, for example, the writer might describe the scene in a dimly lit garage as a student parks her car and then has to walk to an exit alone down shadowy corridors. Parking in the garage might be compared to venturing into a dangerous jungle.

In a proposal to the university administration, on the other hand, the writer might describe past attacks on students in campus garages and the negative publicity and criticism these provoked among students, parents, alumni, and other groups. For the administration, the writer might compare the lighting in the garages to high-risk gambling, arguing that increased lighting would lower the odds of future attacks.

Notice that shaping your appeal to a specific audience calls on you to consider very carefully the language you use. The student arguing for better lighting in campus parking garages, for instance, would probably stick to standard academic English in a proposal to the university administration but might well want to use more informal language, even slang, in a leaflet written for students.

● **EXERCISE 13.9**

Make a list of the common human emotions that might be attached to the following topics, and suggest appropriate ways to appeal to those emotions in a specific audience you choose to address.

1. banning smoking on campus
2. airport security
3. generating nuclear power
4. television evangelism
5. steroid use among athletes

● **EXERCISE 13.10**

Using a working argumentative thesis you formulated for Exercise 13.2 or 13.3, make a list of the emotional appeals most appropriate to your topic and audience. Then spend ten to fifteen minutes brainstorming, looking for descriptive and figurative language to carry out the appeals.

FOR COLLABORATION

Working with two or three classmates, read the following paragraph, and then write a paragraph evaluating its use of description and figurative language, and its appeal to various audiences.

In 1973, all women in the United States became legally entitled to have abortions performed in hospitals by licensed physicians. Before they were legal, abortions were frequently performed by persons who bore more resemblance to butchers than they did to doctors. The all-too-common result was serious complications or death for the woman. Since 1989, states have been able to restrict where and when abortions are performed. Even if the 1973 Supreme Court decision is completely reversed, abortion will not end. Instead, women will again resort to illegal abortions, and there will be a return to the slaughterhouse. Since abortions are going to take place no matter what the law says, why not have them done safely and legally in hospitals instead of in basements, alleys, or dirty compartments in some killing shed? The decision to have an abortion is not an easy one to make, and I believe that a woman who makes it deserves to have her wish carried out in the very safest way possible. Critics of abortion stress the importance of the unborn child's life. At the very least, they should also take the woman's life and safety into consideration.

13h   Using sources in an argument

In constructing a written argument, it is usually necessary — and often essential — to use sources. The key to persuading people to accept your argument is good reasons; and even if your assignment doesn't specify that you must consult outside sources, they are often the most effective way of finding and establishing these reasons. Sources can help you in a number of ways:

- to provide background information on your topic
- to demonstrate your knowledge of the topic to readers
- to cite authority and testimony in support of your thesis
- to find opinions that differ from your own, which can help you sharpen your thinking, qualify your thesis if necessary, and demonstrate fairness to opposing arguments

13i   Using visuals in an argument

Chapters 8 and 9 provide extensive information on using visuals and design effectively in a variety of writing situations — from essays and newsletters to brochures and Web pages. The advice in these chapters is especially important in crafting arguments. As you work toward producing fully developed, strong arguments, then, think carefully about how visuals can help you create the ethical, logical, and emotional appeals presented in 13e, f, and g.

Visuals that make ethical appeals are those that add to your credibility and fairness as a writer. For a Web site, consider including a small, modest picture of yourself as well as a brief statement about your background and credentials. In arguments and in other kinds of writing, whether posted on the Web or not, visuals that reflect authority can help build credibility. That's why so many universities, nonprofit organizations, and government agencies are following the lead of business and creating "brand-name" images for themselves. The U.S. Census Bureau, for example, includes its seal — and usually its motto, "Helping You Make Informed Decisions" — on all of its reports and documents. The

•⋯ For a thorough discussion of finding, gathering, and evaluating sources, both off- and online, see Chapters 14–19.

seal and motto work to establish the ethos or credibility of the bureau
and thus lend authority to the documents it publishes.

A VISUAL THAT MAKES AN ETHICAL APPEAL

U S C E N S U S B U R E A U
Helping You Make Informed Decisions • 1902-2002

For some college work, you may want to use such visual images. If you
are building a Web site that you intend to keep going for some time,
consider developing a logo for it and using that image to unify the site
and help build recognition for it — and for you. Doing so can build credibility for your argument.

Visuals that make logical appeals can be especially useful in arguments,
since they present factual information that can be taken in at a glance.
Charts, graphs, tables, maps, photographs, and so on can help get your
points across. For a report on minority-owned business enterprises, the
U.S. Census Bureau used many charts and graphs, including the pie
chart on p. 285. In the same way, *Business Week* used a simple bar graph
to carry a big message about equality of pay for men and women. A
quick glance will tell you how long it would take to explain all the information in these charts with words alone. In these instances, pictures can
be worth a thousand words.

Visuals that make emotional appeals can add substance to your argument
as well. In fact, many images make powerful arguments all on their own,
as occurred in 1970 when photographers captured National Guard
troops firing on students at Kent State University, or when we saw photographs of the heroic rescuers at Ground Zero in New York City after the
attack on the World Trade Center on September 11, 2001. But you need

For a full dis-
cussion of visual
arguments, see
Chapter 12.

Percent Distribution of American Indian- and Alaskan Native-Owned Firms by Industry Division, 1997

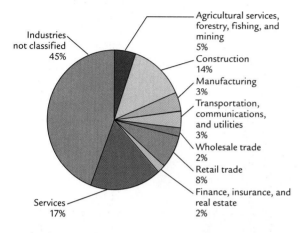

Industries not classified 45%

Agricultural services, forestry, fishing, and mining 5%

Construction 14%

Manufacturing 3%

Transportation, communications, and utilities 3%

Wholesale trade 2%

Retail trade 8%

Finance, insurance, and real estate 2%

Services 17%

THE BIG PICTURE

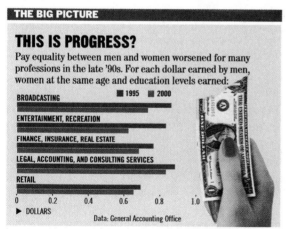

THIS IS PROGRESS?

Pay equality between men and women worsened for many professions in the late '90s. For each dollar earned by men, women at the same age and education levels earned:

■ 1995 ■ 2000

BROADCASTING

ENTERTAINMENT, RECREATION

FINANCE, INSURANCE, REAL ESTATE

LEGAL, ACCOUNTING, AND CONSULTING SERVICES

RETAIL

0   0.2   0.4   0.6   0.8   1.0

► DOLLARS

Data: General Accounting Office

to make sure that the visuals you choose to enhance the emotional appeal of your argument are effective with readers, so test out any photos or other visuals you are thinking of using with several potential readers. In an essay titled "Please Let Me Die with Dignity," for example, one student found that two photos she had intended to use—showing immense suffering in those photographed—were so difficult for her readers to look at that they detracted from the argument she was trying to make.

Magazines often use visuals that add emotional appeal to the arguments being made. In a "My Turn" essay from *Newsweek*, writer and actor Joseph C. Phillips argues that black Americans should claim the American freedom they have fought so long to gain, rather than rejecting America. Accompanying this argument is the following picture of Phillips standing proud and tall in front of an American flag, an image that captures his identification with both flag and country.

A VISUAL THAT MAKES AN EMOTIONAL APPEAL

CONSIDERING DISABILITIES: Description

Remember that some members of your class or peer group may have difficulty seeing visual arguments or recognizing nuances of color or spacing. Be sure to provide verbal descriptions to describe visual image(s).

13j Organizing and designing an argument

cons

13j 287

ARGUMENT
Organizing and
Designing an
Argument

Once you have assembled good reasons and evidence in support of an argumentative thesis, you must organize your material and design your document in order to present the argument convincingly. Although there is no ideal or universally favored organizational framework, you may find it useful to try one of the following patterns.

1 The classical system

The classical system of argument was often followed by ancient Greek and Roman orators. The speaker began with an *introduction,* which stated the thesis and then gave the *background* information. Next came the different *lines of argument* and then the *consideration of alternative arguments.* A *conclusion* both summed up the argument and made a final appeal to the audience. You can adapt this format to written arguments as follows:

1. *Introduction*
   - gains readers' attention and interest
   - establishes your qualifications to write about your topic
   - establishes common ground with readers
   - demonstrates fairness
   - states or implies your thesis
2. *Background*
   - presents any necessary background information, including pertinent personal narrative
3. *Lines of argument*
   - present good reasons and evidence (including logical and emotional appeals) in support of your thesis
   - generally present reasons in order of importance
   - demonstrate ways your argument may be in readers' best interest
4. *Consideration of alternative arguments*
   - examines alternative points of view
   - notes advantages and disadvantages of alternative views
   - explains why one view is better than other(s)
5. *Conclusion*
   - may summarize the argument briefly
   - elaborates on the implication of your thesis
   - makes clear what you want readers to think or do
   - makes a strong ethical or emotional appeal

2 The Toulmin system

For more on the ———•
Toulmin system,
see 11f, 13c, and
13f4.

As you know from earlier discussions, another useful system of argument is the one developed by philosopher Stephen Toulmin. This simplified form of Toulmin's system can help you organize an argumentative essay:

1. Make your claim (a statement that is arguable or controversial).

   The federal government should ban smoking.

2. Qualify your claim if necessary.

   The ban would be limited to public places.

3. Present good reasons to support your claim.

   Smoking causes serious diseases in smokers.

   Nonsmokers are endangered by others' smoke.

4. Explain the warrant(s) (underlying assumptions) that connect your claim and your reasons. If the warrants are controversial, provide additional explanation for them.

WARRANT	The Constitution was established to "promote the general welfare."
WARRANT	Citizens are entitled to protection from harmful actions by others.
ADDITIONAL EXPLANATION	The United States is based on a political system that is supposed to serve the basic needs of its people, including their health.

5. Provide additional evidence to support your claim (facts, statistics, testimony, and the use of other ethical, logical, or emotional appeals).

STATISTICS	Cite the incidence of deaths attributed to second-hand smoke.
FACTS	Cite lawsuits won against large tobacco companies, including one that awarded billions of dollars to states in reparation for smoking-related health care costs.
FACTS	Cite bans on smoking already imposed in many public institutions and places of employment—such as Ohio State University and all restaurants in California.
AUTHORITY	Cite the surgeon general.

cons

13j   289

ARGUMENT

Organizing and
Designing an
Argument

6. Acknowledge and respond to possible counterarguments.

COUNTERARGUMENT   Smokers have rights, too.

RESPONSE   The suggested ban applies only to public places; smokers would be free to smoke in private.

7. Finally, draw your conclusion, stated in the strongest way possible.

● **EXERCISE 13.11**

Using the classical or Toulmin system and the advice in this chapter, draft an argument in support of one of the theses you formulated in Exercise 13.2 or 13.3.

3 Design issues

Like writing of almost every kind today, most arguments no longer appear only in black and white or only in print form. Instead, they are carefully designed to make the best use of space, font style and type size, color, visuals, and contemporary technology. Chapters 8 and 9 provide extensive information on design issues, and it would be wise to consult those chapters as you design an argument. Here are some tips to get you thinking about how to produce and design a document that will add to the ethical, logical, and emotional appeals you are making:

- Before you begin, check out any conventions that may be expected in the kind of argument you are writing. Look for examples of similar arguments, or ask your instructor for information about such conventions. (See 8b.)

- Choose fonts that will help create the overall impression you are trying to achieve, and use a type size that will be readable. (See 8b and c.)

- Think visually as you design your argument, considering the use of white space, titles, and headings and how each page will look (see 8a, b, and c). Choose titles, headings, and subheadings that will guide readers from point to point, and set each one off consistently (see 8c). You may want to set off an especially important part of your argument (such as a list of essential evidence) in a box, carefully labeled.

- Plan where each visual will go, keeping each one as close to the text it illustrates as possible, giving each a title, labeling each as a figure or table, and providing the source for the visual (see pp. 177–182).

- Remember that you may need to request permission to use a visual taken from another source. (See Chapters 17–18 for examples of requests for permission and for a more complete discussion of intellectual property issues related to student work.)

- Choose colors carefully, keeping in mind that colors call up many responses: red for war, for example, or blue for purity. In general, you will probably want to stick to black and white for most of your text, because it is easy to read, reserving color for headings, illustrations, and so on. If you are posting your argument to the Web, remember that you need to have a strong contrast between the background color and print and illustrations. (See 8a and Chapter 9.)

13k A student argument essay

Asked to write an essay addressed to her classmates — one that makes an argumentative claim and supports it with good reasons and evidence — Heather Ricker decided to follow up on her interest in current debates over whether and how video games may affect users' behavior. Her essay is organized according to the classical system and has been annotated to point out the various parts of her argument as well as her use of good reasons and evidence and her appeals to credibility (ethics), logic, and emotion. She also added visuals to help support some of her major reasons.

Heather Ricker

Professor Lunsford

English 167

November 23, 2001

Video Games: Buyers Beware!

"Stay alive at all costs! Find the key! Kill
the bad guys!" This is how one eighth-grader
describes the principles of playing video games.
Such games might seem like harmless fun, but
what if the violence attracts and addicts young
players, affecting their behavior and their view
of reality?

Some say that violent video games have minimal
impact on young teenagers, pointing out that most
video-game players live completely normal lives.
The weaknesses in that argument are almost too
obvious: first, "most" is not "all." More
important, just because a player does not
immediately imitate specific violent acts found
in video games does not mean the games will
have no long-term negative impact on that
player's views and behavior. Because of this
possibility, parents should assume responsibility
for evaluating video games and should prohibit
young teenagers from purchasing those that are
especially violent.

To begin with, a number of authorities claim
that playing a violent video game does present a
threat to the user's psychological health. As early
as 1983, Geoffrey and Elizabeth Loftus, in their

Opening gets
reader's attention
and provides back-
ground information

States argumen-
tative thesis

Introduces good
reason: violent
video games can be
a threat to health

book <u>Mind at Play: The Psychology of Video Games</u>, warned about the dangers of violent video games: "Although we can never be sure in any individual case, a substantial body of evidence indicates that viewing excessive violence on the screen is associated with aggression and violent behavior among children and teenagers" (98). More recently, studies have measured changes in behavior and emotional responses to video games, ranging from "assertiveness" (<u>Journal of Child Study</u> qtd. in Boal, "Shooters") and withdrawal (Jeanne Funk qtd. in Boal, "One Step") to "aggression, anger, and hostility" (A. Mehrabian and W. J. Wixen qtd. in "Social Effects" sec. I). While <u>Mediascope</u>, the publication of a nonprofit research organization, concludes from its survey of research on video game playing that there are not sufficient studies, especially of current games, to make any definitive statements about the dangers of video-game use, parents should be concerned--maybe more so precisely because so few studies have been conducted.

In addition, playing violent video games adversely affects psychological health by actually addicting players. One of the most troubling influences video games have on players is the medium's remarkable ability to fixate a player's attention or, to borrow psychologist Sherry Turkle's term, its "holding power" (30), a state well illustrated in Fig. 1. Addictive reactions in the body can be linked to some of the visual and aural signals found in video games--signals that cause the eyes, for example, to stop blinking for extended periods. This phenomenon triggers the release of dopamine, a neurotransmitter thought by some to be the "master molecule of addiction" (Quittner 3). Is this chemical association the reason forty out of the forty-seven top-rated Nintendo games have violence as their theme (Cesarone)?

Fig. 1. Bill Varie, Boy playing a video game, 12 Nov. 2001, Corbis. Here is a young boy transfixed by a video game.

Admittedly, according to a report in the New York Times, the very best-selling games are nonviolent (Miller). But even without being top sellers, the violent games sell well. The National Coalition on Television Violence (NCTV) rates the violent content of games and concludes that violence is indeed a theme in more than half of the games on the market. As reported by Cesarone, the NCTV rates 55.7 percent of games as unfit or highly violent.

Cites scientific data as evidence

Presents counter-argument

Offers refutation to counterargument

Uses statistic as support

Games that mimic military combat training not only encourage brutality but also totally ignore teaching players about restraint--one more reason violent games should be off-limits. One of the main proponents of this claim has been Lieutenant Colonel David Grossman, an expert witness in federal and state cases dealing with violence. He worries that video games expose young people to combat-style training without teaching them when to put nonviolent alternatives into play (316). As Grossman points out, the military used Pavlovian methods of desensitization during World War II to train soldiers to kill other human beings against their natural tendencies. Repetitive conditioning such as "killing" cadences and unit songs as well as referring to people as "targets" helped to dehumanize the enemy in the soldier's mind. Then there was the positive reinforcement of three-day passes for good marksmanship. It is not hard to see the similarities between military conditioning and desensitization and the conditioning that could come from shooting and harming video-game targets. In fact, the military now uses such games in training its soldiers, as seen in Fig. 2. Though video games may not transform players magically into virtual marines, Grossman's argument stresses that adolescents do learn from the games they play and thus violent games are cause for concern.

Good reason: what games don't teach

Analogy used in support of claim: repetitive conditioning in World War II led to desensitization; it can do so with video games as well

Ricker 5

Fig. 2. Photograph of
combat simulator, 16
Nov. 2001, Abcnews.com.
Soldier shown in
simulation.

In fact, rather than teaching when and where to show restraint, the games and promotion for the games teach that violence can be fun. For instance, the game Resident Evil promotes violence as entertainment. The publishers of the game invite players to "face your fear" using "a vast selection of weapons." The makers of Carmageddon and Grand Theft Auto III imply that preying on the defenseless is acceptable behavior: they market a game that involves killing helpless civilians. Even less violent games like Klingon Honor Guard appeal to the notion that violence carried out honorably is ennobling: ". . . you must fulfill your blood oath--become the ultimate warrior and exact glorious revenge . . ." (Klingon).

Real killing may sometimes be an inevitable evil, but it certainly should not be considered fun or trivial. Parents should not accept violence as entertainment in games--and they should not think that such violence can't affect the way their children look at the world and at other human beings.

Good reason: advertising stresses violence

Introduces examples as evidence

Protests--some coming from senators--against the sale of violent video games to minors have resulted in the formulation of the 21st Century Media Responsibility Act. This bill, if passed, would criminalize selling or lending violent media to children under seventeen years of age. In addition, it would require a common rating system among various media (music, video, TV) and a description of video-game contents. This required package labeling might force retailers to curtail sales to young teenagers.

The video-game industry, however, claims that it can censor itself with its own labels. Its goal, of course, is to prevent restrictive legislation that would cost it "hordes of young gamers" (Boal, "One Step"). The makers of Kingpin, a particularly violent game, have tried to protect the sale of their game by declaring that it was never intended for young audiences. But before the Littleton shootings heightened public awareness of video-game violence, this game could have been purchased easily by young teens like the one described by Salon's Mark Boal: "Once inside [the store], Dave, who is 14 and has spiked hair, makes a beeline for the box with the large yellow [warning] sticker" ("One Step"). Clearly, by leaving enforcement of existing ratings up to retailers, the video-game industry hopes to avoid legislation and protect its own interests.

Video games are not the only contributing
factor to society's tendencies toward violence, but
they are having an influence. For this reason, we
all must take responsibility for the way we use
video games.

Reiterates argumen-
tative thesis

Makes direct appeal
to audience by
using "we"

Works Cited

Boal, Mark. "One Step Ahead of the Law." <u>Salon</u>
19 July 1999. 12 Nov. 2001 <http://
www.salonmagazine.com/tech/feature/1999/07/
19/kingpin/index.htm>.

---. "The Shooters and the Shrinks." <u>Salon</u>
6 May 1999. 12 Nov. 2001 <http://
www.salonmagazine.com/tech/feature/1999/
05/06/game_violence/>.

<u>Carmageddon</u>. Interplay Productions. 1998.

Cesarone, Bernard. "Video Games and Children."
Jan. 1994. 12 Nov. 2001 <http://
www.parenthoodweb.com/articles/phw83.htm>.

<u>Grand Theft Auto III</u>. Rockstar Games. 2001.

Grossman, David. <u>On Killing: The Psychological
Cost of Learning to Kill in War and
Society</u>. New York: Little, 1995.

<u>Kingpin</u>. Interplay Productions. 1999.

<u>Klingon Honor Guard</u>. MacSoft, Microprose, 1998.

Loftus, Geoffrey R., and Elizabeth F. Loftus.
<u>Mind at Play: The Psychology of Video
Games</u>. New York: Basic, 1983.

Miller, Stephen C. "Most-Violent Video Games Are
Not Biggest Sellers." <u>New York Times</u>
29 July 1999, late ed.: G3.

<u>Photograph of combat simulator</u>. 16 Nov. 2001.
Abcnews.com. 18 Nov. 2001 <http://
abcnews.go.com/sectrons/scitech/DailyNews/
pt_STRICOM_01115.html>.

Quittner, Joshua. "Are Video Games Really So
    Bad?" _Time_ 10 May 1999. 10 Nov. 2001
    <http://www.pathfinder.com/time/magazine/
    articles/0,3266,23885,00.html>.

Resident Evil. Capcom Entertainment. 1998.

"The Social Effects of Electronic Interactive
    Games: An Annotated Bibliography."
    Mediascope 10 Nov. 2001 <http://
    www.mediascope.org/pubs/bseeig.htm>.

Turkle, Sherry. _Life on the Screen: Identity in
    the Age of the Internet_. New York: Simon,
    1995.

Varie, Bill. _Boy playing a video game_. Corbis.
    12 Nov. 2001 <http://store.corbis.com/
    search/categoryPOE.asp?navid=create/
    digitalpictures/education>.

cons

13k

ARGUMENT

Constructing
Arguments

Using the questions on p. 265, analyze an argument you've recently written or the draft you wrote for Exercise 13.11. Decide what you need to do to revise your argument, and write out a brief plan for revision.

PART 4

DOING RESEARCH AND USING SOURCES

"Research is formalized curiosity. It is poking and prying with a purpose."
— ZORA NEALE HURSTON

14

⬙ Preparing for a Research Project

14a Understanding the research process

This chapter rests on the assumption that we are all researchers. From this basic assumption come five important premises.

1. *You already know how to do research.* You act as a researcher whenever you investigate something — whether a college, a course, a cosmetic, a computer, or a car — by reading up on it, discussing its features with your friends or with experts, or perhaps checking several stores to see what is in stock and how much it costs. Therefore, you already have essential research skills. You know how to combine experience, observation, and new information when you solve a problem, answer a question, make a decision, analyze a situation, or make an "educated guess."

2. *Good research makes you a genuine expert.* If you approach your research seriously, you may gradually become an expert about a new cancer drug or Jackie Robinson's place in sports history. And you will be able to add your knowledge to the educated conversation taking place all around you.

3. *Research is usually driven by a purpose.* Research is rarely an end in itself. Whether for everyday needs or in an academic setting, researchers seek out facts and opinions for a reason. One writer says that she does research every time she compares nutritional values on cereal boxes, looks at online reviews before ordering a book, or reads about a topic before writing something

new. Why do research? This writer does research for inspiration, to search out details that will make her writing more vivid, to enrich and supplement her memories, and to keep learning new things.

Your main purpose in college research will most often be to fulfill a specific assignment: for example, to compare literary texts, to trace the causes of a war, or to survey and summarize students' feelings about mandatory drug testing of athletes. Sometimes, however, you may be asked to determine your own purpose for research.

4. *Your purpose influences the research you do, which in turn refines your purpose.* When you begin any research, it is impossible to know exactly what you will discover. The evidence you gather, for example, may prove so startling that it calls for you to persuade — to advocate a solution to a problem — when you originally had meant only to explain the problem. In turn, as you refine your purpose, that purpose will help guide you in choosing additional sources and organizing material.

5. *Research rarely progresses in a neat line from start to finish.* You begin with a question that you may or may not be able to answer. Then your background research and investigation may lead you to start all over — or to refer to other sources. This additional research may narrow your idea even more, leading you to more specific sources — or it may lead you to change directions yet again. Wherever the process takes you, however, your overriding goal remains the same: to develop a strong critical understanding of the information you are gathering.

One student's experience illustrates how ideas can change and develop during the research process. Assigned to write an essay on any topic, he began by puzzling over whether modern rock-guitar styles could be traced to the electric-guitar styles developed in the 1940s and 1950s by Chicago blues groups. Starting with background reading about modern rock guitarists such as Eric Clapton and Pete Townshend, he found repeated references to Muddy Waters, Howlin' Wolf, Buddy Guy, Albert King, and other Chicago blues artists. He listened to a number of records and found repeated riffs (musical phrases) and clear derivations. He began to make notes for an essay.

Then, in several sources on the Chicago electric blues tradition, the student found references to country blues and southern race records as influences on the Chicago artists. He was not sure what these terms meant, but then he discovered that blues music harks back to nineteenth-century slave songs, that country blues was nearly always played on a single acoustic guitar, and that the history of country blues guitar styles traces back to the 1920s. Clearly the story was older and the traditions deeper than he had imagined.

304

prep

14b

RESEARCH

Preparing for a
Research Project

The student then searched the Internet using keywords and found a number of Web sites with information about southern and country blues musicians of the 1920s and 1930s like Leadbelly and Mississippi John Hurt. He began to consider the differences between electric and acoustic instruments. Finally, he looked for recordings by some of the early country blues musicians. To his amazement, he heard on these early recordings some of the exact riffs and techniques he so admired in the work of contemporary guitarists.

Thus did this student arrive at a deeper idea to develop, a far better grasp of music history, and more research sources. He had also accumulated enough information to begin crafting a fine essay.

■ *Research for writing*

College research may range from a couple of hours spent gathering background about a topic for a brief essay to weeks or months of full-scale exploration for a term paper. Chapters 14–19 provide guidelines to help you with *any* research done for the purpose of writing. In addition, these chapters show examples of work by Shannan Palma, a student whose complete essay appears in Chapter 20. Additional complete essays appear in Chapters 4, 13, and 64–66.

FOR COLLABORATION

Working with one or two members of your class, come up with a list of some everyday research you have done lately—on what bike or DVD player to buy, on where to take a vacation, on where to go to college, and so on. Choose at least two of these everyday research projects, and detail the processes your group members went through to gather the information. Bring the results of your work to class for discussion. Then identify the steps each group took to find the information they needed. What patterns can you find among these processes?

14b Analyzing a research assignment

Before you begin research in response to a writing assignment, be sure you understand the requirements and limits of the assignment. For an introductory writing course, Shannan Palma received the following assignment:

Choose a subject of interest to you, and use it as the basis for a research essay that makes and substantiates a claim.

In response to questions, Shannan Palma's instructor clarified some requirements of the assignment: the essay was to use information from both print and online sources to support the claim; run roughly ten to fifteen pages in length; and address members of the writing class as audience.

Here are more detailed statements about the context of any research project.

- *Identify the purpose.* Read through the assignment for **cue words,** such as *describe, survey, analyze, persuade, explain, classify, compare,* or *contrast.* Understanding what such words mean in this field will help you identify sources that are appropriate for your purpose.

●— For a definition of *claim*, see 11f.

- *Identify the audience.* Find out whether your assignment specifies an audience other than the instructor. Then answer the following questions:
  - Who will be interested in the information you gather, and why? What will they want to know? What will they already know?
  - What do you know about their backgrounds? What assumptions might they hold about the topic?
  - What response do you want to elicit from them? What kinds of evidence will you need to present to elicit that response?
  - What will your instructor expect in a strong research project on this topic?

●— For a discussion of ways to assess purpose, see 2d.

●— For additional questions to consider about your audience, see 2h.

- *Consider your rhetorical stance.* Think about your own rhetorical stance — the attitude you have toward your topic. Are you just curious about it? Do you like it? dislike it? find it bewildering? What influences have shaped your stance?

- *Gauge the scope of your research.* Consider the kind of research you will need to do. Does the assignment specify how many or what kind(s) of library sources you should use? Does it specify primary *and* secondary sources? Does it suggest any field research — interviewing, surveying, or observing? Will the Web be a good (or bad) place to begin your research? Will you need visuals — charts, maps, photographs, and so on?

●— For additional questions to consider about your rhetorical stance, see 2g.

●— For a discussion of types of sources, see 15a.

- *Note the length of the project.* The amount of research and writing time you need for a five-page essay differs markedly from that for a fifteen-page essay. And you may need more time if materials are not available or if you discover that you must do more research. The best plan is to begin work as soon as possible.

- *Note the deadline—for the project and other items.* When is the project due? Are any preliminary materials—a working bibliography, a thesis, an

outline, a first draft — due before this date? It's never too soon to work
out a schedule for your research project. The sample schedule below is
one you can modify to fit your particular needs.

SCHEDULING A RESEARCH PROJECT

	Try to do by:
Assignment date: _____	
Analyze assignment; decide on primary purpose and audience; choose topic if necessary.	_____
Narrow and focus the topic.	_____
Arrange library time; decide on keywords, and develop search strategy.	_____
Begin research log.	_____
Do background reading and online searches; narrow topic further if necessary.	_____
Decide on research question, tentative hypothesis.	_____
Start working bibliography; track down sources in the library and online.	_____
Develop working thesis and rough outline.	_____
If necessary, conduct interviews, make observations, or distribute and collect questionnaires.	_____
Read and evaluate sources; take notes.	_____
Draft explicit thesis and outline or, for a Web text, a map.	_____
Prepare first draft.	_____
Rough draft due: _____	
Obtain and evaluate critical responses.	_____
Do more research if necessary.	_____
Revise draft; prepare list of works cited.	_____
Edit revised draft; use spell checker if available.	_____
Prepare final draft.	_____
Do final proofreading.	_____
Final draft due: _____	

■ *Keeping a research log*

You might set up a **research log** — either print or electronic — for keeping
track of your work. In the log, jot down thoughts about your topic, lists
of things to do, ideas about possible sources, and details about library
materials (for example, call numbers for specific books and due dates for
books you borrow). (See 14g.)

If your assignment does not specify a topic, you can best begin articulating one by keeping in mind any specifications about purpose, audience, scope, length, and deadline and by considering the following questions:

- What subjects do you already know something about? Which of them would you like to explore in more depth?
- What subjects might you like to become an expert on?
- What subjects evoke a strong reaction from you — intense attraction, puzzlement, or skepticism?

In addition, do some surfing on the Internet, or skim through your textbooks or class notes, current magazines or journals, or standard reference works, looking for some topic or question that intrigues you. You may find the techniques presented in 3a for exploring a topic useful for discovering one. Even if your instructor has assigned a broad topic, these questions and methods may help you decide what aspect of it to research.

■ *Getting responses to your topic*

When you have a topic, describe it in several sentences. Then try to get responses from your instructor and some classmates by asking the following questions:

- Would you be interested in reading about this topic?
- Does the topic seem manageable?
- Can you suggest any interesting angles or approaches?
- Can you suggest any good sources of information on this topic?

● **EXERCISE 14.1**

Using the questions in 14c, come up with at least two topics you would like to carry out research on. Then write a brief response to some key questions about each topic: How much information do you think is available on this topic? What particular angle on the topic would you take? What sources on this topic do you know about or have access to? Who would know about this topic — historians, doctors, filmmakers, psychologists, others?

RESEARCH

Preparing for a
Research Project

Any topic you choose to research must be manageable — must suit the scope, audience, length, and time limits of your assignment. Making a topic manageable often requires narrowing it, but narrowing is not always sufficient in itself. Rather than simply reducing a large subject to a smaller one, then, *focus* on a particular slant, and look for a governing question to guide your research. One good way to work toward such a question is by brainstorming to generate a series of questions you might ask about your topic. You can then evaluate them and choose one or two that seem most interesting and most manageable.

Shannan Palma knew that she wanted to study changes in the image of the hero in U.S. movies, and she originally wanted to discuss this topic in the context of social and economic changes in the United States in the second half of the twentieth century. In working on this angle, however, she realized that doing justice to the social and economic contexts would more than double the length of her essay. She decided, therefore, to narrow her topic and concentrate solely on movies and heroes.

■ *Asking a research question and developing a hypothesis*

The result of the narrowing and focusing process is a **research question** that can be tentatively answered by a **hypothesis,** a statement of what you anticipate your research will show. Like a working thesis, a hypothesis must be not only manageable but also interesting and specific. In addition, it must be arguable, a debatable proposition that can be proved or disproved by research evidence. For example, a statement like this one is not arguable since it merely states a widely known fact: "Senator Joseph McCarthy attracted great attention with his anti-Communist crusade during the 1950s." On the other hand, this statement is an arguable hypothesis since it can be proved or disproved: "Roy Cohn's political views and biased research while he was an assistant to Senator Joseph McCarthy were largely responsible for McCarthy's anti-Communist crusade."

For a discussion of a working thesis, see 3b.

For more on judging whether a hypothesis is arguable, see 13b.

In moving from a general topic of interest, such as Senator Joseph McCarthy's anti-Communist crusade of the 1950s, to a useful hypothesis, such as the one in the previous paragraph, you first narrow the topic to a single manageable issue, such as Roy Cohn's role in the crusade.

After background reading, you then raise a question about that issue ("To what extent did Cohn's political views and research contribute to McCarthy's crusade?") and devise a possible answer, your hypothesis.

Here is how Shannan Palma moved from general topic to hypothesis:

TOPIC	Images of heroes in U.S. films
ISSUE	Changes in the image of heroes in U.S. films
RESEARCH QUESTION	How have the images of heroes changed since heroes found a home in Hollywood?
HYPOTHESIS	As real-life heroes have been dethroned in popular U.S. culture over the last century, so have film heroes, and current films suggest that the hero may not have a future at all.

The hypothesis that tentatively answers the research question is precise enough to be supported or challenged by a manageable amount of research.

14e Investigating what you already know about your topic

Once you have narrowed and focused a topic, you need to marshal everything you already know about it. Here are some strategies for doing so:

For more on investigating a topic, see 15c.

- *Brainstorming.* Take five minutes to list, in words or phrases, everything you think of or wonder about your hypothesis. You may find it helpful to do this in a group with other students. (See 3a1.)

- *Freewriting in favor of your hypothesis.* For five minutes, write about every reason for believing your hypothesis is true. (See 3a2.)

- *Freewriting in opposition to your hypothesis.* For five minutes, write down every argument you can think of, no matter how weak or improbable, that someone opposed to your hypothesis might make.

- *Freewriting about your audience.* Write for five minutes about your readers, including your instructor. What do you think they currently believe about your topic? What sorts of evidence will convince them to accept your hypothesis? What sorts of sources will they respect?

- *Tapping your memory for sources.* List everything you can remember about *where* you learned about your topic: computer bulletin boards, email, books, magazines, courses, conversations, television. Much of what you know may seem like common knowledge, but common knowledge comes from somewhere, and "somewhere" can serve as a starting point for investigation.

● **EXERCISE 14.2**

Using the tips provided in 14e, write down as much as you can about one of the
topics you identified in Exercise 14.1. Then take some time to reread your notes,
and jot down the questions you still need to answer as well as sources you need to
find.

14f Deciding on a preliminary research plan

Once you've considered everything you already know about your topic,
you can begin to plan your research. To do so, answer the following
questions:

- What kinds of sources (books, journal articles, videos, government documents, specialized encyclopedias, maps, illustrations, and so on) will
  you need to consult?
- Do you know the location and availability of the kinds of sources you
  need?
- How current do your sources need to be? (For topical issues, especially
  those related to science, current sources are usually most important. For
  historical subjects, older sources may still offer the best information.)
- Do you need to consult sources contemporary with an event or a person's
  life? If so, how will you get access to those sources?
- How many sources should you consult?

One major goal of your research plan is to begin building a strong working bibliography (see 14i). Carrying out systematic research and keeping
careful notes on the sources you find will make developing your list of
works cited (see Chapters 20–23) much easier later on.

For detailed ⋯⋯⋯•
information on
finding various
kinds of sources,
see Chapter 15.

14g Taking notes and beginning a research log

Keeping a careful and thorough research log will make the job of writing and documenting the sources used for your research project more
efficient and accurate. Since most college students today have access to
word processors, writers can easily set up electronic research logs. Here
are a few guidelines for doing so:

1. Create a new folder, and label it with a name that will be easy to identify: *Research Log for Project on Movie Heroes*.
2. Within this folder, create files or subfolders that will help you manage
   your project. These files might include *Project Deadlines, Notes on*

Hypothesis and Working Thesis, Working Bibliography, Brainstorming Notes, Background Information, Organizational Plan, Images and Visuals, Draft 1, and so on.

3. Make entries into your research log consistently. As you read pertinent material in books, magazine articles, or Web texts, for example, record all the information you will need for your bibliography. (See 14i.)

CONSIDERING DISABILITIES: Try Dictation

> If you have difficulty taking notes either on a computer or in a notebook, consider dictating your notes. You might dictate into a handheld recorder, which you can later play back to yourself, or into a word processor with voice-recognition capability.

If you prefer not to keep your research log on a computer, set up a binder with dividers similar to the subfolders listed above. Whether your log is a computer document or not, be sure to distinguish the notes and comments you make from any quoted passages you record. The screen that follows shows how a student (Laura) has inserted her own comments into the descriptive notes she took in Microsoft Word.

●— For information
on descriptive
annotations,
see 14i.

COMMENT FUNCTION USED IN RESEARCH LOG

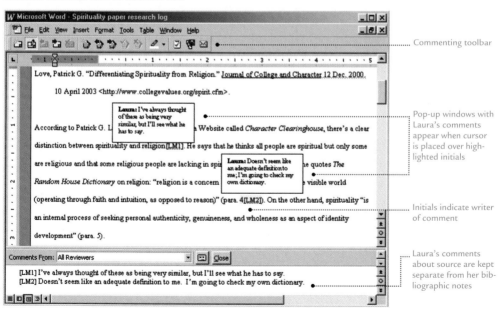

.... Commenting toolbar

Pop-up windows with
Laura's comments
appear when cursor
is placed over high-
lighted initials

.... Initials indicate writer
of comment

Laura's comments
about source are kept
separate from her bib-
liographic notes

14h Moving from hypothesis to working thesis

As you gather information and begin reading sources, your research question is likely to be refined, and your hypothesis is likely to change significantly. Only after you have explored it, tested it, and sharpened it by reading and writing does the hypothesis become a **working thesis.**

In Shannan Palma's case, she found that her hypothesis that the hero has no future in U.S. films did not hold up after her full examination of contemporary films. Thus she shifted her attention to what forms future heroes might take and developed the following working thesis: "Although a case of mistaken identity dealt a near-fatal blow to the image of the hero in U.S. films, a study of recent movies suggests that the hero lives on — in two startlingly different forms."

In doing your own research, you may find that your interest shifts, that a whole line of inquiry is unproductive, that a work you need in order to complete an argument is not available, or that your hypothesis is simply wrong. In each case, the process of research pushes you to learn more and more about your hypothesis, to make it more focused and more precise, to become an expert on your topic.

14i Keeping a working bibliography

Your **working bibliography** — a list of articles, books, Web sites, and other sources that you may ultimately use for your paper — is a key component of your research project, and may be part of your research log. The emphasis here is on *working* because the list will probably include materials that end up not being useful. For this reason, you don't absolutely need to put all entries into the specific documentation style you will use (see Chapters 20–23). If you do style your entries appropriately, however, that part of your work will be done when you prepare the final draft.

For detailed
information on
finding various
kinds of sources,
see Chapter 15.

To start a working bibliography, first decide on a format: a notebook, a computer file you can store on a disc, or index cards. If you use cards or notebook pages, record information on only one side so that you can arrange your entries alphabetically when preparing your final list of works cited. Remember, too, that you should record source information for any material you photocopy or download from an electronic source. Be aware that not every source will provide all the documentation information you may want. For example, a Web page might not list an author. The forms that follow will help you keep track of the information you should try to find. Note that some items listed, such as the volume number for a periodical, won't apply to all sources in that category.

For each *book,* record all the following items that apply:

Call number _____

Author(s) and editor(s) _____

Title and subtitle _____

Place of publication _____

Publisher _____

Year of publication _____

Other (translator, volume, edition) _____

For each *part of a book,* such as a preface, a chapter, or an essay within a collection, record all the following items that apply:

Call number of book _____

Author(s) of part _____

Title of part _____

Author(s) and editor(s) of book _____

Title and subtitle of book _____

Place of publication _____

Publisher _____

Year of publication _____

Inclusive page numbers of part _____

For each *periodical article,* record all the following items that apply:

Call number of periodical _____

Author(s) of article _____

Title of article _____

Name of periodical _____

Volume number _____

Issue number _____

Date of issue _____

Inclusive page numbers of article _____

For each *Internet source,* access the source and print it out or download it if possible. You will eventually need to put the information for any sources you use into the correct documentation style, but the printout or download can save you the interim step of copying the information by hand, and it also serves as a record in case the source changes or disappears. The printout, download, or other form of entry should include all the following items that apply:

Author(s) of document _____

Title of document _____

Title of site _____

Editor(s) of site _____

Sponsor of site _____

Publication information for print version of source _____

Range or total number of pages, paragraphs, or other sections, if numbered _____

Names of database and online service _____

Date of electronic publication or last update _____

Date you accessed the source _____

Electronic address (URL) _____

For other kinds of sources (films, recordings, works of art), list the information required by the documentation style you are using (see Chapters 20–23), and note where you found the information. When you examine print sources you have found in a catalog, bibliography, or index, check the accuracy of your information by consulting the title and copyright page of a book and the table of contents and first page of a journal or magazine. For an electronic source, check the homepage of a Web site or the beginning of the document.

For her research essay, Shannan Palma started out using index cards. When she began having trouble keeping up with the cards, she decided to switch to a computer file. An example of each kind of entry is shown on p. 315. Since her final essay would follow the style of the Modern Language Association (MLA), explained in Chapter 20, Shannan decided to use MLA style for the entries in her working bibliography.

PN1995.9
R57
1995

Rushing, Janice Hocker, and Thomas S. Frentz. Projecting
the Shadow: The Cyborg Hero in American Film.
Chicago: U of Chicago P, 1995.

●⸺ For an explana-
tion of call num-
bers (one of
which is at the
top of Shannan's
card), see 15d1.

COMPUTER FILE ENTRY FOR AN ARTICLE IN AN ONLINE SOURCE

Gallagher, Brian. "Greta Garbo Is Sad: Some Historical Reflections on
the Paradoxes of Stardom in the American Film Industry,
1910–1960." *Images: A Journal of Film and Popular Culture*
3(1997): 7 pts. 7 Aug. 2002 <http://www.imagesjournal.com/
issue03/infocus.htm>.

■ *Preparing annotated bibliographies*

Sometimes an instructor may ask you to compile an **annotated bibliography,** one that includes your description and comments as well as publishing information. Even if annotations aren't required, many students
like to create them because they help students understand and remember what's in the source.

Annotations can be *descriptive,* providing only a bare-bones description of an article, book, Web site, and so on; or they can be *substantive/evaluative,* summarizing the main points in the source and then making an evaluative comment on them. Here are examples of each kind of annotation:

DESCRIPTIVE ENTRY

Gere, Anne Ruggles. "Kitchen Tables and Rented Rooms:
        The Extracurriculum of Composition." Literacy: A
        Critical Sourcebook. Ed. Ellen Cushman, Eugene R.
        Kintgen, Barry M. Kroll, and Mike Rose. Boston:
        Bedford, 2001. 275-89.

This history of writing instruction argues that writing
instruction takes place--and has historically taken
place--in far less formal venues than the writing
classroom. Gere presents numerous examples and comments
on their importance to the study of writing today.

SUBSTANTIVE/EVALUATIVE ENTRY

Gere, Anne Ruggles. "Kitchen Tables and Rented Rooms:
        The Extracurriculum of Composition." Literacy: A
        Critical Sourcebook. Ed. Ellen Cushman, Eugene R.
        Kintgen, Barry M. Kroll, and Mike Rose. Boston:
        Bedford, 2001. 275-89.

This history of how and where writing is learned
includes what's been missing from other accounts: the
history of learning writing outside of the academic
classroom. What Gere calls the "extracurriculum" are the
clubs and groups that have formed since the nineteenth
century and continue to form to help participants
improve their writing--and often to improve their
communities. If writing teachers in academe would take
these groups into account, Gere argues, they could
enrich their understanding and teaching of writing. Like
many other articles in this book, Gere's piece concerns
both the history of literacy and current practices. The
date of her article (1994) precedes the enormous

popularity of contemporary book clubs, but I wonder what
Gere would have to say about those.

■ *Using bibliography software programs*

If you plan to use a bibliography software program such as Research
Assistant or EndNote to help with your working bibliography, you'll
need to become familiar with its forms for entering source information.
These forms usually ask for the same sorts of source information as in
the forms on pp. 313–314. It's a good idea to complete the appropriate
bibliography software form as soon as you find a source. And remember
that accuracy is just as important when you're using software as it is
when formatting a bibliography on your own: although most programs
put the elements in the correct order, you still need to double-check
other items, such as capitalization of titles, names of authors, and accuracy of dates.

THINKING CRITICALLY ABOUT YOUR OWN RESEARCH

If you have done research for an essay or research project before, go back and evaluate the work you did as a researcher and as a writer in light of the principles developed
in this chapter. What was the purpose of the research? Who was your audience? How
did you narrow and focus your topic? What kinds of sources did you use? Did you use
a research log and keep a working bibliography? What about your research and your
essay pleased you most? What pleased you least? What would you do differently if you
were to revise the essay now?

15 ❖ Conducting Research

A few minutes' thought may bring to mind some piece of everyday research you have done. One couple with a passion for ice cream, for instance, wanted to write an article for a local magazine on the best ice cream in their city. Their guiding research questions ("Who has the best ice cream in town, and what makes it the best?") led them first to the library, where they did background reading on the history of ice cream and the way it is made, and later to the World Wide Web, where they searched for discussion groups for ice-cream lovers. Finally, they went into the field, systematically tasting ice cream at many stores and interviewing local ice-cream makers. This chapter offers advice for doing these three basic kinds of research — in the library, on the Internet, and in the field. ■

15a Understanding different kinds of sources

Almost everything around you could conceivably serve as a source for research: even your kid sister's or brother's speech patterns could provide interesting data for a research project on language development. So sources definitely don't come in one shape or size; they include data from interviews, surveys, or observations; books and articles both in print and online; Web homepages and newsgroup postings; film, video, and music; and images of all kinds. Before you begin your research project in earnest, then, it's worth taking time to consider some important differences among sources.

1 Distinguishing between print sources and Internet sources

Making a distinction between print and Internet sources can be tricky because many sources on the Net are electronic versions of texts that also exist in print. Most material on the Internet, however, has no print equivalent. And most print texts, likewise, are never published online. Why is this distinction so important? For one thing, the complex system of peer review and editorial evaluation of print texts that has developed over centuries is not yet in place on the Internet. If you go to a scholarly book or an article in a scholarly journal, you can be fairly sure that the

318

text has been sent out to an expert reader in that particular field of study for peer review—and oftentimes to two or three such readers—before being accepted for publication. Even for books and articles not intended for a scholarly audience, you can easily check on the reputation of the publisher or magazine or newspaper in which an article appears. On the Internet, some journals and magazines that are published only electronically do have peer-review and editorial processes in place. But for most online materials, reviewing and editorial oversight depend solely on the author of the text. As a result, you need to know whether a source exists only in electronic form and, if so, how much you can trust it.

RESEARCH

Understanding Different Kinds of Sources

For more on evaluating Internet sources, see 16b.

Another important distinction between print and Internet sources is that the latter are generally much less stable. Since online sources can easily be changed or deleted from the Internet entirely, you need to make a copy (either print or electronic) so that you have a record of the original; you may need to check the original later for bibliographic information or to verify the accuracy of a quotation in your notes.

Perhaps the most important distinction, though, is the one made originally: most print sources simply do not exist online and vice versa. Even if you limit your research to the most reputable online sources, you are probably missing out on the great majority of potential sources just because they are available only in print. Especially if your topic involves research into events that occurred more than a decade ago, you need to consult print sources as well as electronic ones to avoid getting a superficial and skewed perspective on what's been written about those events.

2 Distinguishing between primary sources and secondary sources

Another important difference in sources is between **primary sources**, or firsthand knowledge, and **secondary sources**, information available from the research of others.

Primary sources are basic sources of raw information, including experiments, surveys, or interviews you conduct; notes from field research; works of art or other objects you examine; literary works you read; and eyewitness accounts, photographs, news reports, and historical documents (such as letters, diaries, household records, speeches, and so on).

Primary sources are literally all around you. Your grandmother's diary, for example, might serve as a powerful primary source in an essay about customs of the era in which she was young; early maps from your library's map collection might serve as primary sources for an essay on changing national borders. Local historical societies and museums also offer good sources of primary materials, and your campus library will hold primary sources in both its regular and special collections and archives. In addition, you can find primary sources online at sites such as American Memory, <www.lcweb2.loc.gov/ammem/>, a project of the Library of Congress that includes over seventy collections of digitized documents, photos, sound recordings, moving pictures, and other items from U.S. history.

Secondary sources are descriptions or interpretations of primary sources, such as researchers' reports, reviews of books and films, biographies, encyclopedia articles, and so on. Often what constitutes a primary or secondary source depends on the purpose of your research. A critic's evaluation of a painting, for instance, is a secondary source for an essay on that painting, but it serves as a primary source for a study of that particular critic's writing.

Most research projects draw on both primary and secondary sources. A research-based essay on the effect of media on Volkswagen advertising patterns, for example, might draw on primary sources such as very early Volkswagen advertisements as well as secondary sources such as articles or books on how media have affected advertising.

3 Distinguishing between scholarly sources and popular sources

While general nonacademic sources like popular magazines can be helpful in getting started on a research project, you will usually want to depend more heavily on the work of scholars who are authorities in a particular field related to your topic. The work of such experts usually appears in specialized scholarly journals. Here are some features that distinguish scholarly journals from popular magazines (many of these distinctions apply to online periodicals as well as to those in print):

SCHOLARLY	POPULAR
Cover lists contents of the issue	Cover features a color picture
Title often contains the word *Journal*	*Journal* usually does not appear in title
Source found at the library	Source found at grocery stores, newsstands, and so on
Few commercial advertisements	Lots of advertisements
Authors identified with academic credentials	Authors are journalists or reporters, not experts
Summary or abstract appears on first page of article; articles are fairly long	No summary or abstract; articles are fairly short
Articles have bibliographies	No bibliographies included

4 Considering older and more current sources

Think about whether your research project calls for the use of older, historical sources or up-to-the-minute information. Most projects can benefit from both kinds of resources. But if you are examining a recent scientific discovery, you will want to depend primarily on contemporary sources; on the other hand, if you are writing about the historical events related to Toni Morrison's novel *Beloved*, you may depend primarily on older sources that come from that time period.

15b Understanding different kinds of searches

Even when you have a general idea of what kinds of sources exist and which kinds you need for your particular research project, you still have to figure out the best ways to look for them. If you go into a big store like Wal-Mart looking for some fuel for your backyard barbecue but are unsure of exactly what you want or where anything in the store is, you have several possible options. If time is short or you have no idea which fuel would work best, you may ask a salesperson to recommend a specific product—and show you where it is—so that you can pay for it fast and get out of the store. But if you aren't in a hurry and want to look at various products, compare prices, and perhaps browse the rest of the store just to see what's on sale, you may choose to roam at your leisure. In the same way, the library and the Internet give you a variety of options for searching for sources, some of which are more efficient and productive than others. All of these options will be explained in more detail later in the chapter, but before you begin your research, it's important to understand some of the basic differences among them.

1 Searches using online library resources

Sometimes beginning researchers assume that all the information they could possibly need is readily available on the Internet. But you must go beyond the Net. Even if you consider only electronic sources, there's a lot more out there than what's on the Net—and more than your own computer can turn up. Your library's computers hold important resources that are either not available on the Web (many are on CD-ROM) or not easily accessible to students except through the library's own system. The most important of these resources is the library's own **catalog** of its holdings (mostly books), but college libraries also pay to subscribe to a large number of **databases**—electronic collections of information, such

res

15b

322

RESEARCH

Conducting
Research

as indexes to journal and magazine articles, texts of news stories and legal cases, lists of sources on particular topics, and compilations of statistics — that students can access for free. Many of these databases offer the additional advantage of having been screened or compiled by editors, reference librarians, or other scholars, a characteristic not true of most of the materials you might find on the Web. Later sections of this chapter will provide detailed information on how to conduct effective Web searches. But as a general rule, you will be wise to work with the electronic sources available to you through your college library before turning to the Web.

2 Catalog and database searches: distinguishing subject headings from keywords

For more on
LCSH, see 15d1.

Searching for sources in your library's online catalog and databases will be much more efficient if you use carefully chosen words to limit the scope of your search. The catalog and databases usually index their contents by author, by title, and by **subject headings** — a standardized set of words and phrases used to classify the subject matter of books and articles. (For books, most U.S. libraries use the *Library of Congress Subject Headings,* or LCSH, for this purpose.) When you search the catalog by subject, then, you are searching only one part of the electronic record of the library's books, and you will need to use the exact wording of the LCSH classifications. Searches using **keywords,** on the other hand, make use of the computer's ability to look for *any* term in *any* field of the electronic record, including not just subject but author, title, and, for articles, perhaps an abstract or summary of the article's content. Keyword searching is less restrictive, but it requires you to put some thought into choosing your search terms in order to get the best results. In addition, you need to learn to use the techniques of combining keywords with the **Boolean operators** AND, OR, and NOT and with parentheses and quotation marks to limit (or in some cases expand) your search.

For an explanation of Boolean operators and other techniques for searching by combining keywords, see 15e5.

3 Internet searches: distinguishing subject directories from search engines

The Internet has no overall index such as the LCSH (yet). Like library catalogs and databases, however, it offers two basic ways for you to search for sources related to a particular topic: one using subject categories and one using keywords. Most Internet search tools, such as Yahoo!, Lycos, and Google, offer both of these options. A **subject** directory organized by categories allows you to choose a broad category like "Entertainment" or "Science" and then to click on increasingly narrow categories like "Movies" or "Astronomy" and then "Thrillers" or "The Solar System" until you reach a point where you are given a list of Web sites or the opportunity to do a keyword search. (In the latter case, the computer searches for keywords appearing in Web sites.) With the second kind of Internet search option, a **search engine,** you start right off with a keyword search. Because the Internet contains vastly more material than even the largest library catalog or database, searching it using a search engine requires even more thought and care in the choice and combining of keywords.

●— For more on
   using search
   tools, see 15e4.

15c Starting your research and gathering background information

When you have a working thesis about your topic and an understanding of some of the kinds of sources you need to look for and some of the ways you can go about searching for them, you are ready to start thinking more specifically about the logistical challenges of your research project. At this point, before you start looking for specific sources in the library and on the Web, it's also a good idea to talk with some other people about what you're looking for and to do some general background research on your topic.

1 Thinking about logistics

For most research projects you will carry out, whether in college or on the job, you will be working against a deadline. Considering logistics can help you complete a project in the time allowed. If you have only two weeks to do research, for instance, you will need to be very selective. If you have several months, however, you can follow a broader course, perhaps conducting some field research. Also consider issues of access: Can you get to the materials, people, works of art, or other items you need in the time allowed? How can you speed up access? For library work, find out whether you can print the results of the searches you conduct (some libraries charge a fee for printing or limit the number of pages you can print on any one day) and whether you can copy these results onto your own disc. Finally, consider any advance contacts you may need to make—to set up an interview, to secure materials through interlibrary loan, to use a friend's computer with a speedy ethernet connection, to see materials in a rare-book room.

●— For guidelines on
   conducting field
   research, see 15f.

Shannan Palma, the student whose research project we followed in Chapter 14, had the entire term to complete her work. Consequently, she decided to include background reading about the history of U.S. film in her set of strategies. In addition, she knew she wanted to conduct a full search of the Web, see a number of movies (either on video or on the big screen), and conduct at least one interview with an expert in film studies.

2 Consulting others

For a discussion ⟶
of the library, see
15d.

One of your most valuable resources for research is the highly trained staff of your library, especially the reference librarians and those skilled in electronic searches. To get the most helpful advice, pose *specific* questions: not "Where can I find information about computers?" but "Where can I find information on the history of computers?" or "Where can I find the *Gale Directory of Databases*?" If you are having difficulty asking clear and precise questions, you probably need to do some general background research on your topic. Then work again on narrowing and focusing your topic, clarifying the issue, asking a more specific research question, formulating a sharper hypothesis. On another trip to the library, you will be able to ask more specific questions and get more helpful answers.

Of course, many people are available beyond the library who can lead you to sources or even serve as sources themselves.

- *Brainstorming* with friends and classmates can help you turn up interesting sources.

For more about ⟶
planning and
conducting inter-
views, see 15f2.

- *Using email* can give you access to experts and others who are interested in and knowledgeable about your topic. If you identify an expert you would like to interview, email that person and ask if she or he would agree to a brief online (or telephone) interview.

**www • bedford
stmartins.com/
smhandbook**

For an index of
electronic mailing
lists and
instructions for
subscribing,
click on

▸ Links
  ▸ Reference
    Resources

- *Using electronic mailing lists and newsgroups* can also provide information about your topic. Before you subscribe to a mailing list related to your topic, though, think about how much email you want to receive: most people find that subscribing to more than one or two lists simply takes up too much time. Your college library likely provides access to a range of public newsgroups, hosted on Usenet, for example. To access a list of Usenet newsgroups, check out <www.groups.google.com>, which offers a twenty-year Usenet archive containing 700 million messages.

3 Consulting reference works

Consulting general reference works like encyclopedias, biographical dictionaries and indexes, atlases, and so on is another good way to get started on your research project, even though the project will eventually take you beyond such general reference sources. These works are especially good for

- getting an overview of a topic
- identifying subtopics of interest to you
- leading you to more specialized sources
- identifying useful keywords for electronic searches

When Shannan Palma began drawing up a research strategy for her project on movie heroes, she consulted an encyclopedia of films as well as biographical dictionaries to find general information about some directors she was interested in.

■ Encyclopedias

For general background on a subject, **encyclopedias** are a good place to begin, particularly because many include bibliographies that can point you to more specialized sources. Though some encyclopedias provide in-depth information, more often they serve as a place to start, not as a major source of information. Note that many general encyclopedias are available, often in elegant multimedia, on CD-ROM or by online subscription from your library's site.

www • bedford
stmartins.com/
smhandbook

For links to
encyclopedias
found online,
click on

▶ Links
  ▶ Reference
    Resources

GENERAL ENCYCLOPEDIAS

Academic American Encyclopedia
The Columbia Encyclopedia
EncyberPedia
Encyclopedia Americana
The New Encyclopaedia Britannica

SPECIALIZED ENCYCLOPEDIAS

Compared with general encyclopedias, **specialized encyclopedias** — on subjects from ancient history to world drama — usually provide more detailed articles by authorities in the field as well as extensive bibliographies for locating sources. Again, you should rely on these books more for background material than as major sources of information. Many specialized encyclopedias are available on CD-ROM or online as well as in print. For more information on specialized encyclopedias in particular fields, see Chapters 64 – 67.

■ *Biographical resources*

The lives and historical settings of famous people are the topics of biographical dictionaries and indexes. Here are a few examples of biographical reference works; many others, particularly volumes specialized by geographic area or field, are available.

> *African American Biographies*
> *American Men and Women of Science*
> *Biography Index*
> *Contemporary Authors*
> *Current Biography*
> *Dictionary of American Biography*
> *Dictionary of National Biography*
> *International Who's Who*
> *Two Thousand Notable American Women*
> *Webster's New Biographical Dictionary*
> *Who's Who in America*
> *World Authors*

■ *Almanacs, yearbooks, and atlases*

Almanacs and **yearbooks** gather data on current events and statistical information.

ALMANACS, YEARBOOKS, NEWS DIGESTS

> *American Annual*
> *Dow Jones–Irwin Business Almanac*
> *Facts on File Yearbook*
> *The Gallup Poll*
> *Information Please Almanac*
> *Statesman's Yearbook*
> *Statistical Abstracts of the United States (U.S. Census Bureau)*
> *UNESCO Statistical Yearbook*
> *World Almanac and Book of Facts*

Atlases provide maps and other geographic data.

ATLASES

> *Atlas of World Cultures: A Geographical Guide to Ethnographic Literature*
> *Encyclopaedia Britannica World Atlas*

National Atlas of the United States
National Geographic Atlas of the World
The New International World Atlas
The New York Times Atlas of the World

15d Using the library

The library is one of a researcher's best friends, especially in an age of electronic communication. Your college library houses a great number of print materials: books, periodicals, and reference works of all kinds. And, as noted earlier, computer terminals there give you access to electronic catalogs and databases — and access to many other libraries (both real and virtual) via the Internet. It is essential, then, to acquaint yourself with the resources in your own college library. The following box includes some of the many resources your library may offer — and indicates where they are discussed in this chapter.

A SAMPLING OF LIBRARY RESEARCH RESOURCES

reference librarians (15c2 and 15d)

online and CD-ROM databases (15b1)

encyclopedias (15c3)

biographical resources (15c3)

almanacs, yearbooks, and atlases (15c3)

library catalog (15d1)

indexes to books and reviews (15d2)

indexes to newspapers, magazines, and journals (15d3)

bibliographies (15d4)

special collections and archives (15d5)

audio and video collections (15d5)

art collections (15d5)

government documents (15d5)

statistical sources (15d5)

interlibrary loans (15d5)

access to Internet and World Wide Web (15e)

res

328

15d

RESEARCH

Conducting
Research

The most efficient way to learn about your library is to make an appointment with a reference librarian, who can introduce you to your library's resources and offer concrete tips on how to access them. If a librarian is not available, ask whether the library has an online self-tutorial that can help you learn about the library's resources. If you have your own computer and an Internet connection, you can do some of your library research from home. In addition, you can no doubt access the library's computerized resources from various computer labs on campus.

One way to start learning about your library's resources is to visit its Web site, which you can usually access directly from your school's main site. Most library homepages will include sections describing collections (often by subject and type), hours of operation, and a floor plan, and the menu will probably also include links to each area of the library and to its databases. Visitors to the main library page at Stanford University, for instance, can learn a lot about Stanford's online catalog (named Socrates) as well as about the many databases that the university's multiple libraries subscribe to. In short, checking out the Web site can give you a good virtual tour of the library that you can then build on with a visit in person.

When Shannan Palma began her research, she spent several hours in the campus library, learning how to use the electronic catalog, how to search the library's databases, and how to access the Internet from the library. She discovered that her library offers students a free online instructional program that provides lessons, examples, and guides for those learning to do electronic searches. In addition, she spoke with a reference librarian about collections in the library related to the history of film. Your college library probably has similar programs and services: check them out.

CONSIDERING DISABILITIES: Web Site Accessibility

While the Americans with Disabilities Act stipulates that all government Web sites must be accessible to those with disabilities, these rules have only recently been expanded to cover educational and other Web sites. If you encounter sites that are not accessible to you, ask the reference librarian to help you identify similar sites that may be more accessible. Also consider clicking on the "Contact Us" button, if there is one, and letting the sponsors of the site know that some potential users can't get ready access to the information.

Working with one or two other classmates, pay a visit to the main library on your campus, and bring back answers to the following questions: How are the library's materials organized? What resources can you use to find out what your library owns and where these materials are located? What electronic encyclopedias, indexes, and databases are available? What electronic journal collections does your library subscribe to? Write up a brief report that answers these questions, and comment on those aspects of the library that your group found most interesting or helpful, most confusing or difficult to use. Bring your report to class for discussion.

1 Using the catalog

The library catalog lists all the library's books as well as its periodical holdings and subscriptions. Some libraries still have their catalogs on cards, but most have transferred (or are in the process of transferring) their files to an electronic catalog you can access easily.

Library catalogs follow a standard pattern of organization. Each holding is identified by three kinds of entries: one headed by the *author's name*, one by the *title*, and one or (usually) more by the *subject*. If you can't find a book under one of these headings, try the others; sometimes entries are lost or misfiled. If your library's catalog is electronic, it can also be searched using a combination of subject headings and keywords.

Here is an author entry from a library catalog. Note that it includes the due date for this book, so you can tell it was checked out of the library.

```
AUTHOR         Rushing, Janice Hocker.
TITLE          Projecting the shadow : the cyborg hero
                  in American film / Janice Hocker Rush-
                  ing, Thomas S. Frentz.
PUBLISH INFO   Chicago : University of Chicago Press,
                  1995.
DESCRIPTION    x, 261 p. : ill. ; 24 cm.
SERIES         New practices of inquiry.
NOTES          Includes bibliographical references
                  (p. 222-244) and index.
SUBJECTS       Cyborgs in motion pictures.
               Myth in motion pictures.
ADD AUTHORS    Frentz, Thomas S.
OCLC #         32737837.
ISBN           0226731669 (cloth : alk. paper)
    LOCATION     CALL NO.        YEAR   STATUS
1 > JOU Stacks   PN1995.9.C9 R57  1995   DUE 01-05-03
```

res

330

15d

RESEARCH

Conducting
Research

■ *Identifying subjects for your search*

Subjects in the library catalog are usually identified and arranged according to the system presented in the *Library of Congress Subject Headings* (LCSH). This multivolume work may be kept at the reference desk and is also available online. (An advantage of accessing an online catalog through the Web is that doing so always allows you to download the information in some way.) In it, you can check the exact wording of subject headings and define key terms of interest to you. You may find that the LCSH identifies headings that have not readily occurred to you. Under most headings, you'll find other subjects that are treated (identified by *UF*, "use for"), broader headings that include the subject (*BT*, "broader topic"), and narrower headings that might be relevant (*NT*, "narrower topic").

For more on searches using subject headings and keywords, see 15b2.

Shannan Palma identified some promising subject headings by using a keyword search in the Library of Congress Web site, <www.loc.gov>. After accessing the site, she clicked on the button "Search Our Catalogs" and then chose the option of a "Guided Search," which allowed her to use more than one keyword, *film* and *hero,* and to limit her search to books written in English. The "Full Record" for one of the sources her search yielded appears on p. 331. Shannan was then able to use the information she found in the "Full Record" to search her own library's holdings for the book.

The "Subjects" listing for this book shows that it is classified under the LCSH heading "Characters and characteristics in motion pictures," which Shannan could use in further subject searches. In fact, the underlining shows that this is a link Shannan could click on; when she did so, she accessed a list of the twenty-five other items in the Library of Congress that are classified under this heading. Another source that her original search turned up led her to the LCSH heading "Myth in motion pictures," which also proved useful.

Searching only for subject entries is likely to be inefficient, however, because the headings are usually so broad. If the best Library of Congress heading you can identify does not match your particular needs or is so broad that your search yields many books but only a few that are useful, use other leads. Look to bibliographies, book indexes, periodical indexes, and notes in other publications for potentially useful authors and titles.

■ *Using call numbers*

Besides identifying a book's author, title, subject, and publication information, each catalog entry also lists a **call number** — the book's identifi-

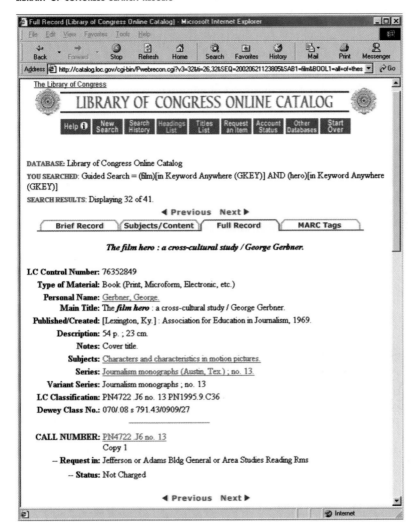

cation number. Most academic libraries now use the Library of Congress system, which begins call numbers with letters of the alphabet.

Take a look at the call number for a book by Lee Drummond, titled *American Dreamtime: A Cultural Analysis of Popular Movies:*

PN1995.9.M96D78 1996. Here's an explanation of what each part of the call number indicates:

P = books on language, literature, motion pictures, and drama

PN = literature (general)

1995.9 = motion pictures (includes 1993 through 1999)

.M96 = more specific aspect of motion pictures

D78 = code for the author's last name

1996 = year of publication

Once you have printed out the catalog entry for the book or written down the call number, look for a library map or shelving plan to tell you where your book is housed. Whether you find your book or not, take the time to browse through the books nearby. Very often you will find the area where your book belongs a more important treasure trove than any bibliography or index.

If the computer tells you that the book is checked out or if your book is not on the shelf, ask about it at the circulation desk. The book may not circulate, or it may be in an area closed to the public. If someone has checked it out, the library might recall it for you. Consider your deadline, and determine whether it is realistic to request a recall.

2 Using indexes to books and reviews

Other useful sources include **book indexes,** which can be helpful for quickly locating complete bibliographic information on a book when you know only one piece of it—the author's last name, perhaps, or the title. These sources can also be valuable for alerting you to other works by a particular author or on a particular subject. Note that such indexes are available as databases online or on CD-ROM as well as in print.

BOOK INDEXES

Books in Print

Cumulative Book Index

OCLC WorldCat

Paperbound Books in Print

Consider also using a **review index** to check the relevance of a source or to get a thumbnail sketch of its contents.

Book Review Digest
Book Review Index
Current Book Review Citations
Index to Book Reviews in the Humanities
Index to Book Reviews in the Social Sciences

3 Using indexes to newspapers, magazines, and journals

Periodical indexes are guides to articles published in newspapers, magazines, and scholarly journals, items that will not appear in your library's catalog. Each index covers a specific group of periodicals, usually identified at the beginning of the index or volume. Originally, many of these indexes were available only in print form, and most libraries still house these volumes. Other indexes, however, are now available as electronic databases. Like print indexes, electronic indexes ordinarily provide author, title, or subject search options, but they also offer the ability to search by keyword, place of publication, publisher, or periodical title.

GENERAL INDEXES

General indexes of periodicals list articles mostly from current general-interest magazines (such as *Time* or *Newsweek*), newspapers, or a combination of these. General indexes usually provide current sources on a topic, but these sources may not treat the topic in sufficient depth for your purposes. In addition to the *Readers' Guide to Periodical Literature,* some of the most-often-used general indexes include the following, all of which are available electronically:

ArticleFirst
Ethnic News Watch
Gale's InfoTrac
LEXIS-NEXIS/Academic Universe
NewsBank
New York Times Index
Periodical Abstracts
Readers' Guide Abstracts

When Shannan Palma began her research, she consulted several general indexes, including the print version of the *Readers' Guide to Periodical Literature* and the electronic version of *Periodical Abstracts,* using the keywords *film* and *hero.* Here are some examples of what she found:

ENTRY FROM READERS' GUIDE TO PERIODICAL LITERATURE

HEROES AND HEROINES IN MOTION PICTURES
Cowardly heroes. il *Premiere* v6 p101-2 Ag '93
Title of article ——From El Cid to Arnold: the superhero in crisis [C. Heston] G.
Fuller. il por *Interview* v23 p98 S '93

Author Title of Volume and Date of
        periodical page number publication

ENTRY FROM PERIODICAL ABSTRACTS

Author	Firstenberg, Jean Picker
Title	**From the Director: On Heroes and the Media**
Appears in	American Film 1987, v13n1, Oct p. 67

Click here to see which OhioLINK libraries have this journal

Abstract	The idea that today's images of **film** and television have had an enormous impact on the evolution of the modern **hero** is expressed in an opinion
Subject	Heroism & heroes Motion picture industry
Note	Availability: American Film Subscription Service, PO Box 966, Farmingdale NY 11737-9866 Article Length: Medium (10-30 col inches) Article Type: Commentary

SPECIALIZED INDEXES AND ABSTRACTS

Many disciplines have **specialized indexes** and **abstracts** to help researchers find detailed information. In general, such works list articles in scholarly journals for that discipline, but they may include other publications as well; check the beginning of the index or the volume. To use these resources most efficiently, ask a reference librarian to help you identify those most likely to address your topic.

For lists of spe-
cialized indexes
and abstracts,
see Chapters
64–67.

Continuing her search, Shannan used the keywords *film* and *hero* to search two specialized electronic indexes available in her library: PsycINFO and ERIC. The PsycINFO search yielded fourty-two entries, the ERIC search thirty-four. Examples of these search results are shown on pp. 335 and 336.

EXERCISE 15.1

Go to your library with your topic carefully defined. Ask a librarian how to identify newspaper, magazine, or journal databases that would include your topic and that might be most helpful. Take notes, and share what you find out about identifying appropriate databases with your class.

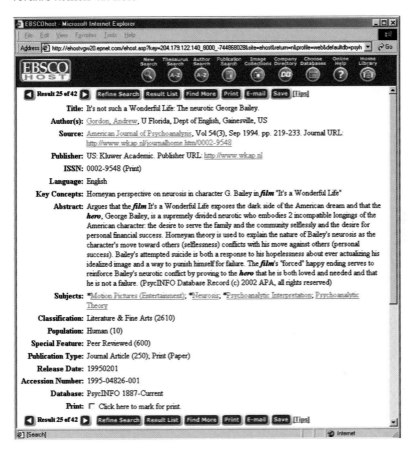

FOR COLLABORATION

Working with a classmate, enter the keywords for each of your research projects in at least three different periodical indexes, and then compare results. How many references did each search yield? What kinds of journals turned up in each different search? What other differences between searches can you note?

res

336   **15d**

RESEARCH

Conducting
Research

ERIC ACCESSED VIA CSA INTERNET DATABASE SERVICE

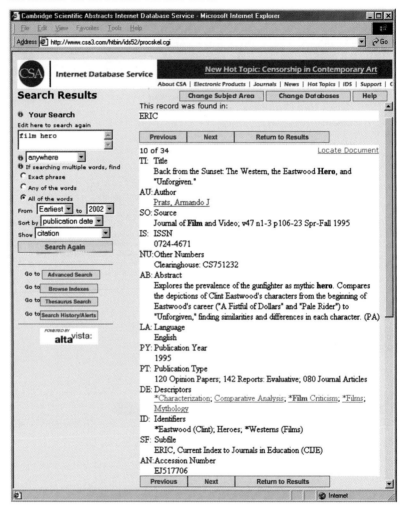

To locate an indexed article that seems promising for your research project, you can check the Web and the online library catalog to see whether the periodical is available electronically and, if so, whether your library offers access to it. By using the library computer network for access, you can often avoid subscription charges or fees for viewing the text of the article. For example, the *New York Times* on the Web, <www.nytimes.com>, a very useful source for many topics currently in the news, charges $3.00 to download most articles that are more than a week old.

If the periodical is not available electronically (as most scholarly journals, for example, are not), if your library does not offer free access to the periodical and downloading from it through a database, or if you simply prefer to look at a print version, the library catalog will tell you whether one is available in the library's periodicals room. This room will probably have recent issues of hundreds or even thousands of newspapers, magazines, and scholarly journals, and it may also contain bound volumes of past issues and microfilm copies of older newspapers. (The *New York Times,* for example, is most likely available in your library on microfilm.)

HOMEPAGE FOR THE NEW YORK TIMES ON THE WEB

res

338 **15d**

4 Using bibliographies

RESEARCH

Conducting
Research

Finding good **bibliographies** (lists of sources) can speed up your research, so it is well worth your time to consider them. Look at any bibliographies in books or articles you are using for your research; they can lead you to other valuable resources. In addition, check with your reference librarian to find out whether the library has more extensive bibliographies devoted to the area of your research. At one time, all such bibliographies were bound in printed volumes; increasingly, however, these resources are available online. When Shannan Palma accessed the *MLA International Bibliography* database (to which her library subscribes), she entered the keywords *film* and *hero,* and the database quickly replied with sixteen initial entries, including the following one:

```
You searched for the WORD: film hero                      MLA
                                                 Record 2 of 81

AUTHOR        Abele, Elizabeth.
TITLE         Rescuing the Hero: Shifting Expectations
                 for Men in the '90s.

APPEARS IN    The Mid-Atlantic Almanac: The Journal of
                 the Mid-Atlantic Popular/American Cul -
                 ture Association, 1996, 5, p. 107-22
                 MAA 1063-1763 Greencastle, PA.

PUB TYPE      journal article.
LANGUAGE      English.

SUBJECT       dramatic arts -- film -- treatment of
                 masculinity -- of hero.
ISSN          1063-1763.
SEQUENCE #    96-4-225.
UPD CODE      9601.
```

5 Using other library resources

In addition to books and periodicals, libraries give you access to many other useful materials that might be appropriate for your research.

• *Special collections and archives.* Your library will probably have one area, often referred to as *special collections,* devoted to rare books and manuscripts. In this area or elsewhere, your library may house **archives,** collections of valuable papers and related materials, which could be helpful to you in your research. Special collections and archives are often available to undergraduate students, so ask your reference librarian whether they contain possible sources on your topic. One student, for example, learned that her university owned a collection of over seventy thousand posters from the early twentieth century to the cold war era, and with help from the librarian, she was able to use a number of these posters as primary sources for her research project on German culture after World War II.

- *Audio, video, and art collections* are also probably available on your campus. Many academic libraries include an area devoted to media, where they collect films and videos as well as sound recordings. Your library may also have a section devoted to art collections — or you may have an art museum on campus that will give you access to primary works for your research. Working with these materials can be very exciting, and it can lead to great research. Shannan Palma made good use of her library's video collection in researching her project on Hollywood movie heroes.

- *Government documents and statistical sources* may take up as much as an entire floor of a library, and many of them may be very helpful to you. You can use the library's or your own networked computer to check the online version of the *Catalog of U.S. Government Publications,* <www.access .gpo.gov/su_docs/locators/cgp/index.html>, to identify publications appropriate to your topic and then see if your library has them.

  For statistical information, consult the sources on p. 326. Some, like the *World Almanac and Book of Facts,* are good for general statistics, whereas others are more specialized. *The Gallup Poll,* for example, provides public opinion statistics, and the *Dow Jones–Irwin Business Almanac* offers business data. Ask your reference librarian to recommend other statistical sources you might need.

- *Interlibrary loans* enable you to borrow books, journals, and video or audio materials from another library. Such loans can take time, however, and may involve some cost to you, so make sure you really need the source and can get it in time to make good use of it.

15e Using the World Wide Web

The World Wide Web, that part of the Internet that is hypertextual, allowing users to leap from link to link with the click of a mouse, is today many college students' favorite way of accessing information. The Web has grown so furiously that estimates of the number of sites and texts available on it (not to mention sights and sounds) stagger the imagination. And since anyone can post a document to the Web, it has been seen as open and highly democratic. Compared with a library, the Web is indeed open to a much wider range of contributors, and this open publishing is one of its most valuable attributes. But openness carries dangers as well: since no one — no librarian, no organization — is responsible for regulating information on the Web, it's possible to find

res

340

15e

RESEARCH
Conducting
Research

anything and everything there, from the most banal and ridiculous statements to outright misinformation, lies, and libel. As a result, you need to use information from the Web with great care.

1 Getting access

Today, most college students have access to the Web from the library, a campus computer center, or the dorms, or via a home computer and connection. Campus-based connections are a lot faster than using a modem, so if you are living off campus, you should check with your school to find out how to connect to the campus network most efficiently. Many colleges now offer students dial-up access to the campus network from home, which is certainly less expensive and less problem-prone than depending on an Internet provider.

2 Reading URLs

Every site on the Net has its own address, called a **Uniform Resource Locator (URL)**. Here, for example, is the URL for a helpful Web site that offers answers to a multitude of questions about computer terminology:

http://www.whatis.com

The first part of this address (*http*) is the **protocol,** in this case "hypertext transfer protocol," which identifies the kind of electronic link that is being made to access the site. The next part (*whatis.com*) is the **domain name,** which identifies the owner of the site and the kind of site it is, in this case a commercial one (*.com*). Other kinds of sites include *.edu* (educational), *.gov* (governmental), and *.org* (nonprofit organization). Some addresses have additional parts, such as a **directory name** that identifies a particular part of a larger site; a **file name** that identifies a particular document; or a **file extension** that identifies the kind of computer language the file is written in.

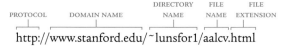

To access a site, you generally have to type the exact URL into the address box, using the precise capital or lowercase letters, spacing, and so on. Depending on the site and on the browser you are using, though, you may not need to include — or may need to leave out — the protocol or the beginning of the domain name.

3 Using Web browsers

Software programs called **browsers** allow you easy access to the Web and let you move swiftly from one Web site to another. The computers in your library or campus computer center no doubt will have one or both of the two most commonly used browsers (Netscape Navigator and Internet Explorer) on the desktops; you just click on one to begin using that browser. These browsers not only give you access to powerful search tools but also can provide lots of help in organizing and keeping track of your research.

RESEARCH
Using the World
Wide Web

●— For an explana-
tion of search
tools, see 15b3
and 15e4.

▓ *Tracking your searches*

In Netscape Navigator, the GO button on the top menu bar shows a list of the Web sites you have accessed during your current Navigator session. In Internet Explorer, use the VIEW button, and then click on GO TO. While this function only keeps track of your steps on the Web in any one session, it can be valuable if you are trying to retrace your steps to find a source you forgot to take notes on or need further information from.

You can track your searches for longer periods of time by using the HISTORY function of your browser. In Internet Explorer, click on the HISTORY button in the standard buttons toolbar to list the sites you have visited, organized by day. In Netscape, go to COMMUNICATOR on the top menu, then to TOOLS, and then to HISTORY, which will list the day and time you visited a site. You can customize the HISTORY function by going to EDIT on the top menu and then to PREFERENCES and then customizing the frame for HISTORY.

▓ *Using bookmarks and favorites*

If you are not already used to bookmarking favorite sites on the Web, take time to learn how to do so now. In Netscape, the BOOKMARK function appears to the left of the location space that lists the URL. When you are at a site whose address you want to save, just click on the BOOKMARK button. The name of the site will appear as a link whenever you click on your full list of bookmarked sites. In Internet Explorer, you can save sites by clicking on the FAVORITES button on the top menu bar and then ADD TO FAVORITES. If you find yourself collecting lots of bookmarked or favorite sites, consider organizing them. In Netscape, you can organize bookmarks into folders by clicking on BOOKMARKS and then EDIT BOOKMARKS and then dragging any bookmark or folder to reposition it. You can also drag and drop bookmarks into folders. In Internet Explorer, click on FAVORITES and then ORGANIZE FAVORITES.

Internet browsers give you access to powerful search engines and subject directories that allow you to carry out research online. Clicking on SEARCH takes you to the search tools programmed into your browser, but you're free to use others as well. Most search tools allow keyword searches as well as subject directory or category searches. If you're using a search engine, you simply type in keywords and get results; some metasearch tools use several search engines at once and compile their findings. In a subject directory, on the other hand, the first screen lists a number of categories you can click on to begin your search, which you can then narrow by clicking on increasingly narrow subcategories. For example, in Yahoo!, you can click on "Entertainment" if you are working on a research project in that area, and then click on "Movies and Film" and then "Theory and Criticism." Each click narrows and focuses your search. And at any point, you can switch to a keyword search to look for specific terms and topics.

Here is a list of some of the most-often-used search tools.

SEARCH TOOLS

AltaVista <*www.altavista.digital.com*> lets you search the entire Web using either a single keyword or multiple keywords.

Excite <*www.excite.com*> allows you to do keyword and subject directory searches.

Google <*www.google.com*> is a popular search tool that is a favorite of many students. Subject directory and keyword searches.

HotBot <*www.hotbot.com*> lets you search using one of several search engines and to narrow the search to specific dates, media, and other criteria. Allows keyword and subject directory searches.

Lycos <*www.lycos.com*> allows you to search a huge catalog of Web sites and includes multimedia documents. Keyword and subject directory searches.

Teoma <*www.teoma.com*> is a search engine that ranks a result's relevance based on the number of same-subject pages that refer to it, not just general popularity.

(Continued on p. 343)

(Continued from p. 342)

Yahoo! *<www.yahoo.com>* allows you either to search directories of sites related to particular subjects (such as entertainment or education) or to enter keywords that Yahoo! gives to a search engine (Google), which sends back the results.

METASEARCH TOOLS

Ixquick *<www.ixquick.com>* is a speedy metasearch tool that allows you to search fourteen other engines or directories at the same time. Uses keywords.

ProFusion *<www.profusion.com>* is another metasearch tool. Uses keywords.

WebCrawler *<www.webcrawler.com>* searches using several search engines (including some that return sponsored listings) and subject directories.

Zworks *<www.zworks.com>* calls itself "the metasearch loved by parents and webmasters alike" because it can be filtered. Also ranks results for relevancy. Uses keywords.

5 Using keywords, Boolean operators, and quotation marks

Since different search tools have different rules for using keywords, it's best to look for the FAQ (frequently asked questions) or information or help section of the search tool you are using and read carefully. You'll need to be careful also in making your keywords as narrow as possible. If you are interested in legal issues regarding the Internet, for example, and you enter *Internet* and *law* as keywords in a search on Google, you will get over three million possible sources. The keywords you choose—names, titles, authors, concepts—need to lead you to more specific sources. In this case, entering the name of a well-known legal theorist, *Lawrence Lessig,* along with another keyword, *speeches,* returns about two hundred responses, which is a much more reasonable number for you to consider.

In order to search using more than one keyword at a time, it is helpful to use your search tool's advanced-search options. Most search engines now offer these options (sometimes on a separate advanced-search page) to help you easily combine keywords, search for an exact phrase, or exclude items containing particular keywords; often they let

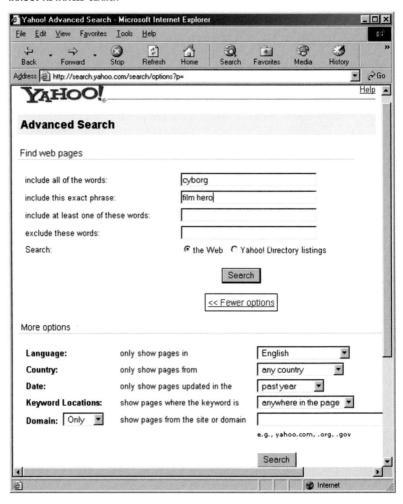

you limit your search in other ways as well, such as by date, language, country of origin, or location of the keyword within a site.

For her research, Shannan Palma found Yahoo! best suited to entertainment-related subjects. By clicking on ADVANCED SEARCH within Yahoo! as shown above, she was able to easily combine keywords and limit her search to only those listings added during the past year, in Eng-

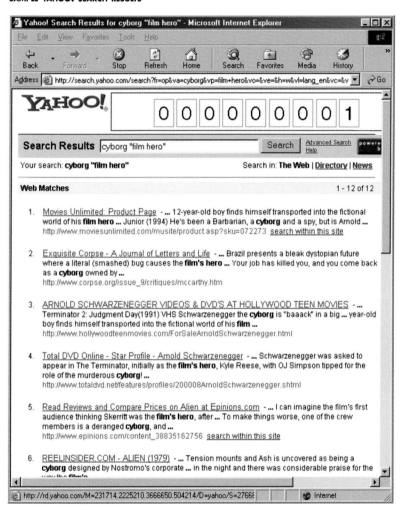

lish. When she entered her keywords *film hero* (as an exact phrase) plus *cyborg*, Yahoo! found twelve sites that matched her request, including one she definitely wanted to follow up. The first page of her search results is shown above.

With many search engines, you can also use quotation marks to create an exact phrase for your search. In addition, many library catalogs

res

346

15e

RESEARCH

Conducting
Research

and some search engines offer a search option using the Boolean operators AND, NOT, and OR as well as parentheses and quotation marks. The Boolean operators work this way:

HOLLYWOOD AND HEROES

AND *limits your search.* If you enter the terms *Hollywood AND heroes,* the search engine will retrieve *only* those items that contain *both* those terms. The following diagram shows how this operator works (the items retrieved using AND are shaded in brown):

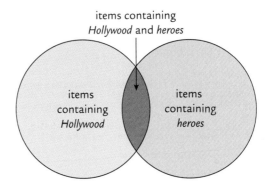

HOLLYWOOD NOT HEROES

NOT *also limits your search.* If you enter the terms *Hollywood NOT heroes,* the search engine will retrieve every item that contains *Hollywood* except those that also contain the term *heroes.* The following diagram shows how NOT works (the items retrieved using NOT are shaded in brown):

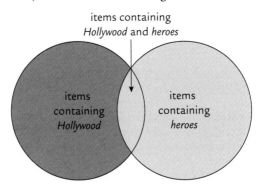

HOLLYWOOD OR HEROES

res

15e   347

RESEARCH

Using the World
Wide Web

OR *expands your search*. If you enter the terms *Hollywood OR heroes*, the computer will retrieve every item that contains the term *Hollywood* and every item that contains the term *heroes*. In this case, the OR stands for MORE, since you will probably get many more sources by using OR than you would by entering either term alone. The following diagram shows how OR works (the items retrieved using OR are shaded in brown):

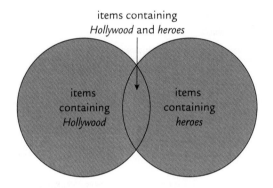

items containing
Hollywood and *heroes*

items
containing
Hollywood

items
containing
heroes

Parentheses can customize your search still further. Entering *Oscar AND (Denzel Washington OR Will Smith)*, for example, will locate items that mention either of those actors in connection with the Academy Awards, while entering *film NOT (western OR thriller)* will exclude those kinds of films from your search.

In one of her searches, Shannan Palma used two keywords, *film AND hero*. She sometimes narrowed her search further by adding a third term, *AND United States* or *AND Hollywood*. Since search engines don't pick up synonyms automatically, she might also have used the terms *movie,* or *America,* or *American*.

Quotation marks around a phrase can also help you narrow your search because they indicate that all the words in the phrase must appear together in the exact order you have typed them. This option is especially important because some search engines assume that when multiple key-words are entered, AND is between them. When Shannan Palma typed in the keywords *Hollywood movie heroes* for a search on Google, it yielded 140,000 hits. But when she put the three terms in one set of quotation marks, Google returned only six sources, as shown on p. 348. (Search engines generally recognize proper names like *George Bush* or *New York* as a unit, however, so you don't need to use quotation marks around them.)

348

res

15e

RESEARCH

Conducting
Research

In general, type the Boolean operators in capital letters. Some search engines use symbols instead of words for them: the plus sign (+) or ampersand (&) for AND, the minus sign or hyphen (-) for NOT, and the | sign for OR (located on the backslash key on most keyboards). To save time (and maybe money), make sure you understand the rules for a particular search engine before you begin using it.

SAMPLE GOOGLE SEARCH RESULTS

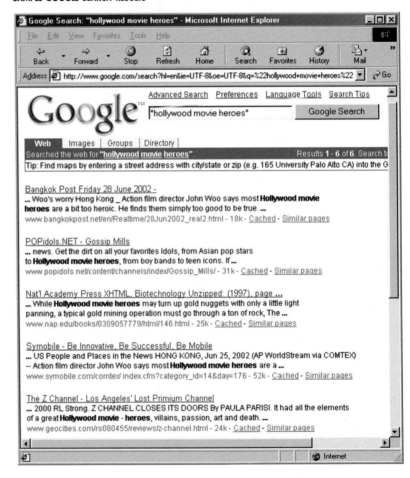

Today, students have online access to some information in libraries other than their own. These **virtual libraries** are sites on the Internet that allow you access to some of another library's collection. The University of California at Berkeley, for example, has a site, <www.sunsite.berkeley.edu>, that allows students at other institutions to access its digital collections of documents and images. A sample screen from that site is shown on p. 350.

Other online collections you may find helpful are housed in governmental sites.

**www • bedford
stmartins.com/
smhandbook**

For more
information on
Virtual Library
sites, click on

▶ **Links**
  ▶ **Reference
    Resources**

Bureau of Labor Statistics <www.bls.gov> provides information by region. Allows you to search by keyword.

Library of Congress <www.lcweb.loc.gov> offers a vast array of information, including legislative information, information on copyright and intellectual property, and collections such as American Memory, which contains more than seven million digital items from over a hundred historical collections. Allows searches by title, author/creator, subject, or keyword.

National Institutes of Health <www.nih.gov> provides data on health and medical issues. Allows keyword searches.

Statistical Abstracts of the United States <www.census.gov/statab/www> provides information on social and economic trends. Allows searches by keyword or place.

U.S. Census Bureau <www.census.gov> provides data on population and other demographic data. Allows you to search by keyword, place, or region.

For current news events, you can consult online versions of newspapers such as the *New York Times* at <www.nytimes.com> or the *Chicago Tribune* at <www.chicagotribune.com>. CNN at <www.cnn.com> and C-SPAN at <www.c-span.org> are among the many other newspapers and news services available electronically. You can also use a search tool like Yahoo!, which has a "News and Media" category you can click on from the main page, <www.yahoo.com>, or you can check daily news at <www.dailynews.yahoo.com>.

Some scholarly journals and at least two general-interest magazines, *Slate* at <www.slate.com> and *Salon,* <www.salon.com>, are now published only on the Web, and many other journals and magazines like *Newsweek,* the *New Yorker,* and the *New Republic* make at least part of their contents available online. In many cases, a paid subscription or a one-time fee is required to view or download articles, but you may be able to avoid these charges by using the library's computers. To access a wide variety of online articles from many different magazines, try the Web sites <www.elibrary.com> and <www.newsdirectory.com>.

res

350

15f

RESEARCH

Conducting
Research

Shannan Palma decided to make use of the UC Berkeley SunSite, where she clicked on "Catalogs and Indexes" on the homepage and found that the collection included a T-Shirt database. There she found a T-shirt featuring *Indiana Jones and the Temple of Doom,* one she considered (but finally did not use) as an illustration in her essay on movie heroes.

UC BERKELEY SUNSITE CATALOGS AND INDEXES PAGE

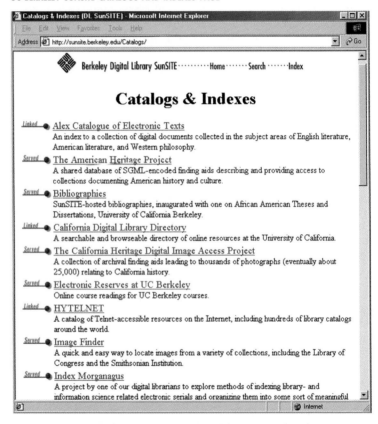

15f Conducting field research

For many research projects, particularly those in the social sciences and business, you will need to collect field data. The "field" may be many things—a classroom, a church, an ice-cream parlor, a laboratory, or the corner grocery store. As a field researcher, you will need to discover *where* you can find relevant information, *how* to gather it, and *who* might provide the best information.

Extensive field research almost certainly lies beyond your grasp as an undergraduate since it requires prolonged observation (often over several years) and complex analysis. Nevertheless, you may be able to use several field-research techniques, including observing and interviewing, to very good advantage.

1 Observing

"What," you might ask, "could be easier than observing something?" You just choose a subject, look at it closely, and record what you see and hear. Yet experience shows that several people who have observed the same scene or phenomenon will most often offer contradictory "evidence." Trained observers tell us that getting down a faithful record of an observation requires intense concentration and mental agility.

Moreover, observation is never neutral. Just as the camera has an angle on its subject and the person behind the camera must choose what to include and what to leave out, so an observer always has an angle on what he or she is looking at. If, for instance, you decide to conduct a formal observation of your writing class, the field notes you take will reflect your status as an insider. Consequently, you will need to question or second-guess your observations to see what your participation in the class may have obscured or led you to take for granted.

In other instances, when you need to observe situations or phenomena in which you are not an insider, you will aim for optimal objectivity, keeping yourself out of the picture and altering as little as possible the phenomena you are looking at — all the while remembering that you will always alter them somewhat. Much professional writing — for example, a doctor's diagnostic notes, a reporter's news article, or a social worker's case study — depends on such careful observation. You can observe anything in this way, from the use of bicycle paths on campus to the kinds of products advertised during Saturday morning television shows to the growth of chicks in an agriculture lab.

Before you conduct any observation, decide exactly what you want to find out, and anticipate what you are likely to see. Are you going to observe an action repeated by many people (such as pedestrians crossing a street), a sequence of actions (such as a medical procedure), or the interactions of a group (such as a church congregation)? Also decide exactly what you want to record and how to do so. In a grocery store, for

res

352

15f

RESEARCH

Conducting
Research

instance, decide whether to observe shoppers or store employees and what you want to note about them — what they say, what they buy, how they are dressed, how they respond to one another, and so on.

CONDUCTING OBSERVATION

1. Determine the purpose of the observation, and be sure it relates to your research question and hypothesis.

2. Make plans as far in advance as possible. Brainstorm about what you are looking for and what you expect to see. Have a sense of what you are looking for, but be flexible.

3. If necessary, make appointments and gain permissions to observe.

4. Develop an appropriate system for recording your data. For field notes taken during observation, consider using a "split" notebook or page: on one side, record your observations directly; on the other, record your own thoughts and interpretations.

5. Gather plenty of materials for note-taking: notebooks, pens, a handheld or laptop computer, camera, tape recorder, or videocassette recorder. Be aware that your way of recording data will inevitably affect your final report, if only in respect to what you include in your notes and what you leave out.

6. Review the steps you plan to take, going through the motions of observing and note-taking. Then conduct a trial run, taking field notes throughout. These activities will help you identify and solve potential problems before your formal observation.

7. After taking field notes, go back and question your observations, remaining open to various interpretations.

2 Interviewing

Some information is best obtained by **interviewing**. If you can talk with an expert in person, on the telephone, or online, you might get information you could not have obtained through any other kind of research. In addition to getting "expert opinion," you might ask for firsthand accounts or suggestions of other places to look or other people to consult. You also may wish to conduct follow-up interviews with some people you've observed.

■ *Finding people to interview*

Check first to see whether your research has generated the names of people you might contact directly. Next, brainstorm for names. In addition to authorities on your topic, consider people in your community— faculty members, war veterans, librarians, government employees, corporate executives, or others. Once you identify some promising possibilities, write, telephone, or email them to see whether interviews might be arranged.

■ *Composing questions*

To prepare useful questions, you need to know your topic well, and you need to know a fair amount about your interviewee. Try to learn as much as you can about his or her experience and opinions. You will probably want to ask several kinds of questions. **Factual questions** elicit specific answers, ones that do not invite expansion or opinion.

What flavors of ice cream does your company produce?

How many people contributed to this year's United Way campaign?

In contrast, **open-ended questions** lead the interviewee to think out loud, to go in directions that interest him or her, and to give additional details.

How would you characterize the atmosphere at the company just before the union went on strike?

How do you feel now about your decision to go to Canada in 1968 rather than be drafted?

Avoid questions that encourage vague or rambling answers (*What do you think of youth today?*) or yes/no answers (*Should the laws governing corporate accounting practices be changed?*). Instead, ask questions that must be answered with supporting details (*Why should the laws governing corporate accounting practices be changed?*).

By looking through the course offerings bulletin, Shannan Palma learned of a professor on her campus who regularly taught film and film criticism courses. She then checked her university homepage to find the email address for this professor, Morris Beja, and wrote to him requesting an interview about her research on the development of the hero in Hollywood films. When he agreed to the interview, she prepared specific questions so that she could be sure of using the hour-long interview efficiently.

PLANNING AND CONDUCTING AN INTERVIEW

1. Determine your exact purpose, and be sure it relates to your research question and hypothesis.

2. Set up the interview in advance by writing, emailing, or calling your interviewee. Specify how long it will take, and if you wish to tape-record the session, ask permission to do so.

3. Confirm your appointment at least one day in advance.

4. Prepare a written list of questions you can use to structure the interview. Brainstorming or freewriting techniques can help you come up with questions. (3a)

5. If possible, try out your questions on one or two people to determine how best to sequence them, how clear and precise they are, and how long answers will take.

6. Make sure your questions relate closely to your research project. You don't want to waste anyone's time.

7. Prepare a final copy of your questions, leaving plenty of space for notes after each one, unless you are conducting the interview online.

8. Check out all equipment beforehand — pens, notebook, tape recorder, laptop, and so on. Record the subject, date, time, and place of the interview at the beginning of all tapes and on all handwritten or typed notes.

9. Be on time!

10. Even if you are taping, take notes. If you take down quotations, ask your interviewee for permission to use them.

11. Offer to send a copy of your research project to the interviewee.

12. Remember to follow up with a thank-you note or email.

Surveys, another common field-research strategy, can take the form of interviews, but more often they depend on **questionnaires.** A student investigating campus parking for motorcycles surveyed his dormitory's residents to learn how many owned motorcycles and how many had difficulty finding parking spaces. Though he sent questionnaires to everyone in the dorm, such extensive surveying is often unwieldy and even unnecessary. All you need is a representative sample of people and a questionnaire with questions that will elicit the information you need.

How do you choose the people you will survey? In some cases, you might want to survey all members of a group, such as everyone in one of your classes. More often, however, you'll aim for a random sample of a large group — the first-year class at your university, for example. While a true random sample is probably unattainable, you can aim for a good cross section by, say, emailing every fifth person in the class directory.

Also important is considering some incentives for people to respond to your survey. If you are surveying students about an issue of importance on campus, you can offer to make the results of your survey available to anyone who wants them; then ask for their names and on-campus or email addresses so that you can send the results to them.

Questions should be clear and easy to understand and designed so that you will be able to analyze the answers easily. For example, questions that ask respondents to say yes or no or to rank something on a five-point scale of most to least desirable are easy to tabulate:

The parking facilities on our campus are adequate.

Strongly agree	Somewhat agree	Unsure	Somewhat disagree	Strongly disagree

As you design your questionnaire, think about possible ways in which respondents could misunderstand you or your questions. Adding a category called "other" to a list of options you are asking people about, for example, allows them to fill in information you would not otherwise get.

Because tabulating the responses takes time and effort and because people often resent being asked to answer more than about twenty questions, especially online, limit the number of questions you ask. After you have done your tabulations, set out your findings in a clear, easily readable fashion, using a chart or spreadsheet if possible.

res

356 **15f**

DESIGNING A SURVEY QUESTIONNAIRE

RESEARCH

Conducting
Research

1. Write out your purpose, and review your research question and hypothesis to determine the kinds of questions to ask.

2. Determine the audience for your questionnaire, and figure out how you will reach the potential respondents.

3. Using brainstorming, freewriting, or another strategy from 3a, draft some potential questions.

4. Check each question to see that it calls for a short, specific answer.

5. Create questions that are as fair and unbiased as you can make them.

6. Test the questions on several people — including your instructor, if possible. Which questions are hard to answer? Do any of them seem biased? How much time do the answers require? Revise the questions as necessary.

7. If the questionnaire is to be mailed, draft a cover letter explaining your purpose, asking the recipient to complete the questionnaire, and thanking him or her in advance. Provide an addressed, stamped return envelope.

8. If the questionnaire is to be distributed electronically, make sure you introduce it and state your purpose clearly. In addition, thank the people or group in advance for their responses, and provide clear instructions on how they should return them to you (to your own email address or some other one?).

9. Be sure to state a deadline.

10. Consider adding a question that asks for comments on the questionnaire itself.

11. Type the questionnaire, or post it to a Web site. Leave adequate space for answers if it is being distributed in print form. Proofread the questionnaire before distributing or posting it.

4 Analyzing, synthesizing, and interpreting data from field research

To make sense of the information you gather and determine its significance, first analyze it to identify what you want to look at: kinds of language? comparisons between men's and women's responses? The point is to find a focus, since you can't pay equal attention to everything. See if your instructor could recommend similar research you could check to see how it was analyzed.

Then synthesize by looking at the relationships among pieces of data. Look for recurring words or ideas that fall into patterns. Establish a system for coding your information, labeling each pattern you identify—a *V* for every use of violent language, for example, or a plus sign for every positive response. Ask one or two classmates to review your notes or data; they may notice other patterns or question your findings in helpful ways. Also consider showing your findings to some of your subjects; their responses might help you revise your analysis and synthesis.

Finally, interpret your data by summing up the meaning of what you have found. What is the significance of your findings? Be careful not to make large generalizations or overstate the importance of your findings.

THINKING CRITICALLY ABOUT CONDUCTING RESEARCH

Begin to analyze the research project you are now working on by examining the ways in which you conducted your research: What use did you make of primary and secondary sources? What library, online, and field work did you carry out? What aspect of the research process was most satisfying? What was most disappointing or irritating? How could you do research more efficiently? Bring your answers to these questions to class.

16

▼ Evaluating Sources and Taking Notes

All research builds on the astute, judicious, and sometimes inspired use of sources — that is, on research done by others. As Isaac Newton noted, those researchers who see the farthest do so "by standing up on the shoulders of giants." And while researchers cannot always count on a giant's shoulders to stand on, the quality of their insights is often directly related to how well they have understood and used the source materials — the shoulders — they have relied on.

As a reader, you will want to make the most of your sources, using the insights you gain from them in creating powerful prose of your own. This chapter offers advice on choosing and evaluating sources and taking useful notes on them. ■

16a Understanding why you should use sources

While all research necessarily draws on sources, it is worth thinking about why writers decide to use one source rather than another. What specifically can sources provide for your research projects?

- background and contextual information that sets the scene for your project or that your audience will need to follow your argument
- explanations of concepts unfamiliar to your audience
- illustrations for points you are making
- authority for the claims you are making, which in turn helps you create your own authority
- evidence to support your claims
- counter-examples or counter-evidence that you need to reflect on and respond to in your own argument
- varying perspectives on your topic

As you begin to work with your sources, spend some time thinking about which ones will provide the most help. Make notes in your research log, working bibliography, or both about why you plan to use a particular source.

FOR COLLABORATION

Working with one or two members of your class, read the following passage, in which MIT psychologist Sherry Turkle questions whether

eval

16b 359

RESEARCH

Evaluating the
Usefulness and
Credibility of
Potential Sources

the state of flux in which we now live may be not a transitional stage but a permanent feature of our existence. Then discuss why the writer may have used each one of the sources cited. What purpose does each source serve? Bring the results of your analysis to class for discussion.

> As we stand on the boundary between the real and the virtual, our experience recalls what anthropologist Victor Turner termed a liminal moment, a moment of passage when new cultural symbols and meanings can emerge (168). Liminal moments are times of tension, extreme reactions, and great opportunity. In our time, we are simultaneously flooded with predictions of doom and predictions of imminent utopia. We live in a crucible of contradictory experience. When Turner talked about liminality, he understood it as a transitional state—but living with flux may no longer be temporary. Donna Haraway's characterization of irony illuminates our situation: "Irony is about contradictions that do not resolve into larger wholes . . . about the tension of holding incompatible things together because both or all are necessary and true" (148).
>
> – SHERRY TURKLE, *Life on the Screen*

16b Evaluating the usefulness and credibility of potential sources

Since you want the information and other ideas you glean from sources to be reliable and persuasive, you must evaluate each potential source carefully.

■ Investigating the purpose of using the source

Begin by asking yourself what this particular source will add to your research project: does it help you support a major point; demonstrate that you have thoroughly reviewed the literature on your topic; help establish your own credibility through its authority? If you can't think of a good reason for using the source, put it aside; you can always come back to it later on if you decide it might be useful.

■ Considering the relevance of the source

How closely related is the source to the narrowed and focused topic you are pursuing? You may find yourself enjoying an article and wanting to use it even if it is only marginally connected to your research question. You may also need to read beyond the title and opening paragraph to check for relevance: the title may be misleading, and the introduction may not adequately foreshadow what is in the source. Even if a source is directly relevant to your topic, you might have good reasons not to use it. For an essay on the impact on young girls of Web sites that encourage anorexia, for example, one student decided to include passages from interviews with girls who spoke directly to this topic but to exclude any references to specific Web sites. These sites were certainly relevant to the topic, but in this case the student decided that she did not want to help advertise them in any way by citing them in her essay.

■ Checking the credentials of the publisher or sponsor

What do you know about the publisher of the source you are using? If it is from a newspaper, is it a major newspaper (such as the *San Francisco Chronicle* or the *Washington Post*) that is known for integrity in reporting, or is it a tabloid? Is it a popular magazine like *People* or a journal sponsored by a professional or scholarly organization like the *Journal of the American Medical Association*? If you're evaluating a book, is the publisher one you recognize or can find described on its own Web site? No hard-and-fast rules exist for deciding what credentials are most appropriate. You may have very good reason to use information from a popular newsmagazine, but remember that these publications are typically commercial, intended to make a profit for the sponsoring publisher. Scholarly journals, on the other hand, carry the authority of their professional or academic sponsors. Books may be published by academic presses (the University of California Press, for example), large commercial presses (such as Viking), or small regional or special-interest presses (such as Algonquin, which concentrates on southern writers, or Alyson, which focuses on gay and lesbian issues). Knowing the sponsor or publisher of a source can help you think carefully about whether its credentials are appropriate for your research project.

Checking the credentials of online sources is also essential. There may be a huge difference between the credibility of a personal page posted by an individual and that of a Web site sponsored by an academic institution, a nonprofit organization, and so on. To start assessing the credentials of an Internet site, look closely at the URL for the site. The domain types, which come after the "dot" in a URL, can tell you something about the sponsor.

For more on reading the parts of a URL, see 15e2.

.com — commercially sponsored site

.edu — education-sponsored site

.gov — government-sponsored site

.mil — military-sponsored site

.net — network-sponsored site

.org — nonprofit organization–sponsored site

You can also tell whether the site originates in another country: .ca indicates Canada; .mx, Mexico; .uk, the United Kingdom; .au, Australia; and so on.

■ Checking the credentials of the author

As you carry out your research, be sure to note the names that keep coming up from one source to another, since these references may indicate that the author is well known to others or is influential in the field. The author's credentials may also be presented in the article, book, or Web site, so be sure to look for a description of the author. In addition, you can go to the Internet to gather information about an author: just open a search tool such as InfoSeek or AltaVista, and type in the name of the person you are looking for. When Shannan Palma (the student whose research we've followed in previous chapters) typed in *Donna Haraway* on AltaVista, she learned that Haraway is professor of the history of consciousness at the University of California at Santa Cruz; she also found a listing of interviews of Haraway, reviews of her books, and links to her speeches. She decided that Haraway would be an excellent source for her essay.

Another way to learn about the credibility of a source is by searching Google/Groups for postings that mention the author. Checking out these references can give you an idea of how others regard the author you are considering.

FOR MULTILINGUAL WRITERS: Understanding Authority

Who or what holds most authority in your native language and culture? a religious text or leader? a political creed? a set of laws? What counts as an authority in one place may not be considered authoritative in another. In the United States, for example, documents like the Constitution, the Bill of Rights, and other time-tested laws tend to hold very great authority. In addition, those who have proven experience in and expertise on a particular subject hold more authority on it: a scientist who specializes in genetics is a much more authoritative source on that subject than a popular film star who may have opinions on genetics but does not have the expertise to back up those opinions.

Considering the currency of the source

Check the date of publication of any book or article as well as the date of posting or updating on a Web source. If you are researching how Shakespeare's *Othello* was reviewed in performances immediately after the Civil War, you will need to rely on sources over a century old. On the other hand, if you are working on research related to a recent medical development, your sources will need to be current. Especially in areas that are changing rapidly, such as those related to science or technology, access to the most recent information is very important.

The publication dates of Internet sites can often be difficult to pin down. And even for sites that include the dates of posting, remember that the material posted may have been composed some time earlier. Most reliable will be those sites that list the dates of updating regularly.

Determining the accuracy of the source

How accurate and complete is the information the source contains? Can it be verified in other sources? While you often may not have the knowledge to judge the full accuracy of potential sources you are considering, looking carefully at a source can help you make this assessment. How thorough is the bibliography or list of works cited that accompanies the source? Especially if the source is electronic, can you find other sources that corroborate what it is saying? What does the author or sponsor do to build the trustworthiness of the content presented in the source?

Identifying the stance of the source

All sources will be presented from a point of view that literally reflects where they're coming from. In evaluating sources, you need to identify this point of view or rhetorical stance and subject it to careful scrutiny. Sometimes the stance will be completely obvious: an article titled "Save the Spotted Owl" strongly suggests that the writer will take a pro-environmental stance, while the Web site for the Republican National Committee will certainly take a more conservative stance. But other times, you will need to read carefully to identify particular stances (see 16c), so that you can then see how or if that stance affects the message the source presents. In addition, ask yourself what the source's goals are. What does the author or sponsoring group want to make happen? to convince you of an idea? sell you something? call you to action in some way? When Shannan Palma was carrying out research on Hollywood movie heroes, one of her sources, Coral Amende, was an outspoken critic of the Hollywood star system. Shannan wanted to use this source, but

eval

16b   363

RESEARCH

Evaluating the
Usefulness and
Credibility of
Potential Sources

she also wanted to put the writer in context, letting her audience know that the comments were coming from someone highly critical of Hollywood. (See p. 451.)

■ *Looking at cross-references to the source*

If you see your source cited by others, looking at how they cite it and what they say about it can provide additional clues to its credibility. So take a look at the bibliographies of all the sources you are using, and see what cross-references you can find.

As you evaluate the usefulness and credibility of potential sources, it is helpful to look quickly at the parts of a source that are listed in the guidelines box that follows. If you decide you want to explore a particular source more thoroughly, these elements can also help you read critically.

SOME GUIDELINES FOR EXAMINING POTENTIAL SOURCES

→ *Title and subtitle.* If you are researching coeducation in the nineteenth century and find a book called *Women in Education,* the subtitle *The Challenge of the 1970s* will tell you that you probably don't need to examine the book.

→ *Title page and copyright page.* In a book, these pages will show you when the book was originally published, whether it is a revised edition, and who published it.

→ *Abstract.* Concise summaries of articles or books, abstracts routinely precede articles in some journals and are included in some periodical or bibliographic guides. They can help you decide whether to read the entire work.

→ *Table of contents.* Part and chapter titles can help you determine whether the chapter topics are specific enough to be useful. In a periodical, the table of contents often includes brief descriptions of articles.

→ *Preface or foreword.* This often details the writer's purposes, range of interests, intended audience, topic restrictions, research limitations, and thesis.

→ *Subheadings.* Subheadings in the text can give you an idea of how much detail is given on a topic and whether that detail would be helpful to you.

→ *Conclusion or afterword.* This summary item could help you decide how appropriate that source is for your project.

(Continued on p. 364)

(Continued from p. 363)

→ *Note on the author.* Check the dust jacket of a book, the first and last few pages of a work, or an article itself for information about the author.

→ *Index.* Check the index for words and topics key to your project. Are the listings for your key terms many or few?

→ *Bibliography and/or footnotes.* Lists of references show how carefully a writer has investigated the subject. They may also help you find other sources.

EXTRA CONSIDERATIONS FOR ELECTRONIC SOURCES

→ *Home- or first page.* This page should tell you about the sponsorship of the source, letting you know who can be held accountable for the information in it. (Sometimes you will need to click on an "About Us" or "About Me" button to learn about the sponsor.) Can you determine the goal of the document or site—to provide information, to express an opinion, to get you to sign up for or buy something?

→ *Links.* The links help you learn how credible and useful the source is. Click on some of them, if necessary, to see if they lead to legitimate and helpful sites.

→ *Design.* The design of the document or site may give you clues to the usefulness of the information it provides. How user-friendly is it? Is it easy to navigate?

→ *Bulletin boards or newsgroup discussions.* Be wary of these sources, which at their best can spark ideas or lead you to investigate an aspect of your topic. Contributors are not likely to be credible experts.

● **EXERCISE 16.1**

Choose two sources that seem well suited to your topic, and evaluate their usefulness and credibility, using the criteria presented in this chapter. If possible, analyze one print source and one electronic source. Bring the results of your analysis to class for discussion.

16c Reading sources with a critical eye

For additional
information on
critical reading,
see 1c.

Because of time constraints and the wealth of material available on most topics, you probably will not have time to read through all of your potential material. For those sources that you do want to analyze more closely, however, reading with a critical eye can make your research process more efficient. The following considerations can guide your critical reading:

▨ *Reading with your research question in mind*

As you read, keep your research question in mind. Use the index and the table of contents (if available) to zero in on the parts of a source that will help you answer your research question. Consider the following questions as you read:

- How does this material address your research question?
- In what ways does it provide support for your hypothesis?
- What quotations from this source might help support your thesis?
- Does the source include counterarguments to your hypothesis that you will need to answer? If so, what answers can you provide?

▨ *Analyzing the author's stance and tone*

As noted earlier, every author holds opinions that affect his or her discussion of an issue, opinions that you as a reader must try to recognize and understand. Even the most seemingly factual report, such as an encyclopedia article, is necessarily filled with judgments, often unstated. Read with an eye for the author's overall rhetorical stance, or perspective on the topic, as well as for facts or explicit opinions. The rhetorical stance is closely related to the author's tone, the way his or her attitude toward the topic and audience is conveyed.

●— For a discussion
of rhetorical
stance, see 2g.

Alertness to perspective and tone will help you more fully understand a source and decide how (or whether) to use it. The following questions can help as well:

- Is the author an enthusiastic advocate of something, a strong opponent, a skeptical critic, an amused onlooker, a confident specialist in the field? Are there any clues to why the author takes this stance? What forces in society may have shaped or influenced it?
- How does this stance affect the author's presentation?
- If the author has a professional affiliation, how might the affiliation affect his or her stance?
- In what ways do you share—or not share—the author's stance?
- What is the author's tone? Is it cautious, angry, flippant, serious, impassioned? What words express this tone?

In the following paragraph, which appeared in a *Parade* magazine essay about nuclear war, the author's stance is obvious from the first sentence: he sees his topic, the possibility of nuclear war, as "an unprecedented human catastrophe." His dismissal of those who disagree with him as "fools and madmen" indicates the depth of his feelings, but his overall tone is restrained and objective because he assumes ("everyone knows") that the great majority of his readers share his view.

> Except for fools and madmen, everyone knows that nuclear war would be an unprecedented human catastrophe. A more or less typical strategic warhead has a yield of 2 megatons, the explosive equivalent of 2 million tons of TNT. But 2 million tons of TNT is about the same as all the bombs exploded in World War II—a single bomb with the explosive power of the entire Second World War but compressed into a few seconds of time and an area 30 or 40 miles across. . . .
>
> – CARL SAGAN, "The Nuclear Winter"

■ *Assessing the author's argument and evidence*

For more on
argument, see
Chapters 11–13.

Just as every author has a point of view, every piece of writing has what may be called an argument, a position it takes. Even a report of scientific data implicitly "argues" that we should accept it as reliably gathered and reported. As you read, then, try to identify the author's argument, the reasons given in support of his or her position. Then try to decide *why* the author takes this position. Considering the following questions as you read can help you recognize — and assess — the points being argued in your sources:

- What is the author's main point?
- How much and what kind of evidence supports that point?
- How persuasive do you find the evidence?
- Can you offer counterarguments to or refutations of the evidence?
- Can you detect any questionable logic or fallacious thinking? (See 11g.)

■ *Questioning your sources*

Because all sources make an explicit or implicit argument, they often disagree with one another. Disagreements among sources arise sometimes from differences about facts, sometimes from differences about how to interpret facts. For instance, if an authoritative source says that the chances of a nuclear power plant melting down are 1 in 100,000, commentators could interpret that statistic very differently. A critic of nuclear power could argue that nuclear accidents are so terrible that this chance is too great to take, while a supporter of nuclear power could argue that such a small chance is essentially no chance at all.

The point is that all knowledge is interpreted subjectively. A writer may well tell nothing but the truth, but he or she can never tell the *whole* truth because people are not all-knowing. Thus you must examine all sources critically, using them not as unquestioned authorities but as contributions to your own informed opinion, your own truth.

16d Interpreting sources: synthesizing data and drawing inferences

Your task as a reader is to identify and understand sources and sets of data as completely as possible. As a writer, your aim must be to present data and sources *to other readers* so that they can readily understand the point you are making. Doing so calls for you to notice patterns in your sources and to develop your own interpretation of them.

Throughout the research process, you are **synthesizing** — grouping similar pieces of data together, looking for patterns or trends, and identifying the gist, or main points, of the data. Doing so enables you to use your sources in pursuit of your own goals, rather than just stacking them up as unconnected bits of information. Shannan Palma began by grouping the movie heroes she was studying into types: the traditional romantic hero, the fantasy hero, the loner or misfit hero, and so on. These categories allowed her to note differences and similarities among them.

As Shannan continued her research, she also began to notice some patterns: the film star both as somehow bigger than life and as a flawed or "damaged human," as she came to call this kind of star. Shannan was able to recognize these patterns because she was thinking critically, synthesizing, and comparing her sources.

Often, such synthesizing will lead you to make **inferences** — conclusions that are not explicitly stated in but that follow logically from the data given. For example, as Shannan looked at the similarities among her categories of heroes, she began to notice another pattern: many of the stars who played the heroes seemed to be viewed by moviegoers as heroes themselves. What started as a hunch turned into an inference she later made, that the Hollywood star system led to a case of "mistaken identity" that blurred the lines between fictional characters and real-life heroes. Shannan began to record her own ideas about these patterns, ideas that could further guide her research.

16e Taking notes and annotating sources

Note-taking methods vary greatly from one researcher to another. Some researchers even have rituals associated with their note-taking: one historian, for example, starts a series of notebooks for every major research project, and the notebooks must be identical except for the color of paper in them. Another scholar insists on taking notes for her projects in different colored ink: each color represents a particular category of her research. Still others now prefer computer files for notes. Whatever method you adopt, your goals will include (1) getting down enough information to help you recall the major points of the source; (2) getting down the information in the form you are most likely to want to incorporate into your text; and (3) getting down all the information you will need in order to cite the source accurately. Taking careful and complete notes will help you digest the source information as you read and incorporate the material into your text without inadvertently plagiarizing the source.

For more information on plagiarism, see Chapter 18.

1 Taking accurate notes

Regardless of your note-taking method — or the kind of note you are writing — following these tips will help ensure that your notes are accurate and useful:

- Using a notebook, index cards, or a computer file, list the author's name and a shortened title of the source — for each note. Your working-bibliography entry for the source should contain full publication information (see 14i), so you don't need to repeat it in the note. If you are combining your working bibliography with your notes, however, be sure to take down all the information you will need before beginning on the notes.

- Record exact page references. If the note refers to more than one page, indicate page breaks so that if you decide to use only part of the note, you will know which page to cite. For online or other sources without page numbers, record the paragraph, screen, or other section number(s) if indicated, as well as section breaks if the note refers to more than one section.

- Label each note with a subject heading or category so you can group similar subtopics together.

- Identify the note as a quotation (see 16e2), a paraphrase (see 16e3), a summary (see 16e4), a combination of these forms, or some other form — such as your own critical comment — to avoid any confusion later. Mark quotations accurately with quotation marks, and paraphrase and summarize completely in your own words to be sure you do not inadvertently plagiarize the source.

- Read over each completed note carefully to recheck the accuracy of quotations, statistics, and specific facts.

●···· For more infor-
mation on work-
ing with quota-
tions, para-
phrases, and
summaries — and
for integrating
them into your
own writing — see
Chapter 17.

2 Taking quotation notes

Some of the notes you take will contain **quotations,** which give the *exact words* of a source. Here, for example, is a note with a quotation Shannan Palma planned to use in her essay:

Cyborg heroes ●·· Subject heading

Haraway, Simians, p. 178. ●··· Author and short title of source (keyed to full entry in working bibliography)

"The replicant Rachel in the Ridley Scott film Blade Runner stands as the image of a cyborg culture's fear, love, and confusion."

Quotation ●·· Label identifies this note as a quotation

The following guidelines will help you take accurate notes that record quotations.

SOME GUIDELINES FOR TAKING QUOTATION NOTES

→ Copy quotations *carefully,* with punctuation, capitalization, and spelling exactly as in the original.
→ Use square brackets if you introduce words of your own into a quotation or make changes in it, and use ellipses if you omit material. If you later incorporate the quotation into your essay, copy it faithfully, brackets, ellipses, and all. (17b4)

(Continued on p. 370)

(Continued from p. 369)

→ It is especially important to enclose the quotation in quotation marks; don't rely on your memory to distinguish your own words from those of the source.

→ Record the author's name, shortened title, and page number(s) on which the quotation appeared. For online sources without page numbers, record the paragraph, screen, or other section number(s) if indicated.

→ Make sure you have a corresponding working-bibliography entry with complete source information. (14i)

→ Label the note with a subject heading.

3 Taking paraphrase notes

Rather than quoting, you will often want to paraphrase a source. A **paraphrase** accurately states all the relevant information from a passage *in your own words and phrasing*, without any additional comments or elaborations.

A paraphrase is useful when the main points of a passage, their order, and at least some details are important but — unlike passages worth quoting — the particular wording is not. Unlike a summary, a paraphrase always restates *all* the main points of a passage in the same order and often in about the same number of words.

In order to paraphrase without plagiarizing inadvertently, *use your own words and sentence structures;* do not simply substitute synonyms, and do not imitate an author's style. If you wish to cite some of an author's words within a paraphrase, enclose them in quotation marks. A good way of assuring your originality is to paraphrase without looking at the source; then check to make sure that the paraphrase accurately presents the author's meaning and that you have used your own words and phrasing.

The following examples of paraphrases resemble the original either too little or too much. Looking at them carefully will help you understand how to take acceptable paraphrase notes. Be aware that even for acceptable paraphrases you must include a citation in your essay identifying the source of the information.

It is not clear who makes and who is made in the relation between human and machine. It is not clear what is mind and what body in machines that resolve into coding practices. In so far as we know ourselves in both formal discourse (for example, biology) and in daily practice (for example, the homework economy in the integrated circuit), we find ourselves to be cyborgs, hybrids, mosaics, chimeras. Biological organisms have become biotic systems, communications devices like others. There is no fundamental, ontological separation in our formal knowledge of machine and organism, of technical and organic. The replicant Rachel in the Ridley Scott film *Blade Runner* stands as the image of a cyborg culture's fear, love, and confusion.   – DONNA J. HARAWAY, *Simians, Cyborgs, and Women*

UNACCEPTABLE PARAPHRASE: STRAYING FROM THE AUTHOR'S IDEAS

Haraway's point is that we can no longer be sure of the distinction between humans and machines. In fact, she argues that we are all already combinations — part body, part mind, part machine. On the other hand, Haraway could be completely wrong: the cyborg metaphor doesn't always work.

Note that this paraphrase starts off well enough, but it moves away from paraphrasing the original to inserting the writer's ideas into the paraphrase of Haraway's text.

UNACCEPTABLE PARAPHRASE: USING THE AUTHOR'S WORDS

As Haraway explains, in a high-tech culture like ours, *who makes and who is made, what is mind or body, becomes unclear.* When we look at ourselves in relation to the real or the mechanical world, we must admit we are cyborgs, and even *biological organisms* are now *communications systems.* Thus our beings can't be separated from machines. A fine example of this cyborg image is Rachel in Ridley Scott's *Blade Runner.*

Because the italicized phrases are either borrowed from the original without quotation marks or changed only superficially, this paraphrase plagiarizes.

UNACCEPTABLE PARAPHRASE: USING THE AUTHOR'S SENTENCE STRUCTURES

As Haraway explains, it is unclear who is the maker and who is the made. It is unclear what in the processes of machines might be the mind and what the body. Thus in order to know ourselves at all, we must recognize ourselves to be cyborgs. Biology then becomes just another device for communicating. As beings, we can't separate the bodily from the mechanical anymore. Thus Rachel in Ridley Scott's *Blade Runner* becomes the perfect symbol of cyborg culture.

Although this paraphrase does not rely explicitly on the words of the original, it does follow the sentence structures too closely. Substituting synonyms for the major words in a paraphrase is not enough to avoid plagiarism. The paraphrase must represent your own interpretation of the material and thus must show your own thought patterns.

Now look at two paraphrases of the same passage that express the author's ideas accurately and acceptably, the first completely in the writer's own words and the second including a quotation from the original.

ACCEPTABLE PARAPHRASE: IN THE WRITER'S OWN WORDS

As Haraway's entire chapter demonstrates, today the line between person and machine is forever blurred, especially in terms of the binary coding systems used by computers to "know." If knowing thyself is still important, we must know ourselves as a mixture of body, mind, and machine. Moviemaker Ridley Scott provides a good example of this mixture in the character of Rachel in *Blade Runner.*

ACCEPTABLE PARAPHRASE: QUOTING SOME OF THE AUTHOR'S WORDS

As Haraway's entire chapter demonstrates, today the line between person and machine is forever blurred, especially in terms of the binary coding systems used by computers to "know." If knowing thyself is still important, we must know ourselves as "cyborgs, hybrids, mosaics, chimeras." Moviemaker Ridley Scott provides a good example of this mixture in the character of Rachel in *Blade Runner.*

Here is another example of an original passage and Shannan Palma's note recording an acceptable paraphrase of the passage:

ORIGINAL

Cyborg imagery can help express two crucial arguments in this essay: first, the production of universal, totalizing theory is a major mistake that misses most of reality, probably always, but certainly now; and second, taking responsibility for the social relations of science and technology means refusing an anti-science metaphysics, a demonology of technology, and so means embracing the skillful task of reconstructing the boundaries of daily life, in partial connection with others, in communication with all of our parts. It is not just that science and technology are possible means of great human satisfaction, as well as a matrix of complex dominations. Cyborg imagery can suggest a way out of the maze of dualisms in which we have explained our bodies and our tools to ourselves. — DONNA J. HARAWAY, *Simians, Cyborgs, and Women* (181)

Cyborg heroes

Haraway, *Simians*, p. 181

Dreams of organic unity and coherence are futile, as are temptations to blame science and machinery for our problems. In place of these dreams and temptations, Haraway recommends the cyborg figure, which can give us a way to reconnect to parts of ourselves as well as others. In addition, it can give us a new dream of ourselves as multiple, surpassing either body or machine.

Paraphrase

On p. 13 of the research essay at the end of Chapter 20 (p. 457), Shannan Palma uses part of this paraphrase: "In one of the essays in her anthology *Simians, Cyborgs, and Women,* historian of science Donna J. Haraway claims that our dreams of organic unity and coherence are futile. In their place, she recommends the cyborg figure, which can give us a new dream of ourselves as multiple, surpassing either body or machine (181)."

Here are some guidelines to help you take accurate paraphrase notes.

SOME GUIDELINES FOR TAKING PARAPHRASE NOTES

→ Include all main points and any important details from the original, in the same order in which they were presented.
→ State the meaning in your own words and sentence structures. If you want to include especially memorable language from the original, enclose it in quotation marks.
→ Leave out your own comments, elaborations, or reactions.
→ Record the author, shortened title, and the page number(s) on which the original material appeared. For online sources without page numbers, record the paragraph, screen, or other section number(s) if indicated.
→ Make sure you have a corresponding working-bibliography entry with complete source information. (14i)
→ Label the note with a subject heading, and identify it as a paraphrase to avoid confusion with a summary.
→ Recheck to be sure that the words and sentence structures are your own and that they express the author's meaning accurately.

eval

374   16e

4 Taking summary notes

RESEARCH

Evaluating Sources
and Taking Notes

A **summary** is a significantly shortened version of a passage, a section, or even a whole chapter or work that *captures main ideas in your own words.* Unlike a paraphrase, a summary uses just enough information to record the main points or the points you wish to emphasize. You needn't include all the author's points or any details, but be sure not to distort his or her meaning. The length of a summary depends on the length of the original and on how much information you will need to use. Your goal is to keep the summary as brief as possible, capturing only the gist of the original.

■ *Summarizing short pieces*

For a short passage, try reading it carefully and, without looking at the text, writing a one- or two-sentence summary. Following is Shannan Palma's note recording a summary of the Haraway passage on p. 371. Notice that it states the author's main points selectively—and without using her words.

> *Cyborg heroes*
>
> *Haraway, Simians, pp. 177–78*
>
> *Haraway says humans today are already part machine, and she cites the Ridley Scott movie Blade Runner as an example.*
>
> *Summary*

Now read the brief article that follows, and then see a student's note summarizing it:

One scientist hoarded a rare virus strain for more than a decade, refusing requests to let other researchers study it. Others refused to share biological materials like cloned genes unless they were included as authors of any resulting discoveries, a nice way to boost a résumé. Hundreds of biologists delay publishing their results by more than six months for reasons like applying for a patent or protecting their lead over competitors. The scientific ideal is openness and sharing—describing your experiments in enough detail that others can evaluate their accuracy, and giving even competitors samples of your cell lines and other material so they can replicate your experiment and thus check it—but "ideal" seems to be the operative word here. Now that genetics is big business, researchers are withholding data, refusing to share materials and delaying publication of results in order to commercialize them, finds a new study in the *Journal of the American Medical Association*. Of the 1,240 geneticists whom Eric G. Campbell and colleagues at the Institute for Health Policy at Massachusetts General Hospital surveyed, 47 percent had been denied information, data or materials in the last three years. "The geneticists told us that such denials were slowing research, preventing replication and causing them to abandon promising leads," says Campbell. Of the geneticists who refused requests for materials, 53 percent said they were protecting their own right to publish more findings before the competition.

– SHARON BEGLEY, "Science Failing to Share"

Genetics / big business

Begley, <u>Science</u>, p. 10

The commercialization of genetics has led scientists, who once aimed to share their findings freely, to withhold information from their research (sometimes for years), thus slowing down the overall progress of science.

Summary

FOR COLLABORATION

Working with another student in your class, prepare a paraphrase note of the brief article "Science Failing to Share." Then prepare a one- or two-sentence summary note of the article, and make sure that it doesn't plagiarize the student's summary above. Bring your completed notes to class for discussion.

eval

376

16e

RESEARCH

Evaluating Sources
and Taking Notes

■ *Summarizing longer pieces*

For a long passage or an entire chapter, skim the headings and topic sentences, and make notes of each; then write your summary in a paragraph or two. For a whole book, you may want to refer to the preface and introduction as well as chapter titles, headings, and topic sentences—and your summary may take a page or more. In general, try to identify the main thesis or claim being made, and then look for the subtopics or supports for that claim. (If you have printed out the source, you might highlight the major thesis and the most important supporting points.)

Here are some guidelines for taking accurate summary notes.

SOME GUIDELINES FOR TAKING SUMMARY NOTES

→ Include just enough information to recount the main points you wish to cite. A summary is usually far shorter than the original.
→ Use your own words. If you include language from the original, enclose it in quotation marks.
→ Record the author, shortened title, and page number(s) on which the original material appeared. For online sources without page numbers, record the paragraph, screen, or other section number(s) if indicated.
→ Make sure you have a corresponding working-bibliography entry with complete source information. (14i)
→ Label the note with a subject heading, and identify it as a summary to avoid confusion with a paraphrase.
→ Recheck to be sure you have captured the author's meaning and that the words are entirely your own.

5 Taking other kinds of notes

Many researchers take notes that don't fall into the categories of quotations, paraphrases, or summaries. Some take **key-term notes,** which might include the topic or subject addressed in the source along with names, dates, or short statements—anything to jog their memories when they begin drafting. Others record **personal** or **critical notes**—thoughts, questions, disagreements, criticisms, or other striking ideas that come to mind as they read. In fact, one very exciting part of research occurs when the materials you are reading spark something in your mind and new ideas take hold, ideas that can become part of your thesis or argument. *Don't let them get away.* While you may later decide not to use these ideas, you need to make notes about them just in case: some of these ideas may even provide a new direction for your research project.

Other researchers adopt systems particular to their own research project. Shannan Palma made a note for each of the visuals she thought she might use. She also kept a separate note for each of the movies that dealt with the themes she pursued in her essay. By labeling these notes with subject headings, she could easily determine how often each theme appeared. Here is one of her notes:

> **Mistaken identity**
>
> *A Star is Born*. Made in 1954. Starred Judy Garland. Garland plays a young actress rising from an unknown to a star. Audiences could easily confuse Garland's own identity with that of the "hero" in the movie.

After she had taken all her notes, Shannan could sort them and see how many related to her theme of mistaken identity; she could then place the notes in the order she would use them in her essay.

Researchers also take **field notes**, which record their firsthand observations or the results of their surveys or interviews.

For more on this kind of field research, see 15f.

Of course, you may find good reason to keep notes of various kinds in addition to those described here. Whatever form your notes take, list the source's title, author, and page number(s) so that you can return to the material easily. In addition, check to make sure you have carefully distinguished your own thoughts and comments from those of the source itself.

6 Annotating sources

Sometimes you may photocopy or download and print out a source you intend to use in your writing. Indeed, nearly all libraries provide machines you can use to photocopy pages, and computerized library catalogs increasingly include databases that allow you to retrieve entire articles and print them out. In such cases, you can annotate the photocopies or printouts with your thoughts and questions and highlight

eval

16e

378

RESEARCH

Evaluating Sources
and Taking Notes

ONE STUDENT'S ANNOTATIONS OF A SOURCE

Title of review

Introduction focuses on movie heroes

Relates this movie to earlier blockbuster — do I agree?

Begins to criticize the film

Backs off from the criticism a bit — so where does he stand on this film?

So in the end, he gives a thumbs down. I need to look for additional reviews before I draw any conclusions

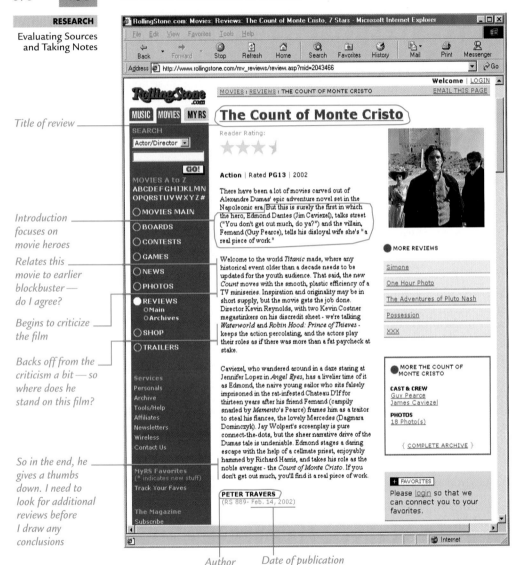

Author   *Date of publication*

interesting quotations and key terms. If you take notes in a computer file, you may be able to copy online sources electronically, paste them into the file, and annotate them there, perhaps even using software designed for this purpose. Try not to rely too heavily on copying or printing out whole pieces, however; you still need to read the material very carefully. And resist the temptation to treat copied material as notes, an action that could lead to inadvertent plagiarizing. (In a computer file, using a different color for text pasted from a source will help prevent this problem.) If you read and take careful notes on your sources rather than relying on copies, your drafting process will be more efficient. If you do copy or print out material, note all the information you need to cite the material in your list of sources cited.

On p. 378 are one student's annotations of a brief online review of the movie *The Count of Monte Cristo,* which she downloaded and printed out. Note that she has circled or underlined the bibliographic information she will need, including the date the review was published on the Web. She has also circled a passage she may want to quote in her text, and she has written her own thoughts in the margins of the review.

● **EXERCISE 16.2**

Choose an online source you are sure you will use in your research project. Then download and print out the source, record all essential publication information for it, and annotate it as you read it.

THINKING CRITICALLY ABOUT YOUR EVALUATION OF SOURCES

Take a careful look at the sources you have gathered for your research project. How many make points that support your own point of view? How many provide counter-arguments to your point of view? Which sources are you relying on most—and why? Which source seems most credible to you—and why? Which sources, if any, are you suspicious of or worried about? Bring the results of this investigation to class for discussion.

17

Integrating Sources into Your Writing

Writer Melissa Goldthwaite points out that "there are multiple sources surrounding you. Take them in, allow them to circulate through you, [and] then transform those sources in your own writing—even as they transform you." This process of absorbing your sources and then integrating them gracefully—what Goldthwaite calls "transforming" them—into your own writing is one of the pleasures of successful research. As you work with these sources and think of using them in your own writing, they become *your* sources. Far from leading the way or in some way taking over your writing, these sources work in support of the thinking they have stimulated, of your own good ideas. This chapter will guide you in thinking carefully about how best to integrate the sources you have found into your research-based writing. ■

17a Deciding whether to quote, paraphrase, or summarize

Deciding what sources to include in your research project and how to use each one is an outgrowth of reading all your sources (including those that are visual images) critically. Some sources may be useful for providing background information, others for supporting your thesis, others for illustrating a point. For print sources, these different purposes may guide you in deciding whether to use a quotation, a paraphrase, a summary, or simply a reference to the source.

You tentatively decided to quote, paraphrase, or summarize material when you took notes on your sources. As you choose which sources to use in your research project and how to use them, however, you may reevaluate those decisions. For example, you may decide to summarize in an essay what you paraphrased in your notes, to use only a quotation you included in the midst of a summary, or not to use a particular quotation at all.

17b Working with quotations

As discussed in Chapter 16, **quoting** involves noting a source's exact words. Direct quotations can be effective for catching your readers' attention—for example, includ-

QUOTE

→ wording that is so memorable or powerful, or expresses a point so perfectly, that you cannot change it without weakening the meaning you need
→ authors' opinions you wish to emphasize
→ authors' words that show you are considering varying perspectives
→ respected authorities whose opinions support your ideas
→ authors whose opinions challenge or vary greatly from those of others in the field

PARAPHRASE

→ passages you do not wish to quote but whose details are important to your point

SUMMARIZE

→ long passages whose main point is important to your point but whose details are not

RESEARCH

Working with Quotations

●— For guidelines on taking quotation, paraphrase, and summary notes, see 16e2, e3, and e4.

ing a memorable phrase in your introduction or giving an eyewitness's account in arresting detail. In a research project, quotations from respected authorities can help establish your credibility as a researcher by showing that you've sought out experts in the field. In addition, allowing authors to speak for themselves, particularly if they hold opinions counter to yours or to those of other experts, helps demonstrate your fairness.

Finally, well-chosen quotations can broaden the appeal of your project by drawing on emotion as well as logic, appealing to the reader's mind and heart. A student writing on the ethical issues of bullfighting, for example, might introduce an argument that bullfighting is not a sport by quoting Ernest Hemingway's striking comment that "the formal bull-fight is a tragedy, not a sport, and the bull is certain to be killed."

●— For more about establishing credibility, see 13e.

●— For more about using logical and emotional appeals in an argument, see 13f and g.

1 Enclosing brief quotations within your text

Prose quotations of no more than four lines (MLA style), fewer than forty words (APA style), or fewer than ten lines or one paragraph (Chicago style) should be worked into your text, enclosed by quotation marks. Such **in-text citations** document material from other sources with both **signal phrases** and **parenthetical references.** Signal phrases introduce the material, often including the author's name. Parenthetical references direct you to full bibliographic entries in a list of works cited at the end of the text. For example:

> In Miss Eckhart, Welty recognizes a character who shares with her "the love of her art and the love of giving it, the desire to give it until there is no more left" (10).

> In Russia, however, the men who took control had hardly any experience in military or administrative fields at all. As Edward Crankshaw explained, "They were a disciplined set of revolutionary conspirators who had spent most of their adult lives in exile in Russia or abroad" (44).

Notice that both examples alert readers to the quotations by using signal phrases that introduce the material and include the author's name. When you cite a quotation in this way, you need to put only the page number in parentheses.

When you introduce a quotation without mentioning the author's name, place the author's last name in parentheses before the page number. Be sure, however, that you always distinguish where someone else's words begin. For example:

> In *The Third Life of Grange Copeland,* Grange's inability to respond to his son is evident "even in private and in the dark and with his son, presumably asleep" when he "could not bear to touch his son with his hand" (Walker 121).

Both MLA and APA styles specify what should appear in parenthetical references, in what circumstances, and how they should be punctuated. See 20a and 21a for guidelines.

2 Setting off long quotations

Prose quotations longer than four lines (MLA style); forty words (APA style); or ten lines, or more than one paragraph (Chicago style), should be set off from the regular text. Begin such a quotation on a new line, and indent every line one inch or ten spaces (MLA) or five to seven spaces (APA) from the left margin. Because this indentation sets off the quotation clearly, no quotation marks are necessary. Type the quotation to the right margin, and double-space it as you do the regular text. Long quotations are usually introduced by a signal phrase or a sentence followed by a colon. The following example shows MLA style:

A good seating arrangement can prevent problems;
however, "withitness," as defined by Woolfolk, works
even better:

> Withitness is the ability to communicate
> to students that you are aware of what is
> happening in the classroom, that you "don't
> miss anything." With-it teachers seem to have
> "eyes in the back of their heads." They avoid
> becoming too absorbed with a few students,
> since this allows the rest of the class to
> wander. (359)

This technique works, however, only if students actually
believe that their teacher will know everything that
goes on.

Note that with long quotations, the parenthetical reference comes after the period at the end of the quotation and does not have a period after it.

Though long quotations are often necessary in research projects, use them cautiously. Too many of them may suggest that you did not rely on your own thinking. In addition, long quotations can make your writing seem choppy, and they can distract from your analysis of the material. If you think you may be overusing long quotations, substitute paraphrases or summaries for some of them.

3 Integrating quotations smoothly into your text

In college writing, quotations need to be smoothly and clearly linked to the surrounding sentences in your essay. In most cases, you need to introduce the source of the quotation and use a **signal verb** to provide such a link. The following sentence fails to introduce the source, identifying the author only in parentheses after the quotation. Therefore, no signal phrase connects the author to the quotation, which simply appears abruptly at the beginning of a sentence.

WITHOUT A SOURCE INTRODUCTION AND SIGNAL VERB

In *Death of a Salesman,* Willy Loman dreams the wrong dreams and idealizes the wrong ideals. "He has lived on his smile and on his hopes, survived from sale to sale, been sustained by the illusion that he has countless friends in his territory, that everything will be all right . . ." (Brown 97).

See how the following revision uses a signal verb (*are well captured*) and introduces the source's author (*by Brown*) to make the link between quotation and text far easier to recognize. Note also how the shift in verb tenses from text to quotation is smoothed out in the revision.

WITH A SOURCE INTRODUCTION AND SIGNAL VERB

In *Death of a Salesman,* Willy Loman dreams the wrong dreams and idealizes the wrong ideals. His misguided perceptions *are well captured by Brown:* "He has lived on his smile and on his hopes, survived from sale to sale, been sustained by the illusion that he has countless friends in his territory, that everything will be all right . . ." (97).

Remember, however, that the signal verb must be appropriate to the idea you are expressing.

As *Richard deCordova notes* in a memorable phrase, the studios wanted to convince millions of moviegoers that "the real hero behave[d] just like the reel hero" (qtd. in Gallagher, pt. 2).

In this sentence from Shannan Palma's essay, her use of the signal verb *notes* makes it clear that the quotation is by deCordova—and that she agrees with it. If she had wanted to indicate that the author's point is more open to disagreement—that other authorities might disagree with it, or that she herself does—she might have used a different verb, such as *claims* or *asserts.* If she had wanted to take a neutral stance, a verb like *says* or *remarks* would have been appropriate.

Verbs like *notes* or *claims* or *says* can be used by themselves following the author's name. But other verbs, like *interprets* or *opposes,* require more complex phrasing.

In her essay, *Haraway strongly opposes* those who condemn technology outright, arguing that we must not indulge in a "demonology of technology" (181).

In any case, the signal verb you choose allows you to characterize the author's viewpoint or perspective as well as your own, so you should choose with care.

SIGNAL VERBS

acknowledges	answers	claims	criticizes
advises	asserts	concludes	declares
agrees	believes	concurs	describes
allows	charges	confirms	disagrees

(Continued on p. 385)

discusses	lists	remarks	says
disputes	objects	replies	states
emphasizes	observes	reports	suggests
expresses	offers	responds	thinks
interprets	opposes	reveals	writes

4 Indicating changes in quotations with square brackets and ellipses

Sometimes, for the sake of clarity or length, you will wish to alter a direct quotation in some way—to make a verb tense fit smoothly into your text, to replace a pronoun with a noun, to eliminate unnecessary detail, to change a capital letter to lowercase or vice versa. Enclose any changed or added words or letters in square brackets, and indicate any deletions with ellipsis points. Because most quotations that you integrate into your essay come from longer passages, you need not use ellipses at the beginning or end of a quotation unless the last sentence as you cite it is incomplete.

Here is an example of an original passage and Shannan Palma's note recording a quotation from it. Notice how she uses ellipses to mark author's words she omitted. She also uses brackets to show an added word, changed capitalization, and which part of the quotation came from which page.

ORIGINAL

It is not clear who makes and who is made in the relation between human and machine. It is not clear what is mind and what body in machines that resolve into coding practices. In so far as we know ourselves in both formal discourse (for example, biology) and in daily practice (for example, the homework economy in the integrated circuit), we find ourselves to be cyborgs, hybrids, mosaics, chimeras. Biological organisms have become biotic systems, communications devices like others. There is no fundamental, ontological separation in our formal knowledge of machine and organism, of technical and organic. The replicant Rachel in the Ridley Scott film *Blade Runner* stands as the image of a cyborg culture's fear, love, and confusion.

— DONNA J. HARAWAY, *Simians, Cyborgs, and Women* (177–78)

Square brackets
identify something you
add to the quotation

Ellipses indicate
material you have
omitted from the
quotation.

Cyborg heroes

Haraway, *Simians*, pp. 177–78

*[177]"In so far as we know ourselves . . . , we find ourselves to be
cyborgs, hybrids . . . . [178][Thus, t]he replicant Rachel in the
Ridley Scott film* Blade Runner *stands as the image of a cyborg
culture's fear, love, and confusion."*

Quotation

Here are some examples of changed quotations integrated smoothly
with the surrounding text:

A farmer, Jane Lee, spoke to the Nuclear Regulatory Commission about
the occurrences. "There is something wrong in the [Three Mile Island]
area. It is happening within nature itself," she said, referring to human
miscarriages, stillbirths, and birth defects in farm animals ("Legacy" 33).

Economist John Kenneth Galbraith has pointed out that "large corporations cannot afford to compete with one another. Their survival is pred-
icated upon . . . market segmentation. In a truly competitive market
someone loses . . . . American big business has finally learned that everybody has to protect everybody else's investment" (Key 17).

Be careful that any changes you make in a quotation do not alter its
meaning. Even if an error occurs in the original, do not correct it, but
alert readers to it by inserting *sic* ("thus") in square brackets after it.

FOR MULTILINGUAL WRITERS: Identifying Sources

While some language communities and cultures expect audiences to
recognize the sources of important documents and texts, thereby eliminating the need to cite them directly, conventions for writing in North
America call for careful attribution of any quoted, paraphrased, or
summarized material. When in doubt, explicitly identify your sources.

As the reviewer for *Gumshoe* remarks, "This absorbing mystery offers an attractively sardonic heroin [*sic*] and a humdinger of a plot" (31).

In any event, use brackets and ellipses sparingly; too many of them make for difficult reading and might suggest that you have changed the meaning by removing some of the context.

RESEARCH

Working with Paraphrases

● For more on using brackets and ellipses to indicate omissions and other changes in quotations, see 53b and f.

● **EXERCISE 17.1**

Take a source-based piece of writing you have done recently or a research project you are working on now, and examine it to see how successfully you have integrated quotations. Have you used accurate signal verbs and introduced the sources of the quotations? Have you used square brackets and ellipses accurately to indicate changes in quotations?

17c Working with paraphrases

As noted in Chapter 16 (see 16e3), when you write a **paraphrase,** you use your own words and sentence structure to state all of the important information from a passage. Paraphrasing material helps you digest a passage, because chances are you can't restate the passage in your own words unless you grasp its full meaning. When you incorporate an accurate paraphrase into your essay, you show readers that you understand that source.

As with quotations, you need to introduce paraphrases clearly into your text, usually with a signal phrase that includes the name of the author of the source. Using the author's name also helps lend authority to the material, especially if you identify the expertise of the author. Here are two original passages from a book that a student integrated into her text, one as a quotation, the other as a paraphrase:

ORIGINAL THAT IS LATER QUOTED

I offer this book to . . . women and men everywhere who are trying their best to talk to each other (19).　　　　　　　　　– DEBORAH TANNEN

ORIGINAL THAT IS LATER PARAPHRASED

Understanding genderlects makes it possible to change — to try speaking differently — when you want to. But even if no one changes, understanding genderlects improves relationships. Once people realize that their partners have different conversational styles, they are inclined to accept differences without blaming themselves, their partners, or their relationships. The biggest mistake is believing there is one right way to listen, to talk, to have a conversation—or a relationship. Nothing hurts more than being told your intentions are bad when you know they are good, or being told you are doing something wrong when you know you're just doing it your way (298).   —DEBORAH TANNEN

In the following passage from the student essay, notice how the writer uses the source to bring authority to the point she makes in the first sentence, first introducing the author by name and title and then quoting and paraphrasing her work. Note also that a page number is included in parentheses for the paraphrase as well as the quotation:

> On the other hand, some observers of the battle of the sexes are trying to arrange cease-fires. Professor of linguistics Deborah Tannen says that she offers her book *You Just Don't Understand: Women and Men in Conversation* to "women and men everywhere who are trying their best to talk to each other" (19). Later in the book, Tannen illustrates how communication between women and men breaks down and then suggests that an awareness of what she calls "genderlects" can help all speakers realize that there are many ways to communicate with others and that these differing styles of communication have their own validity. Understanding this crucial point can keep speakers from accusing others of being wrong in the way they are communicating; instead, they are simply being different (298).

In the following example, the same student writer focuses not on the authors of the sources but on the information paraphrased, identifying the authors only parenthetically. Here the writer's objective is not to cite an expert but to show that the information she presents is valid:

> Three areas of established differences in cognitive abilities are recognized by the majority of researchers: verbal ability, mathematical ability, and spatial ability (Block 517). As shown by current research, a specific cognitive sex difference exists in verbal ability; in general, females are superior to males in this area, starting in early childhood (Weitz 99).

17d Working with summaries

As discussed in Chapter 16 (see 16e4), a **summary** is a brief version of a passage or even a whole work that states its main ideas in your own words. As with quotations and paraphrases, summaries need to be carefully integrated into your text. Because your summary will not include quotation marks (since you aren't quoting!), it is essential that you indicate the source of the summary, including the author's name and page number, if appropriate. Here is how Shannan Palma might have integrated her summary of the passage from a Donna Haraway book (you can see the summary on p. 374 and the entire passage on p. 371):

> In one of the essays in her anthology *Simians, Cyborgs, and Women,* historian of science Donna J. Haraway claims that in fact humans today are already part machine, and she cites the Ridley Scott movie *Blade Runner* as an example (177–78).

Note that in this hypothetical example Shannan introduces her source (Haraway), establishes her expertise by identifying her as a historian of science, and uses the signal verb *claims* to characterize Haraway's passage as argumentative rather than merely informational. Following her summary of Haraway's point, she includes the page numbers in parentheses for the passage she has summarized.

17e Remembering to cite sources for quotations, paraphrases, and summaries

Whenever you include quotations, paraphrases, or summaries in your own writing, it is crucially important that you identify the sources of the material; even unintentional failure to cite material that you drew from other sources constitutes plagiarism. Be especially careful with paraphrases and summaries, where there are no quotation marks to remind you that the material is not your own. Make certain that you have all of the information necessary to identify the sources by author and page number—and that you have full publication information in your working bibliography. If you find that some of your bibliography entries lack this information, go back and find the original sources; reread the appropriate passages; check your quotations, paraphrases, or summaries for accuracy; and take down all the information you need to cite them. If for some reason you cannot find the original sources, it is best to leave this material out rather than risk plagiarizing someone else's work.

For more on respecting the intellectual property of others, see Chapter 18.

17f Working with visuals

Chapter 8 provides information on visual design that you may wish to consult for your research project. In addition, you should think carefully about those visuals you will include in your text.

1 Choosing effective visuals

If a picture is worth a thousand words, then using pictures calls for caution: one picture, in short, could overwhelm — or undermine — the message you are trying to send in your text. In choosing visuals to include in your research project, ask yourself the following questions about each one:

- *Does it make a strong contribution to the written message?* Tangential or decorative visuals just take away from the power of your essay.

- *Is it appropriate and fair to your subject?* A visual that presents a situation or person from an obviously biased perspective may be seen as unfair or manipulative.

- *Is it appropriate for and fair to your audience?* In an essay on recent advances in science, if all five of the illustrations feature men, what impression does that create for your female readers?

With these cautions in mind, you can choose visuals (photographs, cartoons, paintings, drawings, charts and graphs, and other kinds of images) that will enhance your research project, providing concrete illustrations and piquing the interest of your readers.

 You can create visuals yourself using a spreadsheet, for example, or a digital camera, or even old-fashioned crayons and paints. Using a scanner, you can turn these visuals into electronic form so that they can be inserted into your text. Many images are also available on the Web, sometimes free and sometimes for a fee. If you want to use a visual from the Web, make sure you check for copyright information. While it is considered "fair use" for you to use a visual in an essay for a college class, the moment that essay is published to the Web, infringements of copyright may occur. To avoid this possibility, it is a good idea to ask the copyright holder for permission to use the visual. Here is an example of a request to use copyrighted material in college writing:

```
Mail to:   fridanet@aol.com
Cc to:     lunsford.2@osu.edu
Subject:   Request for permission
```

Dear Kimberley Masters:

I am a student at Ohio State University and am writing to request your permission to download and use your photograph of Frida Kahlo in a three-piece suit `<fridanet/suit.htm#top>`. This illustration would be used in a project two other students and I are working on for members of our composition class about the later work of Frida Kahlo. In the report on our project, which we will post on our class's Web page, we will cite `<http://members.aol.com/fridanet/kahlo.htm>` as the URL, unless you want us to use a different source.

Thank you very much for considering our request.

Jennifer Fox `<fox.360@osu.edu>`

2 Integrating visuals into your text and citing them

Treat visuals as you would other sources you integrate into your text. Like quotations, paraphrases, and summaries, visuals need to be introduced and commented on in some way. In addition, label (as figures or as tables) and number (Fig. 1, Fig. 2, and so on) all visuals, provide a caption that includes source information, and cite the source in your bibliography or list of works cited. Keep in mind that even if you create a visual (such as a bar graph) by using information from a source (such as the results of a Gallup Poll), you must cite that source. If you use a photograph you took yourself, you must cite that as well.

On p. 449 is an example of how Shannan Palma integrated a photograph of Mary Pickford, one of the stars she discusses in her essay about Hollywood movie heroes, into her text. Shannan chose this visual, which she found on a photo agency's Web site, because it illustrated her point about how movie studios created public images of their stars as otherworldly, almost mythological beings. She labeled it as "Fig. 1" and included a caption that identified the photographer, provided source information, and explained the point the image was intended to illustrate. In the text, she included a reference to Fig. 1 in an appropriate place.

●··· For an example
of how to cite
a personal
photograph,
see p. 111.

FOR COLLABORATION

Working with a classmate, review Shannan Palma's research-based essay on pp. 441–464. Then analyze how well she has integrated the sources into her text. Identify any areas where that integration could be improved, and bring these to class for discussion.

17g Checking for excessive use of source material

Exactly how much you should use sources in a research project depends on your purpose and your audience. In general, your text should not be a patchwork of quotations, paraphrases, and summaries from other people. You need a rhetorical stance, a perspective that represents you as the author. If you are overquoting and overciting, your own voice will disappear. The following passage illustrates this problem:

> The United States is one of the countries with the most rapid population growth. In fact, rapid population increase has been a "prominent feature of American life since the founding of the republic" (Day 31). In the past, the cause of the high rate of population growth was the combination of large-scale immigration and a high birth rate. As Day notes, "Two facts stand out in the demographic history of the United States: first, the single position as a receiver of immigrants; second, our high rate of growth from natural increase" (31).
>
> Nevertheless, American population density is not as high as in most European countries. Day points out that the Netherlands, with a density of 906 persons per square mile, is more crowded than even the most densely populated American states (33).

Most readers will think that the source, Day, is much too prominent here. If this passage were a background discussion or a survey of the literature on a topic, with each source being different, such a large number of citations might be acceptable. But all these citations are from the same source, and readers are likely to conclude that the source is primary and the author of the essay only secondary.

THINKING CRITICALLY ABOUT YOUR INTEGRATION OF SOURCES

In a research project you have done in the past or from a draft you are working on now, choose three passages that cite sources. Then, using the information in this chapter, examine how well these sources are integrated into your text. Note how you can make that integration smoother.

Acknowledging Sources and Avoiding Plagiarism

18

18a Understanding why you should acknowledge your sources

The sources you use in your own writing add much to the texture of your essays and strengthen your credibility. Most simply, acknowledging these sources offers a polite "thank you" for the work others have done. After all, most of us are happy to share our ideas, our intellectual property, with others—if we feel that our ideas are respected and we are given credit for them. In addition, acknowledging sources says to your reader that you have done your homework, that you have worked to gain expertise on your topic, that you are credible and trustworthy. Acknowledging sources can also demonstrate to readers that you have looked at more than one side of an issue, that you have considered several points of view, again impressing readers with your fairness. Similarly, recognizing your sources can help provide background for your own research by placing it in the context of other thinking and demonstrating that it is part of a larger conversation. Most of all, you want to acknowledge sources in order to help your readers follow your thoughts, understand how they relate to the thoughts of others, and know where to go to find more information on your topic.

In some ways, there really is nothing new under the sun, in writing and research as well as in life. If you think hard, you'll see that whatever writing you do has in some way been influenced by what you have already read and experienced. This chapter discusses how you can acknowledge the work of others and how you can avoid **plagiarism**—using someone else's words and ideas without giving proper credit to the source.

The practice of acknowledging and crediting sources has not always been as explicit as it is today. Shakespeare's audience members might well have known that *King Lear* was based on an earlier drama, *King Leir,* but they did not expect Shakespeare to cite that source. As Western societies came to depend on written texts that were printed and sold, the practice of citing sources grew. Today, writers need to understand the concept of **intellectual property**—one's own ideas or the ideas of others—and to give credit where credit is due. ∎

393

plag

394 **18b**

RESEARCH

Acknowledging
Sources and
Avoiding
Plagiarism

Acknowledging sources fully and generously, then, provides a means of establishing your ethos, or credibility, as a researcher. Failure to credit sources breaks trust with both the research conversation and your readers; as a sign of dishonesty, it can easily destroy the credibility of both you and your research.

18b Knowing which sources to acknowledge

As you carry out research, it is important to understand the distinction between materials that require acknowledgment and those that do not.

1 Materials that don't require acknowledgment

Some of the information you use does not need to be credited to a source because it is well known or because you gathered the data yourself.

- *Common knowledge.* If most readers already know a fact, you probably do not need to cite a source for it. You do not need to credit a source for the statement that George Bush was elected president in 2000, for example. If, on the other hand, you are discussing the very close nature of the election and offering various experts' opinions on the outcome, you should cite the sources of that information.

- *Facts available in a wide variety of sources.* If a number of encyclopedias, almanacs, or textbooks include a certain piece of information, you usually need not cite a specific source for it. For instance, you would not need to cite a source for the fact that the Japanese bombing of Pearl Harbor on December 7, 1941, destroyed most of the base except for the oil tanks and submarines. You would, however, need to credit a source that argued that the failure to destroy the submarines meant that Japan was destined to lose the subsequent war with the United States.

For information
on how to
conduct field
research, see 15f.

- *Your own findings from field research.* If you conduct observations or surveys, simply announce your findings as your own. Do acknowledge people you interview as individuals rather than as part of a survey, however.

When you are not sure whether a fact, an observation, or a piece of information requires acknowledgment, err on the side of safety, and cite the source.

For material that does not fall under the preceding categories, credit sources as fully as possible. Using quotation marks where appropriate, follow the conventions of the citation style you are using (such as MLA or APA), and include each source in a bibliography or list of works cited.

RESEARCH

Knowing Which Sources to Acknowledge

●— For guidelines on documenting sources, see Chapters 20–23.

- *Direct quotations.* Whenever you use another person's words directly, credit the source. If two quotations from the same source appear close together, you can use one parenthetical reference, or note, after the second quotation to refer to both. If you quote some of an author's words within a paraphrase or summary, you need to include a parenthetical reference for the quotation separately, after the closing quotation mark, as one student did when she quoted from Philip G. Hamerton's "One Intellectual Life":

  > Writer Philip G. Hamerton makes an interesting point about quotation when he says that readers "pay much more attention to a wise passage when it is quoted by someone else" (42).

- *Facts that aren't widely known or claims that are arguable.* If your readers would be unlikely to know a fact, or if an author presents as fact a claim that may or may not be true, cite the source. To claim, for instance, that Switzerland is amassing an offensive nuclear arsenal would demand the citation of a source because Switzerland has long been an officially neutral state. If you are not sure whether a fact will be familiar to your readers or whether a statement is arguable, go ahead and cite the source.

- *Judgments and opinions of others.* Whenever you summarize or paraphrase someone else's ideas or opinions, give the source on which you based your summary or paraphrase. Even though the wording is completely your own, you should acknowledge your source.

- *Images, statistics, charts, tables, graphs, and other visuals from any source.* Credit all visual and statistical material not derived from your own field research, even if you yourself create a graph or table from the data provided in a source.

- *Help provided by friends, instructors, and others.* A conference with an instructor may give you the perfect idea for clinching an argument. If so, give credit. Friends may respond to your drafts or help you conduct surveys. Credit them, too.

●— For more on writing accurate and acceptable paraphrases and summaries, see 16e3 and e4.

Here is a quick-reference chart to guide you in deciding whether or not you need to acknowledge a source:

NEED TO ACKNOWLEDGE	DON'T NEED TO ACKNOWLEDGE
quotations	your own words, observations, surveys, and so on
summaries or paraphrases of a source	common knowledge
ideas you glean from a source	facts available in many sources
facts that aren't widely known	graphs or tables you create from statistics you compile on your own
graphs, tables, and other statistical information taken or derived from a source	drawings you create
photographs	
illustrations or other visuals you do not create	
experiments conducted by others	
opinions and judgments of others	
interviews that are not part of a survey	
video or sound taken from sources	
organization or structure taken from a source	

18c Upholding academic integrity and avoiding plagiarism

One of the cornerstones of intellectual work is **academic integrity.** This principle accounts for our being able to trust those sources we use and to demonstrate that our own work is equally trustworthy. While there are many ways to damage academic integrity, two that are especially important are inaccurate or incomplete citation of sources—sometimes called unintentional plagiarism—and plagiarism that is deliberately intended to pass off one writer's work as another's.

Whether it is intentional or not, plagiarism can result in serious consequences. At some colleges, students who plagiarize fail the course automatically; at others, they are expelled. Instructors who plagiarize, even inadvertently, have had their degrees revoked, their books withdrawn from publication. And outside academic life, eminent political, business, and scientific leaders have been stripped of candidacies, positions, and awards because of plagiarism.

● **EXERCISE 18.1**

Spend fifteen minutes or so jotting down your ideas about intellectual property
and plagiarism. Where do you stand, for instance, on the issue of file sharing in
music? on downloading movies free of charge? Do you think these forms of intellectual property should be protected under copyright law? How do you define your
own intellectual property, and in what ways and under what conditions are you
willing to share it?

FOR COLLABORATION

Working with one or two members of your class, come up with your own definitions
of *intellectual property* and *plagiarism*. Take notes on how you arrived at the definitions
and on what points of agreement and disagreement you had. Bring the results of your
investigation to class for discussion.

FOR MULTILINGUAL WRITERS: *Thinking about Plagiarism as a Cultural Concept*

Many cultures do not recognize Western notions of plagiarism, which
rest on a belief that language and ideas can be owned by writers. Indeed,
in many countries outside the United States, and even within some
communities in the United States, using the words and ideas of others
without attribution is considered a sign of deep respect as well as an
indication of knowledge. In academic writing in the United States,
however, you should credit all materials except those that are common
knowledge, that are available in a wide variety of sources, or that are
your own creations (photographs, drawings, and so on) or your own
findings from field research.

1 Inaccurate or incomplete citation of sources

If you use a paraphrase that is too close to the original wording or sentence structure (even if you include a parenthetical reference, or note), if
you leave out the parenthetical reference for a quotation (even if you
include the quotation marks), or if you fail to indicate clearly the source
of an idea that you obviously did not come up with on your own, you
may be accused of plagiarism even if your intent was not to plagiarize.
This kind of inaccurate or incomplete citation of sources often results
either from carelessness or from not trying to learn how to use citations
accurately and fully. Still, because the costs of even unintentional

plagiarism can be severe, it's important to understand how it can happen and how you can guard against it.

In a January 2002 article published in *Time* magazine, historian Doris Kearns Goodwin explains how someone else's writing wound up in her book. The book in question, nine hundred pages long and with thirty-five hundred footnotes, took Goodwin ten years to write. During these ten years, she says, she took most of her notes by hand, organized the notes into boxes, and—once the draft was complete—went back to all her sources to check that all the material from them was correctly cited. "Somehow in this process," Goodwin goes on to say, "a few books were not fully rechecked," and thus she omitted some acknowledgments by mistake. She even left out some necessary quotation marks in material that she did acknowledge, apparently because some notes failed to distinguish clearly among quotations, paraphrases, and Goodwin's own comments. In meditating on this experience, Goodwin says that discovering such carelessness in her own work was very troubling, since "the writing of history is a rich process of building on the work of the past with the hope that others will build on what you have done. Through footnotes [and citations] you point the way to future historians."

As a writer of academic integrity, you—like Goodwin—will want to take responsibility for your research and for citing all sources accurately. Doing so is considerably easier now, when sources can be photocopied and the needed quotations identified right on the copy, and when software programs allow writers to insert footnotes or endnotes into the text as they are writing it. Today, Goodwin says, she can add the citations of her sources on the spot, while she has the source right in front of her, rather than hunting through thousands of handwritten cards looking for the correct note.

2 Intentional plagiarism

Deliberate plagiarism—handing in an essay written by a friend or purchased (or simply downloaded) from an essay-writing company; cutting and pasting passages directly from source materials without marking them with quotation marks and citing sources for them; failing to credit the source of an idea or concept in your text—is what most people think of when they hear the word *plagiarism*.

This form of plagiarism is particularly troubling because it represents dishonesty and deception: those who intentionally plagiarize present the hard thinking and hard work of someone else as their own, and they

plag

18c 399

RESEARCH

Upholding
Academic Integrity
and Avoiding
Plagiarism

claim knowledge they really don't have, thus deceiving their readers. You are probably already convinced that such deception can lead to disaster: how many of us would want to be operated on by a doctor who plagiarized her way through medical school or represented by a lawyer who cheated his way through law school — or drive over bridges engineered by those who downloaded answers to engineering problems, never working out the problems for themselves?

Intentional plagiarism is also fairly simple to spot: your instructor will be very well acquainted with your writing and likely to notice any sudden shifts in the style or quality of your work. In addition, by typing a few words into <www.google.com>, your instructor can identify "matches" very easily.

3 Tips for using sources

Precisely because downloading material from the Web and cutting and pasting from one document to another are so simple today, you need to be even more careful about the sources you work with. Instructor Nick Carbone provides the following advice for students who are working with sources in their writing:

DO

- Share ideas with others, give and get responses to writing, help one another write.
- Edit sections of one another's papers from time to time.
- Expect to make mistakes in managing and citing your sources.
- Expect to correct such mistakes.
- Be careful in downloading sources and in taking notes.
- Find a way to use your sources fairly and wisely, without these sources taking over your essay.
- Learn the many purposes that using and citing sources can have in your writing.
- Use your word processor to help you manage sources (for example, put sources you're quoting or paraphrasing in a different font and font color until your final draft so you don't forget they came from one of your sources).
- See your instructor when you are in doubt about how to use or acknowledge a source.
- Tell your instructor if you feel overwhelmed or fall behind; knowing your predicament will enable the instructor to help you find a solution.

RESEARCH

Acknowledging
Sources and
Avoiding
Plagiarism

DON'T

- Don't cheat, steal, or misrepresent the work of others as your own.
- Don't use online term-paper mills; they aren't worthy of you.
- Don't think that because something is on the Net it doesn't need to be acknowledged in a citation.
- Don't think that simply changing a few words means you don't have to provide a citation and put what is quoted in quotation marks.
- Don't think that because politicians have speechwriters whom they don't acknowledge that you can reasonably get someone else to write a paper for you: the purpose of being in college is to acquire knowledge through your own research and writing.
- Don't procrastinate on assignments so that you put undue pressure on yourself and are tempted to take shortcuts.

**www ● bedford
stmartins.com/
smhandbook**

For exercises
on avoiding
plagiarism, click on

▶ **Recognizing
Plagiarism/
Working with
Sources**
  ▶ **Exercises**

● **EXERCISE 18.2**

Read the brief original passage that follows, and then look closely at the five attempts to quote or paraphrase it. Decide which attempts are acceptable and which plagiarize, prepare notes on what supports your decision in each case, and bring your notes to class for discussion.

The strange thing about plagiarism is that it's almost always pointless. The writers who stand accused, from Laurence Sterne to Samuel Taylor Coleridge to Susan Sontag, tend to be more talented than the writers they lift from.
                    – MALCOLM JONES, "Have You Read This Story Somewhere?"
                    (*Newsweek*, February 4, 2002, p. 10)

1. According to Malcolm Jones, writers accused of plagiarism are always better writers than those they are supposed to have plagiarized.

2. According to Malcolm Jones, writers accused of plagiarism "tend to be more talented than the writers they lift from" (10).

3. Plagiarism is usually pointless, says writer Malcolm Jones.

4. Those who stand accused of plagiarism, such as Senator Joseph Biden, tend to be better writers than those whose work they use.

5. According to Malcolm Jones, "plagiarism is . . . almost always pointless."

18d Considering your own intellectual property

Although you may not have thought much about it, all of your work in college represents a growing bank of intellectual property, and this includes all of the research and writing you do, online and off. In fact, such original work is automatically copyrighted, even if it lacks the © symbol. Here are some tips for making sure that others respect your intellectual property just as you respect theirs:

- Realize that any email you send or anything you post to a listserv or discussion group is public. If you don't want your thoughts and ideas repeated or forwarded, keep them offline. In addition, you may want to let your friends know specifically that you do *not* want your email passed on to any third parties. In turn, remember that you should not use material from email, discussion groups, or other online forums without asking for permission to do so.

● For an example of a request for permission, see 17f.

- Be careful with your passwords and with discs you carry around. Whatever method you use for storing your work should be secure; only you should be able to give someone access to that work.
- Save all your drafts and notes so that you can show where your work has come from should anyone ask you.

18e Collaborating with others

The media's recent focus on plagiarism, the advent of online paper mills and for-hire essay-writing services, and the concern of universities over these services may suggest that you should lock all your work away and refuse even to discuss it with anyone else. That would be a very unfortunate result, however, since much of the learning we do throughout our lives comes as a result of talking with and learning from others. Indeed, many of the projects students undertake in college now call for some form of collaboration: a team of engineering students constructs a project and presents it to the class in writing and orally; a group of business students forms a hypothetical company, invests its assets, and reports on its progress to shareholders; a group of first-year writing students serves as peer editors for one another; and so on.

These are common and effective means of getting work done in writing, and they call for the same kind of acknowledgments you would use in a project you did by yourself. In general, cite all sources used by the group, and acknowledge all assistance provided by others. In some cases, you may decide to do this in an endnote rather than in your bibliography or list of works cited. For an example, see Shannan Palma's note on p. 461 acknowledging the help of her professors and classmates, another professor she interviewed (whom she also included in her list of works cited), and two consultants from her college's writing center.

● For more on collaborating effectively, see Chapter 6.

Look at a recent piece of your writing that incorporates material from sources, and try to determine how completely and accurately you acknowledged them. Did you properly cite every quotation, paraphrase, and summary? every opinion or other idea from a source? every source you used to create visuals? Did you unintentionally plagiarize someone else's words or ideas? Make notes, and bring them to class for discussion.

Writing a Research Project

19

In trying to choose between two jobs in different towns, one person made a long list of questions to answer: Which company offered the best benefits and potential for advancement? Which job location had the lower cost of living? How did the two locations compare in terms of schools, cultural opportunities, major league sports, and so on? After conducting careful and thorough research, he knew it was time to make a decision: he sent a letter of acceptance to one company and a letter of regret to the other.

In much the same way, the research for an academic project winds down: there comes a time to draw the strands of research together and articulate your conclusions in writing. This chapter will guide you through this process. ■

19a Refining your plans

Throughout your research, you have generated notes that answer your research question and reflect on your hypothesis. Your growing understanding of the subject has no doubt led you to gather other information, which may have altered your original question. This somewhat circular process, a kind of research spiral, is at the heart of all research-based writing.

You should by now have a fair number of notes containing facts, opinions, paraphrases, summaries, quotations, and other material; you probably have some visuals as well. You may also have thoughts about the connections among these many pieces of information. And you should have some sense of whether your hypothesis has been established sufficiently to serve as the thesis of an essay. Now it's time to reconsider your purpose, audience, stance, and working thesis.

1 Reconsidering your purpose, audience, stance, and working thesis

Given what you now know about your research question, reconsider questions such as the following:

1. What is your central purpose? What other purposes, if any, do you have?

2. What is your stance toward your topic? Are you an advocate, a critic, a reporter, an observer? (See 2g.)

3. What audience(s) other than your instructor might you be addressing?

4. How much about your research question does your audience know already? How much background will you need to present?

5. What sorts of supporting information are your readers likely to find convincing—examples? precedents? quotations from authorities? statistics? graphs, charts, or other visuals? direct observation? data drawn from interviews?

6. What tone will most appeal to them? Should you present yourself as a colleague, an expert, a student?

7. How can you establish common ground with your readers and show consideration of points of view other than your own? (See 13e2 and Chapter 25.)

8. What is your working thesis trying to establish? How likely is your audience to accept it?

2 Developing an explicit thesis

One useful way of relating your purpose, audience, and thesis before you begin a full draft is by writing out an **explicit thesis statement.** Such a statement allows you to articulate all your major lines of argument and to see how well those arguments carry out your purpose and appeal to your audience. At the drafting stage, try to develop your working thesis into an explicit statement, which might take the following form:

For more on
arguments, see
Chapters 11–13.

> In this research project, I plan to (explain/argue/demonstrate/analyze, and so on) for an audience of _____
>
> that _____
>
> because/if _____, _____,
>
> _____ .

Shannan Palma, the student whose research we've been following in earlier chapters, developed the following explicit thesis statement (see Chapter 20):

> In this research project, I plan to demonstrate for an audience of classmates from my first-year writing class that current trends in Hollywood films signal not the death of the hero but the evolution of the hero into two very different images.

FOR MULTILINGUAL WRITERS: *Asking a Native Speaker to Review Your Thesis*

res
19b   405

RESEARCH
Organizing
Information

You might find it helpful to ask one or two classmates who are native speakers to look at your explicit thesis. Ask if the thesis is as direct and clear as it can be, and revise accordingly.

3 Testing your thesis

Writing out an explicit thesis will often confirm your research and support your hypothesis. It may, however, reveal that your hypothesis is invalid, inadequately supported, or insufficiently focused. In such cases, you must then rethink your original research question, perhaps do further research, and work toward revising your hypothesis and thesis. To test your thesis, consider the following questions:

1. How can you state your thesis more precisely or more clearly (see 3b)? Should the wording be more specific? Could you use more concrete nouns (see 27c) or stronger verbs (see 47a)? Should you add qualifying adjectives or adverbs (see Chapter 36)?
2. In what ways will your thesis interest and appeal to your audience? What can you do to increase that interest (see 2h)?
3. Is your thesis going to be manageable, given your limits of time and knowledge? If not, what can you do to make it more manageable?
4. What evidence from your research supports each aspect of your thesis? What additional evidence do you need?

● EXERCISE 19.1

Take the thesis from your current research project, and test it against the questions provided in 19a3. Make revisions if your analysis reveals weaknesses in your thesis.

19b Organizing information

In discussing her process of writing, writer Marie Winn talks about the challenge of transforming a tangle of ideas and information "into an orderly and logical sequence." This is the task of organization, of grouping information effectively. Experienced writers differ considerably in the ways they go about this task, and you will want to experiment until you find an organizational method that works well for you. This section will discuss two organizing strategies—grouping material by subject headings and outlining.

For guidelines on ⎯•
brainstorming,
see 3a1.

1 Grouping notes by subject headings

During your research, you have been taking notes and listing ideas. To group these materials, examine them for connections, finding what might be combined with what, which notes will be more useful and which less useful, which ideas lend support to the thesis and which should be put aside. Brainstorm about your research question one last time, and add the resulting notes to your other materials, looking to see whether they fit with any of the materials you already have.

If you have been keeping notes on cards, you can arrange the cards in groups by subject headings, putting the ones with your main topics in the center and arranging any related cards around them. If you have been taking notes in a notebook, you can cut the pages apart and group the slips of paper in a similar manner. If your notes are in a computer file, you can sort them by subject headings or search for particular headings — or print them out, cut them up, and group them yourself.

Grouping your notes in this way will help you identify major ideas and see whether you have covered all the areas you need to cover. It will also help you decide whether you have too many ideas, whether you can omit some of your less useful sources, or whether you need to do more research in some area. Most important, it will allow you to see how the many small pieces of your research fit together.

Once you have established initial groups, skim through the notes and look for connections you can use to organize your draft. For example, Shannan Palma noticed that the notes on one of her main topics, contemporary movie heroes, seemed to be related to another set of notes, on movie characters who are only partially human. She thus decided to see whether this connection revealed a new category of hero.

2 Outlining

Outlines can be used in various ways and be done at various stages. Some writers group their notes, write a draft, and then outline the draft to study its tentative structure. Others develop a working outline from their notes, listing the major points in a tentative order with support for each point. Such a working outline may see you through the rest of the process, or you may decide to revise it as you go along. Still other writers prefer to plot out their organization early on in a formal outline.

For further dis- ⎯•
cussion of out-
lines, see 3e.

Shannan Palma drew up an informal outline of her ideas while she was still doing research on her topic, thinking that this simple structure would help keep her focused on the information she still needed to find. Here is that informal outline:

Development of the hero
    in legend, literature, film
    film heroes and "mistaken identity"
    the emerging Hollywood star
    the confusion between the star and the hero/character
    examples
Beyond heroes
    what possibilities??

Because she knew she was required to submit a formal outline with her essay, Shannan Palma kept adding to this informal outline as her research and writing progressed. She did not complete the formal outline (which appears on pp. 442–444) until after her essay was completely drafted, however. At that point, the formal outline served as a way to analyze and revise the draft.

FOR COLLABORATION

Working with a classmate, exchange drafts of your research projects, and then outline each other's drafts, using only the text and not asking questions for clarification. Finally, examine these outlines together. How well does your partner's outline reflect what you thought you were doing in the draft? What points, if any, are left out? What does the outline suggest about the organization of your draft? About the coverage of your topic? In what ways can this outline help you revise your draft?

19c   Drafting

When you are ready to begin drafting, set yourself a deadline for having a draft of your project complete, and structure your work with that deadline in mind. (For most college research projects, the process of drafting a final version should begin *at least* two weeks before the instructor's deadline.) Gather your notes, outline, and sources, and read through them, "getting into" your topic. Most writers find that some sustained work (perhaps two or three hours) pays off at this point. Begin drafting a part of the research project that you feel confident about. For example, if you are not sure how you want to introduce the draft but do know how you want to approach one point, begin with that, and return to the introduction later. The most important thing is to get started.

The drafting process itself varies considerably among researchers, and no one else can determine what will work best for you. The tips offered in 3f, however, can help. No matter what process you use to produce a draft, remember to include sources (for quotations, paraphrases, summaries, and visuals) as you go; doing so during drafting will save time later and help you produce your list of works cited.

Chances are that you will be doing most of your drafting with a word-processing program. If so, remember that most software programs now come with an outlining function as well as capabilities for formatting endnotes, footnotes, and lists of sources cited. You may want to begin by pasting or copying your informal (or formal) outline into a new document and using it to help guide your drafting: you can always jump back and forth from one part of the outline to the next. You can also open up more than one window, putting notes in one window, your draft in another, your bibliography in another, your outline in yet another. If you have been keeping your notes in a computer file, you can copy them directly into your document and then rework them so that they fit appropriately into your draft. And if you have kept your source information in a computer file as well, you can have that file handy as you add entries to your list of sources cited.

1 Drafting a working title and introduction

The title and introduction play special roles, for they set the context for what is to come. Ideally, the title announces your subject in an intriguing or memorable way. To accomplish these goals, Emily Lesk revised the title of her essay on p. 75 from "All-Powerful Coke" to "Red, White, and Everywhere." For her title, Shannan Palma decided that "Hollywood and the Hero" was intriguing and memorable but that it needed to provide more information. Thus she added the subtitle "Solving a Case of Mistaken Identity." The introduction should draw readers in and provide any background they will need to understand the discussion. Consider the following specifics when drafting an introduction to a research project:

For general advice on titles, see 4f1; on introductions, see 4f2 and 5f1.

- It is often effective to *open with a question,* especially your research question. Next, you might explain what you will do to answer the question and then *end with your thesis* — in essence, the answer — which grows out of your working thesis.

- Because you will be bringing together several distinct points from various sources, you will probably want to *forecast your main points* to help readers get their bearings.

- You will want to *establish your own credibility* as a research writer by revealing your experience and demonstrating what you have done to become knowledgeable about your topic.

- In general, you may *not* want to open with a quotation — though it can be a good attention-getter. In a research project, you usually want to quote several sources, and opening with a quotation from one source may give the impression that you will be presenting that writer's ideas rather than using them in support of your own.

Shannan Palma had a good reason to use lyrics from a well-known song at the beginning of her essay, both because she knew that the song and the singer (Jewel) would be known to many of her classmates and because the song poses a provocative question: "where's my hope now that my heroes have gone?" She begins by affirming the importance of this question and then builds interest in its answer by noting the central role heroes have played throughout U.S. history. After establishing that she has conducted extensive research on this question and its possible answers, she provides an overview of her goals for the essay, concluding with her thesis. Because she had to set the scene and provide necessary background information, she decided to use two paragraphs for her full introduction. (See Shannan's introduction on pp. 445–446.)

2 Drafting your conclusion

A good conclusion helps readers know what they have learned. Its job is not to persuade (the body of the essay or project should already have done that), but it can contribute to the overall effectiveness of your argument. The following specific strategies are especially appropriate for conclusions in research projects:

- A specific-to-general pattern frequently works well. Open with a reference to your thesis, and then expand to a more general conclusion that reminds readers of the significance of your discussion.

- If you have covered several main points, you may want to remind readers of them. Be careful, however, to provide more than a mere summary.

- Try to end with something that will have an impact — a provocative quotation or question, a vivid image, a call for action, or a warning. Remember, however, that readers generally don't like obvious preaching.

- Tailor your conclusion to the needs of your readers, in terms of both the information you include and the tone and style you adopt.

For general advice on conclusions, see 4f3 and 5f2.

Shannan Palma's conclusion summarizes the main points of her essay and then ends with an assertion of her topic's importance to our culture. Her use of the pronoun *our* invokes a kinship with readers who are also wondering what kind of heroes the twenty-first century will bring. (See Shannan's conclusion on pp. 459–460.)

19d Incorporating source materials

When you reach the point of drafting your research project, a new task awaits: weaving your source materials into your writing. The challenge is to use your sources yet remain the author—to quote, paraphrase, and summarize other voices while remaining the major voice in your work.

Because learning how to effectively integrate source material is so important, Chapter 17 is devoted entirely to this process. Consult that chapter often as you draft.

19e Reviewing and getting responses to your draft

Because a research project involves a complex mix of your thoughts and materials from outside sources, it calls for an especially careful review before you begin revising. As with most kinds of writing, however, taking a break after drafting is important, so that when you reread the draft, you can bring a fresh eye to the task.

When you return to the draft, read it straight through, without stopping. Then read it again slowly, reconsidering five things: purpose, audience, stance, thesis, and support. You might find that outlining your draft (see 3e and 19b2) helps you analyze it at this point.

- From your reading of the draft, what do you now see as its *purpose?* How does this compare with your original purpose? Does the draft do what your assignment requires?
- What *audience* does your essay address?
- What is your *stance* toward the topic?
- What is your *thesis?* Is it clearly stated?
- What *evidence* supports your thesis? Is the evidence sufficient?

Answer these questions as best you can, since they are the starting point for revision. Next, you need a closer reading of your draft and probably the comments of other readers. Ask friends and classmates to read and respond to your draft, and get a response from your instructor if possible.

The advice from readers may be most helpful if you ask questions specific to your project. If you are unsure about whether to include a particular point, how to use a certain quotation, or where to add more examples, ask readers specifically what they think you should do.

RESEARCH

Revising and Editing

● For more on getting critical responses to a draft, see 4c. For advice on working online to get responses, see 4c3 and 6c.

19f Revising and editing

Using any responses you have gathered and your own analysis, turn now to your final revision. It is advisable to work in several steps.

- *Considering responses.* Have readers identified problems you need to solve? If so, have they made specific suggestions about ways to revise? Have they identified strengths that might suggest ways of revising? For example, if they showed great interest in one point but no interest in another, consider expanding the first and deleting the second.

- *Reconsidering your original purpose, audience, and stance.* Judging from your readers' comments, do you feel confident that you have achieved your purpose? If not, what is missing? How have you appealed to your readers? How have you established common ground with them? How have you satisfied any special concerns they may have? Has your rhetorical stance toward your topic changed in any way? If so, what effect has that change had on your draft?

- *Assessing your own research.* If you conducted experiments, surveys, interviews, observations, or other field research, do the results stand up to your own and readers' analyses? Are all the data accurate and your conclusions warranted? What part did you play in the research, and how could your role have influenced your findings? If your research involved interviewing or surveying other people, how appropriate are their credentials or characteristics to the thesis you are arguing? Have you obtained their permission to quote them (by name if you want to do so)? If you quoted from email, a discussion listserv, or other online forum, did you get permission from the writers to use their words?

- *Gathering additional material.* If you need to strengthen any points, go back to your notes to see whether you have the necessary information. If you failed to consider opposing viewpoints adequately, for instance, you may need to find more material.

- *Deciding on changes you need to make.* Figure out everything you have to do to perfect your draft, and make a list. With your deadline firmly in mind, plan your revision.

- *Rewriting your draft.* Word-processing software has the great advantage of allowing you to move text around and to delete or change passages easily. Experienced writers usually prefer to revise first on hard copy, however, so that they can see the entire document spread out before them. However you revise, be sure to keep copies of each successive draft. And begin with the major work: changing content, adding examples or evidence, addressing section- or paragraph-level concerns. Then turn to sentence-level work and to individual word choice. Also revise for clarity and to sharpen the dominant impression your work creates.

- *Reconsidering your title, introduction, and conclusion.* In light of the reevaluation and revision of your draft, reread these important parts to see whether they still serve their purpose. Does the introduction accurately predict, and the conclusion accurately restate, what the body of the final work discusses? If not, do you need to forecast your main points in the introduction or summarize them in the conclusion? Does your introduction capture readers' attention? Does your conclusion help them see the significance of your argument? Is your title specific enough to let your readers know about your research question and engaging enough to make them want to read your answer to it?

For more on
citing sources,
see Chapters 17
and 20–23.

- *Checking your documentation.* Have you included a citation in your text for every quotation, paraphrase, and summary you incorporated, following consistently the required style? Have you done the same for all visuals (photographs, tables, and so on) that are taken from or based on your sources?

- *Editing your draft.* Now is the time to attend carefully to grammar, usage, spelling, punctuation, and mechanics. If you are using a computer, take the time to use the spell checker—but be aware that it will miss many errors (such as homonyms like *to, two,* and *too*). If you have persistent problems with certain words or phrases, use the FIND command to find them, and then double-check their spelling and usage. If you are using a style or grammar checker, be aware that such programs cannot make rhetorical choices and often miss problem passages or phrases—or identify perfectly acceptable ones as problems—because they aren't yet equal to the complexity of English. Use them with great caution.

For more on
spell, grammar,
and style check-
ers, see 7b.

19g Preparing a list of sources

Once you have a final draft with your source materials in place, you are ready to prepare your list of works cited (according to MLA style), your references (according to the style of APA or the Council of Science Editors [CBE]), or your bibliography (according to the style of the University of Chicago Press [Chicago]). Follow the guidelines for your required

RESEARCH

Preparing and
Proofreading Your
Final Copy

●---- For guidelines on
preparing a list
of sources, see
Chapters 20–23.

style carefully, creating an entry for each source used. Double-check your draft against your list of works cited to see that you have listed every source mentioned in your draft and (unless you are listing all the sources you consulted) that you have not listed any sources not cited in your draft.

Almost all word-processing software programs now provide templates for formatting endnotes, footnotes, or lists of sources. They will alphabetize for you and insert some of the necessary formatting, such as italics.

19h Preparing and proofreading your final copy

Your final rough draft may end up looking very rough indeed. So your next task is to create a final perfectly clean copy. This is the version you will submit to your instructor, the one that will represent all your work and effort.

To make sure that this final version puts your best foot forward, proofread extremely carefully. For proofreading, it is best to work with a hard copy, since reading onscreen often leads to inaccuracies and especially to missed typos. In addition, you may want to read backward, going word for word, or to use a ruler, lowering it as you read each line. Finally, proofread once again for content, for the flow of your argument, to make sure you haven't mistakenly deleted whole lines, sentences, paragraphs, or sections.

Preparing the final copy, especially if you are working with a computer, can allow for interesting possibilities in the layout and design of your work. Be sure to consider issues such as type size and the use of color or boldface headings, which may make your final work more attractive and readable.

●---- For more on
using a com-
puter to format
and design an
essay, see Chap-
ters 7 and 8.

After your manuscript preparation and proofreading are complete, take some time to celebrate your achievement: your research and hard work have paid off and produced a piece of research-based writing you can, and should, take pride in.

THINKING CRITICALLY ABOUT RESEARCH PROJECTS

Reading with an Eye for Research

The research essays in Chapters 20 and 65 were written by two students, the first of whom you've followed since Chapter 14. The first essay, which follows MLA style, was written for a composition class; the second, which follows APA style, was written for a communications class. Read these essays carefully, and study the marginal annotations. Compare your research project with these, noting differences in approach, style, format, and use of sources.

Thinking about Your Own Research Project

Pause now to reflect on the research project you have completed. How did you go about organizing your information? What would you do to improve this process? What problems did you encounter in drafting? How did you solve these problems? How many quotations did you use, and how did you integrate them into your text? When and why did you use summaries and paraphrases? If you used any visuals, how effective were they in supporting the points you were making? What did you learn from revising?

Documenting Sources: MLA Style

No writer since Adam, in other words, has had the luxury of not having to document his or her sources. In your writing, full and accurate documentation is important because it helps build your credibility as a writer and researcher by giving credit to those people whose works influenced your own ideas.

Although all documentation styles require the same basic information, you will want to use the style favored in a particular field or required by a particular instructor. Following specific rules of punctuation and format ensures consistency and helps protect you from plagiarizing because of omitted source information. This chapter discusses the Modern Language Association (MLA) style of documentation, widely used in literature and languages as well as other fields. ■

For more information on MLA style, consult the MLA's Web site, <www.mla.org>, or one of the following books. Both include the MLA's latest guidelines for citing electronic sources. The second is intended primarily for advanced scholars.

Gibaldi, Joseph. *MLA Handbook for Writers of Research Papers.* 6th ed. New York: MLA, 2003.

Gibaldi, Joseph. *MLA Style Manual and Guide to Scholarly Publishing.* 2nd ed. New York: MLA, 1998.

20a MLA format for in-text citations

MLA style requires documentation in the text of an essay for every quotation, paraphrase, summary, or other material that must be cited (see 18b). As discussed in Chapter 17, **in-text citations** document material from other sources with both *signal phrases* and *parenthetical references*. Signal phrases introduce the material, often including the author's name. Parenthetical references direct you to full bibliographic entries in a list of works cited at the end of the text.

In general, make your parenthetical references short, including just enough information for your readers to locate the full reference in the works-cited list. Place a parenthetical reference as near the relevant material as possible without disrupting the flow of the sentence. Note in

MLA

416   **20a**

RESEARCH

Documenting
Sources: MLA Style

DIRECTORY TO MLA STYLE

(Continued on p. 417)

(Continued from p. 416)

2. PERIODICALS

3. ELECTRONIC SOURCES

4. OTHER KINDS OF SOURCES

20d. A student research essay, MLA style

● For examples of
other research
essays using
MLA style, see
13k and 64d.

the following examples *where* punctuation is placed in relation to the parentheses. Except for block quotations, place any punctuation mark *after* the closing parenthesis. If you are referring to a quotation, place the parenthetical reference *after* the closing quotation mark but *before* any other punctuation mark. For block quotations, place the reference one space after the final punctuation mark. Here are examples of the ways to cite various kinds of sources:

1. AUTHOR NAMED IN A SIGNAL PHRASE Ordinarily, use the author's name in a signal phrase to introduce the material, and simply cite the page number(s) in parentheses. Use the full name the first time you cite a source. For later references, use just the last name.

```
Herrera indicates that Kahlo believed in a "vitalistic
form of pantheism" (328).
```

2. AUTHOR NAMED IN A PARENTHETICAL REFERENCE When you do not name the author in the text, include the author's last name before the page number(s) in the parentheses.

```
In places, Beauvoir "sees Marxists as believing in
subjectivity as much as existentialists do" (Whitmarsh
63).
```

3. TWO OR THREE AUTHORS Use all the last names in a signal phrase or parenthetical reference.

```
Gortner, Hebrun, and Nicolson maintain that "opinion
leaders" influence other people in an organization
because they are respected, not because they hold high
positions (175).
```

4. FOUR OR MORE AUTHORS Use the first author's name and *et al.* ("and others") in a signal phrase or parenthetical reference, or, preferably, name all the authors.

```
Similarly, as Belenky, Clinchy, Goldberger, and Tarule
assert, examining the lives of women expands our
understanding of human development (7).
```

5. CORPORATE OR GROUP AUTHOR Give the corporation's name or a shortened form in a signal phrase or parenthetical reference.

In fact, one of the leading foundations in the field of
higher education supports the recent proposals for
community-run public schools (Carnegie Corporation 45).

6. **UNKNOWN AUTHOR** Use the title of the work or a shortened version in
a signal phrase or parenthetical reference.

"Hype," by one analysis, is "an artificially engendered
atmosphere of hysteria" ("Today's Marketplace" 51).

7. **AUTHOR OF TWO OR MORE WORKS** If your list of works cited has more
than one work by the same author, give the title of the work you are citing or a shortened version in a signal phrase or parenthetical reference.

Gardner presents readers with their own silliness
through his description of a "pointless, ridiculous
monster, crouched in the shadows, stinking of dead men,
murdered children, and martyred cows" (Grendel 2).

8. **TWO OR MORE AUTHORS WITH THE SAME SURNAME** If your list of works cited
includes works by authors with the same surname, always include each
author's first name in the signal phrases or parenthetical references for
those works.

Children will learn to write if they are allowed to
choose their own subjects, James Britton asserts, citing
the Schools Council study of the 1960s (37-42).

9. **MULTIVOLUME WORK** In the parenthetical reference, note the volume
number first and then page number(s), with a colon and one space
between them.

Modernist writers prized experimentation and gradually
even sought to blur the line between poetry and prose,
according to Forster (3: 150).

If you name only one volume of the work in your list of works cited, you
need include only the page number in the parentheses.

10. **LITERARY WORK** Because literary works are often available in many
different editions, first cite the page number(s) from the edition you
used followed by a semicolon, and then give other identifying information that will lead readers to the passage in any edition. Indicate the act

and/or scene in a play (*37; sc. 1*). For a novel, indicate the part or chapter (*175; ch. 4*).

> In utter despair, Dostoyevsky's character Mitya wonders
> aloud about the "terrible tragedies realism inflicts on
> people" (376; bk. 8, ch. 2).

For a poem, instead of page numbers cite the part (if there is one) and line(s), separated by a period. If you are citing only line numbers, use the word *line(s)* in the first citation of the poem (*lines 33–34*).

> On dying, Whitman speculates "All goes onward and
> outward, nothing collapses, / And to die is different
> from what any one supposed, and luckier" (6.129-30).

For a verse play, give only the act, scene, and line numbers, separated by periods.

> As Macbeth begins, the witches greet Banquo as "Lesser
> than Macbeth, and greater" (1.3.65).

11. WORK IN AN ANTHOLOGY For an essay, short story, or other piece of prose reprinted in an anthology, use the name of the author of the work, not the editor of the anthology, but use the page number(s) from the anthology.

> Narratives of captivity play a major role in early
> writing by women in the United States, as demonstrated
> by Silko (219).

12. SACRED TEXT To cite a sacred text such as the Qur'an or the Bible, give the title of the edition you used, the book, and the chapter and verse (or their equivalent), separated by a period. In your text, spell out the names of books. In a parenthetical reference, use an abbreviation for books with names of five or more letters (*Gen.* for *Genesis*).

> He ignored the admonition "Pride goes before
> destruction, and a haughty spirit before a fall" (New
> Oxford Annotated Bible, Prov. 16.18).

13. INDIRECT SOURCE Use the abbreviation *qtd. in* to indicate that you are quoting from someone else's report of a conversation, interview, letter, or the like.

As Arthur Miller says, "When somebody is destroyed everybody finally contributes to it, but in Willy's case, the end product would be virtually the same" (qtd. in Martin and Meyer 375).

14. TWO OR MORE SOURCES IN THE SAME REFERENCE Separate the information with semicolons.

Some economists recommend that <u>employment</u> be redefined to include unpaid domestic labor (Clark 148; Nevins 39).

15. ENTIRE WORK OR ONE-PAGE ARTICLE Include the reference in the text without any page numbers or parentheses.

Michael Ondaatje's poetic sensibility transfers beautifully to prose in <u>The English Patient</u>.

16. WORK WITHOUT PAGE NUMBERS If a work has no page numbers but has another kind of numbered sections, include in parentheses the name and number(s) of any specific one(s) you are citing, such as paragraphs (*par.* or *pars.*), parts (*pt.* or *pts.*), or screens. If such a reference includes the author's name, use a comma after the name.

Whitman considered their speech "a source of a native grand opera," in the words of Ellison (par. 13).

17. ELECTRONIC OR NONPRINT SOURCE Give enough information in a signal phrase or parenthetical reference for readers to locate the source in the list of works cited. Usually use the name or title under which you list the source. If you are citing any specific section(s), include the page, part, paragraph, or screen number(s) in parentheses.

Describing children's language acquisition, Pinker explains that "what's innate about language is just a way of paying attention to parental speech" (Johnson, sec. 1).

20b MLA format for explanatory and bibliographic notes

MLA style allows **explanatory notes** for information or commentary that would not readily fit into the text but is needed for clarification or further explanation. In addition, MLA style permits **bibliographic**

For other examples of explanatory and bibliographic notes, see the "Notes" to Shannan Palma's essay (p. 461).

RESEARCH
MLA Format for Explanatory and Bibliographic Notes

notes for citing several sources for one point and for offering thanks to, information about, or evaluation of a source. Superscript numbers are used in the text to refer readers to the notes, which may appear as endnotes (typed under the heading "Notes" on a separate page after the text but before the list of works cited) or as footnotes at the bottom of the page (typed four lines below the last text line). For example:

SUPERSCRIPT NUMBER IN TEXT

Stewart emphasizes the existence of social contacts in Hawthorne's life so that the audience will accept a different Hawthorne, one more attuned to modern times than the figure in Woodberry.[3]

NOTE

[3] Woodberry does, however, show that Hawthorne <u>was</u> often an unsociable individual. He emphasizes the seclusion of Hawthorne's mother, who separated herself from her family after the death of her husband, often even taking meals alone (28). Woodberry seems to imply that Mrs. Hawthorne's isolation rubbed off onto her son.

20c   MLA format for a list of works cited

Works Cited is an alphabetical list of the sources cited in your essay. (If your instructor asks that you list everything you have read as background, call the list "Works Consulted.") Here are some guidelines for preparing such a list:

- Start your list on a separate page after the text of your essay and any notes. (See 20b.)
- Number each page, continuing the page numbers of the text.
- Center the heading *Works Cited* an inch from the top of the page; do not underline or italicize it or enclose it in quotation marks. Double-space between the heading and the first entry, and double-space the entire list.
- Start each entry flush with the left margin, and indent any additional lines one-half inch, or five spaces.
- List your sources alphabetically by author's (or editor's) last name. If the author of a source is unknown, alphabetize the source by the first word of the title, disregarding *A, An,* or *The.*

If you are using software (Microsoft Word, EndNote, Research Assistant) to record and create a list of works cited, double-check that all formatting is accurate.

The sample works-cited entries that follow observe MLA's advice to underline words that are often italicized in print. Although most computers can generate italics easily, the MLA recommends that "you can avoid ambiguity by using underlining" in your research essays where the "type style of every letter and punctuation mark must be easily recognizable." If you wish to use italics instead, first check with your instructor.

1 Books

The basic entry for a book includes three elements, each followed by a period.

- *Author.* List the last name first, followed by a comma and the first name.
- *Title.* Underline or (if your instructor permits) italicize the title and any subtitle, and capitalize all major words.
- *Publication information.* Give the city of publication followed by a colon, a space, and a shortened version of the publisher's name — dropping *Books, Press, Publishers, Inc.,* and so on (*Harper* for *HarperCollins Publishers*); using only the first surname (*Harcourt* for *Harcourt Brace*); and abbreviating *University Press* (*Oxford UP* for *Oxford University Press*). The publisher's name is followed by a comma and the year of publication.

> • For more on
> capitalizing
> titles, see 54c.

Here is an example of a basic entry for a book:

double-space
title (and subtitle, if any),
author, last name first   underlined

Ortiz, Simon. Out There Somewhere. Tucson:

→ U of Arizona P, 2002. ← publisher's city
and name, year
of publication

indent one-half
inch or five spaces

1. ONE AUTHOR

deCordova, Richard. Picture Personalities: The Emergence
   of the Star System in America. Urbana: U of
   Illinois P, 1990.

2. TWO OR THREE AUTHORS List the first author, last name first; then list the name(s) of the other author(s) in regular order, with a comma between authors and an *and* before the last one.

MLA

20c

424

RESEARCH

Documenting
Sources: MLA Style

```
Appleby, Joyce, Lynn Hunt, and Margaret Jacob. Telling
    the Truth about History. New York: Norton, 1994.
```

3. FOUR OR MORE AUTHORS Give the first author listed on the title page, followed by a comma and *et al.* ("and others"), or list all the names, since the use of *et al.* diminishes the importance of the other contributors.

```
Belenky, Mary Field, Blythe Clinchy, Jill Goldberger,
    and Nancy Tarule. Women's Ways of Knowing. New
    York: Basic, 1986.
```

4. CORPORATE OR GROUP AUTHOR Give the name of the group listed on the title page as the author, even if the same group published the book.

```
American Chemical Society. Handbook for Authors of
    Papers in the American Chemical Society
    Publications. Washington: Amer. Chemical Soc.,
    1978.
```

5. UNKNOWN AUTHOR Begin the entry with the title.

```
The New York Times Atlas of the World. New York: New
    York Times, 1980.
```

6. TWO OR MORE BOOKS BY THE SAME AUTHOR(S) Arrange the entries alphabetically by title. Include the name(s) of the author(s) in the first entry, but in subsequent entries, use three hyphens followed by a period.

```
Lorde, Audre. A Burst of Light. Ithaca: Firebrand, 1988.
---. Sister Outsider. Trumansburg: Crossing, 1984.
```

If you cite a work by one author who is also listed as the first coauthor of another work you cite, list the single-author work first, and repeat the author's name in the entry for the coauthored work. Also repeat the author's name if you cite a work in which that author is listed as the first of a different set of coauthors. Use three hyphens only when the work is by *exactly* the same author(s) as the previous entry.

7. EDITOR OR EDITORS Treat an editor as an author, but add a comma and *ed.* (or *eds.* for more than one editor).

```
Wall, Cheryl A., ed. Changing Our Own Words: Essays on
    Criticism, Theory, and Writing by Black Women. New
    Brunswick: Rutgers UP, 1989.
```

8. AUTHOR AND EDITOR If you have cited the body of the text, begin with the author's name, and list the editor's name, introduced by *Ed.,* after the title.

```
James, Henry. Portrait of a Lady. Ed. Leon Edel. Boston:
     Houghton, 1963.
```

If you have cited the editor's contribution to the work, begin with the editor's name followed by a comma and *ed.,* and list the author's name, introduced by *By,* after the title.

```
Edel, Leon, ed. Portrait of a Lady. By Henry James.
     Boston: Houghton, 1963.
```

9. WORK IN AN ANTHOLOGY OR CHAPTER IN A BOOK WITH AN EDITOR List the author(s) of the selection or chapter; its title; the title of the book in which the selection or chapter appears; *Ed.* and the name(s) of the editor(s); the publication information; and the inclusive page numbers of the selection or chapter.

```
Gordon, Mary. "The Parable of the Cave." The Writer on
     Her Work. Ed. Janet Sternburg. New York: Norton,
     1980. 27-32.
```

If the selection was originally published in a periodical and you are asked to supply information for this original source, use the following format. *Rpt.* is the abbreviation for "Reprinted."

```
Didion, Joan. "Why I Write." New York Times Book Review
     9 Dec. 1976: 22. Rpt. in The Writer on Her Work.
     Ed. Janet Sternburg. New York: Norton, 1980. 3-16.
```

For inclusive page numbers up to 99, note all digits in the second number. For numbers above 99, note only the last two digits and any others that change in the second number (*115–18, 1378–79, 296–301*).

●─── For guidelines on citing a periodical article, see 20c2.

10. TWO OR MORE ITEMS FROM AN ANTHOLOGY Include the anthology itself in your list of works cited.

```
Donalson, Melvin, ed. Cornerstones: An Anthology of
     African American Literature. New York: St.
     Martin's, 1996.
```

Also list each selection by its author and title, followed by a cross-reference to the anthology. Be sure to alphabetize all entries.

Baker, Houston A., Jr. "There Is No More Beautiful Way."
    Donalson 856-63.

Ellison, Ralph. "What America Would Be Like without
    Blacks." Donalson 737-41.

11. TRANSLATION Begin the entry with the author's name, and give the
translator's name, preceded by *Trans.* ("Translated by"), after the title.

Zamora, Martha. Frida Kahlo: The Brush of Anguish.
    Trans. Marilyn Sode Smith. San Francisco:
    Chronicle, 1990.

If you cite a translated selection in an anthology, add *Trans.* and the
translator's name before the title of the anthology.

Horace. The Art of Poetry. Trans. Smith Palmer Bovie.
    The Critical Tradition: Classic Texts and
    Contemporary Trends. Ed. David H. Richter. 2nd ed.
    Boston: Bedford, 1998. 68-78.

12. EDITION OTHER THAN THE FIRST Add the information, in abbreviated
form, after the title.

Kelly, Alfred H., Winfred A. Harbison, and Herman Belz.
    The American Constitution: Its Origins and
    Development. 6th ed. New York: Norton, 1983.

13. ONE VOLUME OF A MULTIVOLUME WORK Give the volume number after the
title, and list the number of volumes in the complete work after the date,
using the abbreviations *Vol.* and *vols.*

Foner, Philip S., and Ronald L. Lewis, eds. The Black
    Worker. Vol. 3. Philadelphia: Lippincott, 1980. 8
    vols.

14. TWO OR MORE VOLUMES OF A MULTIVOLUME WORK Give the number of volumes in the complete work after the title, using the abbreviation *vols.*

Foner, Philip S., and Ronald L. Lewis, eds. The Black
    Worker. 8 vols. Philadelphia: Lippincott, 1980.

15. PREFACE, FOREWORD, INTRODUCTION, OR AFTERWORD List the author of the
item, the item title (not underlined, italicized, or in quotation marks),

the title of the book, and its author's name, preceded by the word *By.* If
the same person wrote both the book and the cited item, use just the last
name after *By.* List the inclusive page numbers of the item at the end of
the entry.

> Schlesinger, Arthur M., Jr. Introduction. <u>Pioneer Women:</u>
>   <u>Voices from the Kansas Frontier</u>. By Joanna L.
>   Stratton. New York: Simon, 1981. 11-15.

16. ENTRY IN A REFERENCE WORK List the author of the entry, if known. If
no author is identified, begin with the title. For a well-known work, just
note any edition number and date after the name of the work. If the
entries in the work are in alphabetical order, no volume or page numbers
are needed.

> "Hero." <u>Merriam-Webster's Collegiate Dictionary</u>. 10th
>   ed. 1996.
> Johnson, Peder J. "Concept Learning." <u>Encyclopedia of</u>
>   <u>Education</u>. 1971.

17. BOOK THAT IS PART OF A SERIES Cite the series name as it appears on the
title page, followed by any series number.

> Moss, Beverly J., ed. <u>Literacy across Communities</u>.
>   Written Lang. Ser. 2. Cresskill: Hampton, 1994.

18. REPUBLICATION To cite a modern edition of an older book, add the
original publication date, followed by a period, after the title.

> Scott, Walter. <u>Kenilworth</u>. 1821. New York: Dodd, 1956.

19. GOVERNMENT DOCUMENT Begin with the author, if identified. If no
author is given, start with the name of the government followed by the
agency and any subdivision. Use abbreviations if they can be readily
understood. Then list the title, underlined or italicized. For congressional documents, cite the number, session, and house of Congress
(using *S* for Senate and *H* or *HR* for House of Representatives), and the
type (*Report, Resolution, Document*), in abbreviated form, and number of
the material. If you cite the *Congressional Record,* give only the date and
page number. Otherwise, end with the publication information; the
publisher is often the Government Printing Office (*GPO*).

For advice on
citing online
government doc-
uments, see
p. 434.

New Hampshire. Dept. of Transportation. <u>Right of Way
    Salinity Reports, Hillsborough County, 1985</u>.
    Concord: New Hampshire Dept. of Transportation,
    1986.
United States. Cong. House. <u>Report of the Joint
    Subcommittee on Reconstruction</u>. 39th Cong., 1st
    sess. H. Rept. 30. 1865. New York: Arno, 1969.
United States. Census Bureau. <u>Historical Statistics of
    the United States, Colonial Times to 1970</u>.
    Washington: GPO, 1975.

20. PAMPHLET Treat a pamphlet as you would a book.

<u>Why Is Central America a Conflict Area?</u> Opposing
    Viewpoints Pamphlets. St. Paul: Greenhaven, 1984.

21. PUBLISHED PROCEEDINGS OF A CONFERENCE Treat proceedings as a book, but add information about the conference if it is not part of the title.

Martin, John Steven, and Christine Mason Sutherland,
    eds. <u>Proceedings of the Canadian Society for the
    History of Rhetoric</u>. Calgary: Canadian Soc. for
    the History of Rhetoric, 1986.

22. PUBLISHER'S IMPRINT If a book was published by a publisher's imprint (indicated on the title page), hyphenate the imprint and the publisher's name.

Rose, Phyllis. <u>Parallel Lives: Five Victorian Marriages</u>.
    New York: Vintage-Random, 1984.

23. TITLE WITHIN THE TITLE Do not underline or italicize the title of a book within the title of a book you are citing. Enclose in quotation marks the title of a short work within a book title, and underline or italicize it as you do the rest of the title.

Gilbert, Stuart. <u>James Joyce's</u> Ulysses. New York:
    Vintage-Random, 1955.
Renza, Louis A. <u>"A White Heron" and the Question of a
    Minor Literature</u>. Madison: U of Wisconsin P, 1984.

24. SACRED TEXT To cite individual published editions of sacred books, begin the entry with the title, underlined or italicized. For versions of the Bible in which the version is not part of the title, list the version after the title. If your text does not specify a particular edition or version, the Bible and other sacred writings should not appear in the works-cited list.

```
The Jerusalem Bible. Garden City: Doubleday, 1966.
```

2 Periodicals

The basic entry for a periodical includes three elements, each followed by a period.

- *Author.* List the author's last name first, followed by a comma and the first name.
- *Article title.* Enclose the title and any subtitle in quotation marks, and capitalize all major words. The closing period goes inside the closing quotation mark.

● For more on capitalizing titles, see 54c.

- *Publication information.* Give the periodical title (excluding any initial *A, An,* or *The*), underlined or italicized and with all major words capitalized; the volume number and issue number if appropriate; and the date of publication. For journals, list the year in parentheses followed by a colon, a space, and the inclusive page numbers. For magazines and newspapers, list the month (abbreviated, except for *May, June,* and *July*) or the day and month before the year, and do not use parentheses. Do not use *p.* or *pp.* before the page numbers. For inclusive page numbers, note all digits for numbers 1 to 99, and note only the last two digits and any others that change for numbers above 99 (*24–27, 134–45, 198–201*).

Here is an example of a basic entry for an article in a journal:

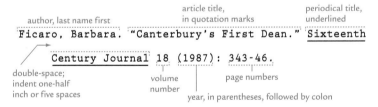

```
author, last name first    article title,            periodical title,
                           in quotation marks        underlined
Ficaro, Barbara. "Canterbury's First Dean." Sixteenth

    Century Journal 18 (1987): 343-46.
double-space;            volume      page numbers
indent one-half          number
inch or five spaces      year, in parentheses, followed by colon
```

25. ARTICLE IN A JOURNAL PAGINATED BY VOLUME Follow the journal title with the volume number in arabic numerals.

```
Norris, Margot. "Narration under a Blindfold: Reading
    Joyce's 'Clay.'" PMLA 102 (1987): 206-15.
```

MLA

20c

430

RESEARCH

Documenting
Sources: MLA Style

26. **ARTICLE IN A JOURNAL PAGINATED BY ISSUE** Put a period and the issue number after the volume number.

```
Loffy, John. "The Politics at Modernism's Funeral."
     Canadian Journal of Political and Social Theory 6.3
     (1987): 89-96.
```

27. **ARTICLE IN A MONTHLY MAGAZINE** Put the month (or months, hyphenated) before the year. Do not include volume or issue numbers.

```
Weiss, Philip. "The Book Thief: A True Tale of
     Bibliomania." Harper's Jan. 1994: 37-56.
```

28. **ARTICLE IN A WEEKLY MAGAZINE** Include the day, month, and year in that order, with no commas between them. Do not include volume or issue numbers.

```
Daly, Steve. "Face to Face." Entertainment Weekly 20
     June 1997: 20-24.
```

29. **ARTICLE IN A NEWSPAPER** Give the name of the newspaper, underlined or italicized, as it appears on the front page but without any initial *A, An,* or *The.* Add the city in brackets after the name if it is not part of the name. Then give the date and the edition (if listed), followed by a colon, a space, the section number or letter (if listed), and the page number(s). If the article appears on discontinuous pages, give the first page followed by a plus sign.

```
Vogel, Carol. "With Huge Gift, the Whitney Is No Longer
     a Poor Cousin." New York Times 3 Aug. 2002, late
     ed.: A1+.
```

30. **EDITORIAL OR LETTER TO THE EDITOR** Use the label *Editorial* or *Letter,* not underlined, italicized, or in quotation marks, after the title or after the author's name if there is no title.

```
Crews, Frederick. "Was Freud a Fraud?" Letter. New York
     Times Book Review 27 Mar. 1994: 27.
Magee, Doug. "Soldier's Home." Editorial. Nation 26 Mar.
     1988: 400-01.
```

31. **UNSIGNED ARTICLE** Begin with the article title, alphabetizing the entry according to the first word after any initial *A, An,* or *The.*

```
"Tipping the Balance." Time 25 June 2001: 34+.
```

32. REVIEW List the reviewer's name and the title of the review, if any, followed by *Rev. of* and the title and author or director of the work reviewed. Then add the publication information for the periodical in which the review appears.

```
Solinger, Rickie. "Unsafe for Women." Rev. of Next Time,
     She'll Be Dead: Battering and How to Stop It, by Ann
     Jones. New York Times Book Review 20 Mar. 1994: 16.
```

33. ARTICLE WITH A TITLE WITHIN THE TITLE Enclose in single quotation marks the title of a short work within an article title. Underline or italicize the title of a book within an article title.

```
Frey, Leonard H. "Irony and Point of View in 'That
     Evening Sun.'" Faulkner Studies 2 (1953): 33-40.
```

3 Electronic sources

Electronic sources such as CD-ROMs, World Wide Web sites, and email differ from print sources in the ease with which they can be — and the frequency with which they are — changed, updated, or even eliminated. In addition, as the *MLA Handbook for Writers of Research Papers* notes, electronic media "so far lack agreed-on means of organizing works." In recommending the following guidelines for some of the most common kinds of electronic sources, the *Handbook* adds, "References to electronic works therefore must provide more information than print citations generally offer." (Further guidelines for citing electronic sources can be found in the *Handbook* and online at <www.mla.org>.)

For example, the most commonly cited electronic sources are from a Web site, such as essays, articles, or poems within a scholarly project, a reference database, a professional site, or an online periodical. The entry for such a source may include up to five basic elements, listed below, but always includes the last two:

www • bedford stmartins.com/ smhandbook

For additional examples of MLA style for electronic sources, click on

▶ Documenting Sources
  ▶ MLA Style

- *Author.* List the author's last name first, followed by a comma and the first name. End with a period. If no author is given, begin with the title.
- *Title.* Enclose the title and subtitle of the work in quotation marks unless you are citing an entire site or an online book, which should be underlined or (if your instructor permits) italicized; capitalize all major words. End with a period inside the closing quotation marks. (For more on capitalizing titles, see 54c.)
- *Print publication information.* Give information about any previous or simultaneous publication in print, using the guidelines on pp. 423–31.

- *Electronic publication information.* List the following items, with a period after each one: the site's title, underlined or italicized, with all major words capitalized; the editor(s) of the site, preceded by *Ed.;* the version number of the site, preceded by *Vers.;* the date of electronic publication or of the latest update, with the month, if any, abbreviated except for *May, June,* and *July;* and the name of any sponsor institution or organization. (The sponsor's name usually appears at the bottom of the site's homepage.)

- *Access information.* Give the most recent date you accessed the work and its URL, enclosed in angle brackets, followed by a period. In general, give the complete URL, including the opening *http, ftp, gopher, telnet,* or *news.* If the URL is very long and complicated, however, give the URL of the site's search page, if there is one, instead. If the site does not provide a usable URL for individual works and citing the search page is inappropriate, give the URL of the site's homepage; if a user can reach the work from the homepage by clicking on a sequence of links, after the URL give the word *Path* followed by a colon and the sequence, with semicolons between the links and a period at the end. If the URL will not fit on one line, break it only after a slash, and do not add a hyphen at the break.

34. WORK FROM A WEB SITE

```
"France." Encyclopaedia Britannica Online. 2003.
     Encyclopaedia Britannica. 13 Mar. 2003
     <http://search.eb.com>.
"Important Dates in the Women's Rights Movement."
     History Channel.com. 2003. History Channel. 13 Mar.
     2003 <http://historychannel.com>. Path: Women's
     History; Special Feature--Women's Suffrage; The
     History of Women's Suffrage in America; Timeline.
Scott, Walter. "Remarks on Frankenstein, or the Modern
     Prometheus: A Novel." Romantic Circles. Ed. Neil
     Fraistat, Steven Jones, Donald Reiman, and Carl
     Stahmer. 1996. 15 Apr. 1998 <http://www.udel.edu/
     swilson/mws/bemrev.html>.
```

35. ENTIRE WEB SITE Follow the guidelines for a specific document, but begin with the title of the site and the name of the editor(s), if any.

```
The Orlando Project: An Integrated History of Women's
     Writing in the British Isles. 1997. U of Alberta.
     9 Oct. 1997 <http://www.ualberta.ca/ORLANDO/>.
Weather.com. 2003. Weather Channel Interactive. 13 Mar.
     2003 <http://www.weather.com>.
```

36. COURSE, DEPARTMENT, OR PERSONAL SITE For the Web site of an academic course, give the name of the instructor, the title of the course, a description such as *Course home page,* the dates of the course, the name of the department, the name of the institution, and the access information. For the site of an academic department, give the name of the department, such as *English;* a description such as *Dept. home page;* the name of the institution; and the access information. Put a period after each item, and do not underline or italicize any items or enclose them in quotation marks.

> Lunsford, Andrea A. Memory and Media. Course home page.
>   Sept.-Dec. 2002. Dept. of English, Stanford U. 13
>   Mar. 2003 <http://www.stanford.edu/class/
>   english12sc>.

For a personal site, include the name of the person who created it; the title, underlined or italicized, or (if there is no title) a description such as *Home page;* the date of the last update, if given; and the access information.

> Lunsford, Andrea A. Home page. 15 Mar. 2003. 17 Mar.
>   2003 <http://www.stanford.edu/~lunsfor1/>.

37. ONLINE BOOK Begin with the name of the author or, if only an editor, a compiler, or a translator is identified, the name of that person followed by a comma and *ed., comp.,* or *trans.* Then give the title, underlined or italicized, and the name of any editor, compiler, or translator not listed earlier, preceded by *Ed., Comp.,* or *Trans.* Include any publication information (city, publisher, and year) for the print version that is given, and end with the date of access and the URL, in angle brackets.

> Riis, Jacob A. How the Other Half Lives: Studies among
>   the Tenements of New York. Ed. David Phillips. New
>   York: Scribner's, 1890. 26 Mar. 1998 <http://
>   www.cis.yale.edu/amstud/inforev/riis/title.html>.

If a book is part of a scholarly project or similar site, after the information about the print version give the information about the project (title, editor, version number, date, and sponsor). If you are citing a poem, essay, or other short work within a book, include its title, in quotation marks, after the author's name. Give the URL of the short work, not of the book, if they differ.

> Dickinson, Emily. "The Grass." Poems: Emily Dickinson.
>   Boston, 1891. Humanities Text Initiative American

For advice on
citing print
government doc-
uments, see
p. 427.

<u>Verse Collection</u>. Ed. Nancy Kushigian. 1995. U of
    Michigan. 9 Oct. 1997 <http://www.planet.net/
    pkrisxle/emily/poemsOnline.html>.

38. ONLINE GOVERNMENT DOCUMENT Cite an online government document as you would a printed government work, adding the electronic publication information, the date of access, and the URL, in angle brackets.

United States. Environmental Protection Agency. Office of
    Emergency and Remedial Response. <u>This Is Superfund</u>.
    Jan. 2000. 16 Aug. 2002 <http://www.epa.gov/
    superfund/whatissf/sfguide.htm>.

39. ARTICLE IN AN ONLINE PERIODICAL To cite an article in an online scholarly journal, magazine, or newspaper, follow the guidelines given on pp. 429–431 for citing articles in print periodicals, but adapt them as necessary to the online medium. Include the author's name; the title, in quotation marks; the name of the periodical, underlined or italicized; the volume, issue, or other identifying number, if any; the date of publication; the range or the total number of pages, paragraphs, parts, or other sections, if they are numbered; the date of access; and the URL, in angle brackets.

For an example
of how to cite an
online periodical
article with num-
bered sections,
see p. 462.

Browning, Tonya. "Embedded Visuals: Student Design in
    Web Spaces." <u>Kairos: A Journal for Teachers of
    Writing</u> 2.1 (1997). 9 Oct. 1997 <http://
    english.ttu.edu/kairos/current/toc.html>.

Gawande, Atul. "Drowsy Docs." <u>Slate</u>. 9 Oct. 1997. 10
    Oct. 1997 <http://www.slate.com/MedicalExaminer/
    97-10-09/MedicalExaminer.asp>.

40. WORK FROM AN ONLINE SUBSCRIPTION SERVICE To cite a work from an online subscription service such as America Online or Lexis-Nexis, follow the guidelines on pp. 432–434 for the appropriate type of work, such as an online book or an article in an online periodical. If possible, end the entry with the URL of the specific work or, if it is very long and complicated, the URL of the service's search page. If, however, the service supplies no URL or one that is not accessible to other subscribers or after the current session, you will need to provide other access information.

If you used a personal subscription service to access a source, include the name of the service before the date of access. After the date, depending on the service's retrieval system, give either the word *Keyword* followed by a colon and the keyword you used or the word *Path* followed by a colon and the sequence of links you followed, with semicolons between links.

```
Weeks, W. William. "Beyond the Ark." Nature Conservancy
     Mar.-Apr. 1999. America Online. 2 Apr. 1999.
     Keyword: Ecology.
```

If you accessed the service through a library's subscription, after the information about the work give the name of the database, underlined or italicized, if you know it; the name of the service; the library; the date of access; and the URL of the service's homepage, in angle brackets.

```
Gordon, Andrew. "It's Not Such a Wonderful Life: The
     Neurotic George Bailey." American Journal of
     Psychoanalysis 54.3 (1994): 219-33. PsycINFO.
     EBSCO. City U of New York, Graduate Center Lib.
     26 Oct. 2003 <http://www.epnet.com>.
```

41. POSTING TO A DISCUSSION GROUP In citing an online posting, begin with the author's name; the title of the document, in quotation marks; the description *Online posting,* not underlined or italicized or in quotation marks; and the date of posting. For a listserv posting, then give the name of the listserv; the date of access; and the URL of the listserv or the email address of its moderator or supervisor. Always cite an archival version of the posting if possible.

```
Chagall, Nancy. "Web Publishing and Censorship."
     Online posting. 2 Feb. 1997. ACW: The Alliance for
     Computers and Writing Discussion List. 10 Oct. 1997
     <http://english.ttu.edu/acw-1/archive.htm>.
```

For a posting to a newsgroup, end with the date of access and the name of the newsgroup, in angle brackets, with the prefix *news*.

```
Martin, Jerry. "The IRA and Sinn Fein." Online posting.
     31 Mar. 1998. 1 Apr. 1998 <news:soc.culture.irish>.
```

42. EMAIL Include the writer's name; the subject line of the message, in quotation marks; a description of the message that mentions the recipient; and the date of the message.

```
Lunsford, Andrea A. "New Texts." Email to Kristin Bowen.
     25 July 2002.
```

43. SYNCHRONOUS COMMUNICATION In citing a posting in a forum such as a MOO, MUD, or IRC, include the name(s) of any specific speaker(s) you are citing; a description of the event; its date; the name of the forum; the date of access; and the URL. Always cite an archival version of the posting if possible.

```
Patuto, Jeremy, Simon Fennel, and James Goss. The
     Mytilene Debate. 9 May 1996. MiamiMOO. 28 Mar. 1998
     <http://moo.cas.muohio.edu/cgi-bin/moo?look+4085>.
```

44. OTHER ELECTRONIC SOURCES In citing other kinds of electronic sources, follow the guidelines given on pp. 437–440, but adapt them as necessary to the electronic medium. Here are examples of citations for a photograph of a work of art, an interview, and a film, accessed online.

```
Aleni, Giulio. K'un-yu t'u-shu. ca. 1620. Vatican, Rome.
     Rome Reborn: The Vatican Library and Renaissance
     Culture. May 1993. 28 Mar. 2003
     <http://archive.ncsa.uiuc.edu/SDG/Experimental/
     vatican.exhibit/exhibit/full-images/
     i-rome_to_china/china02.gif>.
Dyson, Esther. Interview. Hotseat. 23 May 1997 <http://
     www.hotwired.com/packet/hotseat/97/20/index4a.html>.
The Godfather. Dir. Francis Ford Coppola. 28 Mar. 1998
     <http://UK.imdbj.com/Title?Godfather,+The+[1972]>.
```

45. PERIODICALLY REVISED DATABASE ON CD-ROM Include the author's name; publication information for the print version of the text (including its title and date of publication); the title of the database, underlined or italicized; the medium (*CD-ROM*); the name of the company producing it; and the electronic publication date (month and year, if possible).

```
Natchez, Gladys. "Frida Kahlo and Diego Rivera: The
     Transformation of Catastrophe to Creativity."
     Psychotherapy-Patient 4.1 (1987): 153-74. PsycLIT.
     CD-ROM. SilverPlatter. Nov. 1994.
```

46. SINGLE-ISSUE CD-ROM, DISKETTE, OR MAGNETIC TAPE Before the place of publication, include the medium and, if appropriate, the number of the electronic edition, release, or version. If you are citing only a part of the source, end with the page, paragraph, screen, or other section numbers of the part if they are indicated in the source — either the range of numbers (*pp. 78–83*) or, if each section is numbered separately, the total number of sections in the part (*8 screens*).

```
"Communion." The Oxford English Dictionary. 2nd ed.
     CD-ROM. Oxford: Oxford UP, 1992.
```

47. **MULTIDISC CD-ROM** Include either the total number of discs or, if you use material from only one, the number of that disc.

> The 1998 Grolier Multimedia Encyclopedia. CD-ROM. 2
>   discs. Danbury: Grolier Interactive, 1997.
> The 1998 Grolier Multimedia Encyclopedia. CD-ROM. Disc
>   2. Danbury: Grolier Interactive, 1997.

48. **WORK IN AN INDETERMINATE MEDIUM** If you are not sure whether material accessed through a local electronic network is stored on the central computer's hard drive or on a CD-ROM, use the label *Electronic.* Include any publication information that is available, the name of the network or of its sponsoring organization, and the date of access.

> "Communion." The Oxford English Dictionary. 2nd ed.
>   Oxford: Oxford UP, 1992. Electronic. OhioLink,
>   Ohio State U Lib. 15 Apr. 1998.

49. **SOFTWARE OR COMPUTER PROGRAM** To cite downloaded software, replace the publication information with the date of access and the URL, in angle brackets.

> McAfee Office 2000. Vers. 2.0. Santa Clara: Network
>   Associates, 1999.

4 Other kinds of sources

50. **UNPUBLISHED DISSERTATION OR THESIS** Enclose the title in quotation marks. Add the label *Diss.* or *MA thesis, MS thesis,* and so on; the name of the school; a comma; and the year the work was accepted.

> LeCourt, Donna. "The Self in Motion: The Status of the
>   (Student) Subject in Composition Studies." Diss.
>   Ohio State U, 1993.

51. **PUBLISHED DISSERTATION** Cite a published dissertation as a book, adding the identification *Diss.* and the name of the university. If the dissertation was published by University Microfilms International, add *Ann Arbor: UMI,* and the year, and list the UMI number at the end of the entry.

> Botts, Roderic C. Influences in the Teaching of English,
>   1917-1935: An Illusion of Progress. Diss.
>   Northeastern U, 1970. Ann Arbor: UMI, 1971. 71-1799.

52. **ARTICLE FROM A MICROFORM** Treat the article as a printed work, but add the name of the microform and information for locating it.

Sharpe, Lora. "A Quilter's Tribute." <u>Boston Globe</u> 25
     Mar. 1989. <u>Newsbank: Social Relations</u> 12 (1989):
     fiche 6, grids B4-6.

53. INTERVIEW List the person interviewed and then the title of the interview, if any, in quotation marks (or underlined or italicized if the interview
is a complete work). If the interview has no title, use the label *Interview*
(not underlined, italicized, or in quotation marks), and identify the
source. If you were the interviewer, use the label *Telephone interview, Personal
interview,* or *Email interview.* End with the date(s) the interview took place.

Beja, Morris. Personal interview. 2 Oct. 2002.

Schorr, Daniel. Interview. <u>Weekend Edition</u>. Natl. Public
     Radio. WEVO, Concord. 26 Mar. 1988.

54. LETTER If the letter was published, cite it as a selection in a book,
noting the date and any identifying number after the title.

Frost, Robert. "Letter to Editor of the <u>Independent</u>." 28
     Mar. 1894. <u>Selected Letters of Robert Frost</u>. Ed.
     Lawrance Thompson. New York: Holt, 1964. 19.

If the letter was sent to you, follow this form:

Anzaldúa, Gloria. Letter to the author. 10 Sept. 2002.

55. FILM, VIDEO, OR DVD In general, start with the title, underlined or
italicized; then name the director; the company distributing the film,
videocassette, or DVD; and the date of its release. Other contributors,
such as writers or actors, may follow the director. If you cite a particular
person's work, start the entry with that person's name. For a videocassette or DVD, include the original film release date (if relevant) and
the label *Videocassette* or *DVD.*

<u>Face/Off</u>. Dir. John Woo. Perf. John Travolta and
     Nicolas Cage. Paramount, 1997.

<u>The Star</u>. Dir. Lawrence Pitkethly. Videocassette.
     CBS/Fox Video, 1995.

Weaver, Sigourney, perf. <u>Aliens</u>. Dir. James Cameron.
     20th Century Fox, 1986.

56. TELEVISION OR RADIO PROGRAM In general, begin with the title of the
program, underlined or italicized. Then list the narrator, director,
actors, or other contributors, as necessary; the network; the local station

and city, if any; and the broadcast date. If you cite a particular person's work, begin the entry with that person's name. If you cite a particular episode, include any title, in quotation marks, before the program's title. If the program is part of a series, include the series title (not underlined, italicized, or in quotation marks) before the network.

Box Office Bombshell: Marilyn Monroe. Writ. Andy Thomas,
      Jeff Schefel, and Kevin Burns. Dir. Bill Harris.
      Narr. Peter Graves. A&E Biography. Arts and
      Entertainment Network. 23 Oct. 2002.
Gellar, Sarah Michelle, perf. "Once More, with Feeling."
      Buffy the Vampire Slayer. Dir. Joss Whedon. WB.
      WWOR, New York. 6 Nov. 2001.

57. SOUND RECORDING Begin with the name of the composer, performer, or conductor, depending on whose work you are citing. Next give the title of the recording, which is underlined or italicized, or the title of the composition, which is not. End with the manufacturer, a comma, and the year of issue. If you are not citing a compact disc, give the medium before the manufacturer. If you are citing a particular song, include its title, in quotation marks, before the title of the recording.

Grieg, Edvard. Concerto in A minor, op. 16. Cond. Eugene
      Ormandy. Philadelphia Orch. LP. RCA, 1989.
Kilcher, Jewel. "Amen." Pieces of You. A&R, 1994.

58. WORK OF ART OR PHOTOGRAPH List the artist or photographer (if available); the work's title, underlined or italicized; the name of the museum or other location; and the city. If you want to include the date the work was created, add it after the title.

Kahlo, Frida. Self-Portrait with Cropped Hair. 1940.
      Museum of Mod. Art, New York.

To cite a photograph or reproduction of a work—a work you have not seen in person—add the publication information for the source where the photograph appears.

●— For an example
of how to cite
a personal
photograph,
see p. 111.

Peale, Charles Wilson. The Artist in His Museum. 1822.
      Philadelphia Acad. of the Fine Arts. Adcult USA:
      The Triumph of Advertising in American Culture. By
      James B. Twitchell. New York: Columbia UP, 1996.
      214.

59. **LECTURE OR SPEECH** List the speaker, the title in quotation marks, the name of the sponsoring institution or group, the place, and the date. If the speech is untitled, use a label such as *Lecture* or *Keynote speech*.

Lu, Min-Zhan. "The Politics of Listening." Conf. on
      Coll. Composition and Communication. Palmer House,
      Chicago. 3 Apr. 1998.

60. **PERFORMANCE** List the title, underlined or italicized, other appropriate details (such as composer, writer, director), the place, and the date. If you cite a person's work, begin the entry with that person's name.

Frankie and Johnny in the Clair de Lune. By Terrence
      McNally. Dir. Paul Benedict. Westside Arts Theater,
      New York. 18 Jan. 1988.

61. **MAP OR CHART** Cite a map or chart as you would a book with an unknown author, adding the label *Map* or *Chart*.

Pennsylvania. Map. Chicago: Rand, 1985.

62. **CARTOON OR COMIC STRIP** List the artist's name; the title of the cartoon or comic strip (if it has one), in quotation marks; the label *Cartoon* or *Comic strip;* and the usual publication information.

Trudeau, Garry. "Doonesbury." Comic strip. Philadelphia
      Inquirer 9 Mar. 1988: 37.

63. **ADVERTISEMENT** Name the item or organization being advertised, add the label *Advertisement,* and then supply the standard information about the source in which the ad appears.

Dannon Yogurt. Advertisement. TV Guide 4 Dec. 1999: A14.

www • bedford
stmartins.com/
smhandbook

For additional
sample MLA
research essays,
click on

▶ Student Samples
  ▶ Essays

20d A student research essay, MLA style

Shannan Palma's final essay appears on the following pages. In preparing this essay, she followed the MLA guidelines described in this chapter. She was required to prepare a title page. Had she not needed one, she would have followed MLA instructions for a heading at the top of the first page of her essay (see 8e for an example). Note that this essay has been reproduced in a narrow format to allow for annotation.

STUDENT WRITER

Shannan Palma

For the first page of
an essay that does
not use a title page,
see 8e

Hollywood and the Hero:
Solving a Case of Mistaken Identity

Title centered one-
third of way down
page

by Shannan Palma

Writer's name cen-
tered three or four
lines below title

English 167
Professor Lunsford
18 November 2002

Course number,
professor's name,
and date centered
three or four lines
below writer's name

Outline

Thesis statement: Recent films strongly suggest
that the hero of the twenty-first century will most
likely appear not as a Hollywood star or a mythical
manifestation but as a combination of mortal and
machine--in short, a cyborg.

I.   Originally relying on earlier heroes from the
     realms of myth and history, Hollywood studios
     gradually developed a system for transforming
     actors into star-heroes.

     A. Moviegoers began to identify a favorite
        hero-character with the particular actor
        who played him or her.

     B. The studios recognized the financial
        possibilities of the mass idolization of a
        commercialized hero and set out to
        manufacture this "product" efficiently.

        1. The persona that a studio developed to
           turn an actor into a star was the only
           public identity that actor was allowed
           to have.

        2. Early examples of the star-hero included
           Douglas Fairbanks and Mary Pickford.

II. As the studio system disintegrated in the
     1950s and 1960s, and the stars lost the
     publicity shield it had provided, the problems
     of stardom became obvious to the public.

     A. Films from this period show that the movie
        industry was self-mockingly aware of its
        pitfalls.

Student's last name and page number in upper right-hand corner; roman numerals used for outline page numbers

Heading centered

Thesis stated

First major point in support of thesis

Subpoint

Subpoint followed by two supporting details

Second major point in support of thesis

Subpoint followed by two supporting details

    1. <u>Sunset Boulevard</u> showed what happened
       when a hero-image was no longer popular
       and the system abandoned the star it had
       made.

    2. <u>A Star Is Born</u> showed how the system
       created a perfect image and forced a
       human being to become it.

B. Widely publicized scandals like that
   surrounding the death of Marilyn Monroe
   further increased the public's knowledge of
   star-hero failings.   •·········· Subpoint

C. Although scandals seemed only to increase
   public adoration of stars by giving their   •·········· Subpoint
   images an air of tragic martyrdom, public
   perception of star-heroes as <u>ideals</u> began
   to fade.

III. More recent decades have seen the confusion of •·········· Third major point in
   identity between film characters and stars   support of thesis
   take a new form, which has further contributed
   to the decline of the hero.

A. The last vestiges of the studio system's
   image-projection and -protection have   •·········· Subpoint
   vanished, leaving the public with few
   illusions about the lives of star-heroes.

B. Rather than admire stars for their heroic
   achievements and personal qualities, the   •·········· Subpoint
   public envies them for their lifestyle.

C. Profound cynicism toward the hero as ideal
   is reflected in films such as <u>The Ref</u>,   •·········· Subpoint
   which encourage audiences to identify

heroes with the stars that portray them
rather than vice versa.

D. The disappearance of the hero-ideal in film
has led to a lack of lasting empathy with
the hero among movie audiences.

> Subpoint followed by two supporting details

1. After audiences see a movie, they no
longer associate the character with the
film, but rather the actor with the film.

2. To re-create that lasting empathy in a
modern context, we need heroes who can
overcome the problem of mistaken
identity and who are believable and
relevant to today's world.

> Final major point in support of thesis

IV. The 1997 film Face/Off can serve as one
prototype for overcoming these obstacles.

> Subpoint

A. The film turns mistaken identity against
itself, with the two lead actors switching
roles in such a way that the audience has
its preconceptions of the relationships
between star and character challenged and
develops a lasting empathy with the hero.

> Subpoint

B. With its portrayal of a hero who resorts to
advanced technology to take on the face of
his enemy, the film also provides a
prototype for the cyborg hero, a form that
the twenty-first-century hero may take.

Palma 1

Hollywood and the Hero:
Solving a Case of Mistaken Identity

In the song "Amen" from the best-selling album Pieces of You, Jewel Kilcher poses questions about heroes that are worth asking.

> Where are my angels?
>
> Where's my golden one?
>
> Where's my hope
>
> Now that my heroes
>
> have gone?

These questions are important because the hero, what Merriam-Webster's Collegiate Dictionary defines as "a man admired for his achievements and noble qualities" ("Hero," def. 1c), seems to have vanished from American popular culture. From Hercules to Robin Hood, from Joan of Arc to Scarlett O'Hara, male and female heroes alike have reflected the ideals and the most admired traits of their respective times: brute strength or sharply honed cunning, devotion to duty or desire for rebellion. Throughout history, and specifically U.S. history, the hero-ideal has endured in the arts--until now. The twentieth century, which started off with the promising evolution of the hero from figure of legend and literature to star of the silver screen, seems to have ended with the near death of the hero as ideal in popular culture.

The eclipse of the hero in film results from a case of what may be called "mistaken identity," which has caused film heroes' fates to become

Writer's last name and page number in upper right-hand corner

Title centered; announces topic, engages reader interest

Quotation appeals to student readers and poses question that essay will try to answer

First paragraph of introduction provides background

Dictionary definition cited; title of dictionary entry and number of definition given

Second paragraph introduces major theme of "mistaken identity" and explains what writer will do in essay

inextricably intertwined with the fates of the actors who portray them. This research essay will explore whether today's films truly signal the end of the hero-ideal and preview a hero-less future, or whether they instead help the hero evolve to a different, perhaps more realistic, level. If the latter is true, the question then becomes one of what form the new hero will take onscreen. This essay will argue that recent films strongly suggest that the hero of the twenty-first century will most likely appear not as a Hollywood star or a mythical manifestation but as a combination of mortal and machine--in short, a cyborg.[1]

Before either of these questions can be addressed, however, a brief history of Hollywood's relationship with the hero is necessary. Our heroes once came primarily from the fantasy of myth and the remove of history and literature. King Arthur, the Three Musketeers, Jo March of Little Women, Annie Oakley--all have spent time on the hero's pedestal. With the development of motion pictures in the early twentieth century, many of these heroes made the transition from legend to life, or at least to life on the screen. Soon moviegoers were able not only to read about and imagine their heroes in action but also to see them in the most glamorous incarnations Hollywood could create. Fans began to identify a favorite hero-character with the particular actor who played him or her, and this burgeoning case of mistaken identity did not

Explicit thesis stated

Superscript refers readers to bibliographic note

Transition to first main point: Hollywood studios transformed the hero

First subpoint: fans confused characters with actors ("mistaken identity")

go unnoticed for long. Film historian Morris Beja notes that although the studios, then the most powerful force in Hollywood, had originally hoped to give actors as little influence as possible over the studios' operations, it quickly became obvious that "movie stars sold tickets." Recognizing the enormous financial possibilities inherent in the mass idolization of a commercialized hero, the industry set out to manufacture this "product" as efficiently as possible. As a 1995 video on the star system in Hollywood explains:

> In the old days of the studio system there was a structure for developing stars. Players were owned body and soul, signed to long-term contracts. With the powerful publicity machine run by the studio they could reach an audience of millions. But that alone did not guarantee success. The problem for the studio was to find the one persona out of many possible character roles that would boost a character to stardom. (The Star)

Studios found that manufacturing movie stars was not easy. It required an actor with just the right combination of style, charisma, and talent, and it required just the right roles and public persona to make that actor a star. When it succeeded, however, the mistaken identity was complete. The star became an icon--an ideal--a hero. Many fictional hero types (such as the

Quotation from interview

Second subpoint: heroes became "products"

Block quotation introduced by phrase with signal verb

Videocassette title cited in parentheses; for set-off quotation, parenthetical reference follows final punctuation

romantic hero and the western hero) carried over
from the prefilm era; but new kinds of heroes also
emerged, identified even more closely by the public
with the stars who originated them. Early examples
of the star-hero included silent film stars Douglas
Fairbanks and Mary Pickford. "The swashbuckler was
born with . . . Fairbanks," according to Beja,
who also sees Pickford as the prototype of the
brave or "plucky" movie heroine. As Richard
deCordova notes in a memorable phrase, the studios
wanted to convince millions of moviegoers that "the
real hero behave[d] just like the reel hero" (qtd.
in Gallagher, pt. 2). Therefore, the persona that a
studio developed to turn a working actor into a
star was the only public identity that actor would
be allowed to have. Film historians like Beja and
deCordova, who explores this topic in his book
Picture Personalities: The Emergence of the Star
System in America, say that the public's conceptual
link between the hero and the star is the reason
studios tried so hard to encourage the idea that
stars like Fairbanks and Pickford had no private
personalities separate from those of their onscreen
characters. (See Fig. 1.)

As silent films gave way to "talkies" and
Hollywood cinema emerged as a cultural force in and
of itself, new names replaced those of Fairbanks
and Pickford on theater marquees. The star system,
however, only grew more deeply entrenched. As long
as the star-hero stayed separate from the public,

Examples of star-hero

Sentence combining quotation and paraphrase from interview, with ellipses indicating words omitted from quotation

Square brackets enclose material altered so tense of quotation fits into writer's sentence

Indirect online source without page numbers cited using *qtd. in* and part number

No page numbers needed for citation of interview or entire book

Parenthetical reference directs readers to figure

Transition to second main point: public exposure of star-hero failings in the 1950s and 1960s

Fig. 1. Baron De Meyer, <u>Mary Pickford, circa 1915</u>, MPTV Images, Los Angeles. Hollywood studios tried to stage-manage the image of stars like Mary Pickford to create public illusions of heroic, almost mythological beings.

Caption relates figure to text

buffered by studios in order to keep the image intact, his or her fictional self remained safe. But the strain of living up to a legend instead of living a life took a toll on the private, "real" selves. Brian Gallagher cites a remark by Cary Grant that sums up the strain many stars must have felt: "Everybody wants to be Cary Grant. Even I want to be Cary Grant" (pt. 3). As the studio system disintegrated in the 1950s and the 1960s and the stars lost the publicity shield it had provided, this toll became glaringly obvious to their adoring public.

Part number cited for online source without page numbers

Films from this period show that the movie industry was self-mockingly aware of its pitfalls.

Subpoint: movie industry's self-awareness, with two examples

Sunset Boulevard, released in 1950, showed what happened when a hero-image was no longer profitable and the system abandoned the star it had made. Gloria Swanson played the fictional silent film star Norma Desmond, once young and adored, now aging and forgotten, who tries in vain to recapture her lost glory and ends her quest in tragedy. A Star Is Born, remade in 1954 with Judy Garland in the lead role, chronicled the rise of a young woman from nobody to star, showing the reality of how the system created a perfect image and forced a human being to become it (Corey and Ochoa 353, 347). Yet even though these films showed the artificiality and destructiveness of the star system, at the same time they helped to perpetuate it. After all, the fictional star was played by a real-life one--and thus fiction and truth became even further intertwined.

Approximately a decade later, in 1962, Marilyn Monroe died of what was officially ruled an accidental overdose of sleeping pills. And in the words of a television biography, "almost instantly, the lurid circumstances of [her] death made national headlines around the world . . . . Marilyn Monroe was dead. Marilyn the Myth was born" (Box Office Bombshell). The supposedly idyllic life stars lived was being steadily exposed as false through both fictional tragedies and actual scandals, yet paradoxically the public did not turn against the stars but only focused their fascination in a slightly different way. Singer

---

Marginal annotations:

Citation with two page references covers two preceding sentences; comma separates pages

Ironic consequence of star-system exposés pointed out

Subpoint: scandals surrounding stars, with an example

Ellipses indicate words omitted from quotation

and songwriter Elton John immortalized the unique
cult of fame that overshadowed Monroe's death in
his 1973 song "Candle in the Wind," when he wrote
of his own youthful feelings toward her: "Your
candle burned out long before / Your legend ever
did."[2] Rather than serving to separate the hero
from the star, in fact, scandals only bound the two
more closely together, lending a tragic, martyred
cast to the star's image. The public's adoration of
their stars did not diminish. Their perception of
their heroes as <u>ideals</u>, however, began to fade.

> Fast forward from the fifties and sixties to
the present: forty to fifty years later. A brief
excerpt from the celebrity gossip-fest <u>Hollywood
Confidential</u> shows that the last vestiges of the
studio system's image-projection and -protection
have vanished:

> > Well into the throes of drug
> > addiction by the time she was thirteen,
> > Drew Barrymore attempted suicide by
> > cutting her wrists with a kitchen knife.
> > Rosemary Clooney was addicted to
> > prescription drugs and, after two
> > embattled marriages to José Ferrer, was
> > admitted to a psych ward.
> > Francis Ford Coppola takes lithium.
> > Patty (<u>Call Me Anna</u>) Duke is a
> > manic-depressive. (Amende 247)

No longer do stars try to hide their personal lives
from the public, and every scandal, every lie is

Annotations (margin notes):

- Superscript refers readers to explanatory note
- Subpoint: ironic consequence of scandals pointed out; hero-ideal fades
- Transition to next main point
- Imperative sentence with film jargon used to introduce third main point: a new form of mistaken identity and the continued decline of the hero
- Subpoint: disappearance of star's image-protection
- Quotation from popular magazine cites author in parentheses rather than in signal phrase

exposed in the short run. Thus today's public holds very few illusions about the lives of their star-heroes. Although stars are still "living heroes," the relationship between the two terms has changed: rather than admiring stars for their heroic achievements and personal qualities, the public simply envies them for their lifestyle--their immense power, wealth, and fame. Even after the real-life heroism of September 11, a profound cynicism persists toward the hero as ideal, and this cynicism is reflected in the portrayal of the fictional hero in current American films. It is a portrayal that perpetuates the problem of mistaken identity noted earlier, but in reverse, with heroes being identified with the stars that portray them, rather than vice versa.

The 1994 film The Ref offers a fairly recent example of this reversal and of the cynicism it both grows out of and feeds into. As a review on the ABC News Web site Mr. Showbiz notes:

> Judy Davis and Kevin Spacey are a married couple who for the life of them can't stop bickering. Denis Leary is the burglar who's taken them hostage on Christmas Eve. Writers Marie Weiss and Richard LaGravanese have built a . . . platform . . . from which Leary can freely launch himself into the mad stand-up monologues of outrage and spleen that are his trademark [emphasis mine]. (Feeney)

Subpoint: stars are now envied rather than admired

Subpoint: current films reflect cynicism about hero-ideal and perpetuate a new form of mistaken identity

Extended example illustrates cynicism and reversal of mistaken identity

Neutral signal verb introduces description of film

Ellipses indicate omissions in quotation

Bracketed comment indicates underlining added by writer for emphasis

Author's name cited alone for one-page, one-paragraph source

A closer look at this film tells us more. It is Christmas Eve, a traditional time of sharing and harmony among loved ones, yet the married couple in the film and the relatives who descend upon them for the holidays are all so bitter, sarcastic, and self-absorbed that even a hardened criminal is appalled by them. As the values associated with Christmas are turned on their ear and exposed as empty vanity in today's society, the criminal becomes a cynical sort of antihero: unlike his hostages, he at least remembers what a family is supposed to act like. The film's message was emphasized by the casting of comedian Leary in the title role, casting that capitalized on his reputation as a one-man mouthpiece for the Middle-American cynicism or anti-ideals of the nineties. The fictional commentary of Leary's character was made more believable to the audience because the majority of them were familiar with its similarities to the actual commentary made famous by Leary himself. Rather than the hero creating the star, the star now forms the hero.

The disappearance of the hero-ideal as a separate entity from, or as a model for, the star has led to a second and perhaps more complex problem: with most modern films, there is a peculiar absence of lasting empathy of the audience with the hero. Apart from the rare phenomenon such as Luke Skywalker in Star Wars (1977), not only do modern movie heroes not exist apart from actors in

> Concept of antihero introduced

> Transition to next subpoint: absence of lasting audience empathy with most modern film heroes

audiences' minds, but they do not stay there for
long. Think of Sigourney Weaver as Ripley, savior
of humanity from Aliens (1986), Mel Gibson as a
Revolutionary War soldier in The Patriot (2000), or
Will Smith as an alien-hunting secret agent in Men
in Black II (2002). In fact, this wording reveals
just how most moviegoers do think of those heroes--
the roles are indistinguishable from the stars--and
after audiences see a movie, they no longer
associate the character and the film, but rather
the actor and the film. The difference between the
short shelf life of modern heroes and the staying
power of their old-style predecessors is evident if
we look at film remakes of novels like Little Women
and The Three Musketeers, in which the characters
do supersede the actors in importance. But such
films only cater to audience nostalgia for the time
when those heroes gave cause for belief and hope,
when the culture on which they were based held some
ideals. These classic heroes may endure in memory,
but they will never again have the mythic power
that they did once upon a time. To re-create that
lasting empathy in a modern context, we need films
that can overcome mistaken identity and that
contain heroes who are believable and relevant to
today's world. Fortunately, in 1997 such a film,
and such a hero, came to the screen.

Think of the current film hero as, to borrow a
term from The Princess Bride (1987), "mostly dead."
Not having died, the hero needs not rebirth but

Three examples cited

New films contrasted to remakes of novels

Transition to last main point: remakes cater to nostalgia for old heroes, but we need new ones

revival or regeneration. To begin regenerating the hero, then, it is necessary to overcome (1) the audience's preconceptions about the stars' relationships to the characters they play, and (2) the failure of recent hero-characters to invoke a lasting empathy in the public. The 1997 film Face/Off can serve as one prototype for overcoming both of these obstacles and thus for resolving once and for all the problem of mistaken identity.

First, the plot and characterization of this film provide an opportunity to prove that it is possible for a character to exist and be identified apart from the star who plays him or her. During the course of the story, the two main characters, hero Sean Archer and villain Castor Troy, undergo surgery that exchanges their faces. The two stars of the film start off playing particular characters, John Travolta as Archer and Nicolas Cage as Troy; but approximately twenty minutes into the film they switch roles. (See Fig. 2.) In an interview for a magazine article, Travolta described his take on imitating his costar:

> [Cage's walk is] a saunter almost. It's very specific to Nick's natural gait. And I said if you don't mind, maybe we could use that Nick Cage cadence for the bad guy's voice, too, and I could just adapt that. You know, the way Nick slows down and enunciates and pronunciates. He's almost poetic in his talking. (qtd. in Daly 24)

Fig. 2. Stephen Vaughan, <u>Nicolas Cage and John Travolta in</u> Face/Off, 1997, Photofest, New York. The actors switched roles partway through <u>Face/Off</u>, a technique that helped audiences see their characters as figures independent of the actors portraying them.

Director John Woo and others involved in the making of <u>Face/Off</u> seem to have used audience preconceptions about actor-idiosyncrasies being identical to character-idiosyncrasies, purposely emphasized in the beginning of the film, to make the switch-off of actors and roles that much more shocking and real to the audience. They turned mistaken identity against itself. Moviegoers who had seen Cage and Travolta act before, who associated their faces with their body language, found that when the body language remained the same, even with a new face, it was convincing. This disassociation of actor from character negates the second obstacle to regeneration of the hero as well. Without mistaken identity to cloud the issue, Archer was able to create a lasting empathy with the audience. Even after the audience left the darkness of the theater, his character could not be viewed on anything but its own terms.

In 2000, John Woo touched on the theme of mistaken identity again in Mission: Impossible II. Rogue agent Sean Ambrose steals the identity of Ethan Hunt (Tom Cruise) at several points in the film, using technology and elaborate disguises. In these few scenes, Tom Cruise shrugs off some of the actor-idiosyncrasies he plays up throughout the rest of the film.

With the complex problem of mistaken identity overcome, what remains is to create a believable hero who is relevant to today's world. In this context, the major challenge is that the model for the old hero, in Western culture at least, is based on the view that a human being is essentially a unified organic whole and can be labeled in some way: as epic hero, romantic hero, tragic hero, swashbuckling hero, western hero, detective hero, and so on. In the contemporary world, we can no longer believe in such a one-dimensional being. In one of the essays in her anthology Simians, Cyborgs, and Women, historian of science Donna J. Haraway claims that our dreams of organic unity and coherence are futile. In their place, she recommends the cyborg figure, which can give us a

Transition to second subpoint: creating a believable contemporary hero is difficult

Paraphrase of source; signal verbs indicate disputable statements

Concept of cyborg introduced and explained

new dream of ourselves as multiple, surpassing
either body or machine (181). In fact, Haraway
argues that with our thinking computers, our
routine organ transplants and high-technology
prostheses, human beings in the late twentieth
century were already living in a world of cyborgs--
"hybrid[s] of machine and organism, [creatures] of
social reality as well as [creatures] of fiction"
(149). Much of Haraway's analysis can be applied to
the emerging film hero.

The reel hero can no longer exist as a
contained organic whole in today's fractured,
technology-driven society. The human aspect of the
hero has been damaged by mistaken identity to the
extent that moviegoers will no longer put an
extraordinary amount of faith in it. They no longer
want the lie of static perfection given by classic
heroes such as Hercules or Robin Hood and betrayed
by film stars of Monroe's, and later Barrymore's,
generations, but neither will a hero as openly
damaged as such stars suffice in and of itself.
Within their realistic heroes, people still want to
hold firm to a core of something untainted by human
frailties. At just this moment, the cyborg hero has
emerged in film.

Again, Face/Off offers a useful demonstration.
The character of Archer, a tortured FBI agent who
spends years tracking the criminal (Troy) who
gunned down his little boy, is not a hero, in the
classic sense of the word, nor is he an antihero,

in the modern sense of the word. Instead, he is a prototype for the emerging twenty-first-century hero, a figure whose humanity is not perfect but rather is damaged beyond repair (like the American culture's belief in the hero-ideal). To defeat "evil," Archer must use technology to "become" his enemy--literally wear his face and take his place in the world. As Janice Rushing and Thomas Frentz put it in their book <u>Projecting the Shadow: The Cyborg Hero in American Film</u>, "to survive, a man must be technological, and to thrive, he must be technologically adept" (147). The new heroes cannot be sustained without the props of the modern world. Technology supplements their human frailties with cyborg prosthetics that give them an inhuman capacity for human salvation. The cyborg image metaphorically compensates for the modern dissonance between the technological and the organic; it uses technology to weld together the fractured nature of contemporary human beings, creating one inhuman whole that is capable of obtaining a limited perfection precisely because of its inhuman state. Archer achieves this state and triumphs--maybe not an angel, not a "golden one," but certainly a cause for hope.

The emergence of cyborg figures in films is not limited to <u>Face/Off</u>. Over the past two decades, the different facets of the cyborg character have been explored in films as diverse as <u>Blade Runner</u> (1982) and <u>Star Trek: First Contact</u> (1996). These

Signal phrase calls attention to striking quotation and cites source title related to writer's point

Allusions to opening song quotation

Conclusion cites additional examples of cyborgs in films and raises issue of cultural ambivalence toward them

portrayals reflect a deep ambivalence, since many in our culture see the cyborg as a symbol not of hope but of dehumanization, the dead end of the modern world. In <u>Blade Runner</u>, the human hero's job is to hunt down and "cancel" android "replicants" that are "more human than human"; and in <u>First Contact</u>, humans battle to resist "assimilation into the [cy]Borg collective." Steven Spielberg's <u>A.I.</u> (2001) features a twist on the cyborg hero, depicting a robot boy who, like Pinocchio, longs to become "real." In these cases, the films offer positive images of cyborgs as well, suggesting that their future could go either way--or continue to go both ways. Jewel asked the question: "And where's my hope now that my heroes have gone?" Perhaps the 1991 film <u>Terminator 2: Judgment Day</u> provides the answer, one that speaks to the eventual triumph of the cyborg as hero. Turning to human heroes Sarah and John Connor, the cyborg Terminator says simply, "Come with me if you want to live."

Restatement of opening quotation/ question

Closing example suggests answer

Notes

¹ I want to thank those who have contributed to my thinking on this topic, including my professors and classmates, Professor Morris Beja, and two consultants from the Ohio State University Writing Center, Melissa Goldthwaite and Nels Highberg.

² The rewritten version of "Candle in the Wind" that John sang at the funeral of Diana, Princess of Wales, in 1997 is now the best-selling recorded single of all time. Although Diana was not in movies, she was constantly in public view--in newspapers and magazines and on television; she too was caught up in the cult of fame that Monroe experienced. As Diana the person died, Diana the myth was born.

Works Cited

A.I. Dir. Steven Spielberg. Warner Bros., 2001.

Amende, Coral. Hollywood Confidential: An Inside
    Look at the Public Careers and Private Lives
    of Hollywood's Rich and Famous. New York:
    Penguin, 1997.

Beja, Morris. Personal interview. 2 Oct. 2002.

Blade Runner. Dir. Ridley Scott. Warner Bros./
    Ladd, 1982.

Box Office Bombshell: Marilyn Monroe. Writ. Andy
    Thomas, Jeff Schefel, and Kevin Burns. Dir.
    Bill Harris. Nar. Peter Graves. A&E
    Biography. Arts and Entertainment Network.
    23 Oct. 2002.

Corey, Melinda, and George Ochoa. The Dictionary
    of Film Quotations: 6,000 Provocative Movie
    Quotes from 1,000 Movies. New York: Crown,
    1995.

Daly, Steve. "Face to Face." Entertainment Weekly
    20 June 1997: 20-24.

deCordova, Richard. Picture Personalities: The
    Emergence of the Star System in America.
    Urbana: U of Illinois P, 1990.

De Meyer, Baron. Mary Pickford, circa 1915. MPTV
    Images, Los Angeles. 30 Oct. 2002 <http://
    www.netropolisusa.biz/scripts/CUWP_CGI.EXE>.

Face/Off. Dir. John Woo. Perf. John Travolta and
    Nicolas Cage. Paramount, 1997.

Feeney, F. X. Rev. of The Ref, dir. Ted Demme.
    Mr. Showbiz: A World of Entertainment from
    ABCNEWS.com. 18 Oct. 2002 <http://
    www.mrshowbiz.com/reviews/moviereviews/
    movies/32363.html>.

Gallagher, Brian. "Greta Garbo Is Sad: Some
    Historical Reflections on the Paradoxes of

Stardom in the American Film Industry, 1910-
1960." Images: A Journal of Film and Popular
Culture 3 (1997): 7 pts. 7 Aug. 2002
<http://www.imagesjournal.com/issue03/
infocus.htm>.

Gibson, Mel, perf. The Patriot. Dir. Roland
Emmerich. Sony, 2000.

Haraway, Donna J. "A Cyborg Manifesto: Science,
Technology, and Socialist-Feminism in the
Late Twentieth Century." Simians, Cyborgs,
and Women. New York: Routledge, 1991. 149-
81.

"Hero." Merriam-Webster's Collegiate Dictionary.
10th ed. 1996.

John, Elton. "Candle in the Wind." Goodbye Yellow
Brick Road. MCA, 1973.

Kilcher, Jewel. "Amen." Pieces of You. A&R, 1994.

Little Women. Dir. Gillian Armstrong. Columbia
Tri-Star, 1994.

Mission: Impossible II. Dir. John Woo. Perf. Tom
Cruise. Paramount, 2000.

The Princess Bride. Dir. Rob Reiner. 20th
Century Fox, 1987.

The Ref. Dir. Ted Demme. Perf. Denis Leary, Judy
Davis, and Kevin Spacey. Touchstone, 1994.

Rushing, Janice Hocker, and Thomas S. Frentz.
Projecting the Shadow: The Cyborg Hero in
American Film. Chicago: U of Chicago P,
1995.

Smith, Will, perf. Men in Black II. Dir. Barry
Sonnenfeld. Columbia, 2002.

The Star. Dir. Lawrence Pitkethly. Videocassette.
CBS/FOX Video, 1995.

A Star Is Born. Dir. George Cukor. Perf. Judy
Garland. Warner Bros., 1954.

Essay in a collection

Entry in a well-known
A-Z reference work

Sound recordings

Book with two
authors

Videocassette

Star Trek: First Contact. Dir. Jonathan Frakes.
    Paramount, 1996.

Star Wars. Dir. George Lucas. 20th Century Fox,
    1977.

Sunset Boulevard. Dir. Billy Wilder. Perf. Gloria
    Swanson. Paramount, 1950.

Terminator 2: Judgment Day. Dir. James Cameron.
    Tri-Star, 1991.

The Three Musketeers. Dir. Stephen Herek. Disney,
    1993.

Vaughan, Stephen. Nicolas Cage and John Travolta
    in Face/Off. 1997. Photofest, New York.

Weaver, Sigourney, perf. Aliens. Dir. James
    Cameron. 20th Century Fox, 1986.

Performer in a film

Documenting Sources: APA Style

For further reference on APA style, consult the following volume:

> American Psychological Association. *Publication Manual of the American Psychological Association.* 5th ed. Washington, D.C.: APA, 2001.

21a APA format for in-text citations

APA style requires parenthetical references in the text to document quotations, paraphrases, summaries, and other material from a source (see 18b). These citations correspond to full bibliographic entries in a list of references at the end of the text.

1. AUTHOR NAMED IN A SIGNAL PHRASE Generally, use the author's name in a signal phrase to introduce the cited material, and place the date, in parentheses, immediately after the author's name. For a quotation, the page number, preceded by *p.,* appears in parentheses after the quotation. For a long, set-off quotation, position the page reference in parentheses one space after the final punctuation.

```
Key (1983) has argued that the placement of
women in print advertisements is
subliminally important.

As Briggs (1970) observed, parents play an
important role in building children's self-
esteem because "children value themselves to
the degree that they have been valued" (p. 14).
```

It's all "a matter of style," as the old adage suggests, in academic disciplines as in fashion and design. Indeed, the conventions of style vary among disciplines, according to what a discipline values and how it credits work. As a prospective member of one or more academic disciplines, you will have occasion to follow one or more styles, particularly when you need to use their guidelines for citing and documenting sources in your own writing. One of the most important documentation styles is that of the American Psychological Association (APA), which is widely used in psychology and other social sciences. ■

APA

466 **21a**

RESEARCH
Documenting
Sources: APA Style

For an example ·········•
of a research
essay using APA
style, see 65d.

DIRECTORY TO APA STYLE

(Continued on p. 467)

(Continued from p. 466)

APA

21a 467

RESEARCH

APA Format for
In-Text Citations

For electronic texts or other works without page numbers, paragraph numbers may be used instead, preceded by the ¶ symbol or the abbreviation *para.*

> Denes (1980, ¶ 1) claimed that psychotherapy is an art that is "volatile, unpredictable, standardless in its outcome, subjective in its worth."

2. AUTHOR NAMED IN A PARENTHETICAL REFERENCE When you do not name the author in your text, give the name and the date, separated by a comma, in parentheses at the end of the cited material.

> One study has found that only 68% of letters received by editors were actually published (Renfro, 1979).

3. TWO AUTHORS Use both names in all citations. Join the names with *and* in a signal phrase, but use an ampersand (&) instead in a parenthetical reference.

> Murphy and Orkow (1985) reached somewhat different conclusions by designing a study that was less dependent on subjective judgment than were previous studies.

A recent study that was less dependent on subjective
judgment resulted in conclusions somewhat different from
those of previous studies (Murphy & Orkow, 1985).

4. THREE TO FIVE AUTHORS List all the authors' names for the first reference.

Belenky, Clinchy, Goldberger, and Tarule (1986)
suggested that many women rely on observing and
listening to others as ways of learning about
themselves.

In any subsequent references, use just the first author's name plus *et al.*
("and others").

From this experience, observed Belenky et al. (1986),
women learn to listen to themselves think, a step toward
self-expression.

5. SIX OR MORE AUTHORS Use only the first author's name and *et al.* ("and
others") in every citation, including the first.

As Mueller et al. (1980) demonstrated, television holds
the potential for distorting and manipulating consumers
as free-willed decision makers.

6. CORPORATE OR GROUP AUTHOR If the name of the organization or corporation is long, spell it out the first time you use it, followed by an
abbreviation in brackets. In later references, use the abbreviation only.

FIRST CITATION   (Centers for Disease Control [CDC], 1990)

LATER CITATIONS   (CDC, 1990)

7. UNKNOWN AUTHOR Use the title or its first few words in a signal
phrase or in parentheses (in this example, a book's title is italicized).

The school profiles for the county substantiate this
trend (*Guide to secondary schools*, 2003).

8. TWO OR MORE AUTHORS WITH THE SAME SURNAME If your list of references
includes works by different authors with the same surname, include the
authors' initials in each citation.

G. Jones (1994) conducted the groundbreaking study of
retroviruses.

APA

21b

469

RESEARCH

APA Format for
Content Notes

9. TWO OR MORE SOURCES WITHIN THE SAME PARENTHETICAL REFERENCE If you cite more than one source at once, list works in alphabetical order by author's surname, separated by semicolons; list works by the same author in chronological order, separated by commas.

```
(Chodorow, 2001; Gilligan, 2002)
```

```
(Gilligan, 1977, 2002)
```

10. SPECIFIC PARTS OF A SOURCE Use abbreviations (*chap., p.,* and so on) in a parenthetical reference to name the part of a work you are citing.

```
Montgomery (1998, chap. 9) argued that his research
yielded the opposite results.
```

11. EMAIL AND OTHER PERSONAL COMMUNICATION Cite any personal letters, email, electronic postings, telephone conversations, or interviews with the person's initial(s) and last name, with the identification *personal communication* and the date in a parenthetical reference. Note, however, that APA recommends not including personal communications in the reference list.

```
J. L. Morin (personal communication, October 14, 1999)
supported the claims in her article with new evidence.
```

12. WORLD WIDE WEB DOCUMENT To cite a source found on the Web, use the author's name and date as you would for a print source, then indicate the chapter or figure name of the document, as appropriate. If the source's publication date is unknown, use *n.d.* (no date). To document a quotation, include paragraph numbers if page numbers are unavailable.

For an example of citing a source with an unknown author, see p. 468.

```
Shade argued the importance of "ensuring equitable
gender access to the Internet" (1993, p. 6).
```

21b APA format for content notes

APA style allows content notes for information you wish to include to expand or supplement your text. Indicate such notes in the text by superscript numerals. Type the notes themselves on a separate page after the last page of the text, under the heading "Footnotes," centered at the top of the page. Double-space all entries. Indent the first line of each note five to seven spaces, but begin subsequent lines at the left margin.

SUPERSCRIPT IN TEXT

The age of the children involved in the study was an important factor in the selection of items for the questionnaire.[1]

FOOTNOTE

[1]Marjorie Youngston Forman and William Cole of the Child Study Team provided great assistance in identifying appropriate items.

21c APA format for a list of references

For an example of a list of references using APA format, see p. 915.

The alphabetical list of the sources cited in your essay is called **References.** (If your instructor asks that you list everything you have read as background — not just the sources you cite — call the list "Bibliography.") Here are some guidelines for preparing such a list:

- Start your list on a separate page after the text of your document but before any appendices or notes. Number each page, continuing the numbering of the text.
- Type the heading "References," not underlined or italicized or in quotation marks, centered one inch from the top of the page.
- Double-space, and begin your first entry. Unless your instructor suggests otherwise, do not indent the first line of each entry, but indent subsequent lines one-half inch or five spaces (see 21c1). Double-space the entire list.
- List sources alphabetically by authors' (or editors') last names. If a source has no known author or editor, alphabetize it by the first major word of the title, disregarding *A, An,* or *The.* If the list includes two or more works by the same author, see the examples on pp. 473 and 474.

For source materials from books and periodicals, APA style specifies the treatment and placement of four basic elements — author, publication date, title, and publication information. Each element is followed by a period.

- *Author.* List *all* authors last name first, and use only initials for first and middle names. Separate the names of multiple authors with commas, and use an ampersand before the last author's name.

- *Publication date.* Enclose the date in parentheses. Use only the year for books and journals; use the year, a comma, and the month or month and day for magazines. Do not abbreviate the month.

- *Title.* Italicize titles and subtitles of books and periodicals. Do not enclose titles of articles in quotation marks. For books and articles, capitalize only the first word of the title and subtitle and any proper nouns or proper adjectives. Capitalize all major words in a periodical title.

- *Publication information.* For a book, list the city of publication (and the country or postal abbreviation for the state if the city is unfamiliar), a colon, and the publisher's name, dropping any *Inc., Co.,* or *Publishers.* For a periodical, follow the periodical title with a comma, the volume number (italicized), the issue number (if appropriate) in parentheses and followed by a comma, and the inclusive page numbers of the article. For newspaper articles and for articles and chapters in books, include the abbreviations *p.* ("page") or *pp.* ("pages").

If you are using software (Microsoft Word, EndNote, Research Assistant) to record and create a list of references, double-check that all formatting is accurate.

RESEARCH

APA Format for a
List of References

● For more information on capitalization, see 54c.

1 Indentation style

The following sample entries are in a hanging indent format, where the first line aligns on the left and the subsequent lines indent one-half inch or five spaces. This is the customary APA format for final copy, including student papers. Unless your instructor suggests otherwise, it is the format we recommend. Note, however, that for manuscripts being submitted to journals, APA requires the reverse (first lines indented, subsequent lines aligned on the left), assuming that it will be converted by a typesetting system to a hanging indent.

2 Books

1. BOOK BY ONE AUTHOR

```
Lightman, A. P. (2002). The diagnosis. New York: Vintage
     Books.
```

2. BOOK BY TWO OR MORE AUTHORS

```
Newcombe, F., & Ratcliffe, G. (1978). Defining females--
     The nature of women in society. New York: Wiley.
```

3. **BOOK BY A CORPORATE OR GROUP AUTHOR**

Institute of Financial Education. (1983). *Income
property lending.* Homewood, IL: Dow Jones-Irwin.

Use the word *Author* as the publisher when the organization is both the author and the publisher.

American Chemical Society. (1978). *Handbook for authors
of papers in American Chemical Society
publications.* Washington, DC: Author.

4. **BOOK BY AN UNKNOWN AUTHOR**

National Geographic atlas of the world. (1999).
Washington, DC: National Geographic Society.

5. **BOOK PREPARED BY AN EDITOR**

Hardy, H. H. (Ed.). (1998). *The proper study of mankind.*
New York: Farrar, Straus.

6. **SELECTION IN A BOOK WITH AN EDITOR**

West, C. (1992). The postmodern crisis of the black
intellectuals. In L. Grossberg, C. Nelson, & P.
Treichler (Eds.), *Cultural studies* (pp. 689-705).
New York: Routledge.

7. **TRANSLATION**

Durkheim, E. (1957). *Suicide* (J. A. Spaulding & G.
Simpson, Trans.). Glencoe, IL: Free Press of
Glencoe.

8. **EDITION OTHER THAN THE FIRST**

Kohn, M. L. (1977). *Class and conformity: A study in
values* (2nd ed.). Chicago: University of Chicago
Press.

9. **ONE VOLUME OF A MULTIVOLUME WORK**

Baltes, P., & Brim, O. G. (Eds.). (1980). *Life-span
development and behavior* (Vol. 3). New York: Basic
Books.

APA

21c

473

RESEARCH
APA Format for a
List of References

10. ARTICLE IN A REFERENCE WORK

Ochs, E. (1989). Language acquisition. In *International
encyclopedia of communications* (Vol. 2, pp. 390-
393). New York: Oxford University Press.

If no author is listed, begin with the title.

11. REPUBLICATION

Piaget, J. (1952). *The language and thought of the
child.* London: Routledge & Kegan Paul. (Original
work published 1932)

12. GOVERNMENT DOCUMENT

U.S. Census Bureau. (1975). *Historical statistics of the
United States, colonial times to 1970.* Washington,
DC: U.S. Government Printing Office.

● For advice on
citing online
government
documents, see
p. 477.

13. TWO OR MORE BOOKS BY THE SAME AUTHOR(S) List two or more books by
the same author in chronological order. Repeat the author's name in
each entry.

Goodall, J. (1991). *Through a window.* Boston: Houghton-
Mifflin.
Goodall, J. (1999). *Reason for hope: A spiritual
journey.* New York: Warner Books.

3 Periodicals

14. ARTICLE IN A JOURNAL PAGINATED BY VOLUME

Shuy, R. (1981). A holistic view of language. *Research
in the Teaching of English, 15,* 101-111.

15. ARTICLE IN A JOURNAL PAGINATED BY ISSUE

Maienza, J. G. (1986). The superintendency:
Characteristics of access for men and women.
Educational Administration Quarterly, 22(4), 59-79.

16. ARTICLE IN A MAGAZINE

Quinn, J. B. (2002, September 16). Bonds for beginners.
Newsweek, 45.

17. ARTICLE IN A NEWSPAPER

Browne, M. W. (1988, April 26). Lasers for the
battlefield raise concern for eyesight. *The New
York Times*, pp. C1, C8.

18. UNSIGNED ARTICLE

What sort of person reads *Creative Computing*? (1985,
August). *Creative Computing*, 8, 10.

19. EDITORIAL OR LETTER TO THE EDITOR

Russell, J. S. (1994, March 27). The language instinct
[Letter to the editor]. *The New York Times Book
Review*, p. 27.

20. REVIEW

Larmore, C. E. (1989). [Review of the book *Patterns of
moral complexity*]. *Ethics*, 99, 423-426.

21. PUBLISHED INTERVIEW

McCarthy, E. (1968, December 24). [Interview with *Boston
Globe* Washington staff]. *Boston Globe*, p. B27.

22. TWO OR MORE WORKS BY THE SAME AUTHOR IN THE SAME YEAR List two or more
works by the same author published in the same year alphabetically, and
place lowercase letters (*a, b,* etc.) after the dates.

Murray, F. B. (1983a). Equilibration as cognitive
conflict. *Developmental Review, 3*, 54-61.
Murray, F. B. (1983b). Learning and development through
social interaction. In L. Liben (Ed.), *Piaget and
the foundations of knowledge* (pp. 176-201).
Hillsdale, NJ: Erlbaum.

4 Electronic sources

The *Publication Manual of the American Psychological Association,* Fifth Edition, includes guidelines for citing various kinds of electronic resources,
including Web sites; articles, reports, and abstracts; some types of online
communications; and computer software. Updated guidelines are maintained at the APA's Web site, <www.apa.org>.

The basic entry for most sources you access via the Internet should include the following elements:

RESEARCH
APA Format for a
List of References

**www • bedford
stmartins.com/
smhandbook**

For additional
examples of APA
style for electronic
sources, click on

▶ **Documenting
Sources**
▶ **APA Style**

- *Author.* Give the author's name, if available.
- *Publication date.* Include the date of Internet publication or of the most recent update, if available. Use *n.d.* (no date) when the publication date is unavailable.
- *Title.* List the title of the document or subject line of the message, neither underlined nor in quotation marks.
- *Publication information.* For documents from reference databases or scholarly projects, give the city of the publisher or sponsoring organization, followed by the name. For articles from online journals or newspapers, follow the title with a comma, the volume number (italicized), the issue number (if appropriate) in parentheses and followed by a comma, and the inclusive page numbers of the article.
- *Retrieval information.* For most Internet sources, type the word *Retrieved* followed by the date of access, followed by a comma. End with the URL or other retrieval information and no period. For listserv or newsgroup messages and other online postings, type *Message posted to,* followed by the name of the list or group, and archive information if appropriate.

23. WORLD WIDE WEB SITE To cite a whole site, give the address in a parenthetical reference. To cite a document from a Web site, include information as you would for a print document, followed by a note on its retrieval.

American Psychological Association. (2000). DotComSense:
   Commonsense ways to protect your privacy and assess
   online mental health information. Retrieved January
   25, 2001, from http://helping.apa.org/dotcomsense/

Mullins, B. (1995). Introduction to Robert Hass.
   *Readings in Contemporary Poetry at Dia Center for
   the Arts.* Retrieved April 24, 1997, from http://www
   .diacenter.org/prg/poetry/95_96/intrhass.html

If no author is identified, give the title of the document followed by the date (if available), publication information, and retrieval statement.

Media images can spur eating disorders in teens. (2000,
   February 16). *InteliHealth.* Retrieved June 29,
   2001, from http://www.intelihealth.com/IH/ihtIH/
   WSIHW000/333/8014/269144.html

24. **ARTICLE FROM AN ONLINE PERIODICAL** If the article also appears in a print journal, no retrieval statement is required; instead, include the label *[Electronic version]* after the article title. However, if the online article is a revision of the print document (if the format differs or page numbers are not indicated), include the date of access and URL.

> Palmer, K. S. (2000, September 12). In academia, males
>   under a microscope. *Washington Post.* Retrieved
>   January 23, 2001, from http://www.washingtonpost
>   .com
>
> Steedman, M., & Jones, G. P. (2000). Information
>   structure and the syntax-phonology interface
>   [Electronic version]. *Linguistic Inquiry, 31,*
>   649-689.

To cite an online article that did not appear in print, give the date of access and URL.

> Taylor, J. (1998, June). Constructing the relational
>   mind. *Psyche, 4*(10). Retrieved August 11, 2001,
>   from http://psyche.cs.monash.edu.au/v4/
>   psyche-4-10-taylor.html

25. **ARTICLE OR ABSTRACT FROM A DATABASE** Give the information as you would for a print document. List the date you retrieved the article and only the name of the database; you do not need to specify whether you accessed the database through an online library or personal service, the Web, or a CD-ROM. If you are citing an abstract, end by typing *Abstract retrieved* and the date of access and name of the database. End with the document number in parentheses, if appropriate.

> Hayhoe, G. (2001). The long and winding road:
>   Technology's future. *Technical Communication,
>   48*(2), 133-145. Retrieved September 22, 2001, from
>   ProQuest database.
>
> McCall, R. B. (1998). Science and the press: Like oil
>   and water? *American Psychologist, 43*(2), 87-94.
>   Abstract retrieved August 23, 2002, from PsycINFO
>   database (1988-18263-001).

Pryor, T., & Wiederman, M. W. (1998). Personality
features and expressed concerns of adolescents
with eating disorders. *Adolescence, 33,* 291-301.
Retrieved August 26, 2002, from Electric Library
database.

26. ONLINE GOVERNMENT DOCUMENT Cite an online government document
as you would a printed government work, adding the date of access, and
the URL. If there is no date, use *n.d.*

● — For advice on
citing print
government
documents, see
p. 473.

Finn, J. D. (1998, April). *Class size and students at
risk: What is known? What is next?* Retrieved
September 5, 2002, from United States Department
of Education Web site http://www.ed.gov/pubs/
ClassSize/title.html

United States Department of Education. (n.d.). *Progress
of education in the United States of America: 1990
through 1994.* Retrieved September 5, 2002, from
http://www.ed.gov/pubs/Prog95/index.html

27. POSTING TO A DISCUSSION GROUP List an online posting in the references list only if you are able to retrieve the message from a mailing list's
archive. Provide the author's name; the date of posting, in parentheses;
and the subject line from the posting. Include any information that further identifies the message in square brackets. For a listserv message, end
with the retrieval statement, including the name of the list and the URL
of the archived message.

Troike, R. C. (2001, June 21). Buttercups and primroses
[Msg 8]. Message posted to the American Dialect
Society's ADS-L electronic mailing list, archived
at http://listserv.linguistlist.org/archives/
ads-1.html

For a newsgroup posting, end with the name of the newsgroup. (If the
author's real name is unavailable, include the screen name.)

Wittenberg, E. (2001, July 11). Gender and the Internet
[Msg 4]. Message posted to news://comp.edu
.composition

28. EMAIL MESSAGE OR SYNCHRONOUS COMMUNICATION Because the APA stresses that any sources cited in your list of references be retrievable by your readers, you should not include entries for email messages or synchronous communications (MOOs, MUDs); instead, cite these sources in your text as forms of *personal communication* (see p. 469).

29. FTP (FILE TRANSFER PROTOCOL), TELNET, OR GOPHER SITE After the retrieval statement, give the address (substituting *ftp, telnet,* or *gopher* for *http* at the beginning of the URL) or the path followed to access information, with slashes to indicate menu selections.

```
Korn, P. (1994, October). How much does breast cancer
    really cost? Self. Retrieved May 5, 1997, from
    gopher://nysernet.org:70/00/BCIC/Sources/SELF/
    94/how-much
```

30. SOFTWARE OR COMPUTER PROGRAM Begin with the author's name only when an author is listed as owner of the software.

```
McAfee Office 2000. Version 2.0 [Computer software].
    (1999). Santa Clara, CA: Network Associates.
```

5 Other sources

31. TECHNICAL OR RESEARCH REPORTS AND WORKING PAPERS

```
Wilson, K. S. (1986). Palenque: An interactive
    multimedia optical disc prototype for children
    (Working Paper No. 2). New York: Center for
    Children and Technology, Bank Street College of
    Education.
```

32. PAPER PRESENTED AT A MEETING OR SYMPOSIUM, UNPUBLISHED Cite the month of the meeting, if it is available.

```
Engelbart, D. C. (1970, April). Intellectual
    implications of multi-access computing. Paper
    presented at the meeting of the Interdisciplinary
    Conference on Multi-Access Computer Networks,
    Washington, DC.
```

33. UNPUBLISHED DISSERTATION

Leverenz, C. A. (1994). *Collaboration and difference in the composition classroom.* Unpublished doctoral dissertation, Ohio State University, Columbus.

34. POSTER SESSION

Ulman, H. L., & Walborn, E. (1993, March). *Hypertext in the composition classroom.* Poster session presented at the Annual Conference on College Composition and Communication, San Diego, CA.

35. FILM, VIDEO, OR DVD

Hitchcock, A. (Producer & Director). (1954). *Rear window* [Film]. Los Angeles: MGM.

36. TELEVISION PROGRAM, SINGLE EPISODE

Imperioli, M. (Writer), & Buscemi, S. (Director). (2002, October 20). Everybody hurts [Television series episode]. In D. Chase (Executive Producer), *The Sopranos.* New York: Home Box Office.

37. SOUND RECORDING Begin with the writer's name, followed by the date of copyright. At the end of the entry, give the recording date if it is different from the copyright date. Use parentheses for this date but no period.

Colvin, S. (1991). I don't know why. [Recorded by A. Krauss and Union Station]. On *Every time you say goodbye* [Cassette]. Cambridge, MA: Rounder Records. (1992)

22

 Documenting
Sources: CBE Style

In the natural and physical sciences and mathematics, it's often very important to track reported findings to their source. If the study that produced the findings is flawed — or if it cannot be replicated to yield the same results — then the findings are suspect at best. Careful documentation of sources is very important in the sciences, then, and **CBE style** is widely used to do just that. This chapter illustrates CBE style and guides you in the use of such documentation in your own writing. ■

For further reference on CBE style from the Council of Science Editors (formerly the Council of Biology Editors, or CBE), consult the following volume:

> Council of Biology Editors. *Scientific Style and Format: The CBE Manual for Authors, Editors, and Publishers*. 6th ed. New York: Cambridge UP, 1994.

22a CBE formats for in-text citations

In CBE style, citations within an essay follow one of two formats.

- The **citation-sequence format** calls for a superscript number ([1]) or a number in parentheses after any mention of a source.

- The **name-year format** calls for the last name of the author and the year of publication in parentheses after any mention of a source. If the last name appears in a signal phrase, the name-year format allows for giving only the year of publication in parentheses.

Dr. Edward Huth, chairperson of the Council of Science Editors' Style Manual Committee, recommends either the name-year or the superscript (citation-sequence format) system rather than the number-in-parentheses system — and suggests that student writers check a current journal in the field or ask an instructor about the preferred style in a particular course or discipline.

1. IN-TEXT CITATION USING CITATION-SEQUENCE SUPERSCRIPT FORMAT

```
In his lengthy text, Gilman¹ provides the most complete
discussion of this phenomenon.
```

For the citation-sequence format, you would also use a superscript (¹) for each subsequent citation of this work by Gilman.

2. IN-TEXT CITATION USING NAME-YEAR FORMAT

```
In his lengthy text, Gilman provides the most complete
discussion of this phenomenon (1994).
```

```
Maxwell's two earlier studies of juvenile obesity (1988,
1991) examined only children with diabetes.
```

```
The classic examples of such investigations (Morrow
1968; Bridger and others 1971; Franklin and Wayson 1972)
still shape the assumptions of current studies.
```

22b CBE formats for a list of references

The citations in the text of an essay correspond to items on a list called **References.** If you use the citation-sequence superscript format, number and list the references in the sequence in which the references are *first* cited in the text. If you use the name-year format, list the references, unnumbered, in alphabetical order.

For an example
of a list of refer-
ences using CBE
citation-sequence
format, see
p. 931.

In the following examples, you will see that the citation-sequence format calls for listing the date after the publisher's name in references for books and after the periodical name in references for articles. The name-year format calls for listing the date immediately after the author's name in any kind of reference. Notice also the absence of a comma after the author's last name, the absence of a period after an initial, and the absence of underlining or italics in titles of books or journals.

If you are using software (Microsoft Word, EndNote, Research Assistant) to record and create a list of references, double-check that all formatting is accurate.

1. BOOKS

2. PERIODICALS

3. ELECTRONIC SOURCES

For an example of a research proposal using CBE style, see 66c.

1 Books

For a book, the basic entry includes the following items: the author, with the last name first, no comma, and initials without periods for the first and middle names; the title, with only the first word and proper nouns and adjectives capitalized and without underlining, italics, or quotation marks; the place and year of publication; the publisher; and the number of pages in the book. Note the period at the end of each part of the entry.

1. ONE AUTHOR

[1]Freidson E. Profession of medicine. New York: Dodd-Mead; 1972. 802 p.

Freidson E. 1972. Profession of medicine. New York: Dodd-Mead. 802 p.

2. TWO OR MORE AUTHORS

[2]Stalberg E, Trontelj JV. Single fiber electromyography: studies in healthy and diseased muscle. New York: Raven; 1994. 291 p.

Stalberg E, Trontelj JV. 1994. Single fiber electro-
    myography: studies in healthy and diseased muscle.
    New York: Raven. 291 p.

3. ORGANIZATION AS AUTHOR Any organization abbreviation is placed at
the beginning of the name-year entry and is used in the corresponding
in-text citation.

[3]World Health Organization. World health statistics
    annual: 1993. Geneva: World Health Organization;
    1994. 824 p.

[WHO] World Health Organization. 1994. World health
    statistics annual: 1993. Geneva: WHO. 824 p.

4. BOOK PREPARED BY EDITOR(S)

[4]Berge ZL, Collins MP, editors. Computer mediated
    communication and the online classroom. Cresskill,
    NJ: Hampton Pr; 1995. 230 p.

Berge ZL, Collins MP, editors. 1995. Computer mediated
    communication and the online classroom. Cresskill,
    NJ: Hampton Pr. 230 p.

5. SECTION OF A BOOK WITH AN EDITOR

[5]Adler M. Stroke. In: Dulbecco R, editor. Encyclopedia
    of human biology. San Diego: Academic; 1991. p 299-
    308.

Adler M. 1991. Stroke. In: Dulbecco R, editor.
    Encyclopedia of human biology. San Diego: Academic.
    p 299-308.

6. CHAPTER OF A BOOK

[6]Castro J. The American way of health: how medicine is
    changing and what it means to you. Boston: Little,
    Brown; 1994. Chapter 9, Why doctors, hospitals, and
    drugs cost so much; p 131-53.

Castro J. 1994. The American way of health: how medicine
    is changing and what it means to you. Boston:
    Little, Brown. Chapter 9, Why doctors, hospitals,
    and drugs cost so much; p 131-53.

7. PUBLISHED PROCEEDINGS OF A CONFERENCE

```
7[Anonymous]. International Conference on the Bus '86;
    1986 Sep 9-10; London. [London]: Institution of
    Mechanical Engineers; 1986. 115 p.
```

The place of publication was not stated but inferred and placed in brackets.

```
[Anonymous]. 1986. International Conference on the Bus
    '86; 1986 Sep 9-10; London. [London]: Institution
    of Mechanical Engineers. 115 p.
```

2 Periodicals

For a journal article, the basic entry includes the author, with the last name first, no comma, and initials without periods for the first and middle names; the article title, with only the first word and proper nouns and adjectives capitalized; the journal title, abbreviated; the date of the issue; the volume number; the issue number, if any; and the inclusive page numbers. For newspaper and magazine articles, the entry includes the section designation and column number, if any. For rules on abbreviating journal titles, consult *The CBE Manual,* or ask an instructor or librarian to refer you to other examples. Following are examples using both superscript and name-year systems:

8. ARTICLE IN A JOURNAL PAGINATED BY VOLUME

```
8Finkel MJ. Drugs of limited commercial value. New Engl
    J Med 1980;302:643-4.

Finkel MJ. 1980. Drugs of limited commercial value. New
    Engl J Med 302:643-4.
```

9. ARTICLE IN A JOURNAL PAGINATED BY ISSUE

```
9Fagan R. Characteristics of college student
    volunteering. J Vol Admin 1992;11(1):5-18.

Fagan R. 1992. Characteristics of college student
    volunteering. J Vol Admin 11(1):5-18.
```

10. ARTICLE IN A WEEKLY JOURNAL

```
10Kerr RA. How many more after Northridge? Science 1994
    Jan 28;263(5146):460-1.
```

```
Kerr RA. 1994 Jan 28. How many more after Northridge?
    Science 263(5146):460-1.
```

11. ARTICLE IN A MAGAZINE

```
11Jackson R. Arachnomania. Natural History 1995 Mar:28-
    31.
```

```
Jackson R. 1995 Mar. Arachnomania. Natural History:28-
    31.
```

12. ARTICLE IN A NEWSPAPER

```
12Christopher T. Grafting: playing Dr. Frankenstein in
    the garden. New York Times 1995 Feb 19;Sect
    Y:21(col 1).
```

```
Christopher T. 1995 Feb 19. Grafting: playing Dr.
    Frankenstein in the garden. New York Times;Sect
    Y:21(col 1).
```

3 Electronic sources

Although the 1994 edition of *The CBE Manual* includes a few examples for citing electronic sources, the Council of Science Editors now recommends the guidelines provided at its Web site <www.councilscienceeditors .org/pubs_citing_internet.shtml>. The following formats are adapted from the advice on this site. The examples shown follow the citation-sequence format, but you can easily adapt them to the name-year format.

The basic entry for most sources you access through the Internet should include the following elements:

- *Author.* Give the author's name, if available, last name first, followed by the initial(s) and a period.
- *Title.* For book, journal, and article titles, follow the style for print materials. For all other types of electronic material, reproduce the title as closely as possible to the wording that appears on the screen.
- *Medium.* Indicate, in brackets, that the source is not in print format by using designations such as *[Internet]* or *[database on the Internet].*
- *Place of publication.* The city usually should be followed by the two-letter abbreviation for state. If the city is inferred, put the city and state in brackets, followed by a colon. If the city cannot be inferred, use the words

www ● bedford
stmartins.com/
smhandbook

For additional
examples of CBE
style for electronic
sources, click on

▶ Documenting
   Sources
   ▶ CBE Style

place unknown in brackets, followed by a colon. Note that very well-known cities, such as New York or Chicago, may be listed without a state designation.

- *Publisher.* Include the individual or organization that produces or sponsors the work or site. It is sometimes helpful to include a designation for country, in parentheses, after the publisher's name. If no publisher can be determined, use the words *publisher unknown* in brackets.

- *Dates.* Cite three important dates if possible: the date the publication was placed on the Internet or was copyrighted; the latest date of any update or revision; and the date the publication was accessed by you. Dates should be expressed in the format "year month day," and the date of copyright should be preceded by a *c* as in *c2000.* (Because several dates are preferred in citations from electronic sources, the following examples group all dates together after the publisher's name. Since this style is different from what is done with most print materials, check with your instructor to see if this style is acceptable.)

- *Page, document, volume, and issue numbers.* When citing a portion of a larger work or site, list the inclusive page numbers or document numbers of the specific item being cited. For journals or journal articles, include volume and issue numbers.

- *Length.* The length may be shown as a total page count, such as *85 p.* For much electronic material, length is approximate and is shown in square brackets, such as *[12 paragraphs]* or *[about 6 screens].*

- *Address.* Include the URL or other electronic address; use the phrase *Available from:* to introduce the address.

13. ELECTRONIC BOOKS (MONOGRAPHS)

¹³Johnson KA, Becker JA. The whole brain atlas
    [Internet]. Boston: Harvard Medical School; c1995-
    1999 [modified 1999 Jan 12; cited 2001 Mar 7].
    Available from: http://www.med.harvard.edu
    /AANLIB/home.html

To cite a portion of an online book, include the name of the part after the date cited. Include page numbers, if available. If no page numbers are available, include an estimated length for the part, and end with a period: *Chapter 6, Degenerative disease [about 2 screens].*

14. ELECTRONIC JOURNAL ARTICLES
Include the authors' names; the title of the article; the title of the journal; the word *Internet* in brackets; as full a date of publication as possible; the date of access; the volume, issue, and

page numbers (using designations such as *[16 paragraphs]* or *[5 screens]* if traditional page numbering is not available); and the URL.

[14]Tong V, Abbot FS, Mbofana S, Walker MJ. In vitro
      investigation of the hepatic extraction of RSD1070,
      a novel antiarrhythmic compound. J Pharm Pharmaceut
      Sci [Internet]. 2001 [cited 2001 Oct 15]; 4(1):15-
      23. Available from: http://www.ualberta.ca/~csps
      /JPPS4(1)/F.Abbott/RSD1070.pdf

15. WORLD WIDE WEB SITE Include as many of the following dates as possible: the date of publication (or, if this is not available, the copyright date preceded by *c*); the date of the most recent revision; and the date of access.

[15]Animal Welfare Information Center [Internet].
      Beltsville, MD: National Agricultural Library (US);
      [updated 2001 Oct 11; cited 2001 Oct 15]. Available
      from: http://www.nal.usda.gov/awic

[16]Hypertension, Dialysis & Clinical Nephrology
      [Internet]. Hinsdale, IL: Medtext; c1995-2001
      [cited 2001 Oct 15]. Available from:
      http://www.medtext.com/hdcn.htm

16. MATERIAL FROM AN ONLINE DATABASE If the database is open—with records still being added to it—include the beginning date for the database (*2000–*), or include a dash after the date of publication.

[17]Envirofacts Warehouse. Washington, DC: Environmental
      Protection Agency; [updated 2001 Aug 13; cited 2001
      Oct 15]. Toxic releases [about 2 paragraphs].
      Available from: http://www.epa.gov/enviro/html
      /toxic_releases.html

[18]Ovid [Internet]. New York: Ovid Technologies. c2000-
      2001 - [cited 2001 May 3]. Available from:
      http://gateway.ovid.com/. Subscription required.

17. EMAIL MESSAGE Include the author's name; the subject line of the message; the word *Internet* in square brackets; the words *Message to:*

followed by the addressee's name; information about when the message
was sent and when it was cited; and the length of the message.

[19]Voss J. Questions about CBE style [Internet]. Message
    to: Stephanie Carpenter. 2002 Jan 29, 3:34 pm
    [cited 2002 Jan 30]. [about 1 screen]

18. ELECTRONIC DISCUSSION LIST MESSAGE Begin with the author's name, the
subject line, the name of the discussion list, and include as much of the
following information as possible.

[20]Rooyer L. Routing BRM. In: DOCLINE-L [Internet].
    Bethesda, MD: National Library of Medicine (US);
    2001 Apr 2, 21:17:35 [cited 2001 Oct 15]. [about 2
    paragraphs]. Available from: DOCLINE-L@LIST.NIH.GOV
    Archives available from: http://list.nih.gov
    /archives/docline-1.html

23 ◤ Documenting Sources: Chicago Style

The style guide of the University of Chicago Press has long been used in history as well as in other areas of the arts and humanities. The fifteenth edition of *The Chicago Manual of Style,* published in 2003, provides a complete guide to Chicago style. For further reference, you can also consult the following much shorter volume intended for student writers:

> Turabian, Kate L. *A Manual for Writers of Term Papers, Theses, and Dissertations.* 6th ed. Rev. John Grossman and Alice Bennett. Chicago: U of Chicago P, 1996.

For easy reference, examples of how to format both Chicago-style notes and bibliographic entries are shown together in 23b.

The practice of documenting sources is at least as old as ancient libraries, where some kind of systematic listing was desirable. With the explosion of information in print-based societies, more formal kinds of documentation systems became necessary. One of the oldest and most widely respected of such systems is the one referred to simply as **Chicago style,** which has long been used in history as well as in other areas of the arts and humanities. This chapter illustrates Chicago style and guides you in the use of such documentation in your own writing. ■

DIRECTORY TO CHICAGO STYLE

490

Chicago

23a

RESEARCH

Documenting
Sources:
Chicago Style

For an example
of a research
essay using
Chicago style,
see 64e.

23a Chicago format for in-text citations, notes, and bibliography

In Chicago style, you use superscript numbers (^{1}) to mark citations in the text. Place the superscript number for each note near the cited material—at the end of the relevant quotation, sentence, clause, or phrase. Type the number after any punctuation mark except the dash; do not leave space between the superscript and the preceding letter or punctuation mark. Number citations sequentially throughout the text.

The notes themselves can be **footnotes** (each typed at the bottom of the page on which the superscript for it appears in the text) or **endnotes** (all typed on a separate page at the end of the text under the heading "Notes"). Be sure to check your instructor's preference. The first line of each note is indented like a paragraph (five spaces or one-half inch) and begins with a number followed by a period and one space before the first word of the entry. All remaining lines of the entry are typed flush with the left margin. Footnotes should be single-spaced with a double space between each note. All endnotes should be double-spaced.

●— For an example
   of endnotes in
   Chicago format,
   see p. 894.

IN THE TEXT

Sweig argues that Castro and Che Guevara were not the only key players in the Cuban Revolution of the late 1950s.[19]

IN THE FIRST NOTE

19. Julia Sweig, *Inside the Cuban Revolution* (Cambridge: Harvard University Press, 2002), 9.

After giving complete information the first time you cite a work, shorten any additional references to that work: list only the author's name followed by a comma, a shortened version of the title, a comma, and the page number. If the reference is to the same source cited in the previous note, you can use the Latin abbreviation *Ibid.* (for "in the same place") instead of the name and title.

IN SUBSEQUENT NOTES

19. Julia Sweig, *Inside the Cuban Revolution* (Cambridge, MA: Harvard University Press, 2002), 9.

Chicago

492 **23b**

RESEARCH

Documenting
Sources:
Chicago Style

```
20. Ibid., 13.

21. Foner and Lewis, Black Worker, 138-39.

22. Ferguson, "Comfort of Being Sad," 63.

23. Sweig, Cuban Revolution, 21.
```

An alphabetical list of the sources you use in your paper is usually titled **Bibliography** in Chicago style. If "Sources Consulted," "Works Cited," or "Selected Bibliography" better describes your list, however, any of these titles is acceptable.

In the bibliographic entry for a source, include the same information as in the first note for that source, but omit the specific page reference. However, give the *first* author's last name first, followed by a comma and the first name; separate the main elements of the entry with periods rather than commas; and do not enclose the publication information for books in parentheses.

IN THE BIBLIOGRAPHY

```
Sweig, Julia. Inside the Cuban Revolution. Cambridge,
     MA: Harvard University Press, 2002.
```

Start the bibliography on a separate page after the main text and any endnotes. Continue the consecutive numbering of pages. Type the title "Bibliography" (without italics or quotation marks) and center it one inch below the top of the page. Begin each entry at the left margin. Indent the second and subsequent lines of each entry five spaces (or one-half inch). Double-space the entire list.

List sources alphabetically by authors' last names (or by the first major word in the title if the author is unknown). If you use software (Microsoft Word, EndNote, Research Assistant) to collect and format your bibliography, remember to double-check that all formatting is correct.

23b Chicago format for notes and bibliographic entries

For easy reference, the following examples demonstrate how to format both notes and bibliographic entries according to Chicago style.

1. ONE AUTHOR

> 1. James S. Hirsch, *Riot and Remembrance: The Tulsa Race War and Its Legacy* (Boston: Houghton Mifflin, 2002), 119.

Hirsch, James S. *Riot and Remembrance: The Tulsa Race War and Its Legacy.* Boston: Houghton Mifflin, 2002.

2. MULTIPLE AUTHORS

> 2. Margaret Macmillan and Richard Holbrooke, *Paris 1919: Six Months That Changed the World* (New York: Random House, 2003), 384.

Macmillan, Margaret, and Richard Holbrooke. *Paris 1919: Six Months That Changed the World.* New York: Random House, 2003.

When there are more than three authors, it is acceptable in Chicago style to give the first-listed author followed by *et al.* or *and others* in the note. In the bibliography, however, list all the authors' names.

> 2. Stephen J. Blank and others, *Conflict, Culture, and History: Regional Dimensions* (Miami: University Press of the Pacific, 2002), 276.

Blank, Stephen J., Lawrence E. Grinter, Karl P. Magyar, Lewis B. Ware, and Bynum E. Weathers. *Conflict, Culture, and History: Regional Dimensions.* Miami: University Press of the Pacific, 2002.

3. ORGANIZATION AS AUTHOR

> 3. World Intellectual Property Organization, *Intellectual Property Profile of the Least Developed Countries* (Geneva: World Intellectual Property Organization, 2002), 43.

World Intellectual Property Organization. *Intellectual Property Profile of the Least Developed Countries.*

Chicago

494 **23b**

RESEARCH
Documenting
Sources:
Chicago Style

Geneva: World Intellectual Property Organization, 2002.

4. UNKNOWN AUTHOR

4. *Broad Stripes and Bright Stars* (Kansas City, MO: Andrews McMeel Publishing, 2002), 10.

Broad Stripes and Bright Stars. Kansas City, MO: Andrews
McMeel Publishing, 2002.

5. EDITOR

5. James H. Fetzer, ed., *The Great Zapruder Film Hoax: Deceit and Deception in the Death of JFK* (Chicago: Open Court Publishing, 2003), 56.

Fetzer, James H., ed. *The Great Zapruder Film Hoax:
Deceit and Deception in the Death of JFK.* Chicago:
Open Court Publishing, 2003.

6. SELECTION IN AN ANTHOLOGY OR CHAPTER IN A BOOK, WITH AN EDITOR

6. Denise Little, "Born in Blood," in *Alternate Gettysburgs,* ed. Brian Thomsen and Martin H. Greenberg (New York: Berkley Publishing Group, 2002), 245.

Little, Denise. "Born in Blood." In *Alternate
Gettysburgs,* edited by Brian Thomsen and Martin H.
Greenberg, 242-55. New York: Berkley Publishing
Group, 2002.

7. EDITION OTHER THAN THE FIRST

7. Charles G. Beaudette, *Excess Heat: Why Cold Fusion Research Prevailed,* 2nd ed. (South Bristol, ME: Oak Grove Press, 2002), 313.

Beaudette, Charles G. *Excess Heat: Why Cold Fusion
Research Prevailed.* 2nd ed. South Bristol, ME: Oak
Grove Press, 2002.

Chicago

23b 495

RESEARCH
Chicago Format
for Notes and
Bibliographic
Entries

8. MULTIVOLUME WORK

8. John Watson, *Annals of Philadelphia and Pennsylvania in the Olden Time*, vol. 2 (Washington, DC: Ross & Perry, 2003), 514.

Watson, John. *Annals of Philadelphia and Pennsylvania in the Olden Time*. Vol. 2. Washington, DC: Ross & Perry, 2003.

9. REFERENCE WORK

Cite well-known reference works in your notes, but do not list them in your bibliography. Use *s.v.,* the abbreviation for the Latin *sub verbo* ("under the word"), to let your reader know what you looked up in the reference work.

9. *Encarta World Dictionary,* s.v. "carpetbagger."

2 Periodicals

10. ARTICLE IN A JOURNAL PAGINATED BY VOLUME

When a journal's issues are numbered, place a comma after the volume number, insert the abbreviation *no.* and the issue number.

10. Diane Kirkby, "'Beer, Glorious Beer': Gender Politics and Australian Popular Culture," *Journal of Popular Culture* 37, no. 2 (2003): 246.

Kirkby, Diane. "'Beer, Glorious Beer': Gender Politics and Australian Popular Culture." *Journal of Popular Culture* 37, no. 2 (2003): 244-56.

11. ARTICLE IN A JOURNAL PAGINATED BY ISSUE

11. Karin Lützen, "The Female World: Viewed from Denmark," *Journal of Women's History* 12, no. 3 (2000): 36.

Lützen, Karin. "The Female World: Viewed from Denmark." *Journal of Women's History* 12, no. 3 (2000): 34-38.

12. ARTICLE IN A MAGAZINE

> 12. Douglas Brinkley and Anne Brinkley, "Lawyers and Lizard-Heads," *Atlantic Monthly*, May 2002, 56.

Brinkley, Douglas, and Anne Brinkley. "Lawyers and Lizard-Heads." *Atlantic Monthly*, May 2002, 55-61.

13. ARTICLE IN A NEWSPAPER

> 13. Caroline E. Mayer, "Wireless Industry to Adopt Voluntary Standards," *Washington Post*, September 9, 2003, sec. E.

Mayer, Caroline E. "Wireless Industry to Adopt Voluntary Standards." *Washington Post*, September 9, 2003, sec. E.

3 Electronic sources

14. WORLD WIDE WEB SITE

www ● bedford stmartins.com/ smhandbook

For additional examples of Chicago style for electronic sources, click on

► **Documenting Sources**
  ► **Chicago Style**

> 14. Rutgers University, "Picture Gallery," *The Rutgers Oral History Archives of World War II*, http:// fas-history.rutgers.edu/oralhistory/orlhom.htm (accessed November 7, 2003).

Rutgers University. "Picture Gallery." *The Rutgers Oral History Archives of World War II*. http:// fas-history.rutgers.edu/oralhistory/orlhom.htm (accessed November 7, 2003).

15. ONLINE BOOK

> 15. Janja Bec, *The Shattering of the Soul* (Los Angeles: The Simon Wiesenthal Center, 1997), http:// motlc.wiesenthal.com/resources/books/shatteringsoul/ index.html (accessed November 6, 2003).

Bec, Janja. *The Shattering of the Soul.* Los Angeles: The Simon Wiesenthal Center, 1997. http://motlc .wiesenthal.com/resources/books/shatteringsoul/ index.html (accessed November 6, 2003).

16. ARTICLE IN AN ELECTRONIC JOURNAL

Always include the page numbers, if available, when you are citing articles in journals that also have print versions.

> 16. Damian Bracken, "Rationalism and the Bible in Seventh-Century Ireland," *Chronicon* 2 (1998), http://www.ucc.ie/chronicon/bracfra.htm (accessed November 1, 2003).

Bracken, Damian. "Rationalism and the Bible in Seventh-Century Ireland." *Chronicon* 2 (1998). http://www.ucc.ie/chronicon/bracfra.htm (accessed November 1, 2003).

17. ARTICLE IN AN ONLINE MAGAZINE

> 17. Kim Iskyan, "Putin's Next Power Play," *Slate*, November 4, 2003, http://slate.msn.com/id/2090745 (accessed November 7, 2003).

Iskyan, Kim. "Putin's Next Power Play." *Slate*, November 4, 2003. http://slate.msn.com/id/2090745 (accessed November 7, 2003).

18. ARTICLE FROM A DATABASE

> 18. Peter DeMarco, "Holocaust Survivors Lend Voice to History," *Boston Globe*, November 2, 2003, http://www.lexis-nexis.com (accessed November 19, 2003).

DeMarco, Peter. "Holocaust Survivors Lend Voice to History." *Boston Globe*, November 2, 2003. http://www.lexis-nexis.com (accessed November 19, 2003).

19. EMAIL AND OTHER PERSONAL COMMUNICATIONS

Cite email messages and other personal communications, such as letters and telephone calls, in the text or in a note. Do not cite personal communications in your bibliography.

> 19. Kareem Adas, email message to author, February 11, 2004.

Chicago

498 **23b**

RESEARCH

Documenting
Sources:
Chicago Style

4 Other sources

20. PUBLISHED OR BROADCAST INTERVIEW

20. Condoleezza Rice, interview by Charlie Rose, *The Charlie Rose Show*, PBS, October 30, 2003.

Rice, Condoleezza. Interview by Charlie Rose. *The Charlie Rose Show*. PBS, October 30, 2003.

Interviews you conduct are considered personal communications.

21. VIDEO OR DVD

21. Edward Norton and Edward Furlong, *American History X*, DVD, directed by Tony Kaye (1998; Los Angeles: New Line Studios, 2002).

Norton, Edward, and Edward Furlong. *American History X*. DVD. Directed by Tony Kaye. 1998. Los Angeles: New Line Studios, 2002.

22. CD-ROM

22. *The Civil War*, CD-ROM (Fogware Publishing, 2000).

The Civil War. CD-ROM. Fogware Publishing, 2000.

23. PAMPHLET, REPORT, OR BROCHURE

Information about the author or publisher may not be readily available, but give enough information to identify your source.

23. Jamie McCarthy, *Who Is David Irving?* (San Antonio, TX: The Holocaust History Project, 1998).

McCarthy, Jamie. *Who Is David Irving?* San Antonio, TX: The Holocaust History Project, 1998.

24. GOVERNMENT DOCUMENT

24. House Committee on Ways and Means, *Report on Trade Mission to Sub-Saharan Africa*, 108th Cong., 1st

Chicago

23b

499

RESEARCH

Chicago Format
for Notes and
Bibliographic
Entries

sess. (Washington, DC: U.S. Government Printing Office,
2003), 28.

House Committee on Ways and Means. *Report on Trade
Mission to Sub-Saharan Africa.* 108th Cong., 1st
sess. Washington, DC: U.S. Government Printing
Office, 2003.

PART 5

USING LANGUAGE EFFECTIVELY

"A word is dead
When it is said,
Some say.

I say it just
Begins to live
That day."

— EMILY DICKINSON

24

 Writing to the World

When Marshall McLuhan referred to the world in 1967 as a global village, the phrase seemed unfamiliar and highly exaggerated. More than thirty-five years later, his words are practically a cliché, part of our everyday language. People today can communicate, often instantaneously via the Internet, across vast distances and cultures. With speed and ease once unimaginable, businesspeople complete multinational transactions, students take classes at distant universities, and grandmothers check in with family members across four or five — or six — time zones. Now more than ever, it's an everyday act to write to the world. This chapter will help you learn to hone these communicative skills. ■

24a Communicating across cultures

In a time of instantaneous communication, you might find yourself writing to (or with) students throughout the country, or even across the globe — and you may well be in classes with people from other cultures, language groups, and countries. In business, government, and education, writers increasingly operate on an international stage. As the CEO of Tupperware International told a group of new business graduates, "If you want to move into management in this company, you will need knowledge of at least several languages and cultures." Such situations call upon us to think hard about how to write to the world, how to become what might be called *world writers,* able to communicate across cultures.

24b Reconsidering what seems "normal"

How do you decide what is "normal" in a given situation? More than likely, your judgment is based on assumptions you are not even aware of. But remember: behavior that is considered out of place in one community may appear perfectly normal in another. If you want to communicate with people across cultures, you need to try to learn something about the norms in those cultures and, even more important, to be aware of the norms that guide your own behavior.

LANGUAGE

Reconsidering
What Seems
"Normal"

→ Recognize what you consider "normal." Examine your own customary behaviors and assumptions, and think about how they may affect what you think and say (and write). (24b)

→ When speaking with someone from another culture, listen carefully for meaning. Ask for clarification if need be. (24c)

→ Consider your own authority as a writer. Should you sound like an expert? a subordinate? something else? (24d)

→ Think about your audience's expectations. How explicit does your writing need to be? (24e)

→ What kind of evidence will count most with your audience? (24f)

→ Organize your writing with your audience's expectations in mind. (24g)

→ If in doubt, use formal style. (24h)

• Be aware of the values and assumptions that guide your own customary ways of communicating. Remember that most of us tend to see our own way as the normal or right way to do things. Examine your own assumptions, and become aware of the ways they guide your thinking and behavior. Keep in mind that if your ways seem inherently right, then—even without thinking about it—you may assume that other ways are somehow less than right.

• Know that most ways of communicating are influenced by cultural contexts and that they differ widely from one culture to the next.

• Pay close attention to the ways that people from cultures other than your own communicate, and be flexible and open to their ways.

• Pay attention to and respect the differences among individual people *within* a given culture. Do not assume that all members of a community behave in just the same way or value exactly the same things.

• Don't overgeneralize. Even though it's true, for example, that Americans drink millions of gallons of Coca-Cola a year, it is a mistake to think that all Americans drink Coca-Cola. In the same way, knowing that empathy is a more important method of persuasion than explicit criticism for some Asians does not mean this cultural pattern holds true for all Asians. If you have read Amy Tan's books about her life in a Chinese household, you will remember the spirited arguments that took place (though it seems that such arguments occurred only in the home rather than in public). In the final analysis, people argue in every culture, but they do so in very different ways. As a world writer, you need to be aware of and sensitive to differences within—as well as across—cultures.

Listening may be the most underrated communicative art of our time. Certainly, it is seldom taught in U.S. schools. A conversation heard recently suggests how important careful listening is to effective communication. Two students at a writing center were talking about comments their professor had written on their essays. "He keeps telling me to try for more originality!" said one student from the Philippines in exasperation. "I wonder what he really means by 'originality'?" said the other, who was from Massachusetts. In fact, the students came up with two very different definitions of this seemingly simple word. For the Filipina student, *originality* meant going back to the original, whatever it was, and understanding it as thoroughly as possible — and then relating that understanding in her essay. In contrast, the student from Massachusetts understood *originality* to be something she came up with herself, an idea she had on her own. As it turned out, the professor, who was from France, had a third definition: for him, *originality* meant the students were to read multiple sources and then come up with a critical point of their own about those sources. The students listened and then talked about what this all meant. The professor listened, too, and designed a handout for the class providing his own definition of *originality* and giving examples of student work he considered to be original along with an explanation of why he judged them to be so.

This brief example points to the challenges all writers face in trying to communicate across space, across languages, across cultures. While there are no foolproof rules, here are some tips for communicating with people from cultures other than your own:

- Don't hesitate to ask people to explain or even repeat a point if you're not absolutely sure you understand.
- Take care to be explicit about what you mean.
- Invite response — ask whether you're making yourself clear. This kind of back-and-forth is particularly easy (and necessary) in email.

24d Considering your authority as a writer

How should you sound to your readers — like an expert? a beginner? a subordinate? an angry employee or customer? a boss? The answer often depends on how much authority you as a writer have and how that authority relates to others. In the United States, students are often asked to establish authority in their writing—by drawing on certain kinds of personal experience, by reporting on research they or others have conducted, or by taking a position for which they can offer strong evidence and support. But this expectation about writerly authority is by no means universal. Indeed, some cultures view student writers as novices whose job is to reflect what they learn from their teachers—those who hold the most important knowledge, wisdom, and, hence, authority. One Japanese student, for example, said he was taught that it's rude to challenge a teacher: "Are you ever so smart that you should challenge the wisdom of the ages?"

As this student's comment reveals, a writer's tone also depends on his or her relationship with listeners and readers. In this student's case, the valued relationship is one of respect and deference, of what one Indonesian student called "good modesty." Similarly, a Navajo writer explained that he is extremely hesitant to disagree with or criticize a woman who is his elder: in his matriarchal community, he is expected to honor such elders. As a world writer, you need to remember that those you're addressing may hold very different attitudes about authority.

- Whom are you addressing, and what is your relationship to him or her?
- What knowledge are you expected to have? Is it appropriate for or expected of you to demonstrate that knowledge—and, if so, how?
- What is your goal—to answer a question? to make a point? to agree? something else?
- What tone is appropriate? If in doubt, show respect: politeness is rarely if ever inappropriate.

For more information on tone, see Chapter 4.

24e Considering your audience's expectations

In the United States, many audiences (and especially those in the academic and business worlds) expect a writer to get to the point as directly as possible and to take on the major responsibility of articulating that point efficiently and unambiguously. But not all audiences have such expectations. A Chinese student, for instance, who was considered a very good writer in China, found herself struggling in her American classes. Her problem was not with grammar or word choice or sentence structure; she was very proficient in all these. But comments by teachers left her confused: her writing, U.S. teachers said, was "vague" and "indirect,"

506

wtw

24f

LANGUAGE

Writing to the
World

with too much "beating around the bush." As it turned out, this kind of indirectness and subtlety was prized by her teachers in China, where readers and writers are expected to have more shared knowledge—and readers are thus expected to be able to "read between the lines" to understand what is being said.

The point of this story (and note how swiftly that point is made!) is that world writers must think carefully about whether audience members expect the writer to make the meaning of a text explicitly clear or, rather, expect to do some of the work themselves, supplying some of the information necessary to the meaning. A typical BBC news report, for example, provides an example of a writer-responsible text, one that puts the overwhelming responsibility on the writer to present an unambiguous message. Such a report begins with a clear overview of all the points to be covered, follows with a discussion of each of the major points in order, and ends with a brief summary. Many cultures organize information in a different, more reader-responsible, way, expecting that the audience will take more responsibility for understanding what is being said. Here are tips for thinking about reader and writer responsibility:

- What general knowledge do members of your audience have about your topic? What information do they expect—or need—you to provide?
- Do your audience members tend to be very direct, saying explicitly what they mean? Or are they more subtle, less likely to call a spade a spade? Look for cues to determine how much responsibility you have as the writer.

24f Considering what counts as evidence

How do you decide what evidence will best support your ideas? The answer depends, in large part, on how you define *evidence*. Americans generally give great weight to factual evidence. In doing research at a U.S. university, a Chinese student reports she was told time and time again by her instructors that "facts, and facts alone, provide the sure route to truth." While she learned to document her work in ways her U.S. professors found persuasive, she also continued to value the kinds of evidence favored back home, especially those based on authority and on allusion.

Differing concepts of what counts as evidence can lead to arguments that go nowhere. One well-known example of such a failed argument occurred in 1979, when Oriana Fallaci, an Italian journalist, was interviewing the Ayatollah Khomeini. Fallaci argued in a way common in North American and Western European cultures: she presented what she considered strong assertions backed up with facts ("Iran denies freedom to people. . . . Many people we can name have been put in prison and even executed, just for speaking out in opposition"). In his response, Khomeini relied on very different kinds of evidence: analogies ("Just as a finger with gangrene should be cut off so that it will not destroy the whole body, so should people who corrupt others be pulled out like weeds so they will not infect the whole field") and, above all, the authority of the Qur'an. Partly because of these differing beliefs about what counts as evidence, the interview ended in a shouting match, leading not to understanding but to ongoing and serious misunderstanding.

Two lessons all writers can learn from such examples of failed communication are to think carefully about how they use evidence in writing and to pay attention to what counts as evidence to members of other cultures.

- Do you rely on facts? concrete examples? firsthand experience?

- Do you include the testimony of experts? Which experts are valued most, and why?

- Do you cite religious or philosophical texts? proverbs or everyday wisdom? other sources?

- Do you use analogies as support? How much do they count?

- Once you determine what counts as evidence in your own thinking and writing, think about where you learned to use and value this kind of evidence. You can ask these same questions about the use of evidence by members of other cultures.

FOR COLLABORATION

Working with one or two classmates, brainstorm answers to the following questions, and be ready to report your answers to the class.

1. What do you think are the "good manners" of writing? How do you show politeness in writing?

2. In general, what kind of evidence is most persuasive to you?

wtw

508 24g

24g Considering organization

LANGUAGE

Writing to the
World

As you make choices about how to organize your writing, remember that cultural influences are at work here as well: the patterns that you find pleasing are likely to be ones that are deeply embedded in your own culture. The organizational patterns favored by U.S. engineers, for example, hold many similarities to the organizational system recommended by Cicero some two thousand years ago. Indeed, the predominant pattern, highly explicit and leaving little or nothing unsaid or unexplained, is probably familiar to most U.S. students: introduction and thesis, necessary background, overview of the parts to follow, systematic presentation of evidence, consideration of other viewpoints, and conclusion. If a piece of writing follows this pattern, Anglo-American readers ordinarily find it well organized or coherent, and they have been doing so for a very long time.

But writers who value different organizational patterns may not. To some, the writing done by U.S. engineers may seem overly simple. One writer from Chile, for instance, reports that this pattern of writing can even seem childish to those in her country, saying it's like "'This is a watch; the watch is brown; da-da; da-da.' For us, that's funny. I think that, for Americans, it must be funny the way I describe things." Indeed, this writer is accustomed to writing that is more elaborate, that sometimes digresses from the main point, and that is elliptical, not spelling out every connection from point A to point B.

Cultures that value indirection and subtlety tend to use patterns of organization that display these values. One common pattern in Korean writing, for example, includes an introduction; a topic with development; a tangential topic, again with development; and then a conclusion — with the thesis appearing only at the end.

Some cultures especially value repetition. It is common for some Arabic speakers, for example, to reiterate a major point from several different perspectives as a way of making that point.

When writing for world audiences, think about how you can organize material to get your message across effectively. One expert in international business communication recommends, for example, that businesspeople writing to others in Japan should state their requests indirectly — and only after a formal and respectful opening. There are no hard and fast rules to help you organize your writing for effectiveness across cultures, but here are a couple of options for you to consider:

- Determine when to state your thesis—at the beginning? at the end? somewhere else? not at all?
- Consider whether digressions are a good idea, a requirement, or best avoided with your intended audience.

24h Considering style

As with beauty, good style is most definitely in the eye of the beholder—and thus is always affected by language, culture, and rhetorical tradition. In fact, what constitutes effective style varies broadly across cultures and depends on the rhetorical situation—purpose, audience, and so on (see Chapter 2). Even so, there is one important style question to consider when writing across cultures: what level of formality is most appropriate? In the United States, a fairly informal style is often acceptable, even appreciated. Many cultures, however, tend to value more formality. When in doubt, therefore, it may be wise to err on the side of formality, especially in writing to elders or to those in authority.

- Be careful to use proper titles:

  Dr. Beverly Moss   Professor Jaime Mejia

- Avoid slang and informal structures such as fragments.
- Do not use first names in correspondence (even in email) unless invited to do so. Note, however, that an invitation to use a first name could come indirectly; if someone signs an email message or letter to you with his or her first name, you are implicitly invited to do the same.
- For international business email (as with print letters), use complete sentences and words; avoid contractions. Open with the salutation "Dear Mr./Ms. _____." Write dates by listing the day before the month and spelling out the name of the month rather than using a numeral (*7 June 2003*).

•— For more information on style in email messages, see Chapter 7.

Beyond formality, stylistic preferences vary widely. Many writers of Spanish, for example, show a preference for longer sentences than those written by English-speaking writers. Writers of Spanish also use more complex sentences and ornate language (which members of some cultures might find overdone or flowery—and others might find understated!). Japanese writing tends to be very polite and diplomatic, perhaps because the Japanese language has three forms—the honorific, the polite, and the everyday.

Other languages bring other stylistic differences. World writers take nothing about language for granted. To be an effective world writer, you

510

wtw

24h

LANGUAGE

Writing to the
World

will want to work to recognize and respect those differences as you move from culture to culture.

FOR COLLABORATION

Ask a classmate or acquaintance from a cultural and linguistic tradition different from your own to talk with you about the following questions.

1. How do you expect a piece of writing — say, a description — to be organized?

2. What are the characteristics of a pleasing style?

3. How do student writers represent themselves — as experts, novices, peers? in some other way?

Use the information you gather to sum up what you have learned about how others communicate, and bring your notes to class for discussion.

THINKING CRITICALLY ABOUT ASSUMPTIONS IN YOUR WRITING

Choose one or two recent essays or other pieces of writing, and examine them carefully, noting what you assume about what counts as persuasive evidence, good organization, and effective style. How do you represent yourself in relation to your audience? What other unstated assumptions about good writing can you identify?

Considering Others: Building Common Ground

25a Remembering the golden rule

As a child, you may have learned to "do to others what you would have them do to you." To that golden rule, we could add "say to others what you would have them say to you." Language has power. It can praise, delight, inspire. It can also hurt, offend, even destroy. That's one reason we refer to a *stinging* rebuke or a *cutting* remark. Remembering the golden rule of language use thus isn't about being politically correct. Rather, it is about being aware that language that offends others keeps them from identifying with you or even considering your ideas.

In many instances, avoiding such language is simple enough. We can safely assume, for instance, that no readers respond well to being referred to disparagingly — for example, as *slobs* or *nerds*. But other cases are more subtle and perhaps surprising. One student found, for example, that members of a group he had been referring to as *senior citizens* were irritated by that label, preferring more straightforward terms such as *elderly* or even *old*. Similarly, a recent survey of people with physical disabilities reported that most of them resented euphemisms like *physically challenged* because they saw them as trivializing their difficulties.

Because usage changes constantly and preferences vary, few absolute guidelines exist for using language that shows respect for differences and builds common ground. Two general rules, however, can help writers: consider

East is East, and West is West, and never the twain shall meet. . . .

You say toe-may-toe, and I say toe-mah-toe. . . .

These lines suggest a challenge every writer must face: many differences separate us. In the United States today, we are part of a richly diverse population representing just about every social, religious, linguistic, and cultural tradition imaginable — and yet all connected by a common citizenship. How can such different people ever build commonalities? Fortunately, careful language use can help us out. The words we use can and do build common ground, even if you say *toe-may-toe* and I say *toe-mah-toe*.

This chapter will get you started thinking about how your own language can work to respect differences and to build common ground with others. ■

511

→ What unstated assumptions might come between you and your readers? Look, for instance, for language implying approval or disapproval and for the ways you use *we, you,* and *they.* (25a and b)

→ Does any language used to describe others carry offensive stereotypes or connotations? (25b)

→ Have you checked for use of masculine pronouns to refer to members of both sexes and for any other uses of potentially sexist language? (25b1)

→ Are your references to race, religion, gender, sexual orientation, physical ability, age, and so on relevant or necessary to your discussion? If not, consider leaving them out. (25b2 and b3)

→ Are the terms you use to refer to groups accurate and acceptable? Because group labels and preferences are always changing, take care to use the most widely accepted terms. (25b2)

carefully the sensitivities and preferences of others, and watch for words that carry stereotypes and betray unintended assumptions.

25b Watching for stereotypes and other assumptions

Children like to play; U.S. citizens value freedom; people who do not finish high school fare less well in the job market than those who graduate. These broad statements contain **stereotypes,** standardized or fixed ideas about a group. To some extent, we all think in terms of stereotypes, and sometimes they can be helpful in making a generalization. Stereotyping any individual on the basis of generalizations about a group can be dangerous, however, for it can lead to inaccurate and even hurtful conclusions.

Stereotyping becomes especially evident in language, in the words we choose to refer to or describe others. Stereotyped language can, and often does, break the links between writers and readers — or between speakers and listeners. An instructor who notes a male student's absence from her class on the morning after a big frat party and remarks, "Ah, he must be in a frat," is stereotyping the student on the basis of assumptions about fraternity men. But such stereotyping may be far off the mark with this particular student — and with many other fraternity members. By indulging in it, this instructor may well be alienating some of her students and undermining her effectiveness as a teacher.

Very often based on half-truths, misunderstandings, and hand-me-down prejudices, stereotypes can lead to intolerance, bias, and bigotry. Even apparently positive or neutral ones can hurt, for they inevitably ignore the uniqueness of an individual.

Other kinds of unstated assumptions that enter into our thinking and writing destroy common ground by ignoring differences between others and ourselves. For example, a student whose paper for a religion seminar uses *we* to refer to Christians and *they* to refer to members of other religions had better be sure that all the class members and the instructor are Christian, or some of them may feel left out of this discussion and doubt the writer's credibility. In a letter to the editor of a newspaper about a current political issue, language implying that liberals are good and conservatives bad is likely to alienate some readers and prevent them from even considering the writer's argument about the specific issue.

Sometimes assumptions are so deeply ingrained that they have the effect of completely ignoring or "erasing" large groups of people, as students at the University of Kansas realized when they discovered that history books routinely reported only one survivor of General George Custer's Battle of Little Bighorn: Comanche, a horse (now stuffed and on display at their university). Several thousand Sioux survived that battle, yet the history books simply ignored them.

On the other hand, stereotypes and other assumptions often lead writers to mention a group affiliation unnecessarily when it has no relation to the point under consideration, as in *a woman bus driver* or *a Jewish doctor*. Decisions about whether to make a generalization about a group or to describe an individual as a member of a group are often difficult for writers. The following sections invite you to think about how your language can build — rather than destroy — common ground.

● For a discussion of online etiquette, see 7a.

1 Considering assumptions about gender

An elementary teacher in Toronto got increasingly tired of seeing hands go up every time the children sang the line in Canada's national anthem, "true patriot love in all thy sons command." "When do we get to the part about the daughters?" the children inevitably asked. As a result of such questions, the House of Commons voted on a bill to change the line — to "true patriot love in all our hearts command."

These children's questions point to the ways in which powerful and often invisible gender-related elements of language affect our thinking and our behavior. We now know, for instance, that many young women at one time were discouraged from pursuing careers in medicine or engineering at least partially because speakers of our language, following stereotyped assumptions about gender roles in society, always referred to hypothetical doctors or engineers as *he* (and then labeled any woman who worked as a doctor a *woman doctor,* as if to say, "She's an exception; doctors are normally male"). Equally problematic is the traditional use of *man* and *mankind* to refer to people of both sexes and the use of *he, him, his,* and *himself* to refer to people of unknown sex, as in *everyone must bring his own pencils.* Because such usage ignores half the human race — or at least seems to assume that the other half is more important — it hardly helps a writer build common ground. Similarly, labels like *male nurse* or *male secretary* may offend by reflecting stereotyped assumptions about proper roles for males.

■ *Revising sexist language*

Sexist language, those words and phrases that stereotype or ignore members of either sex or that unnecessarily call attention to gender, can usually be revised fairly easily. For example, there are several alternatives to the use of masculine pronouns to refer to persons of unknown sex. One option is to recast the sentence using plural forms.

▶ *Lawyers*
A lawyer must pass the bar exam before he can begin to practice.
                                         they

Another option is to substitute *he or she, him or her,* and so on.

▶ *or she*
A lawyer must pass the bar exam before he can begin to practice.

Yet another way to revise the sentence is to eliminate the pronouns.

▶ *beginning*
A lawyer must pass the bar exam before he can begin to practice.

INSTEAD OF	TRY USING
anchorman, anchorwoman	anchor
businessman	businessperson, business executive
chairman, chairwoman	chair, chairperson
congressman	member of Congress, representative

INSTEAD OF	TRY USING
mailman	mail carrier
male nurse	nurse
man, mankind	humans, human beings, humanity, the human race, humankind
manpower	workers, personnel
mothering	parenting
policeman, policewoman	police officer
salesman	salesperson
woman engineer	engineer

● For more discussion of nonsexist pronouns, see 35d.

EDITING FOR SEXIST LANGUAGE

1. Have you used *man* or *men* or words containing one of them to refer to people who may be female? If so, consider substituting another word — instead of *fireman*, for instance, try *firefighter*.

2. If you have mentioned someone's gender, is your doing so necessary? If you identify someone as a female architect, for example, do you (or would you) refer to someone else as a male architect? And if you then note that the female is an attractive blond mother of two, do you mention that the male is a muscular, square-jawed father of three? Unless gender and related matters — looks, clothes, parenthood — are relevant to your point, don't mention them.

3. Do you use any occupational stereotypes? Watch for the use of female pronouns for nurses, male ones for engineers, for example.

4. Have you used *he, him, his,* or *himself* to refer to people who may be female? Try revising with the help of the advice in 25b1.

5. Have you overused *he or she, him or her,* and so on? Frequent use of these pronoun pairs can bore or even irritate readers.

www ● bedford stmartins.com/ smhandbook

For additional exercises on assumptions about gender, click on

▶ **Exercise Central**
  ▶ **Using Language to Build Common Ground**

● **EXERCISE 25.1**

The following excerpt is taken from the 1968 edition of Dr. Benjamin Spock's *Baby and Child Care*. Read it carefully, noting any language we might today consider sexist. Then try bringing it up-to-date by revising the passage, substituting nonsexist language as necessary.

Feeling his oats. One year old is an exciting age. Your baby is changing in lots of ways—in his eating, in how he gets around, in what he wants to do and in how he feels about himself and other people. When he was little and helpless, you could put him where you wanted him, give him the playthings you thought suitable, feed him the foods you knew were best. Most of the time he was willing to let you be the boss, and took it all in good spirit. It's more complicated now that he is around a year old. He seems to realize that he's not meant to be a baby doll the rest of his life, that he's a human being with ideas and a will of his own.

When you suggest something that doesn't appeal to him, he feels he **must** assert himself. His nature tells him to. He just says No in words or actions, even about things that he likes to do. The psychologists call it "negativism"; mothers call it "that terrible No stage." But stop and think what would happen to him if he never felt like saying No. He'd become a robot, a mechanical man. You wouldn't be able to resist the temptation to boss him all the time, and he'd stop learning and developing. When he was old enough to go out into the world, to school and later to work, everybody else would take advantage of him, too. He'd never be good for anything.

2 Considering assumptions about race and ethnicity

Generalizations about racial and ethnic groups can result in especially harmful stereotyping. Such assumptions can be seen in statements that suggest, for instance, that all African Americans are musically talented, that all Asian Americans excel in math and science, or that all Germans are efficiency experts. Negative stereotypes, of course, are even more damaging. In building common ground, writers must watch for any language that ignores differences not only among individual members of a race or ethnic group but also among subgroups—for instance, the many nations to which American Indians belong or the diverse places from which Americans of Spanish-speaking ancestry have emigrated.

■ *Using preferred terms*

For writers, avoiding stereotypes and other assumptions based on race or ethnicity is only a first step. Beyond that lies the task of attempting to refer to any group in terms that its members actually desire. Doing so is sometimes not an easy task, for preferences change and even vary widely.

The word *colored,* for example, was once widely used in the United States to refer to Americans of African ancestry (in fact, it still appears in the name of the NAACP, the National Association for the Advancement of Colored People). By the 1950s, the preferred term had become

Negro; in the 1960s, however, *Black* came to be preferred by most, though certainly not all, members of that community. Then, in the late 1980s, some leaders of the American Black community urged that *Black* be replaced by *African American,* which is still widely used and respected.

Another example is the word *Oriental,* which was once used to refer to people of East Asian descent but is now often considered offensive. At the University of California at Berkeley, the Oriental Languages Department is now known as the East Asian Languages Department. An advocate of the change explained that *Oriental* is appropriate for objects — like rugs — but not for people.

Once widely preferred, the term *Native American* is being challenged by those who argue that the most appropriate way to refer to indigenous peoples is by the specific name of the tribe or pueblo, such as *Chippewa, Pojoaque, Crow,* or *Diné.* In Alaska and parts of Canada, many indigenous peoples once referred to as *Eskimos* came to prefer *Inuit* or a specific term such as *Tlinget, Haida,* or *Tsimshian.* More recently, many North American indigenous peoples use the term *First Nations.* If you do not know the name of a specific tribe or group, it's probably wise to use *American Indian* or *Indigenous Peoples.*

Among Americans of Spanish-speaking descent, the preferred terms include *Chicano/Chicana, Hispanic, Latin American, Latino/Latina, Mexican American, Dominican,* and *Puerto Rican,* to name a few.

Clearly, then, ethnic terminology changes often enough to challenge the most careful writer. The best advice may be to consider your words carefully, to *listen* for the way members of groups refer to themselves (or *ask* their preferences), and to check any term you are unsure of in a current dictionary. The *Random House Webster's College Dictionary* includes particularly helpful usage notes about racial and ethnic designations.

3 Considering other kinds of difference

Gender, race, and ethnicity are among the most frequent challenges to a writer seeking to find common ground with readers, but you will face many others as well. The following section discusses some of them.

■ *Age*

Mention age if it is relevant, but be aware that age-related terms can carry derogatory connotations (*matronly, teenybopper, well-preserved,* and so on). Although describing Mr. Fry as *elderly but still active* may sound polite to you, chances are Mr. Fry would prefer being called *an active*

518

cg

25b

LANGUAGE

Considering
Others: Building
Common Ground

seventy-eight-year-old — or just *a seventy-eight-year-old,* which eliminates the unstated assumption of surprise that he is active "at his age."

■ *Class*

Because you may not usually think about class as consciously as you do about age or race, for example, you should take special care to examine your words for stereotypes or assumptions about class. Such was the case in a *New York Times* column titled "Young, Privileged, and Unemployed," written by a young woman who had lost her high-paying professional job. Unable to find other "meaningful work," the author wrote, she and others like her had been forced to accept "absurd" jobs like cleaning houses and baby-sitting.

The column provoked a number of angry letters to the *Times,* like this one: "So the young and privileged are learning what we of the working classes have always understood too well: there is no entitlement in life. We have always taken the jobs you label 'absurd.' Our mothers are the women who clean your mothers' houses. . . ." Thus did the column writer destroy common ground with her readers by assuming that cleaning houses is an "absurd" way to make a living and that education or social standing entitles people to more "meaningful" occupations.

As a writer, then, do not assume that all your readers share your background or values — that your classmates' families all own their homes, for instance. And avoid using any words — *redneck, trailer trash,* and the like — that are bound to alienate.

■ *Geographical areas*

Though stereotypes related to geographical areas are not always insulting or even unpleasant, they are very often clichéd and exaggerated. New Englanders are not all thrifty and tight-lipped; Florida offers more than retirement and tourism; Texans do not all wear cowboy boots and Stetson hats; midwesterners are not all hard-working; many Californians neither care about nor participate in the latest trends. Check your writing carefully to be sure it doesn't make such simplistic assumptions.

Check also that you use geographical terms like the following accurately:

> *America, American.* Although many people use these words to refer to the United States alone, be aware that such usage will not necessarily be acceptable to people from Canada, Mexico, and Central or South America.

British, English. British should be used to refer to the island of Great Britain, which includes England, Scotland, and Wales, or to the United Kingdom of Great Britain and Northern Ireland. In general, do not use *English* for these broader senses.

Arab. This term refers only to people of Arabic-speaking descent. Note that Iran is not an Arab nation; its people speak Farsi, not Arabic. Note also that *Arab* is not synonymous with *Muslim* or *Moslem* (a believer in Islam). Most (but not all) Arabs are Muslims, but many Muslims (those in Pakistan, for example) are not Arab.

▪ *Physical ability or health*

One question to ask yourself when writing about a person with a serious illness or disability is whether to mention the disability at all if it is not relevant to your discussion. If you do, consider whether the words you use carry negative connotations. You might choose, for example, to say someone *uses* a wheelchair rather than to say he or she *is confined to* one. Similarly, you might note a subtle but meaningful difference between calling someone a *person with AIDS,* rather than an *AIDS victim.* Mentioning the person first, the disability second — for example, referring to a *child with diabetes* rather than a *diabetic child* or a *diabetic* — is always a good idea. On the other hand, the survey of people with disabilities that was mentioned earlier shows that you also must be careful not to minimize the importance of a disability.

**www ● bedford
stmartins.com/
smhandbook**

For an essay
on how using
computers can help
those with learning
disabilities improve
their writing in
ways not possible
with pen and
paper, click on
▶ Links
  ▶ Considering
    Disabilities

CONSIDERING DISABILITIES: Know Your Readers

The American Council on Education reports that nearly 10 percent of all first-year college students — some 155,000 — identified themselves as having one or more disabilities. As this figure suggests, living with a disability is more the norm than many previously thought. Effective writers learn as much as possible about their readers and any disabilities they may have so that they can find ways to build common ground.

▪ *Religion*

Religious stereotypes are very often inaccurate and unfair. Roman Catholics hold a wide spectrum of views on abortion, for example, Muslim women do not all wear veils, and many Baptists are not fundamen-

520

cg

25b

LANGUAGE

Considering
Others: Building
Common Ground

talists. In fact, not everyone believes in or practices a religion at all, so be careful of such assumptions. As in other cases, do not use religious labels without considering their relevance to your point, and make every effort to get them right — for example, *Reformed* churches but *Reform* synagogues.

■ *Sexual orientation*

Partly because sexual orientation is a topic that was avoided in most public discourse until recent decades, the stereotypes and assumptions that surround it are particularly deep-seated and, often, unconscious. Writers who wish to build common ground, therefore, should not assume that readers all share any one sexual orientation — that everyone is attracted to the opposite sex, for example.

As with any label, reference to sexual orientation should be governed by context. Someone writing about Representative Barney Frank's economic views would probably have little if any reason to refer to his sexual orientation. On the other hand, a writer concerned with diversity in U.S. government might find it important to note that Frank was one of the first members of Congress to make his homosexuality public.

FOR COLLABORATION

Like you, generations of college students have found themselves in classes filled with people both like them and different from them. Take time now to examine where you've come from — your age, ethnicity, hometown, religion, and so on. Then do the same for one or more of your classmates. Write a paragraph about the differences *and* the common ground you see. Then study your paragraph for any assumptions your language reveals. Finally, meet with two other classmates to read your paragraphs and share what you have learned about finding common ground.

THINKING CRITICALLY ABOUT HOW LANGUAGE CAN BUILD COMMON GROUND

The following poem, published in 1949, is partially about finding common ground. Identify those places where the speaker asserts his own individuality and those where he forges common ground with readers. How does the speaker address, perhaps indirectly, issues of racism? How does he deal with issues of difference without insulting readers? Does this poem relate to your experience with others? If so, how?

Theme for English B

The instructor said,

> Go home and write
> a page tonight.
> And let that page come out of you —
> Then, it will be true.

I wonder if it's that simple?

I am twenty-two, colored, born in Winston-Salem.
I went to school there, then Durham, then here
to this college on the hill above Harlem.

I am the only colored student in my class.
The steps from the hill lead down to Harlem,
through a park, then I cross St. Nicholas,
Eighth Avenue, Seventh, and I come to the Y,
the Harlem Branch Y, where I take the elevator
up to my room, sit down, and write this page:

It's not easy to know what is true for you or me
at twenty-two, my age. But I guess I'm what
I feel and see and hear. Harlem, I hear you:
hear you, hear me — we two — you, me talk on this page.
(I hear New York, too.) Me — who?
Well, I like to eat, sleep, drink, and be in love.
I like to work, read, learn, and understand life.
I like a pipe for a Christmas present,
or records — Bessie, bop, or Bach.

I guess being colored doesn't make me not like
the same things other folks like who are other races.
So will my page be colored that I write?
Being me, it will not be white.
But it will be
a part of you, instructor.
You are white —
yet a part of me, as I am a part of you.
That's American.

Sometimes perhaps you don't want to be a part of me.
Nor do I often want to be a part of you.
But we are, that's true!
As I learn from you,
I guess you learn from me —
although you're older — and white —
and somewhat more free.

This is my page for English B.

– LANGSTON HUGHES

26

◥ Considering Varieties of Language

A group of college students gathers outside a deli. "I'm having a hero," says one. "I'm ordering a submarine," says another. "You mean a hoagie?" asks a third. You might know this sandwich as a grinder, a poor boy, a cubano—or some other name. The differences suggest that although all speakers of English share the same language, within this broad category are many differences. Indeed, many varieties of spoken and written English exist, distinguished by pronunciation, vocabulary, and rhetorical and grammatical choices.

In addition to the many varieties of English, many other languages are spoken in the United States. Linguist Dell Hymes suggests that perhaps this multilingualism is what the Founders meant by choosing the Latin motto "E pluribus unum" (out of many, one): "E pluribus unum—bilingualism is . . . only as far away as the nearest nickel."

This chapter will help you consider varieties of English and their use in academic writing. ∎

26a Recognizing different varieties of English

Everyone reading this text uses one or more varieties of English, whether they are those characteristic of particular *geographic regions,* of particular *occupations or professions,* or of particular *social, cultural, or ethnic groups.* In a given day, for example, the author of this textbook might use a midwestern regional variety of English when talking with a group of students on her campus; an occupational variety characterized by highly specialized vocabulary when preparing a scholarly journal article; and an eastern Tennessee regional variety, which is strongly influenced by African American vernacular English, when talking on the phone with her grandmother. In each instance, the chosen language is appropriate. The question becomes, then, *when* to use a particular variety of English or shift from one variety to another—when to insert eastern Tennessee or African American vernacular patterns into a formal essay, for example, or when to use language from work in a conversation with friends.

Sometimes, in fact, our choices are limited or highly circumscribed by various kinds of pressures. An extreme but by no means isolated example is the tendency of many in our society to discriminate against those who fail to use an expected variety of English. Not only is there discrimination against those who don't speak "standard" English; there is also the rejection in other communities of those who sound affected, too proper, or la-di-da. Used appropriately and wisely, however, *all* varieties of English can serve many purposes.

> **FOR MULTILINGUAL WRITERS: Using Appropriate Words**
>
> You may sometimes be hard pressed to know what words are most *appropriate* in U.S. English, and you may not be familiar with many regional, occupational, or social varieties. In such instances, ask your instructor or classmates for advice.

26b Using "standard" varieties of English

One variety of English, often referred to as the "standard," or "standard academic," is that taught prescriptively in schools, used in the national media, and written and spoken widely by those thought to wield the most social and economic power. It is, in addition, the variety of English represented in this and many other textbooks. As the language used in most public institutions and in business, this variety of English is one you will no doubt want to be completely familiar with — all the while recognizing, however, that it is only one of many effective and powerful varieties of our language. As the linguist Steven Pinker says, "It makes sense to have a standard in the same way it makes sense for everyone to drive on the right-hand side of the road. But it's different from saying that the right side is the only true and justified side to drive on." In fact, the right-hand side of the road is not "right" in countries where the standard is to drive on the left. Similarly, what is agreed on as standard in U.S. English will not always be standard elsewhere.

But even standard English is hardly a monolith; the standard varies according to purpose and audience, from the very formal English used in academic writing and in prepared speeches to the informal English characteristic of casual conversation. Thus the notion that there is one absolutely correct and standard way to say or write something is in important ways a myth. Nevertheless, within this variation, a recognizable set of practices and conventions exists. These practices and conventions go by the shorthand name of standard English.

For more on the characteristics of standard academic English, see 2e.

var

26c

524

LANGUAGE

Considering
Varieties of
Language

FOR MULTILINGUAL WRITERS: *Being Aware of Global English*

Like other world languages, English is used in many countries, so it results in many global varieties. For example, if you have studied English outside the United States, you may well have learned a British variety. British English differs somewhat from U.S. English in certain vocabulary (*bonnet* for "hood" of a car), syntax (*to hospital* rather than "to the hospital"), spelling (*centre* rather than "center"), and of course pronunciation. If you have learned a British variety of English, you will want to recognize the ways in which it differs from the U.S. "standard."

26c   Using ethnic varieties of English

Whether you are American Indian or trace your ancestry to Germany, Italy, Ireland, Africa, China, Mexico, or elsewhere, chances are that some part of your heritage lives on in the English language. Take a look, for example, at how a Hawaiian writer uses an ethnic variety of English to paint a picture of young teens hearing a frightening, goose-bump-raising (or what he calls a "chicken skin") story about sharks from their grandmother.

> "—So, rather dan being rid of da shark, da people were stuck with many little ones, for dere mistake."
> Then Grandma Wong wen' pause, for dramatic effect, I guess, and she wen' add, "Dis is one of dose times. Dis is da time of da mano." She wen' look at my kid brother 'Analu and said, "Da time of da sharks."
> Those words ended another of Grandma's chicken skin stories. The stories she told us had been passed on to her by her grandmother, who had heard them from *her* grandmother. Always skipping a generation.
> – RODNEY MORALES, "When the Shark Bites"

**www • bedford
stmartins.com/
smhandbook**

For links to articles
and Web sites on
many language
policy issues, such
as the English Only
movement, click on

▶ Links
   ▶ Language
      Varieties

Notice that the narrator of the story, the brother of 'Analu, uses both standard and ethnic varieties of English—presenting information necessary to the story line mostly in more formal standard English and using a more informal, local ethnic variety to represent spoken language.

This passage comes from fiction, but writers sometimes shift among varieties of English in nonfiction writing as well. Geneva Smitherman is particularly effective at using African American vernacular English to get the reader's attention, to create emphasis, and to make her point, all at the same time.

var

26d 525

LANGUAGE

Using
Occupational
Varieties of English

Before about 1959 (when the first study was done to change black speech patterns), Black English had been primarily the interest of university academics, particularly the historical linguists and cultural anthropologists. In recent years, though, the issue has become a very hot controversy, and there have been articles on Black Dialect in the national press as well as in the educational research literature. We have had pronouncements on black speech from the NAACP and the Black Panthers, from highly publicized scholars of the Arthur Jensen–William Shockley bent, from executives of national corporations such as Greyhound, and from housewives and community folk. I mean, really, it seem like everybody and they momma done had something to say on the subject!

    – GENEVA SMITHERMAN, *Talkin and Testifyin*

In the last sentence of her paragraph, Smitherman shifts into the African American vernacular English she is discussing and lets readers hear what she has been talking about. "Listen up," this shift says to the reader, "I'm making an important point here." And it dramatically illustrates that point by summarizing the content of the preceding academic language.

In each of these examples, the writers have full command of standard academic English, and yet at times they choose to shift to other varieties. In each case, one important reason for the shift is to demonstrate that the writer is a member of the community whose language he or she is representing and thus to build credibility with others in the community.

Take care, however, in using the language of communities other than your own. Used inappropriately, such language can have an opposite effect: that of destroying credibility and alienating your audience.

> **FOR MULTILINGUAL WRITERS: Using the Language of Many Communities**
>
> If English is your second, third, or fourth language, you may often find yourself using the language of communities other than your own. Even writers who are perfectly fluent in several languages remark on the difficulty of switching linguistic gears. For information on how to establish credibility in your writing, see 13d and 24d.

26d Using occupational varieties of English

From the fast-food business to taxi driving, from architecture to zoology, every job has its own special variety of English. Examples abound, from specialized words (*hermeneutics* in literary studies) to invented

var

526

26d

LANGUAGE

Considering
Varieties of
Language

words (*quark* in physics). Here is an example from the computer world about how Extensible Markup Language (XML) is changing the way databases are created and making them more sophisticated:

> Most database servers are on a collision course with XML. The move to XML is a natural tie-in with a new approach to computing—deploying database-enabled Web applications running on application servers in place of stand-alone Windows programs. XML is causing database vendors to rethink their direction from the ground up, and the SQL language itself could well be on the way out in a few years, potentially to be replaced by an XML-based language called *XML Query,* now in development.
>
> —Timothy Dyck, "Clash of the Titans"

The writer here uses technical abbreviations (*XML, SQL*) as well as ordinary words that have special meanings, such as *database-enabled.*

Even within a particular occupation, there is room for variety. The language that sportscasters use, for instance, varies depending on whether the announcer is giving play-by-play commentary or color commentary.

Play-by-Play Announcer:	Second and nine. Brett Favre to throw it. Ahman Green hauls it in and then fumbles. Adam Archuleta recovers for St. Louis.
Color Commentator:	This could be bad news for the Packers if Favre throws interceptions. But remember how well he threw against the Forty-Niners—sixteen of twenty-one. As he said later, "It's do or die in the play-offs."
Play-by-Play Announcer:	And it's a twelve-yard run by Archuleta.

Notice that the play-by-play commentary strings together units of words that exhibit combinations not found in ordinary language but that here are visually and linguistically meaningful to those watching the game. In addition, the play-by-play announcer provides specific technical information (*a twelve-yard run*) and uses technical vocabulary (*second and nine, fumbles*). The color commentator, on the other hand, speaks in nearly complete sentences, provides interesting but tangentially related information, and uses very little technical vocabulary. These differences reflect the purposes of each announcer: one tries to sketch in exactly what is happening on the field, the other to color that sketch by commenting on it and on the players involved.

"Ever'body says words different," said Ivy. "Arkansas folks says 'em different from Oklahomy folks says 'em different. And we seen a lady from Massachusetts, an' she said 'em differentest of all. Couldn' hardly make out what she was sayin'." — JOHN STEINBECK, *The Grapes of Wrath*

Thus does Ivy point to the existence and significance of regional varieties of English. Like Ivy — and every other speaker of English — your language has been affected by region. In writing, such regional language provides an effective means of evoking a character or place.

Garrison Keillor, for instance, has become famous for his Lake Wobegon stories, which are peppered with the English spoken in parts of Minnesota. When Keillor says "Gimme a Wendy's," he refers not to a kind of hamburger but to Saint Wendell's beer, "brewed by the Dimmers family at the Old Dimmers Brewery in nearby Saint Wendell's for five generations."

In writing of her native Vermont, a student writer included the following piece of dialogue:

> "There'll be some fine music on the green tonight, don't ya know?"
> "Well, I sure do want to go."
> "So don't I!"

In both these instances, the regional English creates a homespun effect and captures some of the language used in a particular place.

Selected to capture attention, to amuse, and to evoke the sounds of a particular place, the language in the following passage from a cookbook is characteristic of rural Alabama and other areas of Appalachia:

> Then there's Big Reba Culpepper, big because there's Little Reba also; Big Reba lives in Burnt Corn, Alabama. She is famous countrywide for Reba's Rainbow Icebox Cake. Not too far from Burnt Corn is a place called Flea Hop, Alabama. Big Reba said she has a relative buried "in a small family-type cemetery right out on the edge of town. He was some kind of Civil War hero and when he died he was a very rich man." His grave was richly and clearly marked with a big bronze obelisk "that went way up high," Reba said, "and all his wives (six of them), children, and grandchildren were buried within spittin' distance of his monument. The old cemetery was all growed up with pine trees and needed a whole lot of attention to make it look halfway decent," Reba said. . . . "So I took it on myself to get up a cemetery cleaning party, with rakes, shovels and hoes, fried chicken, Hoppin' John, biscuits, ice tea and, of course, my

var

528 **26f**

LANGUAGE

Considering
Varieties of
Language

famous Rainbow Icebox Cake, enough to kill us all. We loaded down the car and took off like Moody's goose for Flea Hop, Alabama."

– ERNEST MATTHEW MICKLER

In this example, the use of particular terms (*Hoppin' John,* for instance), expressions (*within spittin' distance, like Moody's goose*), and grammatical structures (*all growed up*) depicts regional pronunciations and rhythms, thus helping to capture the flavor of Big Reba's language as well as of Burnt Corn, Alabama. Notice that the regional language here is all *quoted* — that is, it is all spoken language.

● **EXERCISE 26.1**

Try revising one of this chapter's examples of ethnic, occupational, or regional English. First, try to identify the purpose and audience for the original passage. Then rewrite the passage in order to remove all evidence of any variety of English other than the so-called standard. Compare your revised version with the original and with those produced by some of your classmates. What differences do you notice in tone (is it more formal? more distant? something else?) and in overall impression? Which version seems most appropriate for the intended audience and purpose? Which do you prefer — and why?

CONSIDERING DISABILITIES: American Sign Language

One variety of language that is becoming increasingly popular on college campuses is American Sign Language (ASL), a fairly young language that began in this country around 1817. You may have seen ASL performers on television or seen a live ASL poetry performance or workshop. If so, you will have been introduced to this powerful form of expression.

26f Bringing in other languages

Sometimes it may be appropriate for someone writing in English to use another language. You might do so for the same reasons you would use different varieties of English: to represent the actual words of a speaker, to make a point, to connect with your audience, to get the readers' attention.

See how Gerald Haslam uses Spanish to capture his great-grand-mother's words as well as to make a point about his relationship to her.

> *"Expectoran su sangre!"* exclaimed Great-grandma when I showed her the small horned toad I had removed from my breast pocket. I turned toward my mother, who translated: "They spit blood."
>
> *"De los ojos,"* Grandma added. "From their eyes," mother explained, herself uncomfortable in the presence of the small beast.
>
> I grinned, "Awwwwwww."
>
> But my Great-grandmother did not smile. *"Son muy tóxicos,"* she nodded with finality. Mother moved back an involuntary step, her hands suddenly busy at her breast. "Put that thing down," she ordered.
>
> "His name's John," I said.   – GERALD HASLAM, *California Childhood*

On some occasions, a writer may use a particularly apt foreign phrase that doesn't seem easily translatable or one that seems appropriate untranslated. See how the novelist Michele Herman uses Yiddish to evoke another grandmother's world.

> "Skip *shabes*?" Rivke chuckled. "I don't think this is possible. Once a week comes *shabes*. About this a person doesn't have a choice."
>
> "What I *mean*" — Myra's impatience was plain — "is skip the preparation. It's too much for you, it tires you out."
>
> *"Ach,"* Rivke said. "Too much for me it isn't." This wasn't true. For some time she had felt that it really was too much for her. It was only for *shabes* that she cooked; the rest of the week she ate cold cereal, fruit, pot cheese, crackers.   – MICHELE HERMAN, *Missing*

In this passage, Rivke's syntax — the inversion of word order (*Once a week comes shabes,* for example, and *Too much for me it isn't*) — reflects Yiddish rhythms. In addition, the use of the Yiddish *shabes* carries a strong association with a religious institution, one that would be lost if it were translated to "sabbath." It is not "sabbath" to Rivke; it is *shabes*.

FOR COLLABORATION

We all shift regularly among varieties of English, often automatically and especially in speech, in response to changing situations and audiences. Working with a classmate, try listening to yourselves talk — at work, with parents or others in authority, with close friends, and so on. Each of you should take notes on your own use of language by jotting down any words and patterns that are from languages other than English or that are characteristic of a region or a job or a cultural group. Then spend half an hour or so comparing notes, asking which of these you might use in writing as well as in speaking. Why would you use them, and for what effect? Go on to list all the differences you

var

530 **26g**

LANGUAGE

Considering
Varieties of
Language

can find between the two of you, and decide which of these differences are due to regional, occupational, ethnic, or other varieties of English. Bring the results of your exploration to class for discussion.

26g Using varieties of language in academic writing

The key to shifting among varieties of English and among languages is appropriateness: when will such a shift reach your audience and help you make a particular point? Certain common college writing assignments—for example, writing about a person or place; writing based on sources; and oral presentation—might provide the opportunity to bring varieties of English or other languages into your academic writing.

See how an anthropologist weaves together regional and standard academic English in writing about one Carolina community.

> For Roadville, schooling is something most folks have not gotten enough of, but everybody believes will do something toward helping an individual "get on." In the words of one oldtime resident, "Folks that ain't got no schooling don't get to be nobody nowadays."
>
> – SHIRLEY BRICE HEATH, *Ways with Words*

Note how Heath takes care to let a resident of Roadville speak her mind—and in her own words. She does so to be faithful to the person she is quoting as well as to capture some of the flavor of the spoken language.

In the following passage, a linguist uses Spanish in her discussion of literacy in a Mexican community in Chicago:

> *Gracia* (grace, wit) is used to refer to wittiness in talk; people who *tiene gracia* (have grace, are witty) are seen as clever and funny. Not everyone illustrates this quality, but those who do are obvious from the moment they speak. As one middle-aged male said,
>
> > . . . *cuando ellos empiezan a hablar, desde el momento que los oyes hablar, tienen gracia. Entonces, la gente que tiene gracia, se va juntando gente a oírlos. Y hay gente más desabrida, diría yo. No tiene, no le quedan sus chistes. Aunque cuente uno una charrita . . . ya no te vas a reír igual.*
>
> (. . . when they start to speak, from the moment that you hear them speak, they are witty. So then, the people who are witty begin to have a listening crowd gather about them. And then there are people who are more boring, I would say. They don't have, their jokes just don't make it. Even though they may tell a joke . . . you're not going to laugh in the same manner.)
>
> – MARCIA FARR, "Essayist Literacy and Other Verbal Performances"

var
26g 531

LANGUAGE
Using Varieties of
Language in
Academic Writing

Here Farr provides a translation of the Spanish, for she expects that many of her readers will not know Spanish. She evokes the language of the community she describes, however, by presenting the Spanish first.

Remember that using different languages and varieties of English can be a good way to reach out to an audience, as in the pope's use of various languages, but it can also exclude and alienate listeners or readers. Such a danger is particularly great when you shift to language that your audience may not understand or that is not your own. In such cases, you might be seen as attempting to keep others out or to speak for others rather than letting them speak for themselves.

■ *Translating*

The question of whether or not to translate words or passages from another language into English depends on your purpose and audience. In general, you should not assume that all your readers will understand the other language. So in most cases, including a translation (as Marcia Farr does) is appropriate. Occasionally, however, the words from the other language will be clear from the context (as is *shabes* in Michele Herman's passage). A writer might at times leave something untranslated to make a point — to let readers know what it's like not to understand, for example.

To translate, as a general rule, underline or italicize foreign words, and put the translation in roman type, enclosed in parentheses or quotation marks.

THINKING CRITICALLY ABOUT LANGUAGE VARIETY

The following description of a supper features English characteristic of the Florida backwoods in the 1930s. Using this passage as an example, write a description of a memorable meal or other event from your daily life. Try to include some informal dialogue. Then look at the language you used — do you use more than one variety of English, and, if so, which ones? What effect does your use of language have on your description?

> Jody heard nothing; saw nothing but his plate. He had never been so hungry in his life, and after a lean winter and a slow spring . . . his mother had cooked a supper good enough for the preacher. There were poke-greens with bits of white bacon buried in them; sandbuggers made of potato and onion and the cooter he had found crawling yesterday; sour orange biscuits and at his mother's elbow the sweet potato pone. He was torn between his desire for more biscuits and another sandbugger and the knowledge, born of painful experience, that if he ate them, he would suddenly have no room for pone. The choice was plain. — MARJORIE KINNAN RAWLINGS, *The Yearling*

27

⬇ Considering Diction

One restaurant's "down-home beef stew" may look and taste much like another restaurant's "boeuf bourguignon," but in each case the choice of language aims to say something not only about the food but also about the restaurant serving it. The difference is a matter of **diction** — literally, how you say or express something.

Effective diction involves many issues discussed elsewhere in this book, such as being concise, strengthening your vocabulary, and using varieties of English or other languages. This chapter discusses other aspects of good diction including choosing language appropriate to your purpose, topic, and audience; choosing words with the right denotations and connotations; balancing general and abstract words with specific and concrete ones; and using figurative language. ■

27a Choosing words carefully

Musing on the many possible ways to describe a face, Ford Madox Ford notes,

> That a face resembles a Dutch clock has been said too often; to say that it resembles a ham is inexact and conveys nothing; to say that it has the mournfulness of an old smashed-in meat tin, cast away on a waste building lot, would be smart — but too much of that sort of thing would become a nuisance. – FORD MADOX FORD

Ford here implies a major point about diction: effective word choice can be made only on the basis of what is appropriate to the writer's purpose, to the topic, and to the audience. What is appropriate may vary from one region to another, from one occupation to another, and from one social or ethnic group to another. In addition, the level of formality will vary depending on what is appropriate for a particular topic and audience. In an email or letter to a friend or close associate, informal language is often appropriate. For most academic and professional writing, however, more formal language is appropriate because you are addressing people you do not know well. Compare the following responses to a request for information about a job candidate:

→ Check to see that your language reflects the appropriate level of formality for your audience, purpose, and topic. If you use slang or colloquial language (such as *yeah*), is it appropriate? Is your language sufficiently courteous? (27a)

→ Check to be sure your audience will understand any jargon or other technical language. If not, either define the jargon or replace it with words that will be understood. (27a2)

→ Check for any use of pompous language, inappropriate euphemisms, or doublespeak, and revise accordingly. (27a3)

→ Consider the connotations of words carefully to be sure they convey your intended meaning. If you say someone is *pushy*, be sure you mean to be critical; otherwise, use a word like *assertive*. (27b)

→ Be sure to use both general and concrete words. If you are writing about the general category of beds, for example, do you give enough concrete detail (*an antique four-poster bed*)? (27c)

→ Look for clichés, and replace them with fresher language. (27d)

EMAIL TO SOMEONE YOU KNOW WELL

Myisha is great—hire her if you can!

LETTER OF RECOMMENDATION TO SOMEONE YOU DO NOT KNOW

I am pleased to recommend Myisha Fisher. She will bring good ideas and extraordinary energy to your organization.

In deciding on the right words to use in a particular piece of writing, a writer needs to be aware of both the possibilities and the pitfalls of different kinds of language. Some specific kinds to keep in mind are slang and colloquial language; technical language; and pompous language, euphemisms, and doublespeak.

1 Slang and colloquial language

Slang, or extremely informal language, is often confined to a relatively small group and usually becomes obsolete rather quickly. Some slang gains wide use (*duh, dotcoms, face plant*); it is often colorful or amusing (why pay with a dollar bill when you can hand over a *dead president* or a *frogskin?*). **Colloquial language,** such as *a lot, in a bind,* or *snooze,* is less informal, more widely used, and longer lasting than slang.

Slang and colloquial language can expose a writer to the risk of not being understood or of not being taken seriously. If you are writing for a general audience about arms-control negotiations, for example, and you use the term *nukes* to refer to nuclear missiles, some readers may not know what you mean, and others may be distracted or irritated by what they see as a frivolous reference to a deadly serious subject.

● **EXERCISE 27.1**

Choose something or someone to describe — a favorite cousin, a stranger on the bus, an automobile, a musical instrument, whatever strikes your fancy. Describe your subject using colloquial language and slang. Then rewrite the description, this time using neither of these. Read the two passages aloud, and note what different effects each creates.

2 Technical language

Some kinds of technical language originate in particular fields that have created special vocabularies or given common words special meaning. Businesspeople talk about *greenmail* and *upside movement,* biologists about *nucleotides* and *immunodestruction,* and baseball fans about *fielder's choices* and *suicide bunts.* You need to judge any use of technical language very carefully, making sure that your audience will understand your terms and replacing or defining those that they will not. Technical language can be divided into two overlapping categories: neologisms and jargon.

■ *Neologisms*

Defined as new words that have not yet found their way into dictionaries, **neologisms** can be very helpful to writers, especially in the sciences and applied disciplines. Terms like *thermosiphon hypertext,* for example, could not be easily replaced except by a much longer and more complex explanation. Some neologisms, however, do not meet a real need. Words like *deaccess* and *anticipointment* could easily be replaced by existing words or phrases that general readers would understand.

Jargon is the special vocabulary of a trade or profession, enabling members to speak and write concisely to one another. It should be reserved as much as possible for a specific technical audience. Here is an example of jargon used inappropriately in writing addressed to general readers and then revised to eliminate some of the jargon terms and define others:

JARGON

The VDTs in composition were down last week, so we had to lay out on dummies and crop and size the art with a wheel.

REVISED FOR A GENERAL AUDIENCE

The video display terminals were not working last week in the composing room, where models of the newspaper pages are made up for printing, so we had to arrange the contents of each page on a large cardboard sheet and use a wheel, a kind of circular slide rule, to figure out the size and shape of the pictures and other illustrations.

Like all jargon, the terms emerging in the digital age can be irritating and incomprehensible—or extremely helpful. If the jargon is concrete and specific, it can help clarify concepts, providing a useful shorthand for an otherwise lengthy explanation. Saying "Sorry, but for the time being I'm limited to asynchronous communication, primarily email" sends a pretty straightforward message, one that is faster to read than "Sorry, but for the time being I'm limited to the kinds of electronic communication in which there's a delay between the sending and receiving of messages, and primarily to email."

Frequently used terms (such as *asynchronous communication* and *email*) are the ones online writers should know. Other terms, like the jargon in this sentence—*Savvy wavelet compression is the fiber signpost of the virtual chillout room*—may be appropriate for techies talking to one another, but they are not very useful to those trying to communicate with a nontechnical or general audience. Before you use technical jargon, remember your readers: if they will not understand the terms, or if you don't know them well enough to judge, then take the time to say what you need to say in everyday language.

3 Pompous language, euphemisms, and doublespeak

Pompous language is unnecessarily formal for the purpose, audience, or topic. Hence it often gives writing an insincere or unintentionally humorous tone, making the writer's idea seem less significant or believable.

POMPOUS

Pursuant to the August 9 memorandum regarding petroleum supply exigencies, it is incumbent upon us to endeavor to make maximal utilization of telephonic communication in lieu of personal visitation.

REVISED

As of August 9, shortages of petroleum require us to use the telephone rather than make personal visits whenever possible.

EDITING FOR POMPOUS LANGUAGE

While formal language can be useful in many writing situations, sometimes writers use overly formal words in an attempt to sound like experts, and these puffed-up words can easily backfire.

INSTEAD OF	TRY USING
ascertain	find out
commence	begin
finalize	finish or complete
functionality	function
impact (as verb)	affect
methodology	method
operationalize	start; put into operation
optimal	best
parameters	boundaries
peruse	look at
ramp up	increase
utilize	use

Euphemisms are terms designed to make an unpleasant idea more attractive or acceptable. *Your position is being eliminated* seeks to soften the blow of being fired or laid off; the British call this being *declared redundant,* whereas Canadians refer to being *made surplus.* Other euphemisms include *pass on* for *die* and *sanitation engineer* for *garbage collector.*

Use euphemisms with great care. Although they can appeal to readers by showing that the writer is considering their feelings, they can also sound pompous or suggest a wishy-washy, timid, or evasive attitude.

Doublespeak, a word coined from the *newspeak* and *doublethink* of George Orwell's novel *1984*, is language used to hide or distort the truth. During the massive layoffs and cutbacks in the corporate and business worlds in recent years, companies continued to speak of firings and layoffs as *work reengineering, employee repositioning, proactive downsizing,* and *special reprogramming.* The public — and particularly those who lost their jobs — recognized this use of doublespeak.

FOR MULTILINGUAL WRITERS: Avoiding Fancy Diction

In writing standard academic English, which is fairly formal, you may be inclined to use the biggest and newest words in English that you know. Though your intention is good — to put new words to good use — you will be well advised to resist the temptation to use flowery or high-flown diction in your college writing. Academic writing calls first of all for clear, concise prose.

• EXERCISE 27.2

Revise each of these sentences to use formal language consistently. Example:

> Although   be enthusiastic   as soon as
> I can ~~get all enthused~~ about writing, ~~but~~ I sit down to write, ~~and~~ my mind
>   ^   ^   ^
> *immediately*   *blank.*
> goes ~~right to sleep~~.
>   ^   ^

1. Desdemona is a wimp; she just lies down and dies, accepting her death as inevitable.

2. All candidates strive for the same results: you try to make the other guy look pea-brained and to persuade voters that you're okay for the job.

3. Often, instead of firing an incompetent teacher, school officials will transfer the person to another school to avoid hassles.

4. The more she freaked out about his actions, the more he rebelled and continued doing what he pleased.

5. My family lived in Trinidad for the first ten years of my life, and we went through a lot, but when we came to America, we thought we had it made.

www • bedford
stmartins.com/
smhandbook

For additional exercises on levels of formality, click on

▶ Exercise Central
  ▶ Using
    Appropriate,
    Precise Language

27b Understanding denotation and connotation

Think of a stone tossed into a pool, and imagine the ripples spreading out from it, circle by circle. Or think of a note struck clear and clean and the multiple vibrations that echo from it. In such images you can capture the distinction between **denotation,** the general meaning of a word, and **connotation,** the ripples, vibrations, and associations that accompany the word. As a writer, you want to choose words that are both denotatively and connotatively appropriate.

Words with similar denotations may have connotations that vary widely. The words *maxim, epigram, proverb, saw, saying,* and *motto,* for instance, all carry roughly the same denotation. Because of their different connotations, however, *proverb* would be the appropriate word to use in reference to a saying from the Bible; *saw* in reference to the kind of wisdom handed down anonymously; *epigram* in reference to a witty statement by someone well-known, like Mark Twain. *Pushy* and *assertive* also have much the same denotative meaning, but their connotations suggest different attitudes on the part of the writer, one negative, the other neutral or positive.

Because words with the wrong connotations for your intended meaning may not be as obvious as those with wrong denotations, take special care to avoid them. Look at the differences in connotation among the following three statements:

> Students Against Racism (SAR) erected a temporary barrier on the campus oval. They say it symbolizes "the many barriers to those discriminated against by university policies."

> Left-wing agitators threw up an eyesore right on the oval to try to stampede the university into giving in to their every demand.

> Supporters of human rights for all students challenged the university's investment in racism by erecting a protest barrier on campus.

As this example demonstrates, positive and negative connotations can shift meaning significantly. The first statement is the most neutral, merely stating facts (and quoting the assertion about university policy to represent it as someone's words rather than as "facts"); the second, by using words with negative connotations (*agitators, eyesore, stampede*), is strongly critical; the third, by using words with positive connotations (*supporters of human rights*) and presenting assertions as facts (*the university's investment in racism*), gives a favorable slant to the group and its

dict

27b   539

LANGUAGE

Understanding
Denotation and
Connotation

actions. You should always pay attention to the connotations of the words you read or hear—including your own words. Try to use connotation to help make your meanings clear and create the effect you intend.

Many words carry fairly general connotations, evoking similar associational responses in most listeners or readers. But connotations can be personal or distinctive to a particular audience. If you have ever become ill right after eating a particular food, the mere mention of, say, peanut butter cookies carries powerful negative connotations for you.

The power of connotation to a particular audience was notable after the September 11, 2001, suicide attacks on the Pentagon and World Trade Center led to a "war on terrorism." In the weeks following, that war was officially given two different names in succession, each calculated to appeal to a deeply affected worldwide audience. The first name given to the U.S. action, "Operation Infinite Justice," was intended to speak to citizens still reeling from the attacks. Politicians, their speechwriters, and pollsters quickly found, however, that *justice* used in such a way carried negative connotations for many, in particular for the Arab population, who reserve the term *infinite justice* for an action of which only Allah is capable. The effort was soon renamed "Operation Enduring Freedom."

CHECKING FOR WRONG WORDS

Wrong-word errors take so many different forms that it is very difficult to name any foolproof methods of checking for them. If you often find yourself using the wrong words, however, it will be well worth your time to go through each draft looking for them.

1. Check in a dictionary every word you are not absolutely sure of to see that you are using it properly.

2. Look for homonyms, words that sound like other words (such as *to*, *too*, and *two*). Using the information in 30b, make sure you are using the correct form.

3. Keep a list of any words you use incorrectly, including example sentences showing the way you have misused them. Make a point of proofreading carefully for them.

● **EXERCISE 27.3**

From the parentheses, choose the word with the denotation that makes most sense in the context of the sentence. Use a dictionary if necessary.

1. She listened (*apprehensively/attentively*) to the lecture and took notes.

2. Going swimming on a hot day can be a (*rapturous/ravenous*) experience.

3. Mark improved his windsurfing (*dramatically/drastically*) with lessons.

4. Franklin advised his readers to be (*feudal/frugal*) and industrious.

**www ● bedford
stmartins.com/
smhandbook**

For additional
exercises on
denotation and
connotation,
click on

► Exercise Central
  ► Using
     Appropriate,
     Precise
     Language

● **EXERCISE 27.4**

Study the italicized words in each of the following passages, and decide what each word's connotations contribute to your understanding of the passage. Think of a synonym for each word, and see if you can decide what difference the new word would make on the effect of the passage.

1. The Burmans were already *racing* past me across the mud. It was obvious that the elephant would never *rise* again, but he was not dead. He was breathing very rhythmically with long *rattling gasps,* his great *mound* of a side painfully rising and falling. – GEORGE ORWELL, "Shooting an Elephant"

2. If boxing is a sport, it is the most *tragic* of all sports because, more than any human activity, it *consumes* the very excellence it *displays:* Its very *drama* is this consumption. – JOYCE CAROL OATES, "On Boxing"

3. We caught two bass, *hauling* them in *briskly* as though they were mackerel, pulling them over the side of the boat in a *businesslike* manner without any landing net, and stunning them with a *blow* on the back of the head. – E. B. WHITE, "Once More to the Lake"

4. Then one evening Miss Glory told me to serve the ladies on the porch. After I set the tray down and turned toward the kitchen, one of the women asked, "What's your name, *girl?*" – MAYA ANGELOU, *I Know Why the Caged Bird Sings*

5. The Kiowas are a summer people; they *abide* the cold and keep to themselves; but when the season *turns* and the land becomes warm and *vital,* they cannot *hold still.* – N. SCOTT MOMADAY, "The Way to Rainy Mountain"

27c Balancing general and specific diction

Good writers move their prose along and help readers follow the meaning by balancing **general words,** those that refer to groups or classes of things, with **specific words,** those that refer to individual items. One kind of general words, **abstractions,** are words or phrases that refer to qualities or ideas, things we cannot perceive through our five senses. Specific words are often **concrete words;** they name what we can see, hear, touch, taste, or smell. Rarely can we draw a clear-cut line between general or abstract words on the one hand and specific or concrete ones on the other. Instead, most words fall somewhere between these two extremes.

GENERAL	LESS GENERAL	SPECIFIC	MORE SPECIFIC
book	dictionary	abridged dictionary	my 2002 edition of the *American Heritage College Dictionary*

ABSTRACT	LESS ABSTRACT	CONCRETE	MORE CONCRETE
culture	visual art	painting	Van Gogh's *Starry Night*

Because passages that contain mostly general terms or abstractions demand that readers supply most of the specific examples or concrete details with their imaginations, such writing is often hard to read. But writing that is full of specifics can also be tedious and hard to follow if the main point is not made clearly or is lost amid a flood of details. Strong writing must usually provide readers both with a general idea or overall picture and with specific examples or concrete details to fill in that picture. In the following passage, for instance, the author might have simply made a general statement—*their breakfast was always liberal and good*—or simply described the breakfast. Instead, he does both.

> There would be a brisk fire crackling in the hearth, the old smoke-gold of morning and the smell of fog, the crisp cheerful voices of the people and their ruddy competent morning look, and the cheerful smells of breakfast, which was always liberal and good, the best meal that they had: kidneys and ham and eggs and sausages and toast and marmalade and tea.   —THOMAS WOLFE, *Of Time and the River*

Here a student writer balances a general statement with illustrative specific details:

GENERAL   My neighbor is a nuisance.

SPECIFIC   My next-door neighbor is a nuisance, poking and prying into my life, constantly watching me as I enter and leave my house, complaining about the noise when I am having a good time, and telling my parents whenever she sees me kissing my date.

LANGUAGE

Considering
Diction

**www • bedford
stmartins.com/
smhandbook**

For additional
exercises on general
and specific
diction, click on

▶ Exercise Central
  ▶ Using
     Appropriate,
     Precise
     Language

● **EXERCISE 27.5**

Rewrite each of the following sentences to be more specific and concrete.

1. The entryway of the building was dirty.

2. The sounds at dawn are memorable.

3. Our holiday dinner was good.

4. The attendant came toward my car.

5. The child played on the beach.

27d Using figurative language

One good way to communicate with an audience is by using **figurative language**, or **figures of speech**. Such language paints pictures in our minds, allows us to "see" a point and hence understand more readily and clearly. Economists trying to explain the magnitude of the federal deficit use figurative language when they tell us how many hundreds of thousands of dollar bills would have to circle the globe how many times to equal it. Scientists describing the way genetic data are transmitted use figurative language when they liken the data to a messenger that carries bits of information from one generation of cells to another and when they liken certain genetic variants to typographical errors. Far from being mere decoration, figurative language plays a crucial role in helping us understand and share meanings.

In important ways, all language is metaphoric, referring to something beyond the word itself for which the word is a symbol. Particularly helpful in building understanding are specific types of figurative language, including similes, metaphors, and analogies.

FOR MULTILINGUAL WRITERS: Using Idioms

Why do you wear a diamond *on* your finger but *in* your ear? (See 61a.)

■ *Similes*

Similes make explicit the comparison between two things by using *like, as, as if,* or *as though.*

The comb felt as if it was raking my skin off.

– MALCOLM X, "My First Conk"

The Digital Revolution is sweeping through our lives like a Bengali typhoon.   — LOUIS ROSSETTO

■ *Metaphors*

Metaphors are implicit comparisons, omitting the *like, as, as if,* or *as though* of similes.

> Unix is the Swiss Army Knife of the Net.   — THOMAS MANDEL

Often, metaphors are more elaborate.

> Black women are called, in the folklore that so aptly identifies one's status in society, "the mule of the world," because we have been handed the burdens that everyone else — everyone else — refused to carry.
> — ALICE WALKER, *In Search of Our Mothers' Gardens*

> Language is [an] engineering marvel.   — STEVEN PINKER

■ *Analogies*

Analogies compare similar features of two dissimilar things and are often extended to several sentences or paragraphs in length. The following sentence, for example, uses an analogy to help us understand the rapid growth of the computer industry:

For more on analogies, see 13g2.

> If the aircraft industry had evolved as spectacularly as the computer industry over the past twenty-five years, a Boeing 767 would cost $500 today, and it would circle the globe in twenty minutes on five gallons of fuel.

The analogy in the next passage helps us "see" an abstract point.

> One Hundred and Twenty-fifth Street was to Harlem what the Mississippi was to the South, a long traveling river always going somewhere, carrying something.   — MAYA ANGELOU, *The Heart of a Woman*

Before you use an analogy, though, make sure that the two things you are comparing have enough points of similarity to justify the comparison and make it convincing to readers.

■ *Clichés and mixed metaphors*

Just as effective use of figurative language can create the impression the writer wants to create, so *ineffective* figures of speech can create the *wrong* impression by boring, irritating, or unintentionally amusing readers.

544

dict

27d

LANGUAGE

Considering
Diction

Among the most common kinds of ineffective figurative language are clichés and mixed metaphors.

Cliché comes from the French word for "stereotype," a metal plate cast from a page of type and used, before the invention of photographic printing processes, to produce multiple copies of a book or page without having to reset the type. So a **cliché** in language is an expression stamped out in duplicate to avoid the trouble of "resetting" the thought. Many clichés, like *busy as a bee* or *youth is the springtime of life,* are similes or metaphors.

By definition, we use clichés all the time, especially in speech, and the rhythm and alliteration of some continue to please our ears. Like anything else, however, clichés should be used in moderation: if your readers recognize that you are using stereotyped, paint-by-numbers language to excess, they are likely to conclude that what you are saying is not very new or interesting—or true. The person who tells you that you look *pretty as a picture* uses a clichéd simile that may well sound false or insincere. Compare it with a more original compliment a grandmother once paid to her grandchildren: *You all look as pretty as brand-new red shoes.*

How can you check for clichés? Although one person's trite phrase may be completely new to another, one rule of thumb will serve you well: if you can predict exactly what the upcoming word(s) in a phrase will be, it stands a very good chance of being a cliché.

Mixed metaphors are comparisons that are not consistent. Instead of creating a clear and dominant impression, they confuse the reader by pulling against one another, often in unintentionally funny ways. Here is a mixed metaphor revised for consistency:

quickly consumed.

▶ **If you let that sort of thing go on, your bread and butter will be ~~cut right~~**

^

~~out from under your feet.~~ – ERNEST BEVIN

The images of food and shifting ground were inconsistent; in the revised sentence, all of the images relate to food.

■ *Allusions*

Allusions, indirect references to cultural works, people, or events, can bring an entire world of associations to the minds of readers who recognize them. When a sports commentator said, *If the Georgia Tech men have an Achilles heel, it is their inexperience, their youth,* he alluded to the

Greek myth in which the hero Achilles was fatally wounded in his single vulnerable spot, his heel.

You can draw allusions from history, from literature, from sacred texts, from common wisdom, or from current events. Many current movies and popular songs are full of allusions. Remember, however, that allusions work only if your audience recognizes them.

■ Signifying

One distinctive use of figurative language found extensively in African American English is **signifying,** in which a speaker cleverly and often humorously needles or insults the listener. In the following passage, two African American men (Grave Digger and Coffin Ed) signify on their white supervisor (Anderson), who ordered them to discover the originators of a riot:

> "I take it you've discovered who started the riot," Anderson said.
> "We knew who he was all along," Grave Digger said.
> "It's just nothing we can do to him," Coffin Ed echoed.
> "Why not, for God's sake?"
> "He's dead," Coffin Ed said.
> "Who?"
> "Lincoln," Grave Digger said.
> "He hadn't ought to have freed us if he didn't want to make provisions to feed us," Coffin Ed said. "Anyone could have told him that."
>
> – CHESTER HIMES, *Hot Day, Hot Night*

Coffin Ed and Grave Digger demonstrate the major characteristics of effective signifying: indirection, ironic humor, fluid rhythm—and a surprising twist at the end. Rather than insulting Anderson directly by pointing out that he's asked a dumb question, they criticize the question indirectly by ultimately blaming a white man (and not just *any* white man but one they're all supposed to revere). This twist leaves the supervisor speechless, teaching him something *and* giving Grave Digger and Coffin Ed the last word.

You will find examples of signifying in the work of many African American writers. You may also hear signifying in NBA basketball, for it is an important element of trash talking; what Grave Digger and Coffin Ed do to Anderson, Kobe Bryant regularly does to his opponents on the court.

FOR COLLABORATION

Working with a classmate, identify the similes and metaphors in the following passages, and decide how each contributes to your understanding of the passage it appears in. Then try your hands at writing an imitation of one of these sentences, making sure to include an effective simile or metaphor. Bring your explanations and your imitations to class for discussion.

1. John's mother, Mom Willie, who wore her Southern background like a magnolia corsage, eternally fresh, was robust and in her sixties.

   — MAYA ANGELOU, *The Heart of a Woman*

2. I was watching everyone else and didn't see the waitress standing quietly by. Her voice was deep and soft like water moving in a cavern.

   — WILLIAM LEAST HEAT-MOON, "In the Land of 'Coke-Cola'"

3. My horse, when he is in his stall or lounging about the pasture, has the same relationship to pain that I have when cuddling up with a good murder mystery—comfort and convenience have top priority.

   — VICKI HEARNE, "Horses in Partnership with Time"

www • bedford
stmartins.com/
smhandbook

For additional
exercises on
figurative language,
click on

▶ Exercise Central
   ▶ Using
      Appropriate,
      Precise
      Language

● EXERCISE 27.6

Return to the description you wrote in Exercise 27.1. Note any words that carry strong connotations, and identify the concrete and abstract language as well as any use of figurative language. Revise the description for better use of diction.

THINKING CRITICALLY ABOUT DICTION

Read the following brief poem. What dominant feeling or impression does the poem produce in you? Identify the diction, those specific words and phrases, that helps create that impression.

What happens to a dream deferred?

Does it dry up
Like a raisin in the sun?
Or fester like a sore—
And then run?
Does it stink like rotten meat?
Or crust and sugar over—
Like a syrupy sweet?

Maybe it just sags
Like a heavy load.

Or does it explode?

— LANGSTON HUGHES, "Harlem (A Dream Deferred)"

Using Dictionaries

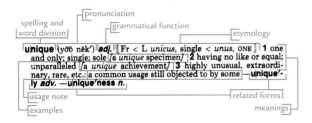

28

28a Exploring the dictionary

A good dictionary packs a surprising amount of information, including much more than correct spelling, into a relatively small space. Look at this entry in *Webster's New World College Dictionary*, Fourth Edition.

spelling and word division | pronunciation | grammatical function | etymology

u|nique (yōō nēk′) *adj.* [Fr < L *unicus*, single < *unus*, ONE] 1 one and only; single; sole [a *unique* specimen/ 2 having no like or equal; unparalleled /a *unique* achievement/ 3 highly unusual, extraordinary, rare, etc.: a common usage still objected to by some —u|nique′- ly *adv.* —u|nique′ness *n.*

usage note | examples | related forms | meanings

In fact, a dictionary entry may contain a dozen or more kinds of information about a word, the most common of which are listed here. The first six normally appear in all entries, the others only when relevant.

1. *Spelling,* including alternative spellings if they exist
2. *Word division,* with bars, dots, or spaces separating syllables and showing where a word may be divided at the end of a line
3. *Pronunciation,* including alternative pronunciations

In the opening scene of Rex Stout's novel *Gambit,* master sleuth Nero Wolfe tears the pages out of a "subversive and intolerably offensive" book—the third edition of *Webster's New International Dictionary.* Wolfe claims that the dictionary threatens the very "integrity of the English language" and is, therefore, burning it page by page.

Dictionaries have, in fact, often been the cause of violent controversy, usually related to a tension between two basic and competing aims: to fix a standard of language by establishing clear "rights" and "wrongs" and, on the other hand, to record a full inventory of the language as it is actually used, without prescribing "right" and "wrong." What enraged Wolfe was one particular dictionary's focus on the second aim. Today, these dual aims persist in dictionaries and may in fact influence your choice of which dictionary to use.

This chapter will help you make the most of a dictionary's offerings and choose the right kind of dictionary for your purposes. ■

4. *Grammatical functions and irregular forms* (if any), including plurals of nouns, principal parts of verbs, and comparative and superlative forms of adjectives and adverbs
5. *Etymology,* the languages and words that the word comes from
6. *Meanings,* in order of either development or frequency of use
7. *Examples* of the word in the context of a phrase or sentence
8. *Usage labels and notes* (See explanation in following section.)
9. *Field labels,* indicating that a word has a special meaning in a particular field of knowledge or activity
10. *Synonyms* and *antonyms*
11. *Related words* and their grammatical functions
12. *Idioms,* phrases in which the word appears and their meanings

FOR MULTILINGUAL WRITERS: Using a Dictionary to Understand Idioms

When you encounter an unfamiliar phrase that appears to involve an idiom, you might find help at the end of a word's dictionary definition, where idioms often are defined.

For more help
with idioms,
see 61a.

◼ *Usage labeling and notes*

For some words, many dictionaries include usage labeling, intended to let readers know that some or all meanings of the word are not considered appropriate in certain contexts. You can generally find such labels identified and described at the beginning of the dictionary. Here are some of the labels *Webster's New World* uses:

1. *Archaic:* rarely used today except in specialized contexts
2. *Obsolete* or *obs.:* no longer used
3. *Colloquial* or *colloq.:* characteristic of conversation and informal writing
4. *Slang:* extremely informal
5. *Dialect:* used mostly in a particular geographical or linguistic area, often one that is specified, such as Scotland or New England

In addition to labels, dictionaries sometimes include notes discussing usage in greater detail. In the *Webster's New World* entry for *unique,* notice that the third meaning includes a note that it is "common" but "still objected to by some."

● **EXERCISE 28.1**

Look up the spelling, syllable division, and pronunciation of the following words in your dictionary. Note any variants in spelling and pronunciation.

1. process (noun)	5. whippet	9. greasy
2. heinous	6. crayfish	10. theater
3. exigency	7. macabre	
4. schedule	8. hurrah	

● **EXERCISE 28.2**

Look up the etymology of the following words in your dictionary.

1. rhetoric	5. apple	9. cinema
2. student	6. sex	10. video
3. curry (noun)	7. okra	
4. whine	8. tortilla	

● **EXERCISE 28.3**

Use your dictionary to find synonyms (and antonyms) of the following words.

1. coerce	3. parameter	5. awesome
2. prevaricate	4. odious	6. obfuscate

28b Distinguishing among dictionaries

Although you may use a portable paperback dictionary most often, you should be familiar with other kinds of dictionaries as well.

**www ● bedford
stmartins.com/
smhandbook**

For links to online
dictionaries,
click on

▶ Links
▶ Reference
Resources

1 Abridged dictionaries

Abridged, or "abbreviated," **dictionaries** are the type most often used by college writers. Though they are not as complete as unabridged dictionaries, they are more affordable and more portable. Among the most helpful abridged dictionaries are *Random House Webster's College Dictionary* and *The American Heritage College Dictionary*.

Random House Webster's College Dictionary, updated annually, has more than 207,000 entries, including words new to the language, from *hotlink* to *identity theft* to *bazillion*. This work is notable for its attempt to eliminate sexist language from definitions, its usage notes intended to warn users when terms may be offensive or disparaging, and its appendix "Avoiding Insensitive and Offensive Language."

The American Heritage College Dictionary, Fourth Edition (Boston: Houghton, 2002), has more than 200,000 listings, augmented by 5,000 scientific and technical terms and over 3,000 illustrations. *The American Heritage* lists meanings in the order of most to least common. Notes on usage are extensive. Introductory essays provide a context for the usage notes in the form of a debate on the issue. The dictionary is also available on CD-ROM.

FOR MULTILINGUAL WRITERS: Using a Learner's Dictionary

In addition to using a good college dictionary, you may want to invest in one of the following dictionaries intended especially for learners of English. The *Longman Dictionary of American English* presents the English spoken in the United States; the *Oxford Advanced Learner's Dictionary* covers British and American English.

These dictionaries provide information about count and noncount nouns, idioms and phrasal verbs, verbs that take a gerund and those that take an infinitive, and other topics important to learners of English. You should in general avoid using a bilingual dictionary, for you'll find more accurate and idiomatic information in an English dictionary than in, for example, a Spanish-English dictionary.

---

2 Unabridged dictionaries

Unabridged, or "unabbreviated," **dictionaries** are the royalty of their species — the most complete, richly detailed, and thoroughly presented dictionaries of English. Whereas good abridged dictionaries may include 200,000 items, unabridged dictionaries far more than double that figure. Because they are large and often multivolume — and hence expensive — you may not own one, but you will want and need to consult one on occasion. You can always find an unabridged dictionary in the library. Among the leading unabridged dictionaries are the *Oxford English Dictionary* and *Webster's Third New International Dictionary of the English Language.*

The Oxford English Dictionary (OED), now available in a twenty-volume second edition, began in Britain in the nineteenth century as an attempt to give a full history of each English word: a record of its entry into the language and the development of the word's various meanings with dated quotations in chronological order. Volunteers all over the English-speaking world contributed quotations, and the first edition was published piecemeal over a period of more than forty years. The second edition traces more than half a million words and is unparalleled in its historical account of changes in word meanings and spellings. It is available on CD-ROM.

Webster's Third New International Dictionary of the English Language (Springfield, MA: Merriam-Webster) contains more entries than any other dictionary except the *OED* — nearly half a million in all, with a special addenda section covering 14,000 new words and meanings. This one-volume work stirred considerable controversy at its publication because of its tendency, as mentioned in the introduction to this chapter, to *describe* rather than to *prescribe* usage. In all, the editors collected 6,165,000 examples of recorded usage, on which they drew for their usage notes. *Webster's Third* lists meanings in order of their entry into the language and quotes from over 14,000 different authors to provide illustrations of words in context.

EXERCISE 28.4

Look up the following words in at least one abridged and one unabridged dictionary, and compare the entries. Record any differences or disagreements you find, and bring this record to class for discussion.

1. dogmatism
2. alienate
3. discriminate
4. hopefully
5. humanism
6. culture

EXERCISE 28.5

Look up one of the following words in the *OED,* and write a paragraph describing any changes in meaning it has undergone since its entry into English.

1. cheerful
2. machine
3. vulgar
4. humor (noun)
5. honest
6. romance

28c Consulting specialized dictionaries

Abridged and unabridged dictionaries will provide you with an enormous amount of information. Sometimes, however, you will need to turn to additional sources for more specialized information. Such sources are available in dictionaries of usage, synonyms, and slang.

■ *Dictionaries of usage*

In cases where usage is disputed or where you feel unsure of your own usage, you may wish to consult a specialized dictionary of usage. The most widely used such work, although it is much more about British than American usage, is *The New Fowler's Modern English Usage,* Third Edition. First published in 1926 and edited by H. W. Fowler, the 1996 third edition has been edited by R. W. Burchfield.

www • bedford
stmartins.com/
smhandbook

For a list of online
thesauri, click on

▶ Links
  ▶ Reference
    Resources

■ *Dictionaries of synonyms and the thesaurus*

All writers are sometimes stuck for just the right word, and at such times, a dictionary of synonyms or a thesaurus is a friend indeed. In these works, each entry is followed by words whose meanings are similar to that of the entry. A useful source is *Webster's Dictionary of Synonyms.*

A **thesaurus** (the word comes from a word meaning "treasure" or "storehouse") provides antonyms as well as synonyms. Two thesauri are particularly helpful: *Webster's Collegiate Thesaurus* and *The New Roget's Thesaurus of the English Language in Dictionary Form.*

Remember, however, to use dictionaries of synonyms and thesauri carefully, because rarely in English are two words so close in meaning that they can be used interchangeably in radically different contexts. As Mark Twain put it, the difference between the right word and the almost right word is the difference between lightning and the lightning bug.

■ *Dictionaries of etymology, regional English, slang, and neologisms*

On some occasions, you may want or need to find out all you can about the origins of a word, to find out about a term used in only one area of the country, or to see whether a term is considered slang or jargon. The following specialized dictionaries can help you:

Dictionary of American Regional English. Ed. Frederic G. Cassidy. Cambridge: Belknap-Harvard UP, Vol. 1, 1985; Vol. 2, 1991; Vol. 3, 1996.

Dictionary of Computer and Internet Words. New York: Houghton, 2001.

NTC's Dictionary of American Slang and Colloquial Expressions. 3rd ed. New York: NTC/McGraw, 2000.

The Oxford Dictionary of English Etymology. Ed. C. T. Onions. New York: Oxford UP, 1966.

FOR COLLABORATION

With a classmate, look up the following words in several specialized dictionaries, and together find out as much as you can about their meanings, origins, and uses.

1. wazoo
2. tip
3. scam
4. jazz
5. whammy
6. advertorial

THINKING CRITICALLY ABOUT WORDS

In his autobiography, Malcolm X says that he taught himself to write by reading and copying the dictionary. Certainly, you can teach yourself to be a better writer by paying careful attention to the way other writers use words that are unfamiliar to you. Choose a writer whose work you admire, and read that author's work for at least thirty minutes, noting six or seven words that you would not ordinarily have thought to use. Do a little dictionary investigative work on these words, and bring your results to class for discussion.

29 ▼ Enriching Vocabulary

In the Bible, how does God create the world? By naming it, creating a vocabulary for what was created. The word *vocabulary* comes, in fact, from a Latin term for "name" (*vocabulum*), which in turn comes from the Latin verb for "call." The connection between vocabulary and calling into being is what led a famous philosopher to declare that "the limits of my language are the limits of my world."

You can apply this insight to your own life by remembering a time when you learned the name of something new. Before that time, this thing did not exist for you; yet curiously enough, once you knew its name, you began to see it all around you. Such is the power of vocabulary in enriching not only our personal language but our lives as well.

This chapter will help you understand a little of the history of the English language and how its words are formed, and also offers tips on how to use that knowledge to enrich your own vocabulary. ■

29a Considering your vocabulary

At its largest, your English vocabulary includes all those words whose meanings you either recognize or can deduce from context. This, your **processing vocabulary**, allows you to interpret the meanings of many passages whose words you might not actively use yourself. Your **producing vocabulary** is more limited, made up of words you actually use in writing or speaking.

Part of what it means to mature intellectually is to broaden your mental horizons by learning how to name more things more accurately, to increase what the hero Beowulf called a "word hoard." Doing so involves consciously strengthening the bridges between your processing vocabulary and your producing vocabulary by beginning to use in your own speech and writing more of the words you recognize and can interpret in context. To accomplish this goal, you must become an investigative reporter of your own language and the language of others.

■ *Charting the history of English*

English has always been a language with a mixed heritage, what Daniel Defoe called "your Roman-Saxon-Danish-Norman English." Where did this language come from, and how did it evolve? English, like one-third of all languages in the world, descends from Indo-European, a language spoken by groups of people whose original home was in some part of north-central Europe. Scholars began to argue for Indo-European as a "common source" and tried to identify its features when they noted striking resemblances among words in a number of languages.

English	Latin	Spanish	French	Greek	German	Dutch	Swedish
three	*tres*	*tres*	*trois*	*treis*	*drei*	*drie*	*tre*

A version of Indo-European was brought to Britain by the Germanic invasions following 449. This early language, called Anglo-Saxon or Old English, was influenced by Latin and Greek when Christianity was reintroduced into England beginning in 597, was later shaped by the Viking invasions beginning in the late 700s, and was transformed by French after the Norman Conquest (1066).

Although English continued to evolve in the centuries after the conquest, Latin and French were then the languages of the learned—of the church and court. In the late 1300s, it was Geoffrey Chaucer, writing *The Canterbury Tales* in the language of the people, who helped establish what is now called Middle English as the political, legal, and literary language of Britain. And after the advent of printing in the mid-1400s, that language became more accessible and more standardized. By about 1600, it had essentially become the Modern English we use today.

The following three versions of a biblical passage will give you an idea of how much English had evolved up to this time:

ANGLO-SAXON GOSPELS, AROUND A.D. 1000

And eft hē ongan hī æt þǣre sǣ lǣran. And him wæs mycel menegu tō gegaderod, swā þæt hē on scip ēode, and on bǣre sǣ wæs; and eall sēo menegu ymbe þē sǣ wæs on lande.

WYCLIFFE BIBLE, ABOUT 1380

And eft Jhesus bigan to teche at the see; and myche puple was gaderid to hym, so that he wente in to a boot, and sat in the see, and al the puple was aboute the see on the loond.

KING JAMES VERSION, 1611

And he began again to teach by the seaside: and there was gathered unto him a great multitude, so that he entered into a ship, and sat in the sea: and the whole multitude was by the sea on the land.

Note that in the Old English text, only a few words—*and, he, him, waes, on, lande*—look at all familiar. By the time of Chaucer and Wycliffe, however, many words are recognizable. And by the time of Shakespeare, the language is easily readable.

In the last four hundred years, English has continued borrowing from many languages and, as a result, now has one of the world's largest vocabularies. Modern English, then, is a plant growing luxuriously in the soil of multiple language sources.

29b Recognizing word roots

As its name suggests, a **root** is a word from which other words grow, usually through the addition of prefixes or suffixes. From the Latin root *-dic-* or *-dict-* ("speak"), for instance, grows a whole range of words in English: *contradict, dictate, dictator, diction, edict, predict, dictaphone,* and others. Here are some other Latin (L) and Greek (G) roots. Recognizing them will help you recognize networks of words.

ROOT	MEANING	EXAMPLES
-audi- (L)	to hear	audience, audio
-bene- (L)	good, well	benevolent, benefit
-bio- (G)	life	biography, biosphere
-duc(t)- (L)	to lead or to make	ductile, reproduce
-gen- (G)	race, kind	genealogy, gene
-geo- (G)	earth	geography, geometry
-graph- (G)	to write	graphic, photography
-jur-, -jus- (L)	law	justice, jurisdiction
-log(o)- (G)	word, thought	biology, logical
-luc- (L)	light	lucid, translucent
-manu- (L)	hand	manufacture, manual
-mit-, -mis- (L)	to send	permit, transmission
-path- (G)	feel, suffer	empathy, pathetic
-phil- (G)	love	philosopher, bibliophile
-photo- (G)	light	photography, telephoto
-port- (L)	to carry	transport, portable
-psych- (G)	soul	psychology, psychopath
-scrib-, -script- (L)	to write	inscribe, manuscript

ROOT	MEANING	EXAMPLES
-sent-, -sens- (L)	to feel	sensation, resent
-tele- (G)	far away	telegraph, telepathy
-tend- (L)	to stretch	extend, tendency
-terr- (L)	earth	inter, territorial
-vac- (L)	empty	vacuole, evacuation
-vid-, -vis- (L)	to see	video, envision, visit

LANGUAGE

Recognizing
Prefixes and
Suffixes

● **EXERCISE 29.1**

Using the preceding list of roots, try to figure out the meaning of each of the following words. Write a potential definition for each one, and compare it with your dictionary's definition.

1. terrestrial
2. scriptorium
3. geothermal
4. lucent

5. beneficent
6. audiology
7. vacuous
8. pathogenic

9. juridical
10. graphology

29c Recognizing prefixes and suffixes

Originally individual words, prefixes and suffixes are groups of letters added to words or to word roots to create new words.

1 Prefixes

The word **prefix** appropriately demonstrates its own meaning: it is made up of a prefix (*pre-*) and a root (*-fix-*) and means literally "fasten before." Fastened to the beginnings of words or roots, prefixes modify and extend meanings. Recognizing common prefixes can often help you decipher the meaning of otherwise unfamiliar words.

■ *Prefixes of negation or opposition*

PREFIX	MEANING	EXAMPLES
a-, an-	without, not	ahistorical, anemia
anti-	against	antibody, antiphonal
contra-	against	contravene, contradict
de-	from, take away from	demerit, declaw

PREFIX	MEANING	EXAMPLES
dis-	apart, away	disappear, discharge
il-, im-, in-, ir-	not	illegal, immature, indistinct, irreverent
mal-	wrong	malevolent, malpractice
mis-	wrong, bad	misapply, misanthrope
non-	not	nonentity, nonsense
un-	not	unbreakable, unable

Prefixes of quantity

PREFIX	MEANING	EXAMPLES
bi-	two	bipolar, bilateral
milli-	thousand	millimeter, milligram
mono-	one, single	monotone, monologue
omni-	all	omniscient, omnipotent
semi-	half	semicolon, semiconductor
tri-	three	tripod, trimester
uni-	one	unitary, univocal

Prefixes of time and space

PREFIX	MEANING	EXAMPLES
ante-	before	antedate, antebellum
circum-	around	circumlocution, circumnavigate
co-, col-, com-, con-, cor-	with	coequal, collaborate, commiserate, contact, correspond
e-, ex-	out of	emit, extort, expunge
hyper-	over, more than	hypersonic, hypersensitive
hypo-	under, less than	hypodermic, hypoglycemia
inter-	between	intervene, international
mega-	enlarge, large	megalomania, megaphone
micro-	tiny	micrometer, microscopic
neo-	recent	neologism, neophyte

PREFIX	MEANING	EXAMPLES
post-	after	postwar, postscript
pre-	before	previous, prepublication
pro-	before, onward	project, propel
re-	again, back	review, re-create
sub-	under, beneath	subhuman, submarine
super-	over, above	supercargo, superimpose
syn-	at the same time	synonym, synchronize
trans-	across, over	transport, transition

LANGUAGE

Recognizing
Prefixes and
Suffixes

FOR COLLABORATION

Working with a classmate, use the preceding list of prefixes and the list of roots in 29b to figure out the meaning of each of the following words. Write a potential definition for each one, and compare it with your dictionary's definition. Bring your collaboratively written definitions to class for discussion.

1. remit
2. subterranean
3. translucent
4. monograph
5. distend
6. superscript
7. deport
8. neologism
9. inaudible
10. apathetic

2 Suffixes

Attached to the ends of words and word roots, **suffixes** modify and extend meanings, many times by altering the grammatical function or part of speech of the original word. Suffixes can, for example, turn the verb *create* into a noun, an adjective, or an adverb.

VERB	create
NOUNS	crea*tor*/crea*tion*/creativi*ty*/creat*ure*
ADJECTIVE	creat*ive*
ADVERB	creative*ly*

▦ *Noun suffixes*

SUFFIX	MEANING	EXAMPLES
-acy	state or quality	democracy, privacy
-al	act of	rebuttal, refusal

560

VOC

29c

LANGUAGE

Enriching
Vocabulary

SUFFIX	MEANING	EXAMPLES
-ance, -ence	state or quality of	maintenance, eminence
-dom	place or state of being	freedom, thralldom
-er, -or	one who	trainer, investor
-ism	doctrine or belief characteristic of	liberalism, Taoism
-ist	one who	organist, physicist
-ity	quality of	veracity, opacity
-ment	condition of	payment, argument
-ness	state of being	watchfulness, cleanliness
-ship	position held	professorship, fellowship
-sion, -tion	state of being or action	digression, transition

■ *Verb suffixes*

SUFFIX	MEANING	EXAMPLES
-ate	cause to be	concentrate, regulate
-en	cause to be or become	enliven, blacken
-ify, -fy	make or cause to be	unify, terrify, amplify
-ize	cause to become	magnetize, civilize

■ *Adjective suffixes*

SUFFIX	MEANING	EXAMPLES
-able, -ible	capable of being	assumable, edible
-al	pertaining to	regional, political
-esque	reminiscent of	picturesque, statuesque
-ful	having a notable quality	colorful, sorrowful
-ic	pertaining to	poetic, mythic
-ious, -ous	of or characterized by	famous, nutritious
-ish	having the quality of	prudish, clownish
-ive	having the nature of	festive, creative, massive
-less	without	endless, senseless

● **EXERCISE 29.2**

Using the preceding list of suffixes, figure out the meaning of each of the following words. (Use your dictionary if necessary.) Then choose two of the words, and use each one in a sentence.

1. contemplative
2. fanciful
3. impairment
4. liquefy

5. barrenness
6. defiance
7. merciless
8. redden

9. standardize
10. satirist

29d Building your vocabulary

Making good use of prefixes and suffixes will increase your vocabulary, but other methods will be even more helpful. These methods include analyzing contexts, reading actively, and learning the vocabulary of your field.

1 Analyzing word contexts

If you have ever run into a person you knew but could not place — until you remembered the place where you normally see the person (at the grocery store, say) — you know firsthand the importance of context in helping you identify people and things. The same principle holds true for words. So if a word is at first unfamiliar to you, look carefully at its context, paying attention to all the clues that the context can give; often you will be able to deduce the meaning.

For instance, if the word *accouterments* is unfamiliar in the sentence *We stopped at a camping-supply store to pick up last-minute accouterments,* the context — *a camping-supply store* and *last-minute* — suggests strongly that *equipment* or some similar word fits the bill. And that is what *accouterments* means.

● **EXERCISE 29.3**

Identify the contextual clues that help you understand any unfamiliar words in the following sentences. Then write paraphrases of three of the sentences.

1. Before Prohibition, the criminal fringe in the United States had been a self-effacing, scattered class with little popular support.

2. The ambiguity of the evidence prevented the jury from determining which parts of it were extraneous. The jury asked for clarification.

3. The community's reaction to the preternatural creature in Shelley's *Frankenstein* shows that people are often more monstrous than a monster is.

4. My fifth-grade teacher was the epitome of what I wanted to be, and I began to imitate him scrupulously.

5. Aristarchus showed that the sun is larger than the earth and proposed a heliocentric model of the solar system. In the second century A.D., however, Ptolemy challenged this theory with his geocentric model, which came to dominate astronomy for the next fourteen hundred years.

SOME GUIDELINES FOR BUILDING YOUR VOCABULARY

As processors of information, we can read words alone, or we can read meanings. Reading meanings means filling in gaps, making connections, leaping ahead, asking questions, taking mental notes. Out of such activity, greater knowledge is born. Here are some tips for building vocabulary:

→ Make a habit of paraphrasing or summarizing unfamiliar words or phrases. Then check the dictionary to see how accurate you were.

→ Practice naming the opposites of words. If you see *abbreviation*, for instance, try supplying its opposite — *enlargement, elaboration,* and so on.

→ Challenge authors by trying to come up with better words than the ones they used.

→ Read aloud to yourself from time to time, noting any words whose pronunciation you are unsure of. Check them in a dictionary.

→ Become a collector of words, choosing those you like best and making them part of your producing vocabulary. Begin by choosing a writer you admire and reading for as long as it takes to identify several words you like but have not yet used in speech or writing. Now analyze what you like about these words — their pronunciation, meaning, or usage.

2 Learning the vocabulary of your field

For more about
learning the
vocabulary of a
discipline, see
Chapter 63.

All occupations, professions, and disciplines rely on characteristic jargon: the vocabulary of medical fields, for example, includes technical terms such as *hematoma* and *carcinoid,* which the layperson might refer to simply as a "bruise" and a "tumor." In physics, the term *charm* indicates the quantum property assigned to the "charmed" quark. And in law, words quite often take on technical meanings associated with earlier legal decisions and precedents. In copyright law, for instance, the word *original* carries meanings and connotations that are much more highly specific and technical than those associated with the word in everyday use. You may want to keep a log of the language of your chosen field, noting both meanings and examples of each term's use.

THINKING CRITICALLY ABOUT VOCABULARY

Reading with Attention to Vocabulary

Read each of the following passages, paying particular attention to the italicized words. See if you can determine the meaning of any words you don't know by using the clues suggested in this chapter — context, prefixes, roots, and suffixes. Check your understanding by looking up each word in a dictionary.

1. Now, I doubt that the imagination can be suppressed. If you truly *eradicated* it in a child, he would grow up to be an eggplant. Like all our evil *propensities,* the imagination will win out.

   – URSULA LeGUIN, "Why Are Americans Afraid of Dragons?"

2. Everything that comes alive seems to be in trade for something that dies, cell for cell. There might be some comfort in the recognition of *synchrony,* in the information that we all go down together, in the best of company.

   – LEWIS THOMAS, "Death in the Open"

Thinking about Your Own Vocabulary

Read over a piece of your writing. Underline any words you think could be improved on, and then come up with several possible substitutes. If you keep a writing log, list them there as a start to your own personal word hoard.

30

⬇ Attending to Spelling

30a The most commonly misspelled words

The thousands of first-year essays used in the research for this book revealed a fairly small number of persistently misspelled words. Look over the list of the fifty most common misspellings on p. 565, and compare it with words you have trouble spelling correctly.

⬤ **EXERCISE 30.1**

Choose the correct spelling from the words in parentheses in each of the following sentences. After checking your answers, make a list of the words you misspelled, and keep it near your computer or on your writing desk.

1. (*Their/There/They're*) going to put (*their/there/they're*) new stereo system over (*their/there/they're*) in the corner.
2. My little brother wants (*to/too*) go swimming (*to/too*).
3. The (*begining/beginning*) of school is (*a lot/alot*) earlier this year than last.
4. The temperature isn't (*noticable/noticeable*) (*until/untill*) the humidity rises.
5. The accident (*occured/occurred*) (*before/befour*) I could step aside.
6. We couldn't (*beleive/believe*) our team could (*loose/lose*) the playoffs.

1. their/there/they're	18. through	35. business/-es
2. too/to	19. until	36. dependent
3. a lot	20. where	37. every day
4. noticeable	21. successful/-ly	38. may be
5. receive/-d/-s	22. truly	39. occasion/-s
6. lose	23. argument/-s	40. occurrences
7. you're/your	24. experience/-s	41. woman
8. an/and	25. environment	42. all right
9. develop/-s	26. exercise/-s/-ing	43. apparent/-ly
10. definitely	27. necessary	44. categories
11. than/then	28. sense	45. final/-ly
12. believe/-d/-s	29. therefore	46. immediate/-ly
13. occurred	30. accept/-ed	47. roommate/-s
14. affect/-s	31. heroes	48. against
15. cannot	32. professor	49. before
16. separate	33. whether	50. beginning
17. success	34. without	

LANGUAGE

The Most Commonly Misspelled Words

7. In making your major life decisions, (*your/you're*) (*definately/definitely*) on (*your/you're*) own.

8. Nothing (*affects/effects*) (*success/sucess*) more (*than/then*) self-confidence or (*its/it's*) absence.

9. We (*received/recieved*) our notice (*threw/through*) the mail.

10. The group hopes to (*develop/develope*) a (*truely/truly*) (*succesful/successful*) fast-food franchise.

11. We (*can not/cannot*) easily (*separate/seperate*) fact and opinion.

12. Please tell me (*wear/where*) (*an/and*) when we should meet.

13. Our (*argumants/arguments*) (*against/aginst*) continuing to pollute the (*enviroment/environment*) fell on deaf ears.

14. Local (*businesses/businesses*) are (*dependant/dependent*) on the tourist trade.

15. (*Heroes/Heros*) are (*necesary/necessary*) to every culture's mythology.

16. Our first (*experiance/experience*) with aerobic (*exercise/exercize*) left us tired.

17. The (*professor/profesor*) agreed to (*accept/except*) our essays late.

www • bedford
stmartins.com/
smhandbook

For additional exercises on the most commonly misspelled words, click on

▶ **Exercise Central**
  ▶ **Spelling**

18. She qualified for three (*catagories/categories*) in the (*final/finel*) gymnastics competition.

19. The two (*roomates/roommates*) would be lost (*without/witout*) each other.

20. We intend to celebrate the (*ocasion/occasion*) (*weather/whether*) or not the (*weather/whether*) cooperates.

21. The plane to Chicago (*may be/maybe*) late; (*therefore/therfore*), we don't need to leave for the airport (*imediately/immediately*).

22. A (*woman's/women's*) place is now wherever she wants it to be.

23. Police departments report (*occurences/occurrences*) of more and more burglaries (*every day/everyday*).

24. (*Its/It's*) not (*all right/alright*) to forgo common (*since/sense*).

25. (*Aparently/Apparently*), the shipment of books never arrived.

**www • bedford
stmartins.com/
smhandbook**

For more
information on
programs that
transcribe dictated
text, click on

▶ Links
  ▶ Considering
     Disabilities

CONSIDERING DISABILITIES: Spelling

While some English spellings are notoriously hard for anyone to learn, spelling is especially difficult for those who have trouble processing letters and/or sounds in sequence. If spelling seems to be particularly difficult or nearly impossible for you, some assistive technologies can help, including "talking pens" that read words aloud when they're scanned or voice-recognition computer programs that take and transcribe dictated text.

30b Recognizing homonyms

Of the words most often misspelled by college students, the largest number are **homonyms**—words that sound alike but have different spellings and meanings. English has many homonyms, but a relatively small number of them—eight pairs or trios—cause student writers frequent trouble. If you tend to confuse any of these words, now is a good time to study them, looking for some twist of memory to help you remember the differences.

accept (to take or receive)
except (to leave out)

affect (an emotion; to have an influence)
effect (a result; to cause to happen)

its (possessive form of *it*)
it's (contraction of *it is* or *it has*)

their (possessive form of *they*)
there (in that place)
they're (contraction of *they are*)

to (in the direction of)
too (in addition; excessive)
two (number between one and three)

weather (climatic conditions)
whether (if)

who's (contraction of *who is* or *who has*)
whose (possessive form of *who*)

your (possessive form of *you*)
you're (contraction of *you are*)

OTHER HOMONYMS AND FREQUENTLY CONFUSED WORDS

advice (suggestion)
advise (to suggest [to])

allude (to refer)
elude (to avoid or escape)

allusion (reference)
illusion (false idea or appearance)

altar (sacred platform or table)
alter (to change)

are (form of *be*)
our (belonging to us)

bare (uncovered)
bear (animal; to carry or endure)

board (piece of lumber)
bored (uninterested)

brake (device for stopping)
break (interruption; to fragment)

buy (to purchase)
by (near; beside; through)

capital (principal city)
capitol (legislators' building)

cite (to refer to)
sight (seeing; something seen)
site (location)

coarse (rough or crude)
course (plan of study; path)

complement (something that completes; to make complete)
compliment (praise; to praise)

(Continued on p. 568)

(Continued from p. 567)

conscience (feeling of right and wrong)
conscious (mentally aware)

council (leadership group)
counsel (advice; to advise)

dairy (source of milk)
diary (journal)

desert (dry area; to abandon)
dessert (sweet course of a meal)

device (something planned or invented)
devise (to plan or invent)

die (to expire)
dye (color; to color)

elicit (to draw forth)
illicit (illegal)

eminent (distinguished)
immanent (inherent)
imminent (expected in the immediate future)

fair (just or right; light in complexion; an exposition)
fare (price of transportation; to go through an experience)

forth (forward; out into view)
fourth (between third and fifth)

gorilla (ape)
guerrilla (irregular soldier)

hear (to perceive with the ears)
here (in this place)

heard (past tense of *hear*)
herd (group of animals)

hoarse (sounding rough or harsh)
horse (animal)

know (to understand)
no (opposite of *yes*)

lead (a metal; to go before)
led (past tense of *lead*)

loose (not tight; not confined)
lose (to misplace; to fail to win)

meat (flesh used as food)
meet (to encounter)

passed (went by; received a passing grade)
past (beyond; events that have already occurred)

patience (quality of being patient)
patients (persons under medical care)

peace (absence of war)
piece (part)

personal (private or individual)
personnel (employees)

plain (simple; flat land)
plane (airplane; tool; flat surface)

presence (condition of being)
presents (gifts; gives)

principal (most important; head of a school)
principle (fundamental truth)

rain (precipitation)
rein (strap to control a horse)
reign (period of rule; to rule)

(Continued on p. 569)

(Continued from p. 568)

right (correct; opposite of *left*)
rite (ceremony)
write (to produce words on a surface)

road (street or highway)
rode (past tense of *ride*)

scene (setting; view)
seen (past participle of *see*)

sense (feeling; intelligence)
since (from the time that; because)

stationary (unmoving)
stationery (writing paper)

than (as compared to)
then (at that time; therefore)

thorough (complete)
threw (past tense of *throw*)
through (in one side of and out the other; by means of)

waist (part of the body)
waste (to squander)

weak (feeble)
week (seven days)

wear (to put onto the body)
were (past tense of *be*)
where (in what place)

which (what; that)
witch (woman with supernatural power)

EXERCISE 30.2

Choose the appropriate word in parentheses to fill each blank.

If _____ (*your/you're*) looking for summer fun, _____ (*accept/except*) the friendly _____ (*advice/advise*) of thousands of happy adventurers: spend three _____ (*weaks/weeks*) kayaking _____ (*thorough/threw/through*) the inside passage _____ (*to/too/two*) Alaska. For ten years, Outings, Inc., has _____ (*lead/led*) groups of novice kayakers _____ (*passed/past*) some of the most breathtaking scenery in North America. _____ (*Their/There/They're*) goal is simple: to give participants the time of _____ (*their/there/they're*) lives. As one of last year's adventurers said, "_____ (*Its/It's*) a trip I will remember vividly, one that _____ (*affected/effected*) me powerfully."

One special group of homonyms often misspelled by college writers is words written sometimes as one word and other times as two words. The correct spelling depends on the meaning. Note the differences illustrated here:

Of course, they did not wear *everyday* clothes *every day* of the year.

All ways of making macaroni and cheese are not *always* easy.

www • bedford
stmartins.com/
smhandbook

For additional
exercises on
homonyms,
click on

▶ **Exercise Central**
  ▶ **Spelling**

By the time we were *all ready* for the game to begin, the coach's patience was *already* exhausted.

We *may be* on time for the meeting, or *maybe* we won't be!

Nobody was surprised when the police officers announced that they had found *no body* at the scene of the crime.

FOR MULTILINGUAL WRITERS: Recognizing American Spellings

Spelling varies slightly among English-speaking countries. If you have learned British or Canadian English, you will want to be aware of some spelling differences in British and American English. For example:

AMERICAN	BRITISH/CANADIAN
analyze	analyse
center	centre
check	cheque
color	colour
criticize	criticise
judgment	judgement

30c Linking spelling and pronunciation

Even for words that are not homonyms, pronunciation often leads spellers astray. Pronunciation can vary considerably from one region to another, and the informality of spoken English allows us to slur or blur letters or syllables. The best way to link spelling and pronunciation is to learn to pronounce words mentally as they look, every letter and syllable included (so that, for example, you hear the *b* at the end of *crumb*) and to enunciate them slowly and clearly when you are trying to spell them.

Learning to "see" words with unpronounced letters or syllables will help you spell them correctly. Here are some frequently misspelled words of this kind with their unpronounced letters or syllables italicized:

can*d*idate	drastic*al*ly	foreign
condem*n*	enviro*n*ment	gover*n*ment
diff*e*rent	Feb*r*uary	int*e*rest

library	probably	separate (adjective)
marriage	quantity	surprise
muscle	restaurant	Wednesday

In English words, *a, i,* and *e* often sound alike in syllables that are not stressed. Hearing the word *definite,* for instance, gives us few clues as to whether the vowels in the second and third syllables should be *i*'s or *a*'s. In this case, remembering how the related word *finite* looks or sounds helps us know that the *i*'s are correct. If you are puzzled about how to spell a word with unstressed vowels, try to think of a related word that will give you a clue to the correct spelling. Then check your dictionary.

30d Taking advantage of spelling rules

Fortunately, English spelling does follow some general rules that can be of enormous help to writers. This section focuses on those rules closely related to commonly misspelled words.

1 Remembering "*i before e*"

Most of you probably memorized the "*i before e*" rule long ago. Here is a slightly expanded version:

i before *e* except after *c*

or when pronounced "ay"

as in *neighbor* or *weigh*

or in *weird* exceptions like *either* and *species*

I BEFORE E   ach*ie*ve, br*ie*f, f*ie*ld, fr*ie*nd

EXCEPT AFTER C   c*ei*ling, conc*ei*vable, dec*ei*t, rec*ei*ve

OR WHEN PRONOUNCED "AY"   *ei*ghth, n*ei*ghbor, r*ei*gn, w*ei*gh

OR IN WEIRD EXCEPTIONS   ancient, caffeine, conscience, either, foreign, height, leisure, neither, science, seize, species, weird

● **EXERCISE 30.3**

Insert either *ei* or *ie* in the blank in each of the following words.

1. sl____gh
2. consc____nce
3. anc____nt
4. l____sure
5. p____rce
6. caff____ne
7. ch____f
8. rec____ve
9. ach____ve
10. h____ress

2 Adding prefixes

Prefixes are verbal elements placed at the *beginnings* of words to add to or qualify their meaning. Prefixes do not change the spelling of the words they are added to, even when the last letter of the prefix and the first letter of the word it is added to are the same.

    dis- + service = disservice   over- + rate = overrate

Some prefixes require the use of hyphens. For a discussion of such usage, see 57c.

3 Adding suffixes

Suffixes are elements placed at the *ends* of words to form related words. This section will provide guidance to spelling words with suffixes.

■ *Words ending in unpronounced* e

For words ending in an unpronounced *e* (*receive, lose, definite*), you must decide whether or not to drop the *e* when adding a suffix. In general, if the suffix starts with a vowel, *drop* the *e*.

    explore + -ation = exploration   exercise + -ing = exercising
    imagine + -able = imaginable   continue + -ous = continuous

If the suffix starts with a consonant, *keep* the *e*.

    force + -ful = forceful   state + -ly = stately
    excite + -ment = excitement   same + -ness = sameness

EXCEPTIONS

    dye + -ing = dyeing   marriage + -able = marriageable
    notice + -able = noticeable   courage + -ous = courageous
    argue + -ment = argument   true + -ly = truly
    judge + -ment = judgment   nine + -th = ninth

● EXERCISE 30.4

Combine each of the following words and suffixes, dropping the unpronounced *e* when necessary.

1. future + -ism	5. malice + -ious	9. exercise + -ing
2. whole + -ly	6. dye + -ing	10. outrage + -ous
3. argue + -ment	7. hope + -ful	
4. lone + -ly	8. continue + -ous	

▧ -ally and -ly

Use *-ally* if the base word ends in *ic*, *-ly* if it does not.

drastic + -ally = drastically	tragic + -ally = tragically
apparent + -ly = apparently	quick + -ly = quickly

EXCEPTION

public + -ly = publicly

▧ -cede, -ceed, and -sede

The suffixes *-cede*, *-ceed*, and *-sede* are easy to use correctly because almost all words ending in the sound pronounced "seed" use the spelling *-cede*. Use *-sede* with only one word: *supersede*. Use *-ceed* with only three words: *exceed, proceed, succeed*. Use *-cede* with all other words ending in the "seed" sound.

accede	intercede	recede
concede	precede	secede

▧ *Words ending in y*

When you add a suffix to some words ending in *y*, you must change the *y* to *i*. In general, if it is preceded by a consonant, change the *y*.

bounty + -ful = bountiful	breezy + -ness = breeziness
try + -ed = tried	busy + -ly = busily
silly + -er = sillier	

Keep the *y* if it is preceded by a vowel, if it is part of a proper name, or if the suffix begins with *i*.

joy + -ous = joyous	dry + -ing = drying
play + -ful = playful	Kennedy + -esque = Kennedyesque

EXCEPTIONS

day + -ly = daily	gay + -ly = gaily
shy + -er = shyer	wry + -ness = wryness
dry + -ly = dryly	

● **EXERCISE 30.5**

Combine each of the following words and suffixes, changing the final *y* to *i* when necessary.

1. lonely + -er
2. carry + -ing
3. defy + -ance
4. study + -ous
5. supply + -ed
6. duty + -ful
7. likely + -hood
8. obey + -ed
9. rainy + -est
10. coy + -ly

■ *Words ending in a consonant*

When a suffix beginning with a vowel is added to a word that ends in a consonant, the consonant is sometimes doubled. In general, if the word ends in consonant + vowel + consonant and the word contains only one syllable or ends in an accented syllable, double the final consonant.

stop + -ing = stopping

slap + -ed = slapped

hot + -est = hottest

run + -er = runner

begin + -ing = beginning

occur + -ence = occurrence

refer + -ing = referring

Do not double the consonant if it is preceded by more than one vowel or by another consonant, if the suffix begins with a consonant, if the word is not accented on the last syllable, or if the accent shifts from the last to the first syllable when the suffix is added.

sleep + -ing = sleeping

ship + -ment = shipment

benefit + -ing = benefiting

infer + -ence = inference

start + -ed = started

fit + -ness = fitness

fasten + -er = fastener

prefer + -ence = preference

www ● bedford
stmartins.com/
smhandbook

For additional
exercises on using
spelling rules,
click on

► Exercise Central
  ► Spelling

● **EXERCISE 30.6**

Combine each of the following words and suffixes, doubling the final consonant when necessary.

1. occur + -ed
2. fast + -est
3. skip + -er
4. refer + -ence
5. commit + -ment
6. regret + -able
7. submit + -ed
8. frantic + -ally
9. benefit + -ed
10. weep + -ing

Making singular nouns plural calls for the use of several different spelling guidelines. For most words, simply add *-s*. For words ending in *s, ch, sh, x,* or *z,* add *-es.*

pencil, pencils	book, books	computer, computers
Jones, Joneses	fox, foxes	flash, flashes
bus, buses	church, churches	buzz, buzzes

● For information on using apostrophes to form certain plurals, see 51c.

▨ Words ending in o

Add *-es* if the *o* is preceded by a consonant. Add *-s* if the *o* is preceded by a vowel.

| potato, potatoes | hero, heroes | veto, vetoes |
| rodeo, rodeos | patio, patios | zoo, zoos |

EXCEPTIONS

| memo, memos | piano, pianos | solo, solos |

▨ Words ending in f or fe

For some words ending in *f* or *fe,* change *f* to *v,* and add *-s* or *-es.*

calf, calves	life, lives	leaf, leaves
half, halves	wife, wives	hoof, hooves
self, selves	shelf, shelves	knife, knives

▨ Words ending in y

For words ending in *y,* change *y* to *i* and add *-es* if the *y* is preceded by a consonant. Keep the *y* and add *-s* if the *y* is preceded by a vowel or if the word is a proper name.

theory, theories	huckleberry, huckleberries
guy, guys	attorney, attorneys
Henry, Henrys	

▨ Irregular plurals

Memorize irregular plurals you do not already know.

man, men	bacterium, bacteria	deer, deer
woman, women	locus, loci	sheep, sheep
child, children	alga, algae	moose, moose
foot, feet	basis, bases	series, series
tooth, teeth	datum, data	species, species

■ Compound words

For compound nouns written as one word, make the last part of the compound plural. For compound nouns written as separate words or hyphenated, make the most important part of the compound plural.

briefcase, briefcases
mailbox, mailboxes
brother-in-law, brothers-in-law
lieutenant governor, lieutenant governors
sergeant major, sergeants major
leap year, leap years
bus stop, bus stops

■ Acronyms and abbreviations without periods

Show the plural by simply adding a lowercase -s.

MOOs   VCRs   SATs   TVs

● **EXERCISE 30.7**

Form the plural of each of the following words.

1. tomato
2. hoof
3. volunteer
4. baby
5. dish
6. spoof
7. beach
8. yourself
9. golf club
10. rose
11. stepchild
12. turkey
13. heir apparent
14. radio
15. phenomenon

30f Using your spell checker

Most writers now have access to a spell checker, a computer program that helps find incorrect spellings. Though these programs can be helpful, a comparison of spelling errors in first-year essays produced these interesting results.

handwritten or typed	1.74 errors per essay
written on a computer *without* spell checker	3.81 errors per essay
written on a computer *with* spell checker	1.60 errors per essay

These findings make an important point about writing on a computer: seeing your words onscreen or in nice, neat typescript may make it difficult to "see" your spelling errors. Indeed, keyboarding often introduces new spelling errors, and the "clean" copy can, in a way, conceal these errors. If you use a computer without a spell checker, you probably need to proofread more carefully than ever before.

These results also tell us that spell checkers alone won't correct all spelling errors. Students using spell checkers misspelled almost as many words as did students who handwrote or typed their essays. To benefit from this tool, therefore, you must understand how to use a spell checker accurately and efficiently, and you must learn to adapt the spell checker to your own needs.

USING A SPELL CHECKER

1. *Use* your spell checker. Keep a dictionary near your computer (or add a dictionary to your word-processing program by going to <www.onelook.com>, where you can download a dictionary for educational use). Look up *any* word the spell checker highlights that you aren't absolutely sure of.

2. Remember that spell-checker dictionaries are limited; they don't recognize most proper names, foreign words, or specialized language. Many spell checkers do, however, allow you to add words so that the program will then recognize them.

3. If your program has a learn option, enter into your spell-checker dictionary any words you use regularly and have trouble spelling. Also create a file for "spelling demons," and keep a special list there.

4. Remember that spell checkers do not recognize homonym errors (misspelling *there* as *their,* for example). If you know that you mix up certain words, check for them after running your spell checker. You may be able to use the search function to identify words you need to check — every *their, there,* and *they're,* for instance.

5. Remember that spell checkers are not sensitive to capitalization. If you write "president bush," the spell checker won't question it.

6. Proofread carefully, even after you have used the spell checker.

30g Building on visualization and memory cues

Before the advent of printing—and photocopying machines—people learned to train their memories extensively. You can activate your memory first by **visualizing** correct spellings or making mental pictures of how a word looks. You can also learn to use memory cues, or **mnemonic devices**, in mastering words that tend to trip you up. Here are one student's memory cues:

WORD; MISSPELLING	CUE
a lot; alot	I wouldn't write *alittle*, would I?
government; goverment	Government should serve those it *governs*.
separate; seperate	*Separate* rates two *a*'s.
definitely; definately	There are a *finite* number of ways to spell *definitely*.

EXERCISE 30.8

Correct each misspelling in the following passage. Whenever possible, classify the misspelling according to one of the guidelines in this chapter. Then draw up three or four spelling tips you could give this particular student.

For me, the ideel ocupation is an arangement in which I would play with a band for six months and tour the other six months of the year. I wouldn't want to teach music because I would probly have to teach in a school where many students are forced by there parrents to take music. When children are forced to do something, its likly that they won't enjoy it. If I were able to both tour an teach, however, I would be happy.

I'm realy glad that I've gotten involved in music; it looks as if I'm destined to be a profesional musician. Surly I don't know what else I could do; I dout I'd be a good administrater or bussiness executive or lawyer. And the idea of being a doctor or denist and probing around people's bodys or looking at teeth that have huge, roting cavities isn't appealing to me. The more I think about it, the happyer I am with my music. I definately plan to pursue that career.

THINKING CRITICALLY ABOUT YOUR SPELLING

If you are keeping a writing log, devote a section of it to a personal spelling inventory. Choose a sample of your recent writing, and identify every misspelling. If you have any drafts saved in a computer, use a spell checker. Then enter the word, your misspelling, and the guideline or pattern that relates to it (such as "homonym" or "final *e* + suffix"). For persistent misspellings, create a memory cue (see 30g), and enter it in the log along with the correct spelling.

PART 6

SENTENCES: MAKING GRAMMATICAL CHOICES

"We learn a great deal about grammar
from reading—and not grammar
books but newspapers, novels,
poetry, magazines, even the labels
on cereal boxes."
—LYNN Z. BLOOM

31

▼ Constructing Grammatical Sentences

31a Understanding the basic grammar of sentences

A **sentence** is a grammatically complete group of words that expresses a thought. To be grammatically complete, a group of words must contain both a subject and a predicate. The **subject** identifies what the sentence is about, and the **predicate** says or asks something about the subject or tells the subject to do something.

SUBJECT	PREDICATE
I	have a dream.
We	shall overcome.
California	is a state of mind.
Harry Potter, wizard extraordinaire,	lives at Hogwarts.

Some sentences contain only a one-word predicate with an implied, or "understood," subject (for example, *Stop!*). Most sentences, however, contain additional words that expand the basic subject and predicate. In the preceding example, for instance, the subject might have been simply *Harry Potter;* the words *wizard extraordinaire* say more about the subject. Similarly, the predicate of that sentence could grammatically be *lives;* the words *at Hogwarts* expand the predicate by telling us where Harry lives.

A good way to examine your own sentences is by studying two or three examples of your own writing and classifying each sentence — grammatically, as simple, compound, complex, or compound-complex (31d1); functionally, as declarative, interrogative, imperative, or exclamatory (31d2); and (where applicable) rhetorically, as periodic or cumulative (46c3). Perhaps keep a tally of how many of each type of sentence you write, and then look for patterns.

→ Are your sentences varied, or do you rely heavily on one or two sentence patterns?

→ If you write mainly simple sentences, see if combining some to make compound or complex sentences makes your writing flow more smoothly.

→ If you have many compound sentences, see if revising some as complex sentences makes your writing easier to read.

→ If your sentences are all declarative, see if you would like to emphasize one, and try rephrasing it as a question or exclamation.

→ If you find several short sentences in a row, try combining them into one cumulative sentence.

● **EXERCISE 31.1**

Identify the subject and predicate in each of the following sentences, underlining the subject once and the predicate twice. Example:

The roaring lion at the beginning of old MGM films is a part of movie history.

1. My foot got tangled in the computer cord.
2. Her first afternoon as a kindergarten teacher had left her exhausted.
3. Dr. Burns is almost certainly going to recommend surgery.
4. Our office manager, a stern taskmaster with a fondness for Chanel suits, has been terrifying interns since 1976.
5. Hearing his petulant voice on the radio always forces me to change the station.

www ● bedford
stmartins.com/
smhandbook

For additional
exercises on
subjects and
predicates, click on

▶ **Exercise Central**
　▶ **Basic Grammar**

31b Recognizing the parts of speech

If the basic sentence parts are subjects and predicates, the central elements of subjects and predicates are nouns and verbs. For example:

582

gram

31b

GRAMMAR

Constructing
Grammatical
Sentences

A solitary figure waited on the platform.

Nouns and verbs are two of the eight **parts of speech,** which are grammatical categories into which words may be classified. The other six parts of speech are pronouns, adjectives, adverbs, prepositions, conjunctions, and interjections. Many English words can function as more than one part of speech. Take the word *book,* for instance: when you *book a plane flight,* it is a verb; when you *take a good book to the beach,* it is a noun; and when you *have book knowledge,* it is an adjective.

1 Recognizing verbs

Verbs are among the most important words, for they move the meaning of sentences along by showing action (*glance, speculate*), occurrence (*become, happen*), or a state of being (*be, seem*). Verbs change form to show *time, person, number, voice,* and *mood.*

TIME	we *work,* we *worked*
PERSON	I *work,* she *works*
NUMBER	one person *works,* two people *work*
VOICE	she *asks,* she *is asked*
MOOD	we *see,* if I *were to see*

See Chapter 33
for a complete
discussion of
verbs; for more
on how verbs
change form to
show person and
number, see 34a.

Auxiliary verbs (also called **helping verbs**) combine with other verbs (often called **main verbs**) to create *verb phrases.* Auxiliaries include the forms of *be, do,* and *have,* which are also used as main verbs, and the words *can, could, may, might, must, shall, should, will,* and *would.*

You *must get* some sleep tonight!

I *could have danced* all night.

She *would prefer* to take Italian rather than Spanish.

www • bedford
stmartins.com/
smhandbook

For additional
exercises on verbs,
click on

▶ Exercise Central
  ▶ Basic Grammar

EXERCISE 31.2

Underline each verb or verb phrase in the following sentences. Example:
    Terence <u>should sing</u> well in Sunday's performance.

1. In April, we will get a new DVD player.

2. The faucet had been leaking all day.

3. I agree; the office does need a new copy machine.

4. One person can collect sap, a second might run the evaporator, and a third should finish the syrup.

5. A job at an animal hospital would be great.

2 Recognizing nouns

Nouns name persons (*aviator, child*), places (*lake, library*), things (*truck, suitcase*), or concepts (*happiness, balance*). **Proper nouns** name specific persons, places, things, or concepts: *Bill, Iowa, Supreme Court, Buddhism.* Proper nouns are capitalized. **Collective nouns** name groups: *team, flock, jury.*

Most nouns can be changed from **singular** (one) to **plural** (more than one) by adding *-s* or *-es: horse, horses; kiss, kisses.* Some nouns, however, have irregular plural forms: *woman, women; alumnus, alumni; mouse, mice; deer, deer.* **Noncount nouns** cannot be made plural because they name something that cannot easily be counted: *dust, peace, prosperity.*

Nouns can also take a possessive form to show ownership. A writer usually forms the possessive by adding an apostrophe plus *-s* to a singular noun or just an apostrophe to a plural noun: *the horse's owner, the boys' department.*

Nouns are often preceded by the **article** *a, an,* or *the: a rocket, an astronaut, the launch.* Articles are also known as **noun markers** or **determiners.**

● For more on proper nouns, see 54b; for more on collective nouns, see 34d and 35b.

● For more on plural forms, see 30e.

● For more on possessives, see 51a.

● For a complete discussion of articles and determiners, see 59c and d.

FOR MULTILINGUAL WRITERS: Using Count and Noncount Nouns

Is the hill covered with grass or grasses? See 59a for a discussion of count and noncount nouns.

● **EXERCISE 31.3**

Identify the nouns, including possessive forms, and the articles in each of the following sentences. Underline the nouns once and the articles twice. Example:

The Puritans' hopes were dashed when Charles II regained his father's throne.

1. After Halloween, the children got sick from eating too much candy.

2. Although plagiarism is dishonest, it does occur.

3. Thanksgiving is a grim season for turkeys.

4. The crocuses' buds dropped when a sudden frost turned the ground into a field of ice.

5. In the front row sat two people, a man with slightly graying hair and a young woman in jeans.

www ● bedford
stmartins.com/
smhandbook

For additional
exercises on nouns,
click on

► Exercise Central
► Basic Grammar

GRAMMAR

Constructing
Grammatical
Sentences

For a complete ··········•
discussion of
pronouns and
antecedents, see
Chapters 32 and
35.

For a discussion ··········•
of the forms of
personal pro-
nouns, see Chap-
ter 32.

Pronouns often function as nouns in sentences and often take the place of nouns, serving as short forms so that we do not have to repeat a noun that has already been mentioned. A noun that a pronoun replaces or refers to is called the **antecedent** of the pronoun. In the following example, the antecedent of *she* is *Caitlin:*

> *Caitlin* refused the invitation even though *she* wanted to go.

Pronouns fall into several categories: personal, possessive, reflexive, intensive, indefinite, demonstrative, interrogative, relative, and reciprocal. **Personal pronouns** refer to specific persons or things.

> I, you, he, she, it, we, they

Each can take several different forms (for example, *I, me, my, mine*) depending on how it functions in a sentence.

> After the scouts made camp, *they* ran along the beach.
>
> Could the scout leaders catch up with *them?*

Possessive pronouns indicate ownership.

> my, mine, your, yours, her, hers, his, its, our, ours, their, theirs
>
> *My* roommate lost *her* keys.

Reflexive pronouns refer to the subject of the sentence or clause in which they appear. They end in *-self* or *-selves.*

> myself, yourself, himself, herself, itself, oneself, ourselves, yourselves, themselves
>
> The seals sunned *themselves* on the warm rocks.

Intensive pronouns have the same form as reflexive pronouns. They are used to emphasize their antecedents.

> He decided to paint the apartment *himself.*

Indefinite pronouns do not refer to specific nouns, although they may refer to identifiable persons or things. They express the idea of a quantity (*all, some, any, none*) or an unspecified person or thing (*somebody, anything*). Indefinite pronouns are one of the largest categories of pronouns; the following is a partial list:

> all, anybody, both, each, everything, few, most, none, one, some
>
> *Somebody* screamed when the lights went out.
>
> We gave them *everything* we had.

Demonstrative pronouns identify or point to specific nouns.

> this, that, these, those
>
> *These* are Peter's books.

Interrogative pronouns are used to ask questions.

> who, which, what
>
> *Who* can help set up the chairs for the meeting?

Relative pronouns introduce dependent clauses and "relate" the dependent clause to the rest of the sentence.

•⸺ For more on
dependent
clauses, see
31c4.

> who, which, that, what, whoever, whichever, whatever
>
> Margaret owns the car *that* is parked by the corner.

The interrogative pronoun *who* and the relative pronouns *who* and *who-ever* have different forms depending on how they are used in a sentence.

•⸺ For a discussion
of the forms of
who and *whoever,*
see 32b.

Reciprocal pronouns refer to the individual parts of a plural antecedent.

> each other, one another
>
> The business failed because the partners distrusted *each other.*

•⸺ www • bedford
stmartins.com/
smhandbook

For additional
exercises on
pronouns, click on

▶ Exercise Central
  ▶ Basic Grammar

● **EXERCISE 31.4**

Identify the pronouns and any antecedents in each of the following sentences, underlining the pronouns once and any antecedents twice. Example:

> As identical twins, they really do understand each other.

1. She thanked everyone for helping.

2. Jane is the only one who understands the telephone system, and she is on vacation.

3. Who is going to buy the jeans and wear them if the designer himself finds them uncomfortable?

4. They have only themselves to blame.

5. People who are extremely fastidious often annoy those who are not.

4 Recognizing adjectives

Adjectives modify (limit the meaning of) nouns and pronouns, usually by describing, identifying, or quantifying those words.

gram

586

31b

GRAMMAR

Constructing
Grammatical
Sentences

The *red* Corvette ran off the road. [describes]

It was *defective.* [describes]

That Corvette needs to be repaired. [identifies]

We saw *several other* Corvettes race by. [quantifies]

In addition to their basic forms, most descriptive adjectives have other forms that are used to make comparisons: *small, smaller, smallest; foolish, more foolish, most foolish, less foolish, least foolish.*

This year's attendance was *smaller* than last year's.

This year's attendance was the *smallest* in ten years.

Many of the pronouns in 31b3 can function as adjectives when they are followed by a noun.

His is the best chili. [pronoun]

His chili is the best in town. [adjective]

Other kinds of adjectives that identify or quantify are articles (*a, an, the*) and numbers (*three, sixty-fifth, five hundred*).

For more on
proper adjec-
tives, see 54b;
for a complete
discussion of
adjectives, see
Chapter 36.

Proper adjectives are adjectives formed from or related to proper nouns (*Egyptian, Emersonian*). Proper adjectives are capitalized.

5 Recognizing adverbs

Adverbs modify verbs, adjectives, other adverbs, or entire clauses. Many adverbs have an *-ly* ending, though some do not (*always, never, very, well*), and some words that end in *-ly* are not adverbs but adjectives (*friendly, lovely*). One of the most common adverbs is *not.*

David and Rebecca *recently* visited Maine. [modifies the verb *visited*]

They had an *unexpectedly* exciting trip. [modifies the adjective *exciting*]

They *very* soon discovered lobster. [modifies the adverb *soon*]

Frankly, they would have liked to stay another month. [modifies the independent clause that makes up the rest of the sentence]

Adverbs often answer the questions *when? where? why? how? to what extent?* In the first example above, for instance, *recently* answers the question *when?* In the third sentence, *very* answers the question *to what extent?*

Many adverbs, like many adjectives, have different forms that are used in making comparisons: *forcefully, more forcefully, most forcefully, less forcefully, least forcefully.*

The senator spoke *more forcefully* than her opponent.

Of all the candidates, she speaks the *most forcefully.*

Conjunctive adverbs modify an entire clause and express the connection in meaning between that clause and the preceding clause (or sentence). Examples of conjunctive adverbs include *however, furthermore, therefore,* and *likewise.*

For more on conjunctive adverbs, see 31b7; for a complete discussion of adverbs, see Chapter 36.

● **EXERCISE 31.5**

Identify the adjectives and adverbs in each of the following sentences, underlining the adjectives once and the adverbs twice. Remember that articles and some pronouns are used as adjectives. Example:

Inadvertently, the two agents misquoted their major client.

1. Because time had grown perilously short, I quickly prepared the final draft.
2. Nevertheless, her teenage son eventually overcame his poor study habits.
3. The somewhat shy author spoke reluctantly to six exuberant admirers.
4. The huge red tomatoes looked lovely, but they tasted disappointingly like cardboard.
5. The youngest dancer in the troupe performed a brilliant solo.

www ● bedford
stmartins.com/
smhandbook

For additional exercises on adjectives and adverbs, click on
▶ Exercise Central
  ▶ Basic Grammar

● **EXERCISE 31.6**

Expand each of the following sentences by adding appropriate adjectives and adverbs. Delete *the* if need be. Example:

Then the three   thoroughly   nervous
The veterinarians examined the patient.

1. A corporation can fire employees.
2. The dog limped along the road.
3. In the painting, a road curves between hills.
4. Candles gleamed on the tabletop.
5. Workers installed a cable.

6 Recognizing prepositions

Prepositions are important structural words that express relationships — in space, time, or other senses — between nouns or pronouns and other words in a sentence.

> We did not want to leave *during* the game.

> The contestants waited nervously *for* the announcement.

> Drive *across* the bridge, go *down* the avenue *past* three stoplights, and then turn left *before* the Gulf station.

■ *Some common prepositions*

about	at	down	near	since
above	before	during	of	through
across	behind	except	off	toward
after	below	for	on	under
against	beneath	from	onto	until
along	beside	in	out	up
among	between	inside	over	upon
around	beyond	into	past	with
as	by	like	regarding	without

Some prepositions, called compound prepositions, are made up of more than one word.

■ *Some compound prepositions*

according to	except for	instead of
as well as	in addition to	next to
because of	in front of	out of
by way of	in place of	with regard to
due to	in spite of	

If you are in doubt about which preposition to use, consult your dictionary. Frederich Wood's *English Prepositional Idioms* is a dictionary devoted to prepositions.

A **prepositional phrase** is made up of a preposition together with the noun or pronoun it connects to the rest of the sentence.

For more on
prepositional
phrases, see
31c3 and Chapter 61.

EXERCISE 31.7

Identify and underline the prepositions. Example:

In the dim interior of the hut crouched an old man.

1. The transportation board of the county is planning to add limited bus service from midnight until five A.M.

2. He ran swiftly through the brush, across the beach, and into the sea.

3. According to reporters, the police arrived promptly at the scene.

4. During our trip down the river, a rivalry developed between us.

5. The nuclear power plant about ten miles from the city has the worst safety record in the country.

**www • bedford
stmartins.com/
smhandbook**

For additional
exercises on
prepositions,
click on

▶ **Exercise Central**
  ▶ **Basic Grammar**

7 Recognizing conjunctions

Conjunctions connect words or groups of words to each other. There are four kinds of conjunctions: coordinating conjunctions, correlative conjunctions, subordinating conjunctions, and conjunctive adverbs.

■ *Coordinating conjunctions*

Coordinating conjunctions join equivalent structures — two or more nouns, pronouns, verbs, adjectives, adverbs, prepositions, conjunctions, phrases, or clauses.

| and | but | or | yet | nor | for | so |

A strong *but* warm breeze blew across the desert.

Please print *or* type the information on the application form.

Her arguments were easy to ridicule *yet* hard to refute.

He did not have much money, *nor* did he know how to get any.

• For a discussion of how to use coordinating conjunctions effectively in writing, see 44a.

■ *Correlative conjunctions*

Correlative conjunctions join equal elements, and they come in pairs.

| both . . . and | just as . . . so | not only . . . but also |
| either . . . or | neither . . . nor | whether . . . or |

gram

31b

590

GRAMMAR

Constructing
Grammatical
Sentences

Both Bechtel *and* Kaiser submitted bids on the project.

Maisha *not only* sent a card *but also* visited me in the hospital.

■ *Subordinating conjunctions*

Subordinating conjunctions introduce adverb clauses and signal the relationship between the adverb clause and another clause, usually an independent clause. For instance, in the following sentence, the subordinating conjunction *while* signals a time relationship, letting us know that the two events in the sentence happened simultaneously:

Sweat ran down my face *while* I frantically searched for my child.

SOME COMMON SUBORDINATING CONJUNCTIONS

after	if	unless
although	in order that	until
as	once	when
as if	since	where
because	so that	while
before	than	
even though	though	

Unless sales improve dramatically, the company will soon be bankrupt.

My grandmother began traveling *after* she sold her house.

■ *Conjunctive adverbs*

Conjunctive adverbs connect independent clauses and often act as transitional expressions (see 48e). As their name suggests, conjunctive adverbs can be considered both adverbs and conjunctions because they modify the second clause in addition to connecting it to the preceding clause. Like many other adverbs yet unlike other conjunctions, they can be moved to different positions in a clause.

The cider tasted bitter; *however,* each of us drank a tall glass of it.

The cider tasted bitter; each of us, *however,* drank a tall glass of it.

The cider tasted bitter. Each of us drank a tall glass of it, *however.*

also	indeed	now
anyway	instead	otherwise
besides	likewise	similarly
certainly	meanwhile	still
finally	moreover	then
furthermore	namely	therefore
however	nevertheless	thus
incidentally	next	undoubtedly

Independent clauses connected by a conjunctive adverb must be separated by a semicolon or a period, not just a comma.

> Some of these problems could occur at any company; *indeed,* many could happen only here.

•— For more on
independent
clauses con-
nected by con-
junctive adverbs,
see 39c.

EXERCISE 31.8

Underline the coordinating, correlative, and subordinating conjunctions as well as the conjunctive adverbs in each of the following sentences. Example:

> We used sleeping bags, even though the cabin had sheets and blankets.

1. After waiting for an hour and a half, both Jenny and I were disgruntled, so we went home.

2. The shops along the waterfront were open, but business was slow.

3. The story was not only long but also dull.

4. Although I live in a big city, my neighborhood has enough trees and raccoons to make me feel as if I live in the suburbs.

5. Enrique was not qualified for the job because he knew one of the programming languages but not the other; still, the interview encouraged him.

**www • bedford
stmartins.com/
smhandbook**

For additional
exercises on
conjunctions,
click on

▸ **Exercise Central**
  ▸ **Basic Grammar**

8 Recognizing interjections

Interjections express surprise or emotion: *oh, ouch, ah, hey.* Interjections often stand alone as fragments. Even when they are included in a sentence, they are not related grammatically to the rest of the sentence. They are used mostly in speaking; in writing, they are used mostly in dialogue.

> *"Yes! All right!"* The fans screamed, jumping to their feet.

> The problem suggested, *alas,* no easy solution.

31c   Recognizing the parts of a sentence

Knowing a word's part of speech helps us understand how to use that word, but we also have to look at the part it plays in a particular sentence. Every sentence has a grammatical pattern or structure, and certain parts of speech — nouns, pronouns, and adjectives — can function in more than one way depending on this structure.

> SUBJECT
> This *description* evokes the ecology of the Everglades.

> DIRECT OBJECT
> I read a *description* of the ecology of the Everglades.

Description is a noun in both of these sentences, yet in the first it serves as the subject of the verb *evokes,* while in the second it serves as the direct object of the verb *read.*

BASIC SENTENCE PATTERNS

1. SUBJECT/VERB

> S   V
> Babies cry.

2. SUBJECT/VERB/SUBJECT COMPLEMENT

> S   V   SC
> Babies seem fragile.

3. SUBJECT/VERB/DIRECT OBJECT

> S   V   DO
> Babies drink milk.

4. SUBJECT/VERB/INDIRECT OBJECT/DIRECT OBJECT

> S   V   IO   DO
> Babies give grandparents pleasure.

5. SUBJECT/VERB/DIRECT OBJECT/OBJECT COMPLEMENT

> S   V   DO   OC
> Babies make parents proud.

This section examines the essential parts of a sentence — subjects, predicates, objects, complements, phrases, and clauses.

As described in 31a, almost every sentence has a stated subject, which identifies whom or what the sentence is about. The **simple subject** consists of one or more nouns or pronouns; the **complete subject** consists of the simple subject (SS) with all its modifiers.

SS
Baseball is a summer game.

COMPLETE SUBJECT — SS
Sailing over the fence, the ball crashed through Mr. Wilson's window.

SS COMPLETE SUBJECT
Stadiums with real grass are popular once again.

SS COMPLETE SUBJECT
Those who sit in the bleachers have the most fun.

A **compound subject** contains two or more simple subjects joined with a coordinating conjunction (*and, but, or*) or a correlative conjunction (*both . . . and, either . . . or, neither . . . nor, not only . . . but also*).

Baseball and softball developed from cricket.

Both baseball and softball developed from cricket.

The simple subject usually comes before the predicate, or verb, but not always. Sometimes writers reverse this order to achieve a particular effect.

Up to the plate stepped *Casey*.

Great was the *anticipation* among Mudville fans.

In **imperative sentences,** which express requests or commands, the subject *you* is usually implied but not stated.

(*You*) Keep your eye on the ball.

In questions and certain other constructions, the subject usually appears between the auxiliary verb and the main verb.

Did *Casey* save the game?

Never have *I* been so angry.

In sentences beginning with *there* or *here* followed by a form of the verb *be,* the subject always follows the verb. *There* and *here* are never the subject.

Here is the sad *ending* of the game.

There was no *joy* in Mudville.

GRAMMAR

Constructing
Grammatical
Sentences

**www • bedford
stmartins.com/
smhandbook**

For additional
exercises on
subjects, click on

▶ **Exercise Central**
  ▶ **Basic Grammar**

● **EXERCISE 31.9**

Identify the complete subject and the simple subject in each sentence. Underline the complete subject once and the simple subject twice. Example:

The tall, powerful woman defiantly blocked the doorway.

1. A shortage of affordable housing near the university makes many students' lives difficult.

2. Has the new elevator been installed?

3. Here are some representative photographs.

4. Japanese animation, with its cutting-edge graphics and futuristic plots, has earned many American admirers.

5. Some women worried about osteoporosis take calcium supplements.

2 Recognizing predicates

In addition to a subject, every sentence has a predicate, which asserts or asks something about the subject or tells the subject to do something. The "hinge," or key word, of most predicates is a verb. A verb can include auxiliary verbs (as in this sentence, where *can* is an auxiliary and *include* is the main verb). The **simple predicate** of a sentence is the main verb and any auxiliaries; the **complete predicate** includes the simple predicate (SP) and any modifiers of the verb and any objects or complements and their modifiers.

COMPLETE
SP PREDICATE
My roommate *seems wonderful.*

COMPLETE PREDICATE
SP
Both of us *are planning to major in history.*

A **compound predicate** contains two or more verbs that have the same subject and that are usually joined by a coordinating or a correlative conjunction.

Omar *shut the book, put it back on the shelf, and sighed.*

The Amish *neither drive cars nor use electricity.*

On the basis of how they function in predicates, verbs can be divided into three categories: linking, transitive, and intransitive.

■ *Linking verbs*

A linking verb links, or joins, a subject with a **subject complement**, a word or word group that identifies or describes the subject. If it identifies the subject, the complement is a noun or pronoun.

> S   V ⌐————— SC —————⌐
> Christine is a single mother.

If it describes the subject, the complement is an adjective.

> S   V   SC
> She is exhausted.

The forms of *be,* when used as main verbs rather than as auxiliary verbs, are linking verbs (like *are* in this sentence). Other verbs, such as *appear, become, feel, grow, look, make, seem, smell,* and *sound,* can also function as linking verbs, depending on the sense of the sentence.

> ⌐————— S —————⌐ ⌐— V —⌐   SC
> The abandoned farmhouse had become dilapidated.

> S   V   ⌐———— SC ————⌐
> It looked ready to fall down.

■ *Transitive and intransitive verbs*

If a verb is not a linking verb, it is either transitive or intransitive. A **transitive verb** expresses action that is directed toward a noun or pronoun, called the **direct object** of the verb.

> S   V   ⌐———— DO ————⌐
> He answered his cellular phone.

A direct object identifies what or who receives the action of the verb. In the preceding example, the direct object says *what* he answered.

A direct object may be followed by an **object complement**, a word or word group that describes or identifies it. Object complements may be adjectives, as in the next example, or nouns, as in the second example.

> S   V   ⌐———————— DO ————————⌐ ⌐— OC —⌐
> I find cell-phone conversations in restaurants very annoying.

> S   V   DO   ⌐— OC —⌐
> Alana considers Harold her best friend.

A transitive verb may also be followed by an **indirect object**, which tells to whom or what, or for whom or what, the verb's action is done. You might say the indirect object is the recipient of the direct object.

$$\overset{\text{S}}{\overbrace{\text{The sound of the traffic all night long}}} \overset{\text{V}}{\text{gave}} \overset{\text{IO}}{\text{me}} \overset{\text{DO}}{\overbrace{\text{a splitting headache.}}}$$

An **intransitive verb** expresses action that is not directed toward an object. Therefore, an intransitive verb does not have a direct object.

$$\overset{\text{S}}{\overbrace{\text{The Red Sox}}} \overset{\text{V}}{\text{struggled.}}$$

$$\overset{\text{S}}{\overbrace{\text{Their fans}}} \overset{\text{V}}{\text{watched}} \text{ helplessly.}$$

The action of the verb *struggled* has no object (it makes no sense to ask, *struggled what?* or *struggled whom?*), and the action of the verb *watched* is directed toward an object that is implied but not expressed.

Some verbs that express action can be only transitive or only intransitive, but most can be used both ways, with or without a direct object.

$$\overset{\text{S}}{\overbrace{\text{A maid wearing a uniform}}} \overset{\text{V}}{\text{opened}} \overset{\text{DO}}{\overbrace{\text{the door.}}} \text{ [transitive]}$$

$$\overset{\text{S}}{\overbrace{\text{The door}}} \overset{\text{V}}{\text{opened}} \text{ silently. [intransitive]}$$

www • bedford
stmartins.com/
smhandbook

For additional
exercises on
predicates, click on

▶ Exercise Central
  ▶ Basic Grammar

● **EXERCISE 31.10**

Underline the predicate in the following sentences. Then label each verb as linking, transitive, or intransitive. Finally, label all subject and object complements and all direct and indirect objects. Example:

$$\text{We } \overset{\text{TV}}{\text{considered}} \overset{\text{DO}}{\overbrace{\text{city life}}} \overset{\text{OC}}{\text{unbearable.}}$$

1. The bus driver is new to this route.
2. The U.S. Constitution made us a nation.
3. A hung jury seems likely in this case.
4. Rock and roll will never die.
5. Advertisers promise consumers the world.

3 Recognizing and using phrases

A **phrase** is a group of words that lacks either a subject or a predicate or both. Phrases can add information to a sentence or shape it effectively.

The new law will restrict smoking *in most public places.*

The basic subject of this sentence is a noun phrase, *the new law;* the basic predicate is a verb phrase, *will restrict smoking.* The prepositional phrase *in most public places* functions here as an adverb, telling *where* smoking will be restricted.

This section will discuss the various kinds of phrases: noun, verb, prepositional, verbal, absolute, and appositive.

■ *Noun phrases*

Made up of a noun and all its modifiers, a **noun phrase** can function in a sentence as a subject, object, or complement.

┌──────────── SUBJECT ────────────┐
Delicious, gooey peanut butter is surprisingly healthful.

┌─ OBJECT ─┐
Dieters prefer *green salad.*

┌─ COMPLEMENT ─┐
A tuna sandwich is *a popular lunch.*

■ *Verb phrases*

A main verb and its auxiliary verbs make up a **verb phrase,** which functions in a sentence in only one way: as a predicate.

Frank *had been depressed* for some time.

His problem *might have been caused* by tension between his parents.

■ *Prepositional phrases*

A **prepositional phrase** includes a preposition, a noun or pronoun (called the **object of the preposition**), and any modifiers of the object. Prepositional phrases usually function as adjectives or adverbs; occasionally they function as nouns.

ADJECTIVE	Our house *in Maine* was a cabin.
ADVERB	*From Cadillac Mountain,* you can see the northern lights.
NOUN	The best time to visit is *after lunch.*

■ *Verbal phrases*

Verbals are verb forms that do not function as verbs. Instead, they function as nouns, adjectives, or adverbs. There are three kinds of verbals: participles, gerunds, and infinitives.

For a list of irregular verbs and their past participles, see 33b.

The **participle** functions as an adjective. The **present participle** is the *-ing* form of a verb: *dreaming, being, seeing*. The **past participle** of most verbs ends in *-ed: dreamed, watched*. But some verbs have an irregular past participle: *been, seen, hidden, gone, set*.

A kiss awakened the *dreaming* princess.

The cryptographers deciphered the *hidden* meaning in the message.

The **gerund** has the same form as the present participle but functions as a noun.

SUBJECT	*Writing* takes practice.
OBJECT	The organization promotes *recycling*.

The **infinitive** is the *to* form of a verb: *to dream, to be, to see*. An infinitive can function as a noun, adjective, or adverb.

NOUN	She wanted *to write*.
ADJECTIVE	They had no more time *to waste*.
ADVERB	The corporation was ready *to expand*.

Verbal phrases are made up of a verbal and any modifiers, objects, or complements.

PARTICIPIAL PHRASES

Participial phrases consist of a present participle or a past participle and any modifiers, objects, or complements. Participial phrases always function as adjectives.

Irritated by the delay, Luisa complained.

A dog *howling at the moon* kept me awake.

GERUND PHRASES

Gerund phrases consist of a gerund and any modifiers, objects, or complements. Gerund phrases function as nouns.

┌─── SUBJECT ───┐
Opening their eyes to the problem was not easy.

┌─── DIRECT OBJECT ───┐
They suddenly heard *a loud wailing from the sandbox.*

Infinitive phrases consist of an infinitive and any modifiers, objects, or complements. They can function as nouns, adjectives, or adverbs.

GRAMMAR
Recognizing the
Parts of a Sentence

    ┌────── NOUN/SC ──────┐
My goal is *to be a biology teacher.*

               ┌────── ADJECTIVE ──────┐
A party would be a good way *to end the semester.*

┌────── ADVERB ──────┐
To perfect a draft, always proofread carefully.

Absolute phrases

An **absolute phrase** usually includes a noun or pronoun and a participle. It modifies an entire sentence rather than a particular word and is usually set off from the rest of the sentence with commas.

●···· For more on
commas with
absolute
phrases, see 48a.

    I stood on the deck, *the wind whipping my hair.*

    My fears laid to rest, I climbed into the plane for my first solo flight.

When the participle is *being,* it is often omitted.

    The ambassador, *her head (being) high,* walked out of the room.

Appositive phrases

A noun phrase that renames the noun or pronoun that immediately precedes it is called an **appositive phrase.**

    The report, *a hefty three-volume work,* included 150 recommendations.

    We had a single desire, *to change the administration's policies.*

EXERCISE 31.11

Read the following sentences, and identify and label all of the prepositional, verbal, absolute, and appositive phrases. Notice that one kind of phrase may appear within another kind. Example:

www ● bedford
stmartins.com/
smhandbook

For additional
exercises on
phrases, click on

► Exercise Central
  ► Basic Grammar

    ┌────── ABSOLUTE ──────┐   ┌── PREP ──┐
    His voice breaking with emotion, Ed thanked us for the award.
              └── PREP ──┘

1. Approaching the rope, I suddenly fell into the icy pond.
2. Chantalle, the motel clerk, hopes to be certified as a river guide.

gram

600 **31c**

GRAMMAR

Constructing
Grammatical
Sentences

3. The figure outlined against the sky seemed unable to move.

4. Floating on my back, I ignored my practice requirements.

5. Jane stood still, her fingers clutching the fence.

6. Learning to drive a car with a manual transmission takes time and patience.

7. Shocked into silence, they kept their gaze fixed on the odd creature.

8. Dancing with abandon, we ignored the band's inability to play their instruments.

9. My brother, a quiet man as a rule, spends his time in the shower singing at the top of his lungs.

10. His favorite form of recreation was taking a nap.

FOR COLLABORATION

Working with a classmate, use prepositional, participial, gerund, infinitive, absolute, or appositive phrases to expand each of the following sentences. Example:

> *In response to my vigorous shake, the*
> ~~The~~ apples dropped from the limb.
>   ^

Make sure that you can explain how you expanded each sentence, and bring the results of your work to class for comparison and discussion.

1. A man waited at the bottom of the escalator.

2. He quickly identified his blind date.

3. Tomas had lost almost all of his hair.

4. The Sunday afternoon dragged.

5. Zakiyyah looked at her mother.

6. The candidates shook hands with the voters.

7. The all-you-can-eat buffet was a bad idea.

8. I may move because my neighbor is too noisy.

9. The plants needed water desperately.

10. They lived in a trailer.

4 Recognizing and using clauses

A **clause** is a group of words containing a subject and a predicate. There are two kinds of clauses: independent and dependent. **Independent clauses** (also known as **main clauses**) can stand alone as complete sentences.

The window is open.

The batter swung at the ball.

Pairs of independent clauses may be joined with a coordinating conjunction and a comma.

The window is open, *so* we'd better be quiet.

The batter swung at the ball, *and* the umpire called her out.

Like independent clauses, **dependent clauses** (also known as **subordinate clauses**) contain a subject and a predicate. They cannot stand alone as complete sentences, however, for they begin with a subordinating word—a subordinating conjunction or a relative pronoun—that connects them to an independent clause.

Because the window is open, the room feels cool.

In this combination, the subordinating conjunction *because* transforms the independent clause *the window is open* into a dependent clause. In doing so, it indicates a causal relationship between the two clauses.

Dependent clauses function as nouns, adjectives, or adverbs.

GRAMMAR

Recognizing the
Parts of a Sentence

● For a discussion
and a list of
coordinating
conjunctions, see
31b7.

● For discussions
and lists of sub-
ordinating con-
junctions and
relative pro-
nouns, see 31b7
and 31b3.

■ *Noun clauses*

Noun clauses can function as subjects, direct objects, subject complements, or objects of prepositions. Thus they are always contained within another clause. They usually begin with a relative pronoun (*that, which, what, who, whom, whose, whatever, whoever, whomever, whichever*) or with *when, where, whether, why,* or *how.*

— S —
That he had a college degree was important to her.

— DO —
She asked *where he went to college.*

— SC —
The real question was *why she wanted to know.*

— OBJ OF PREP —
She was looking for *whatever information was available.*

Notice that in each of these sentences the noun clause is an integral part of the independent clause that makes up the sentence; for example, in the second sentence the independent clause is not just *She asked* but *She asked where he went to college.*

gram

602

31c

GRAMMAR

Constructing
Grammatical
Sentences

■ Adjective clauses

Adjective clauses modify nouns and pronouns in another clause. Usually they immediately follow the words they modify. Most adjective clauses begin with the relative pronouns *who, whom, whose, that,* or *which.* Some begin with *when, where,* or *why.*

> The surgery, *which took three hours,* was a complete success.

> It was performed by the surgeon *who had developed the procedure.*

> The hospital was the one *where I was born.*

Sometimes the relative pronoun introducing an adjective clause may be omitted, as in the following example:

> That is one book *[that] I intend to read.*

■ Adverb clauses

Adverb clauses modify verbs, adjectives, or other adverbs. They begin with a subordinating conjunction. Like adverbs, they usually tell when, where, why, how, or to what extent.

For a discussion
and a list of sub-
ordinating con-
junctions, see
31b7.

> We hiked *where there were few other hikers.*

> My backpack felt heavier *than it ever had.*

> I climbed as swiftly *as I could under the weight of my backpack.*

www ● bedford
stmartins.com/
smhandbook

For additional
exercises on
clauses, click on
▶ Exercise Central
　▶ Basic Grammar

● EXERCISE 31.12

Identify the independent and dependent clauses and any subordinating conjunctions and relative pronouns in each of the following sentences. Example:

┌──────── DEPENDENT CLAUSE ────────┐ ┌─────── INDEPENDENT CLAUSE ───────┐

If I were going on a really long hike, I would carry a lightweight stove.

(If is a subordinating conjunction.)

1. I don't know what happened to my grade school friends because I moved away during middle school.
2. She immediately recognized the officer who walked into the coffee shop.
3. When she was deemed old enough to understand, she was told the truth, and she finally knew why her father had left home.
4. The trip was longer than I had remembered.
5. I could see that he was very tired, but I had to ask him a few questions.

EXERCISE 31.13

Expand each of the following sentences by adding at least one dependent clause to it. Be prepared to explain how your addition improves the sentence. Example:

> *As the earth continued to shake, the*
> ~~The~~ books tumbled from the shelves.
> ^

1. The last guests left.
2. Primo desperately wanted a cup of coffee.
3. The new computer made a strange noise.
4. Rob always borrowed money from friends.
5. The crowd grew louder and more disorderly.

www • bedford stmartins.com/ smhandbook

For additional exercises on clauses, click on

▶ **Exercise Central**
  ▶ **Basic Grammar**

31d Classifying sentences

Like words, sentences can be classified in several different ways: grammatically, functionally, or rhetorically. Grammatical classification groups sentences according to how many and what types of clauses they contain. Functional classification groups them according to whether they make a statement, ask a question, issue a command, or express an exclamation. Rhetorical classification groups them according to where in the sentence the main idea is located. These methods of classification can help you analyze and assess your sentences as you write and revise.

1 Classifying sentences grammatically

Grammatically, sentences may be classified as *simple, compound, complex,* and *compound-complex.*

604

gram

31d

GRAMMAR

Constructing
Grammatical
Sentences

■ *Simple sentences*

A **simple sentence** consists of one independent clause and no dependent clause. The subject or the predicate, or both, may be compound.

> The trailer is surrounded by a wooden deck.

> Both my roommate and I had left our keys in the room.

> At the country club, the head pro and his assistant give lessons, run the golf shop, and try to keep the members content.

■ *Compound sentences*

A **compound sentence** consists of two or more independent clauses and no dependent clause. The clauses may be joined by a comma and a coordinating conjunction, or by a semicolon.

> Occasionally a car goes up the dirt trail, and dust flies everywhere.

> Alberto is obsessed with soccer; he eats, breathes, and lives the game.

■ *Complex sentences*

A **complex sentence** consists of one independent clause and at least one dependent clause.

> ┌────── DEPENDENT CLAUSE ──────┐
> Many people believe that anyone can earn a living.

> ┌────── DEPENDENT CLAUSE ──────┐
> Those who do not like to get dirty should not go camping.

> ┌────── DEPENDENT CLAUSE ──────┐
> As I awaited my interview, I sat with other nervous candidates.

■ *Compound-complex sentences*

A **compound-complex sentence** consists of two or more independent clauses and at least one dependent clause.

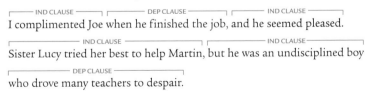

> ┌──── IND CLAUSE ────┐ ┌────── DEP CLAUSE ──────┐ ┌────── IND CLAUSE ──────┐
> I complimented Joe when he finished the job, and he seemed pleased.

> ┌────────── IND CLAUSE ──────────┐ ┌────── IND CLAUSE──────┐
> Sister Lucy tried her best to help Martin, but he was an undisciplined boy
> ┌────────── DEP CLAUSE ──────────┐
> who drove many teachers to despair.

2 Classifying sentences functionally

In terms of function, sentences can be classified as **declarative** (making a statement), **interrogative** (asking a question), **imperative** (giving a command), or **exclamatory** (expressing strong feeling).

DECLARATIVE	Kira plays oboe for the Cleveland Orchestra.
INTERROGATIVE	How long has she been with them?
IMPERATIVE	Get me a ticket for her next performance.
EXCLAMATORY	What a talented musician she is!

3 Classifying sentences rhetorically

Some sentences can be classified rhetorically as either cumulative or periodic sentences. The two patterns create very different rhythms and emphases. See 46c3 for an explanation of periodic and cumulative sentences.

● **EXERCISE 31.14**

Classify each of the following sentences as simple, compound, complex, or compound-complex. In addition, note any sentences that could be classified as interrogative, imperative, or exclamatory.

1. The screen door creaked and banged when she ran into the house.

2. How long would he have to wait for help, or should he try to change the tire himself?

3. Hoping for an end to the rain, we huddled together in the shop doorway, unwilling to get drenched.

4. Keeping in mind the terrain, the weather, and the length of the hike, decide what you need to take.

5. Dreams are necessary, but they can be frustrating unless you have the means to attain them.

www ● bedford
stmartins.com/
smhandbook

For additional
exercises on
classifying
sentences
grammatically
and functionally,
click on

▶ **Exercise Central**
  ▶ **Basic Grammar**

THINKING CRITICALLY ABOUT SENTENCES

The following sentences come from the openings of well-known works. Identify the independent and dependent clauses in each sentence. Then choose one sentence, and write a sentence of your own imitating its structure clause for clause and phrase for phrase. Example:

She is an open and trusting child, unprepared for and unaccustomed to the ambushes of family life, and perhaps it is just as well that I can offer her little of that life.

—JOAN DIDION, "On Going Home"

Nina is an active and alert baby, attracted to and eager for solid foods, so perhaps it is better that we eat our pizza in another room.

1. Most people who bother with the matter at all would admit that the English language is in a bad way, but it is generally assumed that we cannot by conscious action do anything about it. — GEORGE ORWELL, "Politics and the English Language"

2. We observe today not a victory of party but a celebration of freedom, symbolizing an end as well as a beginning, signifying renewal as well as change.

—JOHN F. KENNEDY, Inaugural Address

3. Once in a long while, four times so far for me, my mother brings out the metal tube that holds her medical diploma.

— MAXINE HONG KINGSTON, "Photographs of My Parents"

Understanding Pronoun Case

32

32a Using the three cases

The grammatical term **case** refers to the form a pronoun takes to indicate its function in a sentence. Pronouns functioning as subjects are in the subjective case; those functioning as objects are in the objective case; and those functioning as possessives are in the possessive case.

SUBJECTIVE PRONOUNS

I/we	you	he/she/it	they	who/whoever

OBJECTIVE PRONOUNS

me/us	you	him/her/it	them	whom/whomever

POSSESSIVE PRONOUNS

my/our	your	his/hers/its	their	whose
mine/ours	yours	his/hers/its	theirs	

1 The subjective case

A pronoun should be in the **subjective case** when it is a subject of a clause, a subject complement, or an appositive renaming a subject or subject complement.

SUBJECT OF A CLAUSE

They could either fight or face certain death with the lions.

Who is your closest friend?

During an NCAA men's basketball tournament, an interviewer asked two members of a winning team whether they had "felt a win coming on." One of them responded: "Marcus and me — or Marcus and I, I should say — we definitely knew we could win. All we had to do was play our own game."

This player certainly would have been understood by the TV audience had he stuck with "Marcus and me," but he corrected himself because he realized that *I*, rather than *me*, should be used as a subject. Although most of us know intuitively most of the time when to use *I*, when to use *me*, and when to use *my*, almost everyone becomes confused at least occasionally by choices like those between *who* and *whom*, *we Texans* and *us Texans*, or *Marcus and me* and *Marcus and I*. ■

607

→ Are all pronouns after forms of the verb *be* in the subjective case? (32a1)
→ To check for correct use of *who* and *whom* (and *whoever* and *whomever*), try answering the question or rewriting the clause using *he* or *him*. If *he* is correct, use *who* or *whoever*; if *him*, use *whom* or *whomever*. (32b)
→ In compound structures, make sure pronouns are in the same case they would be in if used alone (*Jake and she were living in Spain*). (32c)
→ When a pronoun follows *than* or *as*, complete the sentence mentally. If the pronoun is the subject of an unstated verb, it should be in the subjective case (*I like her better than he* [*likes her*]). If it is the object of an unstated verb, it should be in the objective case (*I like her better than* [*I like*] *him*). (32d)
→ Circle all the pronouns to see if you rely too heavily on any one pronoun or case, especially *I*. If you find that you do, try rewriting some sentences to change *I* to *me*, *she* to *her*, and so on.

Roberto told the story to Carla, *who* told all her friends.

Our group appealed to *whoever* was willing to listen.

SUBJECT COMPLEMENT

For more about
subject comple-
ments and
appositives, see
31c.

Americans often use the objective case for subject complements, especially in conversation: *Who's there? It's me.* Nevertheless, you should use the subjective case in formal writing.

If I were *she,* I would worry about other things.

If you find the subjective case for a subject complement stilted or awkward, try rewriting the sentence using the pronoun as the subject.

> *She was the*
> ~The first person to see Monty after the awards~ was she.

APPOSITIVE RENAMING A SUBJECT OR SUBJECT COMPLEMENT

Three colleagues—Peter, John, and *she*—worked on the program.

2 The objective case

For more about
objects, see 31c2
and 31c3.

A pronoun should be in the **objective case** when it functions as a direct or indirect object (of a verb or verbal), a subject of an infinitive, an appositive renaming an object, or an object of a preposition.

OBJECT OF A VERB OR VERBAL

The professor surprised *us* with a quiz. [direct object of *surprised*]

The grateful owner gave *him* a reward. [indirect object of *gave*]

Presidents usually rely on advisors *whom* they have known for years. [direct object of *have known*]

The Parisians were wonderful about helping *me*. [direct object of gerund]

SUBJECT OF AN INFINITIVE

The objective case is also used in sentences like the following, where the pronoun is preceded by a verb and followed by an infinitive. Though the pronoun in such constructions is called the subject of the infinitive, it is in the objective case because it is the object of the sentence's verb.

The students convinced *him* to vote for the school bond.

APPOSITIVE RENAMING AN OBJECT

The committee elected two representatives, Joan and *me*.

OBJECT OF A PREPOSITION

Several of his friends went with *him*.

3 The possessive case

A pronoun should be in the **possessive case** when it shows possession or ownership. Notice that there are two forms of possessive pronouns: adjective forms, which are used before nouns or gerunds (*my, your, his, her, its, our, their, whose*), and noun forms, which take the place of a noun (*mine, yours, his, hers, its, ours, theirs, whose*).

ADJECTIVE FORMS

People were buying *their* tickets weeks in advance of the show.

Whose life is it, anyway?

The sound of *his* hammering echoed through the corridor.

NOUN FORMS

The responsibility is *hers*.

Whose is this blue backpack?

A pronoun that appears before a gerund should be in the possessive case (*my/our, your, his/her/its, their*). What can be tricky is distinguishing gerunds from present participles, for both are *-ing* forms of verbs. Notice the difference in meaning in the following examples:

610

case

32b

GRAMMAR

Understanding
Pronoun Case

I remember *his* singing.

I remember *him* singing.

In the first example, the memory is of *singing*, which is a gerund, modified by the possessive pronoun *his*. In the second, the memory is of *him*, which is a direct object of *remember* and thus is in the objective case; *singing* is a present participle modifying *him*. In sentences like these, use the possessive case if you want to emphasize the person; use the objective case if you want to emphasize the action.

32b Using *who, whoever, whom,* and *whomever*

A common problem with pronoun case is deciding whether to use *who* or *whom*. Even when traditional grammar requires *whom*, many Americans use *who* instead, especially in speech. Nevertheless, in formal written English, which includes most college writing, the case of the pronoun should reflect its grammatical function. *Who* and *whoever* are the subjective-case forms and should be used when the pronoun is a subject or subject complement. *Whom* and *whomever* are the objective-case forms and should be used when the pronoun is a direct or indirect object or the object of a preposition.

Most writers find that two particular situations can lead to confusion with *who* and *whom*: when they begin a question and when they introduce a dependent clause. In a dependent clause, you may also have to choose between *whoever* and *whomever*.

For a discussion ·····•
of dependent
clauses, see
31c4.

1 Beginning a question with *who* or *whom*

You can determine whether to use *who* or *whom* at the beginning of a question by answering the question using a personal pronoun. If the answer is in the subjective case, use *who;* if it is in the objective case, use *whom*.

> *Who*
> ▶ ~~Whom~~ do you think wrote the story?

I think *she* wrote the story. *She* is subjective; thus *who* is correct.

> *Whom*
> ▶ ~~Who~~ did you visit?

I visited *them. Them* is objective; thus *whom* is correct.

2 Beginning a dependent clause with *who, whoever, whom,* or *whomever*

The case of a pronoun in a dependent clause is determined by its function in the clause, no matter how that clause functions in the sentence. If the pronoun acts as a subject or subject complement in the clause, use *who* or *whoever*. If the pronoun acts as an object, use *whom* or *whomever*.

> *whoever*
▶ **The center is open to whomever wants to use it.**

> *Whoever* is the subject of the clause *whoever wants to use it*. Though the clause as a whole is the object of the preposition *to,* the pronoun should be in the subjective case.

> *whom*
▶ **The new president was not who she had expected.**

> *Whom* is the object of the verb *had expected* in the clause *whom she had expected.* Though the clause as a whole is the complement of the verb *was,* the pronoun should be in the objective case.

If you are not sure which case to use, try separating the dependent clause from the rest of the sentence and looking at it in isolation. Rewrite the clause as a new sentence with a personal pronoun instead of *who(ever)* or *whom(ever)*. If the pronoun is in the subjective case, use *who* or *whoever;* if it is in the objective case, use *whom* or *whomever.*

> The minister grimaced at (*whoever/whomever*) made any noise.
> [Isolate the clause *whoever/whomever made any noise.* Substituting a personal pronoun gives you *they made any noise. They* is in the subjective case; therefore, *The minister grimaced at whoever made any noise.*]

> The minister smiled at (*whoever/whomever*) she greeted.
> [Isolate and transpose the clause to get *she greeted whoever/whomever.* Substituting a personal pronoun gives you *she greeted them. Them* is in the objective case; therefore, *The minister smiled at whomever she greeted.*]

Ignore such expressions as *he thinks* or *she says* when you isolate the clause.

> The minister grimaced at (*whoever/whomever*) she thought made any noise.
> [The clause is *whoever/whomever made any noise.* Substituting a personal pronoun gives you *they made any noise. They* is in the subjective case; therefore, *The minister grimaced at whoever she thought made any noise.*]

612

case

32c

GRAMMAR

Understanding
Pronoun Case

**www • bedford
stmartins.com/
smhandbook**

For additional
exercises on *who*
and *whom,* click on

▶ **Exercise Central**
  ▶ **Pronouns**

● **EXERCISE 32.1**

Insert *who, whoever, whom,* or *whomever* appropriately in the blank in each of the following sentences. Example:

She is someone _____*who*_____ will go far.

1. _____ shall I say is calling?

2. _____ the committee recommends is likely to receive a job offer.

3. The manager promised to reward _____ sold the most cars.

4. Professor Quiñones asked _____ we wanted to collaborate with.

5. _____ do you trust?

32c Using case in compound structures

When a pronoun is part of a compound subject, object, complement, or appositive, put it in the same case you would use if the pronoun were alone.

SUBJECTS AND SUBJECT COMPLEMENTS

>   *he*
> When Zelda and ~~him~~ were first married, they lived in New York.

>   *she.*
> The next two speakers will be Philip and ~~her~~.

OBJECTS AND SUBJECTS OF INFINITIVES

>   *her*
> The boss invited ~~she~~ and her family to dinner.

>   *her*
> They offered Gail and ~~she~~ a summer internship.

>   *me.*
> This morning saw yet another conflict between my sister and ~~I~~.

>   *her*
> We asked Juan and ~~she~~ to attend the meeting.

To decide whether to use the subjective or the objective case in a compound structure, make each part of the compound into a separate sentence.

>   *me.*
> Come to the park with José and ~~I~~.

Separating the compound structure gives you *Come to the park with José* and *Come to the park with me;* thus, *Come to the park with José and me.*

Pronoun case in a compound appositive is determined by the word the appositive renames. If the word functions as a subject or subject complement, the pronoun should be in the subjective case; if it functions as an object, the pronoun should be in the objective case.

▶ **Both finalists — Tony and ~~me~~ — were stumped by the question.**

I

Finalists is the subject of the sentence, so the pronoun in the appositive *Tony and I* should be in the subjective case.

▶ **The poker game produced two big winners, Aunt Rose and ~~I~~.**

me.

Winners is the direct object of the verb *produced,* so the pronoun in the appositive *Aunt Rose and me* should be in the objective case.

32d Using case in elliptical constructions

Elliptical constructions, in which some words are left out but understood, are often used in comparisons with *than* or *as.* When sentences with such constructions end in a pronoun, the pronoun should be in the case it would be in if the construction were complete.

His brother has always been more athletic than *he* [is].

In some constructions like this, the case depends on the meaning intended. Use the subjective case if the pronoun is actually the subject of an omitted verb; use the objective case if it is an object of an omitted verb.

Willie likes Lily more than *she* [likes Lily].

Willie likes Lily more than [he likes] *her.*

32e Using *we* and *us* before a noun

If you are unsure about whether to use *we* or *us* before a noun, recasting the sentence without the noun will give you the answer. Use whichever pronoun would be correct if the noun were omitted.

GRAMMAR

Understanding
Pronoun Case

> *We*
> **Us fans never give up hope.**
> ^

Fans is the subject, so the pronoun should be subjective.

> *us*
> **The Rangers depend on we fans.**
>   ^

Fans is the object of a preposition, so the pronoun should be objective.

**www • bedford
stmartins.com/
smhandbook**

For additional
exercises on
pronoun case,
click on

▶ **Exercise Central**
  ▶ **Pronouns**

● **EXERCISE 32.2**

Underline the appropriate pronoun from the pair in parentheses in each of the following sentences. Example:

  The possibility of (*their*/*them*) succeeding never occurred to me.

1. Although Paula and Sara are twins, Sara says that few sisters have less in common than Paula and (*she/her*).

2. When I was in high school, I had one teacher (*who/whom*) I truly admired.

3. Riding on the bus with my father and (*they/them*) brought back memories.

4. Our teacher gave the class clowns, Marlys and (*I/me*), repeated detentions.

5. Two of the richest Americans that year were Bill Gates and (*she/her*).

6. We tried to think of an explanation for (*them/their*) winning the game against all odds.

7. The two violinists, Sergei and (*he/him*), played as though they had a single musical mind.

8. Soap operas appeal to (*whoever/whomever*) is interested in intrigue, suspense, joy, pain, grief, romance, fidelity, sex, and violence.

9. Tomorrow (*we/us*) raw recruits will have our first on-the-job test.

10. The only experts (*who/whom*) they can recommend are the two magicians who trained them.

FOR COLLABORATION

Working with a classmate, edit any of the following sentences with errors in pronoun case. Example:

          she
  Of the group, only her and I finished the race.
                    ^

Bring your edited sentences to class, and be prepared to explain why you made each change and why you left some sentences as they were.

1. Waiting for the train, her and him began to talk.

2. If you have any questions, ask Steve or I.

3. The people who Jay worked with were very cold and unsociable.

4. Who would have thought that twenty years later he would be king?

5. One waitress told that customer that she was tired of him forgetting to leave a tip.

6. Only him, a few cabinet members, and several military leaders were aware of the steady advance Japan was making toward Pearl Harbor.

7. No one could feel worse than me about missing your party.

8. Except for Alyssa and her, everyone was on a diet.

9. I never got to play that role in front of an audience, but I am one of the few performers who really did break a leg.

10. Connor always lent money to whomever asked him for it.

THINKING CRITICALLY ABOUT PRONOUN CASE

Reading with an Eye for Pronoun Case

The poet e. e. cummings often broke the standard rules of grammar and word order to create particular effects in his poetry. Read the following poem, and note the function of each pronoun. Then rearrange the words of the poem so that they follow as closely as possible the normal order they would take in an ordinary sentence. How does pronoun case give you a clue to this arrangement?

> Me up at does
>
> out of the floor
> quietly Stare
>
> a poisoned mouse
>
> still who alive
>
> is asking What
> have i done that
>
> You wouldn't have   –E. E. CUMMINGS

Thinking about Your Own Use of Pronoun Case

Research shows that one of the most overused words in any language is the word *I*. Whenever you write anything that includes your own opinions, you probably rely to some degree on first-person pronouns, singular and plural. Read over some of your own paragraphs, paying attention to your use of pronouns. Do you find any patterns? If you find that you rely heavily on any one case—that half your sentences begin with *I*, for example—decide whether your writing seems at all monotonous as a result. If so, try revising some sentences to change *I* to *me* (or vice versa). Do the changes bring greater variety to your writing? If you keep a writing log, you might enter your work in it, noting what you have learned about your use of pronoun case.

33 — Using Verbs

VERB FORMS

Except for *be,* all English verbs have five possible forms.

BASE FORM	PAST TENSE	PAST PARTICIPLE	PRESENT PARTICIPLE	-S FORM
talk	talked	talked	talking	talks
adore	adored	adored	adoring	adores
jog	jogged	jogged	jogging	jogs

The **base form** is the one listed in the dictionary. For all verbs except *be,* it is the form used to indicate an action or condition that occurs in the present when the subject is a plural noun; the pronoun *I, you, we,* or *they;* or a plural pronoun such as *these* or *many.*

During the ritual, the women *go* into trances.

The **past tense** is used to indicate an action or condition that occurred entirely in the past. For most verbs, it is formed by adding -*ed* or -*d* to the base form. Some verbs, however, have irregular past-tense forms. *Be* has two past-tense forms, *was* and *were.* (See 33b.)

The Globe *was* the stage for many of Shakespeare's works.

In 1613, it *caught* fire and *burned* to the ground.

The **past participle** is used to form perfect tenses, the passive voice (pp. 631–633), and adjectives. It usually has the same form as the past tense, though some verbs have irregular past participles. (See 33e–f and 33b.)

→ Circle all forms of *be, do,* and *have* that you used as main verbs. Try in each case to substitute a stronger, more specific verb. (33a)

→ If you have trouble with verb endings, review the rules for using them on pp. 618 and 620.

→ Double-check forms of *lie* and *lay, sit* and *set, rise* and *raise.* See that the words you use are appropriate for your meaning. (33c)

→ If you have problems with verb tenses, use the guidelines on p. 629.

→ If you are writing about a literary work, you should refer to the action in the work in the present tense. (33d)

→ Check all uses of the passive voice for appropriateness. (33g)

→ Check all verbs used to introduce quotations, paraphrases, and summaries. If you rely on *say, write,* and other very general verbs, try substituting more vivid, specific verbs (*claim, insist, wonder,* for instance). (47a)

She *had accomplished* the impossible. [past perfect]

No one *was injured* in the explosion. [passive voice]

Standardized tests usually require *sharpened* pencils. [adjective]

The **present participle** is constructed by adding *-ing* to the base form. Used with auxiliary verbs to indicate a continuing action or condition, it can also function as an adjective or noun (a gerund).

Many students *are competing* in the race. [continuing action]

He tried to comfort the *crying* child. [adjective]

Climbing the mountain took all afternoon. [noun (gerund)]

●— For more about gerunds, see 31c3.

Except for *be* and *have,* the *-s* **form** consists of the base form plus *-s* or *-es.* This form indicates an action or condition in the present for third-person singular subjects. All singular nouns; *he, she,* and *it;* and many other pronouns (such as *this* and *someone*) are third-person singular.

	SINGULAR	PLURAL
FIRST PERSON	I *wish*	we *wish*
SECOND PERSON	you *wish*	you *wish*
THIRD PERSON	he/she/it *wishes*	they *wish*
	Joe *wishes*	children *wish*
	someone *wishes*	many *wish*

The third-person singular form of *have* is *has.*

EDITING FOR -S AND -ES ENDINGS

If you tend to leave off or misuse the *-s* and *-es* verb endings in academic writing, you should check for them systematically.

1. Underline every verb, and then circle all verbs in the present tense.

2. Find the subject of every verb you circled.

3. If the subject is a singular noun; *he, she,* or *it;* or a singular indefinite pronoun, be sure the verb ends in *-s* or *-es.* If the subject is not third-person singular, the verb should not have an *-s* or *-es* ending.

4. Be careful with auxiliary verbs such as *can* or *may.* (60d) These auxiliaries are used with the base form, never with the *-s* or *-es* form.

FORMS OF BE

Be has three forms in the present tense (*am, is, are*) and two in the past tense (*was, were*).

■ *Present tense*

	SINGULAR	PLURAL
FIRST PERSON	I *am*	we *are*
SECOND PERSON	you *are*	you *are*
THIRD PERSON	he/she/it *is*	they *are*
	Jane *is*	children *are*
	somebody *is*	many *are*

■ *Past tense*

	SINGULAR	PLURAL
FIRST PERSON	I *was*	we *were*
SECOND PERSON	you *were*	you *were*
THIRD PERSON	he/she/it *was*	they *were*
	Jane *was*	children *were*
	somebody *was*	many *were*

ABSENCE OF BE; HABITUAL BE

My sister at work. She be there every day 'til five.

These sentences illustrate two common usages of *be.* The first shows the absence of *be;* the same sentence in academic English would read *My sister is at work*. The second shows the use of "habitual *be*," indicating that something is always or almost always the case. The same sentence in academic English would read *She is there every day until five*.

These usages of *be* appear in the discourse of many African American speakers and some southern white speakers. You may have occasion to quote dialogue featuring these patterns in your own writing; doing so can be a good way to evoke particular regions or communities. Most academic writing, however, calls for academic English.

•— For more on using different varieties of English, see Chapter 26.

33a Using auxiliary verbs

Sometimes called *helping verbs,* **auxiliary** verbs are used with a base form, present participle, or past participle to create verb phrases. The base form or participle in a verb phrase is called the **main verb**. The most common auxiliaries are forms of *have, be,* and *do,* which are used to indicate completed or continuing action, the passive voice, emphasis, questions, and negative statements.

We *have considered* all viewpoints. [completed action]

The college *is building* a new dormitory. [continuing action]

We *were warned* to stay away. [passive voice]

I *do respect* your viewpoint. [emphasis]

Do you *know* the answer? [question]

He *does* not *like* wearing a tie. [negative statement]

Modal auxiliaries — *can, could, might, may, must, ought to, shall, will, should, would* — indicate future action, possibility, necessity, obligation, and so on.

They *will explain* the procedure. [future action]

You *can see* three states from the top of the mountain. [possibility]

I *must try* harder to go to bed early. [necessity]

She *should visit* her parents more often. [obligation]

FOR MULTILINGUAL WRITERS: Using Modal Auxiliaries

Why do we not say "Alice can to read Latin"? For a discussion of *can* and other modal auxiliaries, see 60d.

33b Using regular and irregular verbs

A verb is **regular** when its past tense and past participle are formed by adding *-ed* or *-d* to the base form.

BASE FORM	PAST TENSE	PAST PARTICIPLE
love	loved	loved
honor	honored	honored
obey	obeyed	obeyed

EDITING FOR -ED OR -D ENDINGS

Speakers who skip over the *-ed* or *-d* endings in conversation may forget to include them in academic writing. If you tend to drop these endings, make a point of systematically checking for them when proofreading. Underline all the verbs, and then underline a second time any that are past tense or past participles. Check each of these for an *-ed* or *-d* ending. Unless the verb is irregular (see list following), it should end in *-ed* or *-d.*

■ Irregular verbs

A verb is **irregular** when it does not follow the *-ed* or *-d* pattern. If you are unsure about whether a verb is regular or irregular, or what the correct form is, consult the following list or a dictionary. Dictionaries list any irregular forms under the entry for the base form.

SOME COMMON IRREGULAR VERBS

BASE FORM	PAST TENSE	PAST PARTICIPLE
arise	arose	arisen
be	was/were	been
bear	bore	borne, born
beat	beat	beaten

(Continued on p. 621)

(Continued from p. 620)

BASE FORM	PAST TENSE	PAST PARTICIPLE
become	became	become
begin	began	begun
bite	bit	bitten, bit
blow	blew	blown
break	broke	broken
bring	brought	brought
broadcast	broadcast	broadcast
build	built	built
burn	burned, burnt	burned, burnt
burst	burst	burst
buy	bought	bought
catch	caught	caught
choose	chose	chosen
come	came	come
cost	cost	cost
cut	cut	cut
dig	dug	dug
dive	dived, dove	dived
do	did	done
draw	drew	drawn
dream	dreamed, dreamt	dreamed, dreamt
drink	drank	drunk
drive	drove	driven
eat	ate	eaten
fall	fell	fallen
feel	felt	felt
fight	fought	fought
find	found	found
fly	flew	flown
forget	forgot	forgotten, forgot
freeze	froze	frozen

(Continued on p. 622)

(Continued from p. 621)

BASE FORM	PAST TENSE	PAST PARTICIPLE
get	got	gotten, got
give	gave	given
go	went	gone
grow	grew	grown
hang (suspend)[1]	hung	hung
have	had	had
hear	heard	heard
hide	hid	hidden
hit	hit	hit
keep	kept	kept
know	knew	known
lay	laid	laid
lead	led	led
leave	left	left
lend	lent	lent
let	let	let
lie (recline)[2]	lay	lain
lose	lost	lost
make	made	made
mean	meant	meant
meet	met	met
pay	paid	paid
prove	proved	proved, proven
put	put	put
read	read	read
ride	rode	ridden
ring	rang	rung
rise	rose	risen
run	ran	run

---

[1]*Hang* meaning "execute by hanging" is regular: *hang, hanged, hanged.*
[2]*Lie* meaning "tell a falsehood" is regular: *lie, lied, lied.*

(Continued on p. 623)

(Continued from p. 622)

BASE FORM	PAST TENSE	PAST PARTICIPLE
say	said	said
see	saw	seen
send	sent	sent
set	set	set
shake	shook	shaken
shoot	shot	shot
show	showed	showed, shown
shrink	shrank	shrunk
sing	sang	sung
sink	sank	sunk
sit	sat	sat
sleep	slept	slept
speak	spoke	spoken
spend	spent	spent
spread	spread	spread
spring	sprang, sprung	sprung
stand	stood	stood
steal	stole	stolen
strike	struck	struck, stricken
swim	swam	swum
swing	swung	swung
take	took	taken
teach	taught	taught
tear	tore	torn
tell	told	told
think	thought	thought
throw	threw	thrown
wake	woke, waked	waked, woken
wear	wore	worn
win	won	won
wind	wound	wound
write	wrote	written

**www • bedford
stmartins.com/
smhandbook**

For additional
exercises on regular
and irregular verbs,
click on

▶ Exercise Central
  ▶ Verbs

● **EXERCISE 33.1**

Complete each of the following sentences by filling in each blank with the past tense or past participle of the verb listed in parentheses. Example:

They had already __eaten__ (eat) the entree; later they __ate__ (eat) the dessert.

1. The babysitter _____ (let) the children play with my schoolbooks, and before I _____ (come) home, they had _____ (tear) out several pages.

2. After she had _____ (make) her decision, she _____ (find) that the constant anxiety was no longer a factor in her daily life.

3. The process of hazing _____ (begin) soon after fraternities were formed.

4. Grandmother _____ (wind) the clock every year on New Year's Day, but I have often _____ (forget) about it.

5. When Maria Callas _____ (make) her debut at the Metropolitan Opera, some people _____ (know) that music history was being made.

6. I _____ (wake) up with a start because I was convinced that something had _____ (fly) through the window.

7. When the buzzer sounded, the racers _____ (spring) into the water and _____ (swim) toward the far end of the pool.

8. Roberto had _____ (throw) his hat into the ring and had assembled the best advisors he had _____ (be) able to find.

9. When Charles admitted that he had _____ (break) into the apartment, he said that he had _____ (lose) his keys.

10. The wolf _____ (go) back into the woods before the rest of the campers had _____ (see) him.

33c Using *lie* and *lay*, *sit* and *set*, *rise* and *raise*

Three pairs of verbs—*lie* and *lay*, *sit* and *set*, and *rise* and *raise*—cause problems for many writers because both verbs in each pair have similar-sounding forms and somewhat related meanings. In each pair, one of the verbs is **transitive**, meaning that it takes a direct object; the other is **intransitive**, meaning that it does not take an object. The best way to avoid confusing the two is to memorize their forms and meanings—or to use synonyms. All these verbs except *raise* are irregular.

BASE FORM	PAST TENSE	PAST PARTICIPLE	PRESENT PARTICIPLE	-S FORM
lie (recline)	lay	lain	lying	lies
lay (put)	laid	laid	laying	lays
sit (be seated)	sat	sat	sitting	sits
set (put)	set	set	setting	sets
rise (get up)	rose	risen	rising	rises
raise (lift)	raised	raised	raising	raises

Lie is intransitive and means "recline" or "be situated." *Lay* is transitive and means "put" or "place." This pair is especially confusing because *lay* is also the past-tense form of *lie*.

INTRANSITIVE He *lay* on the floor unable to move.

TRANSITIVE I *laid* the package on the counter.

Sit is intransitive and means "be seated." *Set* usually is transitive and means "put" or "place."

INTRANSITIVE She *sat* in the rocking chair.

TRANSITIVE She *set* the vase on the table.

Rise is intransitive and means "get up" or "go up." *Raise* is transitive and means "lift" or "cause to go up."

INTRANSITIVE He *rose* up in bed and glared at me.

TRANSITIVE He *raised* himself to a sitting position.

● **EXERCISE 33.2**

Underline the appropriate verb form in each of the following sentences.

1. Sometimes she just (*lies/lays*) and stares at the ceiling.
2. The chef (*lay/laid*) his knives carefully on the counter.
3. I (*sat/set*) back, closed my eyes, and began to meditate.
4. (*Sitting/Setting*) in the sun too long can lead to skin cancer.
5. The submarine began to (*raise/rise*) to the surface.

www ● bedford
stmartins.com/
smhandbook

For additional
exercises on regular
and irregular verbs,
click on

▶ **Exercise Central**
    ▶ **Verbs**

VERB TENSES

Tenses show when the action or condition expressed by a verb occurs. The three *simple tenses* are present tense, past tense, and future tense.

PRESENT TENSE	I *ask, write*
PAST TENSE	I *asked, wrote*
FUTURE TENSE	I *will ask, will write*

More complex aspects of time are expressed through *progressive, perfect,* and *perfect progressive forms* of the simple tenses. (Although such terminology sounds complicated, you regularly use all these forms.)

PRESENT PROGRESSIVE	she *is asking, is writing*
PAST PROGRESSIVE	she *was asking, was writing*
FUTURE PROGRESSIVE	she *will be asking, will be writing*
PRESENT PERFECT	she *has asked, has written*
PAST PERFECT	she *had asked, had written*
FUTURE PERFECT	she *will have asked, will have written*
PRESENT PERFECT PROGRESSIVE	she *has been asking, has been writing*
PAST PERFECT PROGRESSIVE	she *had been asking, had been writing*
FUTURE PERFECT PROGRESSIVE	she *will have been asking, will have been writing*

The perfect form of each tense expresses the idea of a *completed* action or condition in the present, past, or future; and the progressive form expresses the idea of a *continuing* action or condition. Finally, the perfect progressive form expresses the idea of an action or condition that *continues up to some point* in the present, past, or future.

33d Using the present-tense forms

The **simple present** indicates actions or conditions occurring at the time of speaking as well as those occurring habitually. In addition, with appropriate time expressions, the simple present can be used to indicate a scheduled future event.

They *are* very angry about the decision.

I *eat* breakfast every day at 8:00 A.M.

Love *conquers* all.

Classes *begin* next week.

General truths or scientific facts should be in the simple present, even when the predicate of the sentence is in the past tense.

makes
► **Pasteur demonstrated that his boiling process made milk safe.**

Use the simple present, not the past tense, when writing about action in literary works.

comes *is*
► **Ishmael slowly came to realize all that was at stake in the search for the white whale.**

In general, use the simple present when you are quoting, summarizing, or paraphrasing someone else's writing.

writes
► **Keith Walters wrote that the "reputed consequences and promised blessings of literacy are legion."**

But in an essay using APA (American Psychological Association) style, the reporting of your experiments or another researcher's work should be in the past tense (*wrote, noted*) or the present perfect (*has reported*).

noted
► **Comer (1995) notes that protesters who deprive themselves of food (for example, Gandhi and Dick Gregory) are seen not as dysfunctional but rather as "caring, sacrificing, even heroic" (p. 5).**

The **present progressive** indicates actions or conditions that are ongoing or continuous in the present. It is typically used to describe an action that is happening at the moment of speaking, in contrast to the simple present, which more often indicates habitual actions.

| PRESENT PROGRESSIVE | You *are driving* too fast. |
| SIMPLE PRESENT | I always *drive* carefully. |

With an appropriate expression of time, the present progressive can also be used to indicate a scheduled event in the future.

We *are having* friends over for dinner tomorrow night.

The **present perfect** indicates actions or conditions begun in the past and either completed at some unspecified time in the past or continuing into the present.

Uncontrolled logging *has destroyed* many tropical forests.

verb
33d   627

GRAMMAR
Using the Present-Tense Forms

● For another example of APA style, see the essay in Chapter 65.

The **present perfect progressive** indicates actions or conditions begun in the past and continuing into the present.

The two sides *have been trying* to settle the case out of court.

33e Using the past-tense forms

The **simple past** indicates actions or conditions that occurred at a specific time and do not extend into the present.

Germany *invaded* Poland on September 1, 1939.

The **past progressive** indicates continuing actions or conditions in the past, often with specified limits.

Lenin *was living* in exile in Zurich when the czar was overthrown.

The **past perfect** indicates actions or conditions completed by a specific time in the past or before some other past action occurred.

By the fourth century, Christianity *had become* the state religion.

The **past perfect progressive** indicates continuing actions or conditions in the past that began before a specific time or before some other past action began.

Carter *had been planning* a naval career until his father died.

33f Using the future-tense forms

The **simple future** indicates actions or conditions that have not yet begun.

The exhibition *will come* to Washington in September.

The **future progressive** indicates continuing actions or conditions in the future.

The loans *will be coming* due in the next two years.

The **future perfect** indicates actions or conditions that will be completed by or before some specified time in the future.

In ten years, the original investment *will have doubled*.

The **future perfect progressive** indicates continuing actions or conditions that will be completed by some specified time in the future.

In May, I *will have been living* in Tucson for five years.

EDITING VERB TENSES

Errors in verb tenses take several forms. If you have trouble with verb tenses, make a point of checking for these common errors as you proofread.

→ Errors of verb form: writing *seen* for *saw,* for example, which is an instance of confusing the past participle and past-tense forms (33b)

→ Omission of auxiliary verbs; for example, using the simple past (*Uncle Charlie arrived*) when meaning requires the present perfect (*Uncle Charlie has arrived*) (33d and e)

→ Other errors that result from using a regional or ethnic variety of English (*she nervous*) in situations calling for academic English (*she is nervous*). (See p. 619 and Chapter 26.)

● **EXERCISE 33.3**

Complete each of the following sentences by filling in the blank with an appropriate form of the verb listed in parentheses. Since more than one form will sometimes be possible, be prepared to explain the reasons for your choices.

1. Weather experts _____ (predict) a continuing drought for this area.

2. Ever since the first nuclear power plants were built, opponents _____ (fear) disaster.

3. Thousands of Irish peasants _____ (emigrate) to America after the potato famine of the 1840s.

4. My brother _____ (send) me a package that should arrive today.

5. The committee _____ (meet) again next week.

6. While they _____ (eat) in a neighborhood restaurant, they witnessed a minor accident.

7. By this time tomorrow, Eileen _____ (finish) her last term paper of the semester.

8. By the time a child born today enters first grade, he or she _____ (watch) thousands of television commercials.

9. In one of the novel's most famous scenes, Huck _____ (express) his willingness to go to hell rather than report Jim as an escaped slave.

10. The supply of a product _____ (rise) when the demand is great.

www ● bedford
stmartins.com/
smhandbook

For additional exercises on verb forms, click on

▶ **Exercise Central**
  ▶ **Verbs**

33g Using verb tenses in sequence

Careful and accurate use of tenses is important to clear writing. Even the simplest narrative describes actions that take place at different times; when you use the appropriate tense for each action, readers can follow such time changes easily.

The relationship between the tense of the verb in the independent clause of a sentence and the tense of a verb in a dependent clause or a verbal is called the **sequence of tenses.** Even though in general you can use almost any sequence of tenses, in a particular sentence the tense of the verb in a dependent clause or a verbal is limited by the meaning and by conventions about particular sequences.

By the time he *lent* her the money, she *had declared* bankruptcy.

1 Verb sequence with infinitives

The infinitive of a verb is *to* plus the base form (*to go, to be*). Use the **present infinitive** to indicate actions occurring at the same time as or later than the action of the predicate verb.

I *wanted to swim* in the ocean last summer.
[The wanting and the (imagined) swimming occurred at the same time in the past.]

I *expect to swim* in the ocean next summer.
[The expecting is present; the swimming is in the future.]

Use the **perfect infinitive** (*to have* plus the past participle) to indicate actions occurring before the action of the predicate verb.

He *was reported to have left* his fortune to his cat.
[The leaving of the fortune took place before the reporting.]

2 Verb sequence with participles

Use the **present participle** (base form plus *-ing*) to indicate actions occurring at the same time as that of the predicate verb.

Seeking to relieve unemployment, Roosevelt *established* several public-works programs.

Use the **past participle** or the **present perfect participle** (*having* plus the past participle) to indicate action occurring before that of the predicate verb.

Flown to the front, the troops *joined* their hard-pressed comrades.

Having crushed all opposition at home, he *launched* a war of conquest.

3 Verb sequence and habitual actions

In conversation, people often use *will* or *would* to describe habitual actions. In writing, however, stick to the present and past tenses for this purpose.

▶ When I have a deadline, I ~~will~~ work all night.

▶ While we sat on the porch, the children ~~would play.~~ *played.*

EXERCISE 33.4

Edit each of the following sentences to create the appropriate sequence of tenses. Example:

have sent
He needs to ~~send~~ in his application before today.

1. When he was twenty-one, he wanted to have become a millionaire by the age of thirty.
2. Leaving England in December, the settlers arrived in Virginia in May.
3. They hoped to plant their garden by now.
4. Working with great dedication as a summer intern at the magazine, Roberto called his former supervisor in the fall to ask about a permanent position.
5. When we walked home from school, we would often stop for ice cream.

VOICE

Voice tells whether the subject is acting (*he questions us*) or being acted upon (*he is questioned*). When the subject is acting, the verb is in the **active voice**; when the subject is being acted upon, the verb is in the **passive voice**. The passive voice is formed, as in this sentence, by using the appropriate form of the auxiliary verb *be* followed by the past participle

www • bedford
stmartins.com/
smhandbook

For additional
exercises on verb
sequence, click on

▶ **Exercise Central**
  ▶ **Verbs**

of the main verb: he *is being questioned,* he *was questioned,* he *will be questioned,* he *has been questioned.*

ACTIVE VOICE

Marianne *avoided* elevators.

PASSIVE VOICE

Elevators *were avoided* by Marianne.

Most contemporary writers use the active voice as much as possible because it makes prose more *active,* more lively. When passive-voice verbs pile up in a passage, that passage is generally hard to understand and remember. In addition, writers sometimes use the passive voice to try to avoid taking responsibility for what they have written. A university president who announces that "it is recommended that fees rise substantially" skirts the pressing question: recommended by whom?

In spite of such questionable uses, however, the passive voice can work to good advantage in some situations. Reporters often use the passive voice to protect the confidentiality of their sources, as in the familiar phrase *it is reported that.* The passive voice is also appropriate when the performer of an action is unknown or less important than the recipient, as in the following passage:

DALLAS, Nov. 22 — President John Fitzgerald Kennedy was shot and killed by an assassin today.
He died of a wound in the brain caused by a rifle bullet that was fired at him as he was riding through downtown Dallas in a motorcade.
Vice President Lyndon Baines Johnson, who was riding in the third car behind Mr. Kennedy's, was sworn in as the 36th President of the United States 99 minutes after Mr. Kennedy's death.
— TOM WICKER, *New York Times*

Wicker uses the passive voice with good reason: to focus on Kennedy, not on who killed him, and on Johnson, not on who swore him in.

Much technical and scientific writing uses the passive voice effectively to highlight what is being studied rather than who is doing the studying. Look at the following example, from a description of geological movement:

For more about active and passive voice, see 38c and 47b.

The Earth's plates are created where they separate and are recycled where they collide, in a continuous process of creation and destruction.
— FRANK PRESS AND RAYMOND SIEVER, *Understanding Earth*

If you use the passive voice a great deal, however, practice shifting some of your sentences to the active voice. To do so, convert the subject of the verb into a direct or indirect object, and make the performer of the action into the subject.

> *The alarm clock*   *me*
> ▶ I̶ w̶a̶s̶ awakened promptly at seven. by the alarm clock.
>   ^   ^   ^

www ● bedford
stmartins.com/
smhandbook

For additional
exercises on active
and passive voice,
click on

▶ Exercise Central
  ▶ Verbs

● **EXERCISE 33.5**

Convert each sentence from active to passive voice or from passive to active, and note the differences in emphasis these changes make. Example:

> *The*   *is advised by Machiavelli*
> Machiavelli advises the prince to gain the friendship of the people.
>   ^   ^

1. Huge pine trees were uprooted by the storm.

2. The comic-book artist drew a superhero with amazing crime-fighting powers.

3. For months, the baby kangaroo is protected, fed, and taught how to survive by its mother.

4. The lawns and rooftops were covered with the first snow of winter.

5. A team of architects designed a sleek new building to house a modern art collection.

FOR COLLABORATION

Working with one or two classmates, look at several pieces of writing that all of you particularly like, and find examples of both the active voice and the passive voice. Convert each of the examples to the other voice, and note the difference in emphasis and rhythm the changes make. Bring your results to class for discussion.

MOOD

The **mood** of a verb indicates the attitude of the writer toward what he or she is saying or writing. Different moods are used to express a fact, opinion, or inquiry (**indicative mood**); a command or request (**imperative mood**); or a wish, suggestion, requirement, or condition contrary to fact (**subjunctive mood**).

INDICATIVE   I *did* the right thing.

IMPERATIVE   *Do* the right thing.

SUBJUNCTIVE   If I *had done* the right thing, I would not be in trouble now.

33h Using the subjunctive

The **present subjunctive** uses the base form.

It is important that children *be* psychologically ready for a new sibling.

The **past subjunctive** is the same as the past tense except for the verb *be*, which uses *were* for all subjects.

He spent money as if he *had* infinite credit.

If the store *were* better located, it would attract more customers.

Because the subjunctive can create a rather formal tone, many people today tend to substitute the indicative in informal conversation.

If I *was* a better typist, I would type my own papers.

Nevertheless, formal writing still requires the use of the subjunctive in the following kinds of dependent clauses:

■ *Clauses expressing a wish*

He wished that his mother *were* still living nearby.

■ *If clauses expressing a condition that does not exist*

If the sale of tobacco *were* banned, tobacco companies would suffer a great loss.

One common error is to use *would* in both clauses. Use the subjunctive in the *if* clause and *would* in the main clause.

> ▶ If I ~~would have~~ played harder, I would have won.

had

■ *As if and as though clauses*

He started down the trail as if he *were walking* on thin ice.

FOR MULTILINGUAL WRITERS: Using the Subjunctive

"If you were to practice writing every day, it would eventually seem much easier to you." For a discussion of this and other uses of the subjunctive, see 62f.

verb
33h   635

GRAMMAR
Using the
Subjunctive

www ● bedford
stmartins.com/
smhandbook

For additional
exercises on mood,
click on

► Exercise Central
  ► Verbs

■ **That** *clauses expressing a demand, request, requirement, or suggestion*

The job demands that the employee *be* in good physical condition.

● **EXERCISE 33.6**

Revise any of the following sentences that do not use the appropriate subjunctive verb forms required in formal writing. Example:

> I saw how carefully he moved, as if he ~~was~~ caring for an infant.
> ^{were}

1. Her stepsisters treated Cinderella as though she was a servant.

2. Marvina wished that she was able to take her daughter along on the business trip.

3. The instructor insisted that the student get a note from her doctor.

4. If more money was available, we would be able to offer more scholarships.

5. It is necessary that the manager knows how to do any job in the store.

THINKING CRITICALLY ABOUT VERBS

Reading with an Eye for Verbs

Some years ago a newspaper in San Francisco ran the headline "Giants Crush Cardinals, 3 – 1," provoking the following friendly advice from John Updike about the art of baseball-headline verbs:

> The correct verb, San Francisco, is *whip*. Notice the vigor, force, and scorn obtained. . . . [These examples] may prove helpful: 3 – 1 — *whip*, 3 – 2 — *shade*, 2 – 1 — *edge*. 4 – 1 gets the coveted verb *vanquish*. Rule: Any three-run margin, *provided the winning total does not exceed ten*, may be described as a vanquishing.

Double-digit scores, Updike continues, merit such verbs as *annihilate*, *obliterate*, and *humiliate*. (Thus, *A's Annihilate O's, 13 – 2*.) And if the home team is on the short end of the score, *shade* should become *squeak by*. Finally, Updike advises, use of *bow* (*A's bow to O's*) can allow the home team, while losing, "to be given the active position in the sentence and an appearance of graciousness as well."

Take the time to study a newspaper with an eye for its verbs. Copy down several examples of strong verbs as well as a few examples of weak or overused verbs. For the weak ones, try to come up with better choices.

Thinking about Your Own Use of Verbs

Writing that relies too heavily on the verbs *be, do,* and *have* almost always bores readers. Look at something you've written recently to see whether you rely too heavily on these verbs, and revise accordingly.

34

▼ Maintaining Subject-Verb Agreement

In everyday terms, the word *agreement* refers to an accord of some sort: you reach an agreement with your boss about salary; friends agree to go to a movie; the members of a family agree to share household chores; the United States and Russia negotiate an agreement about reducing nuclear arms. This meaning covers grammatical agreement as well. In academic varieties of English, verbs must agree with their subjects in number (singular or plural) and in person (first, second, or third). In practice, only a very few subject-verb constructions cause confusion. This chapter will look at those constructions in some detail. ■

34a Making verbs agree with third-person singular subjects

To make a verb in the present tense agree with a third-person singular subject, add *-s* or *-es* to the base form.

A vegetarian diet *lowers* the risk of heart disease.

To make a verb in the present tense agree with any other subject, use the base form of the verb.

I *miss* my family.

They *live* in another state.

Have and *be* do not follow the *-s* or *-es* pattern with third-person singular subjects. *Have* changes to *has; be* has irregular forms in both the present and past tenses and in the first person as well as the third person. (See Chapter 33.)

War *is* hell.

The soldier *was* brave beyond the call of duty.

In some varieties of African American English and some regional white English, third-person singular verb forms do not end with *-s* or *-es*.

She *go* to work seven days a week.

He *don't* take it to heart.

→ Check your drafts verb by verb, and identify the subject that goes with each verb.

  ▸ **The players on our side *is* sure to win.** *(are)*

Because the simple subject here is *players,* the verb needs to be *are.* When you take away the words between the subject and the verb, it is easier to identify agreement problems. (34b)

→ Check compound subjects. Those joined by *and* usually take a plural verb form. With those subjects joined by *or* or *nor,* however, the verb agrees with the part of the subject closest to the verb. *Neither the parents nor Claire plans to vote.* (34c)

→ Check collective-noun subjects. These nouns take a singular verb form when they refer to a group as a single unit but a plural form when they refer to the multiple members of a group. *The crowd screams its support. The team are arriving at the camp on different days.* (34d)

→ Check indefinite-pronoun subjects. Most take a singular verb form. *Both, few, many, others,* and *several* take a plural form; and *all, any, enough, more, most, none,* and *some* can be either singular or plural, depending on the noun they refer to. *Each of the singers rehearses for three hours daily. Most of the land was forested. Most of the people were farmers.* (34e)

In academic English, these verb forms are *(she) goes* and *(he) doesn't.* You will often see verb forms such as those in the two preceding examples in African American literature, especially in dialogue, and you may quote passages using these varieties of English in your own writing. In most academic writing, however, add *-s* or *-es* to third-person singular verb forms.

34b Making subjects and verbs agree when separated by other words

Sometimes the simple subject is separated from the verb by other words. Make sure the verb agrees with the subject and not with another noun that falls in between.

A vase of flowers makes a room attractive.

638

s-v

34c

GRAMMAR

Maintaining
Subject-Verb
Agreement

have

▶ **Many books on the best-seller list ~~has~~ little literary value.**

The simple subject is *books,* not *list.*

Be careful when you use phrases beginning with *as well as, along with, in addition to, together with,* or similar prepositions. They do not make a singular subject plural.

The president, along with many senators, *opposes* the bill.

was

▶ **A passenger, as well as the driver, ~~were~~ injured in the accident.**

Though this sentence has a grammatically singular subject, it suggests the idea of a plural subject. The sentence makes better sense with a compound subject: *The driver and a passenger were injured in the accident.*

www • bedford
stmartins.com/
smhandbook

For additional
exercises on words
between the subject
and verb, click on

▶ Exercise Central
  ▶ Subject-Verb
    Agreement

EXERCISE 34.1

Underline the appropriate verb form in each of the following sentences. Example:

The benefits of family planning (*is/are*) not apparent to many peasants.

1. People who live in high-rise apartments seldom (*knows/know*) their neighbors.

2. The dog, along with his owner, (*races/race*) wildly down the street every afternoon.

3. A sky full of stars (*rewards/reward*) me each time I camp in the mountains.

4. The system of sororities and fraternities (*supplies/supply*) much of the social life on some college campuses.

5. The buck (*stops/stop*) here.

6. The police officer, in addition to a couple of pedestrians, (*was/were*) pinned to the wall as the crowd rushed by.

7. In many species, the male as well as the female (*cares/care*) for the offspring.

8. He (*holds/hold*) a controlling interest in the company.

9. The pictures in this book often (*frightens/frighten*) small children.

10. Current research on AIDS, in spite of the best efforts of hundreds of scientists, (*leaves/leave*) serious questions unanswered.

34c Making verbs agree with compound subjects

Two or more subjects joined by *and* generally require a plural verb form.

Tony and his friend *commute* from Louisville.

were
▶ **A backpack, a canteen, and a rifle was issued to each recruit.**
⌃

When subjects joined by *and* are considered a single unit or refer to the same person or thing, they take a singular verb form.

George W. Bush's close friend and political ally *is* his brother.

remains
▶ **Drinking and driving remain a major cause of highway fatalities.**
⌃

In this sentence, *drinking and driving* is considered a single activity, and a singular verb is used.

If the word *each* or *every* precedes subjects joined by *and,* the verb form is singular.

Each boy and girl *chooses* one gift to take home.

With subjects joined by *or* or *nor,* the verb agrees with the part closest to the verb.

Neither my roommate nor my neighbors *like* my loud music.

is
▶ **Either the witnesses or the defendant are lying.**
⌃

If you find this sentence awkward, put the plural noun closest to the verb: *Either the defendant or the witnesses are lying.*

am
▶ **Either you or I are wrong.**
⌃

34d Making verbs agree with subjects that are collective nouns or fractions

Collective nouns—such as *family, team, audience, group, jury, crowd, band, class,* and *committee*—refer to a group. Collective nouns can take either singular or plural verb forms, depending on whether they refer to the group as a single unit or to the multiple members of the group. The meaning of a sentence as a whole is your guide to whether a collective noun refers to a unit or to the multiple parts of a unit.

After deliberating, the jury *reports* its verdict.

The jury acts as a single unit.

The jury still *disagree* on a number of counts.

The members of the jury act as multiple individuals.

>   *scatter*
> **The family of ducklings scatters when the cat approaches.**

Family here refers to the many ducks; they cannot scatter as one.

Treat fractions that refer to singular nouns as singular and those that refer to plural nouns as plural.

SINGULAR	Two-thirds of the park *has* burned.
PLURAL	Two-thirds of the students *were* commuters.

Treat phrases starting with *the number of* as singular and with *a number of* as plural.

SINGULAR	The number of applicants for the internship *was* unbelievable.
PLURAL	A number of applicants *were* put on the waiting list.

34e Making verbs agree with indefinite-pronoun subjects

Indefinite pronouns are those that do not refer to specific persons or things. Most take singular verb forms.

SOME COMMON INDEFINITE PRONOUNS

another	each	much	one
any	either	neither	other
anybody	everybody	nobody	somebody
anyone	everyone	no one	someone
anything	everything	nothing	something

Of the two jobs, neither *holds* much appeal.

>   *depicts*
> **Each of the plays depict a hero undone by a tragic flaw.**

Both, few, many, others, and *several* are plural.

Though many *apply,* few *are* chosen.

contain
▶ Several of the articles in that paper contains references to the deficit.

All, any, enough, more, most, none, and *some* can be singular or plural, depending on the noun they refer to.

All of the cake *was* eaten.

All of the candidates *promise* to improve the schools.

34f   Making verbs agree with the antecedents of *who, which,* and *that*

When the relative pronouns *who, which,* and *that* are used as a subject, the verb agrees with the antecedent of the pronoun.

Fear is an ingredient that *goes* into creating stereotypes.

Guilt, jealousy, and fear are ingredients that *go* into creating stereotypes.

Problems often occur with the words *one of the.* In general, *one of the* takes a plural verb, while *only one of the* takes a singular verb.

work
▶ Carla is one of the employees who always works overtime.

Some employees always work overtime. Carla is among them. Thus *who* refers to *employees,* and the verb is plural.

works
▶ Sam is the only one of the employees who always work overtime.

Only one employee always works overtime, and that employee is Sam. Thus *one,* and not *employees,* is the antecedent of *who,* and the verb form is singular.

34g   Making linking verbs agree with their subjects, not their complements

A linking verb should agree with its subject, which usually precedes the verb, not with the subject complement, which follows it.

● For an explanation of subject complements, see 31c2.

642

s-v

34h

GRAMMAR

Maintaining
Subject-Verb
Agreement

▶ The signings of three key treaties *is* the topic of my talk.
(are)

The subject is *signings*, not *topic*.

▶ Nero Wolfe's passion *were* orchids.
(was)

The subject is *passion*, not *orchids*.

34h Making verbs agree with subjects that are plural in form but singular in meaning

Some words that end in -*s* seem to be plural but are singular in meaning and thus take singular verb forms.

▶ Measles still *strike* many Americans.
(strikes)

Some nouns of this kind (such as *statistics* and *politics*) may be either singular or plural, depending on context.

SINGULAR   Statistics *is* a course I really dread.

PLURAL   The statistics in that study *are* highly questionable.

34i Making verbs agree with subjects that follow them

In English, verbs usually follow subjects. When this order is reversed, it is easy to become confused. Make the verb agree with the subject, not with a noun that happens to precede it.

▶ Beside the barn *stands* silos filled with grain.
(stand)

The subject is *silos;* it is plural, so the verb must be *stand*.

In sentences beginning with *there is* or *there are* (or *there was, there have been,* and so on), *there* serves only as an introductory word; the subject follows the verb.

There *are* five basic positions in classical ballet.

The subject, *positions,* is plural, so the verb must also be plural.

FOR COLLABORATION

Working with a classmate, write a paragraph about a movie you have seen recently, making sure to use the present tense as you describe some of the action, special effects, or other elements you admire. Then go through your paragraph, identifying every subject and its verb. Using the information provided in this chapter, make sure all your subjects and verbs agree. Bring your paragraph to class to read aloud.

34j Making verbs agree with titles and words used as words

When the subject is the title of a book, film, or other work of art, the verb form is singular even if the title is plural in form.

One Writer's Beginnings describes Eudora Welty's childhood.

Similarly, a word referred to as a word requires a singular verb form even if the word itself is plural.

Steroids is a little word that packs a big punch in the world of sports.

EXERCISE 34.2

Revise any of the following sentences as necessary to establish subject-verb agreement. (Some of the sentences do not require any change.) Example:

darts
Into the shadows ~~dart~~ the frightened raccoon.
          ^

1. The old library and the train station is two of my favorite downtown buildings.

2. Talking and getting up from my seat was my crime.

3. If rhythm and blues is your kind of music, try Mary Lou's.

4. Sleek furniture and the gleaming marble floor tell customers that this is a classy office.

5. *The vapors* were a Victorian term for hypochondria.

6. Neither the escape attempt nor the prisoners' lawsuit convince taxpayers of the prison's problems.

7. On the sidewalk sits tables and chairs.

8. Most of the voters support reducing real-estate taxes.

9. Each of the security workers are considered trained after viewing a twenty-minute videotape.

10. Neither her manner nor her tantrums intimidates the staff.

11. A jury rarely make a decision based on evidence alone.

12. My grandmother is the only one of my relatives who still goes to church.

www • bedford
stmartins.com/
smhandbook

For additional
exercises, click on

▶ **Exercise Central**
  ▶ **Subject-Verb
    Agreement**

13. *Our Tapes* were one of Fitzgerald's earlier titles for *Tender Is the Night*.

14. Sweden was one of the few European countries that was neutral in 1943.

15. Physics reveal the natural laws of the universe.

THINKING CRITICALLY ABOUT SUBJECT-VERB AGREEMENT

Reading with an Eye for Subject-Verb Agreement

The following passage, from a 1990 essay questioning suggestions that our society is returning to more traditional values, especially marriage, includes several instances of complicated subject-verb agreement. Read the passage, paying close attention to the subjects and verbs and noting the rules governing subject-verb agreement in each case.

> For me, none of [these assumptions about marriage] add up. Between the public statistic and the private reality lies a sea of contradiction in which these pronouncements drown. Marriage seems to me more conflict-ridden than ever, and the divorce rate — with or without new babies in the house — remains constant. The fabric of men-and-women-as-they-once-were is so thin in places no amount of patching can weave that cloth together again. The longing for connection may be strong, but even stronger is the growing perception that only people who are real to themselves can connect. Two shall be as one is over, no matter how lonely we get.
>
> – VIVIAN GORNICK, "Who Says We Haven't Made a Revolution?"

Thinking about Your Own Use of Subject-Verb Agreement

Visiting relatives is/are treacherous. Either of these verbs makes a grammatically acceptable sentence, agreeing with a subject, yet they result in two very different statements. Write a brief explanation of the two possible meanings. Then write a paragraph or two about visiting relatives. Using the information in this chapter, examine each subject and its verb. Have you maintained subject-verb agreement throughout? Revise to correct any errors you find, and then look for any patterns in your writing. If you find any, make a note to yourself (in a writing log, if you keep one) of things to look for routinely as you revise your writing.

35 Maintaining Pronoun-Antecedent Agreement

35a Making pronouns agree with compound antecedents

A compound antecedent whose parts are joined by *and* requires a plural pronoun.

My parents and I tried to resolve *our* disagreement.

When a compound antecedent is preceded by *each* or *every*, however, it takes a singular pronoun.

Every plant and animal has *its* own ecological niche.

With a compound antecedent whose parts are joined by *or* or *nor*, the pronoun agrees with the nearest antecedent. If the parts of the antecedent are of different genders or persons, however, this kind of sentence can be awkward.

AWKWARD	Neither Annie nor Barry got *his* work done.
REVISED	Annie didn't get *her* work done, and neither did Barry.

With compound antecedents containing both singular and plural parts, the sentence may sound awkward unless the plural part comes last.

▶ Neither the ~~radio stations~~ *newspaper* nor the ~~newspaper~~ *radio stations* would reveal ~~its~~ *their* sources.

Pronouns "are tricky rather than difficult," says H. W. Fowler in *A Dictionary of Modern English Usage.* The "trickiness" Fowler notes results primarily because a pronoun usually stands in for another word, a noun or some other pronoun, called the *antecedent.* Making sure that the pronoun and its antecedent match up, or agree, is a task every writer faces.

Like a verb with its subject, a pronoun must agree with its antecedent in person and number. In addition, a third-person singular pronoun must agree with its antecedent in *gender* — masculine, feminine, or neuter. Fortunately, only a few kinds of antecedents cause problems with agreement. ■

→ Check all subjects joined by *and, or,* or *nor* to be sure they are treated as singular or plural as appropriate. Recast any sentence in which agreement creates awkwardness. (35a)

→ Check all uses of *anyone, each, everybody, many,* and other indefinite pronouns (see list in 34e) to be sure they are treated as singular or plural as appropriate. (35c)

→ If you find *he, his,* or *him* used to refer to persons of either sex, revise the pronouns, or recast the sentences altogether. (35d)

35b Making pronouns agree with collective-noun antecedents

When a collective-noun antecedent (*herd, team, audience*) refers to a single unit, it requires a singular pronoun.

> The audience fixed *its* attention on center stage.

When such an antecedent refers to the multiple parts of the unit, however, it requires a plural pronoun.

> The director chose this cast because *they* had experience in the roles.

Remember that collective nouns referring to single units require not only singular pronouns but also singular verb forms in the present tense. Collective nouns referring to separate individuals in a unit, on the other hand, require plural pronouns and plural verb forms.

> Each generation *has its* own slang. [*generation* as single unit]
>
> That generation *have* sold *their* souls for money. [*generation* as individuals]

35c Making pronouns agree with indefinite-pronoun antecedents

Indefinite pronouns are those that do not refer to specific persons or things. A pronoun whose antecedent is an indefinite pronoun should agree with it in number. Many indefinite pronouns are always singular (as with *one*); a few are always plural (as with *many*). Some can be singular or plural depending on the context.

For more on indefinite pronouns, see 34e.

One of the ballerinas lost *her* balance.

Many in the audience jumped to *their* feet.

Some of the furniture was showing *its* age. [singular meaning for *some*]

Some of the farmers abandoned *their* land. [plural meaning for *some*]

35d Checking for sexist pronouns

Indefinite pronouns often refer to antecedents that may be either male or female. Writers used to use masculine pronouns, known as the generic *he*, in such cases. In recent decades, however, many people have pointed out that such wording ignores or even excludes females — and thus should be avoided.

● For a list of indefinite pronouns, see 34e; for more on ways to avoid sexist language, see 25b.

EDITING OUT THE GENERIC USE OF HE, HIS, *OR* HIM

Look at the following sentence:

Every citizen should know *his* rights under the law.

Here are three ways to express the same idea without *his*:

1. Revise to make the antecedent plural.

   All citizens should know their legal rights.

2. Revise the sentence altogether.

   Every citizen should have some knowledge of basic legal rights.

3. Use both masculine and feminine pronouns.

   Every citizen should know his or her legal rights.

The last option, using both masculine and feminine pronouns, can be awkward, especially when repeated several times in a passage.

When an antecedent is an indefinite pronoun, such as *anybody* or *each*, some people avoid the generic *he* by using a plural pronoun. You will probably hear, and perhaps use, such sentences in conversation, but be careful about using them in writing.

USED IN CONVERSATION

Everybody had *their* own theory about Jennifer's resignation.

Although this usage—*everybody* with the plural pronoun *their*—is fast gaining acceptance, many readers still consider it excessively informal or even incorrect. *Everybody* is grammatically singular and hence calls for a singular pronoun.

PREFERRED IN WRITING

The employees had their own theory about Jennifer's resignation.

**www ● bedford
stmartins.com/
smhandbook**

For additional
exercises on
pronoun-
antecedent
agreement, click on

▶ **Exercise Central**
  ▶ **Pronouns**

● **EXERCISE 35.1**

Revise the following sentences as needed to create pronoun-antecedent agreement and to eliminate the generic *he* and any awkward pronoun references. Some can be revised in more than one way, and some do not require any changes. Example:

or her
Every graduate submitted his diploma card.
^

All graduates   *their*   *cards.*
~~Every graduate submitted his diploma card.~~
^   ^   ^

1. With tuition on the rise, a student has to save money wherever they can.

2. Not everyone gets along with his roommate, but the two can usually manage to tolerate each other temporarily.

3. Congress usually resists presidential attempts to encroach on what they consider their authority.

4. We voted on whether Carlos or Lucille would have their chance to join the club.

5. If there is a doctor in the house, he should step forward and offer his assistance.

6. Every dog and cat has their own personality, which could never be cloned.

7. Neither the scouts nor their leader knew their way out of the forest.

8. The committee offered its recommendations, but the choices were all rejected.

9. A celebrity can sometimes convince themselves that they really are special and talented.

10. I often turn on the fan and the light and neglect to turn it off.

THINKING CRITICALLY ABOUT PRONOUN AGREEMENT

Following is a paragraph from *Democracy in America,* Alexis de Tocqueville's classic critique of American institutions and culture, which was first published in 1835. Read the paragraph with an eye for pronouns. Does the use of the masculine pronoun to refer to both men and women seem odd to you? Revise the paragraph to eliminate this generic use of masculine pronouns.

After the birth of a human being, his early years are obscurely spent in the toils or pleasures of childhood. As he grows up, the world receives him, when his manhood begins, and he enters into contact with his fellows. He is then studied for the first time, and it is imagined that the germ of the vices and the virtues of his maturer years is then formed. This, if I am not mistaken, is a great error. We must begin higher up; we must watch the infant in his mother's arms; we must see the first images which the external world casts upon the dark mirror of his mind, the first occurrences which he witnesses; we must hear the first words which awaken the sleeping powers of thought, and stand by his earliest efforts — if we would understand the prejudices, the habits, and the passions which will rule his life. The entire man is, so to speak, to be seen in the cradle of the child.   — ALEXIS DE TOCQUEVILLE, *Democracy in America*

36

◥ Using Adjectives and Adverbs

As words that describe other words, adjectives and adverbs add liveliness and color to the flat gray surface of writing, helping writers *show* rather than just tell. See how much Dorothy West relies on them:

With a long blackened fireplace *stick Mama* carefully *tilted the lid of the* three-legged *skillet to see if her cornbread was* done. . . . Gently *she let the lid drop. . . .*

— DOROTHY WEST
The Living Is Easy

Adjectives such as *blackened* and *three-legged* and adverbs such as *carefully* and *gently* create vivid images for the reader.

In addition, adjectives and adverbs often provide indispensable meanings to the words they modify. In basketball, for example, there is an important difference between a *flagrant* foul and a *technical* foul, a layup and a *reverse* layup. In each instance, the modifiers are crucial to accurate communication. ■

36a Distinguishing adjectives from adverbs

Although adjectives and adverbs both modify other words, each modifies different parts of speech. **Adjectives** modify nouns and pronouns, answering the question *which? how many?* or *what kind?* **Adverbs** modify verbs, adjectives, other adverbs, or entire clauses; they answer the question *how? when? where?* or *to what extent?* Many adverbs are formed by adding *-ly* to adjectives (*slight, slightly*), but many are not (*outdoors, very*). And some words that end in *-ly* are adjectives (*lovely, homely*). Since adjectives and adverbs both act as modifiers, often have similar or even the same forms, and in some cases can occupy the same positions in sentences, sometimes the only way of identifying a word as one or the other is to identify its function in the sentence.

36b Using adjectives after linking verbs

When adjectives come after linking verbs, they usually serve as a subject complement, to describe the subject: *I am patient.* Note that in specific sentences, some verbs may or may not act as linking verbs—*look, appear, sound, feel, smell, taste, grow,* and *prove,* for instance. The advice here is

1. Scrutinize each adjective and adverb to see whether it is the best word possible. Considering one or two synonyms for each one might help you decide.

2. Is each adjective and adverb really necessary? See if a more specific noun would eliminate the need for an adjective (*mansion* rather than *enormous house*, for instance); do the same with verbs and adverbs.

3. Are there places where adding an adjective or adverb might make your writing more vivid or specific?

4. Do all adjectives modify nouns or pronouns and all adverbs modify verbs, adjectives, or other adverbs? (36a) Check especially for proper use of *good* and *well, bad* and *badly, real* and *really.* (36c)

5. Are all comparisons complete? (36d4)

6. If English is not your first language, check that adjectives are in the right order. (59e)

when a word following one of these verbs modifies the subject, use an adjective; when the word modifies the verb, use an adverb.

ADJECTIVE   Kobe Bryant looked *angry.*

ADVERB   He looked *angrily* at the referee.

Linking verbs suggest a state of being, not an action. In the preceding examples, *looked angry* suggests the state of being angry; *looked angrily* suggests an angry action.

FOR MULTILINGUAL WRITERS: Using Adjectives with Plural Nouns

In Spanish, Russian, and many other languages, adjectives agree in number with the nouns they modify. In English, however, adjectives do not change number this way: *her dogs are small* (not *smalls*).

36c Using adverbs to modify verbs, adjectives, and adverbs

In everyday conversation, you will often hear (and perhaps use) adjectives in place of adverbs. When you write in standard academic English, however, use adverbs to modify verbs, adjectives, and other adverbs.

▶ You can feel the song's meter if you listen ~~careful.~~ *carefully.*

▶ The audience was ~~real~~ *really* disappointed by the show.

FOR MULTILINGUAL WRITERS: Determining Adjective Sequence

Should you write *these beautiful blue kitchen tiles* or *these blue beautiful kitchen tiles*? See 59e for guidelines on adjective sequence.

■ Good *and* well, bad *and* badly

The modifiers *good, well, bad,* and *badly* cause problems for many writers because the distinctions between *good* and *well* and between *bad* and *badly* are often not observed in conversation. Problems also arise because *well* can function as either an adjective or an adverb. *Good* and *bad* are adjectives, and both can be used after a linking verb. Do not use them to modify a verb, an adjective, or an adverb; use *well* or *badly* instead.

The weather looks *good* today.

I feel *bad* for the Chicago fans.

▶ He plays the trumpet ~~good~~ *well* and the trombone not ~~bad.~~ *badly.*

Badly is an adverb and can be used to modify a verb, an adjective, or another adverb.

In her first recital, the soprano sang *badly.*

Do not use it after a linking verb; use *bad* instead.

▶ The clams tasted ~~badly.~~ *bad.*

As an adjective, *well* means "in good health"; as an adverb, it means "in a good manner" or "thoroughly."

> **ADJECTIVE**   After a week of rest, Julio felt *well* again.
>
> **ADVERB**   She plays *well* enough to make the team.

■ Right *smart,* way *cool*

Most regions have certain characteristic adjectives and adverbs. Some of the most colorful are intensifiers, adverbs meaning *very* or *absolutely*. In parts of the South, for example, and particularly in Appalachia, you are likely to hear the following:

> He paid a *right* smart price for that car.
>
> She was *plumb* tuckered out.

In each case, the adverb (*right, plumb*) acts to intensify the meaning of the adjective (*smart, tuckered out*). Consider two other examples, the first overheard in New York City, the second in Oakland, California:

> It seems like *way* long ago that we were on vacation.
>
> They looked *way* cool in their new sneakers.

As with all language, use of regional adjectives and adverbs is governed by appropriateness. In writing about a family member who lives in Minnesota, for example, you might well quote her, thus bringing some midwestern expressions into your writing. For most academic writing, however, you should use academic English.

●⋯ For guidelines on using different varieties of language, see Chapter 26.

● EXERCISE 36.1

Revise each of the following sentences to maintain correct adverb and adjective use. Then identify each adjective or adverb that you have revised, and point out the word each modifies. Example:

> superbly
> The attorney delivered a ~~superb~~ conceived summation.
>   ^

1. Honest lawyers are not complete obsessed with status or money.
2. The young man was embarrassed because he behaved ridiculous at the party.
3. Hypochondriacs call a doctor whenever they feel badly.
4. The summers are real hot and humid here, but in the winter the wind chill is frequent below zero.
5. He talked loud about volunteering, but he was not really interested.

6. Regrettably, the youngster was hurt bad in the accident.
7. The skater performed good despite the intense competition.
8. Aneil felt terrifically about his discussion with Professor Greene.
9. After we added cinnamon, the stew tasted really well.
10. They brought up their children very strict.

36d Using comparatives and superlatives

In addition to their simple, or positive, form, many adjectives and adverbs have two other forms, the **comparative** and **superlative**, that are used for making comparisons.

POSITIVE	COMPARATIVE	SUPERLATIVE
large	larger	largest
early	earlier	earliest
careful	more careful	most careful
delicious	more delicious	most delicious

Canada is *larger* than the United States.

My son needs to be *more careful* with his money.

This is the *most delicious* coffee we have tried.

As the first example shows, the comparative and superlative of most short (one-syllable and some two-syllable) adjectives are usually formed by adding *-er* and *-est. More* and *most* are sometimes used with short adjectives, however, to create a more formal tone. With some two-syllable adjectives, with longer adjectives, and with most adverbs, use *more* and *most: scientific, more scientific, most scientific; elegantly, more elegantly, most elegantly.* If you are not sure whether a word has *-er* and *-est* forms, consult the dictionary entry for the simple form, where any *-er* and *-est* forms are usually listed.

1 Irregular forms

Some adjectives and adverbs have irregular comparative and superlative forms. Here is a list of them:

POSITIVE	COMPARATIVE	SUPERLATIVE
good, well	better	best
bad, badly, ill	worse	worst
little (quantity)	less	least
many, some, much	more	most

2 Comparatives vs. superlatives

The comparative is used to compare two things; the superlative, to compare three or more.

> Rome is a much *older* city than New York.

> Damascus is one of the *oldest* cities in the world.

In conversation, you will often hear the superlative form used even when only two things are being compared: *Of the two paintings, the one by Klee is the most interesting.* In college writing, however, use the comparative: *Of the two paintings, the one by Klee is the more interesting.*

3 Double comparatives and superlatives

Double comparatives and superlatives unnecessarily use both the *-er* or *-est* ending and *more* or *most.* Occasionally they can act to build a special emphasis, as in the title of Spike Lee's movie *Mo' Better Blues.* In college writing, however, make sure not to use *more* or *most* before adjectives or adverbs ending in *-er* or *-est.*

▶ Paris is the ~~most~~ loveliest city in the world.

▶ Rome lasted ~~more~~ longer than Carthage.

4 Incomplete comparisons

In speaking, we sometimes use incomplete comparisons—ones that specify only one of the things being compared—because the context makes the rest of the comparison clear. If after comparing your CD player with a friend's you say *Yours is better,* the context makes it clear that you mean *Yours is better than mine.* In writing, that context may not exist. So take time when editing to check for incomplete comparisons—and to complete them if they are unclear.

than those receiving a placebo.

▶ The patients taking the drug appeared healthier/ₐ

of all composers.

▶ I consider Mozart the greatest/ₐ

5 Absolute concepts

Some adjectives and adverbs—such as *perfect, final,* and *unique*—are absolute concepts, so it is illogical to form comparatives or superlatives of these words.

▶ Max felt compelled to have ~~more~~ perfect control over his thoughts.

        a

▶ Anne has ~~the most~~ unique sense of humor.

6 Multiple negatives

Speakers of English sometimes use more than one negative at a time—saying, for instance, *I can't hardly see you.* Emphatic double negatives—and triple, quadruple, and more—are used by many speakers of African American vernacular English, who may say, for instance, *Don't none of you know nothing at all.*

Even though double negatives occur in many varieties of English (and in many other languages, including French and Russian), in academic or professional writing, you will play it safe if you avoid them—unless you are quoting regional dialogue.

For more on
multiple nega-
tives, see 47c.

36e Using nouns as modifiers

Sometimes a noun can function as an adjective by modifying another noun, as in *chicken soup* or *money supply.* If noun modifiers pile up, however, they can obscure meaning and should thus be revised.

AWKWARD	The cold war–era Rosenberg espionage trial and execution continues to arouse controversy.
REVISED	The Rosenbergs' trial and execution for espionage during the cold war continues to arouse controversy.

● **EXERCISE 36.2**

Revise each of the following sentences to use modifiers correctly, clearly, and effectively. Many of the sentences can be revised in more than one way. Example:

GRAMMAR

Using Nouns as Modifiers

www ● bedford stmartins.com/ smhandbook

For additional exercises on comparatives and superlatives, click on

▶ **Exercise Central**
  ▶ **Adjectives and Adverbs**

bill to approve a financial plan for the

He is sponsoring a housing project. ~~finance plan approval bill.~~
                                 ^   ^

1. Aidan reads both science fiction and mysteries, but he likes science fiction best.

2. The article argued that walking is more healthier than jogging.

3. The crown is set with some of the preciousest gemstones in the world.

4. Most of the elderly are women because women tend to live longer.

5. Minneapolis is the largest of the Twin Cities.

6. She came up with the most perfect plan for revenge.

7. My graduation day will be the most happiest day of my life.

8. The student cafeteria is operated by a college food service system chain.

9. Commuting by train or bus is more energy efficient.

10. Seeing grizzly bears in Glacier National Park was a excitinger experience for the children than going to Disneyland.

THINKING CRITICALLY ABOUT ADJECTIVES AND ADVERBS

Reading with an Eye for Adjectives and Adverbs

Gwendolyn Brooks "describes the 'graceful life' as one where people glide over floors in softly glowing rooms, smile correctly over trays of silver, cinnamon, and cream, and retire in quiet elegance."

– MARY HELEN WASHINGTON, "Taming All That Anger Down"

Identify the adjectives and adverbs in the preceding passage, and comment on what they add to the writing. What would be lost if they were removed? What can you conclude about using adjectives and adverbs in your own writing?

Thinking about Your Own Use of Adjectives and Adverbs

Think of something you can observe or examine closely, and take a few minutes to study it. In a paragraph or two, describe your subject for someone who has never seen it. Using the guidelines at the beginning of the chapter, check your use of adjectives and adverbs, and revise your paragraphs. How would you characterize your use of adjectives and adverbs — do you overuse them? Put these thoughts in your writing log if you keep one.

PART 7

SENTENCES: MAKING CONVENTIONAL CHOICES

"When you start writing—and I think it's true for a lot of beginning writers— you're scared to death that if you don't get that sentence right that minute it's never going to show up again. And is isn't. But it doesn't matter—another one will, and it'll probably be better."

—TONI MORRISON

37

Maintaining Clear Pronoun Reference

Take the Interstate until you come to Exit 3 and then Route 313. Go past it, and take the next exit, which will be Broadway.

These directions, intended to lead an out-of-towner to her friend's house, provide a good example of why it's important for most pronouns to refer clearly to another word, called the antecedent. The word *it* in this example could mean either Exit 3 or Route 313 — or are they perhaps the same thing? If the visitor doesn't already know, or if the exit *and* Route 313 aren't both clearly marked, she could have difficulty finding her way.

Avoiding such problems in your own writing is a fairly simple matter — of identifying each pronoun, finding the word(s) it substitutes for, or supplying such a word and making sure the pronoun cannot mistakenly refer to any other word as well. ■

37a Matching pronouns clearly to one antecedent

If more than one possible antecedent for a personal pronoun appears in a passage, the pronoun should refer clearly and unambiguously to only *one* of them. Look at the following examples:

▶ The meeting between Bowman and Sonny makes him̲ *Bowman*

compare his own unhappy life with one that is more

emotionally secure.

Who is the antecedent of *him* and *his:* Bowman or Sonny? The revision makes the reference clear by replacing a pronoun (*him*) with a noun (*Bowman*).

▶ Kerry told Ellen s̲h̲e̲ ̲s̲h̲o̲u̲l̲d̲ be ready soon. *to*

37b Keeping pronouns and antecedents close together

If a pronoun is too far from its antecedent, readers will have trouble making the connection between the two.

1. Find all the pronouns in your draft, and then identify the specific noun that is the antecedent of each one.

2. If you cannot find a noun antecedent, replace the pronoun with a noun, or supply an antecedent to which the pronoun clearly refers. (37a)

3. Look to see if any pronoun could be misunderstood to refer to a noun other than its antecedent. If so, replace the pronoun with the appropriate noun, or revise the sentence so that the pronoun can refer to only one possible antecedent. (37a)

4. Look at any pronoun that seems far from its antecedent. If a reader might have trouble relating the pronoun to its antecedent, replace the pronoun with the appropriate noun. (37b)

5. Check, in particular, any use of *it, this, that,* and *which* to be sure each pronoun refers to a specific antecedent. (37c)

6. Be sure that any use of *you* refers to your specific reader or readers. (37e)

CONVENTIONS

Checking for Vague Use of *It, This, That,* and *Which*

▶ The right-to-life coalition believes that a *zygote,* an egg at the moment of fertilization, is as deserving of protection as is the born human being and thus that abortion is as much murder as is the killing of a child. The coalition's focus is on what ~~it~~ *the zygote* will become as much as on what it is now.

37c Checking for vague use of *it, this, that,* and *which*

Writers are often tempted to use *it, this, that,* or *which* as a quick and easy way of referring to something mentioned earlier. But such shortcuts can often cause confusion. Make sure that these pronouns refer clearly to a specific antecedent.

▶ When they realized the bill would be defeated, they tried to postpone the vote. However, ~~it~~ *the attempt* failed.

662

ref

37d

CONVENTIONS

Maintaining Clear
Pronoun Reference

▶ Nancy just found out that she won the lottery, ~~which~~ explains her

an event that

sudden resignation from her job.

If *that* or *which* opens a clause that refers to a specific noun, put *that* or *which* directly after the noun, if possible.

▶ We worked all night on the float ~~for the Rose Parade~~ that our club was

for the Rose Parade

going to sponsor.

Does *that* refer to the float or the parade? The editing makes the meaning clear.

37d Checking for appropriate use of *who, which,* and *that*

Be careful to use the relative pronouns *who, which,* and *that* appropriately. *Who* refers primarily to people or to animals with names. *Which* refers to animals or to things, and *that* refers to animals, things, and occasionally anonymous or collective groups of people.

For more on *that*
and *which,* see
the Glossary of
Usage.

Julia Child, *who* is known as "the French chef," is actually from England.

The whale, *which* has only one baby a year, is subject to extinction because it reproduces so slowly.

Laboratories *that* harm animals have become controversial.

FOR MULTILINGUAL WRITERS: Using Pronoun Subjects

In some languages — Spanish, for instance — personal-pronoun subjects are largely unnecessary because the verb ending shows person and number. In other languages, such as Arabic, personal pronouns are added to the verbs as suffixes or prefixes. Native speakers of these languages sometimes "overcorrect" in English by doubling the subject, as in *My cousin he lives next door.* Such a double subject is inappropriate in English. Therefore, if you are using a pronoun as a subject, make sure that you have not used a second noun subject: *He lives next door.*

37e Checking for indefinite use of *you* and *they*

In conversation, we frequently use *you* and *they* in an indefinite sense, as in such expressions as *you never know* and *on television, they said*. In college writing, however, use *you* only to mean "you, the reader," and *they* only to refer to a clear antecedent.

▶ Commercials try to make ^people^ you buy without thinking.

▶ ^Most restaurants in^ In France, they allow dogs in most restaurants.

37f Checking for implied antecedents

Though an adjective or possessive may clearly imply a noun antecedent, it does not serve as a clear antecedent.

▶ In ^her^ Welty's story, ^Welty^ she characterizes Bowman as a man unaware of his own isolation.

● EXERCISE 37.1

Revise each of the following items to clarify pronoun reference. Most of the items can be revised in more than one way. If a pronoun refers ambiguously to more than one possible antecedent, revise the sentence in at least two different ways, reflecting each possible meaning. Example:

www ● bedford
stmartins.com/
smhandbook

For additional exercises on pronoun reference, click on

▶ **Exercise Central**
  ▶ **Pronouns**

> ^Miranda found Jane's keys after^
> ~~After~~ Jane left, ~~Miranda found her keys.~~

> ^Miranda found her own keys after^
> ~~After~~ Jane left, ~~Miranda found her keys.~~

1. Sasha hurried to call her sister before she flew to Brazil.

2. Lear divides his kingdom between the two older daughters, Goneril and Regan, whose extravagant professions of love are more flattering than the simple affection of the youngest daughter, Cordelia. The consequences of this error in judgment soon become apparent, as they prove neither grateful nor kind to him.

3. New England helped shape many aspects of American culture, including education, religion, and government. As New Englanders moved west, they carried its institutions with them.

4. When drug therapy is combined with psychotherapy, the patients relate better to their therapists, are less vulnerable to what disturbs them, and are more responsive to them.

5. Before the restaurant opened for business next to the cleaners, it burned down.

6. In Texas, you often hear about the influence of big oil corporations.

7. Jonathan had an interview with a person that convinced him to keep looking for a job in advertising.

8. She dropped off a friend which had gone to the party with her.

9. Company policy prohibited smoking, which many employees resented.

10. In Derek Walcott's poems, he often describes the landscape of St. Lucia.

EXERCISE 37.2

Revise to establish a clear antecedent for every pronoun that needs one.

In Paul Fussell's essay "My War," he writes about his experience in combat during World War II, which he says still haunts his life. Fussell confesses that he joined the infantry ROTC in 1939 as a way of getting out of gym class, where he would have been forced to expose his "fat and flabby" body to the ridicule of his classmates. However, it proved to be a serious miscalculation. After the United States entered the war in 1941, other male college students were able to join officer training programs in specialized fields that kept them out of combat. If you were already in an ROTC unit associated with the infantry, though, you were trapped in it. That was how Fussell came to be shipped to France as a rifle-platoon leader in 1944. Almost immediately they sent him to the front, where he soon developed pneumonia because of insufficient winter clothing. He spent a month in hospitals; because he did not want to worry his parents, however, he told them it was just the flu. When he returned to the front, he was wounded by a shell that killed his sergeant, which had been with him since basic training.

FOR COLLABORATION

Working with a group of three classmates, have one person read the following poem out loud, and then see if the other two can provide the poem's two-word title. How did your group members know what the title should be? Next, have each member of the group try writing a poem (perhaps three or four verses) like this one, using pronouns and other words to give clues to the title. Read your poems aloud to each other. Can group members guess each title? Bring the results of your collaboration to class for discussion.

His art is eccentricity, his aim
How not to hit the mark he seems to aim at,

His passion how to avoid the obvious,
His technique how to vary the avoidance.

The others throw to be comprehended. He
Throws to be a moment misunderstood.

Yet not too much. Not too errant, arrant, wild,
But every seeming aberration willed.

Not to, yet still, still to communicate
Making the batter understand too late.

–ROBERT FRANCIS

CONVENTIONS

Checking for
Implied
Antecedents

THINKING CRITICALLY ABOUT YOUR USE OF PRONOUN REFERENCE

Turn to something you've written, and analyze your use of pronouns. Do any pronouns not refer clearly and directly to the correct antecedent? Could any antecedents be ambiguous? Using the guidelines on p. 661, revise as necessary. Note any patterns in your use of pronouns — in a writing log, if you keep one.

38

◥ Recognizing Shifts

A shift in writing is an abrupt change of some sort that results in inconsistency. Sometimes writers shift deliberately, as Dave Barry does in saying he "would have to say that the greatest single achievement of the American medical establishment is nasal spray." Barry's shift in tone from the serious (the American medical establishment) to the banal (nasal spray) makes us laugh, as Barry wishes us to. Although writers sometimes deliberately make such shifts for good reasons, unintentional shifts can be jolting and confusing to readers. Among the most common kinds of unintentional shifts are those in tense, in mood, in voice, in person and number, between direct and indirect discourse, and in tone and diction. ∎

38a Checking for unnecessary shifts in tense

If the verbs in a passage refer to actions occurring at different times, they may require different tenses. Be careful, however, not to change tenses for no reason.

> ▶ While I was staring into space, I ~~notice~~ my missing
>   ^noticed^
>   notebook on the windowsill.

> ▶ The director of admissions reads each application
>   twice. She ~~will reflect~~ on each for at least half an hour.
>   ^reflects^

FOR MULTILINGUAL WRITERS: Shifting Tenses in Speech

If Al said to Maria, "I will marry you," why did she then correctly tell her mom, "He said that he *would* marry me"? For guidelines on reporting speech, see 60b.

38b Checking for unnecessary shifts in mood

Be careful not to shift from one mood to another without good reason. The mood of a verb can be indicative (he *closes* the door), imperative (*close* the door), or subjunctive (if the door *were closed*). (See Chapter 33.) Notice how the

→ Shift from one verb tense to another only when you have a reason for doing so. (38a)

→ In your sentences, do you see any shifts in mood—perhaps from an indicative statement to an imperative—and if so, are they necessary? (38b)

→ Check for shifts from active (*She asks questions*) to passive voice (*Questions are asked*). Are they intentional—and if so, for what reason? (38c)

→ Do you see any shifts in person or number—from *we* to *you*, for example—and if so, what are the reasons for the shifts? (38d)

→ Do any of your sentences sound like direct discourse when they are supposed to be indirect discourse? (38e)

→ Check your writing for consistency in tone and diction. If your tone is serious, is it consistently so? Does your word choice match your tone? (38f)

CONVENTIONS

Checking for
Unnecessary Shifts
in Person and
Number

original version of the following sentence shifts unnecessarily from the imperative to the indicative:

▶ Keep your eye on the ball, and ~~you should~~ bend your knees.

The writer's purpose is to give orders, and the editing makes both verbs imperative.

38c Checking for unnecessary shifts in voice

Do not shift without reason between the active voice (she *sold* it) and the passive voice (it *was sold*). Sometimes a shift in voice makes sense, but often it may only confuse readers.

•⸳⸳ For more about voice, see Chapter 33 and 47b.

▶ Two youths approached me, and ~~I was~~ asked for my wallet.
　　　　　　　　　　　　　　　　　^*me*

The original sentence shifts from the active (*youths approached*) to the passive (*I was asked*), so it is unclear who asked for the wallet. Making both verbs active clears up the confusion.

38d Checking for unnecessary shifts in person and number

Unnecessary shifts between first person (*I, we*), second person (*you*), and third person (*he, she, it, one,* or *they*) or between singular and plural subjects can confuse readers.

You
▶ One can do well on this job if you budget your time.
  ^

In the original, it is not clear whether the writer is making a general statement or giving advice to someone in particular. Eliminating the shift eliminates this confusion.

nurses have
▶ Nurses receive much less pay than doctors, even though a nurse has the
                                                          ^
primary responsibility for daily patient care.

The writer had no reason to shift from third-person plural (*nurses*) to third-person singular (*a nurse*).

For a complete discussion of pronoun-antecedent agreement, see Chapter 35.

Many shifts in number are actually problems with pronoun-antecedent agreement.

INCONSISTENT	I have difficulty seeing another *person's* position, especially if *their* opinion contradicts mine.
REVISED	I have difficulty seeing other *people's* positions, especially if *their* opinions contradict mine.
REVISED	I have difficulty seeing another *person's* position, especially if *his* or *her* opinion contradicts mine.

38e Checking for unnecessary shifts between direct and indirect discourse

For more on direct and indirect discourse, see 60b.

When you quote someone's exact words, you are using **direct discourse:** *She said, "I'm an editor."* When you report what someone says without repeating the exact words, you are using **indirect discourse:** *She said she is an editor.* Shifting between direct and indirect discourse in the same sentence can cause problems, especially with questions.

he
▶ Bob asked what could he do to help?
                      ^   ^

The editing eliminates an awkward shift by rephrasing what Bob said. The sentence could also be edited to quote him: Bob asked, *"What can I do to help?"*

www • bedford
stmartins.com/
smhandbook

For additional exercises on shifts in tense, click on

▶ Exercise Central
  ▶ Shifts

● EXERCISE 38.1

Revise the following sentences to eliminate unnecessary shifts in tense, mood, voice, or person and number and between direct and indirect discourse. Most of the items can be revised in more than one way. Example:

When a person goes to college, you face many new situations.

When a person goes to college, he or she faces many new situations.

When people go to college, they face many new situations.

CONVENTIONS

Checking for
Confusing Shifts in
Tone and Diction

1. The greed of the 1980s gave way to the occupational insecurity of the 1990s, which in turn gives way to reinforced family ties in the early 2000s.

2. The dean asked that we close the door and that we should then sit down.

3. The editor thought she had eliminated all the errors when she was struck by yet another misplaced modifier.

4. She studied the package, wondered what could it be, and tore off the wrapping.

5. Suddenly, we heard an explosion of wings off to our right, and you could see a hundred or more ducks lifting off from the water.

6. After the suspect was searched, he ate at taxpayers' expense.

7. He was irritated by the upstairs noise until he figured out its source — a kitten.

8. A cloud of snow powder rose as skis and poles fly in every direction.

9. The instructor told us, "Please read the next two stories before the next class" and that she might give us a quiz on them.

10. Workers with computer skills were in great demand, and a programmer could almost name their salary.

11. I think it is better that Grandfather die painlessly and with dignity than that he continues to live in terrible pain.

12. I liked the sense of individualism, the crowd yelling for you, and the feeling that I was in command.

13. Oscar Wilde wrote that books cannot be labeled moral and immoral but "books are either well written or badly written."

14. Put the ground beans in the filter cone, pour in the water, turn on the coffee machine, and then you must sit back and enjoy the smell of the coffee.

15. The aroma, which wafts through the house, lured the adults from their beds.

38f Checking for confusing shifts in tone and diction

Tone, the way a writer's attitude toward a topic or audience is expressed in writing, is related to **diction,** or word choice, and to the writer's overall level of formality or informality. Watch out for tone or diction shifts that could confuse readers and leave them wondering what your real attitude is. (See 4g4.)

INCONSISTENT TONE

The question of child care forces a society to make profound decisions about its economic values. Can most families with children actually live adequately on only one salary? If some conservatives had their way, June Cleaver would still be stuck in the kitchen baking cookies for Wally and the Beaver and waiting for Ward to bring home the bacon, except that with only one income, the Cleavers would be lucky to afford hot dogs.

In the preceding version, the first two sentences set a serious, formal tone as they discuss child care in fairly general, abstract terms. But in the third sentence, the writer shifts suddenly to sarcasm, to references to television characters, and to informal language like *stuck* and *bring home the bacon*. Readers cannot tell whether the writer is presenting a serious analysis or preparing for a humorous satire. See the revision, which makes the tone consistent.

REVISED

The question of child care forces a society to make profound decisions about its economic values. Can most families with young children actually live adequately on only one salary? Some conservatives believe that women with young children should not work outside the home, but many must do so for financial reasons.

THINKING CRITICALLY ABOUT SHIFTS

Reading with an Eye for Shifts

The following paragraph includes several *necessary* shifts in person and number. Read the paragraph carefully, marking all such shifts. Notice how careful the author must be as he shifts back and forth among pronouns.

It has been one of the great errors of our time to think that by thinking about thinking, and then talking about it, we could possibly straighten out and tidy up our minds. There is no delusion more damaging than to get the idea in your head that you understand the functioning of your own brain. Once you acquire such a notion, you run the danger of moving in to take charge, guiding your thoughts, shepherding your mind from place to place, *controlling* it, making lists of regulations. The human mind is not meant to be governed, certainly not by any book of rules yet written; it is supposed to run itself, and we are obliged to follow it along, trying to keep up with it as best we can. It is all very well to be aware of your awareness, even proud of it, but never try to operate it. You are not up to the job.   – LEWIS THOMAS, "The Attic of the Brain"

Thinking about Any Shifts in Your Own Writing

Find an article about a well-known person you admire. Then write a paragraph or two about him or her, making a point of using both direct and indirect discourse. Using the information in 38e, check your writing for any inappropriate shifts between direct and indirect discourse, and revise as necessary.

39

Identifying Comma Splices and Fused Sentences

39a Separating the clauses into two sentences

The simplest way to revise comma splices or fused sentences is to separate them into two sentences.

COMMA SPLICE	My mother spends long hours every spring tilling the soil and moving manure, this part of gardening is nauseating.
FUSED SENTENCE	My mother spends long hours every spring tilling the soil and moving manure. this part of gardening is nauseating.

If the two clauses are very short, making them two sentences may sound abrupt and terse, and some other method of revision would probably be preferable.

39b Linking the clauses with a comma and a coordinating conjunction

If the ideas in the two clauses are fairly closely related and equally important, an alternative for revision is to use a comma and a coordinating conjunction: *and, but, or, nor,*

A **comma splice** results from placing only a comma between two independent clauses. We often see comma splices in advertising, where they can give slogans a catchy rhythm.

Life's short, play hard.
      – NIKE ADVERTISEMENT

A related construction is a **fused,** or run-on, **sentence,** which results from joining two independent clauses with no punctuation or connecting word between them. The Nike advertisement as a fused sentence would be "Life's short play hard."

Despite the powerful effects comma splices or fused sentences can create in certain contexts, you should seldom use these constructions in academic writing. In fact, such use will almost always draw an instructor's criticism. ■

671

If you find no punctuation between two of your independent clauses—groups of words that can stand alone as sentences—you have identified a fused sentence. If you find two such clauses joined only by a comma, you have identified a comma splice. Here are six methods of editing comma splices and fused sentences. To choose among these methods, look at the sentences before and after the ones you are revising. Doing so will help you determine how a particular method will affect the rhythm of the passage.

1. Separate the clauses into two sentences. (39a)

    ► *Education* is an elusive word, ⟨*It*⟩ it often means different things to different people.

For more on
using commas,
see Chapter 48.

2. Link the clauses with a comma and a coordinating conjunction (*and, but, or, nor, for, so,* or *yet*). (39b)

    ► *Education* is an elusive word, ⟨*for*⟩ it often means different things to different people.

3. Link the clauses with a semicolon. (39c)

    ► *Education* is an elusive word,⟨;⟩ it often means different things to different people.

If only a comma and a conjunctive adverb—a word like *however, then, therefore*—link the clauses, add a semicolon.

    ► *Education* is an elusive word,⟨;⟩ indeed, it often means different things to different people.

4. Recast the two clauses as one independent clause. (39d)

    ⟨*An elusive word, education*⟩
    ► ~~*Education* is an elusive word, it often means different things to~~ different people.

5. Recast one independent clause as a dependent clause. (39e)

    ⟨*because*⟩
    ► *Education* is an elusive word, it often means different things to different people.

6. Link two short independent clauses with a dash. (39f)

    ► *Education* is an elusive word,⟨—⟩ its meaning varies.

for, so, or yet. The conjunction helps indicate what kind of link exists between the two clauses. For instance, *but* and *yet* signal opposition or contrast (*I am strong, but she is stronger*); *for* and *so* signal cause-effect relationships (*The cabin was bitterly cold, so we built a fire*).

                    and
COMMA   I got up feeling bad, I feel even worse now.
SPLICE   ^

                    but
FUSED   I should pay my tuition, I need a new car.
SENTENCE   ^

39c Linking the clauses with a semicolon

If the ideas in two spliced or fused clauses are closely related and you want to give them equal weight, you can link them with a semicolon.

• For more on semicolons, see Chapter 49.

COMMA   This photograph is not at all realistic; it uses
SPLICE   ^

            dreamlike images to convey its message.

FUSED   The practice of journalism is changing dramatically;
SENTENCE   ^

            technology has sped up news cycles.

Be careful when you link clauses with a conjunctive adverb or a transitional phrase. You *must* use such words and phrases with a semicolon, with a period, or with a comma combined with a coordinating conjunction. (See 31b7.)

SOME CONJUNCTIVE ADVERBS AND TRANSITIONAL PHRASES

also	in contrast	next
anyway	indeed	now
besides	in fact	otherwise
certainly	instead	similarly
finally	likewise	still
furthermore	meanwhile	then
however	moreover	therefore
in addition	namely	thus
incidentally	nevertheless	undoubtedly

Note the new punctuation in the following revisions.

COMMA SPLICE   He's getting too old for the crowd,¦ in fact, he has spent

                spring break in San Padre for fourteen consecutive years.

FUSED SENTENCE   Some developing countries still have very high
                          and,

                birthrates, therefore, most of their citizens are young.

FOR MULTILINGUAL WRITERS: Judging Sentence Length

If you speak a language that uses and values very long sentences—Arabic, Farsi, or Chinese, for instance—you may string together independent clauses in English in a way that results in comma-splice errors. Note that in standard academic English, a sentence should contain only one independent clause *unless* you join the clauses with a comma and a coordinating conjunction, or with a semicolon.

39d Recasting the two clauses as one independent clause

Sometimes you can reduce two spliced or fused clauses to a single independent clause that is more direct and concise.

               Most   *and*

COMMA SPLICE   A~~large part~~ of my mail is advertisements, ~~most of the~~

                ~~rest is~~ bills.

               Most   *and*

FUSED SENTENCE   A~~large part~~ of my mail is advertisements ~~most of the~~

                ~~rest is~~ bills.

39e Recasting one independent clause as a dependent clause

For a discussion
of dependent
clauses, see
31c4.

When one of the spliced or fused clauses is less important than the other, try converting the less important one to a dependent clause.

COMMA
SPLICE

, *which reacted against mass production,*

The arts and crafts movement called for handmade
⌃

objects, ~~it reacted against mass production.~~
⌃

Both original clauses discuss related aspects of the arts and crafts movement. In the revision, the writer chooses to emphasize the first independent clause, the one describing what the movement advocated, and to make the second independent clause, the one describing what the movement reacted against, into a dependent clause.

CONVENTIONS
Linking Two Independent Clauses with a Dash

FUSED
SENTENCE

Although

Zora Neale Hurston is regarded as one of America's
⌃

major novelists, she died in obscurity.
⌃

In the original, the first clause stands in contrast to the second one — that is, in contrast to Hurston's importance today (she is held in high esteem) are the circumstances of her death (obscurity). In the revision, the writer chooses to emphasize the second clause and to make the first one into a dependent clause by adding the subordinating conjunction *although.*

● For a list of subordinating conjunctions, see 31b7.

39f Linking two independent clauses with a dash

In informal writing, you can use a dash to join two independent clauses, especially when the second clause elaborates on the first.

COMMA
SPLICE

Exercise has become too much like work, — it's a bad trend.
⌃

FUSED
SENTENCE

Exercise trends come and go — this year yoga is hot.
⌃

EXERCISE 39.1

Using *two* of the methods in this chapter, revise each item to correct its comma splice or fused sentence. Use each of the methods at least once. Example:

so

I had misgivings about the marriage, I did not attend the ceremony.
⌃

Because

I had misgivings about the marriage, I did not attend the ceremony.
⌃

1. Listeners prefer talk shows to classical music, the radio station is changing its programming.

www ● bedford
stmartins.com/
smhandbook

For additional exercises on comma splices and fused sentences, click on

▸ **Exercise Central**
  ▸ **Comma Splices and Fused Sentences**

cs/fs

676   **39f**

CONVENTIONS

Identifying Comma
Splices and Fused
Sentences

2. Clothing designers recycle styles nothing is original anymore.

3. Some students read more online than in print, some do the opposite.

4. Mexicans observe Day of the Dead it is not a mournful holiday.

5. A Hollywood actor played a dog in three movies, indeed, he became typecast.

6. He acquired life skills via the canine world he learned the value of persistence.

7. You adopted the rabbit now you feed him.

8. The West Indian woman has lived in New England for years, nevertheless she always feels betrayed by winter.

9. The restaurant on the roof of the Pompidou Center is colorful in fact it looks like a set for the Jetsons.

10. A popular restaurateur opened a barbecue joint in a jazz club critics applauded the new venture.

● EXERCISE 39.2

Revise the following paragraph, eliminating all comma splices by using a period or a semicolon. Then revise the paragraph again, this time using any of the other methods in this chapter. Comment on the two revisions. What differences in rhythm do you detect? Which version do you prefer, and why?

My sister Mary decided to paint her house last summer, thus, she had to buy some paint. She wanted inexpensive paint, at the same time, it had to go on easily and cover well, that combination was unrealistic to start with. She had never done exterior painting before, in fact she did not even own a ladder. She was a complete beginner, on the other hand, she was a hard worker and was willing to learn. She got her husband, Dan, to take a week off from work, likewise she let her two teenage sons take three days off from school to help. Mary went out and bought the "dark green" paint for $6.99 a gallon, it must have been mostly water, in fact, you could almost see through it. Mary and Dan and the boys put one coat of this paint on the house, as a result, their white house turned a streaky light green. Dan and the boys rebelled, declaring they would not work anymore with such cheap paint. Mary was forced to buy all new paint, even so, the house did not really get painted until September.

FOR COLLABORATION

Working with another classmate, revise the following paragraph, eliminating the comma splices and fused sentences by using any of the methods discussed in this chapter. Then revise the paragraph again, this time eliminating each comma splice and fused sentence by a *different* method. Decide which paragraph is more effective, and why. Finally, compare the revision you prefer to the revisions of other pairs of students. Discuss the ways in which the versions differ in meaning.

CONVENTIONS

Linking Two
Independent
Clauses with
a Dash

Gardening can be very satisfying, it is also hard work people who just see the pretty flowers may not realize this. My mother spends long hours every spring tilling the soil, she moves many wheelbarrow-loads of disgusting cow manure and chicken droppings, in fact, the whole early part of gardening is nauseating. The whole garden area has to be rototilled every year, this process is not much like the ad showing people walking quietly behind the rototiller, on the contrary, my father has to fight that machine every inch of the way, sweating so much he looks like Hulk Hogan after a hard bout. Then the planting all must be done by hand, my back aches, my hands get raw, my skin gets sunburned. I get filthy whenever I go near that garden my mother always asks me to help, though. When harvest time comes the effort is *almost* worth it, however, there are always extra zucchinis I give away at school everybody else is trying to give away zucchinis, too. We also have tomatoes, lettuce, there is always more than we need and we feel bad wasting it wouldn't you like this nice bag of cucumbers?

THINKING CRITICALLY ABOUT COMMA SPLICES AND FUSED SENTENCES

Reading with an Eye for Special Effects

Roger Angell is known as a careful and correct stylist, yet he often deviates from the "correct" to create special effects. Look, for example, at the way he uses a comma splice in the following passage about pitcher David Cone:

> And then he won. Next time out, on August 10th, handed a seven-run lead against the A's, he gave up two runs over six innings, with eight strike-outs. He had tempo, he had poise. – ROGER ANGELL, "Before the Fall"

Angell uses a comma splice in the last sentence to emphasize parallel ideas; any conjunction, even *and,* would change the causal relationship he wishes to show. Because the splice is unexpected, it attracts just the attention that Angell wants for his statement.

Look through some stories or essays to find some comma splices and fused sentences. Copy down one or two and enough of the surrounding text to show context, and comment in writing on the effects they create.

Thinking about Any Comma Splices and Fused Sentences in Your Own Writing

Go through some essays you have written, checking for comma splices and fused sentences. Revise any you find, using one of the methods in this chapter. Comment on your chosen methods—in your writing log if you are keeping one.

40

◥ Recognizing Sentence Fragments

40a Revising phrase fragments

Phrases are groups of words that lack a subject, a verb, or both (see 31c3). When phrases are punctuated like a sentence, they become fragments. To revise these fragments, attach them to an independent clause, or make them a separate sentence.

▶ NBC is broadcasting the debates, ^w^With discussions afterward.

The word group *with discussions afterward* is a prepositional phrase, not a sentence. The editing combines the phrase with an independent clause.

▶ Our nation's cherished ideal, may be in danger. ^a^A good education for every child, *, may be in danger.*

A good education for every child is a noun phrase. It is also an appositive phrase renaming the noun *ideal*. It is not a sentence. The editing attaches the fragment to the sentence containing the noun.

▶ Vivian stayed out of school for three months after she gave birth to Linda. *She did so to* To recuperate and to take care of her.

To recuperate and to take care of her includes verbals, not verbs. The revision—adding a subject (*she*) and a verb (*did*)—turns the fragment into a separate sentence.

A group of words must meet the following three criteria to form a complete sentence. If it does not meet all three, it is a fragment. Revise a fragment by combining it with a nearby sentence or by rewriting it as a complete sentence.

1. A sentence must have a subject. (31a)

2. A sentence must have a verb, not just a verbal. A verbal needs an auxiliary verb in order to function as a sentence's verb. (31c3)

> **VERBAL** The terrier *barking.*
>
> **VERB**   The terrier *is barking.*

3. Unless it is a question, a sentence must have at least one clause that does *not* begin with a subordinating word. Following are some common subordinating words:

although	if	when
as	since	where
because	that	whether
before	though	who
how	unless	why

▶ *In his*
His editorial making a plea for better facilities for severely handicapped
^   *, he pointed*
children, Pointed out that rundown facilities are always located in poor
          ^

areas.

The first fragment lacked a verb (*making* is a verbal); the second lacked a subject. The editing gives us a long introductory phrase followed by an independent clause.

■ Fragments beginning with transitions

Transitional expressions sometimes lead to fragments. If you introduce an example or explanation with one of the following transitions, be

frag

680 **40b**

CONVENTIONS

Recognizing
Sentence
Fragments

certain you write a sentence, not a fragment. Transitional words and phrases include:

again	but	like
also	finally	or
and	for example	specifically
as a result	for instance	such as
besides	instead	that is

▶ **Joan Didion has written on many subjects, Such as the Hoover Dam and migraine headaches.**

In the original, the second word group is a phrase, not a sentence. The editing combines it with an independent clause.

40b Revising compound-predicate fragments

A compound predicate consists of two or more verbs, along with their modifiers and objects, that have the same subject. Fragments occur when one part of a compound predicate is punctuated as a separate sentence although it lacks a subject. These fragments usually begin with *and, but,* or *or.* You can revise them by attaching them to the independent clause that contains the rest of the predicate.

▶ **They sold their house, And moved into an apartment.**

**www • bedford
stmartins.com/
smhandbook**

For additional
exercises on
sentence fragments,
click on

▶ **Exercise Central**
  ▶ **Sentence
    Fragments**

● **EXERCISE 40.1**

Revise each of the following items to eliminate any sentence fragments, either by combining fragments with independent clauses or by rewriting them as separate sentences. Example:

~~Zoe looked close to tears.~~ Standing with her head bowed, *, Zoe looked close to tears.*

Zoe looked close to tears. *She was* Standing with her head bowed.

1. Small, long-veined, fuzzy green leaves. Add to the appeal of this newly developed variety of carrot.

2. Living with gusto. That is what many Americans yearn for.

3. The region has dry, sandy soil. Blown into strange formations by the ever-present wind.

4. Paul McCartney has gone beyond music. Exploring sculpture and video.

5. Hong Kong offers numerous museums. And celebrates all the performing arts.

6. Diners in Creole restaurants might try shrimp gumbo. Or order turtle soup.

7. Tupperware parties go back to the late 1940s. Parties where the hosts are salespersons.

8. Trying to make his friend feel better. He joked that time heals all haircuts.

9. Joan Didion has investigated politics. Besides having explored human emotions.

10. Mary Wollstonecraft believed in universal public education. Also, in education that forms the heart and strengthens the body.

CONVENTIONS

Revising
Dependent-Clause
Fragments

40c Revising dependent-clause fragments

Dependent clauses contain both a subject and a verb, but they cannot stand alone as sentences because they depend on an independent clause to complete their meaning. Dependent clauses usually begin with words such as *after, because, before, if, since, though, unless, until, when, where, while, who, which,* and *that.* You can usually combine dependent-clause fragments with a nearby independent clause.

●— For more on
    dependent
    clauses, see
    31c4.

▶ One win and six losses was a dismal record. ^w^Which made the manager's

next move a surprise.

If you cannot smoothly attach a dependent clause to a nearby independent clause, try deleting the opening subordinating word and turning the dependent clause into a sentence.

▶ Injuries in automobile accidents occur in two ways. ~~When~~ ^A^an occupant

either is hurt by something inside the car or is thrown from the car.

● **EXERCISE 40.2**

Identify all the sentence fragments in the following items, and explain why each is grammatically incomplete. Then revise each one in at least two ways. Example:

Controlling my temper, ~~That~~ has been one of my goals this year.

One of my goals this year has been
Controlling my temper. ~~That has been one of my goals this year.~~

1. As soon as the seventy-five-year-old cellist walked onstage. The audience burst into applause.

682

frag

40c

CONVENTIONS

Recognizing
Sentence
Fragments

2. The patient has only one goal. To smoke behind the doctor's back.

3. Lust, an emotion that someone famously said he had felt in his heart.

4. The director lowered his fee. Which had started out in the stratosphere.

5. In the United States of all places. Genealogy is a very popular hobby.

6. Forster stopped writing novels after *A Passage to India*. One of the greatest novels of the twentieth century.

7. Sylvia Plath achieved new status. Because of *Ariel,* her final book of poems.

8. I loved *Beloved*. And knew Toni Morrison deserved the Nobel Prize.

9. The president appointed five members. Who drew up a set of bylaws.

10. Parents eventually realize that rebellion is normal. Because the younger generation often rejects the ways of its elders.

THINKING CRITICALLY ABOUT FRAGMENTS

Reading with an Eye for Fragments

Identify the fragments in the following passage. What effect does the writer achieve by using fragments rather than complete sentences?

> On Sundays, for religion, we went up on the hill. Skipping along the hexagon-shaped tile in Colonial Park. Darting up the steps to Edgecomb Avenue. Stopping in the candy store on St. Nicholas to load up. Leaning forward for leverage to finish the climb up to the church. I was always impressed by this particular house of the Lord.
>
> – KEITH GILYARD, *Voices of the Self*

Thinking about Any Fragments in Your Own Writing

Read through some essays you have written. Using the guidelines on p. 679, see whether you find any sentence fragments. If so, do you recognize any patterns? Do you write fragments when you're attempting to add emphasis? Are they all dependent clauses? phrases? Note any patterns you discover (in your writing log, if you keep one), and make a point of routinely checking your writing for fragments. Finally, revise any fragments to form complete sentences.

Placing Modifiers Appropriately

41

Modifiers enrich writing by making it more concrete or vivid, often adding important or even essential details. To be effective, however, modifiers should refer clearly to the words they modify and be positioned close to those words. Consider, for example, a sign seen recently in a hotel:

DO NOT USE
THE ELEVATORS
IN CASE OF FIRE.

Should we really avoid the elevators altogether for fear of causing a fire? Repositioning the modifier *in case of fire* eliminates such confusion— and makes clear that we are to avoid the elevators only if there is a fire: IN CASE OF FIRE, DO NOT USE THE ELEVATORS. This chapter examines three types of problem modifiers— misplaced, disruptive, and dangling—and ways of revising them. ■

41a Revising misplaced modifiers

Misplaced modifiers are words, phrases, and clauses that cause ambiguity or confusion because they are not close enough to the words they modify or because they seem to point both to words before and to words after them. For example, in the sentence *Clearly I could hear the instructor lecturing,* the adverb *clearly* may mean "obviously," as in "Clearly, I could hear the instructor lecturing." Yet the writer might have meant it to modify *could hear* or *lecturing.* A writer can avoid such confusion by placing a modifier as close as possible to the word or words it actually describes.

I could hear the instructor lecturing *clearly.*

I could *clearly* hear the instructor lecturing.

Be especially careful with the placement of **limiting modifiers** like *almost, even, hardly, just, merely, nearly, only, scarcely,* and *simply.* In general, these modifiers should be placed right before or after the words they limit. Putting them anywhere else may produce not just ambiguity but a completely different meaning.

AMBIGUOUS	The court only hears civil cases on Tuesdays.
CLEAR	The court hears *only* civil cases on Tuesdays.
CLEAR	The court hears civil cases on Tuesdays *only.*

1. Identify all the modifiers in each of your sentences, and draw an arrow from each modifier to the word it modifies.

2. If a modifier is far from the word it modifies, try to move the two closer together. (41a)

3. Does any modifier seem to refer to a word other than the one it is intended to modify? If so, move the modifier so that it refers clearly to only the intended word. (41a, 41b)

4. If you cannot find the word to which a modifier refers, revise the sentence: supply such a word, or revise the modifier itself so that it clearly refers to a word already in the sentence. (41c)

In the first sentence, placing *only* before the verb makes the meaning ambiguous. Does the writer mean that civil cases are the only cases heard on Tuesdays or that those are the only days when civil cases are heard? Each of the revised sentences expresses one of these meanings clearly.

Phrases also should ordinarily be close to the words they modify. The most common type of phrase modifier, the prepositional phrase, usually belongs right after the word it modifies.

> *on voodoo*
> ► She teaches a seminar this term ~~on voodoo~~ at Skyline College.

Surely the voodoo was not at the college.

Participial phrases usually appear right before or after the words they modify.

> *to my guests*
> ► I pointed out the moose head ~~to my guests~~ mounted on the wall.

The unedited sentence implies that the guests were mounted on the wall.

> W   *billowing from every window.*
> ► ~~Billowing from every window,~~ we saw clouds of smoke.

People cannot billow from windows.

Although you have more flexibility in the placement of dependent clauses than in the placement of modifying words and phrases, try whenever possible to place them close to what you wish them to modify. If you do not, unintended meanings can result.

that line the walks are   *and*

▶ **The trees trimmed in the shapes of animals ~~that line the walks~~**
  ^   ^

delight visitors.

Do animals line the walks?

After he lost the 1962 race,
▶ **Nixon said he would get out of politics. ~~after he lost the 1962 race.~~**
   ^

The unedited sentence implies that Nixon planned to lose the race.

● **EXERCISE 41.1**

Revise each of the following sentences by moving any misplaced modifiers so that
they clearly modify the words they are intended to. Example:

  When they propose sensible plans, politicians
  ~~Politicians~~ are supported by the people. ~~when they propose sensible plans.~~
  ^   ^

1. The comedian had the audience in stitches relating his amusing stories.

2. The tanks almost toppled all the government buildings on the square.

3. The victim apparently died from friendly fire.

4. While helping my father clean his attic, I found and offered to frame the cita-
    tion for outstanding service that the mayor had given him.

5. Public transportation running all night, which connects the university and
    downtown, is a new service.

6. Doctors recommend a new test for cancer, which is painless.

7. I went through the process of taxiing and taking off in my mind.

8. I knew that the investment would pay off in a dramatic way before I decided
    to buy the stock.

9. The bank offered flood insurance to the homeowners underwritten by the fed-
    eral government.

10. Revolving out of control, the maintenance worker shut down the turbine.

www ● bedford
stmartins.com/
smhandbook

For additional
exercises on
misplaced
modifiers, click on

▶ **Exercise Central**
  ▶ **Modifier**
    Placement

■ *Squinting modifiers*

If a modifier can refer to *either* the word(s) before it *or* the word(s) after
it, it is called a **squinting modifier.** For example:

   AMBIGUOUS   Students who practice writing *often* will benefit.

Does the writer mean that students often benefit from practice or that
they benefit from practicing often? Two revisions are possible, depending on the meaning:

| CLEAR | Students who *often practice* writing will benefit. |
| CLEAR | Students who practice writing *will often benefit*. |

If a sentence could be read more than one way because of your place-ment of a modifier, put the modifier where it clearly relates to only a sin-gle term.

**www • bedford
stmartins.com/
smhandbook**

For additional
exercises on
misplaced
modifiers, click on

▶ Exercise Central
  ▶ Modifier
    Placement

● EXERCISE 41.2

Revise each of the following sentences in at least two ways. Move the squinting modifier so that it unambiguously modifies either the word(s) before it or the word(s) after it. Example:

completely
The course we hoped would engross us ~~completely~~ bored us.
                                   ^

                                                    completely.
The course we hoped would engross us ~~completely~~ bored us/
                                                           ^

1. The candidate promised quickly to reduce class size.

2. She suggested after graduation she would take the summer off.

3. The collector who owned the painting originally planned to leave it to a museum.

4. Doctors can now restore limbs that have been severed partially to a function-ing condition.

5. The speaker said when he finished he would answer questions.

41b Revising disruptive modifiers

Disruptive modifiers interrupt the parts of a sentence or a grammatical structure, making it hard for readers to follow the progress of the thought. Most disruptive modifiers are adverbial clauses or phrases. In general, do not place such modifiers between the parts of a verb phrase, between a subject and a verb, or between a verb and an object.

If they are cooked too long, vegetables will
▶ **Vegetables will, if they are cooked too long, lose most of their**
  ^
  nutritional value.

Separating the parts of the verb phrase, *will* and *lose,* disrupts the flow of the sentence.

> *were discarded*
▶ The books, because the librarians had decided they were no longer
   ∧

useful, ~~were discarded.~~
       ∧

It was awkward to separate the subject *books* from the verb *were discarded*.

> *a secondhand car*
▶ He bought with his first paycheck. ~~a secondhand car.~~
          ∧   ∧

Separating the verb *bought* from the object *a secondhand car* makes it hard to
follow the thought.

▦ *Modifiers splitting an infinitive*

In general, do not split an infinitive by placing a modifier between the *to*
and the base form of the verb. Doing so makes it hard for readers to recognize that the two go together.

>   *surrender*
▶ Hitler expected the British to fairly quickly. ~~surrender.~~
                                ∧   ∧

In some cases, however, a modifier sounds awkward in any other position. To avoid a split infinitive in such cases, it may be best to reword the
sentence and eliminate the infinitive altogether.

SPLIT	I hope *to* almost *double* my income from last year.
REWRITTEN	I hope that I will earn almost twice as much as I did last year.

● EXERCISE 41.3

Revise each of the following sentences by moving the disruptive modifier so that
the sentence reads smoothly. Example:

> *During the recent economic depression, many*
> Many unemployed college graduates attended ~~during the recent economic~~
> ∧
> ~~depression~~ graduate school.

1. Strong economic times have, statistics tell us, led to increases in the college dropout rate.

2. Sometimes a radical proposal, due to its shock value in negotiations, stimulates creative thinking by labor and management.

3. The architect wanted to eventually design public buildings.

4. Bookstores sold, in the first week after publication, fifty thousand copies.

5. The stock exchange became, because of the sudden trading, a chaotic circus.

www ● bedford
stmartins.com/
smhandbook

For additional
exercises on
disruptive
modifiers,
click on

▶ Exercise Central
  ▶ Modifier
    Placement

688

mod

41c

CONVENTIONS

Placing Modifiers
Appropriately

41c Revising dangling modifiers

Dangling modifiers are words that modify nothing in particular in the rest of a sentence. They often seem to modify something that is suggested or implied but not actually present in the sentence. Attached to no specific element, such modifiers dangle, or hang loosely from the sentence. They frequently appear at the beginnings or ends of sentences.

> **DANGLING**   Driving nonstop, Shalishan Lodge is two hours from Portland.

Who is driving? This sentence inadvertently suggests that Shalishan Lodge is the driver.

To revise a sentence with a dangling modifier, add a subject that the modifier clearly refers to, or change the dangling modifier itself into a phrase or a clause that clearly modifies an existing part of the sentence. You could revise the sentence above in two ways:

> **REVISED**   Driving nonstop from Portland, you can reach Shalishan Lodge in two hours.
>
> **REVISED**   If you drive nonstop, Shalishan Lodge is two hours from Portland.

Here are additional problem sentences and ways to fix them:

▶ Bankrupt, the land ~~was sold~~ to a neighboring farmer.
  family sold the

Land cannot be bankrupt.

▶ As a young boy, his aunt told stories of her years as a country doctor.
  When he was

His aunt was never a young boy.

▶ ~~Thumbing through the magazine,~~ my eyes automatically noticed the perfume ads.
  M   *as I was thumbing through the magazine.*

Eyes cannot thumb through a magazine.

▶ ~~A rabbit's teeth are never used for defense even when cornered.~~
  Even when cornered, a rabbit never uses its teeth for defense.

The teeth are not cornered.

▶ Although a reserved and private man, everyone enjoyed his company.
  he was

The original, elliptical clause does not refer to *everyone* or to *his company*. It needs its own subject and verb.

● **EXERCISE 41.4**

Revise each of the following sentences to correct the dangling phrase. Example:

CONVENTIONS

Revising Dangling
Modifiers

         a viewer gets
Watching television news,∧an impression is given of constant disaster.

1. Determined to increase its audience share, news may become entertainment.

2. Craving instant updates, all-news stations gain in popularity.

3. To provide comic relief, heat waves and blizzards are attributed to the weather forecaster.

4. Chosen for their looks, newscasters' journalistic credentials may be weak.

5. As a visual medium, complex issues are hard to present on television.

**www ● bedford
stmartins.com/
smhandbook**

For additional
exercises on
dangling modifiers,
click on

▶ **Exercise Central**
  ▶ **Modifier
    Placement**

FOR COLLABORATION

Working with a classmate, revise each of the following sentences to correct the dangling elliptical clause. Provide more than one revision wherever possible. Example:

    I was
While cycling through southern France, the Roman ruins impressed me.
       ∧

1. However unhappy, my part-time job helps pay my rent.

2. While drinking eight glasses of water a day, Ben's weight often drops.

3. A waiter's job can become very stressful when faced with a busy restaurant full of hungry people.

4. Although careful of their pronunciation, Parisians cannot understand Americans' French.

5. No matter how costly, my family travels for two weeks every summer.

THINKING CRITICALLY ABOUT MODIFIERS

Reading with an Eye for Modifiers

E. B. White was a master of precise wording. He chose and positioned his words with great care. Read the following sentences by White, and pay attention to the limiting modifier italicized in each one. Identify which word or words each one modifies. Then try moving the modifier to some other spot in the sentence, and consider how the meaning of the sentence changes as a result.

1. When we got back for a swim before lunch, the lake was exactly where we had left it, the same number of inches from the dock, and there was *only* the mere suggestion of a breeze.   – "Once More to the Lake"

2. It was, among other things, the sort of railroad you would occasionally ride *just* for the hell of it, a higher existence into which you would escape unconsciously and without hesitation. — "Progress and Change"

Thinking about Your Own Use of Modifiers

As you examine two pages of a draft, check for clear and effective modifiers. Can you identify any misplaced, disruptive, or dangling modifiers? Using the guidelines in this chapter, revise as need be. Then look for patterns — in the kinds of modifiers you use and in any problems you have placing them. Make a note of what you find.

Maintaining Consistent and Complete Grammatical Structures

42

42a Making grammatical patterns consistent

One inconsistency that poses problems for writers and readers is a **mixed structure**, which results from beginning a sentence with one grammatical pattern and then switching to another one. For example:

MIXED   The fact that I get up at 5:00 A.M., a wake-up time that explains why I'm always tired in the evening.

The sentence starts out with a subject (*The fact*) followed by a dependent clause (*that I get up at 5:00 A.M.*). The sentence needs a predicate to complete the independent clause, but instead it moves to another phrase followed by a dependent clause (*a wake-up time that explains why I'm always tired in the evening*). Thus the independent clause is never completed, and what results is a fragment, or incomplete sentence. (See Chapter 40.)

REVISED   The fact that I get up at 5:00 A.M. explains why I'm always tired in the evening.

Deleting *a wake-up time that* changes the rest of the sentence into a predicate.

REVISED   I get up at 5:00 A.M., a wake-up time that explains why I'm always tired in the evening.

Deleting *The fact that* turns the beginning of the sentence into an independent clause.

About twenty-five years ago, a writing instructor who had studied thousands of student essays came to a simple but profound conclusion about many of the sentences in the essays. Though at first glance the sentences seemed incoherent or nonsensical, they actually fell into certain patterns. They could be better characterized, the instructor decided, either as (1) unsuccessful attempts to combine sentence structures that did not fit together grammatically or sensibly or as (2) sentences missing some element necessary to complete meaning.

In fact, many writers who produce garbled sentences do so in an attempt to use complex and sophisticated structures. What look like "errors," then, may be stepping-stones on a writer's way to greater stylistic maturity. This chapter will help you be sure your own sentences are consistent and complete. ■

CONVENTIONS

Maintaining
Consistent and
Complete
Grammatical
Structures

→ If you find an especially confusing sentence, check to see whether it has a subject (*The athletes swam and ran*) and a predicate (*The athletes swam and ran*). If not, revise as necessary. (42a) If you find both a subject and a predicate and you are still confused, see whether the subject and verb make sense together. If not, revise so that they do. (42b)

→ Revise any *is when, is where,* and *reason . . . is because* constructions. (42b)

　　　　　　　　　a practice in which
▶ **Spamming is ~~where~~ companies send electronic junk mail.**
　　　　　　　　　^

→ Check all comparisons for completeness. (42e)

　　　　　　　　　we like
▶ **We like Marian better than Margaret.**
　　　　　　　　　　　　　　　^

Here is another example of a mixed structure:

▶ **Because hope was the only thing left when Pandora finally closed up the**

　mythical box, ~~explains why~~ even today we never lose hope.
　　　　　　　　　　^

The adverb clause beginning with *Because* is followed by a predicate (beginning with *explains*) that lacks a subject. Deleting *explains why* changes the original predicate into an independent clause to which the adverb clause can be attached.

42b Making subjects and predicates consistent

Another kind of mixed structure, called **faulty predication,** occurs when a subject and predicate do not fit together grammatically or simply do not make sense together.

　　　　　　　　　　　　　　generosity.
▶ **A characteristic that I admire is ~~a person who is generous.~~**
　　　　　　　　　　　　　　　　　　　^

A person is not a characteristic.

　　　　　　　　　　　　　require that
▶ **The rules of the corporation ~~expect~~ employees ~~to~~ be on time.**
　　　　　　　　　　　　　　　^

Rules cannot expect anything.

Is when, is where, *and* reason . . . is because

These constructions are inappropriate in academic writing because they use an adverb clause rather than a noun as a subject complement.

CONVENTIONS

Using Elliptical Structures Carefully

an unfair characterization of
▶ A stereotype is ~~when someone characterizes a group~~ unfairly.
                                                              ^

a place
▶ A confluence is ~~where~~ two rivers join to form one.
                  ^

▶ ~~The reason~~ I like to play soccer ~~is because~~ it provides aerobic exercise.

● **EXERCISE 42.1**

Revise each of the following sentences in two ways to make its structures consistent in grammar and meaning. Example:

> The fact that our room was cold we put a heater between our beds.
>
> <u>Because</u> our room was cold, we put a heater between our beds.
>
> The fact that our room was cold <u>led us</u> to put a heater between our beds.

1. My interest in a political career would satisfy my desire for public service.

2. The reason air-pollution standards should not be relaxed is because many people would suffer.

3. By not prosecuting white-collar crime as vigorously as violent crime encourages white-collar criminals to think they can ignore the law.

4. Irony is when you expect one thing and get something else.

5. One common side effect of the medication is women with hair on their faces.

www ● bedford stmartins.com/ smhandbook

For additional exercises on inconsistent structures, click on

▶ **Exercise Central**
  ▶ **Consistency and Completeness**

42c Using elliptical structures carefully

Sometimes writers omit a word in a compound structure. They succeed with an **elliptical structure,** as Eudora Welty does below, when the word they omit is exactly the same as the word in the other part(s) of the compound.

> That bell belonged to the figure of Miss Duling as though it grew directly out of her right arm, as wings grew out of an angel or a tail out of the devil.   – EUDORA WELTY, *One Writer's Beginnings*

The omitted word, *grew,* is the exact same verb that follows *it* and *wings* in the other parts of the compound. If the omitted word does not match

inc

694   **42d**

CONVENTIONS

Maintaining
Consistent and
Complete
Grammatical
Structures

a word used in the other part(s) of the compound, the omission is inappropriate.

is
▶ His skills are weak, and his performance only average.
                                              ^

The verb *is* does not match the verb in the other part of the compound (*are*), so the writer must include it.

42d Checking for missing words

The best way to catch inadvertent omissions is to proofread carefully, reading each sentence slowly — and aloud.

                                           it   *to*
▶ The professor's heavy German accent made difficult for the class
                                          ^   ^

understand her lectures.

FOR MULTILINGUAL WRITERS: Deciding When Articles Are Necessary

Do you say "I'm at university now" or "I'm at *the* university now"? Deciding when to use the articles *a, an,* and *the* can be challenging for multilingual writers since many languages have nothing directly comparable to them. See 59d for help using articles.

42e Making comparisons complete, consistent, and clear

Check comparisons. When you compare two or more things, the comparison must be complete, logically consistent, and clear.

                                                 from my friends' parents.
▶ I was embarrassed because my parents were so different/
                                                        ^

Different from what? Adding *from my friends' parents* tells readers with what the comparison is being made.

                                         the one by
▶ Woodberry's biography is better than Fields.
                                      ^

This sentence illogically compares a book with a person. The editing makes the comparison logical.

inc

42e   **695**

CONVENTIONS

Making
Comparisons
Complete

UNCLEAR   Ted felt more affection for his brother than his sister.

Did Ted feel more affection for his brother than his sister did — or more affection for his brother than he felt for his sister?

CLEAR   Ted felt more affection for his brother than *he did for* his sister.

CLEAR   Ted felt more affection for his brother than his sister *did.*

www • bedford
stmartins.com/
smhandbook

For additional
exercises on
incomplete
structures, click on

► **Exercise Central**
  ► **Consistency and
   Completeness**

● **EXERCISE 42.2**

Revise each of the following sentences to eliminate any inappropriate elliptical constructions; to make comparisons complete, logically consistent, and clear; and to supply any other omitted words that are necessary for meaning. Example:

   Most of the candidates are bright, and one ᴵˢ brilliant.

1. My new stepmother makes my father happier.
2. Argentina and Peru were colonized by Spain, and Brazil by Portugal.
3. She argued that children are even more important for men than women.
4. Were the traffic jams in Texas any worse than many other states in the South and West?
5. The personalities of firstborn offspring are different from middle children.

FOR COLLABORATION

Working with a classmate, revise this paragraph to make every sentence grammatically and logically consistent and complete. Bring the results of your revision to class, and be ready to explain each change you made.

   The reason I believe the United States should have a military draft is because draft would make us better citizens. By requiring the same sacrifice from every young person would make everyone feel part of a common effort. In addition, a draft is fairer. When an army is made up of volunteers come mostly from the poor and minority groups. During the Persian Gulf War, news reports showed blacks were overrepresented among the troops, largely because their economic options were more limited than young whites and the military thus more attractive as a career. I also feel that women should be subject to the draft. A quality that the military needs is soldiers who are dedicated, and women soldiers have shown that they are more dedicated to their jobs than men. The requirements of a modern army also need skills that more women possess. Equality is when both sexes have equal responsibilities as well as equal opportunity.

THINKING CRITICALLY ABOUT CONSISTENCY AND COMPLETENESS

CONVENTIONS

Maintaining
Consistent and
Complete
Grammatical
Structures

Read over three or four paragraphs from a draft or completed essay you have written recently. Check for mixed sentences and incomplete or missing structures. Revise the paragraphs to correct any problems you find. If you find any, do you recognize any patterns? If so, make a note of them for future reference (in your writing log, if you keep one).

PART 8

SENTENCES: MAKING STYLISTIC CHOICES

"A university student asked [a well-known writer], 'Do you think I could be a writer?' 'Well,' the writer said, 'do you like sentences?'"
— ANNIE DILLARD

43

▼ Constructing Effective Sentences

Put most simply, effective sentences have two main characteristics: they emphasize ideas clearly, and they do so as concisely as possible. We can see the importance of emphasis and conciseness in many sets of instructions. Look, for instance, at those found on one common prescription drug:

Take one tablet daily. Some non-prescription drugs may aggravate your condition, so read all labels carefully. If any include a warning, check with your doctor. Refill prescription only until 12/12/04.

Squeezing important information onto a three-inch label probably won't be a task you'll confront regularly, but more often than not, you will want to write as emphatically and concisely as you can — especially in academic contexts. This chapter will help you to do so. ■

43a Emphasizing main ideas

When we speak, we achieve **emphasis** by raising our voices, putting extra stress on an important word, or drawing out a phrase. And much of the writing we see around us — in advertisements, on Web sites, in magazines — gains emphasis in similar fashion, with color or graphics or bold type, for instance. Much academic writing can't rely on such graphic devices for emphasis. Luckily, however, writers have other ways to let readers know which parts of their sentences are most important.

1 Using closing and opening positions for emphasis

When you read a sentence, what do you remember? Other things being equal, you remember the ending. This is the part of the sentence that moves the writing forward by providing new information, as it does in the following example:

> We hear language through a powerful filter of *social values and stereotypes.*

A less emphatic but still important position in a sentence is the opening, which often hooks up the new sentence with what has come before.

> *As a precise example of linguistic stereotypes,* consider the following fragment from a classroom lesson.
> – MICHAEL STUBBS, "Some Basic Sociolinguistic Concepts"

698

FOR EMPHASIS

→ Identify the words you want to give special emphasis. If you've buried those words in the middle of a sentence, edit the sentence to change their position. Remember that the end and the beginning are generally the most emphatic positions. (43a1)

→ Note any sentences that include a series of three or more words, phrases, or clauses. Can you arrange the items in the series in climactic order, with the most important item last? (43a2)

FOR CONCISENESS

→ Look for redundant words. If you are unsure about a word, read the sentence without it; if the meaning is not affected, leave the word out. (43b1)

→ Look for empty words — words like *aspect* and *factor, definitely* and *very.* Unless your meaning is unclear without them, leave them out. (43b2)

→ Do you use any wordy phrases? If so, try to replace them with a single word — instead of *because of the fact that,* try *because;* rather than *for the purpose of,* try *for.* (43b3)

→ Look for grammatical structures to simplify: adjective clauses that you can reduce to appositive phrases, expletive constructions that you can eliminate, passive-voice verbs that you can change to the active voice, consecutive sentences with the same subject or predicate that you can combine into one sentence. (43b4)

The second sentence uses the opening position to hook up to the sentence before it, which is about stereotypes and language. The phrase in the ending position emphasizes what will come next — the precise example. If you place relatively unimportant information in the memorable closing position of a sentence, you may undercut what you want to emphasize or give more emphasis to the closing words than you intend.

▶   *Last month, she*   *$500,000.*
    She gave $500,000 to the school capital campaign ~~last month.~~

Moving *$500,000* to the end of the sentence emphasizes the amount.

2 Using climactic order

Presenting ideas in **climactic order** means arranging them in order of increasing importance, power, or drama so that your writing builds to a climax.

> Dissidents risk social rejection, forced relocation, long imprisonment, and almost certain death.

> After they've finished with the pantry, the medicine cabinet, and the attic, [neat people] will throw out the red geranium (too many leaves), sell the dog (too many fleas), and send the children off to boarding school (too many scuffmarks on the hardwood floors).
> – SUSANNE BRITT, "Neat People vs. Sloppy People"

Each of these statements saves its most dramatic item for last, making its point forcefully. The original version of the next sentence fails to achieve strong emphasis because its verbs are not sequenced in order of increasing power; the editing provides climactic order.

>   *offend our ears,*   *and*
> ▶ Soap operas assault our eyes, damage our brains, ~~and offend our ears~~.

**www • bedford
stmartins.com/
smhandbook**

For additional
exercises on main
ideas, click on

▶ Exercise Central
   ▶ Effective
     Sentences

● **EXERCISE 43.1**

Revise each of the following sentences to highlight what you take to be the main or most important ideas. Example:

>   *hybrids of cold-blooded capabilities,*
> Theories about dinosaurs have run the gamut — simple lizards, fully adapted warm-blooded creatures, ~~hybrids of cold-blooded capabilities~~.

1. The producers were pleased with their film at the festivals, at the box office, and in the reviews.

2. More important than who wins Best Actress is what she wears to accept the award if we are to judge by reports in newspapers the next morning.

3. From the sightseeing boat, we saw a whale dive toward us and then, before crashing its tail on the waves, lift itself out of the water.

4. The presence of the Indian in these movies always conjures up destructive stereotypes of bloodthirsty war parties, horse thieves, and drunkenness.

5. Victorian women were warned that if they smoked, they would become sterile, grow a mustache, die young, or contract tuberculosis.

Usually you'll want to be **concise** — to make your point in the fewest possible words. Look at the following sentence:

> Her constant and continual use of vulgar expressions with obscene meanings indicated to her pre-elementary supervisory group that she was rather deficient in terms of her ability to interact in an efficient manner with peers in her potential interaction group.

Why write that sentence when you could instead write the following one?

> Her constant use of four-letter words told the day-care workers she might have trouble getting along with other four-year-olds.

1 Eliminating redundant words

Sometimes writers say that something is large *in size* or red *in color* or that two ingredients should be combined *together*. The italicized words are **redundant**, or unnecessary for meaning, as are the deleted words in these examples:

▶ ~~Compulsory~~ Attendance at assemblies is required.

▶ The auction featured ~~contemporary~~ "antiques" made recently.

2 Eliminating empty words

Empty words are so general and so overused that they contribute no real meaning to a sentence.

EMPTY WORDS

angle, area, aspect, case, character, element, factor, field, kind, nature, scope, situation, thing, type

Many modifiers are so common that they have become empty words.

MEANINGLESS MODIFIERS

absolutely, awesome, awfully, central, definitely, fine, great, literally, quite, really, very

When you cannot simply delete empty words, try to think of a more specific way to say what you mean.

▶ ~~The~~ housing situation can ~~have a really significant impact on the~~

~~social aspect of~~ a student's life.

> *H* (above "housing")
> *strongly influence* (above "significant impact")
> *social* (above "aspect of")

3 Replacing wordy phrases

Wordy phrases are those that can be reduced to a word or two with no loss in meaning.

WORDY	CONCISE
at all times	always
at the present time	now/today
at that point in time	then
due to the fact that	because
for the purpose of	for
in order to	to
in spite of the fact that	although
in the event that	if

4 Simplifying sentence structure

Using the simplest grammatical structures possible will strengthen your sentences considerably.

▶ Kennedy, ~~who was~~ only the second Roman Catholic ~~to be nominated~~

for the presidency by a major party, had to handle the religion issue

~~in a delicate manner.~~
> *delicately.*

Reducing a clause to an appositive, deleting unnecessary words, and replacing four words with one tighten the sentence and make it easier to read.

▶ When ~~she was~~ questioned about her previous job, she seemed nervous~~.~~

~~She~~ also tried to change the subject.
> *and*

Reducing an adverb clause to an elliptical form and combining two sentences produces one concise sentence.

Other ways to simplify grammatical structures include using strong verbs and nouns, avoiding expletive constructions, and using the active rather than the passive voice. These methods are discussed in Chapter 47.

FOR COLLABORATION

Working with a classmate, make each of the following sentences clear and concise by eliminating unnecessary words and phrases. Come up with more than one revision whenever possible. Example:

> *summarize.*
> Let me ~~fill you in on the main points of the overall picture.~~
>   ^

1. At the present time, many different forms of hazing occur, such as various forms of physical abuse and also mental abuse.

2. Many people have a tendency toward the expansion of their sentences by the superfluous addition of extra words that are not really needed for the meaning of the sentences.

3. One of the major problems that is faced at this point in time is that there is world hunger.

4. The tourist, who had come to New York for the first time and who was really proud of finishing the *Times* crossword puzzle on Monday, had no idea at all that Monday was the day of the week when the puzzle is easiest in order to give everyone who tries it kind of a sense of accomplishment.

5. The stock market seems to be a source of anxiety to some investors due to the fact that they don't understand the very important principle of repetitive cycles.

www • bedford stmartins.com/ smhandbook

For additional exercises on conciseness, click on

▶ Exercise Central
  ▶ Effective
    Sentences

43c   Writing concisely online

Brevity is particularly important in online contexts — email, postings, MOOs and MUDs, and homepages. Since readers of online writing have to scroll down and back up, they don't want to waste time looking for what is not there or moving in the wrong direction.

Keep in mind that an effective homepage needs to provide necessary information via images and words and to anticipate where users will want to go next. Although linked documents may be lengthy, the homepage leading to them needs to be concise.

●—— For more about writing online, see Chapters 7 and 9.

STYLE

Constructing
Effective Sentences

Reading with an Eye for Sentence Style

Here are two sentences from "A Sweet Devouring," Eudora Welty's essay about the pleasures of reading. Each sentence makes a powerful statement. Read each sentence, and decide how Welty achieves such strong emphasis. Then, in a piece by a favorite writer, look for strong, emphatic sentences. Bring in one or two sentences to compare with those chosen by your classmates.

1. The pleasures of reading itself—who doesn't remember?—were like those of a Christmas cake, a sweet devouring.

2. And then I went again to the home shelves and my lucky hand reached and found Mark Twain—twenty-four volumes, not a series, and good all the way through.

Thinking about Your Own Sentences

Find two or three paragraphs you have written recently, and study them with an eye for empty words. Using 43b2 for guidance, eliminate meaningless words such as *aspect, factor, quite,* and *very.* Compare notes with one or two classmates to see what empty words, if any, you all tend to use. Finally, make a note (in your writing log, if you keep one) of empty words you use, and try to avoid them in the future.

44 Creating Coordinate and Subordinate Structures

44a Using coordination to relate equal ideas

When used well, **coordination** relates separate but equal ideas. The element that links the ideas, usually a coordinating conjunction (*and, but, for, nor, or, so, yet*) or a semicolon, makes the precise relationship clear. The following sentences all use coordination, but note that the precise relationship between independent clauses differs in each sentence, as expressed in the connecting element (a coordinating conjunction or a semicolon):

> They acquired horses, *and* their ancient nomadic spirit was suddenly free of the ground.

> There is perfect freedom in the mountains, *but* it belongs to the eagle and the elk, the badger and the bear.

> No longer were they slaves to the simple necessity of survival; they were a lordly and dangerous society of fighters and thieves, hunters and priests of the sun.
> — N. Scott Momaday, *The Way to Rainy Mountain*

Coordination can help make more explicit the relationship between two sentences, as the following revision shows:

▶ My son watches *The Simpsons* religiously; Forced to choose, he would probably choose Homer Simpson over his sister.

If you think about how you build sentences, you may notice a difference between your spoken and your written language. In speech, people tend to use *and* and *so* as all-purpose connectors.

I'm going home now, and I'll see you later.

The meaning of this sentence may be perfectly clear in speech, which provides clues through voice, facial expressions, and gestures. But in writing, it could, for instance, have either of two rather different meanings.

Because I'm going home now, I'll see you later.

I'm going home now because I'll see you later.

These examples show two different tools for combining ideas in a sentence: coordinating conjunctions like *and* give the ideas equal weight, and subordinating conjunctions like *because* emphasize one idea over another. As a writer, you must often decide whether to use coordinate structures, subordinate ones, both, or neither, depending on the emphasis and effect you want to achieve. ■

705

How do your ideas flow from one sentence to another? Do they connect smoothly and clearly? Are the more important ideas emphasized over the less important ones? These guidelines will help you edit with such questions in mind.

→ How often do you link ideas with *and*? If you use *and* a great deal in this way, consider whether the linked ideas are equally important. If they are not, edit to subordinate the less important ones. (44b)

→ Look for strings of short sentences that might be combined to join related ideas. (44a)

► The report was short*, but it* It was persuasive*; it* It changed my mind.

→ Are the most important ideas in independent clauses? If not, edit so that they are. (44b)

► *Even though the* The report was short, ~~even though~~ it changed my mind.

When you use coordination to connect ideas within a sentence, make sure that the connecting element clearly and accurately expresses the relationship between the ideas.

► Watching television is a common way to spend leisure time, and *but* it makes viewers apathetic.

The relationship between the two ideas in the original sentence is unclear: what does television's being a common form of leisure have to do with viewers' being apathetic? Changing *and* to *but* better relates the two ideas.

■ *Using coordination for special effect*

Coordination can create special effects, as in a passage by Carl Sandburg describing the reaction of the American people to Abraham Lincoln's assassination.

Men tried to talk about it and the words failed and they came back to silence.

To say nothing was best.

Lincoln was dead.

Was there anything more to say?

Yes, they would go through the motions of grief and they would take part in a national funeral and a ceremony of humiliation and abasement and tears.

But words were no help.

Lincoln was dead.   –CARL SANDBURG, *Abraham Lincoln: The War Years*

Together with the other short simple sentences, the coordinate clauses, phrases, and words in the first and fifth sentences create a powerful effect. Everything in the passage is grammatically equal, flattened out by the pain and shock of the death. In this way, the sentence structure and grammar mirror the dazed state of the populace. The short sentences and independent clauses are almost like sobs that illustrate the thought of the first sentence, that "the words failed."

In the next example, the use of *and* and *but* helps the writer catalog many colorful, if somewhat unsavory, details. The writer presents the images in a heap, which contributes to the overall impression of the motel chain.

Are you familiar with Motel 7? It's a chain of cheesy cheap motels across the South—twenty dollars a night gets you peeling beaverboard walls *and* thin pink blankets. There's no phone in the room, *but* a TV set that's always tuned to the Nashville Channel, *and* an air conditioner that's always got a screw or three loose *and* vibrates like a 747 on takeoff. You see piles of emptied cigarette butts in the parking lot, *and* always cigarette burns on the table, *and* more cigarette burns on the carpet, *and* a poorly repaired hole in the wall where some good old boy put his fist through it in anger at his pregnant sixteen-year-old wife who didn't wanna go out to the Ponderosa.

● EXERCISE 44.1

Using the principles of coordination to signal equal importance or to create special effects, combine and revise the following twelve short sentences into several longer and more effective ones. Add or delete words as necessary.

The bull-riding arena was fairly crowded.
The crowd made no impression on me.
I had made a decision.

It was now time to prove myself.
I was scared.
I walked to the entry window.
I laid my money on the counter.
The clerk held up a Stetson hat filled with slips of paper.
I reached in.
I picked one.
The slip held the number of the bull I was to ride.
I headed toward the stock corral.

44b Using subordination to distinguish main ideas

Subordination allows you to distinguish major points from minor points or bring in supporting details. If, for instance, you put your main idea in an independent clause, you might then put any less significant ideas in dependent clauses. Look at the following sentence, which shows the subordinated point in italics:

> Mrs. Viola Cullinan was a plump woman *who lived in a three-bedroom house somewhere behind the post office.*   – MAYA ANGELOU, "My Name Is Margaret"

The dependent clause adds information about Mrs. Cullinan, but it is grammatically subordinate to the independent clause, which carries the main idea: *Mrs. Viola Cullinan was a plump woman.*

Notice that the choice of what to subordinate rests with the writer and depends on the intended meaning. Angelou might have given the same basic information differently: *Mrs. Viola Cullinan, a plump woman, lived in a three-bedroom house somewhere behind the post office.* Subordinating the information about Mrs. Cullinan's size to that about her house would have resulted in a slightly different meaning, of course. As a writer, you must think carefully about where you want your emphasis to be and subordinate accordingly.

Besides adding information, subordination also helps establish logical relationships among ideas. These relationships are often specified by subordinating conjunctions — words such as *after, because,* and *so that* — and relative pronouns, words such as *which, who,* and *that.* Look, for example, at another sentence by Angelou. The subordinate clause is italicized, and the subordinating conjunction is underlined.

For more about
subordinating
conjunctions,
see 31b7.

> She usually rested her smile until late afternoon *when her women friends dropped in and Miss Glory, the cook, served them cold drinks on the closed-in porch.*   – MAYA ANGELOU, "My Name Is Margaret"

sub

44b   709

STYLE

Using
Subordination
to Distinguish
Main Ideas

Finally, subordination can provide a useful alternative to coordination. Using too many coordinate structures can sound monotonous to your readers and can make it hard for them to recognize your most important ideas. By subordinating some of the less important ideas in the following passage, the editing makes clear to the reader that some of the ideas are more important than others.

▶ Many people come home tired in the evening, and so they turn on the
    Though they
television to relax. ~~They~~ may intend to watch just the news, ~~but then~~
                                                        which
a game show comes on next, ~~and~~ they decide to watch ~~it~~ for just a short
Eventually,
while~~,~~ ~~and they~~ get too comfortable to get up, and they end up

spending the whole evening in front of the television.

Like coordination, however, subordination can become excessive. When too many subordinating structures, usually dependent clauses, fall one after another, readers have trouble keeping track of the main idea expressed in the independent clause. Look, for example, at the following:

TOO MUCH SUBORDINATION

Philip II sent the Spanish Armada to conquer England, which was ruled by Elizabeth, who had executed Mary because she was plotting to overthrow Elizabeth, who was a Protestant, whereas Mary and Philip were Roman Catholics.

The long string of subordinate clauses makes the relationships among the ideas hard to follow—and makes the main idea (in the independent clause at the beginning) hard for readers to remember. See how changing one of the dependent clauses to the independent clause in a new sentence and reducing two others to appositive phrases makes the meaning clearer.

REVISED

Philip II sent the Spanish Armada to conquer England, which was ruled by Elizabeth, a Protestant. She had executed Mary, a Roman Catholic like Philip, because Mary was plotting to overthrow her.

You can use a variety of grammatical structures—not only dependent clauses—to subordinate a less important element within a sentence:

For more about ⬤
types of phrases,
see 31c3.

The parks report was persuasively written. It contained five typed pages. [no subordination]

The parks report, *which contained five typed pages,* was persuasively written. [dependent clause]

The parks report, *containing five typed pages,* was persuasively written. [participial phrase]

The *five-page* parks report was persuasively written. [adjective]

The parks report, *five typed pages,* was persuasively written. [appositive]

The parks report, *its five pages neatly typed,* was persuasively written. [absolute]

**www ⬤ bedford
stmartins.com/
smhandbook**

For additional
exercises on
subordination,
click on

▶ **Exercise Central**
  ▶ **Coordination
    and
    Subordination**

⬤ **EXERCISE 44.2**

Combine each of the following sets of sentences into one sentence that uses subordination to signal the relationships among ideas. Example:

> I was looking over my books.
>
> I noticed that *Paradise* was missing.
>
> This book is a favorite of my roommate's.
>
> *While I was looking over my books, I noticed that* Paradise, *one of my roommate's favorite books, was missing.*

1. The *Hindenburg* was gigantic.
   It was an airship.
   It was destroyed in an explosion.

2. In South Africa, you can explore a savannah.
   Magnificent wildlife roam there.
   The country also has world-class cities.

3. Stephen King was arrested in 1970.
   He had stolen traffic cones.
   His fine was one hundred dollars.

4. The mayor tells about selling Christmas wreaths.
   At the same time, he was studying for his bar mitzvah.
   He is still a man of paradoxes.

5. Skateboarding originated in Venice, California.
   The time was the mid-seventies.
   There was a drought.
   The swimming pools were empty.

▧ *Using subordination for special effect*

Subordination can create powerful effects. Some particularly fine examples come from Martin Luther King Jr. In the following passage, he piles up dependent clauses beginning with *when* to build up suspense for his main statement, given in the independent clause:

> Perhaps it is easy for those who have never felt the stinging darts of segregation to say, "Wait." But *when* you have seen vicious mobs lynch your mothers and fathers at will and drown your sisters and brothers at whim; *when* you have seen hate-filled policemen curse, kick, and even kill your black brothers and sisters; . . . *when* you have to concoct an answer for a five-year-old son who is asking: "Daddy, why do white people treat colored people so mean?"; *when* you take a cross-country drive and find it necessary to sleep night after night in the uncomfortable corners of your automobile because no motel will accept you; . . . *when* your first name becomes "nigger," your middle name becomes "boy" (however old you are) and your last name becomes "John," and your wife and mother are never given the respected title "Mrs."; . . . *when* you are forever fighting a degenerating sense of "nobodiness" — then you will understand why we find it difficult to wait.
> — MARTIN LUTHER KING JR., "Letter from Birmingham Jail"

Look now at a student example that uses subordination.

> *Though* dogs are messy and hard to train, *though* they chew up my shoes and give me the blues, *though* they howl like wolves but jump at their own shadows, *though* they eat me out of house and home — still, I love them all.

A dependent clause can also create an ironic effect if it somehow undercuts the independent clause. Probably no American writer was better at using this technique than Mark Twain. In a tongue-in-cheek commencement address, Twain once opened a paragraph with this sentence.

> Always obey your parents, *when they are present.*
> — MARK TWAIN, "Advice to Youth"

Now look at a student writer's use of the same technique.

> Never eat fattening foods — *unless you are hungry.*

FOR COLLABORATION

Together with one or two classmates, revise the following paragraph, using coordination and subordination where appropriate to clarify the relationships between ideas.

> I stayed with my friend Louise. She owns a huge, mangy wolf. It is actually a seven-eighths wolf cross. The poor creature is allergic to everything. It looks like a shabby, moth-eaten exhibit of a stuffed wolf in a third-rate museum. Louise and Bill feed it rice and raw potatoes. It slavers all over everything. It never goes out of the house. It sleeps on the beds. They are covered with animal hair. It makes no sounds. It just looks at you

sub

712 **44b**

STYLE

Creating
Coordinate and
Subordinate
Structures

with those sunken, wild eyes. It is not dangerous or ferocious. It is just completely miserable. This animal should never have been born. It's trying to tell you that with every twitch.

THINKING CRITICALLY ABOUT COORDINATION AND SUBORDINATION

Reading with an Eye for Coordination and Subordination

Read over the first draft of "All-Powerful Coke," in 3f4, paying special attention to the coordination and subordination. Do you notice any patterns—is there some of each? more of one than the other? Identify the coordination and subordination in one paragraph. Are they used appropriately? If not, revise the paragraph by following the guidelines in this chapter. Bring the results to class for discussion.

Thinking about Your Own Use of Coordination and Subordination

Analyze two paragraphs from one of your drafts. Do the independent clauses contain the main ideas? How many dependent clauses do you find? Should the ideas in the dependent clauses be subordinate to the ones in the independent clauses? Following the advice in this chapter, revise the paragraphs to use coordination and subordination effectively. What conclusions can you draw about your use of coordination and subordination? Note them down (in your writing log, if you keep one).

Creating and Maintaining Parallel Structures

45

45a Using parallel structures in series, lists, outlines, and headings

All items in a series should be in parallel form — all nouns, all prepositional phrases, all adverb clauses, and so on. Such parallelism makes a series both graceful and easy to follow. In the sentences below, note how the revisions make all items in a series parallel.

▶ The quarter horse skipped, pranced, and ~~was sashaying~~. *sashayed.*

▶ The children ran down the hill, skipped over the lawn, and ~~into~~ the swimming pool. *jumped*

▶ The duties of the job include baby-sitting, house-cleaning, and ~~preparation of~~ meals. *preparing*

Items in a list should be parallel.

▶ Kitchen rules: (1) Coffee to be made only by

library staff. (2) Coffee service to be closed at

4:00 P.M. (3) Doughnuts to be kept in cabinet.
Coffee materials not to be handled by faculty.
(4) ~~No faculty members should handle coffee materials.~~

Parallel structures stand out in tried-and-true expressions such as *sink or swim*. But parallel structures also characterize elegant prose. See how Jonathan Franzen uses parallelism in describing a job:

My job in the basement consisted of assembling cardboard cartons, filling them with smaller boxes and excelsior, checking the invoices to be sure the orders were complete, and sealing the cartons with paper tape that I wetted with a sea sponge. Since I was paid better than the minimum wage, and since I enjoyed topological packing puzzles, and since the Geyers liked me and gave me lots of cake, it was remarkable how fiercely I hated the job — how I envied even those friends of mine who manned the deep-fry station at Long John Silver's or cleaned the oil traps at Kentucky Fried Chicken.

The parallelism indicated by the underscores give the job description a sense of orderliness. This chapter will help you use parallelism to create pleasing effects. ■

→ Look for any series of three or more items, and make all of the items parallel in structure. If you want to emphasize one particular item, try putting it at the end of the series. (45a and d)

→ Be sure items in lists are parallel in form. (45a)

→ Be sure all headings are parallel in form. (45a)

→ Check for sentences that compare, contrast, or otherwise pair two ideas. Often these ideas will appear on either side of *and, but, or, nor, for, so,* or *yet,* or after each part of *both . . . and, either . . . or, neither . . . nor, not only . . . but also, whether . . . or,* or *just as . . . so.* Edit to make the two ideas parallel in structure. (45b)

→ Check all parallel structures to be sure you have included all necessary words — articles, prepositions, the *to* of the infinitive, and so on. (45c)

For a discussion
of formal out-
lines, see 3e.

Items on a formal outline and headings in a paper should be parallel. This chapter, for example, uses verbal phrases for all its main headings and, on p. 715, prepositional phrases for each of its two lower-level headings.

45b Using parallel structures with pairs

One effective use of parallel structures occurs when a writer pairs two ideas. The more nearly parallel the two structures are, the stronger the connection between the ideas will be. Parallel structures are especially appropriate when two ideas are compared or contrasted, as in the following examples:

> History became popular, and historians became alarmed.   –WILL DURANT

> We die. That may be the meaning of life. But we *do* language. That may be the measure of our lives.   –TONI MORRISON

When two clauses in a sentence compare or contrast ideas in exactly or almost exactly parallel structures, they produce a **balanced sentence,** one with two parts that "mirror" each other. Balanced sentences create an especially forceful impression.

Mankind must put an end to war, or war will put an end to mankind.

— JOHN F. KENNEDY

There is much in your book that is original and valuable — but what is original is not valuable, and what is valuable is not original.

— SAMUEL JOHNSON

▨ *With coordinating conjunctions*

In general, use the same grammatical structure on both sides of any of the coordinating conjunctions — *and, but, or, nor, for, so, yet.*

> We performed *whenever folks would listen* and *wherever they would pay.*

> *who is*
> ► Consult a friend in your class or ‸ who is good at math.

▨ *With correlative conjunctions*

Use the same structure after both parts of a correlative conjunction — *either . . . or, both . . . and, neither . . . nor, not . . . but, not only . . . but also, just as . . . so, whether . . . or.*

> The organization provided both *scholarships for young artists* and *grants for established ones.*

> *not only*
> ► Eating a bigger lunch than dinner ‸ gives you ~~not only~~ more energy for
>
> the afternoon but also allows you more time to burn off calories.

The edited sentence is more balanced. Both parts of the correlative conjunction (*not only . . . but also*) precede a verb.

◉ EXERCISE 45.1

Complete the following sentences, using parallel words or phrases in each case. Example:

The wise politician *promises the possible*, *effects the unavoidable*, and *accepts the inevitable*.

1. Before we depart, we must _____, _____, and _____.

2. My favorite pastimes include _____, _____, and _____.

3. We must either _____ or _____.

4. I want not only _____ but also _____.

5. Graduates find that the job market _____, _____, and _____.

www • bedford
stmartins.com/
smhandbook

For additional exercises on parallelism, click on

► Exercise Central
   ► Parallelism

● **EXERCISE 45.2**

Revise the following sentences as necessary to eliminate any errors in parallel structure. Example:

sending
I enjoy skiing, playing the guitar, and ~~I send~~ email to my friends.
　　　　　　　　　　　　　　　　　　^

1. I remember watching it the first time, realizing I'd never seen anything like it, and immediately vowed never to miss an episode of *Saturday Night Live.*

2. Just as my parents grew up devoted to *I Love Lucy,* so *Buffy the Vampire Slayer* had a lot of meaning for me.

3. *Lucy* often concerned white lies, how a wife could fool a husband, and getting into and out of jams.

4. It is impossible to watch *The Simpsons* and not seeing a little of yourself in one of the characters.

5. TV networks now face the question of either coming up with new situations, or they'll have to acknowledge the death of the sitcom.

45c Including all necessary words

In addition to making parallel elements grammatically similar, be careful to include all words — prepositions, articles, verb forms, and so on — that are necessary for clarity or grammar.

to
▶ **We'll move to a town near the ocean or ^Mexico.**

To a town *near* Mexico or *to* Mexico? The editing makes the meaning clear.

seen
▶ **I had never before ^and would never again see such a sight.**

In the unedited version, *had . . . see* is not grammatical.

For more examples that add
missing words,
see 42e.

those in
▶ **I prefer the beaches in Brazil to ^the United States.**

The revision clearly compares beaches with beaches.

45d Using parallel structures for emphasis and effect

Parallel structures can help a writer emphasize the most important ideas in a sentence. Look at the following sentence:

//
45d   **717**

STYLE

Using Parallel
Structures for
Emphasis and
Effect

I would like to promise her that she will grow up with a sense of her cousins and of rivers and of her great-grandmother's teacups, would like to pledge her a picnic on a river with fried chicken and her hair uncombed, would like to give her *home* for her birthday, but we live differently now and I can promise her nothing like that.

—Joan Didion, "On Going Home"

The first two parallel phrases, *would like to promise her . . . , would like to pledge her . . . ,* provide a series of specific, concrete details and images that leads up to the general statement in the last phrase, that Didion would like to give her daughter a sense of home. Although Didion could have stated this general point first and then gone on to illustrate it with concrete details, she achieves greater emphasis by making it the last in a series of parallel structures arranged in climactic order.

Besides emphasizing an idea, parallel structures can create a stylistic effect.

> At work, he may have time to gulp down a cup of coffee if the dining halls are running smoothly, if all the workers show up, and if the boss is not asking questions.

This sentence creates an impression of somewhat desperate activity as it piles up the three parallel *if* clauses.

● For more on ways to emphasize particular parts of a sentence, see 43a.

FOR COLLABORATION

Working with one or two classmates, revise the following paragraph to maintain parallelism and to supply all words necessary for clarity and grammar in parallel structures.

> Growing up in a large city provides a very different experience from a suburban childhood. Suburban children undoubtedly enjoy many advantages over those who live in a city, including lawns to play ball on, trees for climbing, and often the schools are better. However, in recent years many people raised in the suburbs but who moved to large cities as young adults are deciding to bring up their own children in an urban setting. Their reasons for doing so include what they consider the cultural advantages of the city, the feeling that they will be able to spend more time with their children if they do not have to commute so far to work, and also they want to expose the children to a greater diversity of social and economic groups than most suburbs offer. Just as their own parents left the city for the space and calm of suburbia, so crowds and excitement are why today's parents are returning to it. Wherever they bring up their children, though, parents have never nor will they ever find utopia.

Reading with an Eye for Parallelism

Read the following paragraph about a bareback rider practicing her circus act, and identify all the parallel structures. Consider what effect they create on you as a reader, and try to decide why the author chose to put his ideas in such overtly parallel form. Try imitating the next-to-last sentence, the one beginning *In a week or two*.

> The richness of the scene was in its plainness, its natural condition—of horse, of ring, of girl, even to the girl's bare feet that gripped the bare back of her proud and ridiculous mount. The enchantment grew not out of anything that happened or was performed but out of something that seemed to go round and around and around with the girl, attending her, a steady gleam in the shape of a circle—a ring of ambition, of happiness, of youth. (And the positive pleasures of equilibrium under difficulties.) In a week or two, all would be changed, all (or almost all) lost: the girl would wear makeup, the horse would wear gold, the ring would be painted, the bark would be clean for the feet of the horse, the girl's feet would be clean for the slippers that she'd wear. All, all would be lost.   – E. B. WHITE, "The Ring of Time"

Thinking about Your Own Use of Parallelism

Read carefully several paragraphs from a draft you have recently written, noting any series of words, phrases, or clauses. Using the guidelines at the beginning of this chapter, determine whether the series are parallel, and if not, revise them for parallelism. Then reread the paragraphs, looking for places where parallel structures would add emphasis or clarity, and revise accordingly. Can you draw any conclusions about your use of parallelism? Make a note of them (in your writing log, if you keep one).

Varying Sentence Structures

46a Varying sentence length

Varying sentence length not only makes prose more read-able and interesting but also creates a pleasing rhythmic effect, what some writers call "flow." Deciding how and when to vary sentence length is not always easy, however. How short is too short? How long is too long? Is there a "just right" length for a particular sentence or idea?

These questions are difficult because the answers depend on, among other things, the writer's purpose, intended audience, and topic. A children's story, for instance, may call for mostly short sentences whereas an article on nuclear disarmament in the *Atlantic* may call for considerably longer ones. Many technical writers, particu-larly those who write manuals that will be translated into numerous languages, must follow stringent rules for sen-tence length and structure.

Although both series of short and of long sentences can be effective in individual situations, frequent alterna-tion in sentence length characterizes much memorable writing. After one or more long sentences that express complex ideas or images, the pith of a short sentence can be refreshing and arresting. For example:

> The fire of, I think, five machine-guns was pouring upon us, and there was a series of heavy crashes caused by the Fascists flinging bombs over their own parapet in the most idiotic manner. It was intensely dark.
>
> – GEORGE ORWELL, *Homage to Catalonia*

Row upon row of trees identical in size and shape may appeal at some level to a sense of orderliness, but those identical rows can soon become boring. If vari-ety is the spice of life, it is also the spice of sentence structure, where sameness can result in dull, listless prose. One instructor saw this principle in action in a particular college classroom. Although a peer-response group had worked on an essay for almost an hour, they felt stumped: it still seemed boring. Finally, one student exclaimed, "I've got it! Look at these sentences. They all look about the same length!"

And they were: every sentence in the essay was between twenty-two and twenty-five words long. Once the group realized this, they went to work again, carving some sentences into short ones and combining others to create new rhythms. With the resulting sentence vari-ety, the essay took on new life. ■

Count the words in each of your sentences, and underline the longest and shortest sentences in each paragraph. If the difference between the longest and shortest sentences is fairly small — say, five words or fewer — consider revising the paragraph to create greater variety in length. Do not, however, change sentences arbitrarily. Think about the ideas you want to emphasize, and try to arrange your sentence lengths in a way that emphasizes them. Start by asking the following questions:

→ Do two or more short sentences in a row express closely related ideas? If so, could you make the relationship between these ideas clearer or more precise by combining them into a single longer sentence?

→ Is there a long sentence that contains two or three important ideas? Would these ideas be more emphatic if each was expressed in a short sentence of its own?

Similarly, a long sentence after several short ones can serve as a climax or summation that relaxes the tension or fulfills the expectation created by the series. For example:

> But it is under siege, too. Santa Fe, so recently hardly more than a remote and rather secretive village, is chic these days. The smart, the modish, the merely rich move in. The haven is embattled. The old hands watch thoughtfully as Santa Fe, *dear* Santa Fe, slowly but inexorably changes its character — as the condominiums spring up over the foothills, as the Soak Hot-Tub Club offers its twelve hot-tub suites with individual stereo and mood lighting, as downtown land reaches $100,000 an acre — as the triviality of things, the cuteness, the sham and the opportunism, spreads like a tinsel stain across the town.
>
> – JAN MORRIS, "Capital of the Holy Faith"

◉ EXERCISE 46.1

The following paragraph can be improved by varying sentence length. Read it aloud to get a sense of how it sounds. Then revise it, creating some short, emphatic sentences and combining other sentences to create more effective long sentences. Add words or change punctuation as you need to.

Before beginning to play bridge, it is necessary to have the proper materials, the correct number of people, and a knowledge of the rank of suits and cards. The necessary materials include a full deck of playing cards (minus the jokers) and a score pad, along with a pen or pencil. Bridge is played by four people grouped into two partnerships, which are usually decided by drawing cards from a shuffled deck. The two players who draw the highest cards and the two who draw the lowest are partners, and the partners sit across from each other. The person who draws the highest card during partnership is the first dealer. Starting with the person on his or her left and going clockwise, the dealer deals each person one card at a time, face down. The deal continues until all four players have thirteen cards apiece. After the deal, the players sort their cards by suit, usually alternating black and red suits. The players then arrange the cards in ranking order from the highest, the ace, to the lowest, the deuce. The five highest cards, the ace, king, queen, jack, and ten, are referred to as honors. There is one suit that has great power and outranks every other one, the trump suit, which is designated at the start of the game.

46b Varying sentence openings

In making prose readable and interesting, beginning sentences in different ways is just as important as writing sentences of different lengths. For instance, when each sentence begins with the subject of an independent clause, a passage may become monotonous or even hard to read.

▶ The way football and basketball are played is as interesting as the
    Because football
players. ~~Football~~ is a game of precision., Each play is diagrammed to
                                              however,
accomplish a certain goal. Basketball, is a game of endurance.
In fact, a
A basketball game looks like a track meet; the team that drops of

exhaustion first loses. Basketball players are often compared to artists.;
their
~~The players'~~ moves and slam dunks are their masterpieces.

The editing adds variety by using a subordinating word (*Because* in the second line) and a transitional phrase (*In fact* in the fourth line) and by linking sentences. Varying sentence openings prevents the passage from seeming to jerk or lurch along.

You can add variety to your sentence openings by using transitions, various kinds of phrases, and introductory dependent clauses.

Underline the subject of each sentence. If most of your sentences begin with the subject, revise some of them to open in other ways. Consider the following suggestions:

→ Look for sentences that relate to the preceding sentence in a specific chronological, spatial, or logical way that you can signal by a transitional expression. (5d4 and 46b1)
→ Try rewording some sentences to begin with a phrase. (31c3 and 46b2)
→ If two consecutive sentences are closely related, see if it would be logical to combine them into one sentence, making one of the original sentences a dependent clause. (31c4 and 46b3)

1 Using transitional expressions

See how transitions bring variety and clarity to this passage.

> In order to be alert Friday morning in New York, I planned to take the shuttle from Washington Thursday night. *On Thursday morning* it began to snow in Washington and to snow even harder in New York. *By mid-afternoon* I decided not to risk the shuttle and caught a train to New York. *Seven hours later* the train completed its three-hour trip. I arrived at Penn Station to find a city shut down by the worst blizzard since 1947.
>
> – LINDA ELLERBEE, "And So It Goes"

Many other transitional expressions can be used to vary sentence openings. For a detailed list, see 5d4.

Here the transitional words establish chronology and help carry us smoothly through the paragraph.

2 Using phrases

Prepositional, verbal, and absolute phrases can also provide variety in sentence openings.

PREPOSITIONAL PHRASES

At each desk, a computer printout gives the necessary data.

From a few scraps of wood in the Middle Ages to a precisely carved, electrified instrument in our times, the guitar has gone through uncounted changes.

VERBAL PHRASES

Frustrated by the delays, the drivers started honking their horns.

To qualify for flight training, one must be in good physical condition.

Having qualified for flight training, the student began by learning turns.

Our hopes for snow shattered, we started home.

Baton raised in a salute, the maestro readied the orchestra.

In general, use a comma after these phrases when they open a sentence.

STYLE
Varying Sentence
Types

●— For more about
commas after
introductory
phrases, see 48a.

●— For more about
commas after
adverb clauses,
see 48a.

3 Using dependent clauses

Dependent clauses are another way to open a sentence.

While the boss sat on his tractor, I was down in a ditch, pounding in stakes and leveling out the bottom.

What they want is a place to call home.

In general, use a comma after an adverb clause that opens a sentence.

46c Varying sentence types

In addition to using different lengths and openings, you can help vary your sentence structures by using different *types* of sentences. Sentences can be classified in three different ways: grammatically, functionally, and rhetorically.

●— For more on
grammatical and
functional classi-
fication of sen-
tences, see 31d1
and d2.

EDITING TO VARY SENTENCE TYPES

→ Mark each sentence as simple, compound, complex, or compound-complex. If any one or two patterns predominate, combine, divide, and otherwise revise sentences to vary the grammatical types. (46c1)

→ Consider whether the ideas in any declarative sentences might be effective as commands, questions, or exclamations. (46c2)

→ Look for ideas that could use greater emphasis: would they get such emphasis in periodic sentences? Also look for ideas with significant detail or with colorful images: would they work best as cumulative sentences? (46c3)

1 Grammatical types

Grammatically, sentences fall into four categories—**simple, compound, complex,** and **compound-complex**—based on the number of independent

●— For more on
these four sen-
tence categories,
see 31d.

var

and dependent clauses they contain. Varying your sentences among these grammatical types can help you create readable, effective prose.

2 Functional types

Functional types of sentences are **declarative** (making a statement), **interrogative** (asking a question), **imperative** (giving a command), and **exclamatory** (expressing strong feeling). Most sentences are declarative, but occasionally a command, a question, or an exclamation of some kind is appropriate for your purpose. Note how those three are used in the following examples:

COMMAND

Coal-burning plants undoubtedly harm the environment in various ways; for example, they contribute to acid rain. *But consider the alternatives.*

QUESTION

We kept pressing on. *And why? Why would sixteen middle-aged people try to backpack thirty-seven miles?* At this point, I was not at all sure.

EXCLAMATION

Divorcés! They were everywhere! Sometimes he felt like a new member of an enormous club, the Divorcés of America, that he had never before even heard of.

3 Rhetorical types

Periodic and cumulative sentences spotlight sentence endings and beginnings and can be especially helpful in achieving sentence variety. Although not all sentences can be classified as cumulative or periodic, these types can create strong effects.

■ *Periodic sentences*

Periodic sentences postpone the main idea (usually in an independent clause) until the very end of the sentence. Effectively written periodic sentences are especially useful for creating tension or building toward a climactic or surprise ending. Note in each of the following examples how the writer holds back the main idea, thus using the end of the sentence to shock or inspire:

Early one morning, under the arc of a lamp, carefully, silently, in smock and leather gloves, *old Doctor Manza grafted a cat's head onto a chicken's trunk.*   — DYLAN THOMAS

Even though large tracts of Europe and many old and famous states have fallen or may fall into the grasp of the Gestapo and all the odious apparatus of Nazi rule, *we shall not flag or fail.*   — WINSTON CHURCHILL

Look at the following sentence and its revision to see how periodic order can provide emphasis:

ORIGINAL SENTENCE

The nations of the world have no alternative but coexistence because another world war would be unwinnable and because total destruction would certainly occur.

REVISED AS A PERIODIC SENTENCE

Because another world war would be unwinnable and because total destruction would certainly occur, the nations of the world have no alternative but coexistence.

Nothing is wrong with the first sentence, which conveys the information clearly. But to put greater emphasis on the idea in the independent clause of the sentence — *no alternative but coexistence* — the writer chose to revise using the periodic pattern.

▪ *Cumulative sentences*

Cumulative sentences, which begin with an independent clause and then add details in phrases and in dependent clauses (as does the preceding sentence labeled *original*), are far more common than periodic sentences. They are useful when you want to provide both immediate understanding of the main idea and a great deal of supporting detail. The writers of the following sentences use the cumulative pattern not only to add important detail but also to end with a strong image:

From boyhood to manhood, *I have remembered him in a single image* — seated, asleep on the sofa, his head thrown back in a hideous corpselike grin, the evening newspaper spread out before him.

— RICHARD RODRIGUEZ, "My Parents"

Powther threw small secret appraising glances at the coffee cup, lipstick all around the edges, brown stains on the side where the coffee had dripped and spilled over, the saucer splotched with a whole series of dark brown rings.   — ANN PETRY, *The Narrows*

var

46c

726

STYLE

Varying Sentence
Structures

● **EXERCISE 46.2**

Revise each of the following sentences twice. First make each a periodic sentence and then a cumulative sentence.

1. Obviously not understanding reporters, the politician did not know their names, did not answer their questions, and did not read their stories.

2. I became the best salesperson in our store once I mastered the problems that I had encountered at the beginning and once I became thoroughly familiar with the stock.

FOR COLLABORATION

The following is an introductory paragraph from an essay. Working with a classmate, analyze the paragraph carefully, noting for each sentence its length, its kind of opening, its grammatical type. Then revise the paragraph to add variety in sentence length, sentence openings, and sentence types.

> When we arrived at the accident scene, I could tell that the injuries were not minor. I walked up to the car nearest me to check the injuries of the people inside. I looked through the driver's window and saw the woman's body entangled in the steering wheel. I told dispatch, via two-way radio, to send medics "code red, lights and siren." I then went to see how the passenger in the car was. The passenger appeared to be in shock and had a broken leg. The officer walked over and checked the other vehicle. The driver of the other vehicle had received no injuries at all.

THINKING CRITICALLY ABOUT SENTENCE VARIETY

Reading with an Eye for Sentence Variety

Read something by an author you admire. Analyze two paragraphs for sentence length, opening, and type. Compare the sentence variety in these paragraphs with that in one of your paragraphs. What similarities or differences do you recognize, and what conclusions can you draw about sentence variety?

Thinking about Your Own Sentence Variety

Choose a piece of writing you have recently completed, and analyze two or three pages for sentence variety. Note sentence length, opening, and type (grammatical, functional, and rhetorical). Choose a passage you think can be improved for variety, and make those revisions.

Creating Memorable Prose

47

47a Choosing strong verbs

The greatest writers in any language are those with a genius for choosing the precise words that will arrest and hold a reader's attention. In your own writing, you can help gain this attention by using precise nouns and adjectives instead of vague, empty ones (see 43b2). Perhaps even more important, however, you can use strong, precise verbs instead of weak, catchall verbs and instead of nouns.

1 Using precise verbs

Verbs serve as the real workhorses of our language. Take a look, for instance, at the strong, precise verbs in the following passage:

> A fire engine, out for a trial spin, *roared* past Emerson's house, hot with readiness for public duty. Over the barn roofs the martens *dipped* and *chittered*. A swarthy daughter of an asparagus grower, in culottes, shirt, and bandanna, *pedalled* past on her bicycle.   –E. B. WHITE, "Walden"

Instead of the italicized verbs, White could have used more general verbs such as *drove, flew, called,* and *rode.* But the more precise verbs are stronger because they give readers vivid sensory impressions of the actions they express. In White's verbs, readers can hear the roar of the fire engine, see the martens swooping downward and hear

How many times have you read something so striking that you wanted immediately to share it with a friend? And how many times have you remembered the exact words of something you have read or heard? All of us recognize, and can even quote, certain passages from literature or history or music — the opening of Jane Austen's *Pride and Prejudice*, perhaps, or passages from Martin Luther King's "I Have a Dream," or lyrics to a well-known song. As writers, we can profit by examining some of the elements that help make such pieces memorable: strong verbs, active voice, and special effects such as repetition, antithesis, and inversion. This chapter will help you to use these elements in your own work, to make your writing not only worth reading but also worth remembering. ∎

1. Underline all verbs, and look to see whether you rely too much on *be, do,* and *have*. If so, try to substitute more specific verbs. (47a1)

2. Note nouns whose meaning could be expressed by a verb. Try revising using the verbs instead of the nouns. (47a2)

3. Identify all expletives, and delete any that do not create special emphasis. (47a1)

4. Look for passive verbs, and decide whether they obscure the performer of the action or dull the sentence. If so, recast the sentence in the active voice. (47b)

them chirping shrilly, and feel the young woman pushing on the pedals of her bicycle.

Some of the most common verbs in English — especially *be, do,* and *have* — carry little or no sense of specific action, but many writers tend to overuse them in situations where more precise verbs would be clearer and more effective. Look at how the following sentences are strengthened when precise verbs are used:

> *stunts and distorts*
> **Constant viewing of rock videos is harmful to children's development.**

> *etch*
> **In front of the hotel, an artist would do your portrait on glass.**

> *sweated through*
> **We had basic training at Fort Ord.**

■ *Expletives*

One potentially weak verb construction to watch out for is the **expletive,** which begins with *there* or *it* followed by a form of *be* or another linking verb (*there are, it seems,* and so on). However, a writer can use an expletive effectively to introduce an idea with extra emphasis, as Samuel Johnson does in 45b and as June Jordan does in the following sentence:

It is for us, the living, to ensure that We the People shall become the powerful.
— JUNE JORDAN, "Inside America"

Here the *it is* slows down the opening of the sentence and sets up an appropriate formal rhythm that adds emphasis to what follows. Often, however, writers do not use expletive openings to add emphasis. Instead, they merely overuse them, creating sentences that needlessly bury action in nouns, verbals, or dependent clauses. Note how the following sentences are strengthened by deleting the expletives:

▶ ~~There are~~ *M*any people ~~who~~ fear success because they believe they do

  not deserve it.

▶ ~~It is necessary for~~ *P*residential candidates *must* perform well on television.

2 Changing nouns to verbs

Much modern writing expresses action through nouns formed from verbs, a process called **nominalization**. Although nominalization can help make prose clearer and more concise — for example, using *abolition* instead of *the process of abolishing* — it can also produce the opposite effect, making a sentence unnecessarily wordy and hard to read. Nominalization reduces the *active* quality of a sentence by burying the action in an abstract noun and forcing the writer to use weak, generalized verbs and too many prepositional phrases. Too often, writers use nominalizations not to make a complex process easier to talk about but to make an idea *sound* more complex and abstract than it is. Bureaucratic writing, in particular, tends to use nominalization in this way.

You can decide when to use a nominalized form and when to use the verb from which it derives by asking one question: which is more readily understandable? Look at the following sentence:

The firm is now engaged in an assessment of its procedures for the development of new products.

This sentence scarcely impresses itself on our memories, and it sounds pretentious and stuffy as well. In contrast, note the more easily understood and forceful version.

The firm is now assessing its procedures for developing new products.

47b Choosing between active and passive voice

In addition to choosing strong, precise verbs, you can help make your prose memorable by alternating those verbs appropriately between active and passive voice. Look at the following paragraph:

> A young man might go into military flight training believing that he was entering some sort of technical school in which he was simply going to acquire a certain set of skills. Instead, he found himself all at once enclosed in a fraternity. And in this fraternity, even though it was military, men were not rated by their outward rank as ensigns, lieutenants, commanders, or whatever. No, herein the world was divided into those who had it and those who did not. This quality, this *it*, was never named, however, nor was it talked about in any way.   – TOM WOLFE, *The Right Stuff*

For more about
active and pas-
sive voice, see
33g and 38c.

In this paragraph, Wolfe introduces the indefinable quality that he has made the title of his book. Note that the first sentence focuses on some-one *doing* things: going into flight training, entering a school, acquiring skills. All of the verbs are in the active voice.

In the second sentence, the verb is still active. But note that because the subject and the object are the same person, because the subject of the verb *found* also receives the action of the verb, the sentence has the *feel* of being in the passive voice, as if *was enclosed* were the verb. And in the independent clauses of the last three sentences, the focus clearly shifts to things *being done* (or not done): men not being rated, the world being divided, and a quality never being named or talked about. The persons doing these things are unimportant or unknown; in fact, like the quality itself, they are never named, and the verbs are in the passive voice. However, Wolfe uses the active voice when he focuses on the persons "who had it and those who did not."

Try to use the active voice whenever possible. Because the passive diverts attention from the performer of an action and because it is usually wordier than the active voice, its excessive use makes for dull and difficult reading. But as Wolfe's paragraph indicates, the passive works effectively in certain situations: when the performer is unknown, unwilling to be identified, or less important than the recipient of the action. In the last sentence, for example, Wolfe could have written *No one ever named this quality, this* it, *however, nor did anyone talk about it in any way*. By using the passive voice, however, he focuses attention on the quality itself rather than on the persons who do not name or talk about it; in fact, by not mentioning them, he heightens the sense of a mysterious quality that cannot be defined.

Here is an example of how to edit an unnecessary passive construction:

his   *Gower*
▶ In ~~Gower's~~ research, ~~it was found~~ that pythons often dwell in trees.

www • bedford
stmartins.com/
smhandbook

For additional exercises on active and passive voice, click on

▶ **Exercise Central**
  ▶ **Verbs**

● EXERCISE 47.1

Look at the following sentences, in which some of the verbs are active and some passive. Then rewrite each sentence in the other voice, and decide which version you prefer and why. Example:

I   *you*
~~You are~~ hereby relieved of your duties. ~~by me.~~

1. Mistakes have been made.
2. The first lady was helped with her decor by a Dallas design team.
3. When the soldiers denied murdering civilians, journalists questioned that denial.
4. The leader of the rebels was assassinated by his long-time enemy.
5. In a patient with celiac disease, intestinal damage can be caused by the body's immunological response to gluten.

● EXERCISE 47.2

Revise the following paragraph to eliminate weak verbs, unnecessary nominalizations and expletives, and inappropriate use of the passive voice.

There has long been resistance to the proposition that the effectiveness of educational methods and teachers must be measured in terms of the results secured. Those responsible for the evaluation of teachers have put emphasis on procedures in teaching and have seldom made an examination of the products—that is, the efficiency of the teacher as indicated by what can be done by his or her pupils following instruction. However, we are beginning to see an increasing number of bold proposals founded on the assumption that the American public has expectations of improved results from schooling. As public support of education increases, there will be greater insistence on making judgments about a teacher in the light of his or her ability to enhance the learning of pupils.

47c Creating special effects

Contemporary movies often succeed on the basis of their special effects. Similarly, special effects like repetition, antithesis, and inversion can animate your prose and help make it memorable.

pr

47c

1 Using repetition

Carefully used, repetition of sounds, words, phrases, or other grammatical constructions serves as a powerful stylistic device. Orators in particular have long known its power. Here is a famous use of repetition from one of Sir Winston Churchill's addresses to the British people during World War II:

> We shall not flag or fail, we shall go on to the end. We shall fight in France, we shall fight on the seas and oceans, we shall fight with growing confidence and growing strength in the air, we shall defend our island, whatever the cost may be; we shall fight on the beaches, . . . we shall fight in the fields and in the streets, . . . we shall never surrender.
>
> –WINSTON CHURCHILL

In this passage, the constantly hammering of *we shall* accompanied by the repetition of *f* sounds (*flag, fail, fight, France, confidence, defend, fields*) has the effect of strengthening British resolve.

Though we may not be prime ministers, we can use repetition to equally good effect. Here are additional examples:

> So my dream date turned into a nightmare. Where was the quiet, considerate, caring guy I thought I had met? In his place appeared this jerk. He strutted, he postured, he preened — and then he bragged, he bellowed, he practically brayed — just like the donkey he so much reminded me of.

> We need science, more and better science, not for its technology, not for leisure, not even for health or longevity, but for the hope of wisdom which our kind of culture must acquire for its survival.
>
> – LEWIS THOMAS, "Medical Lessons from History"

Be careful, however, to use repetition only for a deliberate purpose.

▓ *Multiple negatives*

One common way in which people use repetition for emphasis is to use more than one negative term in a negative statement. In *I can't hardly see you*, for example, both *can't* and *hardly* carry negative meanings. Emphatic double negatives — and triple, quadruple, and more — are especially common in the South and among speakers of African American vernacular English, who may say, for example, *Don't none of my people come from up North.*

Multiple negatives have a long history in English and can be found in the works of Chaucer and Shakespeare, as well as in other languages. In the eighteenth century, however, in an effort to make English more "logical," double negatives came to be labeled as incorrect. In college writing, you may well have reason to quote passages that include them (whether from Shakespeare, Toni Morrison, or your grandmother), but it would be safer to avoid other uses of double negatives in academic writing.

FOR MULTILINGUAL WRITERS: Avoiding Double Negatives

Many languages other than English, such as French and Russian, commonly use more than one negative word to make negative statements. In French, for example, "never" is expressed by putting *ne* before the verb and *jamais* after the verb. If you are a native speaker of one of these languages, be especially careful in English to use only one negative word to express a negative meaning.

EXERCISE 47.3

Go through the examples in 47c1, identifying the uses of repetition. Using one example as a model, write a passage of your own with effective repetition.

---

2 Using antithesis

Another special effect that can contribute to memorable writing is **antithesis,** the use of parallel structures to highlight contrast or opposition. Like other uses of parallelism, antithesis provides a pleasing rhythm that calls readers' attention to the contrast, often in a startling or amusing way.

For a complete discussion of parallelism, see Chapter 45.

Love is an ideal thing, marriage a real thing.

The congregation didn't think much of the new preacher, and what the new preacher thought of the congregation she didn't wish to say.

It is a sin to believe evil of others — but it is not a mistake.
— H. L. MENCKEN

EXERCISE 47.4

Using one of the preceding examples as a guide, create a sentence of your own that uses antithesis. You might begin by thinking of opposites you could build on: hope/despair, good/evil, fire/ice. Or you might begin with a topic you want to write about: success, greed, generosity, and so on.

3 Using inverted word order

Inversion of the usual word order, such as putting the verb before the subject or the object before the subject and verb, can make writing memorable by creating surprise or emphasizing a particular word or phrase.

> ▶ ~~Two dead birds~~ *Out* ~~plummeted out~~ of the tree. *plummeted two dead birds.*

The inverted word order creates a more dramatic sentence by putting the emphasis at the end, on *two dead birds*.

As with any unusual sentence pattern, use inverted word order sparingly, only to create occasional special effects.

Into this grey lake plopped the thought, I know this man, don't I?
– Doris Lessing

In a hole in the ground there lived a hobbit.   – J. R. R. Tolkien

Into her head flowed the whole of the poem she had found in that book.
– Eudora Welty

EXERCISE 47.5

Look at something you have written, and find a sentence that might be more effective with inverted word order. Experiment with the word order. Read the results aloud, and compare the effects.

FOR COLLABORATION

Prose can be memorable for reasons quite different from those presented in this chapter. The Bulwer-Lytton Competition, known less formally as the Wretched Writing contest, challenges writers to produce an opening sentence to a novel, a sentence that will celebrate the possibilities of "deliberate wretchedness" without hurting anyone's feelings. Here are two finalists.

1. It was the eve of the yearly whale-slaughtering festival, thought Mamook as her horny fingers relentlessly pushed the whalebone needle through the sole of the mukluk; and suddenly, unaccountably, uncontrollably, she began to blubber.

2. When the last of the afterglow faded and the air was still, John liked to sit in the porch swing, in the dark, and test his night vision by spitting through the banisters.

Working with a classmate, write a "wonderfully bad" sentence for a story. Then work together to write an equally "bad" closing sentence. Bring the sentences to class for comparison with those of the rest of the class, and be ready to explain what features make your sentences exquisitely bad.

Reading with an Eye for Prose Style

Chapters 43–47 have presented many elements that mark effective prose. One amusing way to practice these elements is to imitate them. Choose a writer you admire — Virginia Woolf, Chaucer, Leslie Marmon Silko, Stephen King, Tupac Shakur, whoever. Reread this writer's work, getting a feel for the rhythms, the structures, the special effects. Make a list of the elements that contribute to the distinctive style. Then choose a well-known story, and retell it in that style. Following is the opening of "The Three Little Pigs" as one student imagined Edgar Allan Poe might have done it.

> It began as a mere infatuation. I admired them from afar, with a longing that only a wolf may know. Soon, these feelings turned to torment. Were I even to set eyes upon their porcine forms, the bowels of my soul raged, as if goaded by some festering poison. As the chilling winds of November howled, my gullet yearned for them. I soon feasted only upon an earnest and consuming desire for the moment of their decease.

Thinking about Your Own Prose Style

Read over something you have written, looking for memorable sentences. If few sentences catch your eye, choose some that show promise — ones with strong verbs or a pleasing rhythm, perhaps. Using this chapter for guidance, try revising one or two sentences to make them more effective and memorable. Finally, note some ways in which your writing is effective and some strategies for making it more effective. If you keep a writing log, make your notes there.

PART 9

PUNCTUATION CONVENTIONS

"You can show a lot with a look. . . .
It's punctuation."
—CLINT EASTWOOD

◤ Using Commas

48a Using commas after introductory elements

A comma usually follows an introductory word, expression, phrase, or clause.

▶ Slowly, Drue became conscious of her predicament.

▶ Nevertheless, the hours of a programmer are flexible.

▶ In fact, only Ajani was prepared.

▶ Frustrated, he wondered whether he should change jobs.

▶ In Fitzgerald's novel, the color green takes on great symbolic qualities.

▶ Sporting a pair of specially made running shoes, Logan prepared for the race.

▶ To win the contest, Connor needed luck.

▶ Pens poised in anticipation, the students waited for the test to be distributed.

▶ Since my mind was not getting enough stimulation, I decided to read some good literature.

Research for this book shows that five of the most common errors in college writing involve commas. Check your writing for these five errors:

1. Check every sentence that doesn't begin with the subject to see whether it opens with an introductory element (a word, phrase, or clause that tells when, where, how, or why the main action of the sentence occurs). Separate the introductory material with a comma. (48a)

2. Look at every sentence that contains one of the conjunctions *and, but, or, for, nor, so,* or *yet.* If the group of words before and after the conjunction each functions as a complete sentence, you have a compound sentence. Make sure to use a comma before the conjunction. (48b)

3. Look at all adjective clauses beginning with *which, who, whom, whose, when,* or *where,* and at phrases and appositives. (31c3 and 31c4) Consider each element, and decide whether it is essential to the meaning of the sentence. If the rest of the sentence would be unclear without it, you should *not* set off the element with commas. (48c)

4. Identify all adjective clauses beginning with *that,* and make sure they are *not* set off with commas. (48c and j)

5. Check every *and* and *or* to see if it comes before the last item in a series of three or more words, phrases, or clauses. Be sure that each item in a series (except the last) is followed by a comma. (48d)

Some writers omit the comma if the introductory element is short and does not seem to require a pause after it.

At the racetrack Henry lost nearly his entire paycheck.

However, you will seldom be wrong if you use a comma after an introductory element. If the introductory element is followed by inverted word order, with the verb preceding the subject, do not use a comma except if misreading might occur.

▶ **From directly behind my seat‚ came huge clouds of cigar smoke.**

▶ **Before he went‚ on came the rains.**
  ^

www • bedford stmartins.com/ smhandbook

For additional exercises on using commas after introductory elements, click on

▶ **Exercise Central**
　▶ **Commas**

● **EXERCISE 48.1**

In the following sentences, add any commas that are needed after the introductory element.

1. At the worst possible moment a computer crash made me lose my document.
2. Unfortunately the door to the kennel had been left open.
3. Certain of her ability to earn a high score on the test Katrina got a good night's sleep.
4. Whenever someone unexpectedly rings the doorbell his dog goes berserk.
5. Therefore answering the seemingly simple question is very difficult.
6. With the fifth century came the fall of the Roman Empire.
7. A tray of cheese canapes in one hand and a pile of napkins in the other the waiter moved slowly around the room.
8. To find a good day-care provider parents usually need plenty of time and money.
9. After the hurricane moved on the citizens of the town assessed the damage.
10. Startled by the explosion the workers dropped to the ground.

48b Using commas in compound sentences

A comma usually precedes a coordinating conjunction (*and, but, or, for, nor, so,* or *yet*) that joins two independent clauses in a compound sentence.

▶ The title may sound important, but *administrative clerk* is only a
　euphemism for *photocopier.*

▶ The show started at last, and the crowd grew quiet.

With very short clauses, writers sometimes omit the comma before *and* or *or.* You will never be wrong to include it, however.

She saw her chance and she took it.

She saw her chance, and she took it.

Always use the comma if there is any chance the sentence will be misread without it.

▶ The game ended in victory, and pandemonium erupted.

You may want to use a semicolon rather than a comma when the clauses are long and complex or contain other punctuation.

> When these early migrations took place, the ice was still confined to the lands in the far north; but eight hundred thousand years ago, when man was already established in the temperate latitudes, the ice moved southward until it covered large parts of Europe and Asia.
> – ROBERT JASTROW, *Until the Sun Dies*

Be careful not to use *only* a comma between independent clauses. Doing so is usually considered a serious grammatical error, called a comma splice. Either use a coordinating conjunction after the comma, or use a semicolon.

● For more about
comma splices,
see Chapter 39.

COMMA SPLICE	Do not say luck is responsible for your new job, give yourself the credit you deserve.
REVISED	Do not say luck is responsible for your new job, *but* give yourself the credit you deserve.
REVISED	Do not say luck is responsible for your new job; give yourself the credit you deserve.

EXERCISE 48.2

Use a comma and a coordinating conjunction (*and, but, or, for, nor, so,* or *yet*) to combine each of the following pairs of sentences into one sentence. Delete or rearrange words if necessary. Example:

I had finished studying for the test, I went to bed.
_{so}

www ● bedford
stmartins.com/
smhandbook

For additional
exercises on
using commas
in compound
sentences, click on

▶ **Exercise Central**
  ▶ **Commas**

1. The chef did not want to serve a heavy dessert. She was planning to have a rich stew for the main course.
2. The children are usually well behaved. They forgot their manners at their grandmother's house.
3. I studied ten of Verdi's operas. I have only begun to appreciate the wealth of his creativity.
4. The playwright disliked arguing with directors. She avoided rehearsals.
5. Tropical fish do not bark. They are not cuddly pets.

48c Using commas to set off nonrestrictive elements

Nonrestrictive elements — clauses, phrases, and words that do *not* limit, or restrict, the meaning of the words they modify — are set off from the rest of the sentence with commas. **Restrictive elements** *do* limit meaning and are *not* set off with commas.

RESTRICTIVE   Drivers *who have been convicted of drunken driving* should lose their licenses.

NONRESTRICTIVE   The two drivers involved in the accident, *who have been convicted of drunken driving,* should lose their licenses.

In the first sentence, the clause *who have been convicted of drunken driving* is essential to the meaning because it limits the word it modifies, *Drivers,* to only those drivers who have been convicted of drunken driving. Therefore, it is not set off by commas. In the second sentence, the same clause is not essential to the meaning because it does not limit what it modifies, *The two drivers involved in the accident,* but merely provides additional information about these drivers. Therefore, it *is* set off with commas.

Notice how using or not using commas to set off such an element can change the meaning of a sentence.

The bus drivers rejecting the management offer remained on strike.

The bus drivers, rejecting the management offer, remained on strike.

In the first sentence, not using commas to set off the phrase *rejecting the management offer* makes the phrase restrictive, limiting the meaning of *The bus drivers.* This sentence says that only some of the total group of bus drivers, the ones who rejected the offer, remained on strike, implying that other drivers went back to work. In the second sentence, the commas around the phrase make it nonrestrictive, implying that *The bus drivers* refers to all of the drivers and that all of them remained on strike.

To decide whether an element is restrictive or nonrestrictive, mentally delete the element, and then decide whether the deletion changes the meaning of the rest of the sentence or makes it unclear. If it does, the element is probably restrictive and should not be set off with commas. If it does not, the element is probably nonrestrictive and requires commas.

1 Adjective and adverb clauses

For more about adjective clauses, see 31c4.

For more about subordinating conjunctions, see 31b7; for more about adverb clauses, see 31c4.

Adjective clauses begin with *who, whom, whose, which, that, when, where,* or *why.* Adverb clauses begin with *when, where,* or another subordinating conjunction, such as *because, although,* or *before.* Adverb clauses are usually essential to the meaning of the sentence; in general, do not set them off with commas unless they precede the independent clause or begin with *although, even though, while,* or another conjunction expressing the idea of contrast.

▶ **The city renovated Straus Park, which soon became a popular gathering place.**

The adjective clause beginning with *which* is not essential to the meaning of *Straus Park* and therefore is set off with a comma.

▶ **The park soon became a popular gathering place, although some nearby residents complained about the noise.**

The adverb clause *although some nearby residents complained about the noise* expresses the idea of contrast; therefore, it is set off with a comma.

RESTRICTIVE CLAUSES

I grew up in a house *where the only regular guests were my relations.*
                              – RICHARD RODRIGUEZ, "Aria: Memoir of a Bilingual Childhood"

The claim *that men like seriously to battle one another to some sort of finish* is a myth.   – JOHN MCMURTRY, "Kill 'Em! Crush 'Em! Eat 'Em Raw!"

An adjective clause that begins with *that* is always restrictive and is not set off with commas. An adjective clause beginning with *which* may be either restrictive or nonrestrictive; however, some writers prefer to use *which* only for nonrestrictive clauses.

2 Participles and phrases

Participles and participial phrases may be either restrictive or nonrestrictive. Prepositional phrases are usually restrictive but sometimes are not essential to the meaning of a sentence and are therefore set off with commas.

●— For more about
participles and
participial and
prepositional
phrases, see
31c3.

NONRESTRICTIVE PHRASES

▶ **Stephanie, amazed, stared at the strange vehicle.**

The participle *amazed* does not limit the meaning of *Stephanie*.

▶ **Many baby boomers, fearing that Social Security funds will run out, are saving for their future retirement through company investment plans.**

The participial phrase beginning with *fearing* does not limit the meaning of *Many baby boomers* or change the central meaning of the sentence.

▶ The bodyguards, in dark suits and matching ties, looked quite
   ⌃   ⌃
intimidating.

The prepositional phrase *in dark suits and matching ties* does not limit the meaning of *The bodyguards*.

RESTRICTIVE PHRASES

A penny *saved* is a penny *earned*.
[Without *saved* and *earned*, the sentence does not say much.]

Wood *cut from living trees* does not burn as well as dead wood.
[The participial phrase *cut from living trees* is essential to the meaning.]

The bodyguards were the men *in dark suits and matching ties*.
[The prepositional phrase *in dark suits and matching ties* is essential to the meaning.]

3 Appositives

An **appositive** is a noun or noun substitute that renames a nearby noun or noun substitute. When an appositive is not essential to identify what it renames, it is set off with commas.

NONRESTRICTIVE APPOSITIVES

▶ Ms. Baker, my high school chemistry teacher, inspired my love of science.
   ⌃   ⌃

Ms. Baker's name identifies her; the appositive simply provides extra information.

▶ Beethoven's opera, *Fidelio*, includes the famous "Prisoners' Chorus."
   ⌃   ⌃

Beethoven wrote only one opera, so its name is not essential.

RESTRICTIVE APPOSITIVES

The editorial cartoonist *Thomas Nast* helped bring about the downfall of the Tweed ring in New York City.
[The appositive *Thomas Nast* identifies the specific cartoonist.]

Mozart's opera *The Marriage of Figaro* was considered revolutionary.
[The appositive is restrictive because Mozart wrote more than one opera.]

EXERCISE 48.3

Use commas to set off nonrestrictive clauses, phrases, and appositives in any of the following sentences that contain such elements.

1. Anyone who is fourteen years old faces strong peer pressure every day.

2. Embalming is a technique that preserves a cadaver.

3. I would feel right at home in the city dump which bears a striking resemblance to my bedroom.

4. The rescue workers exhausted and discouraged stared ahead without speaking.

5. The building across the street from Julio's apartment is the only one on the block with a door attendant.

6. The Zunis an ancient tribe live in New Mexico.

7. The marsh is completely surrounded by brand-new homes.

8. Genevieve de Gaulle-Anthonioz a niece of the former president of France spent time in a Nazi concentration camp during World War II.

9. Birds' hearts have four chambers whereas reptiles' have three.

10. My grandfather always picked up pennies if he saw them lying on the sidewalk.

PUNCTUATION

Using Commas to Separate Items in a Series

www ● bedford stmartins.com/ smhandbook

For additional exercises on using commas with nonrestrictive elements, click on

▶ **Exercise Central**
  ▶ **Commas**

48d Using commas to separate items in a series

A comma is used between items in a series of three or more words, phrases, or clauses.

I bumped into professors, horizontal bars, agricultural students, and swinging iron rings.   –JAMES THURBER, "University Days"

He has plundered our seas, ravaged our coasts, burnt our towns, and destroyed the lives of our people.
    – THOMAS JEFFERSON, Declaration of Independence

You may see a series with no comma after the next-to-last item, particularly in newspaper writing. Occasionally, however, omitting the comma can cause confusion, and you will never be wrong if you include it.

▶ **Diners had a choice of broccoli, green beans, peas, and carrots.**
          ^

Without the comma after *peas,* you wouldn't know if there were three choices (the third being a *mixture* of peas and carrots) or four.

When the items in a series contain commas of their own or other punctuation, separate them with semicolons rather than commas.

For more about using semicolons to separate items in a series, see 49b.

Coordinate adjectives, those that relate equally to the noun they modify, should be separated by commas.

The *long, twisting, muddy* road led to a shack in the woods.

In a sentence like *The cracked bathroom mirror reflected his face,* however, *cracked* and *bathroom* are not coordinate because *bathroom mirror* is the equivalent of a single word, which is modified by *cracked.* Hence they are *not* separated by commas.

You can usually determine whether adjectives are coordinate by inserting *and* between them. If the sentence makes sense with the *and,* the adjectives are coordinate and should be separated by commas.

They are sincere *and* talented *and* inquisitive researchers.
[The sentence makes sense with the *and*'s, so the adjectives should be separated by commas: *They are sincere, talented, inquisitive researchers.*]

▶ **Byron carried an elegant *and* gold *and* pocket watch.**

The sentence does not make sense with the *and*'s, so the adjectives should not be separated by commas: *Byron carried an elegant gold pocket watch.*

www • bedford stmartins.com/ smhandbook

For additional exercises on using commas with items in a series, click on

▶ **Exercise Central**
 ▶ **Commas**

EXERCISE 48.4

Revise any of the following sentences that require commas to set off words, phrases, or clauses in a series.

1. They found employment in truck driving farming and mining.

2. We bought zucchini peppers and tomatoes at the market.

3. A high center of gravity a narrow wheel base and the fact that a typical owner drives the vehicle at highway speeds all contribute to SUV rollovers.

4. Anouk enrolled in courses in history statistics and geometry.

5. The tiny brown-eyed Lafayette twins were the only children in the kindergarten class who could already read.

6. Supermarket cashiers need to know several skills: how to bag groceries properly how to make correct change and how to identify dozens of different fruits and vegetables.

7. The ball sailed over the fence across the road and through the Wilsons' living room window.

8. I timidly offered to help a loud overbearing lavishly dressed customer.

9. The restaurant continued to advertise for an experienced pizza chef.

10. These Dick Vitale clones insist on calling every play judging every move and telling everyone within earshot exactly what is wrong with the team.

Parenthetical expressions are added comments or information. Because they often interrupt or digress, they are usually set off with commas. Transitional expressions are also usually set off with commas. They include conjunctive adverbs such as *however* and *furthermore* and other words and phrases used to connect parts of sentences.

> Some studies, *incidentally*, have shown that chocolate, *of all things*, helps prevent tooth decay.

> Roald Dahl's stories, *it turns out*, were often inspired by his own childhood.

> Ceiling fans are, *moreover*, less expensive than air conditioners.

> Ozone is a by-product of dry cleaning, *for example*.

●⸳⸳ For full lists of transitional expressions, see 5d4 and 31b7.

48f Using commas to set off contrasting elements, interjections, direct address, and tag questions

▦ Contrasting elements

> On official business it was she, *not my father*, one would usually hear on the phone or in stores.
>
> – RICHARD RODRIGUEZ, "Aria: A Memoir of a Bilingual Childhood"

●⸳⸳ For information on using a dash to set off material, see 53c.

▦ Interjections

> *My God*, who wouldn't want a wife?   – JUDY BRADY, "I Want a Wife"

> We had hiked for, *say*, seven miles before stopping to rest.

▦ Direct address

> *My friends*, I must say to you that we have not made a single gain in civil rights without determined legal and nonviolent pressure.
>
> – MARTIN LUTHER KING JR., "Letter from Birmingham Jail"

▦ Tag questions

> The governor did not veto the unemployment bill, *did she?*

**www • bedford
stmartins.com/
smhandbook**

For additional
exercises on using
commas with
parenthetical
and transitional
expressions,
click on

▶ Exercise Central
  ▶ Commas

● **EXERCISE 48.5**

Revise each of the following sentences, using commas to set off parenthetical and transitional expressions, contrasting elements, interjections, words used in direct address, and tag questions.

1. One must consider the society as a whole not just its parts.
2. Many of the parents and students did in fact support the position of the teacher who resigned.
3. Her friends did not know about her illness did they?
4. The drought this year will it appears prevent him from watering his garden.
5. Ladies and gentlemen I bid you farewell.

48g Using commas with dates, addresses, titles, and numbers

Commas are used according to established rules with dates, addresses and place-names, and numbers. Commas are also used to separate personal and professional titles from the names preceding them.

■ Dates

Use a comma between the day of the week and the month, between the day of the month and the year, and between the year and the rest of the sentence, if any.

> The attacks on the morning of *Tuesday, September 11, 2001,* took the United States by surprise.

Do not use commas with dates in inverted order or with dates consisting of only the month and the year.

> 18 October 2002

> Thousands of Germans swarmed over and through the wall in *November 1989* and effectively demolished it.

■ Addresses and place-names

Use a comma after each part of an address or place-name, including the state if no ZIP code is given. Do not precede a ZIP code with a comma.

> Forward my mail to the Department of English, The Ohio State University, Columbus, Ohio 43210.

> Portland, Oregon, is much larger than Portland, Maine.

■ *Titles*

Use commas to set off a title such as *M.D.*, *Esq.*, and so on from the name preceding it and from the rest of the sentence. The titles *Jr.* and *Sr.*, however, are often *not* set off by commas.

Jaime Mejia, *Ph.D.*, will speak about his anthropological research.

Martin Luther King *Jr.* was one of the twentieth century's greatest orators.

■ *Numbers*

In numbers of five digits or more, use a comma between each group of three digits, starting from the right.

The city's population rose to *17,126* in the 2000 census.

The comma is optional within numbers of four digits but is never used in years with four digits. Use a comma with numbers of more than four digits.

The college has an enrollment of *1,789* [or *1789*] this semester.

The French Revolution began in *1789*.

Do not use a comma within house or building numbers, ZIP codes, or page numbers.

My parents live at *11311* Wimberly Drive, Richmond, Virginia *23233*.

Turn to page *1566*.

EXERCISE 48.6

Revise each of the following sentences, using commas appropriately with page numbers, dates, addresses and place-names, titles, and numbers.

1. The abridged version of the assigned novel is 1200 pages long.

2. More than 350000 people gathered for the protest on the Washington Mall.

3. The *Titanic* hit an iceberg on April 14 1912 and sank in about two hours, drowning 1503 people.

4. MLA headquarters are at 10 Astor Place New York New York 10003.

5. The nameplate read *Donald Good R.N.* and looked quite impressive.

www ● bedford
stmartins.com/
smhandbook

For additional
exercises on using
commas with
dates, addresses,
titles, and numbers,
click on

► Exercise Central
► Commas

48h Using commas with quotations

Commas set off a quotation from words used to introduce or identify the source of the quotation. A comma following a quotation goes *inside* the closing quotation mark.

"No one becomes depraved all at once," wrote Juvenal.

A German proverb warns, "Go to law for a sheep, and lose your cow."

"All I know about grammar," said Joan Didion, "is its infinite power."

For information on using colons to introduce quotations, see 53d.

Do not use a comma after a question mark or exclamation point.

▶ "What's a thousand dollars?," asks Groucho Marx in *Cocoanuts*. "Mere chicken feed. A poultry matter."

▶ "Out, damned spot!," cries Lady Macbeth.

Do not use a comma to introduce a quotation with *that*.

▶ The writer of Ecclesiastes concludes that, "all is vanity."

Do not use a comma with a quotation when the rest of the sentence includes more than the words used to introduce or identify the source of the quotation.

▶ People who say, "Have a nice day" irritate me.

Do not use a comma before an indirect quotation, one that does not use the speaker's exact words.

▶ In a famous speech, Patrick Henry declared, that he wanted either liberty or death.

▶ Abigail Adams said, all men would like to be tyrants.

www • bedford stmartins.com/ smhandbook

For additional exercises on using commas to set off quotations, click on

▶ Exercise Central
  ▶ Commas

EXERCISE 48.7

Insert a comma in any of the following sentences that require one.

1. "The public be damned!" William Henry Vanderbilt was reported to have said. "I'm working for my stockholders."

2. My professor insisted "The cutting edge gets dull very quickly."

3. Who remarked that "youth is wasted on the young"?

4. "Neat people are lazier and meaner than sloppy people" according to Suzanne Britt.

5. "Who goes there?" shouted the soldier nervously.

48i Using commas to facilitate understanding

Sometimes a comma is necessary to make a sentence much easier to read or understand.

▶ The members of the dance troupe strutted in, in matching tuxedos and top hats.

▶ Before, I had planned to major in biology.

48j Checking for unnecessary commas

Excessive use of commas can spoil an otherwise fine sentence.

■ Around restrictive elements

Do not use commas to set off restrictive elements, which limit, or define, the meaning of the words they modify or refer to.

●— For more about restrictive elements, see 48c.

▶ I don't let my children watch TV shows, that are violent.

▶ A law, reforming campaign financing, was passed in 2002.

▶ My only defense, against my allergies, is to stay indoors.

▶ The actor, Russell Crowe, has played in a rock band for many years.

■ Between subjects and verbs, verbs and objects or complements, and prepositions and objects

Do not use a comma between a subject and its verb, a verb and its object or complement, or a preposition and its object. This rule holds true even if the subject, object, or complement is a long phrase or clause.

▶ Watching movies on my VCR late at night, has become an important way for me to relax.

▶ Parents must decide, how much TV their children may watch.

▶ The winner of, the trophy for outstanding community service stepped forward.

■ *In compound constructions*

Do not use a comma before or after a coordinating conjunction joining the two parts of a compound construction (other than a compound sentence).

▶ Meridel Le Sueur worked as a stuntwoman, and trained as an actress and a writer.

■ *In a series*

Do not use a comma before the first or after the last item in a series.

▶ The auction included, furniture, paintings, and china.

▶ The swimmer took slow, powerful, strokes.

www ● bedford
stmartins.com/
smhandbook

For additional
exercises on
unnecessary
commas, click on

▶ Exercise Central
  ▶ Commas

FOR COLLABORATION

Working with one other person in your class, revise each of the following sentences, deleting unnecessary commas. Bring an explanation to class for every change you decide to make.

1. Awards are given for, best actor, best actress, best supporting actor, and best supporting actress, every year.

2. Observers watch facial expressions and gestures, and interpret them.

3. We could see nothing, except jagged peaks, for miles around.

4. Everyone in the high school auditorium that night, felt strongly about the proposed zoning changes.

5. Clothes, that had to be ironed, were too much trouble.

6. Before we got into the sun-baked car, we opened the doors, and waited for a few minutes.

7. Students, with high scores on standardized tests, do not necessarily get high grades in college.

8. The photographer, Edward Curtis, is known for his depiction of the West.

9. We all took panicked, hasty, looks at our notebooks.

10. An invitation to buy prescription drugs online, and an offer for golf balls, were two of the junk email messages waiting in my computer's mailbox.

THINKING CRITICALLY ABOUT COMMAS

Reading with an Eye for Commas

The following poem uses commas to create rhythm and guide readers. Read the poem aloud, listening especially to the effect of the commas at the end of the first and fifth lines. Then read it again as if those commas were omitted, noting the difference. What is the effect of the poet's decision *not* to use a comma at the end of the third line?

Some say the world will end in fire,
Some say in ice.
From what I've tasted of desire
I hold with those who favor fire.
But if it had to perish twice,
I think I know enough of hate
To say that for destruction ice
Is also great
And would suffice.
   – ROBERT FROST, "Fire and Ice"

Thinking about Your Own Use of Commas

The following passage has had all of the author's commas removed. Punctuate the passage with commas as seems appropriate to you, and then explain in writing why you put commas where you did. Finally, check over your use of commas, consulting this chapter for guidance and noting any problems or observations.

And here was another strange thing about Myers. He not only did nothing for a living but he appeared to have no history. He came from Elkhart Indiana but beyond this fact nobody seemed to know anything about him—not even how he had met my aunt Margaret. Reconstructed from his conversation a picture of Elkhart emerged for us that showed it as a flat place consisting chiefly of ball parks poolrooms and hardware stores. Aunt Margaret came from Chicago which consisted of the Loop Marshall Field's assorted priests and monsignors and the black-and-white problem. How had these two worlds impinged? Where our family spoke freely of its relations real and imaginary Myers spoke of no one not even a parent. At the very beginning when my father's old touring car which had been shipped on still remained in our garage Myers had certain seedy cronies whom he took riding in it or who simply sat in it in our driveway as if anchored in a houseboat; but when the car went they went or were banished. Uncle Myers and Aunt Margaret had no friends no couples with whom they exchanged visits — only a middle-aged black-haired small emaciated woman with a German name and a yellowed skin whom we were taken to see one afternoon because she was dying of cancer. . . .   – MARY McCARTHY, *Memories of a Catholic Girlhood*

▼ Using Semicolons

49a Using semicolons to link independent clauses

You can join independent clauses in several ways: with a comma and a coordinating conjunction (see 48b), with a colon (see 53d), with a dash (see 53c), or with a semicolon. Semicolons provide writers with subtle ways of signaling closely related clauses. The clause following a semicolon often restates an idea expressed in the first clause, and it sometimes expands on or presents a contrast to the first. As a writer, you must choose when and where to use semicolons to signal such relationships.

> Immigration acts were passed; newcomers had to prove, besides moral correctness and financial solvency, their ability to read.   – MARY GORDON, "More Than Just a Shrine"

> They were bigger; he was quicker. Their bench was deeper; he was in better shape. They struggled shooting; he was dead-eyed.
> – JOE DRAPE
> "Even without Much Help, Barkley Halts Hoyas"

In the first sentence, Gordon uses a semicolon to lead to a clause that expands on the statement made in the first clause. She might have joined the two clauses with *and* or *so*, but the semicolon gives the sentence an abrupt, clipped rhythm that suits the topic: laws that imposed strict requirements. In the second example, the semicolons link

If you've ever pored over the fine print at the bottom of an ad for a big sale, looking for the opening hours or the address of the store nearest you, then you've seen plenty of semicolons in action. Here's an example from a Bloomingdale's ad:

Store Hours —
Short Hills: SUN., 12 – 6;
MON., 10 – 9:30;
TUES., 10 – 5; WED. through
FRI., 10 – 9:30; SAT., 10 – 8.

The semicolons separate the information for one day's hours from the next. Semicolons, which create a pause stronger than that of a comma but not as strong as that of a period, are used primarily to link independent clauses and to separate items in a series.
   This chapter will help you use semicolons effectively in your own writing. ■

1. Note any semicolons. If you find few or none, look at each sentence together with the one that follows. Are there any pairs of sentences that express closely related ideas that would be stronger if combined into one sentence using a semicolon? (49a)

2. Make sure semicolons are used only between independent clauses or between items in a series. If you have used a semicolon between an independent clause and a dependent clause or a phrase, change it to a comma. If you have used a semicolon before the *first* item in a series, change it to a colon. (49b and d)

3. Do semicolons separate more than three independent clauses in a sentence, or do they separate clauses in more than two consecutive sentences? If so, would making some clauses into separate sentences make the writing smoother or less monotonous? (49c)

contrasting clauses; the contrasts between the clauses are far more immediate than if Drape had used *but* to join the clauses.

A semicolon can also be used to link independent clauses joined by conjunctive adverbs such as *therefore, however,* and *indeed* or transitional expressions such as *in fact, in addition,* and *for example.*

For more about
conjunctive
adverbs and
transitional
expressions,
see 39c.

> The circus comes as close to being the world in microcosm as anything I know; in a way, it puts all the rest of show business in the shade.
> – E. B. WHITE, "The Ring of Time"

If two independent clauses joined by a coordinating conjunction contain commas, you may use a semicolon instead of a comma before the conjunction to make the sentence easier to read.

> Every year, whether the Republican or the Democratic Party is in office, more and more power drains away from the individual to feed vast reservoirs in far-off places; and we have less and less say about the shape of events which shape our future.
> – WILLIAM F. BUCKLEY JR., "Why Don't We Complain?"

FOR COLLABORATION

Working with another member of your class, use the four examples in 49a as models for sentences you write collaboratively. Bring your sentences to class, and compare them with those written by your classmates.

PUNCTUATION

Checking for
Overused
Semicolons

**www • bedford
stmartins.com/
smhandbook**

For additional
exercises on using
semicolons with
independent
clauses, click on

▸ **Exercise Central**
  ▸ **Semicolons**

● **EXERCISE 49.1**

Combine each of the following pairs of sentences into one sentence by using a semicolon. Example:

>   *m*
> Take the bus to Henderson Street,; Meet me under the clock.
>   ^

1. Joining the chorus was a great experience for Will. It helped him express his musical talent and gave him a social life.
2. City life offers many advantages. In many ways, however, life in a small town is much more pleasant.
3. Florida's mild winter climate is ideal for bicycling. In addition, the terrain is very flat.
4. The voting machines in poorer counties were most likely to reject correctly punched ballots. Therefore, the voting system favors people in wealthier areas.
5. The debate over political correctness affects more than the curriculum. It also affects students' social relationships.

49b   Using semicolons to separate items in a series

Ordinarily, commas separate items in a series. But when the items themselves contain commas or other punctuation, using semicolons to separate the items will make the sentence clearer and easier to read. Such a series is best placed at the *end* of a sentence.

> Anthropology encompasses several fields: archaeology, the study of ancient civilizations through artifacts; linguistics, the study of the structure and development of language; and cultural anthropology, the study of the way of life of various peoples, especially small, nonindustrialized societies.

Note that a semicolon should never be used to *introduce* a series; use a colon instead.

● For more about
using commas
with items in a
series, see 48d.

49c   Checking for overused semicolons

If semicolons are used too often, they distract readers by calling attention to themselves instead of to what the writer is saying. In addition, sentence upon sentence punctuated with semicolons will sound monotonous and jerky.

www ● bedford
stmartins.com/
smhandbook

For additional
exercises on
semicolons and
other punctuation,
click on

► Exercise Central
  ► Semicolons

► Like many people in public life, he spoke with confidence; perhaps he even spoke with arrogance; yet I noted a certain anxiety; it touched and puzzled me; he seemed too eager to demonstrate his control of a situation and his command of the necessary data.

EXERCISE 49.2

Revise the following passage, substituting other punctuation for some of the semicolons. Add or delete words if necessary.

Remember when the neighborhood kids played football out in the vacant lot; they were there every Saturday, having a good time. Whatever happened to just playing for a good time? Now uniformed coaches yell at young players to win; they put more and more pressure on them; and parents join in the chant of win, win, win; in fact, if the child is not a winner, he or she must be—that's right—a loser. The young athlete is constantly told that winning is everything; what used to be fun is now just like a job; play to win, the adults say, or do not play at all.

49d Checking for misused semicolons

A comma, not a semicolon, should separate an independent clause from a dependent clause or a phrase.

► The police found a set of fingerprints; which they used to identify the thief.

A colon, not a semicolon, should introduce a series.

► The tour includes visits to the following art museums; the Prado, in Madrid; the Louvre, in Paris; and the Rijksmuseum, in Amsterdam.

49e Using semicolons with quotation marks

Ordinarily, a semicolon goes *outside* closing quotation marks.

Shirley Jackson's most famous story is "The Lottery"; it is a horrifying allegory about the power of tradition and the search for scapegoats.

Reading with an Eye for Semicolons

The author of the following paragraph describes a solar eclipse in elaborate detail, using semicolons to separate many parts of her description. Read the paragraph with attention to the use of semicolons. What different effect would the paragraph have if the author had used periods instead of semicolons? Imagine also that she had used commas and coordinating conjunctions. What is the effect of all the semicolons?

> You see the wide world swaddled in darkness; you see a vast breadth of hilly land, and an enormous, distant, blackened valley; you see towns' lights, a river's path, and blurred portions of your hat and scarf; you see your husband's face looking like an early black-and-white film; and you see a sprawl of black sky and blue sky together, with unfamiliar stars in it, some barely visible bands of cloud, and over there, a small white ring. The ring is as small as one goose in a flock of migrating geese — if you happen to notice a flock of migrating geese. It is one 360th part of the visible sky. The sun we see is less than half the diameter of a dime held at arms' length.
>
> – ANNIE DILLARD, "Solar Eclipse"

Thinking about Your Own Use of Semicolons

Think of something you might take five or ten minutes to observe — a football game, a brewing storm, an ant awkwardly carrying a crumb — and write a paragraph describing your observations point by point and using semicolons to separate each point, as Annie Dillard does in the preceding paragraph. When you have finished, look at the way you used semicolons. Are there places where a period or a comma and a coordinating conjunction would better serve your meaning? Revise appropriately. What can you conclude about effective ways of using semicolons? If you keep a writing log, record your thoughts there.

50

◥ Using End Punctuation

50a Using periods

Use a period to close sentences that make statements or give mild commands.

> After six years in the NBA, I've learned how to play through struggles. — ALLEN IVERSON

A period also closes indirect questions, which report rather than ask questions.

> I asked how old the child was.

> Many parents ask if autism is an inherited disorder.

In American English, periods are also used with most abbreviations.

Mr.	B.C.E.	Jr.
Ms.	A.D.	Ph.D.
Mrs.	ibid.	M.D.
A.M./a.m.	Dr.	M.B.A.
P.M./p.m.	Sen.	R.N.

Some abbreviations do not require periods. Among them are the postal abbreviations of state names, such as *FL* and *TN* (though the traditional abbreviations, such as *Fla.* and *Tenn.,* do call for periods), and most groups of initials

→ If you find that all or almost all of your sentences end with periods, see
if any of them might be phrased more effectively as questions or exclamations. (50a, b, and c)
→ Check to be sure you use question marks appropriately. (50b)
→ Do you use exclamation points? If so, consider carefully whether they
are justified. Does the sentence call for extra emphasis? If in doubt, use
a period instead. (50c)

(*MLA, CIA, AIDS, UNICEF*). If you are not sure whether a particular
abbreviation should include periods, check a dictionary.

●—— For more about
abbreviations,
see Chapter 55.

● **EXERCISE 50.1**

Revise each of the following sentences by inserting periods in the appropriate
places. Example:

Ms. Maria Ortiz received both a Ph.D. in chemistry and an M.Ed.
‸   ‸ ‸   ‸ ‸

1. Please attend the meeting on Tuesday at 10:00 AM in Room 401.

2. Cleopatra committed suicide in 30 BCE when she was about thirty-nine years
old

3. "Have you lost something, Charles?" I inquired

4. Trish asked the receptionist if Dr Margolies had office hours that afternoon

5. A voluntary effort by the AMA could help contain hospital costs

**www ● bedford
stmartins.com/
smhandbook**

For additional
exercises on
periods, click on

▶ **Exercise Central**
  ▶ **End Punctuation**

50b Using question marks

A question mark closes sentences that ask direct questions.

If you own things, what's their effect on you?
> – E. M. FORSTER, "My Wood"

Who will be left to celebrate a victory made of blood and fire?
> – THICH NHAT HANH, "Our Green Garden"

Question marks do not close *indirect* questions, which report rather than ask questions. Indirect questions close with a period.

▶ **She asked whether I opposed his nomination?.**

Do not use a comma or a period after a question mark that ends a direct quotation.

▶ **"Am I my brother's keeper?," Cain asked.**

▶ **Cain asked, "Am I my brother's keeper?,"**

For more on
question marks
and quotation
marks, see 52e.

A polite request phrased as a question can be followed by a period rather than a question mark.

Would you please close the door.

Questions in a series may have question marks even when they are not separate sentences.

I often confronted a difficult choice: should I go to practice? finish my homework? spend time with my friends?

A question mark in parentheses can be used to indicate that a writer is unsure of a date, a figure, or a word.

Quintilian died in A.D. 96 (?).

www • bedford
stmartins.com/
smhandbook

For additional
exercises on
question marks,
click on

▶ Exercise Central
  ▶ End Punctuation

● **EXERCISE 50.2**

Revise each of the following sentences, adding question marks and substituting them for other punctuation where appropriate. Not all of the sentences require question marks. Example:

She asked the travel agent, "What is the air fare to Greece/?"

1. Social scientists face difficult questions: should they use their knowledge to shape society, merely describe human behavior, or try to do both.
2. Did the employees realize that the company was in danger of bankruptcy.
3. "Can I play this" asked Manuel.
4. The interviewer asked why the actor had taken such a demanding role.
5. The judge asked, "What is your verdict."

Exclamation points show surprise or strong emotion.

> In those few moments of geologic time will be the story of all that has happened since we became a nation. And what a story it will be!
>
> —JAMES RETTIE, "But a Watch in the Night"

Ouch!

Look out!

Use exclamation points sparingly because they can distract your readers or suggest that you are exaggerating the importance of what you are saying. Do not, for instance, use them with mild interjections or to suggest sarcasm or criticism. In general, try to create emphasis through diction and sentence structure rather than with exclamation points.

● For more on creating emphasis through diction and sentence structure, see Chapter 27 and 43a.

▶ **This university is so large, so varied, that attempting to tell someone**

  everything about it would take three years!.
                                              ^

Do not use a comma or a period after an exclamation point that ends a direct quotation.

▶ **"Happiness hates the timid!" according to Eugene O'Neill, who went**

  on to add, "So does Science!",

● **EXERCISE 50.3**

Revise each of the following sentences, adding or deleting exclamation points where appropriate and removing any other unnecessary punctuation you find. Example:

  Look out,/! The tide is coming in fast,/!
           ^   ^

1. The court denied a New Jersey woman's petition to continue raising tigers in her backyard!

2. I screamed at Jamie, "You rat. You tricked me."

3. "This time we're starting early!," she shouted.

4. Help. I can't swim.

5. Oh, no. We've lost the house.

www ● bedford
stmartins.com/
smhandbook

For additional exercises on exclamation points, click on

▶ **Exercise Central**
  ▶ **End Punctuation**

Reading with an Eye for End Punctuation

Consider the use of end punctuation in the following paragraph. Then experiment with the end punctuation. What would be the effect of deleting the exclamation point from the quotation by Cicero or of changing it to a question mark? What would be the effect of changing Cicero's question to a statement?

> To be admired and praised, especially by the young, is an autumnal pleasure enjoyed by the lucky ones (who are not always the most deserving). "What is more charming," Cicero observes in his famous essay *De Senectute,* "than an old age surrounded by the enthusiasm of youth! . . . Attentions which seem trivial and conventional are marks of honor—the morning call, being sought after, precedence, having people rise for you, being escorted to and from the forum. . . . What pleasures of the body can be compared to the prerogatives of influence?" But there are also pleasures of the body, or the mind, that are enjoyed by a greater number of older persons.
>
> – MALCOLM COWLEY, *The View from 80*

Thinking about Your Own Use of End Punctuation

Look through something you have written recently, noting its end punctuation. Using the guidelines at the beginning of this chapter, see if your use of end punctuation follows any patterns. Try revising the end punctuation in a paragraph or two to emphasize (or de-emphasize) some point. What conclusions can you draw about ways of using end punctuation to draw attention to (or away from) a sentence? If you keep a writing log, note your observations there.

51 ▾ Using Apostrophes

51a Using apostrophes to signal possessive case

The possessive case denotes ownership or possession of one thing by another (see 32a3). Apostrophes are used in the possessive case of nouns and some pronouns.

▬ Singular nouns and indefinite pronouns

Add an apostrophe and *-s* to form the possessive of most singular nouns, including those that end in *-s,* and of indefinite pronouns.

▶ Marilyn Monroe's early movies are considered classics.

▶ *Star Wars* made George Lucas's fortune.

▶ Anyone's guess is as good as mine.

Apostrophes are not used with the possessive forms of *personal* pronouns: *yours, his, hers, its, ours, theirs.*

▬ Plural nouns

For plural nouns that do not end in *-s,* add an apostrophe and *-s.*

▶ Most suits in the mens' department are appropriate business attire.

[margin note]

The little apostrophe can sometimes make a big difference in meaning. One man found that out when he agreed to look after a neighbor's apartment while she was out of town. "I'll leave instructions on the kitchen counter," the neighbor said as she gave him her key. Here are the instructions he found: "(1) Please water the plants in the living room—once will be fine. (2) The cat's food is on the counter. Once a day on the patio. Thanks. I'll see you Friday."

Because the note said *cat's,* he expected one cat—and when he saw one, he put it and the food outside on the patio. When the neighbor returned, she found one healthy cat—and a second, very weak one that had hidden under the bed. The difference between *cat's* and *cats'* in this instance almost cost his neighbor a cat. This chapter will help you use apostrophes carefully. ▬

For plural nouns ending in *-s*, add only the apostrophe.

clowns'
▶ **The three c͟l͟o͟w͟n͟'͟s͟ costumes were bright green and orange.**

■ *Compound words*

For compound words, make the last word in the group possessive.

> The *secretary of state's* speech was televised.

> Both her *daughters-in-law's* birthdays fall in July.

> My *in-laws'* disapproval dampened our enthusiasm for the new house.

■ *Two or more nouns*

To signal individual possession by two or more owners, make each noun possessive.

> The differences between Ridley Scott's and Jerry Bruckheimer's action films are enormous.
> [Scott and Bruckheimer make different films.]

To signal joint possession, make only the last noun possessive.

> Wallace and Gromit's creator is Nick Park.
> [Wallace and Gromit have the same creator.]

EDITING FOR POSSESSIVE APOSTROPHES

1. Circle all the nouns that end in *-s*. Then check each one that shows ownership or possession to see that it has an apostrophe in the right place, either before or after the *-s*.

2. Then underline all the indefinite pronouns, such as *someone* and *nobody*. (See 31b3 for a list.) Any that end in *-s* should have an apostrophe before the *-s*.

● **EXERCISE 51.1**

Write a brief paragraph, beginning "I've always been amused by my neighbor's (or roommate's) _____." Then note every use of an apostrophe.

● **EXERCISE 51.2**

Complete each of the following sentences by inserting 's or an apostrophe alone to form the possessive case of the italicized words.

1. Grammar is *everybody* favorite subject.
2. *Britney Spears* musical career may not last as long as *Madonna* has.
3. She insists that her personal life is *nobody* business.
4. *Carol and Jim* income dropped drastically after Jim lost his job.
5. Parents often question their *children* choice of friends.
6. Many smokers disregard the *surgeon general* warnings.
7. *A.J.* older *brother* name is Griffin.
8. The *trees* leaves were turning brown all over the county during the long drought.
9. This dog has a *beagle* ears and a *St. Bernard* nose and feet.
10. *Michelle Kwan and Sarah Hughes* performances in the long program brought Hughes a gold medal and Kwan a bronze.

**www • bedford
stmartins.com/
smhandbook**

For additional
exercises on
forming
possessives,
click on

▶ **Exercise Central**
  ▶ **Apostrophes**

51b Using apostrophes to signal contractions and other omissions

Contractions are two-word combinations formed by leaving out certain letters, which are indicated by an apostrophe.

it is, it has/it's	I would, I had/I'd	will not/won't
was not/wasn't	he would, he had/he'd	let us/let's
I am/I'm	would not/wouldn't	who is, who has/who's
he is, he has/he's	do not/don't	cannot/can't
you will/you'll	does not/doesn't	

Contractions are common in conversation and informal writing. Some academic and professional work, however, calls for greater formality.

■ *Distinguishing its and it's*

Do not confuse the possessive pronoun *its* with the contraction *it's*. *Its* is the possessive form of *it*. *It's* is a contraction for *it is* or *it has*.

▶ **This disease is unusual; it's symptoms vary from person to person.**

▶ It's a difficult disease to diagnose.

▶ Waving goodbye, Zainab said, "It's been great to meet you."

EDITING FOR CORRECT USE OF ITS AND IT'S

> 1. Check each *its*. Does it show possession? If not, add an apostrophe before the *-s*.
>
> 2. Check each *it's*. Does it mean "it is" or "it has"? If not, remove the apostrophe.

■ **Signaling omissions**

An apostrophe signals omissions in some common phrases:

ten of the clock	rock and roll	class of 2003
ten o'clock	rock 'n' roll	class of '03

In addition, writers can use an apostrophe to signal omitted letters in approximating the sound of speech or some specific dialect. Note the way Mark Twain uses the apostrophe to form contractions and signal omitted letters in the following passage, in which Huckleberry Finn tells Jim about King Henry VIII:

> S'pose people left money laying around where he was—what did he do? He collared it. S'pose he contracted to do a thing; and you paid him, and didn't set down there and see that he done it—what did he do? He always done the other thing. S'pose he opened his mouth—what then? If he didn't shut it up powerful quick, he'd lose a lie, every time. That's the kind of a bug Henry was; and if we'd 'a' had him along 'stead of our kings, he'd 'a' fooled that town a heap worse than ourn done.
>
> – MARK TWAIN, *The Adventures of Huckleberry Finn*

51c Using apostrophes to form certain plurals

An apostrophe and *-s* are used to form the plural of abbreviations that take periods and of numbers, letters, symbols, and words referred to as such.

The gymnasts need marks of *8*'s and *9*'s to qualify for the finals.

Several Cessna *150*'s were lined up for takeoff.

Many *Ph.D.*'s cannot find jobs as college teachers.

The computer prints *e*'s whenever there is an error in the program.

I marked special passages with a series of three *'s.

The five *Shakespeare*'s in the essay were spelled five different ways.

The plural of years is usually written without an apostrophe (*1990s*). However, when the century is omitted from a decade, an apostrophe marks the omission (*the music of the '80s*).

● EXERCISE 51.3

The following sentences, from which all apostrophes have been deleted, appear in Langston Hughes's "Salvation." Insert apostrophes where appropriate. Example:

"Sister Reed, what is this child's name?"
                                   ^

1. There was a big revival at my Auntie Reeds church.
2. I heard the songs and the minister saying: "Why dont you come?"
3. Finally Westley said to me in a whisper: "Im tired o sitting here. Lets get up and be saved."
4. So I decided that maybe to save further trouble, Id better lie. . . .
5. That night, . . . I cried, in bed alone, and couldnt stop.

FOR COLLABORATION

All apostrophes have been deleted from the following sentences. Working with a class-mate, insert apostrophes where appropriate. Bring the results of your work to class for comparison with others. Example:

Who's
~~Whos~~ in charge here?
   ^

1. His Great-Uncle Rays contribution helped him pay off his auto loan.
2. Zillah couldnt finish painting the garage before dark.
3. Each of the dogs in the shelter has its own charm, but theres no way to find a home for every one.
4. If you went to Hollywood, youd have to forget about how difficult itd be to get a job in the film industry.
5. Its late; lets go out for pizza instead of making supper.

Reading with an Eye for Apostrophes

In the following rhyme, Zora Neale Hurston uses apostrophes to form contractions and signal omitted letters. They help create the rhythms and cadences of African American vernacular English. To get a sense of this effect, try reading the lines aloud with the missing letters filled in.

> Ah got up 'bout half-past fo'
> Forty fo' robbers wuz 'round mah do'
> Ah got up and let 'em in
> Hit 'em ovah de head wid uh rollin' pin.   – ZORA NEALE HURSTON, *Jonah's Gourd Vine*

Thinking about Your Own Use of Apostrophes

As a tool for presenting contractions and omitted letters, apostrophes play a larger role in informal writing than in formal writing. You may need to learn to write with few or no contractions, a task that requires some effort because we all use contractions in conversation. To get an idea of the difference between spoken and written language, try transcribing a "paragraph" or so of your own spoken words. Use apostrophes whenever you use a contraction or otherwise omit a letter. Look over your paragraph to see how many apostrophes you used, and then revise the piece to make it more formal, eliminating all or most apostrophes. What conclusions can you draw about ways you should and should not use apostrophes?

52 ▼ Using Quotation Marks

52a Using quotation marks to signal direct quotations

In American English, double quotation marks signal a direct quotation.

> Bush referred to an "axis of evil" in his speech.

> She smiled and said, "Son, this is one incident I will never forget."

Single quotation marks enclose a quotation within a quotation. Open and close the quoted passage with double quotation marks, and change any quotation marks that appear *within* the quotation to single quotation marks.

> In "The Uses of the Blues," James Baldwin says, "The title 'The Uses of the Blues' does not refer to music; I don't know anything about music."

Do not use quotation marks for *indirect* quotations, which do not repeat someone's exact words.

▶ **Dad smiled and said that "he would never forget the incident."**

1 Quoting longer passages

If the prose passage you wish to quote exceeds four typed lines, set it off from the rest of the text by starting it on a

---

As a way of bringing other people's words into our own, quotation can be a powerful writing tool. For example:

Mrs. Macken urges parents to get books for their children, to read to them when they are "li'l," and when they start school to make certain they attend regularly. She holds herself up as an example of a "millhand's daughter who wanted to be a schoolteacher and did it through sheer hard work."
— SHIRLEY BRICE HEATH
Ways with Words

The writer could have paraphrased, but by quoting, she lets her subject speak for herself—and lets us as readers hear that person's voice.

Quotation marks are also used to mark certain titles, to set off definitions, to quote poetry, to signal dialogue, and to highlight words used ironically. ∎

→ Use quotation marks around direct quotations and titles of short works. (52a and b)

→ Do not use quotation marks around set-off quotations of more than four lines of prose or three lines of poetry or around titles of long works. (52a and b)

→ Check other punctuation used with closing quotation marks. (52e)
  • Periods and commas should be *inside* the quotation marks.
  • Colons, semicolons, and footnote numbers should be *outside*.
  • Question marks, exclamation points, and dashes should be *inside* if they are part of the quoted material, *outside* if they are not.

→ Never use quotation marks around indirect quotations. (52a)

  ▶ **Keith said that "he was sorry."**

→ Do not rely on quotation marks to add emphasis to words. (52d)

FOR MULTILINGUAL WRITERS: Quoting in American English

American English and British English offer opposite conventions for double and single quotation marks. Writers of British English use single quotation marks first and, when necessary, double quotation marks for quotations within quotations. If you have studied British English, be careful to follow the U.S. conventions governing quotation marks: double quotation marks first and, when necessary, single quotation marks within double.

---

new line and indenting each line ten spaces from the left margin. This format, known as **block quotation**, does not require quotation marks.

> In *Winged Words: American Indian Writers Speak,* Leslie Marmon Silko describes her early education:
>
>> I learned to love reading, and love books, and the printed page, and therefore was motivated to learn to write. The best thing ... you can have in life is to have someone tell you a story ... but in lieu of that ... I learned at an early age to find comfort in a book, that a book would talk to me when no one else would. (145)

66 99

52a   773

PUNCTUATION

Using Quotation
Marks to Signal
Direct Quotations

This block quotation, including the ellipses and the page number in parentheses at the end, follows the Modern Language Association's (MLA) style. Other organizations that publish style guides, such as the American Psychological Association (APA), have different guidelines for ellipses and block quotations. (See Chapters 20–23.)

2 Quoting poetry

If the quotation is fewer than four lines, include it within your text, enclosed in double quotation marks. Separate the lines of the poem with slashes, each preceded and followed by a space.

> In one of his best-known poems, Robert Frost remarks, "Two roads diverged in a wood, and I— / I took the one less traveled by, / And that has made all the difference."

If the poetic quotation is longer, start it on a new line, indent each line ten spaces from the left margin, and do not use quotation marks.

> The duke in Robert Browning's "My Last Duchess" is clearly a jealous, vain person, whose arrogance is illustrated through his statement:
>
> > She thanked men—good! but thanked
> > Somehow—I know not how—as if she ranked
> > My gift of a nine-hundred-years-old name
> > With anybody's gift.

When you quote poetry, take care to follow the indention, spacing, capitalization, punctuation, and other features of the original passage.

● **EXERCISE 52.1**

Quoting someone else's words can contribute authority, texture, and even irony to your writing in that it adds other voices and images to your own. See how one writer uses a quotation in the following passage about Wyoming:

> Most characteristic of the state's landscape is what a developer euphemistically describes as "indigenous growth right up to your front door"—a reference to waterless stands of salt sage, snakes, jackrabbits, deerflies, red dust, a brief respite of wildflowers, dry washes, and no trees.   –GRETEL EHRLICH, *The Solace of Open Spaces*

Spend a few minutes reading an article on a topic you know something about. Then write a paragraph on that topic, quoting the article at least once. Choose

www ● bedford
stmartins.com/
smhandbook

For additional
exercises on direct
quotation, click on

▶ Exercise Central
  ▶ Quotation
    Marks

something worded in a memorable way or someone whose voice will lend weight to your own words. Finally, check your use of quotation marks against the guidelines in this chapter.

FOR MULTILINGUAL WRITERS: Using Quotation Marks

Remember that the way you mark quotations in English (" ") may not be the same as in other languages. In French, for example, quotations are marked with *guillemets* (« »), while in German, quotations take split-level marks (" " or " ").

3 Signaling dialogue

When you write dialogue or quote a conversation, enclose the words of each speaker in quotation marks, and mark each shift in speaker by beginning a new paragraph, no matter how brief the quoted remark may be.

> "But I can see you're bound to come," said the father. "Only we ain't going to catch us no fish, because there ain't no water left to catch 'em in."
> "The river!"
> "All but dry." — EUDORA WELTY, "Ladies in Spring"

Beginning a new paragraph with each change in speaker helps readers follow the dialogue. In the preceding example, we know when the father is speaking and when the child is speaking without the author's having to repeat *said the father, the child said,* and so on.

52b Using quotation marks to signal titles and definitions

Quotation marks are used to enclose the titles of short poems, short stories, articles, essays, songs, sections of books, and episodes of television and radio programs.

"Dover Beach" moves from calmness to sadness. [poem]

Alice Walker's "Everyday Use" is about more than just quilts. [short story]

Sinéad O'Connor's "Nothing Compares 2 U" brought her to worldwide attention. [song]

66 99

52c   775

PUNCTUATION

Using Quotation
Marks to Signal
Irony and Coinages

The *Atlantic* published an article titled "Illiberal Education." [article]

In the chapter called "Complexion," Richard Rodriguez describes his sensitivity about his skin color. [section of book]

The domestic violence plot on *ER* came to a head in the episode called "A Simple Twist of Fate." [television series episode]

Use italics rather than quotation marks for the titles of longer works, such as books and magazines. Do not use either in titling your own writing unless your title is or includes another title or a quotation.

Definitions are sometimes set off with quotation marks.

The French phrase *idée fixe* means literally "fixed idea."

●— For a discussion
of the use of
italics for titles,
see 56a.

52c Using quotation marks to signal irony and coinages

One way of showing readers that you are using a word or a phrase ironically is to enclose it in quotation marks.

The "banquet" consisted of dried-out chicken and canned vegetables. [The quotation marks suggest that the meal was anything but a banquet.]

Quotation marks are also used to enclose words or phrases made up by the writer, as is *forebirth* in the following example:

Your whole first paragraph or first page may have to be guillotined in any case after your piece is finished: it is a kind of "forebirth."

—JACQUES BARZUN, "A Writer's Discipline"

● **EXERCISE 52.2**

Revise each of the following sentences, using quotation marks appropriately to signal titles, definitions, irony, or coinages.

1. Kowinski uses the term *mallaise* to mean physical and psychological disturbances caused by mall contact.

2. My favorite article in *People* magazine every year is The Sexiest Man Alive.

3. "The little that is known about gorillas certainly makes you want to know more," writes Alan Moorehead in his essay A Most Forgiving Ape.

4. The fun of surgery begins before the operation ever takes place.

5. Should America the Beautiful replace The Star-Spangled Banner as the national anthem?

" "

52d

6. Sylvia Nasar describes the brilliant mathematician's youth and early career in the book's first section, which is called A Beautiful Mind.

7. Many viewers were stunned when Jackie Jr. was killed in The Army of One, the last episode of *The Sopranos'* third season.

8. The Beatles song Love Me Do catapulted the band to international stardom.

9. My dictionary defines *isolation* as the quality or state of being alone.

10. When my teacher assigned Chaucer's *Canterbury Tales*, I never expected to read a poem as hilarious and bawdy as The Miller's Tale.

52d Checking for misused quotation marks

Use quotation marks only when there is a reason for them. Do not use them just to emphasize particular words or phrases.

▶ **Michael said that his views may not be "politically correct" but that he wasn't going to change them for anything.**

▶ **Much time was spent speculating about their "relationship."**

For a discussion of slang and colloquial language, see 27a.

Do not use quotation marks with slang or colloquial language; they create the impression that you are apologizing for using such language. Instead, try to express the idea in formal language. If you have a good reason to use a slang or colloquial term, use it without quotation marks.

▶ **After their twenty-mile hike, the campers were** *exhausted* **"wiped out" and ready to "hit the sack."** *go to bed.*

52e Using quotation marks with other punctuation

Periods and commas go *inside* closing quotation marks.

"Don't compromise yourself," said Janis Joplin. "You are all you've got."

Colons and semicolons go *outside* closing quotation marks.

Everything is dark, and "a visionary light settles in her eyes"; this vision, this light, is her salvation.

I felt only one emotion after finishing "Eveline": pity.

66 99
52e 777

PUNCTUATION
Using Quotation
Marks with Other
Punctuation

Question marks, exclamation points, and dashes go *inside* closing quotation marks if they are part of the quotation, *outside* if they are not.

PART OF THE QUOTATION

Gently shake the injured person while asking, "Are you all right?"

"Jump!" one of the firefighters shouted.

"Watch out — watch out for —" Jessica began nervously.

NOT PART OF THE QUOTATION

What is the theme of "The Birth-Mark"?

How tired she must be of hearing "God Save the Queen"!

"Break a leg" — that phrase is supposed to bring good luck to a performer.

Footnote numbers go *outside* closing quotation marks.

Tragedy is defined by Aristotle as "an imitation of an action that is serious and of a certain magnitude."[1]

●— For help using
quotation marks
in MLA and CMS
documentation,
see Chapters 20
and 23.

FOR COLLABORATION

Working with a classmate, revise the following paragraph to use quotation marks appropriately. Bring your revision to class for discussion.

An article called Their Game, Their Gold appeared in the *New York Times* the morning after Canada won the gold medal in men's hockey at the 2002 winter Olympics in Park City, Utah. Sportswriter George Vecsey described the final match as 'so fast, so furious, so full of skill that it will live in the memories of all who witnessed it' and noted, "The game itself deserved a gold medal". The Canadian men's hockey team had not won a gold medal at the Olympics since 1952, fifty years "to the day" before their winning match in Utah. Wayne Gretzky, one of the "all-time greats" of the sport and the executive director of the winning team, said that "his country desperately needed to win this tournament."

**www ● bedford
stmartins.com/
smhandbook**

For additional
exercises on using
quotation marks
with other
punctuation,
click on

▶ **Exercise Central**
  ▶ **Quotation
    Marks**

THINKING CRITICALLY ABOUT QUOTATION MARKS

Reading with an Eye for Quotation Marks

Read the following passage about the painter Georgia O'Keeffe, and pay particular attention to the use of quotation marks. What effect is created by the author's use of quotation marks with *hardness, crustiness,* and *crusty*? How do the quotations by O'Keeffe help support the author's description of her?

"Hardness" has not been in our century a quality much admired in women, nor in the past twenty years has it even been in official favor for men. When hardness surfaces in the very old we tend to transform it into "crustiness" or eccentricity, some tonic pepperiness to be indulged at a distance. On the evidence of her work and what she has said about it, Georgia O'Keeffe is neither "crusty" nor eccentric. She is simply hard, a straight shooter, a woman clean of received wisdom and open to what she sees. This is a woman who could early on dismiss most of her contemporaries as "dreamy," and would later single out one she liked as "a very poor painter." (And then add, apparently by way of softening the judgment: "I guess he wasn't a painter at all. He had no courage and I believe that to create one's own world in any of the arts takes courage.") This is a woman who in 1939 could advise her admirers that they were missing her point, that their appreciation of her famous flowers was merely sentimental. "When I paint a red hill," she observed coolly in the catalogue for an exhibition that year, "you say it is too bad that I don't always paint flowers. A flower touches almost everyone's heart. A red hill doesn't touch everyone's heart."   —JOAN DIDION, "Georgia O'Keeffe"

Thinking about Your Own Use of Quotation Marks

Choose a topic that is of interest on your campus, and interview one of your friends about it for ten or fifteen minutes. On the basis of your notes from the interview, write two or three paragraphs about your friend's views, using several direct quotations that support the points you are making. Then look to see how closely you followed the conventions for quotation marks explained in this chapter. Note any usages that caused you problems — in your writing log, if you keep one.

53 Using Other Punctuation Marks

Parentheses, brackets, dashes, colons, slashes, and ellipses are all around us. Pick up the television listings, for instance, and you will find all these punctuation marks in abundance, helping viewers preview programs in a clear and efficient way.

7 8 *College Football* 3:30
501019/592361 — Northwestern Wildcats at Ohio State Buck-eyes. The Buckeyes are looking for their 20th straight win over Northwestern. (Live) [Time approximate.]

This chapter will guide you in deciding when you can use these marks of punctuation to signal relationships among sentence parts, to create particular rhythms, and to help readers follow your thoughts. ■

53a Using parentheses

Parentheses enclose material that is of minor or secondary importance in a sentence or passage—material that supplements, clarifies, comments on, or illustrates what precedes or follows it. Parentheses also enclose numbers or letters that precede items in a list, and sometimes they enclose source citations or publication information.

■ Enclosing less important material

Normal children do not confuse reality and fantasy—they confuse them much less often than we adults do (as a certain great fantasist pointed out in a story called "The Emperor's New Clothes").

> – URSULA LE GUIN
> "Why Are Americans Afraid of Dragons?"

Of course, Nike is powerful enough to muscle its way into any market it chooses. (If Nike started selling light bulbs, someone would buy them.) But Nike isn't powerful enough both to muscle in and to make a lot of money doing so. — JAMES SUROWIECKI, "Turf War"

As the preceding examples demonstrate, a period may be placed either inside or outside a closing parenthesis, depending on whether the parenthetical text is part of a

( )

→ Be sure that any material set off with dashes or enclosed in parentheses requires special treatment. Then check to see that the dashes or parentheses don't make the sentence difficult to follow. (53a and c)

→ Decide whether you have chosen the right punctuation: parentheses tend to de-emphasize material they enclose, whereas dashes add emphasis.

→ Check to see that you use square brackets to enclose parenthetical elements in material that is already within parentheses and to enclose words or comments inserted into a quotation. (53b)

→ Check to see that you have not used a colon between a verb and its object or complement, between a preposition and its object, or after such expressions as *such as, especially,* or *including.* (53d)

→ Check to be sure you've used slashes to mark line divisions in poetry quoted within text. (53e)

→ Make sure you've used ellipses (three equally spaced dots) to indicate omissions from quoted passages. (53f)

→ Check email and Internet addresses to make sure you've copied the punctuation within them precisely. If you're using them within a sentence or with other punctuation, enclose them in angle brackets. (53b, e, and g) Make sure you use emoticons sparingly. (53g)

larger sentence. A comma, however, is always placed *outside* a closing parenthesis (and never before an opening one).

> Gene Tunney's single defeat in an eleven-year career was to a flamboyant and dangerous fighter named Harry Greb ("The Human Windmill"), who seems to have been, judging from boxing literature, the dirtiest fighter in history.   —JOYCE CAROL OATES, "On Boxing"

If the material in parentheses is a question or an exclamation, use a question mark or exclamation point inside the closing parenthesis.

> Our laughing (so deep was the pleasure!) became screaming.
> —RICHARD RODRIGUEZ
> "Aria: A Memoir of a Bilingual Childhood"

Use parentheses judiciously, for they break up the flow of a sentence or passage, forcing readers to hold the original train of thought in their minds while considering a secondary one.

Enclosing numbers or letters in a list

Five distinct styles can be distinguished: (1) Old New England, (2) Deep South, (3) Middle American, (4) Wild West and (5) Far West or Californian.
—ALISON LURIE, *The Language of Clothes*

Enclosing textual citations or publication information

The following in-text citation shows the style of the American Psychological Association (APA):

A recent study that was less dependent on subjective judgment resulted in conclusions somewhat different from those of previous studies (Murphy & Orkow, 1985).

The following note for a book shows the citation style recommended by *The Chicago Manual of Style:*

1. John A. Garraty, *Quarrels That Have Shaped the Constitution* (New York: Harper and Row, 1987), 7-14.

53b Using brackets

Square brackets are used to enclose parenthetical elements in material that is within parentheses and to enclose explanatory words or comments that are inserted into a quotation.

Setting off material within parentheses

Eventually the investigation had to examine the major agencies (including the previously sacrosanct National Security Agency [NSA]) that were conducting covert operations.

Inserting material within quotations

In the following sentence, the bracketed words clarify the words *He* and *it* in the original quotation and tell the reader that *Johnson* and *the war* do not appear in the original:

As Curtis argues, "He [Johnson] saw it [the war] as a game or wrestling match in which he would make Ho Chi Minh cry 'uncle.'"

In the following sentence, the bracketed material explains what the *that* in the quotation means:

In defending his station's inferior children's programs, a network executive states, "If we were to do that [supply quality programs in the afternoon, one of the demands of ACT], a lot of people might say: 'How dare they lock the kids up for another two and a half hours.'"

— MARIE WINN
The Plug-in Drug: Television, Children, and the Family

In the quotation in the following sentence, the artist Gauguin's name is misspelled. The bracketed Latin word *sic,* which means "so," tells readers that the person being quoted — not the writer — made the mistake.

One admirer wrote, "She was the most striking woman I'd ever seen — a sort of wonderful combination of Mia Farrow and one of Gaugin's [*sic*] Polynesian nymphs."

Use angle brackets to enclose email and Internet addresses in other text. (See 53g.)

I told her she could get more census information at <www.census.gov>.

www • bedford
stmartins.com/
smhandbook

For additional
exercises on
parentheses,
click on

▶ Exercise Central
  ▶ Other
    Punctuation

● **EXERCISE 53.1**

Revise the following sentences, using parentheses and brackets correctly. Example:

She was in fourth grade (or was it third?) when she became blind.
                        ^   ^

1. While doing online research on the Federal Communications Commission, Mario found the links at www.google.com very helpful.

2. During my research, I found that a flat-rate income tax a single-rate tax with no deductions has its problems.

3. The health care expert informed readers that "as we progress through middle age, we experience intimations of our own morality *sic.*"

4. The speaker pointed out that some hospitals train nurses in this pseudoscientific technique he was referring to therapeutic touch TT, which had been discredited by many rigorous studies.

5. Albert made the following suggestions: 1 clean the dishes as soon as they are used, 2 put items away when they are no longer needed, and 3 make a schedule for vacuuming, dusting, doing laundry, and other household chores.

53c Using dashes

Use dashes to insert a comment or to highlight particular material. In contrast to parentheses, dashes give more rather than less emphasis to the material they enclose. On most typewriters and with some computer software, a dash is made with two hyphens (--) with *no* spaces before, between, or after. In some software, a solid dash can be typed as it is in this book (—). Many word-processing programs automatically convert two typed hyphens into a solid dash.

■ *Inserting a comment*

The pleasures of reading itself—who doesn't remember?—were like those of Christmas cake, a sweet devouring.

— EUDORA WELTY, "A Sweet Devouring"

■ *Emphasizing explanatory material*

Mr. Angell is addicted to dashes and parentheses—small pauses or digressions in a narrative like those moments when the umpire dusts off home plate or a pitcher rubs up a new ball—that serve to slow an already deliberate movement almost to a standstill.

— JOEL CONARROE, *New York Times Book Review*

A single dash sets off a comment or emphasizes material at the end of a sentence. It may also mark a sudden shift in tone, indicate a hesitation in speech, or introduce a summary or explanation of what has come before.

■ *Emphasizing material at the end of a sentence*

In the twentieth century it has become almost impossible to moralize about epidemics—except those which are transmitted sexually.

— SUSAN SONTAG, *AIDS and Its Metaphors*

■ *Marking a sudden change in tone*

New York is a catastrophe—but a magnificent catastrophe.

— LE CORBUSIER

■ *Indicating a hesitation in speech*

As the officer approached his car, the driver stammered, "What—what have I done?"

■ *Introducing a summary or explanation*

In walking, the average adult person employs a motor mechanism that weighs about eighty pounds—sixty pounds of muscle and twenty pounds of bone.   — EDWIN WAY TEALE

In introducing a summary or explanation, the difference between a single dash and a colon is a subtle one. In general, however, a dash is less formal. In fact, you should use dashes very carefully in college writing because too many of them create a jerky, disconnected effect that makes it hard for readers to follow your thought.

**www ● bedford
stmartins.com/
smhandbook**

For additional
exercises on dashes,
click on

▶ Exercise Central
  ▶ Other
    Punctuation

● **EXERCISE 53.2**

Punctuate the following sentences with dashes where appropriate. Example:

> He is quick, violent, and mean — they don't call him Dirty Harry for
> nothing — but appealing nonetheless.

1. Many people would have ignored the children's taunts but not Ace.

2. Even if marijuana is dangerous an assertion disputed by many studies it is certainly no more harmful to human health than alcohol and cigarettes, which remain legal.

3. If you want to do well on a test and why wouldn't you? remember that a little anxiety can improve your performance.

4. Union Carbide's plant in Bhopal, India, sprang a leak a leak that killed more than 2,000 people and injured an additional 200,000.

5. Fair-skinned people and especially those with red hair should use a strong sunscreen.

53d Using colons

A colon is used to introduce something: an explanation, an example, an appositive, a series, a list, or a quotation. Colons also separate elements such as hours, minutes, and seconds; biblical chapter numbers and verses; and titles and subtitles.

■ *Introducing an explanation, an example, or an appositive*

And we are all on our own when it comes to keeping those lines open to ourselves: your notebook will never help me, nor mine you.

–JOAN DIDION, "On Keeping a Notebook"

The men may also wear the getup known as Sun Belt Cool: a pale beige suit, open-collared shirt (often in a darker shade than the suit), cream-colored loafers and aviator sunglasses.

–ALISON LURIE, *The Language of Clothes*

At the baby's one-month birthday party, Ah Po gave him the Four Valuable Things: ink, inkslab, paper, and brush.

– Maxine Hong Kingston, *China Men*

We began a series of workshops on nonviolence, and we repeatedly asked ourselves: "Are you able to accept blows without retaliation?"

– Martin Luther King Jr., "Letter from Birmingham Jail"

Separating elements

SALUTATIONS IN FORMAL LETTERS

Dear Dr. O'Brien:

HOURS, MINUTES, AND SECONDS

4:59 P.M.
2:15:06

RATIOS

a ratio of 5:1

BIBLICAL CHAPTERS AND VERSES

I Corinthians 3:3–5

TITLES AND SUBTITLES

The Joy of Insight: Passions of a Physicist

CITIES AND PUBLISHERS IN BIBLIOGRAPHIC ENTRIES

Boston: Bedford, 2003

Checking for misused colons

A colon should be used only at the end of an independent clause (except when it is used to separate the standard elements discussed in the preceding section). Do not put a colon between a verb and its object or complement, unless the object is a quotation. Do not put a colon between a preposition and its object or after such expressions as *such as*, *especially*, or *including*.

▶ Some natural fibers are⫶ cotton, wool, silk, and linen.

▶ In poetry, additional power may come from devices such as⫶ simile, metaphor, and alliteration.

**www • bedford
stmartins.com/
smhandbook**

For additional exercises on colons, click on

▶ Exercise Central
  ▶ Other
    Punctuation

● **EXERCISE 53.3**

Insert a colon or colons in each of the following items that needs them. Some of the items do not require a colon. Example:

Images: My Life in Film includes revealing material written by Ingmar Bergman.

1. The article made one point forcefully and repeatedly the United States must end its dependence on foreign oil.

2. Another example is taken from Psalm 139 16.

3. Ajani tried to make healthier choices, such as eating organic food, walking to work, and getting plenty of rest.

4. The president declared "Not over my dead body will they raise your taxes."

5. Watching television in the wee hours of the morning had given me just two things lines under my eyes and an irrational desire to purchase hair-care and cleaning products.

6. Gandhi urged four rules tell the truth even in business, adopt more sanitary habits, abolish caste and religious divisions, and learn English.

7. Solid vocal technique is founded on the correct use of head position, diaphragm control, muscle relaxation, and voice placement.

8. According to *The Birds of Heaven Travels with Cranes,* eleven of the fifteen crane species on earth are endangered.

9. Even more important was what money represented success, prestige, and power.

10. Two buses go to Denver: one at 9 38 A.M. and one at 2 55 P.M.

53e Using slashes

Slashes are used to mark line divisions in poetry quoted within text (see 52a2), to separate two alternative terms, and to separate the parts of fractions and Internet addresses. When used to separate lines of poetry, the slash should be preceded and followed by a space.

■ *Marking line divisions in poetry*

In "Digging," Seamus Heaney observes, "Between my finger and my thumb / The squat pen rests; snug as a gun."

■ *Separating alternatives*

"I'm not the typical wife/girlfriend of a baseball player—those women you see on TV with their hair done up and their Rose Bowl Parade wave to the crowds."   – ROGER ANGELL, "In the Country"

■ *Separating parts of fractions*

The structure is 138½ feet high.

■ *Separating parts of Internet addresses*

http://www.bedfordstmartins.com/smhandbook

Ellipses, or ellipsis points, are three equally spaced dots. Most often used to indicate that something has been omitted from a quoted passage, they can also be used to signal a pause or hesitation in speech in the same way that a dash can.

▣ Indicating omissions

Just as you should carefully use quotation marks around any material that you quote directly from a source, so you should carefully use ellipses to indicate that you have left out part of a quotation that otherwise appears to be a complete sentence.

ORIGINAL TEXT

The quasi-official division of the population into three economic classes called high-, middle-, and low-income groups rather misses the point, because as a class indicator the amount of money is not as important as the source.   – PAUL FUSSELL, "Notes on Class"

WITH ELLIPSES

As Paul Fussell argues, "The quasi-official division of the population into three economic classes . . . rather misses the point . . . ."

In this example, the ellipses are used to indicate two different omissions — one in the middle of the sentence and one at the end. When you omit the last part of a quoted sentence, add a period after the ellipses — for a total of four dots. Be sure a complete sentence comes before and after the four points. If your run-in quotation ends with a source documentation (such as a page number, a name, or a title), follow these steps:

1. Use three ellipsis points but no period after the quotation.
2. Add the closing quotation mark, closed up to the third ellipsis point.
3. Add the source documentation in parentheses.
4. Use a period to indicate the end of the sentence.

Hawthorne writes, "My friend, whom I shall call Oberon — it was a name of fancy and friendship between him and me . . ." (575).

▣ Indicating a pause or a hesitation

Then the voice, husky and familiar, came to wash over us — "The winnah, and still heavyweight champeen of the world . . . Joe Louis."
                                    – MAYA ANGELOU, *I Know Why the Caged Bird Sings*

Certain punctuation marks are essential parts of electronic addresses. Be careful to include them *exactly* as you find them in email addresses and URLs—if they are changed or omitted, the address or URL will be incorrect.

- **/** The **forward slash** separates parts of URLs.
- **•** The **dot** separates parts of email addresses and URLs.
- **@** The **"at" sign** is part of every email address, indicating that you are "at" an electronic address.
- **<>** **Angle brackets** can be used to frame email addresses and URLs, making it possible to use them within sentences and with other punctuation.
- **_** The **underscore** is used in many URLs (and around titles in online text in place of italics).
- **~** The **tilde** appears in many URLs as an indicator of the user or owner of the directory path.

For more about
online communi-
cation, see
Chapter 7.

If you participate in any computer bulletin boards, discussion groups, or other electronic forms of communication, you will already have come in contact with **emoticons**, also known as *smileys*. These are combinations of keyboard characters that, when looked at sideways, "punctuate" a passage by indicating the mood of the sender. Following are some commonly used emoticons:

the smile:	:-)	the wink:	;-)
the frown:	:-(	the laugh:	:-D

These marks are sometimes also used to express something about the sender's appearance. How, for instance, might a writer indicate that she or he wears glasses, has a mustache, or wears a turban? As these questions suggest, many emoticons are used simply for fun, to tease and puzzle readers. Their growing use, however, suggests that some of these symbols may well become standard punctuation marks.

In the meantime, if you are using emoticons in your writing, follow the same rules you would use for other marks: Are they appropriate to your topic and purpose? Will they be readily understood and accepted by your audience? In general, you will probably not use them in most college writing. Take a look at how the following Arlo and Janis cartoon uses one of these emoticons to make a particularly funny point.

● **EXERCISE 53.4**

Complete the following sentence by incorporating two parts of one of the sentences in the passage below, using ellipsis points to indicate what you omit: "In 'Shopping and Other Spiritual Adventures,' Phyllis Rose says of Americans' attitudes toward shopping, _____."

We Americans are beyond a simple, possessive materialism. We're used to abundance and the possibility of possessing things. The things, and the possibility of possessing them, will still be there next week, next year. So today we can walk the aisles calmly.   – PHYLLIS ROSE, "Shopping and Other Spiritual Adventures"

● **EXERCISE 53.5**

The following sentences use the punctuation marks presented in this chapter very effectively. Read the sentences carefully; then choose one, and use it as a model for writing a sentence of your own, making sure to use the punctuation marks in the same way in your sentence.

1. The dad was—how can you put this gracefully?—a real blimp, a wide load, and the white polyester stretch-pants only emphasized the cargo.
          – GARRISON KEILLOR, "Happy to Be Here"

2. Monet has been transformed into a human virus bomb. He walks slowly into the airport terminal and through the building and out to a curving road where taxis are always parked. The taxi drivers surround him— "Taxi?" "Taxi?"
   "Nairobi . . . Hospital," he mumbles.   – RICHARD PRESTON, *The Hot Zone*

3. Not only are the distinctions we draw between male nature and female nature largely arbitrary and often pure superstition: they are completely beside the point.   – BRIGID BROPHY, "Women"

4. If no one, including you, liked the soup the first time round (and that's why you've got so much left over), there is no point in freezing it for some hopeful future date when, miraculously, it will taste delicious. But bagging leftovers— say, stews—in single portions can be useful for those evenings when you're eating alone.   – NIGELLA LAWSON, *How to Eat*

:-)

FOR COLLABORATION

The following paragraph uses many parentheses and dashes. Working with a class-mate, use the guidelines in this chapter to revise the paragraph to make it flow more smoothly, and emphasize appropriate elements by deleting some of the parentheses and dashes, replacing one with the other, or substituting other punctuation. Bring your collaborative revisions to class for discussion.

By the time we reached Geneva, we had been traveling more than seven weeks—it seemed like seven months!—and were getting rather tired of one another's company. (We had been only casual acquaintances before the trip.) Since there was not a great deal to see in the city—especially on Sunday—we decided to take the train to Chamonix (France) to see Mont Blanc—Europe's second-highest mountain (a decision that proved to be a disaster). After an argument about the map (the kind of argument we were having more and more often), we wandered around endlessly before finding the train station, only to discover that it was the wrong one. So we had to walk even farther—back to the other train station. Despite an exhausting pace, we just missed the train—or so we thought—until we learned that there was no train to Chamonix that day—because it was Sunday. I have never (for obvious reasons) gone back to Geneva.

THINKING CRITICALLY ABOUT PUNCTUATION

Reading with an Eye for Punctuation

In the following passage, Tom Wolfe uses dashes, parentheses, ellipses, and a colon to create rhythm and build momentum in a very long (178-word) sentence. The editorial comment inserted in brackets calls attention to the fact that the "right stuff" was, in the world Wolfe describes here, always male. Look carefully at how Wolfe and the editors use these punctuation marks, and then try writing a description of something that effectively uses as many of them as possible. Your description should be about the same length as Wolfe's passage, but it need not be all one sentence.

Likewise, "hassling"—mock dogfighting—was strictly forbidden, and so naturally young fighter jocks could hardly wait to go up in, say, a pair of F-100s and start the duel by making a pass at each other at 800 miles an hour, the winner being the pilot who could slip in behind the other one and get locked in on his [never *her* or *his or her!*] tail ("wax his tail"), and it was not uncommon for some eager jock to try too tight an outside turn and have his engine flame out, whereupon, unable to restart it, he has to eject . . . and he shakes his fist at the victor as he floats down by parachute and his million-dollar air-craft goes *kaboom!* on the palmetto grass or the desert floor, and he starts thinking about how he can get together with the other guy back at the base in time for the two of them to get their stories straight before the investigation: "I don't know what happened, sir. I was pulling up after a target run, and it just flamed out on me."

— TOM WOLFE, *The Right Stuff*

Thinking about Your Own Use of Punctuation

Look through a draft you have recently written or are working on, and check your use of parentheses, brackets, dashes, colons, slashes, and ellipses. Have you followed the conventions presented in this chapter? If not, revise accordingly. Then read through the draft again, looking especially at all the parentheses and dashes. Are there too many? Check the material in parentheses to see if it could use more emphasis and thus be set off instead with dashes. Then check any material in dashes to see if it could do with less emphasis and thus be punctuated with commas or parentheses. If you keep a writing log, enter some examples of this work in your log.

PUNCTUATION

Using Online
Punctuation

MECHANICAL CONVENTIONS

"If writing must be a precise form of communication, it should be treated like a precision instrument. It should be sharpened, and it should not be used carelessly."
—THEODORE M. BERNSTEIN

54

◣ Using Capitals

54a Capitalizing the first word of a sentence or line of poetry

Capitalize the first word of a sentence.

> Posing relatives for photographs is a challenge.

> Could you move to the left a little?

If you are quoting a full sentence, capitalize its first word.

> Everyone was asking, "What will I do after I graduate?"

Capitalization of a sentence following a colon is optional.

> Gould cites the work of Darwin: The [*or* the] theory of natural selection incorporates the principle of evolutionary ties between all animals.

Capitalize a sentence within parentheses unless the parenthetical sentence is inserted into another sentence. A sentence set off within another sentence by dashes should not be capitalized.

> Those assigned to transports were not humiliated like washouts — *somebody* had to fly those planes — nevertheless, they, too, had been *left behind* for lack of the right stuff. Or a man could go for a routine physical one fine day, feeling like a million dollars, and be grounded for *fallen arches.* It happened! — just like that! (And try raising them.)
> — TOM WOLFE, *The Right Stuff*

→ Make sure to capitalize the first letter of each sentence. If you quote a poem, follow its original capitalization. (54a)
→ Check to make sure you have appropriately capitalized proper nouns and proper adjectives. (54b)
→ If you have used titles of people or of works, see that they are capitalized correctly. (54b and c)
→ Double-check the capitalization of geographic directions (*north* or *North?*), family relationships (*dad* or *Dad?*), and seasons of the year (*spring,* never *Spring*). (54e)
→ In email, check to see that you have capitalized words as you would in print and have followed other email conventions. (54f)

When citing poetry, follow the capitalization of the original poem. Though most poets capitalize the first word of each line of a poem, some poets do not.

> Morning sun heats up the young beech tree
> leaves and almost lights them into fireflies
>
> I wish I could dig up the earth to plant apples
> pears or peaches on a lazy dandelion lawn
>
> I am tired from this digging up of human bodies
> no one loved enough to save from death   –JUNE JORDAN, "Aftermath"

54b Capitalizing proper nouns and proper adjectives

Capitalize **proper nouns** (those naming specific persons, places, and things) and most **proper adjectives** (those formed from proper nouns). All other nouns are common nouns and are not capitalized unless they begin a sentence or are used as part of a proper noun: *a street,* but *Elm Street.* Do not capitalize articles (*a, an,* or *the*) or prepositions preceding or within proper nouns or proper adjectives.

PROPER	COMMON
Alfred Hitchcock, Hitchcockian	the director, directorial
Brazil, Brazilian	the nation, national
Golden Gate Bridge	the bridge

SOME COMMONLY CAPITALIZED TERMS

NAMES OF INDIVIDUALS

Morgan Freeman   Condoleezza Rice
Aristotelian logic   Freudian slip

GEOGRAPHIC NAMES

Asia   Pacific Ocean
Nepal   Sugarloaf Mountain
St. Louis   Michigan Avenue
African art   Parisian fashions

STRUCTURES AND MONUMENTS

Flatiron Building   Gateway Arch
Fort McHenry Tunnel   Coit Tower

SHIPS, TRAINS, AIRCRAFT, AND SPACECRAFT

S.S. *Titanic*   Metroliner
Spirit of St. Louis   *Mir*

INSTITUTIONS, ORGANIZATIONS, AND BUSINESSES

Library of Congress   National Organization for Women
St. Martin's Press   United Auto Workers
General Motors Corporation   Democratic Party

HISTORICAL EVENTS, ERAS, AND CALENDAR ITEMS

Shays's Rebellion   Saturday
Great Depression   July
Middle Ages   Memorial Day

RELIGIONS AND RELIGIOUS TERMS

Buddhism, Buddhists   Allah
Catholicism, Catholics   Jesus Christ
Islam, Muslims *or* Moslems   God
Judaism, Jews   the Bible
United Methodist Church,   the Qur'an
  Methodists   Bhagavad Gita

(Continued on p. 797)

(Continued from p. 796)

ETHNIC GROUPS, NATIONALITIES, AND LANGUAGES

African American	Arab	Iraqi
Chicano/Chicana	English	Latin
Slavic	Chinese	

TRADE NAMES

Reebok	Cheerios	Levi's
Xerox	Quicken	Walkman

■ *Titles of individuals*

Capitalize titles used before a proper name. Used alone or following a proper name, most titles are not capitalized. The only exceptions are titles of some very high officials — for example, many writers capitalize the word *president* when it refers to the President of the United States.

Mayor Michael Bloomberg	Michael Bloomberg, mayor of New York City
Professor Lisa Ede	Lisa Ede, an English professor
Doctor Edward A. Davies	Edward A. Davies, our doctor

■ *Academic institutions and courses*

Capitalize the names of specific schools, departments, or courses but not the common nouns referring to institutions or subject areas, unless that subject is a language.

University of California (*but* a California university)

the History Department (*but* a history department)

Political Science 102 (*but* a political science course)

Japanese 201 (*and* a Japanese course)

54c Capitalizing titles of works

Capitalize most words in titles of books, articles, stories, essays, plays, poems, documents, films, paintings, and musical compositions. Do not capitalize articles (*a, an, the*), prepositions, conjunctions, and the *to* in an infinitive unless they are the first or last words in a title or subtitle.

Walt Whitman: A Life   "Where I'm Calling From"
"Oops, I Did It Again"   Declaration of Independence
"Shooting an Elephant"   *Harry Potter and the Sorcerer's Stone*
The Producers   *Me without You*

54d Capitalizing *I*

Always capitalize the pronoun *I*.

In fact, I don't know the answer.

54e Checking for unnecessary capitalization

Do not capitalize a compass direction, unless the word designates a specific geographic region.

The nation was at that time divided into three competing economic sections: the Northeast, the South, and the West.

▶ John Muir headed ^w^West, motivated by the need to explore.

Do not capitalize a word indicating a family relationship, unless the word is used as part of the name or as a substitute for the name.

I could always tell when Mother was annoyed with Aunt Rose.

▶ When she was a child, my ^m^Mother shared a room with her ^a^Aunt.

Do not capitalize seasons of the year and parts of the academic year.

spring   fall semester
winter   winter term
autumn   spring quarter

54f Capitalizing in email

For more on writing email, see 7a.

In general, capitalize online as you would in print. Some writers treat email almost like talk, writing hurriedly and not using any capital letters. This practice can be hard on your readers, however, and can result in text that looks unprofessional if it is printed out. Since email *is* often

> Capitalization systems vary considerably among languages, and some languages (Arabic, Chinese, and Hebrew, for example) do not use capital letters at all. English may be the only language to capitalize the first-person singular pronoun (*I*), but Dutch and German capitalize some forms of the second-person pronoun (*you*). German capitalizes all nouns; English used to capitalize more nouns than it does now (see the Declaration of Independence for one good example). As a result, the system of capitalization commonly used in standard academic English may pose challenges for speakers of other languages.

printed out, you should ordinarily follow the print conventions of capitalization.

For electronic addresses, follow the capitalization *exactly* in address lines, since systems that are case sensitive may not recognize the address otherwise: *LJM.dd@aol.com.*

Capitalizing whole words or phrases for emphasis comes across to readers as SHOUTING. So instead of uppercase letters, use italics, underlining, or asterisks to add emphasis.

> Sorry for the abrupt response, but I am *very* busy.

Some contemporary companies use capitals called *InterCaps* in the middle of their own or their products' names, often turning two words into one. Leave the capitals in, following the style you see in company advertising or on the product itself — *eBay, FedEx, EasyWriter.*

● **EXERCISE 54.1**

Capitalize words as needed in the following sentences. Example:

        T S E   T W   L   F   F
    t. s. eliot, who wrote the waste land, was an editor at faber and faber.

1. the town in the south where i was raised had a statue of a civil war soldier in the center of main street.

2. we had a choice of fast-food, chinese, or italian restaurants.

3. reporters speculated about the secret location where vice president cheney had remained for several weeks.

4. the council of trent was convened to draw up the catholic response to the protestant reformation.

www ● bedford stmartins.com/ smhandbook

For additional exercises, click on

▶ **Exercise Central**
  ▶ **Capitalization**

5. We drove east over the hudson river on the tappan zee bridge.

6. every artist on a major label seems to want a lexus or a lincoln navigator and a chauffeur to drive it.

7. accepting an award for his score for the film *the high and the mighty,* dmitri tiomkin thanked beethoven, brahms, wagner, and strauss.

8. my french teacher in high school showed us films by françois truffaut, including *small change* and *the 400 blows,* but i could hardly understand a word.

9. u.s. soldiers went to afghanistan in the fall of 2001, after the attacks on the world trade center and the pentagon.

10. in the back seat, the children sang "the itsy bitsy spider" over and over until their mother thought she would scream.

THINKING CRITICALLY ABOUT CAPITALIZATION

The following poem uses capitalization in an unconventional way. Read it over a few times, at least once aloud. What effect does the capitalization have on your understanding and recitation of the poem? Why do you think the poet chose to use capitals as she did?

A little Madness in the Spring
Is wholesome even for the King,
But God be with the Clown —
Who ponders this tremendous scene —
This whole Experiment of Green —
As if it were his own!

– EMILY DICKINSON

55 Using Abbreviations and Numbers

ABBREVIATIONS

55a Abbreviating titles and academic degrees

When used before or after a name, some personal and professional titles and academic degrees are abbreviated, even in academic writing.

Ms. Steinem	Henry Louis Gates Jr.
Mr. Guenette	Paul Irvin, M.D.
Dr. Cheryl Gold	Jamie Barlow Kayes, Ph.D.

Other titles, including religious, military, academic, and government titles, should always be spelled out in academic writing. In other writing, they may be abbreviated when they appear before a full name but should be spelled out if they appear before a last name alone.

Gen. Colin Powell	General Powell
Prof. Beverly Moss	Professor Moss
Sen. Diane Feinstein	Senator Feinstein

Academic degrees may be abbreviated when used alone, but personal or professional titles used alone are never abbreviated.

She received her *Ph.D.* this year.

professor,
▶ He was a demanding ~~prof.,~~ and we worked hard.

Anytime you open up a telephone book, you see an abundance of abbreviations and numbers, as in the following movie theater listing from the telephone book in California's Bay Area:

Oaks Theater 1875 Solano Av Brk

Abbreviations and numbers allow writers to present detailed information in a small amount of space and allow readers to process information quickly and efficiently. In academic writing, you will want to follow certain conventions in using abbreviations and numbers, conventions that vary from field to field.

This chapter provides guidelines and examples to help you use abbreviations and numbers appropriately, especially in English and other humanities courses. ∎

→ Make sure you use abbreviations and numbers according to the conventions of a specific field. For example, *57%* might be acceptable in a math paper, but *57 percent* may be more appropriate in a sociology essay. (55d)

→ If you use an abbreviation readers might not understand, make sure you spell out the term the first time you use it, and give the abbreviation in parentheses. (55c)

→ If you use an abbreviation more than once, make sure you use it consistently.

→ When writing online, be sure to use appropriate monetary or measurement units. (55h)

Use either a title or an academic degree, but not both, with a person's name.

INAPPROPRIATE	Dr. James Dillon, Ph.D.
REVISED	Dr. James Dillon
REVISED	James Dillon, Ph.D.

55b Using abbreviations with years and hours

The following abbreviations are acceptable when used with numerals. Notice that A.D. precedes the numeral; all other abbreviations follow the numeral.

399 B.C. ("before Christ")

A.D. 49 (*anno Domini*, Latin for "year of our Lord")

210 B.C.E. ("before the common era")

49 C.E. ("common era")

11:15 A.M. *or* a.m. (*ante meridiem*, Latin for "before noon")

9:00 P.M. *or* p.m. (*post meridiem*, Latin for "after noon")

Note that B.C.E. and C.E. are becoming preferred abbreviations with dates.

55c Using acronyms and initial abbreviations

Abbreviations that can be pronounced as words are called **acronyms:** OPEC, for example, is the acronym for the Organization of Petroleum Exporting Countries. **Initial abbreviations** are those that are pronounced as separate initials: NRA for National Rifle Association, for instance. Many well-known acronyms and initial abbreviations come from business, government, and science: NASA, PBS, DNA, GE, UNICEF, AIDS, SAT.

As long as you can be sure your readers will understand them, you can use such abbreviations in much of your college writing. If you are using a term only once or twice, you should spell it out; but when you need to use a term repeatedly, abbreviating it will serve as a convenience for you and your readers alike. If the abbreviation may be unfamiliar to your readers, however, spell out the term at the first use, and give the abbreviation in parentheses. After that, you can use the abbreviation by itself.

> The Comprehensive Test Ban (CTB) Treaty was first proposed in the 1950s. For those nations signing it, the CTB would bring to a halt all nuclear-weapons testing.

www • bedford
stmartins.com/
smhandbook

For links to Web
sites that list
popular Internet
acronyms,
click on

▶ Links
  ▶ Language

55d Using other kinds of abbreviations

The following guidelines will help you use some other common abbreviations. Especially in science courses, however, you may also want to check with your instructor about special conventions for abbreviations in a particular field. In general, in an academic writing assignment, you should not use any type of abbreviation not discussed in this chapter.

>   *biology*   *Friday*
> ▶ **The bio lab was deserted on Fri. nights.**

■ *Company names*

Use such abbreviations as *Inc., Co.,* and *Corp.* and the ampersand (&) if they are part of a company's official name. You should not, however, use them in most other contexts.

>   *corporation*
> ▶ **Sears, Roebuck & Co. was the only big corp. in town.**

■ *Reference information*

Though it is conventional to abbreviate such words as *chapter* (ch.), *edition* (ed.), *page* (p.), or *pages* (pp.) in source citations, it is not conventional to do so in the body of a paper.

> *edition*
> ▶ The preface to the 1851 ed. of *Twice-Told Tales* states that the stories
> are not autobiographical.

■ *Latin abbreviations*

In general, avoid these abbreviations except when citing sources:

cf.	compare (*confer*)
e.g.	for example (*exempli gratia*)
et al.	and others (*et alia*)
etc.	and so forth (*et cetera*)
i.e.	that is (*id est*)
N.B.	note well (*nota bene*)

> *for example,*
> ▶ Many firms have policies to help working parents — e.g., flexible hours,
> parental leave, day care.

■ *Geographic terms and months*

For examples of
abbreviations in
bibliographic
references, see
Chapters 20–23.

Place-names and months of the year are often abbreviated in source citations, but they should always be written out within sentences.

> *August,*   *California,* *Los Angeles.*
> ▶ In Aug., I moved from Lodi, Calif., to L.A.

Common exceptions are *Washington, D.C.,* and *U.S.* The latter is acceptable as an adjective but not as a noun.

> The *U.S. delegation* negotiated the treaty.

> *United States.*
> ▶ The exchange student enjoyed the U.S.

■ *Symbols*

Except in some technical and scientific writing, symbols such as ¢, #, %, +, and = should generally not be used in the body of a paper, though they are commonly used in graphs and tables. The dollar sign ($) is acceptable before specific figures, and the "at" sign (@) is used in Internet addresses.

▶ Only fifty *percent* % of applicants are accepted.

■ *Units of measure*

Except in scientific and technical writing, most units of measure should not be abbreviated in the body of a paper.

▶ The ball sailed 425 *feet* ft. over the fence.

● **EXERCISE 55.1**

Revise each of the following sentences to eliminate any abbreviations that would be inappropriate in most academic writing. Example:

The population of the *United States* U.S. grew about ten *percent* % in the 1980s.

1. The Thurs. night NBC show set in an E.R. remains popular even though cast members have changed over the years.

2. An MX missile, which is 71 ft. long and 92 in. around, weighs 190,000 lbs.

3. Almost every P.M., my neighbor stops by and borrows things she never returns — e.g., milk, coffee, or a couple of onions.

4. Enron officials met with the V.P. of the U.S. to discuss the admin.'s energy policy, but soon afterward the Tex. co. declared bankruptcy.

5. A large corp. like AT&T may help finance an employee's M.B.A.

6. Unfortunately, the five-¢ candy bar is a relic of the past.

7. The Grammy Awards are sometimes held in NYC, but the Oscars always take place in L.A.

8. The local NPR station has a broadcast range of seventy-five mi.

9. After less than a yr. at U.Va., Poe left and joined the U.S. Army.

10. In spite of its old-fashioned name, the NAACP is a thoroughly modern org.

www ● bedford
stmartins.com/
smhandbook

For additional
exercises on
abbreviations,
click on

▶ Exercise Central
  ▶ Abbreviations

55e Spelling out numbers

If a number can be written as one or two words, spell it out.

The victim's screams were ignored by *thirty-eight* people.

Police arrested the assailant *six* days later.

When a sentence begins with a number, either spell out the number or rewrite the sentence.

INAPPROPRIATE   277,000 hours (or 119 years) of CIA labor cost taxpayers sixteen million dollars.

HARD TO READ   Two hundred seventy-seven thousand hours (or 119 years) of CIA labor cost taxpayers sixteen million dollars.

REVISED   Taxpayers spent sixteen million dollars for 277,000 hours (or 119 years) of CIA labor.

55f Using figures for numbers

Numbers that cannot be written in one or two words should be expressed in figures.

Did you know that a baseball is wrapped in 174 yards of blue-gray wool yarn and is held together by 216 red stitches?

If one of several numbers *of the same kind* in the same sentence needs to be expressed in figures, all the numbers should be expressed that way.

▶ A complete audio system can range in cost from ~~one hundred dollars~~ *$100*
    to $2,599; however, a reliable system can be purchased for approximately
    ~~five hundred dollars.~~ *$500.*

55g Using figures according to convention

Conventions for expressing numbers vary from field to field, and you will want to make sure you understand the conventions of your own field — and follow them closely. For rules on using numbers in a partic-

The term *hundred* is used idiomatically in English. When it is linked with numbers like *two, eight,* and so on, the word *hundred* remains singular: *Eight hundred years have passed, and still old animosities run deep.* Add the plural *-s* to *hundred* only when no number precedes the term: *Hundreds of priceless books were lost in the fire.*

ular discipline, the *MLA Handbook for Writers of Research Papers* or *The Chicago Manual of Style* is usually followed in the humanities; the *Publication Manual of the American Psychological Association,* in the social sciences; and *Scientific Style and Format: The CBE Manual for Authors, Editors, and Publishers,* in the natural sciences. (CBE stands for Council of Biology Editors, which changed its name in 2000 to Council of Science Editors.) The following examples show *MLA Handbook* style for running prose:

ADDRESSES

23 Main Street; 175 Fifth Avenue, New York, NY 10010

DATES

September 17, 1951; the 1860s; the sixties; the '60s; the twentieth century

DECIMALS, FRACTIONS, AND PERCENTAGES

65.34; 8½; seventy-seven percent

DIVISIONS OF BOOKS AND PLAYS

volume 5, pages 81–85 (*not* 81–5)
Act III, Scene ii (*or* Act 3, Scene 2), lines 3–9

SPECIFIC AMOUNTS OF MONEY

$7,348; $1.46 trillion; $2.50; thirty-five cents

SCORES AND STATISTICS

an 8–3 Red Sox victory; a verbal score of 600
a mean of 53; a ratio of 3 to 1

TIME OF DAY

6:00 a.m.; 5:45 p.m.; 12:01
five in the morning; four o'clock; four-thirty

55h Expressing numbers online

Because the Internet reaches readers around the globe, you may some-times need to use non-U.S. units. When using monetary figures online, use the currency of the nation you are writing about or to. For weights and measures, remember that the system of inches and pounds is largely limited to the United States; use metric measurements (meters, grams) when they are appropriate for the nation you are discussing. Begin phone numbers with a plus sign (+) followed by the international access code; then add the area, province, or city code in parentheses; and then add the local number, with spaces between.

+1 (212) 846 3119
+81 (5) 9232 6722

www • bedford stmartins.com/ smhandbook

For additional exercises on numbers, click on

▶ **Exercise Central**
  ▶ **Numbers**

● **EXERCISE 55.2**

Revise the numbers in the following sentences as necessary for correctness and consistency. If a sentence is correct, circle its number. Example:

> *twenty-first*
> Did the ~~21st~~ century begin in 2000 or 2001?
>   ^

1. 307 miles long and 82 miles wide, the island offered little of interest.

2. In the seventies, teenagers watched television shows about the '50s, and in the late '90s, a show about the seventies was popular.

3. You could travel around the city for only 65 cents.

4. As far as she knew, nothing of interest had happened on June eight, 1982, except her birth.

5. The senator who voted against the measure received 6817 angry emails and only twelve in support of her decision.

6. He was pleased that he had scored in the seventy-ninth percentile in math.

7. Walker signed a three-year, $4.5-million contract.

8. In that age group, the risk is estimated to be about 1 in 2,500.

9. During the birthday party, it took all eight parents to herd the six overstimu-lated four-year-olds out the door.

10. The amulet measured one and one-eighth by two and two-fifths inches.

Reading with an Eye for Abbreviations and Numbers

The paragraph by Roger Angell at the end of Chapter 57 follows the style of the *New Yorker* magazine, which often spells out numbers in situations where this chapter recommends using figures. Read the paragraph carefully, and then consider whether it would have been easier to read if figures had been used for some of the numbers. If so, which ones? Then consider how the paragraph would have been different if Angell had used *semi-professional* instead of *semi-pro*. What effect does the abbreviated form create?

Thinking about Your Own Use of Abbreviations and Numbers

Look over an essay or two that you have written, noting all abbreviations and numbers. Check your usage for correctness, consistency, and appropriateness. If you discover anything you have done wrong, make a note of it (in your writing log, if you are keeping one) so that you will do it correctly the next time.

56 ▼ Using Italics

The slanted type known as *italics* is more than just a pretty typeface. Indeed, italics give words special meaning or emphasis. In the sentence "Many people read *People* on the subway every day," the italics (and the capital letter) tell us that *People* is a publication.

You may use a computer that produces italic type; if not, underline words that you would otherwise italicize. But remember not to overdo the use of italics to emphasize important words: doing so will get *very boring* to readers *very quickly*.

This chapter will introduce you to conventional uses of italics. ■

56a Using italics for titles

In general, italics are used for the titles of long or complete works; use quotation marks for shorter works or sections of works. (See 52b.)

BOOKS	*Beloved*
CHOREOGRAPHIC WORKS	Agnes de Mille's *Rodeo*
FILMS AND VIDEOS	*Star Wars*
LONG MUSICAL WORKS	*Brandenburg Concertos*
LONG POEMS	*The Waste Land*
MAGAZINES AND JOURNALS	*Newsweek,* the *New England Journal of Medicine*
NEWSPAPERS	the Cleveland *Plain Dealer,* the *New York Times*
PAINTINGS AND SCULPTURE	Georgia O'Keeffe's *Black Iris*
PAMPHLETS	Thomas Paine's *Common Sense*
PLAYS	*The Producers*
RADIO SERIES	*All Things Considered*
RECORDINGS	Eminem's *Marshall Mathers LP*
SOFTWARE AND WEB SITES	*Dreamweaver, Purdue Online Writing Lab*
TELEVISION SERIES	*The Simpsons*

→ Check that all titles of long or complete works are italicized. (56a)
→ If you refer to any words, letters, or numbers as words, make sure they are in italics. (56b)
→ Italicize any non-English words or phrases that are not in an English dictionary. (56c)
→ If you use italics to emphasize words, check to be sure you really need them. If so, use them sparingly. (56e)
→ In online communication, use asterisks or the underline mark if italics are not available. (56f)

Note that sacred books, such as the Bible and the Qur'an, and public documents, such as the Constitution and the Magna Carta, are *not* italicized. Notice also with magazines and newspapers that an initial *the* is neither italicized nor capitalized, even if part of the official name.

56b Using italics for words, letters, and numbers referred to as terms

Italicize words, letters, or numbers referred to as terms.

> What's vulgar? Some people might say that the contraction of the words *what* and *is* itself is vulgar.   –JOSEPH EPSTEIN, "What Is Vulgar?"

> One characteristic of some New York speech is the absence of postvocalic *r*, with some New Yorkers, for example, pronouncing *four* as "fouh."

> The first four orbitals are represented by the letters *s, p, d*, and *f*.

> On the back of his jersey was the famous *24*.

56c Using italics for foreign words and phrases

Italicize words and phrases from other languages unless they are so frequently used by English speakers that they have come to be considered a part of English, such as the French word *bourgeois* and the Italian *pasta*. As a rule, if the word is in an English dictionary, it need not be italicized.

At last one of the phantom sleighs gliding along the street would come to a stop, and with gawky haste Mr. Burness in his fox-furred *shapka* would make for our door. —VLADIMIR NABOKOV, *Speak, Memory*

Note that Latin genus and species names are always italicized.

The caterpillars of *Hapalia,* when attacked by the wasp *Apanteles machaeralis,* drop suddenly from their leaves and suspend themselves in air by a silken thread. —STEPHEN JAY GOULD, "Nonmoral Nature"

56d Using italics for the names of vehicles

Italicize names of specific aircraft, spacecraft, ships, and trains. Do not italicize types and classes, such as Learjet, space shuttle, and Concorde.

AIRCRAFT AND SPACECRAFT	*Spirit of St. Louis, Discovery*
SHIPS	the *Santa Maria,* U.S.S. *Iowa*
TRAINS	the *Orient Express,* Amtrak's *Lakeshore Limited*

56e Using italics for special emphasis

Italics can help create emphasis in writing, but use them sparingly for this purpose. It is usually better to create emphasis with sentence structure and word choice.

Great literature and a class of literate readers are nothing new in India. What is new is the emergence of a gifted generation of Indian writers *working in English.* —SALMAN RUSHDIE

56f Using italics online

For programs that don't allow you to use italics, as is sometimes the case in online communication, you can substitute other devices. To add emphasis to a word or phrase, use asterisks.

The company homepage simply *must* be updated.

To indicate a title, use the underline mark before and after the title.

Thanks for the copy of _EasyWriter_, which arrived today.

Because underlining on the World Wide Web signals an active hypertext link, you should not underline text to signal italics in Web documents.

MECHANICS
Using Italics Online

**www • bedford
stmartins.com/
smhandbook**

For additional
exercises on italics,
click on

▶ **Exercise Central**
  ▶ **Italics**

● **EXERCISE 56.1**

In each of the following sentences, underline any words that should be italicized, and circle any italicized words that should not be. Example:

Critics debated whether <u>Thelma & Louise</u> was a feminist film.

1. Guests often stayed in the bathroom for long periods reading Spamku, a book of *haiku* about luncheon meat.

2. While shopping at Poverty Records, a secondhand store, Joan found a copy of The Velvet Underground and Nico with its banana sticker still intact.

3. Georgetown offers a *potpourri* of cultures and styles.

4. The word veterinary comes from the Latin *veterinarius*.

5. Niko Tinbergen's essay *The Bee-Hunters of Hulshorst* is a diary of experiments on *Philanthus triangulum Fabr,* the *bee-killer wasp.*

6. Flying the Glamorous Glennis, named for his wife, Chuck Yeager was the first pilot to fly faster than the speed of sound.

7. The Washington Post provides extensive coverage of Congress.

8. The monster in the Old English epic Beowulf got to tell his own side of the story in John Gardner's novel Grendel.

9. W. H. Auden wrote a poem describing Brueghel's painting Landscape with the Fall of Icarus.

10. While listening to Prairie Home Companion on my local public radio station, I heard the singers who perform *I Am a Man of Constant Sorrow* in the movie O Brother, Where Art Thou?

THINKING CRITICALLY ABOUT ITALICS

Reading with an Eye for Italics

The following passage about a graduate English seminar uses italics in several different ways—for emphasis, for a foreign phrase, and for a title. Read the passage carefully, particularly noting the effects created by the italics. How would it differ without any italic emphasis? What other words or phrases might the author have italicized?

To get into this seminar, you had to submit to a grilling wherein you renounced all former allegiance to the then-current literary religion, New Criticism, which considered that only the text existed, not the world. I passed the interview by lying—cunningly, and against my real convictions. I said that probably the world *did* exist—and walked triumphantly into the seminar room.

There were four big tables arranged in a square, with everyone's feet sticking out into the open middle of the square. You could tell who was nervous, and how much, by watching the pairs of feet twist around each other. The Great Man presided awesomely from the high bar of the square. His head was a majestic granite-gray, like a centurion in command; he *looked* famous. His clean shoes twitched only slightly, and only when he was angry.

It turned out he was angry at me a lot of the time. He was angry because he thought me a disrupter, a rioter, a provocateur, and a fool; also crazy. And this was twenty years ago, before these things were *de rigueur* in the universities. Everything was very quiet in those days: there were only the Cold War and Korea and Joe McCarthy and the Old Old Nixon, and the only revolutionaries around were in Henry James's *The Princess Casamassima.*   – CYNTHIA OZICK, "We Are the Crazy Lady"

Thinking about Your Own Use of Italics

Write a paragraph or two describing the most eccentric person you know. Make a point of italicizing some words for special emphasis. Read your passage aloud to hear the effect of the italics. Consider italicizing any other words you wish to emphasize. Now explain each use of italics, stating in words the reason for it. If you find yourself unable to give a reason, ask yourself whether the word should be italicized at all.

Then revise the passage to eliminate *all but one* use of italics. Try revising sentences and choosing more precise words to convey emphasis without italics. Compare the two versions, and decide which is more effective. Can you reach any conclusions about using italics for emphasis?

▼ Using Hyphens

57a Using hyphens to divide words at the end of a line

It is best not to divide words between lines, but when you must do so, break words between syllables. The word *metaphor,* for instance, is made up of three syllables (*met-a-phor*), and you could break it after either the *t* or the *a.* All dictionaries show syllable breaks, so the best advice for dividing words correctly is simply to look them up. In addition, you should follow certain other conventions.

- *Never divide one-syllable words,* even relatively long words.
- *Divide compound words, if possible, between the parts.* Try to hyphenate words such as *anklebone* or *mother-in-law* between the parts that make up the compound (*ankle-bone*) or at their hyphens (*mother-in-law*).
- *Divide words with hyphenated prefixes and suffixes, if possible, at the hyphen.* Try to divide *self-righteous* and *mayor-elect,* for example, at the hyphen rather than within *righteous* or *mayor.*
- *Never divide abbreviations, contractions, or figures.* Though such "words" as *NASA, didn't,* and *150,000* have audible syllables, do not divide them in writing.
- *Leave at least two letters on each line when dividing a word.* Words such as *acorn* (*a-corn*) or *scratchy* (*scratch-y*) may not be divided at all, and a word such as *Americana* (*A-mer-i-can-a*) can be broken only after the *r* or *i.*
- *Never use a hyphen when you break a URL across two or more lines.* For MLA style on breaking URLs, see 20c3.

Hyphens show up every time you listen to hip-hop, wear a T-shirt, make a left-hand turn, eat Tex-Mex food, get one-on-one tutoring, or worry about a long-term relationship. Sometimes the dictionary will tell you whether to hyphenate a word. Other times, you will have to apply some general rules or think about your intended meaning.

As Hall of Fame pitcher Jim Palmer once said, "The difference between *re-sign* and *resign* is a hyphen." This statement, heard on a televised baseball game, shows how important a hyphen can be. This chapter will help you use hyphens appropriately and correctly. ■

EDITING FOR HYPHENS

→ Check that words broken at the end of a line are divided at an appropriate point. (57a)
→ Double-check compound words to be sure they are properly closed up, separated, or hyphenated. If in doubt, consult a dictionary. (57b)
→ Check all terms that have prefixes or suffixes to see whether you need hyphens. (57c)

● **EXERCISE 57.1**

Divide each of the following words into syllables, first referring to your dictionary. Then indicate with a hyphen the places where you might break each word at the end of a line. Indicate any words that cannot be divided into syllables or broken at the end of a line.

1. passable
2. echo
3. stripped
4. necessity
5. antechamber

6. well-liked
7. haven't
8. hoping
9. anonymous
10. breathe

57b Using hyphens with compound words

Compound words are made up of more than one word. Some compounds are written as one word (*rowboat*), some as separate words (*floppy disc*), and some with hyphens (*up-to-date*). In general, consult a dictionary if you have any doubt about how to spell a compound. There are, in addition, some conventions that can guide you in using hyphens with compound words.

■ Compound adjectives

Often you will use adjectives made up of word combinations that are not listed in a dictionary. The guiding principle, then, is to hyphenate most compound adjectives that precede a noun but not those that follow a noun.

a *well-liked* boss   My boss is *well liked*.
a *six-foot* plank   The plank is *six feet* long.

In general, the reason for hyphenating such compound adjectives is to facilitate reading.

▶ **The designers used potted palms as living-room dividers.**

Without the hyphen, *living* may seem to modify *room dividers*.

Commonly used compound adjectives do not usually need to be hyphenated for clarity — *income tax reform* or *first class mail* would seldom if ever be misunderstood. Never hyphenate a combination of an adverb ending in *-ly* and an adjective: *a radically different approach*.

Compound adjectives formed from compound proper nouns are hyphenated if the noun is hyphenated: *Austro-Hungarian history*, but *Latin American literature*.

■ *Coined compounds*

You may sometimes want to use hyphens to link words that would not normally be hyphenated but that you are using in an unexpected way, especially as an adjective. Such combinations are called **coined compounds.**

It was an established *Daddy-said-so* fact. . . .

Before it reached the top of the porch it went off, a piece of tin shot *God-is-whipping-you* straight for Eddy's eye.   – MAXINE CLAIR, "Cherry Bomb"

■ *Fractions and compound numbers*

To write out fractions, use a hyphen to join the numerator and denominator. Also use hyphens to spell out whole numbers from twenty-one to ninety-nine, both when they stand alone and when they are part of larger numbers. (Usually such larger numbers should be written as numerals.)

one-seventh   thirty-seven
seven-sixteenths   three hundred fifty-four thousand

■ *Suspended hyphens*

A series of compound words that share the same base word can be shortened by the use of suspended hyphens.

Each student should do the work *him-* or *herself.*

■ *New compound words pertaining to technology*

New compounds may not appear in the dictionary right away. Many new compounds, especially those pertaining to technology, appear as one word, without hyphenation. Helpful advice comes from *Wired* magazine's *Wired Style:* "When in doubt, close it up." Hence *firewall, pageview,* and *imagemap.*

Following its own advice, *Wired* closed up the abbreviated form of *electronic mail,* writing it *email.* The magazine then famously changed its mind and used *e-mail,* unleashing a storm of controversy on both sides of the question. So it's still possible for the little hyphen to cause plenty of trouble. This book continues to use *email* since that term has become a word in its own right.

57c Using hyphens with prefixes and suffixes

Most words containing prefixes or suffixes are written without hyphens: *antiwar, gorillalike.* Only in the following cases do you need a hyphen:

WITH CAPITALIZED BASE WORDS

pro-Bush, un-American, non-Catholic

WITH FIGURES

pre-1960, post-1945

WITH CERTAIN PREFIXES AND SUFFIXES

all-state, self-possessed, quasi-legislative, mayor-elect, fifty-odd

Hyphens are also used with *ex-* and *-some* when these mean "former" and "approximately," respectively: *ex-husband, twenty-some.*

WITH COMPOUND BASE WORDS

pre-high school, pro-civil rights, post-cold war

FOR CLARITY OR EASE OF READING

re-cover, anti-inflation, troll-like

Re-cover means "cover again"; the hyphen distinguishes it from *recover,* meaning "get well." In *anti-inflation* and *troll-like,* the hyphens separate confusing clusters of vowels and consonants.

MECHANICS

Using Hyphens
with Prefixes and
Suffixes

Working with a classmate and using the dictionary as a reference, insert hyphens as needed.

1. antiinflammatory
2. pre Industrial Revolution
3. pro and anti handgun lobbyists
4. happily married couple
5. a what me worry look
6. self important
7. bride to be
8. seven hundred thirty three
9. bumper to bumper traffic
10. a politician who is fast talking

EXERCISE 57.2

www • bedford
stmartins.com/
smhandbook

For additional
exercises on
hyphens, click on

▶ Exercise Central
  ▶ Hyphens

Insert or delete hyphens as necessary, and correct any incorrect word divisions in the following sentences. Use your dictionary if necessary.

1. Stress can lead to hypertension and ulcers.

2. The drum-beating and hand-clapping signaled that the parade was near.

3. I bought a five pound bag of sugar and two and three quarter pounds of ground turkey.

4. After he spent four weeks in an alcohol re-habilitation program, he apologized to his wife for twenty two years of heavy drinking.

5. We urged him to be open minded and to temper his insensitive views.

6. Both pro and antiState Department groups registered complaints.

7. The employees found John difficult to work for because of his rudeness and huge e-go.

8. In the early years of the western frontier, people had no-one to turn to for help when lawless-ness got out of hand.

9. The governor elect joked about the preelection polls.

10. Her heavily-rouged cheeks and blue eye-shadow made her look like a circus clown.

THINKING CRITICALLY ABOUT HYPHENATION

The following paragraph uses many hyphens. Read it carefully, and note how the hyphens make the paragraph easier to read. Why do you think *semi-pro* is hyphenated? Why is *junior-college* hyphenated in the last sentence?

All semi-pro leagues, it should be understood, are self-sustaining, and have no farm affiliation or other connection with the twenty-six major-league clubs, or with the seventeen leagues and hundred and fifty-two teams . . . that make up the National Association — the minors, that is. There is no central body of semi-pro teams, and semi-pro players are not included among the six hundred and fifty major-leaguers, the twenty-five-hundred-odd minor-leaguers, plus all the managers, coaches, presidents, commissioners, front-office people, and scouts, who, taken together, constitute the great tent called organized ball. (A much diminished tent, at that; back in 1949, the minors included fifty-nine leagues, about four hundred and forty-eight teams, and perhaps ten thousand players.) Also outside the tent, but perhaps within its shade, are five college leagues, ranging across the country from Cape Cod to Alaska, where the most promising freshman, sophomore, and junior-college ballplayers . . . compete against each other. . . .   – ROGER ANGELL, "In the Country"

PART 11

FOR MULTILINGUAL WRITERS

"The story of the American people . . . is told in the rich accents of Cherokee, Spanish, German, Dutch, Yiddish, French, Menomenie, Japanese, Norwegian, Arabic, Aleut, Polish, Navajo, Thai, Portuguese, Caribbean creoles, and scores of other tongues."
—HARVEY DANIELS

58

◥ Learning U.S. Academic Conventions

How often have you been in a situation in which you were unfamiliar either with the language or with the conventions of speaking and writing that others were using? Many U.S. citizens and students studying in this country have difficulty as they seek to negotiate their ways among several languages, including the standard academic English expected in most college classes. Learning to be successful at such negotiations always involves some conflict, but, as writer/teacher Min-Zhan Lu notes, it can also lead to growth: "In spite of the frustration and confusion I experienced growing up caught between two conflicting [linguistic and cultural] worlds," she says, "the conflict ultimately helped me grow as a reader and writer."

The chapters that follow aim to help you grow as a reader and writer and to better negotiate the demands of standard academic written English. ■

58a Writing U.S.A. style

Xiao Ming Li, now a college teacher, says that before she first came to the United States, she had been a "good writer" in China—in both English and Chinese. Once in the United States, however, she struggled to grasp what her teachers expected of her college writing in English. While she could easily use grammar books and dictionaries, her instructors' unstated expectations seemed to go far beyond such grammatical issues, calling for her to take a stance on issues and to write in, for her, a new way.

This experience is shared by many students in the United States, whether monolingual or multilingual, for the expectations that Li encountered are often taken for granted by instructors. As a result, instructors may not think to explain them to students. These unspoken expectations are what many students have in mind when they ask Writing Center tutors or instructors how to produce effective academic writing in their college classes, which they often refer to as writing "U.S.A. style." Though all students face challenges in trying to become proficient writers of academic prose, this style of writing can be particularly troublesome for multilingual students.

Of course, there is no one style of writing in any culture, and surely not in the United States. Even the variety of English often referred to as "standard" covers a wide range of styles, as Chapter 26 demonstrates. In addition, effective oral styles differ from effective written styles, and written styles vary considerably from field to field. In spite of this wide variation, multilingual students want to learn the style that is most often associated with college writing in general and described briefly in Chapter 2. United States academic writing has the following characteristics:

MULTILINGUAL
Understanding
Expectations about
Readers

●— For information
on writing styles
of the world's
majorities, see
Chapter 24.

- conventional use of grammar, spelling, punctuation, and mechanics (that is, those features that meet U.S. conventions, as detailed throughout this text)
- organization that links ideas explicitly (See Chapter 5.)
- easy-to-read type size and typeface, conventional margins, and double-spacing (See Chapter 8.)
- explicitly stated claims supported by examples, statistics, anecdotes, and authorities of various kinds (See Chapter 13.)
- careful documentation of all sources (See Chapters 20–23.)
- consistent use of the appropriate level of formality (See 24h and 27a.)
- conventional use of idioms (See Chapter 61.)
- conventional academic formats, such as literature reviews, research essays, lab reports, and research proposals (See Chapters 64–66.)

This brief list begins to get at features of the kind of writing students identify as "U.S.A. style," yet these characteristics can create even more questions, such as *What does* conventional *mean?* This chapter aims to help answer such questions.

As you become a good writer in American English as well as in the other languages you write, you can add to your understanding by considering some of the basic expectations prevalent in the United States about readers, writers, and texts.

58b Understanding expectations about readers

When you receive reading assignments in your college classes, how do you go about completing them? It might be worth jotting down the strategies you use as a college reader: Do you read primarily to extract the information in the assignment? Do you take notes as you read? Do you read quickly through an assignment and then go back, rereading slowly?

Perhaps the most important expectation college instructors have about good reading is that it calls for active engagement. In other words,

●— For information
on reading
strategies that
work well in U.S.
college classes,
see Chapters 1,
11, and 16.

For more on
critical-thinking
skills, see 11a;
for an example
of one student's
critical response
to a text, see
Milena Ateyea's
essay in 11h.

as a reader you're expected to be assertive, to talk back to the reading, and to offer your informed opinions on what the reading has to say. This kind of highly active reading may seem impolite or even rude to you, but it will not seem so to your college instructors and many of your classmates. In other words, the kind of critique your instructors expect is not negative or combative. Rather, by talking back, you signal your constructive engagement with and respect for the text.

In addition, here are some other expectations many of your college instructors will have about what good reading involves.

SOME GUIDELINES FOR READING

→ Good reading calls for understanding the content of the assignment and being able to provide a brief summary of it.

→ Good reading calls for thinking critically and analyzing what you read. In other words, you need to do more than understand the content: you need to make direct and explicit connections between sentences and paragraphs, keep track of recurrent themes or images, and figure out how they contribute to the entire piece of writing. You should also note the author's attitude toward and implied assumptions about the subject of the reading so that you can then speculate on how that attitude and those assumptions may affect the author's thinking.

→ Good reading calls for distinguishing carefully between the author's stance in a piece of writing and the author's representation of the stances of others. To signal an opposing argument, authors often use key phrases such as *while some have argued that* or *in the past.* Keeping an eye open for these kinds of words or phrases will help you become a better reader.

→ Good reading calls for being attentive not only to *what* a text says but also to *how* it says it — that is, to organizational patterns, use of sources, choice of words, and so on.

For more on
analyzing an
author's stance,
see 16c.

FOR COLLABORATION

Working with another person in your class, read one of your assignments together, first silently, making notes for yourself about what you are doing as you read. Then talk about the reading assignment and about your and your classmate's approaches to it, noting similarities as well as differences in the reading strategies you used. Finally, work together to write a summary of the reading you did, and bring your summary to class for discussion and comparison with those of others. See 16e4 if you need more information on writing summaries.

College audiences also hold some definite, if unstated, expectations about how writers will present themselves in their writing.

■ *Establishing authority*

Students in the United States are expected to be in the process of establishing themselves as authorities, as writers who are capable of creating new knowledge based on their own thinking and on what others have written and said. In reality, this emphasis on newness — on what is often referred to as *creativity* or *originality* — is a bit of a fiction: writing is possible only by using and building on the work of others. Rather than creating something totally original, writers most often discover and share new ways of understanding and expressing information and ideas. What, then, does "establishing authority" mean in practice?

- Assume that your individual opinions count (as long as they are informed rather than merely tossed out with little or no thought) and that your audience will expect you to present these opinions.

- Feel free to draw conclusions based on what you have read about your subject and to offer those conclusions on your own authority. In a book review for a course in political science, for example, you might begin with a summary of a book you read on voting trends but then go on to relate the book to some of the themes discussed in class and to draw your own conclusions about how effectively the book treats those themes.

- Build your authority by showing — in writing — that you have done the necessary research for the assignment. By citing the works of others, you show your readers that you are familiar with these works and with how they relate to your subject. In the book review just mentioned, for instance, you might cite an article you've read about voting trends among young adults or statistics you've found in a Gallup Poll.

- Don't hesitate to criticize the ideas of others as long as you explain your criticism thoroughly. Remember that good criticism is constructive rather than negative or destructive: being critical does not indicate a lack of respect.

■ *Being direct*

Your college instructors will most often expect you to be very direct in your approach to your topic. In practice, this means getting to the main point sooner rather than later and making sure that everything that follows is in some way tied to that point. To achieve directness in your written English, try the following strategies:

- Avoid overqualifying your statements. Instead of saying *I think the data reveal* or *The data possibly reveal,* it's all right to say *The data reveal.*
- Watch out for using a number of prepositional phrases in a row; they can often detract from the point you are trying to make or can confuse readers. Instead of saying *The effect of the overuse of prepositional phrases in writing is to place too much strain on an inadequate number of verbs,* with its string of five prepositional phrases, simply say *Overusing prepositional phrases places too much strain on verbs.*
- Avoid digressions. If you use an anecdote, story, or example, be sure that it relates directly to your main point. For instance, a story about your brother, who happens to be a firefighter, may or may not be appropriate in an essay you're writing about current fire-fighting techniques, depending on how closely it is tied to the main point you want to make.
- Speak to your readers confidently, as one who has done the work necessary to prepare for this piece of writing.

58d Understanding expectations about your texts

Your readers will also hold some expectations about the texts you produce and the features of those texts.

■ Considering kinds of texts

Research shows that the most common writing students do in college occurs in class, in short-answer questions and very brief essays (usually on exams). For this kind of writing, you will almost always be expected to display knowledge you have learned in the course. In this setting, demonstrating that you know the material is more important than developing new or original ideas about it. For many multilingual students, the major problem presented by in-class writing is running out of time. You can overcome this problem by preparing carefully in advance.

For further
advice on writing
in-class essays,
see Chapter 68.

- Review all the material carefully.
- Anticipate the questions, and write practice answers to them. (Do not, however, memorize answers to questions you think might be on the exam, since doing so might lead you to rely on answers that don't fit the questions on the actual test.)
- Explain the material you will be tested on — either orally or in writing — to someone unfamiliar with it.

- Do some timed writing right before class to get your writing muscles warmed up.

Finally, prepare a very brief outline to guide you once the test begins. Such an outline can help you organize your thoughts and keep you on track.

The most common out-of-class writing assignments in college classes include (1) research-based papers that draw on sources from your library or from online searches (see 20d); (2) reports, which include some interpretation (see 66b); (3) summaries, which may or may not call for analysis (see 16e4); (4) proposals (see 66c); (5) book reviews or critiques (see 64b); and (6) close reading or explication of a text (see 64c and d). This textbook provides some basic information on all these kinds of writing.

■ *Considering features of texts*

In college writing, you will be expected to provide every piece of information readers need to follow your train of thought, even if some details and links seem redundant to you. Researchers call this kind of writing *low context* because it doesn't rely on anything outside of the writing — the **context** of the writing — to provide information. In contrast, *high-context* writing often leaves quite a lot of information out because either the physical context or the readers of the text will provide that information. Since college writing in the United States is low context, you should work to fill in every blank and stop up every gap, again leaving as little as possible to the imagination. How can you meet this expectation?

First, assume that your audience will expect you to make your main point explicit and to offer it early on in your piece of writing — whether you are taking an in-class essay exam or writing an out-of-class project. Here is an example of one student's statement of his main point in an out-of-class essay:

> While the United States decries human rights abuses in many other countries, most notably China, the government turns away from the abuses occurring right here and right now in the United States.

In some kinds of writing, such as arguments or proposals, you may want to make your main point in a statement of intent, like the one this student wrote:

> In this proposal, I intend to begin by reviewing the three failed attempts to solve the problem of overcrowding and will then present a solution that, based on my analysis, will succeed where the others have failed.

For more on
transitions, see
5d4.

If you need to provide background information before getting to your main point, keep it as brief as possible, and make sure to show how that information relates *directly* to your main point.

For all kinds of college writing, make your transitions from paragraph to paragraph and point to point obvious and clear. You might think of such transitions from paragraph to paragraph as a handshake between the paragraphs: the first sentence of a new paragraph reaches back to the paragraph before and then looks forward to what is to come, like two hands coming together in a handshake. Sometimes you will also want to use summary statements, especially if your paper is longer than two or three pages. You can add a summary statement, for example, at the end of each section of your paper. A student who was writing a paper on the pros and cons of taking vitamin C as a diet supplement used the following summary statement at the end of the first section of her paper:

> We can see, then, that vitamin C supplements may help prevent some diseases. Let's look at the other side now—how too much vitamin C can be harmful.

For long essay questions and, especially, your formal papers, be sure to provide plenty of specific details in support of your points. These details can include examples, precedents, statistics, definitions, or occasionally even anecdotes, but to be effective these details need to be as specific as possible and be directly related to the point you are making.

For an example
of an essay that
uses detail well,
see Emily Lesk's
essay in 4j.

Finally, be careful to cite all your sources and document them meticulously. You may be used to weaving together sources without mentioning them, and while that is an old and time-honored tradition in some cultures, in U.S. academic writing it almost always results in a charge of plagiarism. Your instructors will expect you to acknowledge every source you use, even if you are only paraphrasing or summarizing it rather than quoting it directly.

For more on
using sources
correctly, see
Chapters 17
and 18.

THINKING CRITICALLY ABOUT USING U.S. ACADEMIC CONVENTIONS

Reading with an Eye for U.S. Academic Conventions

This chapter has attempted to put expectations about U.S. academic writing in plain view, to help you understand this particular context. But why is it worthwhile to gain this understanding in the first place? Will doing so in some way discount the good writing you do in other languages, or will it impose U.S. cultural values on your thinking? In what ways might learning about a U.S. academic style of writing help you in other kinds of writing you do? On a piece of paper or in your writing log, if you keep one, write out your thoughts in response to these questions, and bring them to class to compare with others.

Thinking about Your Own Use of U.S. Academic Conventions

Read very carefully a piece of writing you have done recently for one of your college classes. Using the information in this chapter, determine how well your piece of writing meets the expectations about writers and about texts in the United States. Then trade with a member of your class, and analyze each other's writing to see how well your partner has met the expectations about writers and texts in the United States. Bring the results of your analysis to class for discussion.

Understanding Nouns and Noun Phrases

59a Distinguishing count and noncount nouns

Look at the following sentences:

The hill was covered with trees.

The hill was covered with grass.

Trees is a count noun, and *grass,* a noncount noun. **Count nouns** refer to separate individuals or things: *a doctor, a book, a tree; doctors, books, trees.* **Noncount nouns** refer to masses or collections without distinctly separate parts: *milk, ice, clay, blood, grass.* These terms do not mean that grass cannot be counted but only that English grammar requires that if we count grass, we express it indirectly: *one blade of grass, two blades of grass,* not *one grass, two grasses.*

Count nouns usually have singular and plural forms: *tree, trees.* Noncount nouns usually have only a singular form: *grass.*

COUNT	NONCOUNT
people (plural of *person*)	humanity
tables, chairs, beds	furniture
letters	mail
pebbles	gravel
beans	rice
facts	information
suggestions	advice

Some nouns can be either count or noncount, depending on meaning.

COUNT   Before there were video games, children played with *marbles.*

NONCOUNT The floor of the palace was made of *marble.*

When you learn a noun in English, you need to learn whether it is count, noncount, or both. Two dictionaries that supply this information are the *Oxford Advanced Learner's Dictionary* and the *Longman Dictionary of American English.*

59b Stating plural forms explicitly

Look at this sentence from a traffic report:

All four bridges into the city are crowded with cars right now.

This sentence has three count nouns; one is singular (*city*), and two are plural (*bridges, cars*). If you speak a language with nouns that generally have no distinct plural forms (for example, Chinese, Japanese, or Korean), you might think that no information would be lost if the sentence were *All four bridge into the city are crowded with car right now.* After all, *four* indicates that *bridge* is plural, and obviously there would have to be more than one car if the bridges are crowded. But English requires that every time you use a count noun, you ask yourself whether you are talking about one item or more than one and that you choose a singular or a plural form accordingly.

Since noncount nouns usually have no plural forms, they can be quantified only with a preceding phrase: *one quart of milk, three pounds of rice, several bits of information.* The noun in question remains singular.

59c Using determiners appropriately

A noun together with all its modifiers constitutes a **noun phrase,** and the noun around which the modifiers cluster is called the **head.** For example, in *My adventurous sister is leaving for New Zealand tomorrow,* the noun phrase *my adventurous sister* consists of two modifiers (*my* and *adventurous*) and the head *sister.*

Words like *my, our,* and *this* are **determiners,** which are common and important words in the English language. Determiners identify or quantify the noun head.

COMMON DETERMINERS

- *a/an, the*
- *this, these, that, those*
- *my, our, your, his, her, its, their*
- possessive nouns and noun phrases (*Sheila's, my friend's*)
- *whose, which, what*
- *all, both, each, every, some, any, either, no, neither, many, much, (a) few, (a) little, several,* and *enough*
- the numerals *one, two,* etc.

■ *Using determiners with singular count nouns*

Every noun phrase with a singular count-noun head must begin with a determiner.

> *my*
> **adventurous sister**
> ^

> *the*
> **big, bad wolf**
> ^

> *that*
> **old neighborhood**
> ^

If there is no reason to use a more specific determiner, use *a* or *an*: *a big, bad wolf; an old neighborhood.*

Notice that every noun phrase need not begin with a determiner, only those whose head is a singular count noun. Noncount and plural count nouns sometimes have determiners, sometimes not: *This grass is green* and *Grass is green* are both acceptable, though different in meaning.

■ *Remembering which determiners go with which types of noun*

- *This* and *that* go with singular count or noncount nouns: *this book, that milk.*
- *These, those, (a) few, many, both,* and *several* go with plural count nouns: *these books, those plans, a few ideas, many students, both hands, several trees.*
- *(A) little* and *much* go with noncount nouns: *a little milk, much affection.*
- *Some* and *enough* go with noncount or plural count nouns: *some milk, some books; enough trouble, enough problems.*
- *A, an, every,* and *each* go with singular count nouns: *a book, every child, each word.*

59d Choosing articles appropriately

noun

59d 833

MULTILINGUAL

Choosing Articles
Appropriately

The definite article *the* and the indefinite articles *a* and *an* are challenging to multilingual speakers. Many languages have nothing directly comparable to them, and languages that do have articles differ from English in the details of their use.

▣ *Using* the

Use the definite article *the* with nouns whose identity is known or is about to be made known to readers. The necessary information for identification can come from the noun phrase itself, from elsewhere in the text, from context, from general knowledge, or from a superlative.

> ▶ Let's meet at *the* fountain in front of Dwinelle Hall.

The phrase *in front of Dwinelle Hall* identifies the specific fountain.

> ▶ Last Saturday, a fire that started in a restaurant spread to a neighboring clothing store. ~~Store~~ *The store* was saved, although it suffered water damage.

The word *store* is preceded by *the*, which directs our attention to the information in the previous sentence, where the store is identified.

> ▶ Professor to student in her office: "Please shut *the* door when you leave."

The professor expects the student to understand that she is referring to the door in her office.

> ▶ ~~Pope~~ *The pope* is expected to visit Africa in October.

Since there is only one living pope, his identity is clear.

> ▶ Will is now *the* best singer in the choir.

The superlative *best* identifies the noun *singer*.

▣ *Using* a *or* an

Use *a* before a consonant sound: *a car.* Use *an* before a vowel sound: *an uncle.* Pay attention to sounds rather than to spelling: *a house, an hour.*

A or *an* tells readers they do not have enough information to identify what the noun refers to. The writer may or may not have a particular thing in mind but in either case will use *a* or *an* if the reader lacks the information necessary for identification. Compare these sentences:

I need *a* new *coat* for the winter.

I saw *a coat* that I liked at Dayton's, but it wasn't heavy enough.

The coat in the first sentence is hypothetical rather than actual. Since it is indefinite to the writer, it clearly is indefinite to the reader and is used with *a*, not *the*. The second sentence refers to a very specific actual coat, but since the writer cannot expect the reader to know which one it is, it is used with *a* rather than *the*.

If you want to speak of an indefinite quantity, rather than just one indefinite thing, use *some* with a noncount noun or a plural count noun.

This stew needs *some* more *salt*.

I saw *some plates* that I liked at Gump's.

■ *Using the zero article*

If a noun appears without *the, a* or *an,* or any other determiner (even if it is preceded by other adjectives), it is said to have a zero article. The zero article is used with noncount and plural count nouns: *cheese, hot tea, crackers, ripe apples* (but not with *cracker* or *ripe apple*). Use the zero article to make generalizations.

In this world nothing is certain but *death* and *taxes*.   –BENJAMIN FRANKLIN

The zero article indicates that Franklin refers not to a particular death or specific taxes but to death and taxes in general.

Here English differs from many other languages — Greek or Spanish or German, for example — that would use the definite article to make generalizations. In English, a sentence like *The snakes are dangerous* can refer only to particular, identifiable snakes, not to snakes in general.

You can also sometimes make general statements with *the* or *a/an* and singular count nouns.

First-year college students are confronted with many new experiences.

A first-year student is confronted with many new experiences.

The first-year student is confronted with many new experiences.

These sentences all make the same general statement, but the last two are more vivid than the first. The second focuses on a hypothetical student taken at random, and the third sentence, which is characteristic of formal written style, projects the image of a typical student as representative of the whole class.

59e Arranging modifiers

Some modifiers precede the noun head, and others follow, and you need to learn both the required and the preferred positions for modifiers in order to know what can go where.

- Phrases or clauses follow the noun head: *the tiles on the wall, the tiles that we bought in Brazil.*
- Determiners go at the very beginning of the noun phrase: *these old-fashioned tiles. All* or *both* precedes any other determiners: *all these tiles.* Numbers follow any other determiners: *these six tiles.*
- Noun modifiers go directly before the noun head: *these kitchen tiles.*
- All other adjectives go between determiners and noun modifiers: *these old-fashioned kitchen tiles.* If there are two or more of these adjectives, their order is variable, but there are strong preferences, described below.
- Subjective adjectives (those that show the writer's attitude) go before objective adjectives (those that merely describe): *these beautiful old-fashioned kitchen tiles.*
- Adjectives of size generally come early: *these beautiful large old-fashioned kitchen tiles.*
- Adjectives of color generally come late: *these beautiful large old-fashioned blue kitchen tiles.*
- Adjectives derived from proper nouns or from nouns that refer to materials generally come after color terms and right before noun modifiers: *these beautiful large old-fashioned blue Portuguese ceramic kitchen tiles.*
- All other objective adjectives go in the middle, and adjectives for which a preferred order does not exist are separated by commas: *these beautiful large decorative, heat-resistant, old-fashioned blue Portuguese ceramic kitchen tiles.*

As you probably realize, the endless noun phrase presented as an illustration in the last bulleted item would be out of place in almost any conceivable kind of writing. You should always budget your use of adjectives.

MULTILINGUAL

Understanding
Nouns and
Noun Phrases

EXERCISE 59.1

Each of the following sentences contains an error. Rewrite each sentence correctly.

1. Before a middle of the nineteenth century, surgery was usually a terrifying, painful ordeal.

2. Because anesthesia did not exist yet, only painkiller available for surgical patients was whiskey.

3. The pain of surgical procedures could be so severe that much people were willing to die rather than have surgery.

4. In 1846, one of the hospital in Boston gave ether to a patient before he had surgery.

5. The patient, who had a large on his neck tumor, slept peacefully as doctors removed it.

**www • bedford
stmartins.com/
smhandbook**

For additional
exercises, click on

▶ **Exercise Central**
▶ **Nouns and
Noun Phrases**

EXERCISE 59.2

Insert articles as necessary in the following passage from *The Silent Language*, by Edward T. Hall.

Hollywood is famous for hiring _____ various experts to teach _____ people technically what most of us learn informally. _____ case in point is _____ story about _____ children of one movie couple who noticed _____ new child in _____ neighborhood climbing _____ tree. _____ children immediately wanted to be given _____ name of his instructor in _____ tree climbing.

Understanding Verbs and Verb Phrases

60

60a Forming verb phrases

Verb phrases can be built up out of a main verb (MV) and one or more auxiliaries. (See 33a.)

My cat *drinks* milk.

My cat *is drinking* milk.

My cat *has been drinking* milk.

My cat *may have been drinking* milk.

Verb phrases have strict rules of order. If you try to rearrange the words in any of these sentences, you will find that most alternatives are impossible. You cannot say *My cat drinking is milk* or *My cat have may been drinking milk.* The only permissible rearrangement is to move the first auxiliary to the beginning of the sentence in order to form a question: *Has my cat been drinking milk?*

■ Auxiliary and main verbs

In *My cat may have been drinking milk,* the main verb *drinking* is preceded by three auxiliaries: *may, have,* and *been.*

- *May* is a modal, which must be followed by the base form (*have*).
- *Have* indicates that the tense is perfect, and it must be followed by a past participle (*been*).

Verbs can be called the heartbeat of prose in every language, but in English the metaphor is especially meaningful. With rare exceptions, you cannot deprive an English sentence of its verb without killing it. If you speak Russian or Arabic, you might wonder what is wrong with a sentence like *My teacher very intelligent.* But unlike those and many other languages, English requires that sentences have a verb (for example, *My teacher impresses me as very intelligent*), and if no other verb is chosen, a form of the verb *be* must be used: *My teacher is very intelligent.*

English also differs from some other languages in its use of verb phrases, including perfect tenses, progressive forms, and modals. This chapter discusses some of the distinctive features of English verbs. ■

- *Been* (or any other form of *be*), when it is followed by a present participle (such as *drinking*), indicates that the tense is progressive.
- When a form of *be* is followed by a past participle, as in *My cat may have been bitten by a dog*, it indicates passive voice.

Auxiliaries must be in the following order: modal + perfect *have* + progressive *be* + passive *be*.

>   ┌PERF PASS┐   MV
> Sonya *has been invited* to stay with a family in Prague.

>   ┌PERF PROG┐   MV
> She *has been taking* an intensive course in Czech.

>   MOD
>   ┌─ PROG ─┐   MV
> She *must be looking* forward to her trip.

Only one modal is permitted in a verb phrase.

>   *will be able to speak*
> ▶ She ~~will can speak~~ Czech much better soon.
>   ^

Every time you use an auxiliary, you should be careful to put the next word in the appropriate form.

■ *Modal + base form*

Use the base form of a verb after *can, could, will, would, shall, should, may, might,* and *must.*

> Alice *can read* Latin.

> Sanjay *should have* studied for the test.

> They *must be* going to a fine school.

In many other languages, modals such as *can* or *must* are followed by an infinitive (*to* + base form). In English, use only the base form.

> ▶ Alice can ~~to~~ read Latin.

■ *Perfect* have + past participle

To form the perfect tenses, use *have, has,* or *had* with a past participle.

> Everyone *has gone* home.

> They *have been* working all day.

■ *Progressive* **be** *+ present participle*

A progressive form of a verb is signaled by two elements, a form of the auxiliary *be* (*am, is, are, was, were, be,* or *been*) and the *-ing* form of the next word: *The children are studying.* Be sure to include both elements.

▶ The children $\overset{are}{\underset{\wedge}{\text{studying}}}$ in school.

▶ The children are $\overset{studying}{\underset{\wedge}{\text{study}}}$ in school.

Some verbs are rarely used in progressive forms. These are verbs that express unchanging conditions or mental states rather than deliberate actions: *believe, belong, hate, know, like, love, need, own, resemble, understand.*

■ *Passive* **be** *+ past participle*

Use *am, is, are, was, were, being, be,* or *been* with a past participle to form the passive voice.

   Tagalog *is spoken* in the Philippines.

Notice that with the progressive *be* the following word (the present participle) ends in *-ing,* but with the passive *be* the following word (the past participle) never ends in *-ing.*

   Meredith *is* studying music.

   Natasha *was* taught by a famous violinist.

If the first auxiliary in a verb phrase is *be* or *have,* it must show either present or past tense, and it must agree with the subject: *Meredith has played in an orchestra.*

   Although a modal auxiliary may also show present or past tense (for example, *can* or *could*), it never changes form to agree with the subject.

▶ Michiko $\overset{can}{\underset{\wedge}{\text{cans}}}$ play two instruments.

60b Using present and past tenses

Every English sentence must have at least one verb or verb phrase that is not an infinitive, a gerund, or a participle without any auxiliaries. Furthermore, every such verb or verb phrase must have a tense.

In some languages, such as Chinese and Vietnamese, the verb form never changes regardless of when the action of a verb takes place, and the time of the action is simply indicated by other expressions such as *yesterday, last year,* and *next week.* In English, the time of the action must be clearly indicated by the tense form of each and every verb, even if the time is obvious or indicated elsewhere in the sentence.

▶ During the Cultural Revolution, millions of young people ~~cannot~~ go to [could not] school and ~~are~~ sent to the countryside. [were]

In some languages (Spanish, for example), words end in either a vowel sound or a single consonant sound, not in one consonant sound followed by another. If you speak such a language, remember to add the *-s* of the present-tense third-person singular and the *-ed* of the past tense.

▶ Last night I ~~call~~ my aunt who ~~live~~ in Santo Domingo. [called] [lives]

■ *Direct and indirect discourse*

Changing direct quotations to indirect quotations can sometimes lead to inappropriate tense shifts. If the verb introducing the indirect discourse is in the present tense, the verb in the indirect discourse should also be in the present tense.

DIRECT   She said, "My work *is* now complete."

INDIRECT   She *tells* me that her work *is* now complete.

In most instances, if the verb introducing the indirect discourse is in the past tense, stick with tenses that refer to past time in the indirect discourse.

▶ She told me that her exams were over and that she ~~receives~~ the highest [had received] score in her class.

If, however, the introductory verb is in the past tense, but the information that follows holds true in the present, then shifting to a present-tense verb is acceptable.

She *told* me that her work *is* as exciting as ever.

The perfect and progressive auxiliaries combine with the present or past tense, or with modals, to form complex verb phrases with special meanings. In particular, you should learn to recognize sentences in which the perfect or progressive rather than a simple tense must be used.

■ *Distinguishing the simple present and the present perfect*

My sister *drives* a bus.

The simple present (*drives*) merely tells us about the sister's current occupation. But if you were to add the phrase *for three years,* it would be incorrect to say *My sister drives a bus for three years.* Instead, you need a time frame that includes both the past and the present, and therefore you should use the present perfect or the present perfect progressive.

My sister *has driven* a bus for three years.

My sister *has been driving* a bus for three years.

■ *Distinguishing the simple past and the present perfect*

Since she started working, she *has bought* a new car and a VCR.

The clause introduced by *since* sets up a time frame that runs from past to present and requires the present perfect (*has bought*) in the following clause. Furthermore, the sentence does not say exactly when she bought the car or the VCR, and that indefiniteness also calls for the perfect. It would be less correct to say *Since she started working, she bought a new car and a VCR.* But what if you should go on to say when she bought the car?

She *bought* the car two years ago.

It would be incorrect to say *She has bought the car two years ago* because the perfect cannot be used with definite expressions of time. In this case, use the simple past (*bought*).

■ *Distinguishing the simple present and the present progressive*

When an action is in progress at the present moment, use the present progressive. Use the simple present for actions that frequently occur during a period of time that might include the present moment (though the simple present does not necessarily indicate that the action is taking place now).

My sister *drives* a bus, but she *is taking* a vacation now.

My sister *drives* a bus, but she *takes* a vacation every year.

Many languages, such as French and German, use the simple present (*drives, takes*) for both types of sentences. In English, however, the first sentence above would be incorrect if it said *but she takes a vacation now.*

■ *Distinguishing the simple past and the past progressive*

Sally *spent* the summer in Italy.

You might be tempted to use the past progressive (*was spending*) here instead of the simple past, since spending the summer involves a continuous stretch of time of some duration, and duration and continuousness are typically associated with the progressive. But English speakers use the past progressive infrequently and would be unlikely to use it in this case except to describe actions that are simultaneous with other past actions. For example:

Sally *was spending* the summer in Italy when she *met* her future husband.

Use the past progressive to focus on duration or continuousness and especially to call attention to past action that went on at the same time as something else.

60d Using modals appropriately

The nine basic modal auxiliaries are *can, could, will, would, shall, should, may, might,* and *must.* There are a few others as well, in particular *ought to,* which is close in meaning to *should.* Occasionally *need* can be a modal rather than a main verb.

The nine basic modals fall into the pairs *can/could, will/would, shall/should, may/might,* and the loner *must.* In earlier English, the second member of each pair was the past tense of the first. To a limited degree, the second form still functions as a past tense, especially in the case of *could.*

Ingrid *can* ski.

Ingrid *could* ski when she was five.

But for the most part, in present-day English, all nine modals typically refer to present or future time. When you want to use a modal to refer to the past, you follow the modal with a perfect auxiliary.

If you have a fever, you *should* see a doctor.

If you had a fever, you *should have seen* a doctor.

In the case of *must,* refer to the past by using *had to.*

You *must* renew your visa by the end of this week.

You *had to* renew your visa by the end of last week.

■ Using modals to make requests or to give instructions

Modals are often used in requests and instructions. Imagine making the following request of a flight attendant:

Will you bring me a pillow?

You have expressed your request in a demanding manner, and the flight attendant might resent it. A more polite request acknowledges that fulfilling the request may not be possible.

Can you bring me a pillow?

Another way of softening such a request is to use the past form of *will,* and the most discreet choice is the past form of *can.*

Would you bring me a pillow?

Could you bring me a pillow?

Using the past of modals is considered more polite than using their present forms because it makes any statement or question less assertive.
Now consider each of the following instructions:

1. You *can* submit your report electronically.
2. You *may* submit your report electronically.
3. You *should* submit your report electronically.
4. You *must* submit your report electronically.
5. You *will* submit your report electronically.

Instructions 1 and 2 give permission to submit the paper electronically but do not require it; of these, 2 is more formal. Instruction 3 adds a strong recommendation; 4 allows no alternative; and 5 implies, "Don't even think of doing otherwise."

■ Using modals to indicate doubt and certainty

Modals can also indicate how confident the writer is about the likelihood that what is being asserted is true. Look at the following set of examples, which starts with a tentative suggestion and ends with full assurance:

Please sit down; the show *might* be about to begin.

Please sit down; the show *may* be about to begin.

Please sit down; the show *must* be about to begin.

60e Using participial adjectives appropriately

Many verbs refer to feelings — for example, *bore, confuse, excite, fascinate, frighten, interest.* The present and past participles of such verbs can be used as ordinary adjectives (see 31c3). Use the past participle to describe a person having the feeling.

The *frightened* boy started to cry.

Use the present participle to describe the thing (or person) causing the feeling.

The *frightening* dinosaur display gave him nightmares.

Be careful not to confuse the two types of adjectives.

> *interested*
> I am ~~interesting~~ in African literature.
>   ^

> *interesting.*
> African literature seems ~~interested.~~
>   ^

www • bedford
stmartins.com/
smhandbook

For additional
exercises, click on

► Exercise Central
  ► Verbs and Verb
    Phrases

● **EXERCISE 60.1**

Each of the following sentences contains an error. Rewrite each sentence correctly.

1. Over the last forty years, average temperatures in the Arctic increase by several degrees.

2. A few years ago, a robin was observe in Inuit territory in northern Canada.

3. Inuit people in previous generations will never have seen a robin near their homes.

4. The Inuit language, which called *Inuktitut,* has no word for *robin.*

5. Many Inuits are concerning that warmer temperatures may change their way of life.

EXERCISE 60.2

Rewrite the following passage, adapted from "Cold Comfort" by Atul Gawande (*New Yorker*, March 11, 2002), adding appropriate auxiliaries and verb endings where necessary. The total number of words required in each case is indicated in parentheses.

The notion that a chill _____put (1)_____ you at risk of catching a cold is nearly universal. Yet science _____find (2)_____ no evidence for it. One of the first studies on the matter _____lead (2)_____ by Sir Christopher Andrewes. He _____take (1)_____ a group of volunteers and _____inoculate (1)_____ them with a cold virus; previously, half of the group _____keep (3)_____ warm, and the other half _____make (3)_____ to take a bath and then to stand for half an hour without a towel while the wind _____blow (2)_____ on them. The chilled group _____get (1)_____ no more colds than the warm group.

61

▼ Understanding Prepositions and Prepositional Phrases

If you were traveling by rail and asked for directions, it would not be helpful to be told to "take the Chicago train." You would need to know whether to take the train *to* Chicago or the one *from* Chicago. Words such as *to* and *from*, which show the relations between other words, are prepositions. Not all languages use prepositions to show such relations, and English differs from other languages in the way prepositions are used. This chapter will help you in deciding which preposition to use for your intended meaning and in using verbs that include prepositions, such as *take off*, *pick up*, and *put up with*. ■

61a Using prepositions idiomatically

Even if you usually know where to use prepositions, you may have difficulty from time to time knowing which preposition to use. Each of the most common prepositions, whether in English or in other languages, has a wide range of different applications, and this range never coincides exactly from one language to another. See, for example, how English speakers use *in* and *on*.

The peaches are *in* the refrigerator.

The peaches are *on* the table.

Is that a diamond ring *on* your finger?

■ *If you speak Spanish*

The Spanish translations of these sentences all use the same preposition (*en*), a fact that might lead you astray in English.

on
▶ Is that a ruby ring ̭in your finger?

There is no easy solution to the challenge of using English prepositions idiomatically, but the following strategies can make it less troublesome.

MULTILINGUAL

Using Prepositions
Idiomatically

1. Keep in mind typical examples of each preposition.

   IN   The peaches are *in* the refrigerator.

          There are still some pickles *in* the jar.

   Here the object of the preposition *in* is a container that encloses something.

   ON   The peaches are *on* the table.

          The book you are looking for is *on* the top shelf.

   Here the object of the preposition *on* is a horizontal surface that supports something with which it is in direct contact.

2. Learn other examples that show some similarities and some differences in meaning.

   IN   You shouldn't drive *in* a snowstorm.

   Here there is no container, but like a container, the falling snow surrounds and seems to enclose the driver.

   ON   Is that a diamond ring *on* your finger?

   A finger is not a horizontal surface, but like such a surface it can support a ring with which it is in contact.

3. Use your imagination to create mental images that can help you remember figurative uses of prepositions.

   IN   Michael is *in* love.

   Imagine a warm bath in which Michael is immersed (or a raging torrent, if you prefer to visualize love that way).

   ON   I've just read a book *on* computer science.

   Imagine a shelf labeled "Computer Science" on which the book you have read is located.

4. Try to learn prepositions not in isolation but as part of a system. For example, in identifying the location of a place or an event, the three prepositions *at, in,* and *on* can be used.

   At specifies the exact point in space or time.

   AT   There will be a meeting tomorrow *at* 9:30 A.M. *at* 160 Main Street.

(Continued on p. 848)

(Continued from p. 847)

Expanses of space or time within which a place is located or an event takes place might be seen as containers and so require *in*.

IN   I arrived *in* the United States *in* January.

On must be used in two cases: with the names of streets (but not the exact address) and with days of the week or month.

ON   The airline's office is *on* Fifth Avenue.
          I'll be moving to my new apartment *on* September 30.

FOR COLLABORATION

Working with another student, insert prepositions as necessary in the following paragraph.

Haivan skated gracefully _____ the pond, enjoying the brisk weather and looking _____ her new engagement ring. As she skated, she thought about the plans for her forthcoming wedding. Should it be _____ September or October? Could the caterer _____ her neighborhood do a good job? Would her sister arrive late for the ceremony or manage to be _____ time?

61b Using two-word verbs idiomatically

Some words that look like prepositions do not always function as prepositions. Consider the following two sentences:

The balloon rose *off* the ground.

The plane took *off* without difficulty.

In the first sentence, *off* is a preposition that introduces the prepositional phrase *off the ground*. In the second sentence, *off* neither functions as a preposition nor introduces a prepositional phrase. Instead, it combines with *took* to form a two-word verb with its own meaning. Such a verb is called a **phrasal verb,** and the word *off,* when used in this way, is called an **adverbial particle.** Many prepositions can function as particles to form phrasal verbs.

The verb + particle combination that makes up a phrasal verb is a tightly knit entity that usually cannot be torn apart.

MULTILINGUAL
Using Two-Word
Verbs Idiomatically

▶ **The plane took ~~with difficulty.~~ off.** *off*

The exceptions are the many phrasal verbs that are transitive, meaning that they take a direct object. Some transitive phrasal verbs have particles that may be separated from the verb by the object.

●— For more about
transitive verbs,
see 31c2.

   I *picked up my baggage* at the terminal.

   I *picked my baggage up* at the terminal.

If a personal pronoun is used as the direct object, it *must* separate the verb from its particle.

   I *picked it up* at the terminal.

Some idiomatic two-word verbs, however, do not operate like phrasal verbs.

   We *ran into* our neighbor on the train.

In such verbs, the second word *is* a preposition, which cannot be separated from the verb: *We ran our neighbor into on the train* would be unacceptable. *Ran into* seems to consist of the verb *ran* followed by the preposition *into,* which introduces the prepositional phrase *into our neighbor.* Yet *to run into our neighbor* is different from a normal verb + prepositional phrase, such as *to run into the room.* If you know the typical meanings of *run* and *into,* you can interpret *to run into the room.* Not so with *to run into our neighbor;* the combination *run* + *into* has a special meaning ("find by chance") that could not be determined from the typical meanings of *run* and *into.* Therefore, *run into* must be considered a two-word verb but one that has much more in common with verbs followed by prepositions than with phrasal verbs. Such verbs as *run into* are called **prepositional verbs.**

Prepositional verbs include such idiomatic two-word verbs as *take after,* meaning "resemble" (usually a parent or other older relative); *get over,* meaning "recover from"; and *count on,* meaning "trust." They also include verb + preposition combinations in which the meaning is predictable, but the specific preposition that is required is less predictable and must be learned together with the verb (for example, *depend on, look at, listen to, approve of*). There are also **phrasal-prepositional verbs,** which

●— For dictionaries
that distinguish
verb + particle
from verb +
preposition,
see 28c.

MULTILINGUAL

Understanding
Prepositions and
Prepositional
Phrases

**www • bedford
stmartins.com/
smhandbook**

For additional
exercises, click on

▶ **Exercise Central**
  ▶ **Prepositions and
    Prepositional
    Phrases**

are verb + adverbial particle + preposition sequences (for example, *put up with, look forward to, give up on, get away with*).

● **EXERCISE 61.1**

Each of the following sentences contains a two-word verb. In some, the verb is used correctly; in some, incorrectly. Identify each two-word verb, indicate whether it is a phrasal or prepositional verb, and rewrite any incorrect sentences correctly.

1. Soon after I was hired at my last job, I learned that the company might lay off me.

2. I was counting on the job to pay my way through school, so I was upset.

3. I decided to pick up a newspaper and see what other jobs were available.

4. As I looked the newspaper at, I was surprised to see that I was qualified for a job that paid much better than mine.

5. I gave my old job up and took the new one, which made attending school much easier.

Forming Clauses and Sentences

62

62a Expressing subjects and objects explicitly

English sentences consist of a subject and a predicate. This simple statement defines a gulf separating English from many other languages that leave out the subject when it can easily be inferred. With few exceptions, English demands that an explicit subject accompany an explicit predicate in every sentence. Though you might write *Went from Yokohama to Nagoya* on a postcard to a friend, in most varieties of spoken and written English, the extra effort of explicitly stating who went is not simply an option but an obligation.

In fact, every independent and every dependent clause must have an explicit subject.

> ► They took the Acela Express to Boston because *it* was fast.

English even requires a kind of "dummy" subject to fill the subject position in certain kinds of sentences. Consider the following sentences:

It is raining.

There is a strong wind.

Transitive verbs typically require that objects also be explicitly stated, and in some cases even other items of information as well (see 31c2). For example, it is not

Sound bites surround us, from Avis' "We try harder" to Apple's "Think different." These short simple sentences may be memorable, but they don't tell us very much. Ordinarily, we need more complex sentences to convey meaning. The sentences of everyday discourse are not formed in the same way in every language, however, and English has its own rules. Among the features of English sentences that give multilingual writers the most trouble are explicit subjects and objects, word order, noun clauses, infinitives and gerunds, adjective clauses, and conditional sentences. This chapter will offer some guidance in dealing with these issues. ■

enough to tell someone *Give!* even if it is clear what is to be given to whom. You must say *Give it to me* or *Give her the passport* or some other such sentence. Similarly, saying *Put!* or *Put it!* is insufficient when you mean *Put it on the table*.

■ *If you speak Spanish*

Speakers of Spanish might be inclined to leave out dummy subjects. In English, however, *it* and *there* are indispensable.

▶ *It is*
  ̭Is raining.

▶ *There is*
  ̭Has a strong wind.

62b Using English word order

In general, you should not move subjects, verbs, or objects out of their normal positions in a sentence. In the following sentence, each element is in an appropriate place:

SUBJECT VERB OBJECT   ADVERB
▶ Mario left Venice reluctantly.

This sentence would also be acceptable if written as *Mario reluctantly left Venice* or as *Reluctantly Mario left Venice,* but note that only the adverb can be moved. The three key elements of subject, verb, and object should be moved out of their normal order only to create special effects.

For more about
changing word
order for special
effects, see 47c3.

■ *If you speak Turkish, Korean, or Japanese*

In these languages, the verb must come last. Even if you have no difficulty adjusting to a different position for the verb in English, your recognition of the fact that word order can vary from one language to another should alert you to other possible problems.

For more on
subjects and
objects, see 31c1
and c2; for more
on disruptive
modifiers, see
41b.

■ *If you speak Russian*

Because Russian permits a great deal of freedom in word order, you must remember never to interchange the position of subject and object (*Venice left Mario reluctantly* is not acceptable English). In general, also avoid separating the verb from its object (*Mario left reluctantly Venice*).

62c Using noun clauses appropriately

Examine the following sentence:

In my last year in high school, my advisor urged that I apply to several colleges.

This is built up out of two sentences, one of them (B) embedded in the other (A):

A. In my last year in high school, my advisor urged B.

B. I (should) apply to several colleges.

When these are combined as in the original sentence, sentence B becomes a **noun clause** introduced by *that* and takes on the role of object of the verb *urged* in sentence A. Now look at the following sentence:

It made a big difference that she wrote a strong letter of recommendation.

Here the two component sentences are C and D:

C. D made a big difference.

D. She wrote a strong letter of recommendation.

In this case, the noun clause formed from sentence D functions as the subject of sentence C so that the combination reads as follows:

That she wrote a strong letter of recommendation made a big difference.

This is an acceptable sentence but somewhat top-heavy. Usually when a lengthy noun clause is the subject of the sentence, it is moved to the end. The result is *Made a big difference that she wrote a strong letter of recommendation.* If you speak Italian, Spanish, or Portuguese, you might see nothing wrong with such a sentence. In English, however, the subject must be stated. The dummy element *it* comes to the rescue.

> *It made*
> ▶ ~~Made~~ **a big difference that she wrote a strong letter of recommendation.**
>   ^

62d Choosing between infinitives and gerunds

Knowing whether to use an infinitive or a gerund in a particular sentence may be a challenge to multilingual writers. Though no simple explanation will make it an easy task, some hints will help you.

My advisor urged me *to apply* to several colleges.

Her *writing* a strong letter of recommendation made a big difference.

Why was an infinitive chosen for the first and a gerund for the second? In general, **infinitives** tend to represent intentions, desires, or expectations, and **gerunds** tend to represent facts. The gerund in the second sentence calls attention to the fact that a letter was actually written; the infinitive in the first sentence conveys the message that the act of applying was something desired, not an accomplished fact.

▦ Using gerunds to state facts

Jerzy *enjoys going* to the theater.

We *resumed working* after our coffee break.

Kim *appreciated getting* candy from Sean.

In all of these cases, the second verb form is a gerund, and the gerund indicates that the action or event that it expresses has actually happened. Verbs like *enjoy, resume,* and *appreciate* can be followed only by gerunds, not by infinitives. In fact, even when these verbs do not convey clear facts, the verb form that follows must still be a gerund.

Kim *would appreciate getting* candy from Sean, but he hardly knows her.

▦ Using infinitives to state intentions

Kumar *expected to get* a good job after graduation.

Last year, Fatima *decided to become* a math major.

The strikers have *agreed to go* back to work.

Here it is irrelevant whether the actions or events referred to by the infinitives did or did not materialize; at the moment indicated by the verbs *expect, decide,* and *agree,* those actions or events were merely intentions. These three verbs, as well as many others that specify intentions (or negative intentions, like *refuse*), must always be followed by an infinitive, never by a gerund.

▦ Understanding other rules and guidelines

A few verbs can be followed by either an infinitive or a gerund. With some, such as *begin* and *continue,* the choice makes little difference in meaning. With others, however, the difference in meaning is striking.

Carlos was working as a medical technician, but he *stopped to study* English. [The infinitive indicates that Carlos intended to study English when he left his job. We are not told whether he actually did study English.]

Carlos *stopped studying* English when he left the United States. [The gerund indicates that Carlos actually did study English but later stopped.]

The distinction between fact and intention is not a rule but only a tendency, and it can be superseded by other rules. Use a gerund — never an infinitive — directly following a preposition.

▶ **This fruit is safe for ~~to eat~~.**
   eating.

▶ **This fruit is safe ~~for~~ to eat.**

▶ **This fruit is safe for to eat.**
   us

A full list of verbs that can be followed by an infinitive and verbs that can be followed by a gerund can be found in the *Index to Modern English* by Thomas Lee Crowell Jr. (McGraw-Hill, 1964).

62e Using adjective clauses carefully

Adjective clauses can be a challenge to multilingual writers. Look at the following sentence:

The company *Yossi's uncle invested in* went bankrupt.

The subject is a noun phrase in which the noun *company* is modified by the article *the* and the adjective clause *Yossi's uncle invested in*. The sentence as a whole says that a certain company went bankrupt, and the adjective clause identifies the company more specifically by saying that Yossi's uncle had invested in it.

One way of seeing how the adjective clause fits into the sentence is to rewrite it like this: *The company (Yossi's uncle had invested in it) went bankrupt*. This is not a normal English sentence, but it helps demonstrate a process that leads to the sentence we started with. Note the following steps:

- Change the personal pronoun *it* to the relative pronoun *which: The company (Yossi's uncle had invested in which) went bankrupt.* That still is not acceptable English.

- Move either the whole prepositional phrase *in which* to the beginning of the adjective clause, or move just the relative pronoun: *The company in which Yossi's uncle had invested went bankrupt* or *The company which Yossi's uncle had invested in went bankrupt.* Both of these are good English sentences, the former somewhat more formal than the latter.

- If no preposition precedes the relative pronoun, substitute *that* for *which* or leave out the relative pronoun entirely: *The company that Yossi's uncle had invested in went bankrupt* or *The company Yossi's uncle had invested in went bankrupt.* Both of these are good English sentences, not highly formal but still acceptable in much formal writing.

Speakers of some languages find adjective clauses difficult in different ways. Following are some guidelines that might help.

■ If you speak Korean, Japanese, or Chinese

If you speak Korean, Japanese, or Chinese, the fact that the adjective clause does not precede the noun that it modifies may be troublesome, both because such clauses precede nouns in the East Asian languages and because other modifiers, such as determiners and adjectives, *do* precede nouns in English.

■ If you speak Farsi, Arabic, or Hebrew

If you speak Farsi, Arabic, or Hebrew, you may expect the adjective clause to follow the noun as it does in English, but you might need to remind yourself to change the personal pronoun (*it*) to a relative pronoun (*which* or *that*) and then to move the relative pronoun to the beginning of the clause. You may put a relative pronoun at the beginning but mistakenly keep the personal pronoun, thus producing incorrect sentences such as *The company that Yossi's uncle invested in it went bankrupt.*

■ If you speak a European or Latin American language

If you are a speaker of some European or Latin American languages, you are probably acquainted with adjective clauses very much like those of English, but you may have difficulty accepting the possibility that a relative pronoun that is the object of a preposition can be moved to the beginning of a clause while leaving the preposition stranded. You might, therefore, move the preposition as well even when the relative pronoun is *that*, or you might drop the preposition altogether, generating such incorrect sentences as *The company in that Yossi's uncle invested went bankrupt* or *The company that Yossi's uncle invested went bankrupt.*

Finally, the fact that the relative pronoun can sometimes be omitted may lead to the mistaken notion that it can be omitted in all cases. Remember that you cannot omit a relative pronoun that is the subject of a verb.

who
▶ **Everyone invested money in that company lost a great deal.**
            ^

62f   Understanding conditional sentences

English pays special attention to whether or not something is a fact or to the degree of confidence we have in the truth or likelihood of an assertion. Therefore, English distinguishes among many different types of **conditional sentences** — that is, sentences that focus on questions of truth and that are introduced by *if* or its equivalent. The following examples illustrate a range of different conditional sentences. Each of these sentences makes different assumptions about the likelihood that what is stated in the *if* clause is true; each then draws the corresponding conclusion in the main clause.

If you *practice* (or *have practiced*) writing frequently, you *know* (or *have learned*) what your chief problems are.

This sentence assumes that what is stated in the *if* clause may very well be true; the alternatives in parentheses indicate that any tense that is appropriate in a simple sentence may be used in both the *if* clause and the main clause.

If you *practice* writing for the rest of this term, you *will* (or *may*) *understand* the process better.

This sentence makes a prediction about the future and again assumes that what is stated may very well turn out to be true. Only the main clause uses the future tense (*will understand*) or some other modal that can indicate future time (*may understand*). The *if* clause must use the present tense, even though it, too, refers to the future.

If you *practiced* (or *were to practice*) writing every single day, it *would* eventually *seem* much easier to you.

This sentence casts some doubt on the likelihood that what is stated will be put into effect. In the *if* clause, the verb is either past—actually, past subjunctive—or *were to* + the base form, though it refers to future time (see 33h). The main clause has *would* + the base form of the main verb.

> If you *practiced* writing on Mars, you *would find* no one to read your work.

This sentence contemplates an impossibility at present or in the foreseeable future. As with the preceding sentence, the past subjunctive is used in the *if* clause, although past time is not being referred to, and *would* + the base form is used in the main clause.

> If you *had practiced* writing in ancient Egypt, you *would have used* hieroglyphics.

This sentence shifts the impossibility back to the past; obviously you are not going to find yourself in ancient Egypt. But since past forms have already been used in the preceding two sentences, this one demands a form that is "more past": the past perfect in the *if* clause and *would* + the perfect form of the main verb in the main clause.

www • bedford
stmartins.com/
smhandbook

For additional
exercises, click on

▶ Exercise Central
  ▶ Clauses and
     Sentences

● **EXERCISE 62.1**

Revise the following sentences as necessary. Not all sentences contain an error.

1. The scholar who deciphered finally hieroglyphics was Jean François Champollion.

2. Champollion enjoyed to study the languages of the Middle East.

3. By comparing the Greek and Egyptian inscriptions on the Rosetta Stone, he made a great deal of progress in understanding hieroglyphics.

4. Was of great importance that he knew Coptic, a later form of the Egyptian language.

5. In 1822 Champollion wrote a paper which he presented his decipherment of hieroglyphics in it.

6. If the Rosetta Stone was not discovered, it would have been much more difficult to decipher hieroglyphics.

PART 12

ACADEMIC AND PROFESSIONAL WRITING

"Once one can write, one can write on many topics. . . . Indeed, writing may be a chief survival skill."
— HOWARD GARDNER

63

▼ Understanding Disciplinary Discourse

A recent survey confirmed that good writing plays an important role in almost every profession, and in some it is crucial to success. As one MBA wrote, "Those who advance quickly in my company are those who write and speak well." But writing works in different ways in different disciplines, and you may begin to get a sense of such differences as you prepare essays or other written assignments for various courses. Certainly, by the time you choose a major, you should be somewhat familiar with the expectations, vocabularies, styles, methods of proof, and conventional formats used in your field. This chapter will help you begin this process of familiarization. It will also help you develop the critical-thinking skills (see 11a) that are essential for success in life, whatever your profession. ■

63a Recognizing the critical role that writing plays in all disciplines

Students in the humanities tend to expect that writing will play a central role in their education; students in other areas sometimes imagine that writing will be of secondary importance to them. Yet faculty working in the sciences, social sciences, business, and other areas have a different understanding. Here, for example, is what some faculty members in chemistry have to say:

> Is writing important in chemistry? Don't chemists spend their time turning knobs, mixing reagents, and collecting data? They still get to do those things, but professional scientists also make presentations, prepare reports, publish results, and submit proposals. Each of these activities involves writing. If you remain skeptical about the need for writing skills, then ask your favorite professor, or any other scientist, to track the fraction of one workday spent using their word-processing program. You (and they) may be surprised at the answer.
> – OREGON STATE UNIVERSITY, *Writing Guide for Chemistry*

As this statement suggests, writing is central to learning regardless of the discipline you are in.

Since academic assignments vary widely from course to course and even from professor to professor, the tips this section offers can only be general. The best advice, however, is really very simple: make sure you are in control of the assignment rather than letting the assignment be in control of you. To take control, you need to understand the assignment fully and to understand what professors in the particular discipline expect in response.

When you receive an assignment in *any* discipline, your first job is to make sure you understand what that assignment is asking you to do. Some assignments may be as vague as "Write a five-page essay on one aspect of the Civil War" or "Write an analysis of the group dynamics at play in your recent collaborative project for this course." (See 65d for one student's essay in response to this last assignment.) Others, like this psychology assignment, will be fairly specific: "Collect, summarize, and interpret data drawn from a sample of letters to the editor published in two newspapers, one in a small rural community, and one in an urban community, over a period of three months. Organize your research report according to APA requirements." Whatever the assignment, you must take charge of analyzing it. Answering the following questions can help you do so.

ANALYZING AN ASSIGNMENT IN ANY DISCIPLINE

1. *What is the purpose of the assignment?* Does it serve an informal purpose, as a basis for class discussion or as a way to brainstorm about a topic? Or is the purpose more formal, a way to demonstrate your mastery of certain material and your competence as a writer?

2. *What is the assignment asking you to do?* Are you to summarize, explain, evaluate, interpret, illustrate, define? If the assignment asks you to do more than one of these things, does it specify the order in which you are to do them?

3. *Do you need to ask for clarification of any terms?* Students responding to the preceding psychology assignment might well ask the instructor, for instance, to discuss the meaning of *collect* or *interpret* and perhaps to give examples. Or they might want further clarification of the term *urban community* or the size of a suitable *sample*.

(Continued on p. 862)

For more on the ·····•
expectations for
various disci-
plines, see Chap-
ters 64–67.

**www • bedford
stmartins.com/
smhandbook**

For information on
invention techniques
that can be applied
across disciplines
and discourse
communities,
click on

► Links
  ► Art and Craft
  of Writing

(Continued from p. 861)

4. *What do you need to know or find out to do the assignment?* Students doing the psychology assignment need to develop a procedure—a way to analyze or categorize the letters to the editor. Furthermore, they need to know how to do simple statistical analyses of the data.

5. *Do you understand the expectations regarding background reading and preparation, use of sources (both written and visual), method of organization and development, format, and length?* The psychology assignment mentions no reading, but in this field an adequate statement of a problem usually requires setting that problem in the context of other research. A student might well ask how extensive this part of the report is to be.

6. *Can you find an example of an effective response to a similar assignment?* If so, you can analyze it and perhaps use it as a model for developing your own approach to the current assignment.

7. *Does your understanding of the assignment fit with that of other students?* Talking over an assignment with classmates is one good way to test your understanding.

EXERCISE 63.1

Here is an assignment from a communications course. Read it carefully, and then use the seven questions in 63b to analyze the assignment.

Assignment: Distribute a questionnaire to twenty people (ten male, ten female) asking these four questions: (1) What do you expect to say and do when you meet a stranger? (2) What don't you expect to say and do when you meet a stranger? (3) What do you expect to say and do when you meet a very close friend? (4) What don't you expect to say and do when you meet a very close friend? When you have collected your twenty questionnaires, read them over and answer the following questions.

- What, if any, descriptions were common to all respondents' answers?

- How do male and female responses compare?

- What similarities and differences were found between the responses to the stranger and to the very close friend?

- What factors (environment, time, status, gender, and so on) do you think have an impact on these responses?

- Discuss your findings, using concepts and theories explained in your text.

The rhetorician Kenneth Burke describes how people become active participants in the "conversation of humankind" in the following way. Imagine, he says, that you enter a crowded room in which everyone is talking and gesturing animatedly. You know no one there and cannot catch much of what is being said. Slowly you move from group to group listening, and finally you take a chance and interject a brief statement into the conversation. Others listen to you and respond. Thus, slowly but surely, do you come to *participate* in, rather than to observe, the conversation.

Entering into an academic discipline or a profession is much like entering into such a conversation. At first you feel like an outsider, and you do not catch much of what you hear or read. Trying to enter the new "conversation" takes time and careful attention. Eventually, however, the vocabulary becomes familiar, and participating in the conversation seems easy and natural.

Of course, this chapter cannot introduce you to the vocabulary of every field. The point is that *you* must make the effort to enter into the conversation, and that again means taking charge of the situation. To get started, one of the first things you need to do is to study the vocabulary of the field you are most interested in.

Try to determine how much of what you are hearing and reading depends on specialized or technical vocabulary by highlighting key terms in your reading or your notes to help you distinguish the specialized vocabulary. If you find little specialized vocabulary, try to master the new terms quickly by reading your textbook carefully, by asking questions of the instructor and other students, and by looking up key words or phrases.

If you find a great deal of specialized vocabulary, however, you may want to familiarize yourself with it somewhat methodically. Any of the following procedures may prove helpful:

- Keep a log of unfamiliar or confusing words *in context*. To locate definitions, check the terms in your textbook's glossary or index or consult a specialized dictionary.
- Review your class notes each day after class. Underline important terms, review their definitions, and identify anything that is unclear. Use your textbook or ask questions to clarify anything confusing before the class moves on to a new topic.
- Check to see if your textbook has a glossary of terms or sets off definitions in italics or boldface type. Study pertinent sections to master the terms.

dis

864 **63d**

ACADEMIC WRITING

Understanding
Disciplinary
Discourse

- Try to start using or working with key concepts. Even if they are not yet entirely clear to you, working with them will help you come to understand them. For example, in a statistics class, try to work out (in words) how to do an analysis of *covariance,* step by step, even if you are not sure of the precise definition of the term. Or try to plot the narrative progression in a story even if you are still not entirely sure of the definition of *narrative progression.*

- Find the standard dictionaries or handbooks of terms for your field. Students beginning the study of literature, for instance, can turn to such guides as *A Handbook to Literature,* Ninth Edition, or *A Handbook of Critical Approaches to Literature.* Those entering the discipline of sociology may refer to the *Dictionary of the Social Sciences,* while students beginning statistical analysis may turn to *Statistics without Tears.* Ask your instructor or a librarian for help finding the standard references in your field.

- If you belong to online listservs or discussion groups — or even if you are browsing sites on the Internet and World Wide Web related to a particular field — take special note of the ways technical language or disciplinary vocabulary is used there. Sometimes, you can find definitions of terms on a Web site's FAQ page, if one exists.

Whatever your techniques for learning a specialized vocabulary, begin to use the new terms whenever you can — in class, in discussions with instructors and other students, and in your assignments. This ability to *use* what you learn in speaking and writing is crucial to your full understanding of and participation in the discipline.

63d Identifying the style of a discipline

Becoming familiar with technical vocabulary is one important way to initiate yourself into a discipline or field of study. Another method is to identify stylistic features of the writing in that field. You will begin to assimilate these features automatically if you immerse yourself in reading and thinking about the field. To get started, study some representative pieces of writing in the field with the following questions in mind:

- How would you describe the overall *tone* of the writing? Is it very formal, somewhat formal, informal? (See 4g.)

- To what extent do writers in the field strive for a somewhat distanced, objective stance? (See 16c.)

- In general, how long are the sentences? How long are the paragraphs? (See Chapter 5; 46a)

- Are verbs generally active or passive — and why? (See 33g.)
- Do the writers use first person (*I*) or prefer terms such as *one* or *the investigator*? What is the effect of this choice?
- Does the writing use visual elements such as graphs, tables, charts, computer-based graphics, visuals, or maps? How are these integrated into the text?
- What role, if any, do headings and other formatting elements play in the writing? (See Chapter 8.)
- What bibliographic style (such as MLA, APA, CBE, or Chicago) is used? (See Chapters 20–23.)

Of course, writings within a single discipline may have different purposes and different styles. Although a research report is likely to follow a conventional form, a speech greeting specialists at a convention may well be less formal and more personal no matter what the field. Furthermore, answering questions such as the preceding ones will not guarantee that you can produce a piece of writing similar to the ones you are analyzing. Nevertheless, looking carefully at writing in the field brings you one step closer to writing effectively in that discipline.

63e Understanding the use of evidence

"Good reasons" form the core of any writing that argues a point; they provide the launching pad for the specific *evidence* for the argument. Chapter 13 explains how to formulate good reasons and back them up with evidence. However, what is acceptable and persuasive evidence in one discipline may be more or less so in another. Observable, quantifiable data may constitute the very best evidence in, say, experimental psychology, but the same kind of data may be less appropriate — or even impossible to come by — in a historical study. As you grow familiar with any area of study, you will develop a sense of just what it takes to prove a point in that field. You can speed up this process, however, by doing some investigating and questioning of your own. As you read your textbook and other assigned materials, make a point of noticing the use of evidence. The following questions are designed to help you do so:

- How do writers in the field use precedent and authority? What or who counts as an authority in this field? How are the credentials of an authority established? (See 13e.)

dis

63f

866

ACADEMIC WRITING

Understanding
Disciplinary
Discourse

- What use is made of quantitative data (items that can be counted and measured)? What kinds of data are used? How are such data gathered and presented?

- What use is made of qualitative data (items that can be systematically observed)?

- How are statistics used and presented? Are tables, charts, or graphs common? How much weight do they carry?

- How is logical reasoning used? How are definition, cause and effect, analogy, and example used in this discipline?

- How does the field use primary and secondary sources? What are the primary materials — the firsthand sources of information — in this field? What are the secondary materials — the sources of information derived from others? How is each type of source likely to be presented? (See 15a2 and 64a.)

- What other kinds of textual evidence are cited? Web sites? electronic journals or databases? video or audio? visual images? personal experiences or personal correspondence?

- How are quotations used and integrated into the text? (See Chapter 17.)

In addition to carrying out your own investigation, ask your instructor how you can best go about making a case in this field.

● **EXERCISE 63.2**

Do some reading in books and journals associated with your prospective major or a discipline of particular interest to you, using the preceding questions to study the use of evidence in that discipline. If you are keeping a writing log, make an entry in it summarizing what you have learned.

63f Using conventional disciplinary patterns and formats

You can gather all the evidence in the world and still fail to produce effective writing in your discipline if you do not know the field's generally accepted formats for organizing and presenting evidence. Again, these formats vary widely from discipline to discipline and sometimes from instructor to instructor, but patterns do emerge. The typical laboratory report, for instance, follows a fairly standard organizational framework whether it is in botany, chemistry, or parasitology. A case study in sociology or education or anthropology likewise follows a typical organizational plan.

For more on the
formats typical
of the major
academic disci-
plines, see Chap-
ters 64–66.

Your job in any discipline is to discover its conventional formats and organizing principles so that you can practice using them. This task is easy enough to begin. Ask your instructor to recommend some excellent examples of the kind of writing you will do in the course. Then analyze these examples in terms of format and organization. You might also look at major scholarly journals in the field to see what types of formats seem most common and how each is organized. Study these examples, and keep in mind these questions about organization and format:

- What types of essays, reports, or documents are common in this field? What is the purpose of each type? Are these types produced mainly in print or mainly online?

- What can a reader expect to find in each type? What does each type assume about its readers?

- How is a particular type of text organized? What are its main parts? Are they labeled with conventional headings? What logic underlies this sequence of parts?

- How does a particular type of essay, report, or document show the connections among ideas? What assumptions of the discipline does it take for granted? What points does it emphasize?

Remember that there is a close connection between the writing patterns and formats a particular area of study uses and the work that scholars in that field undertake. Here are statements from two writing guides that were developed for students by faculty members in philosophy and microbiology. What do these statements suggest about disciplinary patterns and formats?

PHILOSOPHY

Like baking a pie, planning a vacation, or raising a child, good writing in philosophy requires creativity, thought, and a set of basic skills. This section . . . identifies and exemplifies eight skills that you will frequently make use of in your philosophy writing assignments. These include (1) identifying a philosophical problem; (2) organizing ideas; (3) defining concepts; (4) analyzing arguments; (5) comparing and contrasting; (6) giving examples; (7) applying theory to practice; and (8) testing hypotheses.

– OREGON STATE UNIVERSITY
Writing Philosophy Papers: A Student Guide

MICROBIOLOGY

The main purpose of most scientific writing is to inform and educate other people about research that has been performed. A scientific report should explain clearly how the research was performed and what results

dis

868   **63f**

ACADEMIC WRITING

Understanding
Disciplinary
Discourse

were observed. "Good science" must be repeatable—other scientists should be able to repeat the experiment in order to see if they come up with the same results or not. And, lastly, an argument or opinion might be proposed based on the results obtained.

— OREGON STATE UNIVERSITY, *Writing for Microbiology Majors*

FOR COLLABORATION

Pair up with a classmate or friend who intends to major in the same field you are considering. Then do some investigating on your college Web site to identify a faculty member in that field and learn about that professor's scholarly work. Next, call or email the professor, asking for an appointment to conduct an interview. (Have a couple of backup professors on your list in case the first one is not available.) Before the interview, check section 15f2 on conducting an interview. Then draw up some questions about what doing research in this field is like. You might use the information in this chapter. Conduct the interview, and, afterward, write a brief report for your class about what you have learned.

THINKING CRITICALLY ABOUT THE DISCOURSE OF A DISCIPLINE

Reading with an Eye for Disciplinary Discourse

The following abstract (see 15d3) introduces an article titled "Development of the Appearance-Reality Distinction." This article appeared in *Cognitive Psychology*, a specialized academic journal for researchers in the subfield of psychology that focuses on human cognition. Read this abstract carefully to see what you can infer about the discourse of cognitive psychology—about its characteristic vocabulary, style, use of evidence, and so on.

Young children can express conceptual difficulties with the appearance-reality distinction in two different ways: (1) by incorrectly reporting appearance when asked to report reality ("phenomenism"); (2) by incorrectly reporting reality when asked to report appearance ("intellectual realism"). Although both phenomenism errors and intellectual realism errors have been observed in previous studies of young children's cognition, the two have not been seen as conceptually related and only the former errors have been taken as a symptom of difficulties with the appearance-reality distinction. Three experiments investigated 3- to 5-year-old children's ability to distinguish between and correctly identify real versus apparent object properties (color, size, and shape), object identities, object presence-absence, and action identities. Even the 3-year-olds appeared to have some ability to make correct appearance-reality discriminations and this ability increased with age. Errors were frequent, however, and almost all children who erred made both kinds. Phenomenism errors predominated on tasks where the appearance versus reality of the three object properties were [*sic*] in question; intellectual realism errors predominated on the other three types of tasks. Possible reasons for

dis

63f   869

ACADEMIC WRITING

Using Conventional
Disciplinary
Patterns and
Formats

this curious error pattern were advanced. It was also suggested that young children's problems with the appearance-reality distinction may be partly due to a specific metacognitive limitation, namely, a difficulty in analyzing the nature and source of their own mental representations.

–JOHN H. FLAVELL, ELEANOR R. FLAVELL, AND FRANCES L. GREEN
Cognitive Psychology

Thinking about Your Own Writing in a Discipline

Choose a piece of writing you have produced for a particular discipline — a hypertext history essay, a laboratory report, a review of the literature in some particular field, or any other written assignment. Examine your writing closely for its use of that discipline's vocabulary, style, methods of proof, and conventional formats. How comfortable are you writing a piece of this kind? In what ways are you using the conventions of the discipline easily and well? What conventions give you difficulty, and why? You might talk to an instructor in this field about the conventions and requirements for writing in the discipline. Make notes about what you learn about being a better writer in the field.

64

Writing for the Humanities

Have you ever wondered why your idea of good art often differs from the ideas of past generations? Are you fascinated by the history of Asia—or of the western United States? Have you always loved stories—from Maurice Sendak's *In the Night Kitchen* to Shakespeare's *Tempest* to Toni Morrison's *Beloved*? If you share these or similar fascinations, you are an instinctive student of the humanities.

Whatever their specific focus, disciplines in the humanities are concerned with what it means to be *human*. Historians study and reconstruct the past. Literary critics analyze and interpret texts, often to help others explore a text's meaning. Philosophers raise questions about truth, knowledge, beauty, and justice. Scholars of Spanish, Russian, Chinese, and other languages learn not just to speak but to inhabit other languages and cultures. In these and other ways, those in the humanities strive to explore, interpret, and reconstruct the human experience. This chapter will help you read and write more proficiently in these disciplines. ■

64a Becoming a strong reader of texts in the humanities

In humanities disciplines, the interpretation and creation of texts are central. The nature of these texts may vary: an art historian may "read" a painting by Leonardo Da Vinci; a literary critic may interpret a poem, play, novel, or cultural artifact such as a TV show or magazine advertisement; and a philosopher may analyze a treatise by John Locke or Emmanuel Kant. But whether the text being studied is ancient or modern, literary or historical, verbal or visual, textual analysis plays a critical role in the reading and writing that people in the humanities undertake. Sometimes their purpose is to inform: a historian studying census records from the period when the Black Plague devastated Europe hopes to gain helpful information about the development of this catastrophic disease. In many instances, information learned by reading may lead to argument. The historian working with centuries-old census records, for example, may eventually argue that one or more practices played a particularly important role in the spread of the plague. How, then, do you become a strong reader of the humanities so that you can join in creating and interpreting texts?

Strong readers of texts in the humanities are active, engaged readers who know the value of reading critically (see 11a). That is, they consistently pose questions and construct hypotheses as they read. They ask themselves, for instance, why a writer might be making some points or developing some examples but omitting others. They understand that, rather than finding meaning only in the surface information texts convey, strong readers create fuller meanings through their questions and hypotheses. In this sense, strong readers construct the significance of what they read.

Strong readers of texts in the humanities also understand the differences between primary and secondary sources. *Primary sources* typically are firsthand accounts, records of events, and artifacts. Diaries, letters, data from experiments, and historical documents are common primary sources. *Secondary sources* are texts written about a primary source or are in some other way one step removed from the main source. Encyclopedias, scholarly books, and biographies are typical secondary sources. Whether a source is primary or secondary can vary, depending on your purpose. If you use Barry Lopez's *Arctic Dreams: Imagination and Desire in a Northern Landscape* in a history class to provide background information for an essay you are writing on arctic history, Lopez's book would be considered a secondary source. If you read Lopez's work in a class on contemporary nonfiction prose in order to carry out an analysis of the text itself, it would be considered a primary source. As this example suggests, your purpose for reading—whether to learn more about the history of the arctic or to understand the intricacies of Lopez's prose style—will influence the way you approach a text.

●— For more on
primary and sec-
ondary sources,
see 15a2.

64b Becoming a strong writer of texts in the humanities

Texts in the humanities reflect writers' concerns with the related skills of self-expression, analysis, and argument. Common assignments that make use of these skills include summaries, response pieces, position papers, critical analyses, and research-based projects. To take a more specific example, consider this list of assignments given in a philosophy department: class journals, summaries, analytic essays, case studies, dialogues, and research papers. Some of the assignments, such as summaries and analytic essays, encourage looking very closely at a particular text, while others, such as research projects and case studies, call for going well beyond a primary text.

Many humanities assignments (in disciplines such as the modern languages, literature, and philosophy) will call for you to format your documents according to the style of the Modern Language Association (MLA style). Other disciplines, such as history, use formats prescribed by the University of Chicago Press (Chicago style). If you have questions about which formats to use, consult your instructor.

●— For more on
MLA style, see
Chapter 20; for
more on Chicago
style, see Chap-
ter 23.

Although you are most likely to read and write about literature in English classes, you may encounter stories, poems, and essays in a number of disciplines in the humanities. The ability to interpret and analyze literary texts is a key skill in the humanities. To successfully engage such texts, you must recognize that you are not a neutral observer, not an empty cup into which the meaning of a literary work is poured. If such were the case, literary works would have exactly the same meanings for all of us, and reading would be a fairly boring affair. If you have ever gone to a movie with a friend and each come away with a completely different understanding or response, you already have ample evidence that a story never has just one meaning.

Nevertheless, you may have been willing to accept the first meaning to occur to you, or to take a literary work at face value. The following guidelines aim to help you exercise your interpretive powers, to build your strengths as a reader of literature.

SOME GUIDELINES FOR READING LITERATURE

1. *Read the work first for an overall impression.* Read it straight through, and jot down your first impressions. How did the work make you feel? What about it is most remarkable or memorable? Are you confused about anything in it?

2. *Reread the work, annotating* in the margins to "talk back," asking questions, pointing out anything that seems out of place or ineffective.

3. *What is the genre* — gothic fiction? tragic drama? hypertext fiction? lyric poetry? creative nonfiction? What is noteworthy about the form of the work?

4. *What is the point of view, and who is (are) the narrator(s)?* How reliable and convincing does the narrator seem? What in the work makes the narrator seem reliable or unreliable? How does the narrator's point of view affect your response to the work?

5. *What do you see as the major themes* of the work, the points the author seems to want to make? What evidence in the text supports these themes? Consider plot, setting, character, point of view, imagery, and sound.

(Continued on p. 873)

6. *What may have led the author to address these themes?* Consider the time and place represented in the work as well as when and where the writer lived. Also consider social, political, or even personal forces that may have affected the writer.

7. *Who are the readers the writer seems to address?* Do they include you? Do you sympathize with a particular character — and if so, why?

8. *Review your notes,* and highlight the ideas that most interest you. Then freewrite for fifteen minutes or so about your overall response to this work and about the key point you would like to make.

■ *One student's annotation of a poem*

We Real Cool

*The Pool Players.
Seven at the Golden Shovel.*

*Here's my clue
to setting — a
pool hall!*

We real cool. We
Left school. We

*Putting "we" at
the end of the line
makes for a kind of
syncopated sound.
Cool. Jazz, maybe?*

Lurk late. We
Strike straight. We

Sing sin. We
Thin gin. We

*This word acts like a
drumbeat. But it makes
me wonder who this "we"
is. Me? Who is talking here?*

*Not sure what this and the
next line mean. Look up in
a slang dictionary?*

*Yes — I was right.
Jazz for sure.*

Jazz June. We
Die soon.

– Gwendolyn Brooks

*What's the link between
being "cool," jazz, and dying
soon? Leaving school is cool,
maybe — but also a kind of
death? Is this connection
overstated? I'll have to think
some more.*

This student went on to freewrite about the way the poem draws her into the "we," in spite of the fact that she felt little connection to the pool players at first.

In writing about literature, you may need to use a number of special terms. The following list includes terms that are frequently used in the close reading of literary works.

A GLOSSARY OF LITERARY TERMS

To analyze the sounds in a literary work, you might use the following terms:

alliteration   the repetition of an initial sound to create special emphasis or rhythm, as in this sentence from Eudora Welty: *Monsieur Boule inserted a delicate dagger in Mademoiselle's left side and departed with a posed immediacy.*

meter   the rhythm of verse, as determined by the kind and number of feet (groups of syllables) in a line. Iambic pentameter indicates five feet of two syllables, with the stress falling on the second of the two, as in *An aged man is but a paltry thing.*

onomotopoeia   the use of words whose sounds call up or echo their meaning: *hiss* or *sizzle*, for example.

rhyme scheme   the pattern of end rhymes in a poem, usually designated by the letters *a, b, c.* The Emily Dickinson poem at the end of Chapter 54 has a rhyme scheme of *aabccd.* A Shakespearean sonnet typically follows a rhyme scheme of *abab cdcd efef gg.*

rhythm   in metrical poetry, the beat or pattern of stresses; in prose, the effect created by repetition, parallelism, and variation of sentence length and structure. Robert Frost's "Fire and Ice" (at the end of Chapter 48) uses a basic iambic rhythm, with every other syllable stressed: ˊ/ˇ/ˊ/ˇ/.

stanza   a division of a poem: a four-line stanza is called a *quatrain;* a two-line stanza, a *couplet.* Robert Francis's poem at the end of Chapter 37 contains five two-line stanzas.

Literary language is sometimes distinguished from the nonliterary by its intensely purposeful use of imagery, vivid descriptions that evoke a picture or appeal to other senses. Often imagery is used to defamiliarize or

(Continued on p. 875)

(Continued from p. 874)

hum

64c 875

ACADEMIC WRITING

Reading and
Writing about
Literature

"make strange" the ordinary so that readers can look at it in new ways. In discussing imagery, you might use the following terms:

allusion   an indirect (that is, unacknowledged) reference in a work to another work, such as a biblical passage, or to a historical event, a contemporary issue, a mythological character, and so on.

analogy   a comparison of two things that are alike in some respect, often to explain one of the things or to represent it more vividly by relating it to the second. A *simile* is an explicit analogy; a *metaphor,* an implied one. At the end of Chapter 34, Vivian Gornick compares traditional relationships between men and women to a thin fabric that *no amount of patching can weave . . . together again.*

figurative language   metaphor, simile, signifying, and other figures of speech that enrich description and create meaning. (13g2 and 27d)

symbolism   the use of one thing to represent other things or ideas, as the flag symbolizes patriotism or as ice symbolizes hate in Frost's "Fire and Ice." (Chapter 48)

The codes and structures of narrative are very important to literary interpretation. You might want to examine the complexities that arise from representations of the author, the characters and their relationships, or the structures of time and space in a work. Some helpful terms for doing so include the following:

characters   the people in a story, who may act, react, and change accordingly during the course of a story.

dialogism   a term associated with the critic Mikhail Bakhtin, describing the rich social, cultural, and historical context surrounding any word or phrase, which is inevitably *in dialogue with* and responding to that context. The word *democracy,* for instance, carries a whole history of meanings and usages that any writer using the word must contend with.

dialogue   the conversation among characters, which can show how they interact and suggest why they act as they do. The passage from Eudora Welty in 52a3 is some dialogue from a story. A *monologue* is a long speech by one character, spoken to himself or herself or aloud to another character.

(Continued on p. 876)

876

hum

64c

ACADEMIC WRITING

Writing for the
Humanities

(Continued from p. 875)

heteroglossia   a term referring to the many voices present in a work of literature. In Charles Dickens's *Hard Times*, for example, the "voice" of mass education speaks alongside the voices of fictional characters.

implied author   the author that is inferred from or implied by the text, as distinct from the real person/author. In *The Adventures of Huckleberry Finn*, for example, the real author is the flesh-and-blood Samuel Clemens (or Mark Twain); the implied author is the author we imagine as Clemens presents himself in the text.

intertextuality   the system of references in one text to other texts through quotations, allusions, parodies, or thematic references. Gary Larson's *The Far Side* Frankenstein cartoons refer intertextually to the original novel, *Frankenstein*, as well as to many movie versions and to other works focusing on the rewards — and limits — of science.

irony   the suggestion of the opposite, or nearly the opposite, of what the words usually mean, as in saying that being caught in a freezing downpour is "delightful."

narrator   the person telling a story, who may be a character or an omniscient voice with a viewpoint outside the story itself. In *The Adventures of Huckleberry Finn*, the narrator is Huck himself. In poetry, the narrator is known as the speaker. Both narrator and speaker may be referred to as the *persona*. See also *point of view*.

parody   an imitation intended for humorous or satiric effect, as in a takeoff on the magazine *Martha Stewart Living* titled *Is Martha Stewart Living?* At the end of Chapter 47 is an example of a student parody of Edgar Allan Poe's style.

plot   the events selected by a writer to reveal the conflicts among or within the characters, often arranged in chronological order but sometimes including flashbacks to past events or even using episodic or spiraling progressions. Traditionally, the plot begins with *exposition*, which presents background information; rises to a *climax*, the point of greatest tension; and ends with a *resolution* and *denouement*, which contain the outcome.

point of view   the perspective from which a work is presented — in fiction, by a narrator outside the story or a character speaking in first or third person; in poetry, by the poet or a role assumed by the poet.

(Continued on p. 877)

(Continued from p. 876)

In "Theme for English B" (at the end of Chapter 25), the point of view is that of the student.

protagonist the hero, or main character, often opposed by an *antagonist*, as Othello is opposed by Iago in Shakespeare's play *Othello*.

setting the scene of a literary work, including the time, physical location, and social situation. "Theme for English B" (in Chapter 25) is set in Harlem during the 1950s.

style a writer's choice of words and sentence structures. Two devices characteristic of John F. Kennedy's style are repetition and inverted word order.

theme a major and often recurring subject or topic. The predominant theme often reveals the larger meaning of the work, including any thoughts or insights about life or people in general.

tone a writer's attitude, conveyed through specific word choices and structures.

2 Developing a critical stance and a thesis

A good grasp of literary terminology will help you begin to analyze a particular work. To do so, you need to develop a **critical stance** that can help you develop a **thesis**—the major point or claim you wish to make about the work. In general, student writers tend to adopt one of three primary stances: a *text-based stance* that builds an argument by focusing on specific features of the literary text in question; a *context-based stance* that builds an argument by focusing on the context in which a literary text exists; a *reader-based stance* that focuses on the personal response of a particular reader to the text and the interpretation that grows out of that response; or a combination of these approaches. For context-based or combined approaches, you may draw on one or more critical perspectives, such as feminism, which examines how gender is represented in a work and how it is related to power; cultural studies, which examine how an aspect or aspects of culture affects a literary work; postcolonial studies, which examine how imperialism affects people and themes in a work; or poststructural analysis, which examines the relationship between power and language in a work. (If you would like more

www • bedford
stmartins.com/
smhandbook

For more
information on
critical approaches
to literature,
click on

▶ Writer's Almanac

information about approaches such as these, consult your instructor or a work such as David H. Richter's *Falling into Theory.*)

Whatever stance you take, be sure to ground your analysis in one or more important questions that you have about the work. For example, a student writing about Shakespeare's *Macbeth* might find her curiosity piqued by the many comic moments that appear in this tragedy. She could eventually build on her curiosity by turning the question of why Shakespeare uses so much comedy in *Macbeth* into the following thesis statement, which proposes an answer to the question: "The many unexpected comic moments in *Macbeth* emphasize how disordered the world becomes for murderers like Macbeth and his wife."

64d A student literary analysis using MLA style

STUDENT WRITER

Melissa Schraeder

For another
student essay
in MLA style,
see 20d.

In an Introduction to American Literature class, Melissa Schraeder was asked to "analyze some aspect of one of the works read this term." In thinking about the text she liked best, Toni Morrison's *Beloved,* Melissa found herself returning again and again to the relationships between women and men in the text. To explore the relationships, she knew she would have to read the text very carefully, but she also wanted to explore the historical and cultural contexts of the relationships. Since the assignment was fairly open-ended, she checked with her instructor to make sure that her chosen topic — gender relations in Toni Morrison's *Beloved* — would qualify as an aspect of a work to be analyzed. Note that because the assignment called for an analysis of a work that had been read by the entire class, Melissa did not need to review the plot in detail. Moreover, as a student in a literature class, Melissa could assume that analyzing characters and themes would be an appropriate form of interpretation. She also knew her instructor would want her to put her essay in MLA style, the primary style for essays in literature and languages. (See Chapter 20.) Note that this essay has been reproduced in a narrow format to allow for annotation.

Schraeder 1

Melissa Schraeder
Professor Cheryl Glenn
English 205 Essay 3
April 24, 2003

Name, instructor's
name, title of
course and assign-
ment, and date are
all at left margin,
double-spaced

"He Wants to Put His Story Next to Hers":
Gender in Toni Morrison's Beloved

Title centered

Double space
between title and
first paragraph

Toni Morrison's Beloved is a novel about
transformation--a transformation of individual
identities and of the communal identity of African
American Ohioans. This transformation is most
closely connected to a new understanding of gender
relations. As part of her retelling of the history
of slavery, Morrison explores the complicated power
relations between male and female masters and male
and female slaves, paralleling the individual
stories of two former slaves--Sethe and Paul D--
in order to highlight the common pain in their
experiences. Morrison then brings their stories
together so that Sethe and Paul D may overcome
that pain through common understanding. Linking
these stories together through the common threads
of sexual exploitation and exclusion from the
typical gender roles of whites, Morrison criticizes
the traditional values of white male dominance.
Out of this critique, she offers a new model of
gender for African Americans, a model based on
shared suffering of an enslaved past and the
shared struggle for a future of freedom and
equality.

Indent first sentence
of paragraph

Opening paragraph
concludes with
thesis statement

The history that Morrison offers in Beloved crosses geography and generations. In the first chapters of the novel, Morrison brings two new characters into an African American community in Ohio, where Sethe is attempting to start a new life. First, Paul D--a former slave at the Sweet Home plantation where Sethe was also enslaved-- returns to Ohio after being imprisoned at a forced labor camp reserved for runaway slaves. Second, Beloved appears and is soon discovered to be the matured ghost of Sethe's infant daughter (the baby girl that Sethe first rescued from slavery and then murdered rather than see her re-enslaved). Sethe and Paul D begin to recall their memories of slavery, as Sethe attempts to explain her murder of Beloved to Paul D and, more important, to Beloved herself. Morrison's complex history of slavery unfolds as characters reenact everything from the horrifying events of the Middle Passage to the continued racial terror of Reconstruction.

Much of the history of racial suffering that Morrison retells includes episodes of sexual violence, as Pamela Barnett's work on Beloved has emphasized (73-75). This history is consistent with the larger body of literature written about and by enslaved African American women, which shows clearly that sexual exploitation was part of the women's daily struggle to maintain their safety, their lives, and their self-respect. For example, Harriet Jacobs's Incidents in the Life of a Slave

Fig. 1. Virginian Luxuries, Abby Aldrich
Rockefeller Folk Art Center, Williamsburg. This
painting illustrates the combined gender and race
power that white males had over African American
women and men like Sethe and Paul D.

Girl, which according to PBS Online's Africans in
America Web site was "one of the first open
discussions about the sexual harassment and abuse
endured by slave women," offers a firsthand account
of the sufferings caused by sexual exploitation.
The anonymous, colonial-era painting called
Virginian Luxuries depicts sexual harassment and
physical violence as common liberties taken by
slave owners (see Fig. 1). Thus, the descriptions

of sexual violence in <u>Beloved</u>, such as Sethe's recollection of her African mother who had been "taken up many times by the crew" on her Middle Passage journey, or her neighbor Ella's imprisonment "in a house where she was shared by father and son, whom she called 'the lowest yet,'" have very real historical precedents (Morrison 74, 301).

In the lives of African American women, violence made motherhood a double burden: they not only had to watch their children suffer under slavery or see them sold off at young ages, but they also knew that many of their children were conceived through hate instead of love. While Beloved is not conceived through rape, Sethe does offer the fear of white rape and the desire to protect her children from it as an explanation for her decision to kill the infant Beloved: "The best thing she was, was her children. Whites might dirty <u>her</u> all right, but not her best thing, her beautiful magical best thing-- the part of her that was clean" (Morrison 296). Morrison suggests, however, that motherhood is only one aspect of women's lives that slavery made at best difficult and at worst unbearable for African American women. Morrison offers Sethe's story as an illustration of how participation in most conventional gender roles was denied to African American women. As a female slave, Sethe experiences frustration and dehumanization as her race keeps her from the full experiences of her gender. To the whites who enslaved her, Sethe appears as a female

but not as a woman; that is, she bears the double
burden of productive and reproductive labor, but
will never be a daughter to her parents, a wife to
her husband, or a mother to her children. Indeed,
the white people surrounding Sethe mock her attempts
to fulfill these roles. When Sethe first approaches
Mrs. Garner about marrying Halle, Mrs. Garner laughs
at Sethe's disbelief that there would be no ceremony
or celebration marking the marriage of two slaves.
Mrs. Garner dismisses Sethe's wishes as childish
naiveté, saying, "'You are one sweet child'"
(Morrison 31). Finally, Morrison highlights the
contradictory way in which Sethe's white male
enslavers alternately deny and affirm her identity
as a woman in order to satisfy their own desires.
While she remembers that the white men of Sweet
Home were constantly telling her that she was a
beastly, uncivilized woman, Sethe also recalls
that "[they never thought] I was too nasty to
cook their food or take care of Mrs. Garner"
(Morrison 237).

Through her depiction of Paul D, the main male
character in Beloved, Morrison points out that
African American males suffered similar abuse.
Morrison's portrayal of Paul D as a male victim of
sexual abuse is somewhat more shocking because we
often think of women as the sole victims of rape.
Paul D's memory of the homosexual favors he and the
forty-five African American men were forced to
perform upon the three white labor prison guards in

Discussion of male
gender role begins

Schraeder 6

Georgia suggests that the dominant male role has often depended on racial difference instead of mere sexual difference. In other words, Paul D's encounters with sexual violence illustrate that in a white-male-to-black-male scenario, the black male is often gendered feminine while the white male takes on the dual position of male dominance and white supremacy.

Unlike Sethe's struggle with womanhood under slavery, which focuses on exclusion from specific feminine roles, Paul D's struggle is marked by a confusion over the idea of gender itself, over what constitutes manhood. When the guards from the prison camp lead Paul D away from Sweet Home wearing an iron bit in his mouth, it occurs to him that a rooster the slaves called Mister was more of a man than he was. Paul D recalls this emasculating and dehumanizing experience for Sethe, telling her, "Mister, he looked so . . . free. Better than me. Stronger, tougher. . . . Mister was allowed to be and stay what he was. But I wasn't allowed to be and stay what I was" (Morrison 86). Through much of Beloved, Paul D struggles with his title as "the last of the Sweet Home men." Recalling the pride that Garner, the slave owner who owned Paul D and Sethe, took in being "tough enough and smart enough to make and call his own niggers men," Paul D confronts the conditions surrounding his title, asking himself, "Is that where the manhood lay? In the naming done by a whiteman who was supposed to

Male and female slaves' struggles contrasted

Bracketed ellipses indicate omission in quotation

know?" (Morrison 13, 147). Paul D increasingly questions the worth of Garner's ideals of manhood--such as independent action, self-sufficiency, physical strength, and eloquence--since these are denied to him by the dehumanizing tools of slavery.

In recalling the maxim of the slave owner named schoolteacher that "definitions belonged to the definers--not the defined," Paul D decides to define his own conditions for manhood instead of allowing a white man to name them for him (Morrison 225). First, Paul D decides to turn inward, shutting out the white-dominated world that threatens and diminishes his existence, thereby protecting his feelings by "lov[ing] small," forming few attachments, and locking away all of his pain in his "tobacco tin heart" (Morrison 191, 133). Soon, however, Paul D's love for Sethe begins to soften these protective measures as he imagines that they might be able to live a conventional married life together. Yet the power that the supernatural Beloved has over both him and Sethe destroys his resolve and disrupts his plans. The confusion caused by Beloved and the anger and pain caused by Sethe's story of murdering Beloved force Paul D to reconsider both white ideals of manhood and his own self-protective attempts to maintain a separate sense of African American manhood.

Struggling under the power that Beloved has over him, while trying to build a life with Sethe, Paul D realizes that "[The point] was not being

Elements of plot recounted as evidence of Paul D's transformation

Bracketed words clarify beginning of quotation to fit writer's introduction

able to stay or go where he wished in [Sethe's house], and the danger was losing Sethe because he was not man enough to break out, so he needed her, Sethe, to help him, to know about it, and it shamed him to have to ask the woman he wanted to protect to help him to do it" (Morrison 149). This shame is too much for Paul D to face, and he attempts to convince Sethe to bear a child with him, as "a solution: a way to hold on to her, document his manhood and break out of the girl's spell--all in one" (Morrison 151). For Sethe, however, the idea of pregnancy is a sign of Paul D's jealousy and a desire to expand his control over her, her daughter Denver, and Beloved.

When Paul D finally can accept Sethe's actions and Beloved begins to disappear back into the supernatural world, Sethe and Paul D undergo a final transformation that resolves these conflicts over gender power. In the end, when Paul D returns to Sethe to offer his new terms of their relationship--terms that call for him both to care for her and to listen to her--Morrison writes that "his coming is the reverse route of his going," a phrase suggesting both a careful retracing of steps or revisiting of mistakes and a healing erasure of pain (Morrison 318).

Beloved's final depiction of Sethe and Paul D is remarkable for the two ways it reenvisions gender. First, Morrison establishes a plane of gender equality and mutual respect, as suggested by

the narrator's voicing of Paul D's thoughts: "He
wants to put his story next to hers" (Morrison
322). Second, Morrison enfolds the values of self-
knowledge, self-worth, self-love, and self-respect
into the gender roles of Sethe and Paul D. After
their long journey through the past, Paul D
realizes that "only this woman Sethe could have
left him his manhood," and Sethe finally stops
fighting her past as she hears the words that only
Paul D would speak: "You your best thing, Sethe.
You are" (Morrison 322). Through these deeper
understandings of one another's gendered histories,
Sethe and Paul D transform the pain of the past
into the knowledge necessary to order the present
and the power to shape the future.

> Summary of argu-
> ment and restate-
> ment of thesis

Works Cited

Work in an
anthology

Barnett, Pamela. "Figurations of Rape and the
Supernatural in Beloved." Toni Morrison:
Beloved. Ed. Carl Plasa. New York: Columbia
UP, 1998. 73-85.

Document within
an information
database

"Judgment Day." Africans in America. 1998. PBS
Online. 16 Apr. 2003 <http://www.pbs.org/
wgbh/aia/part4/4p2923.html>.

Republished book

Morrison, Toni. Beloved. 1987. New York: Knopf,
1998.

Anonymous
painting found
on Internet

Virginian Luxuries. n.d. Abby Aldrich Rockefeller
Folk Art Center, Williamsburg. Common Place.
18 Apr. 2003 <http://www.common-place.org/
vol-01/no-04/slavery/bontemps.shtml>.

Working with a classmate, analyze Melissa Schraeder's essay on *Beloved,* using the principles and guidelines presented in this chapter. Then write a two- or three-paragraph peer response to Schraeder's essay, and bring it to class for discussion.

EDITING YOUR WRITING ABOUT LITERATURE

→ What is your thesis? What critical point does it make about the literary work? How could it be stated more clearly?

→ What support do you offer for your thesis? Check to be sure you include concrete instances drawn from the text you are writing about.

→ How do you organize your essay? Do you move chronologically through the work of literature? Do you consider major elements such as images or themes or characters one by one? If you cannot discern a clear relationship among your points, you may have to rearrange them, revise your materials, or substitute better evidence in support of your thesis.

→ Check all quotations to make sure each supports your thesis and that you have properly used signal phrases, indentations (necessary for longer quotations), and parenthetical references.

→ If you quote, paraphrase, or summarize secondary sources, do you cite and document thoroughly and accurately following MLA guidelines? (Chapters 17 and 20)

→ Use present-tense verbs to discuss works of literature: *A strange girl who calls herself Beloved is soon discovered.* Use past tense only to describe historical events: *Slave women were particularly vulnerable to assaults by white masters.*

→ Check all visual images you have included in your text, and make sure you have labeled them accurately and referred to them in the text.

ACADEMIC WRITING

A Student Position Paper in History Using Chicago Style

For more information on writing an effective peer response, see 4c.

64e A student position paper in history using Chicago style

Here is another essay, this one written by Kelly Darr for an introductory history course on U.S. civilization to 1877. The assignment called on students to write an essay "of no more than six pages focusing on a controversial issue related to the First Amendment." Darr chose to review the 1803 *Marbury v. Madison* decision and to relate that decision to the growth of the Supreme Court's powers. Following are the first four paragraphs of her essay, excerpted, and her endnotes and bibliography, which follow Chicago style, the primary style for essays in history and some other humanities. (See Chapter 23.) Note that this essay has been reproduced in a narrow format to allow for annotation.

www • bedford stmartins.com/ smhandbook

For another student history essay, click on

► Student Samples
  ► Essays

Marbury v. Madison and the

Origins of Judicial Review

The Supreme Court of the United States is a very prestigious and powerful branch of American government today. Perhaps the most notable demonstration of the Court's power was its decision concerning the presidential election of 2000, a decision that resulted in George W. Bush becoming president.[1] The Court has not always held this position, however. When the government system was developed in the late eighteenth century, the powers of the judicial branch were fairly undefined. In 1803, Chief Justice John Marshall, with his decision in *Marbury v. Madison*, began to define the duties of the Court by claiming for the Supreme Court the power of judicial review. Judicial review has been upheld ever since, and many people take the practice for granted. There is controversy around Marshall's decision, however, with some claiming that judicial review was not the intent of the Framers. Two questions must be asked: Did Marshall overstep his bounds when he declared judicial review for the Court? If so, why has his decision been upheld for two hundred years? An examination of the actual case, *Marbury v. Madison*, and of Marshall's reasons for his decision is the first step to answering these questions.

This case was surrounded by personal and political opposition. It was brought to Court by William Marbury, whose commission as justice of the

---

All pages except title page numbered in upper right-hand corner

Source cited using superscript numeral

Opening paragraph concludes with thesis in the form of two questions

peace by John Adams was withheld by Thomas
Jefferson when he became president. Jefferson's act
was prompted by Adams's attempt to fill the
national judiciary with Federalist judges on the
eve before Jefferson took office. Due to a mistake
by John Marshall himself (at the time the secretary
of state under Adams), however, the commissions
were not delivered. Jefferson, who did not
appreciate the last-minute attempt to fill the
offices with Federalists, refused to deliver the
commissions after he took office. Marbury and a few
other men sued James Madison, secretary of state
under Jefferson. Marshall, now the chief justice,
was eager to try the case and attack Jefferson, his
political enemy.[2]

By the time the case went to trial in 1803,
two of the five years of the term for justice of
the peace had expired. It was no longer a case over
undelivered commissions; it was a case testing the
power of the courts against the executive. . . . If
Marshall issued a writ of mandamus requiring
Madison to hand over the commissions, Jefferson
could have him impeached.[3] If Marshall ruled in
favor of Jefferson, he would make the judicial
branch look even more powerless than it already
did. Marshall was in a no-win situation, and he was
aware of this predicament when he set out to make
his decision.[4]

He finally made his decision on February 24,
1803, and it was based on two concerns: the ethics

of withholding Marbury's commission, and the right
of the Supreme Court to issue a writ of mandamus to
the president.[5] Marshall broke the issue into three
questions. The first question addressed whether
Marbury had a right to the commission. Marshall
said that he did have the right to it because it
had been signed by the president at the time and
sealed with the seal of the United States. Second,
Marshall asked, if Marbury had a right to the
commission, did the laws of the land protect his
right to the appointment? Marshall reasoned that
withholding his commission would be in violation of
his personal rights, so the laws must protect those
rights. Third, Marshall asked if the laws protected
Marbury in the form of a writ of mandamus from the
Supreme Court. Marshall reasoned that the Court
could not issue a writ of mandamus even though the
Judiciary Act of 1789 said that it could. According
to this law, the Supreme Court could issue writs
of mandamus to people under the authority of the
United States, which Marbury clearly was; however,
if the Court could not issue a writ of mandamus,
then this law was unconstitutional. He went on to
say that the Supreme Court only had appellate
jurisdiction (except in a few specific cases) and
this case had been brought before the Court for
original jurisdiction. Therefore he declared that
the law stating that the Supreme Court could issue
writs of mandamus was unconstitutional. In other
words, Congress did not have the legal power to

Darr 5

give the Court that right. He went on to say that
the Constitution is the supreme law of the land,
and since it was the judicial branch's duty to say
what the law is, the Court had the power to declare
acts unconstitutional. Thus Marshall denied
mandamus for Marbury and ruled in favor of Madison.
At the same time, however, he took a big step
toward strengthening the judicial branch by
establishing judicial review for the Supreme
Court.[6]

[In the next paragraphs, Darr sums up the strengths and weaknesses of Marshall's decision. She then discusses the effects of
Marbury v. Madison and its status today.]

Notes

1. *Bush v. Gore,* 531 U.S. 98 (2000), http://
supct.law.cornell.edu/supct/html/00-949.ZPC.html
(accessed February 8, 2003).

Web source for court decision

2. John A. Garraty, *Quarrels That Have Shaped
the Constitution* (New York: Harper and Row, 1987),
7-14.

First line of each note indented five spaces

3. Ibid., 19.

4. William C. Louthan, *The United States
Supreme Court: Lawmaking in the Third Branch of
Government* (Englewood Cliffs, NJ: Prentice-Hall,
1991), 51.

Book

5. Thomas J. Higgins, *Judicial Review Unmasked*
(West Hanover, MA: Christopher Publishing House,
1981), 40-41.

6. *Marbury v. Madison,* 5 U.S. 137 (1803).

Court decision

7. Louthan, *Supreme Court,* 51.

Author's last name and shortened title used for source already cited

8. Ibid.

9. Ibid., 50-51.

10. Higgins, *Judicial Review,* 40-41.

Ibid. used to cite same source as in previous note

11. Ibid., 32.

12. Ibid., 34.

Bibliography

Bush v. Gore. 531 U.S. 98 (2000). http://supct
.law.cornell.edu/supct/html/00-949.ZPC.html
(accessed February 8, 2003).

Garraty, John A. *Quarrels That Have Shaped the
Constitution.* New York: Harper and Row, 1987.

Higgins, Thomas J. *Judicial Review Unmasked.* West
Hanover, MA: Christopher Publishing House,
1981.

Louthan, William C. *The United States Supreme
Court: Lawmaking in the Third Branch of
Government.* Englewood Cliffs, NJ: Prentice-
Hall, 1991.

Marbury v. Madison. 5 U.S. 137 (1803).

First line of each
source flush left,
subsequent lines
indented five spaces

**www • bedford
stmartins.com/
smhandbook**

For additional
resources in the
humanities,
click on

▶ Writer's Almanac

● **EXERCISE 64.1**

Looking carefully at the essays of Melissa Schraeder and Kelly Darr, make a list of their similarities and differences. Take note of the kinds of evidence each paper uses and the critical stance each writer takes, for instance. What conclusions can you draw about these two disciplines based on your analysis?

64f Research sources for the humanities

The following lists contain print and Web resources for students of the humanities. Many of the Web sites include links to other Web resources, so they are doubly helpful.

■ *Art*

GENERAL REFERENCE SOURCES

Encyclopedia of World Art. 15 vols. plus supplements. 1959–68; 1983; 1987.
Oxford Dictionary of Art. 1997.

INDEXES AND DATABASES

ARTBibliographies Modern. 1974–. (Online)
Art Index. 1929–. (Online, CD-ROM)
Art Information: Research Methods and Resources. 1990.
Avery Index to Architectural Periodicals. 1965–. (Online, CD-ROM)
BHA: Bibliography of the History of Art. 1991–. (Online as *Art Literature International*)
Fine Arts: A Bibliographic Guide to Basic Reference Books. 1990.

WEB RESOURCES

Art History Resources on the Net <witcombe.sbc.edu/ARTHLinks.html>
Virtual Library Museums Pages <vlmp.museophile.com>
World Wide Arts Resources <world-arts-resources.com>

■ *Classics*

GENERAL REFERENCE SOURCES

Oxford Classical Dictionary. 1996.
Oxford Companion to Classical Civilization. 1998.

INDEXES AND DATABASES

L'Année Philologique. 1928–. (CD-ROM)

WEB RESOURCES

Ancient World Web <www.julen.net/ancient/>

Classics at Oxford <www.classics.ox.ac.uk/resources/index.html>

Internet Resources for Classical Studies and Classical Languages <www.brynmawr.edu/Library/Test/classics.html>

■ *History*

GENERAL REFERENCE SOURCES

Cambridge Ancient History. 12 vols. 1939–82, with later revisions.

Cambridge Encyclopedia of Latin America and the Caribbean. 1992.

Cambridge History of Africa. 8 vols. 1975–86.

Cambridge Medieval History. 9 vols. 1911–75.

Dictionary of Concepts in History. 1986.

Dictionary of the Middle Ages. 13 vols. 1982–89.

Encyclopedia of American Social History. 3 vols. 1993.

Encyclopedia of Asian History. 4 vols. 1988.

Encyclopedia of the Renaissance. 1987.

Timeless Atlas of World History. 1993.

INDEXES AND DATABASES

America: History and Life. 1964–. (Online, CD-ROM)

Historical Abstracts. 1955–. (Online, CD-ROM)

Reference Sources in History: An Introductory Guide. 1990.

WEB RESOURCES

History @ Bedford/St. Martin's <www.bedfordstmartins.com/history>

The Library of Congress: American Memory <memory.loc.gov/ammem/amhome.html>

World History Archives <www.hartford-hwp.com/archives/index.html>

WWW-VL History Central Catalogue <history.cc.ukans.edu/history/VL>

■ *Literature and linguistics*

GENERAL REFERENCE SOURCES

Dictionary of Literary Biography. 1978–.

Encyclopedia of World Literature in the Twentieth Century. 5 vols. 1981–93.

International Encyclopedia of Linguistics. 4 vols. 1991.

Oxford Companion to American Literature. 1995.

Oxford Companion to English Literature. 2000.

INDEXES AND DATABASES

Dictionary of Literary Biography. 1978–.

MLA International Bibliography of Books and Articles on the Modern Languages and Literature. 1921–. (Online, CD-ROM)

Reference Works in British and American Literature. 2 vols. 1990–91.

WEB RESOURCES

English Language and Literature Resources <www.lib.vt.edu/subjects/engl>

Linguistic Society of America <www.lsadc.org>

Literary Research Tools on the Net <andromeda.rutgers.edu/~jlynch/Lit>

The Voice of the Shuttle <vos.ucsb.edu>

■ *Music*

GENERAL REFERENCE SOURCES

New Grove Dictionary of Music and Musicians. 20 vols. 2001. (Online)

New Oxford Companion to Music. 2 vols. 1983.

New Oxford History of Music. 9 vols. 1986–90.

INDEXES AND DATABASES

Music: A Guide to the Reference Literature. 1987.

Music Index: A Subject-Author Guide to Current Music Periodical Literature. 1949–. (CD-ROM)

Music Reference and Research Materials: An Annotated Bibliography. 1993.

RILM Abstracts of Music Literature. 1966–. (Online, CD-ROM as *Muse*)

WEB RESOURCES

hum
64f 899

ACADEMIC WRITING
Research Sources
for the Humanities

Internet Resources for Music Scholars <hcl.harvard.edu/loebmusic/online-ir-intro.html>

Worldwide Internet Music Resources <www.music.indiana.edu/music_resources>

The WWW Virtual Library: Music <www.vl-music.com>

▨ *Philosophy, religion, and ethics*

GENERAL REFERENCE SOURCES

Dictionary of Philosophy. 1984.

Encyclopedia of Philosophy. 4 vols. 1973.

Encyclopedia of Religion. 16 vols. 1987.

INDEXES AND DATABASES

Philosopher's Index. 1967–. (Online, CD-ROM)

Philosophy: A Guide to the Reference Literature. 1986.

Religion Index. 1975–. (Online, CD-ROM)

Religious and Theological Abstracts. 1958–. (CD-ROM)

WEB RESOURCES

The Analects <www.human.toyogakuen-u.ac.jp/~acmuller/contao/analects.htm>

The Avesta <www.avesta.org/avesta.html>

Bhagavad-Gita <www.bhagavad-gita.org>

The Bible <www.bible.org>

The Book of Mormon <www.hti.umich.edu/m/mormon>

The Dhammapada <www.ciolek.com/WWWVL-Buddhism.html>

The Holy Book of the Sikhs <www.sikhs.org/transl.htm>

Internet Resources: Religion and Philosophy <wally.rit.edu/internet/subject/philosophy.html>

Kitab-I-Aqdas <www.bahai.org>

Philosophy in Cyberspace <www-personal.monash.edu.au/~dey/phil>

The Qur'an <www.unn.ac.uk/societies/islamic/index.htm>

The Talmud (in Hebrew) <www1.snunit.k12.il/kodesh/kodesh.html> Another source on Judaism and Jewish resources: <shamash.org/trb/judaism.html#learning>

Tao Te Ching <www.human.toyogakuen-u.ac.jp/~acmuller/contao/laotzu.htm>

The Vedas <hindubooks.org/scriptures>

The WWW Virtual Library: Philosophy <www.bris.ac.uk/Depts/Philosophy/VL>

Theater and film

GENERAL REFERENCE SOURCES

Film Encyclopedia. 1994.

McGraw-Hill Encyclopedia of World Drama. 5 vols. 1984.

INDEXES AND DATABASES

Film Literature Index. 1973–.

International Index to Film Periodicals. 1972–. (Online)

WEB RESOURCES

The Internet Movie Database <us.imdb.com>

McCoy's Brief Guide to Internet Resources in Theatre and Performance Studies <www.stetson.edu/departments/csata/thr_guid.html>

World Wide Arts Resources: Theater <wwar.com/categories/Theater>

The WWW Virtual Library: Theatre and Drama <vl-theatre.com>

THINKING CRITICALLY ABOUT WRITING IN THE HUMANITIES

Choose at least two papers you have written for different disciplines in the humanities—say, literature and history. Reread these papers with an eye to their similarities. What features do they have in common? Do they use similar methods of analysis and value similar kinds of evidence, for instance? In what ways do they differ? Based on your analysis, what conclusions can you draw about these two disciplines?

65 Writing for the Social Sciences

65a Becoming a strong reader of texts in the social sciences

Like readers in other subject areas, strong readers in the social sciences are engaged, active, and critical. They understand that whether they are reading a theoretical paper (which sets forth a theoretical premise or overall theory and defends it), a case study (which describes in detail a particular case and draws out inferences and implications from it), or a research report (which presents the results of research aimed at answering an important question in the field), they must not just read but analyze and interpret the text before them. They realize, as well, that social-science disciplines often use special terms for basic concepts. In the abstract to the article titled "Development of the Appearance-Reality Distinction" on pp. 868–869, for example, the author uses the terms *phenomenism* and *intellectual realism* as shorthand for complex ideas that otherwise would take paragraphs to explain.

When you read social-science texts, you should try to become familiar with each discipline's basic terms, concepts, and formats. As you read, remember that a term you might use in everyday speech, such as *identity,* can have a specialized meaning in the social sciences. You should recognize as well that different texts in the social sciences may call for different reading strategies. For example, texts that report the results of *quantitative*

When do most workers begin to save toward retirement, and how do they make decisions about this process? What constitutes an effective meeting, and how can team members improve a meeting's effectiveness? What role do television ads play in the decision-making process of potential voters?

The social sciences—which include psychology, anthropology, political science, speech communication, sociology, economics, and education—try to answer such questions by looking both to the humanities and to the sciences. The social sciences share with the humanities an interest in what it means to be human. But unlike the humanities, the social sciences share with the sciences the goal of engaging in a systematic, observable study of human behavior. Whatever their particular focus, all the social sciences attempt to identify and explain patterns of human behavior. This chapter will help you read and write effectively in the social sciences. ■

902

soc

65b

ACADEMIC WRITING

Writing for the
Social Sciences

studies emphasize statistical evidence based on surveys, polls, experiments, and tests. Thus an analysis of voting patterns in southern states would rely on statistical data that readers should analyze with care: do the statistics, for example, apply to all voters in each state — or to a particular group of voters? Texts that report the results of *qualitative* studies, however, are more subjective: they do not aim for scientific objectivity but rather rely on interviews and observations to reveal social patterns. A study of the way children in one kindergarten class develop rules of play, for instance, would draw on qualitative data — observations of social interaction, interviews with students and teachers, and so on.

Readers of both quantitative and qualitative studies need to interpret and analyze what they read, but they may use these reading skills somewhat differently, depending on the nature of the material. Someone reading a quantitative study, for instance, might spend a great deal of time analyzing the information presented in graphs and charts since these often summarize a quantitative study's findings. A qualitative study makes different demands on readers because its findings are usually not so easily recognizable. Moreover, researchers undertaking qualitative studies base their analyses on interpretations of the phenomenon they have studied. Thus readers need to pay attention to the soundness and consistency of these interpretations, and to the appropriateness of the theories that help guide them. Finally, readers will make use of conventional disciplinary formats to help guide them. In the social sciences, many texts conform to the format and documentation style of the American Psychological Association (APA). In addition, articles often include standard features — an abstract that gives an overview of the findings, followed by an introduction, review of literature, methods, results, discussion, and references. Readers who become familiar with such a format and others advocated by the APA can easily find the information they need.

For more on •······
APA style, see
Chapter 21.

65b Becoming a strong writer of texts in the social sciences

Perhaps because the social sciences share concerns with both the humanities and the sciences, the forms of writing within the social sciences are particularly varied, including summaries, abstracts, literature reviews, reaction pieces, position papers, radio scripts, briefing notes, book reviews, briefs, research papers, quantitative research reports, case studies, and ethnographic analyses. Such an array of writing assignments could seem overwhelming, but in fact these assignments can be organized under five main categories:

Writing that encourages student learning (reaction pieces, position papers)

Writing that demonstrates student learning (summaries, abstracts, research papers)

Writing that reflects common on-the-job communication tasks undertaken by graduates of a discipline (radio scripts, briefing notes)

Writing that requires students to analyze and evaluate the writings of others (literature reviews, book reviews, briefs)

Research reports that ask students to replicate the work of others or to engage in original research (quantitative research reports, case studies, ethnographic analyses)

As is the case with most academic disciplines, many forms of writing in the social sciences call either explicitly or implicitly for argument. Suppose, for example, that you develop a survey on students' attitudes toward physician-assisted suicide for your sociology class and then email the survey to a sample of students on your campus. When you write an essay reporting on your results, you will make an explicit argument about the significance of your data. But even other forms of writing, such as summaries and book reports, have an argumentative edge because you are implicitly arguing that your description and analysis provide a clear, thorough overview of the text(s) you have read.

One important form of writing in the social sciences is the **literature review**, which usually comes at the beginning of a report. Students of the social sciences carry out literature reviews to find out the most current thinking about a topic, to learn what research has already been carried out on that topic, and to set any research they will do on that topic in the context of earlier work. In the social sciences, a literature review does not have to do with novels or poetry but rather with analyzing the social-science literature that is related to a research topic. The following questions lead students working on literature reviews to explore and question the sources they are reviewing, looking for flaws, false claims, or gaps. Such a critical review then leads to a discussion of how the student's research will avoid such flaws and will advance knowledge. Hence the final question in the list below for students working on literature reviews in sociology: what's new in *your* research?

What is your dependent variable or topic of interest?

What are the theories used to explain the dependent variable?

For a discussion of constructing arguments, see Chapter 13.

What populations have been studied?

How have variables been measured?

Have things changed over time?

Could relationships found in previous research be spurious, or vary depending on another (control) variable?

What's new in your research?

– OREGON STATE UNIVERSITY
Writing within Sociology: A Guide for Undergraduates

65c Addressing issues of style in the social sciences

Students sometimes assume that the writing they do in the social sciences should be dry and jargon-ridden. This is hardly the case. While you need to understand the conventions, concepts, and habits of mind typical of these disciplines, you can still write clear prose that engages readers. Here, for instance, is an introduction to a literature review written by sociologist Mark Edwards. Note that he is reviewing quantitative research that is related to his own paper on the employment of parents with children. Also note the stylistic strategies he uses to engage readers: parallel sentence structures (sentences 1 and 2), everyday language ("kids," "missing out"), active voice verbs as often as possible, clear statement of purpose, and so on. Even the verb tenses he uses conform to APA style: when discussing research sources, he uses past or present perfect tense.

> Nearly 60% of mothers of preschoolers are in the labor force. Over 90% of fathers of preschoolers are in the labor force. While many families appear to be juggling the work/family conflict adequately, others claim to feel guilty about leaving their kids in the care of other adults and perhaps missing out on important events in the young child's life. Meanwhile, the potential setbacks in their careers make it difficult for young parents to consider taking time out of the labor force. Employers are also concerned about this issue as the state continues to pass and consider new laws providing family leave and as they seek to retain skilled workers.
>
> Most previous research has emphasized the human capital arguments for new mothers' rapid return to work. However, little effort has been made at understanding how the order of events such as parents' educational attainment, cohabitation, marriage, first job, promotions, and the like are related to the decision of mothers to remain in the labor force. And no research has explored how these characteristics influence the likelihood of new fathers to take time off to be with their new children.

This paper identifies the characteristics of families and young mothers and fathers which are associated with full- and part-time employment while the first child is still an infant. Unlike earlier studies that rely on cross-sectional data, this analysis follows the early life histories of young families to locate not only how demographic characteristics but also the timing and order of events [influence] the likelihood of a new mother or father returning quickly to paid work.

– MARK EDWARDS

Writing within Sociology: A Guide for Undergraduates

● **EXERCISE 65.1**

Read the introduction to Mark Edwards's literature review carefully, and take notes on how it addresses the questions on pp. 903–904. Note what seems effective — or ineffective — about this review, and bring your notes to class for discussion.

www ● bedford
stmartins.com/
smhandbook

To read a formal social science research report, click on

▶ Student Samples
  ▶ Essays

65d A student essay in the social sciences using APA style

Here is another example of effective writing in the social sciences, an essay written by Merlla McLaughlin for a communications class. Merlla and a group of her peers had completed a substantial collaborative project on parking problems on campus. In carrying out this project, the group designed and conducted a survey of students who used parking services and interviewed business owners in the surrounding area to find out how the lack of campus parking affected them. The group presented their research findings in class and then carried out one more assignment: to write individual reports, describing what they had learned about small-group dynamics as a result of their project. Although the following essay is not a formal social-science research report, it does conform to the APA style of documentation. Note that this essay has been reproduced in a narrow format to allow for annotation.

STUDENT WRITER

Merlla McLaughlin

●⸳⸳⸳ For more on
APA style, see
Chapter 21.

Leadership Roles in a Small-Group Project

Merlla McLaughlin

Professor Bushnell

Communications 102

February 22, 2003

Abstract

Using the interpersonal communications research of
J. K. Brilhart and G. J. Galanes, and W. Wilmot and
J. Hocker, along with T. Hartman's personality
assessment, I observed and analyzed the leadership
roles and group dynamics of my project collaborators in a communications course. Based on results
of the Hartman personality assessment, I predicted
that a single leader would emerge. However,
complementary individual strengths and gender
differences encouraged a distributed leadership
style, in which the group experienced little
confrontation and conflict. Conflict, because it
was handled positively, was crucial to the group's
progress.

·

soc

65d   907

Title centered

No indentation

Double spacing used

Key points of report
discussed

Leadership Roles in a Small-Group Project

College lectures provide students with volumes of information. Many experiences, however, cannot be understood well solely by *learning about* them in a classroom. Instead, these experiences can only be understood by *living* them. So it is with the workings of a small, task-focused group. What observations would I make after working with a group of peers on a class project? And what have I learned personally as a result of my involvement with our collaborative project?

Leadership Expectations and Emergence

Our six group members were selected by the instructor; half were male and half were female. We had already performed the Hartman Personality Assessment (Hartman, 1998) in class, an assessment that can also be found online (Hayden). Hartman has associated key personality traits with the colors red, blue, white, and yellow (see Table 1).

The assessment identified most of us as "Blues," concerned with intimacy and caring. Because of the bold qualities associated with "Reds," I expected that Nate, our only "Red," might become our leader. (Kaari, the only "White," seemed poised to become the peacekeeper if need be.) However, after Nate missed the first two meetings, it seemed that Pat, who contributed often during our first three real meetings, might emerge as leader. Pat has strong communications skills, and he is a tall male (and thus a commanding presence).

Full title, centered

Paragraphs indented

Essay double-spaced throughout

Questions clearly indicate the focus of the essay

Headings help organize the report

APA style parenthetical reference

Background information about team members' personality types

Minimum of one-inch margin on all sides

Table 1

Hartman's Key Personality Traits

Trait category	Color			
	Red	Blue	White	Yellow
Motive	Power	Intimacy	Peace	Fun
Strengths	Loyal to tasks	Loyal to people	Tolerant	Positive
Limitations	Arrogant	Self-righteous	Timid	Uncommitted

Note. Table is adapted from information found at *The Hartman Personality Profile,* by N. Hayden. Retrieved February 24, 2003, from http://students.cs.byu.edu/~nhayden/Code/index.php

Pat is also sensitive to others. I was somewhat surprised, then, when our group developed a *distributed style* of leadership (Brilhart & Galanes, 1998). The longer we worked together, however, the more convinced I became that this approach to leadership was best for our group.

As Brilhart and Galanes have noted, "distributed leadership explicitly acknowledges that the leadership of a group is spread among members, with each member expected to perform the communication behaviors needed to move the group toward its goal" (p. 175). These researchers have divided positive communicative actions into two types: task functions that affect a group's productivity,

and maintenance functions that influence the interactions of group members. Our group members enacted
many task- and maintenance-focused communication
roles. One of our most immediate task-function
needs was decision-making, and as we made our
first major decision--what topic to pursue--our
group's distributed-leadership style began to
emerge.

Decision-Making Methods

Our decision to do an investigative report on
the parking services at Oregon State University
(OSU) was not the result of a majority vote but was
achieved instead through negotiated consensus. Nate
was absent on the day we made our decision, but we
felt that we needed to move from brainstorming--
which we had already done--to action. Several of us
argued that a presentation on parking services at
OSU would interest most students, and after more
discussion the others agreed. At our next meeting,
Nate seemed happy to go along with our collaborative decision.

Although we spent a good deal of time debating
the topic for our project, once we decided on one,
other decisions came naturally. At one point, for
instance, we considered producing a videotape for
part of our final presentation to the class. But
after we discussed whether we had the resources and
skills to shoot, edit, and produce a videotape, we
quickly realized that it was not feasible. By using
slides instead (which Pat and Nate prepared), we

Discussion of the
group's decision-
making supports
claim of distributed
leadership style

Transition sentence

were still able to tie the whole presentation
together through visual images.

Roles Played

Thanks in part to the distributed leadership
that our group developed, the strengths of
individual group members became increasingly
apparent. While early in our project Pat had been
the key initiator and Nate had acted largely as an
information seeker, all group members eventually
took on these task functions. We took turns serving
as recorders, and we all gathered information and
worked on our questionnaire. McKenzie, Kaari, Pat,
and I all coordinated the group's work at some
point. Kaari, Joe, and I traded off as gatekeeper--
the role of ensuring that everyone could speak and
be heard. Joe was especially good at catching
important details the rest of us were apt to miss.
At one meeting, for instance, he pointed out that
parking problems on campus could affect surrounding
businesses and that interviewing business owners
and employees could be informative. Joe, McKenzie,
Kaari, and I frequently clarified or elaborated on
information. Pat, Kaari, and Nate were particularly
good at contributing ideas during brainstorming
sessions. Nate, Joe, and McKenzie kept humor in the
group by providing tension-relieving jokes and
dramatic "what if" scenarios.

Just as each group member brought individual
strengths to the group, gender differences also
made us effective as a whole. For example, the

> Another example of distributed leadership style

> Transition to gender influences

women all seemed to take a holistic approach to the project--to look at the big picture--and to make intuitive leaps in ways that the men generally did not. The men preferred a more systematic process. Brilhart and Galanes have suggested that men working in groups dominated by women may display "subtle forms of resistance to a dominant presence of women" (p. 98). Although the men in our group did not attend all the meetings and the women did, I do not believe that the men's nonattendance implied male resistance any more than the women's attendance implied female dominance. Our differing qualities complemented each other and enabled us to work effectively as we conducted research, organized the information we gathered, and prepared for and gave a successful presentation.

Social Environment

As previously noted, our group primarily consisted of Blues, who value altruism, intimacy, appreciation, and having a moral conscience (Hayden, "Blues"). At least three of the four Blues had White as their secondary color; peace, kindness, independence, and sacrifice are important to Whites (Hayden, "Whites"). The presence of these traits may explain why our group had little confrontation and conflict. Nate, the Red, was most likely to speak bluntly, but everyone was careful to self-monitor during group interactions. The one time that Nate seemed put off, at the third meeting, it was not his words but his body language

Writer returns to categories defined earlier

that expressed his discomfort. Nate sat at the far
end of the group and leaned back in his chair with
his arms crossed, his legs stretched out, and his
ankles crossed. By contrast, everyone else in the
group had scooted in close together. This was an
awkward moment, but a rare one given our group's
generally positive handling of conflict. Because
obstacles were treated not as one person's problems
but rather as a group problem, we approached
difficulties from a united position instead of
forming opposing camps among ourselves.

Conclusion

Perhaps my most important personal understanding as a result of this project has to do with
conflict. I have always found conflict difficult
and have believed, as Wilmot and Hocker (1998) have
suggested, that most people think "harmony is
normal and conflict is abnormal" (p. 9). Now I
recognize that some kinds of conflict are essential
for increasing understanding between group members
and creating an effective collaborative product. It
was essential, for instance, that our group explore
different members' ideas about possible topics for
our project, and this process inevitably required
some conflict. The end result, however, was a
positive one.

As Wilmot and Hocker have argued, conflict (in
the sense of a discussion of multiple possibilities) is essential to the full exploration of
ideas. Good conflict, they say, requires an open

In her concluding section, writer clearly answers assignment question

and engaging attitude among group members and encourages personal growth. Good conflict ends when the issue at hand is resolved. And most important for our group, good conflict encourages cooperation (pp. 47-48). When group members handle conflict positively, they increase the group's cohesiveness. I think all the members of our group felt, for instance, that their ideas about possible topics were considered. Once we decided on a topic, everyone fully committed to it. Thus our group identity was enhanced by constructive conflict.

As a result of this project, I have a better sense of when conflict is--and isn't--productive. My group used conflict productively when we hashed out our ideas, and we avoided the kind of conflict that creates morale problems and wastes time. I realize that each group operates somewhat differently. But with the grounding this class has provided, I feel more prepared to understand and participate in future small-group projects.

Conclusion looks toward future

Leadership Roles   10

References

Brilhart, J. K., & Galanes, G. J. (1998). *Effective group discussion* (9th ed.). Boston: McGraw-Hill.

Hartman, T. (1998). *The color code: A new way to see yourself, your relationships, and your life.* New York: Scribner.

Hayden, N. (n.d.). *The Hartman Personality Profile.* Retrieved February 15, 2003, from http://students.cs.byu.edu/~nhayden/Code/index.php

Wilmot, W., & Hocker, J. (1998). *Interpersonal conflict* (5th ed.). Boston: McGraw-Hill.

Heading centered on new page

Entries listed alphabetically by author, last name first; initials used for first and middle names

First line of each entry is flush left with margin

Subsequent lines indent

ACADEMIC WRITING
Writing for the
Social Sciences

**www • bedford
stmartins.com/
smhandbook**

For additional
resources in the
social sciences,
click on

▶ Writer's Almanac

The following lists contain many print and Web resources for students of the social sciences. Many of the Web sites include links to other Web resources, so they are doubly helpful.

▪ *Anthropology*

GENERAL REFERENCE SOURCES

Encyclopedia of Anthropology. 1976.

INDEXES AND DATABASES

Abstracts in Anthropology. 1970–.
Anthropological Literature. 1979–. (Online)

WEB RESOURCES

Anthro.Net <www.anthro.net>
UCSB Anthropology Web Links <www.anth.ucsb.edu/links/pages>
The WWW Virtual Library: Anthropology <vlib.anthrotech.com>

▪ *Communication and journalism*

GENERAL REFERENCE SOURCES

Communication Yearbook. 1977–.
International Encyclopedia of Communication. 4 vols. 1989.
International Encyclopedia of Linguistics. 4 vols. 1991.
Webster's New World Dictionary of Media and Communications. 1990.

INDEXES AND DATABASES

Communication Abstracts. 1978–. (Online)

WEB RESOURCES

International Communication Association <www.icahdq.org>
Kidon Media-Link <www.kidon.com/media-link>
National Communication Association <www.natcom.org>
News on the Net <www.reporter.org/news>
Society of Professional Journalists <www.spj.org>
World Wide Web Resources: Journalism <www.uky.edu/subject/journalism.html>

GENERAL REFERENCE SOURCES

Encyclopedia of Education. 10 vols. 1971.

Encyclopedia of Educational Research. 4 vols. 1992.

International Encyclopedia of Education: Research and Studies. 10 vols. 1992.

INDEXES AND DATABASES

Current Index to Journals in Education (CIJE). 1969–. (Online, CD-ROM in ERIC)

Education: A Guide to Reference and Information Sources. 1989.

Education Index. 1929–. (Online, CD-ROM)

ERIC (Educational Resources Information Center). 1966–. (Online, CD-ROM)

WEB RESOURCES

AskERIC <ericir.syr.edu>

EdWeb <www.edwebproject.org>

U.S. Department of Education <www.ed.gov>

The World Lecture Hall <www.utexas.edu/world/lecture>

■ **Ethnic studies**

GENERAL REFERENCE SOURCES

The American Indian: A Multimedia Encyclopedia. 1993. (CD-ROM)

Blackwell Companion to Jewish Culture: From the Eighteenth Century to the Present. 1989.

Dictionary of Asian American History. 1986.

Dictionary of Mexican American History. 1981.

Encyclopedia of Native American Tribes. 1988.

Encyclopedia of World Cultures. 10 vols. 1990–1995.

Harvard Encyclopedia of American Ethnic Groups. 1980–.

The Hispanic-American Almanac. 1993.

The Negro Almanac: A Reference Work on the African American. 1990.

Sourcebook of Hispanic Culture in the United States. 1982.

The State of Black America. 1976–.

INDEXES AND DATABASES

Afro-American Reference: An Annotated Bibliography of Selected Sources. 1985.

Asian American Studies: An Annotated Bibliography and Research Guide. 1989.

Chicano Index. 1989–. (Online and CD-ROM)

Ethnic News Watch. (CD-ROM)

Guide to Research on North American Indians. 1983.

Hispanic American Periodicals Index (HAPI). 1970–. (Online, CD-ROM)

Index to Black Periodicals. 1984–.

Native Americans: An Annotated Bibliography. 1991.

Women of Color in the United States: A Guide to the Literature. 1989.

WEB RESOURCES

Africa Web Links: An Annotated Resource List <www.sas.upenn.edu/African_Studies/Home_Page/WWW_Links.html>

Columbia University: Latino Studies Links <www.columbia.edu/cu/latino/mags/index2.htm>

NativeWeb <www.nativeweb.org>

The WWW Virtual Library: Asian Studies <coombs.anu.edu.au/WWWVL-AsianStudies.html>

The WWW Virtual Library: Migration and Ethnic Relations <www.ercomer.org/wwwvl>

■ *Political science*

GENERAL REFERENCE SOURCES

Almanac of American Politics: The President, the Senators, the Representatives, the Governors: Their Records and Election Results, Their States and Districts. 1972–. Biennial. (Online)

Congressional Quarterly Almanac. 1945–.

Political Handbook of the World. 1927–.

State Legislative Sourcebook: A Resource Guide to Legislative Information in the 50 States. Annual.

INDEXES AND DATABASES

ABC Pol Sci: A Bibliography of Current Contents: Political Science and Government. 1969–. (CD-ROM)

Political Science: A Guide to Reference and Information Sources. 1990.

Population Index. 1935–.
United States Political Science Documents. 1975–. (Online)

SOC
65e 919

ACADEMIC WRITING
Research Sources
for the Social
Sciences

WEB RESOURCES

Fedworld <www.fedworld.gov>
The Gallup Organization <www.gallup.com>
Legal Information Institute <www.law.cornell.edu>
Political Resources on the Net <www.politicalresources.net>
Political Science Resources on the Web <www.lib.umich.edu/govdocs/polisci.html>
Thomas: Legislative Information on the Internet <thomas.loc.gov>
United Nations <www.un.org>

Psychology

GENERAL REFERENCE SOURCES

Encyclopedia of Psychology. 8 vols. 2000.
Oxford Companion to the Mind. 1987.

INDEXES AND DATABASES

Bibliographic Guide to Psychology. 1974–.
Mental Health Abstracts. 1969–. (Online)
Psychological Abstracts. 1927–. (Online as *PsycINFO,* CD-ROM as *PsycLIT*)

WEB RESOURCES

American Psychological Association <www.apa.org>
American Psychological Society <www.psychologicalscience.org>
Internet Mental Health <www.mentalhealth.com>
PsychWeb <www.psywww.com>
Social Psychology Network <www.socialpsychology.org>

Sociology

GENERAL REFERENCE SOURCES

Encyclopedia of Social Work. 3 vols. 1990.

INDEXES AND DATABASES

Social Work Research and Abstracts. 1977–. (Online, CD-ROM)

Sociological Abstracts. 1952–. (Online, CD-ROM as *SocioFile*)

WEB RESOURCES

Social Science Sites <www2.tntech.edu/history/socsci.html>

A Sociological Tour through Cyberspace <www.trinity.edu/~mkearl/index.html>

SocioSite <www.pscw.uva.nl/sociosite>

The Socioweb <www.socioweb.com/~markbl/socioweb>

U.S. Census Bureau <www.census.gov>

FOR COLLABORATION

Working with a classmate, reread Merlla McLaughlin's essay, and then evaluate it: what features (concrete examples, active verbs, clearly stated points, careful presentation of data, for example) of this essay represent especially effective social-science writing? Use your finding as the basis for a brief peer response to McLaughlin's work, and bring your response to class for discussion.

THINKING CRITICALLY ABOUT WRITING IN THE SOCIAL SCIENCES

Reading with an Eye for Writing in the Social Sciences

Using the preceding list of sources to help you, choose two readings from a social-science discipline that interest you, and read them with an eye toward issues of style. Does the use of disciplinary terms and concepts seem appropriate? In what ways do the texts attempt to engage readers? If the texts are not clear and understandable, how might they be improved?

Thinking about Your Own Writing in the Social Sciences

Choose a paper you like that you have written for a social-science discipline. Then examine your style in this paper to see how well you have engaged your readers. Note variation in sentence length and type (do you, for example, use any questions?), number of active and passive verbs, use of concrete examples and everyday language, and so on.

Writing for the Natural and Applied Sciences

66

When we think of scientists, we often imagine them engaged in action-oriented research—a botanist tending an experiment in a greenhouse, a biologist or chemist working in a lab, a vulcanologist exploring a newly active volcano. More than many scholars, scientists are likely to leave the privacy of their office or lab to engage in fieldwork and experimentation. Whether done in the lab or the field, however, writing is central to the scholarly work of scientists. Writing plays a key role in the sciences, from the first grant proposal written to fund a project to the final report or scientific paper.

Whether they are studying geological faults or developing a stronger support structure for suspension bridges, scientists in the natural and applied sciences want to understand how the physical and natural worlds work. This chapter will aid your understanding of the sciences by helping you read and write more effectively in your science courses. ■

66a Becoming a strong reader of texts in the natural and applied sciences

While English majors may base an argument about *Jane Eyre* on their own interpretation of the book and on other writers' commentaries, scientists prefer to work with the kind of evidence that can be observed, verified, and controlled. Though scientists cannot avoid interpretation, they strive for objectivity by using the *scientific method*—a system of observing or in other ways studying phenomena, formulating a hypothesis about these phenomena, and testing that hypothesis through controlled experiments. Scientists also create and manufacture instruments (from specialized microscopes to linear accelerators to computer programs and models) that enable them to generate precise, standardized, replicable data. And they develop experiments that enable them to account for extraneous factors. In this careful, precise way, scientists test and write about particular theories relating to the world. What, then, should you pay attention to as you read in the sciences?

When you read texts in the sciences, try to become familiar with various disciplinary terms, concepts, and formats as soon as possible, and practice reading for detail. Charts, graphs, illustrations, models, and other visuals often play an important role in scientific writing,

sci
66a

ACADEMIC WRITING

Writing for the
Natural and
Applied Sciences

so be sure to read these with special care. As in other fields, different kinds of texts may call for different reading strategies. If you are reading an introductory textbook for a class in physics or first-year biology, for example, you can draw upon general critical-reading strategies, making sure to preview your reading, ask questions as you read, annotate and summarize key points, and so on.

As you advance in your course work, you will need to develop additional reading strategies for increasingly specialized texts. Imagine, for instance, that your advanced microbiology instructor has asked you to read a number of journal articles on a particular topic. Most often, scientific journal articles are divided into the following sections: title, author(s), abstract, introduction, literature review, materials and methods, results, discussion, and references. It might seem commonsensical to read these articles from start to finish, giving equal weight to each section. Experienced readers, however, read with specific purposes in mind. A microbiologist or other experienced scientist might well skim a title and abstract to see if an article warrants further reading. If it does — and this is an individual judgment call based on the reader's own research interest — the scientist might then read the introduction to understand the rationale for the experiment and then skip to the results section. Only if the scientist has a specific interest in the methods or wants to replicate the work might he or she read the materials and methods section.

Other important differences exist between introductory and specialized texts in the sciences. When you read an introductory textbook, you can assume that the information presented there is authoritative and as objective as possible. Such textbooks are reviewed by numerous scholars and editors who read them to ensure that they are accurate and up-to-date. When you read more specialized materials, however, you need to recognize that although scholarly reports undergo significant peer review, they nevertheless represent arguments. Thus the connection between facts and claims in the sciences, as in all subject areas, is created by the author rather than simply revealed by the data. It is important, then, to read both facts and claims with a questioning eye. Did the scientist choose the most appropriate method to test his or her hypothesis? Are there other reasonable interpretations of the experiment's results? Do other studies contradict the conclusions of this experiment? When you read specialized texts in the sciences with questions like these in mind, you are reading — and thinking — like a scientist.

For more on reading arguments, see Chapter 11.

ACADEMIC WRITING

Becoming a Strong
Writer of Texts in
the Natural and
Applied Sciences

● **EXERCISE 66.1**

Choose a respected journal in a scientific discipline that interests you. (Ask your instructor or a reference librarian if you need help identifying a journal.) Then read quickly through two articles, taking notes on what headings and/or subheadings are used, what specialized vocabulary you note, and what kinds of evidence the authors use. Bring the results of your investigation to class for discussion.

66b Becoming a strong writer of texts in the natural and applied sciences

It is hardly surprising that scientists particularly value clarity in written prose, as noted in the following statement by chemistry professors:

> Although the exchange of information in science usually focuses on content rather than writing style, it is important that work be presented using accepted conventions and in an appropriate style. Whether your audience consists of readers, reviewers, seminar attendees, or the boss, a clear, concise writing style can help gain their confidence, maintain their interest, and convince them of your work's value.
>
> – OREGON STATE UNIVERSITY DEPARTMENT OF CHEMISTRY
> *A Writing Guide for Chemistry*

Like others in college, students in the sciences must be able to respond to a diverse range of writing tasks. Often, they must maintain **lab notebooks** that include careful records of ongoing experiments. They also write essays, literature reviews, and progress reports; in addition, they may develop print and Web-based presentations for both technical and lay audiences. Particularly common writing assignments in the sciences are the literature review, research proposal, and research report.

Scientists undertake **literature reviews** so that they can keep up with and evaluate developments in their field. As such, literature reviews are an essential first step in any research effort, for they enable scientists to discover what research has already been completed and how they might build on earlier efforts. Successful literature reviews demonstrate a student's ability to identify relevant research on a topic and to summarize and (in some instances) also evaluate that research. When instructors in the sciences assign literature reviews, they generally do not expect that students will conduct an exhaustive review of the literature on a particular topic. Rather, they hope the review will help students learn more about a specific topic – and about scientific work in general. Note that the past tense is used when citing research previously performed.

www ● bedford stmartins.com/ smhandbook

For an example of a scientific literature review, click on

▸ **Student Samples**
  ▸ **Essays**

Most scientists spend a great deal of time writing **research proposals** aimed at securing funds to support their research. Undergraduate writers often have an opportunity to make similar proposals — to an office of undergraduate research or to a science-based firm that supports innovative student research, for example. Such funding agencies will often have guidelines for preparing a proposal. If not, you can organize and write your proposal by building in the general sections that appear in many proposals for research funding: title page, introduction, purpose(s) and significance of the study, methods, timeline, budget, and references. You may also need to submit an abstract, especially if the research proposal is longer than several pages. As with most scientific writing, you want to provide precise details and use the past tense to refer to research carried out (by you or others) in the past.

Research reports, another common writing form in the sciences, typically include literature reviews as one of their components. But since research reports are based on primary research — most often an experiment — they are more extensive than literature reviews. Both research reports and published journal articles generally follow the form specified earlier: title, author(s), abstract, introduction, literature review, materials and methods, results, discussion, and references. When writing research reports, be aware that specific conventions govern the use of tense in these reports. In general, use the present tense for research reports. Use the past tense, however, when you are describing specific experimental methods and observations or citing research published in the past.

Sometimes, instructors ask students to write **lab reports,** which are briefer versions of research reports. Lab reports generally include the following sections: title, purpose, methods, results, discussion/conclusion, references.

Whether you are writing a literature review, research proposal, research report, or lab report, you will likely face several challenges. Much scientific writing, for instance, is collaborative. As students move from introductory to advanced courses and then to the workplace, they increasingly find themselves working as part of teams or groups. Indeed, in such areas as engineering, collaborative research and writing projects are often the norm.

For suggestions
on working col-
laboratively, see
Chapter 6.

Most students in the sciences also need to know how to produce complex figures, tables, images, and models and how to use software designed to analyze data or run computer simulations. As a result, the ability to work with complex computer programs is increasingly part of what it means to write well in the sciences.

In addition, remember that the presentation of data is very important in the sciences. If you are developing a graph, be sure to provide headings for columns, to label axes with numbers or units, and to identify data points. Be sure as well to caption figures and tables with a number and descriptive title. And remember that your research should not include *orphan data*—data that you present in figure or table form but don't comment on in your report.

66c A student research proposal using CBE style

The following piece of student writing uses the CBE style (citation-sequence format) of documentation, which is commonly used in the sciences. The paper is a proposal for a summer research fellowship by Tara Gupta, a student at Colgate University. Note that this essay has been reproduced in a narrow format to allow for annotation.

ACADEMIC WRITING

A Student Research Proposal Using CBE Style

●— For more on using charts, graphs, and other visuals, see Chapter 8.

STUDENT WRITER

Tara Gupta

●— For more on CBE style, see Chapter 22.

www • bedford stmartins.com/ smhandbook

For an additional student research proposal, click on

▶ **Student Samples**
   ▶ **Essays**

Field Measurements of
Photosynthesis and Transpiration
Rates in Dwarf Snapdragon
(*Chaenorrhinum minus* Lange):
An Investigation of Water Stress
Adaptations

Tara Gupta

Proposal for a
Summer Research
Fellowship
Colgate University
February 25, 2003

Introduction

Dwarf snapdragon (*Chaenorrhinum minus*) is a weedy pioneer plant found growing in central New York during spring and summer. Interestingly, the distribution of this species has been limited almost exclusively to the cinder ballast of railroad tracks[1] and to sterile strips of land along highways.[2] In these harsh environments, characterized by intense sunlight and poor soil water retention, one would expect *C. minus* to exhibit anatomical features similar to those of xeromorphic plants (species adapted to arid habitats).

However, this is not the case. T. Gupta and R. Arnold (unpublished) have found that the leaves and stems of *C. minus* are not covered by a thick, waxy cuticle but rather with a thin cuticle that is less effective in inhibiting water loss through diffusion. The root system is not long and thick, capable of reaching deeper, moister soils; instead, it is thin and diffuse, permeating only the topmost (and driest) soil horizon. Moreover, in contrast to many xeromorphic plants, the stomata (pores regulating gas exchange) are not found in sunken crypts or cavities in the epidermis that retard water loss from transpiration.

Despite a lack of these morphological adaptations to water stress, *C. minus* continues to grow and reproduce when morning dew has been its only source of water for up to five weeks

(R. Arnold, personal communication). Such growth
involves fixation of carbon by photosynthesis and
requires that the stomata be open to admit
sufficient carbon dioxide. Given the dry, sunny
environment, the time required for adequate carbon
fixation must also mean a significant loss of water
through transpiration as open stomata exchange
carbon dioxide with water. How does *C. minus*
balance the need for carbon with the need to
conserve water?

Purposes of the Proposed Study

The above observations have led me to an
exploration of the extent to which *C. minus* is able
to photosynthesize under conditions of low water
availability. It is my hypothesis that *C. minus*
adapts to these conditions by photosynthesizing in
the early morning and late afternoon, when leaf and
air temperatures are lower and transpirational
water loss is reduced. During the middle of the
day, its photosynthetic rate may be very low,
perhaps even zero, on hot, sunny afternoons.
Similar diurnal changes in photosynthetic rate in
response to midday water deficits have been
described in crop plants.[3,4] There appear to be no
comparable studies on noncrop species in their
natural habitats.

Thus, the research proposed here aims to help
explain the apparent paradox of an organism that
thrives in water-stressed conditions despite a lack
of morphological adaptations. This summer's work

Unpublished source cited in parentheses within text but not included in references

States purposes and scope of proposed study

Significance of the study noted

Water Stress Adaptations 4

will also serve as a basis for controlled experiments in a plant growth chamber on the individual
effects of temperature, light intensity, soil water
availability, and other environmental factors on
photosynthesis and transpiration rates. These
experiments are planned for the coming fall
semester.

Methods and Timeline

Simultaneous measurements of photosynthesis
and transpiration rates will indicate the balance
C. minus has achieved in acquiring the energy it
needs while retaining the water available to it.
These measurements will be taken daily from June
22 to September 7, 2003, at field sites in the
Hamilton, NY, area, using an LI-6220 portable
photosynthesis system (LICOR, Inc., Lincoln, NE).
Basic methodology and use of correction factors
will be similar to that described in related
studies.[5-7] Data will be collected at regular
intervals throughout the daylight hours and
will be related to measurements of ambient air
temperature, leaf temperature, relative humidity,
light intensity, wind velocity, and cloud cover.

Budget

1 kg soda lime, 4-8 mesh $70
   (for absorption of CO_2 in photosynthesis
   analyzer)
1 kg anhydrous magnesium perchlorate $130
   (used as desiccant for photosynthesis
   analyzer)

Relates the pro-
posed research
project to future
research

Briefly describes
methodology to be
used

Provides timeline
for the study

Budget provides
itemized details

SigmaScan software (Jandel Scientific $195
  Software, Inc.)
  (for measurement of leaf areas for which
  photosynthesis and transpiration rates
  are to be determined)

Estimated 500 miles travel to field sites $140
  in own car @ $0.28/mile

CO_2 cylinder, 80 days rental @ $0.25/day $20
  (for calibration of photosynthesis
  analyzer)

                       TOTAL REQUEST $555

Water Stress Adaptations 6

References

[1]Wildrlechner MP. Historical and phenological observations of the spread of *Chaenorrhinum minus* across North America. Can J Bot 1983; 61:179-87.

[2]Dwarf Snapdragon [Internet]. Olympia, WA: Washington State Noxious Weed Control Board; [updated 2001 July 7; cited 2003 Jan 25]. Available from: http://www.wa.gov/agr /weedboard/weed_info/dwarfsnapdragon.html

[3]Boyer JS. Plant productivity and environment. Science 1982;218:443-8.

[4]Manhas JG, Sukumaran NP. Diurnal changes in net photosynthetic rate in potato in two environments. Potato Res 1988;31:375-8.

[5]Doley DG, Unwin GL, Yates DJ. Spatial and temporal distribution of photosynthesis and transpiration by single leaves in a rainforest tree, *Argyrodendron peralatum*. Aust J Plant Physiol 1988;15:317-26.

[6]Kallarackal J, Milburn JA, Baker DA. Water relations of the banana. III. Effects of controlled water stress on water potential, transpiration, photosynthesis and leaf growth. Aust J Plant Physiol 1990;17:79-90.

[7]Idso SB, Allen SG, Kimball BA, Choudhury BJ. Problems with porometry: measuring net photosynthesis by leaf chamber techniques. Agron 1989;81:475-9.

Includes all published works cited; numbers correspond to order in which sources were first mentioned in the text; CBE citation-sequence format is shown

The following lists contain many print and Web resources for students of the natural and applied sciences. Many of the Web sites include links to other Web resources, so they are doubly helpful.

■ *Astronomy*

GENERAL REFERENCE SOURCES

Encyclopedia of Astronomy and Astrophysics. 2001.

INDEXES AND DATABASES

Astronomy and Astrophysics Abstracts. 1969–.

WEB RESOURCES

The Astronomy Cafe <itss.raytheon.com/cafe/cafe.html>

The Astronomy Net <www.astronomy.net>

NASA <www.nasa.gov>

The WWW Virtual Library: Astronomy and Astrophysics & AstroWeb <webhead.com/wwwvl/astronomy>

■ *Biology and biosciences*

GENERAL REFERENCE SOURCES

Encyclopedia of Bioethics. 2 vols. 1982.
Encyclopedia of Human Biology. 8 vols. 1997.
Encyclopedia of Microbiology. 4 vols. 1992.
Grzimek's Animal Life Encyclopedia. 13 vols. 1972–74.
Mammals: A Multimedia Encyclopedia. (CD-ROM)

INDEXES AND DATABASES

Biological Abstracts. 1926–. (Online, CD-ROM)
Biological and Agricultural Index. 1964–. (Online, CD-ROM)

WEB RESOURCES

Biosciences Index <mcb.harvard.edu/BioLinks.html>
Links to the Genetic World <www.ornl.gov/hgmis/links.html>
Scott's Botanical Links <www.ou.edu/cas/botany-micro/bot-linx>
The WWW Virtual Library: Bio Sciences <vlib.org/Biosciences.html>

GENERAL REFERENCE SOURCES

Kirk-Othmer Encyclopedia of Chemical Technology. 27 vols. 1991–.

INDEXES AND DATABASES

Chemical Abstracts. 1907–. (Online)

WEB RESOURCES

ACS Resources <www.chemistry.org>

CHEMINFO <www.indiana.edu/~cheminfo/cisindex.html>

The WWW Virtual Library: Chemistry <www.liv.ac.uk/Chemistry/Links/
   links.html>

Computer science

GENERAL REFERENCE SOURCES

Encyclopedia of Computer Science. 1993.
Encyclopedia of Computer Science and Technology. 2003.
McGraw-Hill Multimedia Encyclopedia of Science and Technology. 1997.

INDEXES AND DATABASES

ACM Guide to Computing Literature. 1980–. (Online as ACM Portal)

WEB RESOURCES

MIT Laboratory for Computer Science <lcs.mit.edu>

PC Webopedia <www.pcwebopedia.com>

The WWW Virtual Library: Computing <www.vlib.org/
   Computing.html>

Earth science

GENERAL REFERENCE SOURCES

Encyclopedia of Earth Sciences. 24 vols. 1966–.
Encyclopedia of Earth System Science. 4 vols. 1992.
Encyclopedia of Minerals. 1974–.
McGraw-Hill Dictionary of Earth Sciences. 1997.

sci
66d

ACADEMIC WRITING
Writing for the
Natural and
Applied Sciences

INDEXES AND DATABASES

Bibliography and Index of Geology. 1969–. (Online, CD-ROM)

WEB RESOURCES

Internet Resources in the Earth Sciences <www.lib.berkeley.edu/EART/ EarthLinks.html>

NASA's Global Change Master Directory (GCMD) <gcmd.gsfc.nasa.gov>

The WWW Virtual Library: Earth Sciences <www.vlib.org/ EarthScience.html>

■ *Engineering*

GENERAL REFERENCE SOURCES

Annual Book of ASTM Standards. 1990–.

CRC Handbook of Tables for Applied Engineering Science. 1973.

Encyclopedia of Materials Science and Engineering. 8 vols. 1986.

Handbook of Engineering Fundamentals. 1990.

Handbook of Industrial Engineering. 2001.

Marks' Standard Handbook for Mechanical Engineers. 1987–.

McGraw-Hill Encyclopedia of Engineering. 1993.

Perry's Chemical Engineer's Handbook. 1997.

Standard Handbook for Civil Engineers. 1996.

Standard Handbook for Electrical Engineers. 1986.

Standard Handbook of Environmental Engineering. 1990.

INDEXES AND DATABASES

Engineering Index Monthly. 1884–. (Online, CD-ROM)

INSPEC. 1969–.

WEB RESOURCES

EEVL: The Internet Guide to Engineering, Mathematics, and Computing <www.eevl.ac.uk>

IEEE Spectrum <www.spectrum.ieee.org>

■ *Environmental studies*

GENERAL REFERENCE SOURCES

Dictionary of Energy. 1988.

Encyclopedia of Environmental Science and Technology. 2000.

sci

66d   935

ACADEMIC WRITING
Research Sources
for the Natural and
Applied Sciences

Facts on File Dictionary of Environmental Science. 1991.
Grzimek's Encyclopedia of Ecology. 1976–.
McGraw-Hill Encyclopedia of Environmental Science and Engineering. 1993.
United States Energy Atlas. 1986.

INDEXES AND DATABASES

Ecological Abstracts. 1980–. (Online by subscription, CD-ROM)
Environment Abstracts. 1971–. (CD-ROM in *ENVIRO/ENERGYLINE*)
Environmental Periodicals Bibliography. 1972–. (Online, CD-ROM)
Pollution Abstracts. 1970–. (Online, CD-ROM)

WEB RESOURCES

EnviroInfo: Environmental Information Sources <www.deb.uminho.pt/
fontes/enviroinfo>

EnviroLink <www.envirolink.org>

The WWW Virtual Library: Environment <earthsystems.org/
virtuallibrary/vlhome.html>

■ *Mathematics*

GENERAL REFERENCE SOURCES

CRC Handbook of Mathematical Sciences. 1987.
Encyclopedic Dictionary of Mathematics. 4 vols. 1987.

INDEXES AND DATABASES

Mathematical Reviews. 1940–. (Online as *Math on the Web,* CD-ROM as
MathSciDisc)

WEB RESOURCES

American Mathematical Society, Math on the Web <www.ams.org/
mathweb>

Math Archives Undergrads' Page <archives.math.utk.edu/
undergraduates.html>

Math Forum Internet Mathematics Library <mathforum.org/library>

NIST (National Institute of Standards and Technology) Virtual
Library <nvl.nist.gov>

▪ *Medicine/nursing*

GENERAL REFERENCE SOURCES

Cecil Textbook of Medicine. 2000.

Conn's Current Therapy 2001. 2001.

Gale Encyclopedia of Medicine. 5 vols. 1999.

Handbook of Clinical Nursing Research. 1999.

INDEXES AND DATABASES

The CINAHL Database. 1977–.

Cumulative Index to Nursing and Allied Health Literature. 1961–. (Online, CD-ROM)

Index Medicus. 1899–1926; 1960–. (Online, CD-ROM in *MEDLINE*)

WEB RESOURCES

HealthWorld Online <www.healthy.net>

National Institutes of Health <www.nih.gov>

National Science Foundation: Biology <www.nsf.gov/home/bio/start.htm>

Nursing Net <www.nursingnet.org>

Virtual Hospital <www.vh.org>

Weill Cornell Medical Library <www.med.cornell.edu>

▪ *Physics*

GENERAL REFERENCE SOURCES

American Institute of Physics Handbook. 1972.

Encyclopedia of Physics. 1991.

McGraw-Hill Dictionary of Physics. 1997.

INDEXES AND DATABASES

Information Sources in Physics. 1985.

Physics Abstracts. 1898–. (Online, CD-ROM)

WEB RESOURCES

AIP Physics Information <www.aip.org>

Contemporary Physics Education Project <www.cpepweb.org>

PhysLINK.com <www.physlink.com>

The WWW Virtual Library: Physics <www.vlib.org/Physics.html>

FOR COLLABORATION

Team up with a classmate who is interested in the same scientific field or major you are. Then go to the library and identify (or ask your instructor to help you identify) an article in that field that is clearly argued and well written. Read the article individually, and then go through it again together, taking notes on how it is organized, on its tone and style, on its use of evidence and sources. Determine how effective this article is in presenting its information, and bring the results of your analysis to class for discussion.

THINKING CRITICALLY ABOUT WRITING FOR THE SCIENCES

Reading with an Eye for Writing in the Sciences

It's easy to take the conventions of scientific writing for granted — to assume that scientists have always written in this way. But they have not. Indeed, the habits that characterize current scientific practice took centuries to develop. In the Middle Ages, for instance, the only records that physicians kept were of charges to patients. And only in the seventeenth century did such early Western scientists as Francis Bacon, Robert Boyle, and Isaac Newton recognize that in order to conduct valid scientific experiments they would need to develop a clear, consistent vocabulary that other scientists could understand.

In order to better understand why current conventions in scientific writing continue to be effective, identify one or more features of scientific texts and consider their usefulness. Why, for instance, do research reports always include a discussion of materials and methods? Why does an abstract precede the actual article? How do scientific nomenclatures, classification systems, and other features of scientific writing aid the work of scientists? In considering questions such as these, try to identify the functions that textual elements such as these play in the ongoing work of science.

Thinking about Your Own Writing in the Sciences

Choose a piece of writing you did for a natural or applied science class — a lab report, a research report, a proposal — and read it carefully. Note the format and headings you used, how you presented visual data, what kinds of evidence you used, and what citation system you used. Compare your piece of writing with a similar piece of writing published in a journal in the field. How well does your writing compare?

67

While some may claim that "love makes the world go round," many others would say that it's actually business that turns the world today. The information revolution has brought many changes to business in North America and throughout the world. Yet in the midst of these changes one constant remains: written communication is essential in identifying and solving the complex problems of today's companies. To succeed in business, you need to know how to manage many kinds of writing—from negotiating an ever-increasing number of emails to communicating effectively with readers from Manhattan to Malaysia, Mexico, Mali, and Madagascar. This chapter will help you read and write more effectively in a business environment. ■

67a Becoming a strong reader of texts in business

Readers in today's Information Age face a dizzying array of demands. Thanks to computer hardware and software, a team of businesspeople researching a topic has almost unlimited access to information. Somehow, the members of this team need to negotiate a huge stream of print, electronic, and online information and to evaluate that information for its usefulness. To meet demands such as these, you can draw on the general strategies for effective reading presented in Chapter 11, which will remind you that effective readers have a clear purpose in mind when they read. This general principle is particularly important when you are engaged in work-related reading. Are you reading to solve a problem? to gather and synthesize information? to make a recommendation? Having a clear purpose will increase your productivity as a reader.

Those in business are aware that time constraints and deadline pressures affect decisions about *what* to read as well as about *how* to read. Increasingly, good readers recognize that the ability to use search tools effectively is an important way to improve their reading online. Thus they often use interdocument links, bookmarks, and other tools to annotate electronic and online texts.

Finally, good readers in business realize that they are working increasingly in a global context. As a result, they need to consider the cultural contexts of what they read and respond sensitively to those contexts. Even email conventions can vary from culture to culture, as what is considered polite in one culture may be considered rude in another. For more on reading in a global context, see Chapter 24.

67b Becoming a strong writer of texts in business

Writing assignments in business classes serve two related functions. While their most immediate goal is to help students master the theory and practice of business, these assignments also try to prepare students for the kinds of writing they will face when they enter the world of work after college. For this reason, students in *every* discipline need to know how to write effective business memos, emails, letters, résumés, and reports (see 67c).

www • bedford
stmartins.com/
smhandbook

For an example of
business writing
done for a business
class, click on

▸ **Student Samples**
   ▸ **Essays**

■ *Understanding general business-writing skills*

No matter what medium they are working within, writers in business — like writers everywhere — need to ask themselves the following questions:

- What is my purpose in writing?
- Who is my intended audience? Might my audience grow to include others (in the case of forwarded email, for instance)? Will my audience include people accessing my writing through a Web site?
- What medium (print, electronic, online) provides the most effective means of communicating with my audience?
- What principles of document design do I need to consider, given the medium in which I choose to communicate?
- What major points do I want to make in the text I am composing?
- Does my writing situation call for me to follow a conventional format, such as that of the memo or report?
- What style and tone best suit my overall situation?
- How can my text be enhanced by the use of figures, tables, or other visual images?

●···· For a fuller dis-
cussion of these
writing issues, see
Chapter 2; for
more on visuals
and document
design, see Chap-
ters 8 and 9.

Business writers who ask questions such as these can respond more effectively to the challenges of communication in the twenty-first century.

67c Writing business memos, emails, letters, and résumés

In most business classes, writing assignments reflect the situations students might experience on the job. **Memos,** for instance, are a common form of print or electronic correspondence sent within and between organizations. Memos tend to be brief, often dealing with only one subject.

SOME GUIDELINES FOR WRITING EFFECTIVE MEMOS

→ Write the date, the name of the recipient, your name, and the subject on separate lines at the top.

→ Begin with the most important information: depending on the memo's purpose, you may have to provide background information, define the task or problem, or clarify the memo's goal.

→ Try to involve readers in your opening paragraph by focusing on how the information you convey affects them.

→ In each subsequent paragraph, discuss one idea pertaining to the subject. Present information concisely and from the readers' perspective.

→ Emphasize specific action—exactly what you want readers to do, and when.

→ Use attachments for detailed supporting information.

→ For print memos, initial your memo next to your name.

→ Adjust your style and tone to fit your audience. You would probably use a more formal tone in a memo to a supervisor or someone in another company than you would in a memo to a coworker.

→ Attempt to build goodwill in your conclusion.

STUDENT WRITER

Michelle Abbott

STUDENT WRITER

Carina Abernathy

Here is a memo, written by Michelle Abbott and Carina Abernathy, that presents an analysis and recommendation to help an employer make a decision.

Date: January 30, 2003
To: Rosa Donahue, Sales Manager
From: Michelle Abbott & Carina Abernathy,   *MA CA*
           Sales Associates
Subject: Taylor Nursery Bid

As you know, Taylor Nursery has requested bids on a 25,000-pound order of private-label fertilizer. Taylor Nursery is one of the largest distributors of our Fertikil product. The following is our analysis of Jenco's costs to fill this special order and a recommendation for the bidding price.

The total cost for manufacturing 25,000 pounds of the private-label brand for Taylor Nursery is $44,075. This cost includes direct material, direct labor, and variable manufacturing overhead. Although our current equipment and facilities provide adequate capacity for processing this special order, the job *will* involve an excess in labor hours. The overtime labor rate has been factored into our costs.

The absolute minimum price that Jenco could bid for this product without losing money is $44,075 (our cost). Applying our standard markup of 40% results in a price of $61,705. Thus, you could reasonably establish a price anywhere within that range.

In making the final assessment, we advise you to consider factors relevant to this decision. Taylor Nursery has stated that this is a one-time order. Therefore, the effort to free this special order will not bring long-term benefits.

Finally, Taylor Nursery has requested bids from several competitors. One rival, Eclipse Fertilizers, is submitting a bid of $60,000 on this order. Therefore, our recommendation is to slightly underbid Eclipse with a price of $58,000, representing a markup of approximately 32%.

Please let us know if we can be of further assistance in your decision on the Taylor Nursery bid.

Initials of sender added in ink

Paragraphs not indented

Opening paragraph provides necessary background and clearly states memo's purpose

Most important information clearly emphasized

Double-space between paragraphs

Options presented to employer

Factors explained to help in employer's decision

Final recommendation

Closing builds goodwill by offering further help

bus

942 **67c**

FOR COLLABORATION

ACADEMIC WRITING

Writing for
Business

Working with one or two classmates, analyze the Abbott and Abernathy memo. Use the guidelines on p. 940 to help you with your analysis. Make a list of the memo's strengths, and note any weaknesses you find. Also jot down any additional topics you think the memo should have discussed—or any information that should have been deleted. Bring the results of your analysis to class for discussion, making sure you are prepared to explain all of your ideas.

Email is a form of brief communication used continuously in business, industry, and the professions. Traveling instantaneously to individuals and groups anywhere in the world at any hour, an email message follows a format much like that of a memo, with lines for the sender, recipient, and subject. (For guidelines for and an example of effective email, see Chapter 7.)

Despite the popularity of email, **letters** remain an important form of communication. When you send a business or professional letter, you are writing either as an individual or as a representative of an organization. In either case, and regardless of your purpose, a letter should follow certain conventions.

SOME GUIDELINES FOR WRITING EFFECTIVE LETTERS

→ Consider your audience. Who should be addressed in the letter? Should others receive copies? Who else might be given your letter to read? Keep this information in mind as you draft your letter.

→ Use a conventional format. Many letters use the block format, in which all text aligns at the left margin. Some writers prefer a modified block format, aligning the return address, date, close, and signature on the right. When using letterhead, you also have the option of centering the return address, as the student writer on p. 944 does.

→ Whenever possible, write to a specific person (*Dear Alfredo Lujan* or *Dear Ms. Otuteye*) rather than to a general *Dear Sir or Madam*.

→ Open cordially and be polite—even if you have a complaint.

→ State the reason for your letter clearly. Include whatever details will help your reader see your point and respond.

→ If appropriate, make clear what you hope your reader will do.

→ Express appreciation for your reader's attention.

→ Make it easy for your reader to respond by including your telephone or fax number or email address and, if appropriate, a self-addressed, stamped envelope.

One particular type of letter, the **letter of application** or cover letter, often accompanies a résumé. The purpose of a letter of application is to demonstrate how the experiences and skills you outline in your résumé have prepared you for a particular job. In a letter of application, then, it is important to focus on how you can benefit the company, not how the company can help you. If you are responding to a particular advertisement, mention it in the opening paragraph. Finally, be sure to indicate how you can be reached for an interview.

In the letter of application for a summer job on p. 944, note that Nastassia Lopez uses a block format along with the personal letterhead she has created for her correspondence.

As noted previously, a letter of application and a **résumé** often travel together. While a letter of application usually emphasizes specific parts of the résumé, telling how your background is suited to a particular job, a résumé summarizes your experience and qualifications and provides support for your letter. An effective résumé is brief, usually one or two pages.

Research shows that employers generally spend less than a minute reading a résumé. Remember that they are interested not in what they can do for you but what you can do for them. They expect a résumé to be printed neatly on high-quality paper or formatted neatly on a Web page or in an electronic file. In all cases, your aim is to use clear headings, adequate spacing, and conventional formats that will make your résumé easy to read. Although you may be tempted to use colored paper or unusual type because you want your résumé to stand out, avoid such temptations. A well-written résumé with a standard format is the best way to distinguish yourself.

Your résumé may be arranged chronologically (in reverse chronological order) or functionally (around skills or expertise). Either way, you will probably include the following information:

1. *Name, address, phone and fax numbers, and email address,* often centered at the top.
2. *Career objective(s).* List immediate or short-term goals and specific jobs for which you realistically qualify.
3. *Educational background.* Include degrees, diplomas, majors, and special programs or courses that pertain to your field of interest. List honors and scholarships and your grade-point average if it is high.
4. *Work experience.* Identify each job — whether a paying job, an internship, or military experience — with dates and names of organizations.

Writing for
Business

Nastassia creates a
letterhead for her let-
ter and provides con-
tact information

Block format with left
justified margin

Double spacing
between date and
inside address

Single spacing of
inside address with
full name, title, and
address

Salutation addresses
a specific person

Double spacing
between inside address
and salutation and
between salutation
and opening sentence

Opening provides
information about
Nastassia and lists her
major goals

Side margins at one
inch

Provides background
information to illus-
trate her skills and
the strength of her
interest

Closing phrase

Four line spaces left
for signature

1"

Nastassia Rose Lopez
523 Brown Avenue
Stanford, CA 94305
650-326-6790 / nrl87@hotmail.com

February 1, 2003

Mr. Price Hicks
Director of Educational Programs and Services
Academy of Arts and Sciences
5220 Lankersheim Blvd.
North Hollywood, CA 91601

Dear Mr. Hicks:

I am an enthusiastic Stanford student who is keenly interested in the entertainment industry and who believes that a Development Internship at the
Academy of Arts and Sciences would greatly benefit both the Academy and
me. A Los Angeles native in my first year at Stanford, I'm a serious student
who is a hard worker. My current goal is to comprehend the full scope of the
entertainment industry and to learn the ropes of the craft.

As an experienced writer, I am attracted to the Development Department
because I am curious to learn the process of television production from paper
to screen. In high school, I was enrolled in Advanced Placement Writing,
and I voluntarily took a creative writing class. At Stanford, I received High
Honors for maintaining an excellent grade-point average across all my
classes, including several writing-intensive courses.

My passion for writing, producing, directing, and most of all *learning* is
enormous. If my application is accepted, I will bring a strong work ethic,
proficiency, and creativity to the workplace.

Thank you very much for your time and consideration. My résumé is
enclosed, and I look forward to hearing from you.

Sincerely yours,

Nastassia Rose Lopez

Nastassia Rose Lopez

Describe your duties by carefully selecting strong action verbs. Highlight any of your activities that improved business in any way.

5. *Skills, personal interests, activities, awards, and honors.* Identify your technology skills. List hobbies, offices held, volunteer work, and awards.

6. *References.* List two or three people who know your work well, first asking their permission. Give their titles, addresses, and phone or fax numbers. Or simply say that your references are available on request.

7. *Keywords.* Labels and terms that an employer might use to search for a job candidate are important to include if your résumé is submitted electronically and might become part of a database.

Scannable résumés can be used in both online and electronic (database) environments. Since employers increasingly search these environments, take careful note of how to prepare a scannable résumé.

- Choosing and positioning keywords are particularly important in preparing scannable résumés. The keywords enable those searching databases or Web sites to identify job candidates whose skills match their needs.

- In general, *nouns* function as keywords by which a résumé is scanned by Web search engines and organized in databases. For this reason, look for places where you can convert verbs (*performed laboratory tests*) to nouns (*laboratory technologist*).

- Place the most important keywords toward the beginning of the résumé: the program scanning your résumé may have a limited number of items it can scan for, and many programs start scanning at the top of the document.

- Use a standard typeface, such as Times New Roman, and type size throughout. Do not use underlining, italics, boxes, borders, or columns.

www • bedford
stmartins.com/
smhandbook

For an example of an online résumé, click on

▶ **Student Samples**
 ▶ **Academic and
  Professional
  Writing**

Be aware that the conventions involving scannable résumés are in flux. In recent years, it has been common to develop a scannable résumé that could be scanned for both online and electronic databases. Increasingly, though, job seekers who want to target the Internet are composing online résumés as hypertext screen documents, which make keywords more visible to search engines and thus tend to produce more **hits**. In addition, some companies ask applicants to fill out résumé forms on their own Web sites.

The following pages show Dennis Tyler's résumé in two formats, one in conventional print style, the other formatted for scanning.

STUDENT WRITER

Dennis Tyler Jr.

ACADEMIC WRITING

Writing for Business

Name in boldface and larger type size

Position being sought

Educational background

Work experience relevant to position being sought

Talents and honors not listed above

DENNIS TYLER JR.

CURRENT ADDRESS	PERMANENT ADDRESS
P.O. Box 12345	506 Chanelle Court
Stanford, CA 94309	Baton Rouge, LA 70128
Phone: (650) 498-4731	Phone: (504) 246-9847
Email: dtyler@yahoo.com	

CAREER OBJECTIVE   Position on editorial staff of a major newspaper

EDUCATION

9/98–6/02   **Stanford University,** Stanford, CA
B.A., ENGLISH AND AMERICAN STUDIES, June 2002

9/00–12/00   **Morehouse College,** Atlanta, GA
STANFORD STUDY EXCHANGE PROGRAM

EXPERIENCE

6/01–9/01   **Business Scholar Intern,** Finance, AOL Time Warner, New York, NY
Responsible for analyzing data for strategic marketing plans. Researched the mergers and acquisitions of companies to which Time Inc. sells advertising space.

1/00–6/01   **Editor-in-Chief,** *Enigma* (a literary journal), Stanford University, CA
Oversaw the entire process of Enigma. Edited numerous creative works: short stories, poems, essays, and interviews. Selected appropriate material for the journal. Responsible for designing cover and publicity to the greater community.

8/00–12/00   **Community Development Intern,** University Center Development Corporation (UCDC), Atlanta, GA
Facilitated workshops and meetings on the importance of home buying and neighborhood preservation. Created UCDC brochure and assisted in the publication of the center's newsletter.

6/00–8/00   **News Editor,** *Stanford Daily,* Stanford University, CA
Responsible for editing stories and creating story ideas for the newspaper. Assisted with the layout for the newspaper and designs for the cover.

SKILLS AND HONORS

- Computer Skills: MS Word, Excel, PageMaker, Microsoft Publisher; Internet research
- Language: Proficient in Spanish
- Trained in making presentations, conducting research, acting, and singing
- Mellon Fellow, Gates Millennium Scholar, Public Service Scholar, National Collegiate Scholar
- Black Community Service Arts Award. 2001–2002

REFERENCES   Available upon request

Dennis Tyler Jr.

Current Address
P.O. Box 12345
Stanford, CA 94309
Phone: (650) 498-4731
Email: dtyler@yahoo.com

Permanent Address
506 Chanelle Court
Baton Rouge, LA 70128
Phone: (504) 246-9847

Keywords: journalist; journal editor; literary publishing; finance; community development; design; leadership; newspaper writer; PageMaker; Spanish; editor-in-chief

Education
B.A. in English and American Studies, June 2002, Stanford University, Stanford, CA
Morehouse College Study Exchange, fall 2000, Atlanta, GA

Experience
Business Scholar Intern, summer 2001
Finance, AOL TimeWarner, New York, NY
Data analyst for strategic marketing plans. Researcher for the mergers and acquisitions of companies to which Time Inc. sells advertising.

Editor-in-Chief, 2000-2001, Enigma (a literary journal), Stanford University, CA
Oversaw the entire process of Enigma. Editor for numerous creative works: short stories, poems, essays, and interviews. Content selection for the journal. Cover design and publicity to the greater community.

Community Development Intern, fall 2000
University Center Development Corporation (UCDC), Atlanta, GA
Workshops on the importance of home buying and neighborhood preservation. Publication responsibility for UCDC brochure and the center's newsletter.

News Editor, summer 2000, Stanford Daily, Stanford University, CA
Story editor for the newspaper. Layout and cover design for the newspaper.

Skills and Honors
Computer skills: MS Word, Excel, PageMaker, Microsoft Publisher; Internet research
Language: Proficient in Spanish
Trained presenter, researcher, actor, singer
Mellon Fellow, Gates Millennium Scholar, Public Service Scholar, National Collegiate Scholar
Black Community Service Arts Award, 2001-2002

References
Available upon request

Writing Business Memos, Emails, Letters, and Résumés

Each phone number or email address on a separate line

Standard typeface (Times Roman) and type size used throughout

Keywords listed to aid in computer searches by employers

No underlining, italics, boxes, borders, or columns

White space used to mark off sections

Verbs converted to nouns wherever possible

Keywords used in body of résumé wherever possible

● **EXERCISE 67.1**

Take a close look at the two versions of Dennis Tyler's résumé on pp. 946–947, and note the differences in presentation and content. What purposes might these differences serve? Can you identify differences in the audience — and audience expectations — for these résumés?

■ *Special considerations in business writing*

In the contemporary work environment, **collaboration,** or the ability to work with team members, is a highly valued skill. Thanks to electronic networks, email, and so on, much business writing is easily undertaken collaboratively. Such collaboration happens when a salesperson drafts a letter to a potential client and emails it to a manager, asking her for editorial advice. It happens when an important document such as an IPO (initial public offering) or company brochure is reviewed online by a number of individuals or offices for its accuracy and effectiveness. And it happens when members of a team handle different responsibilities for a document and communicate with each other via email — with one person collecting data, another composing the text, another preparing visuals, and yet another editing the resulting document.

For more advice
on collab-
oration, see
Chapter 6.

Precisely because new information technologies are enabling people throughout the world to work and write together, people in business increasingly find themselves working as members of transnational teams. The ability to communicate effectively across cultures requires both knowledge and sensitivity. The more knowledge you have about different cultural norms, the more effectively you can communicate with someone working in a country other than your own. And since the United States is very diverse, you need to recognize that not all people working and writing in this country will have the same understanding of communication.

For advice on
how to commu-
nicate effectively
across cultures,
see Chapter 24.

Finally, business writers face a number of complex ethical questions. Imagine, for instance, that you are part of a team of writers responsible for a newsletter for company employees. How do you determine the priorities for your newsletter? To what extent should these priorities reflect the party line of top officials in your company? To what extent should they reflect the concerns of the majority of its workers? Or imagine that you work in a consumer-relations department. Clearly, the texts you write must serve the interests and goals of the business for which you work. But what about the needs of the consumer and of the general public? Other ethical issues can arise in business writing. What if your supervisor encourages you to manipulate data to enhance the desirability of your product or to make a problematic situation look more posi-tive? What if an advertising team presents you with an ad that uses dis-torted or slanted visuals to enhance the visual appeal of a product?

Fortunately, some guidelines for ethics in business already exist. If preexisting local, state, or federal regulations apply to the work you do, you have an ethical obligation to follow them. Many professions and companies also have their own codes or standards of ethics. These guide-lines can help you make decisions about day-to-day writing. Even so, you will undoubtedly encounter situations where the "right" decision is rather murky. Someone who regularly responds to complaints, for instance, may have to decide whether to reply with a form letter or an original letter — and this decision could have serious consequences for the person who initiated the complaint. On a more global level, the lan-guage that companies use in annual reports and other public docu-ments can, as the much-publicized Enron/Arthur Andersen case indi-cates, have significant consequences not only for investors and workers but also for the country at large.

67d Research sources for business

The following lists contain print and Web resources for students of busi-ness and economics. Many of the Web sites include links to other Web resources, so they are doubly helpful.

www • bedford
stmartins.com/
smhandbook

For additional resources in business and economics, click on

▶ Writer's Almanac

GENERAL REFERENCE SOURCES

Encyclopedia of Banking and Finance. 1991.
McGraw-Hill Dictionary of Modern Economics. 1994.
The New Palgrave: A Dictionary of Economics. 1987.
Occupational Outlook Handbook. 1949–. (Online, CD-ROM)

INDEXES AND DATABASES

Business Index. 1979–. (Online, CD-ROM)
Business Periodicals Index. 1958–. (Online, CD-ROM as *Wilson Business Abstracts*)
Encyclopedia of Business Information Sources. 1988.
International Bibliography of Economics. 1955–.
Predicasts F&S Index: United States. 1972–. (Online, CD-ROM)

WEB RESOURCES

Business and Economics Resources <www.ipl.org/div/subject/browse/bus00.00.00>

Center for International Business Education and Research <ciber.bus.msu.edu>

Federal Reserve Board <www.federalreserve.gov>

Internet and Marketing <www.ntu.edu.sg/library/mktg/int-mktg.htm>

Rutgers Accounting Web <accounting.rutgers.edu>

SEC EDGAR Database <www.sec.gov/edgar.shtml>

Webec <www.helsinki.fi/WebEc>

World Trade Organization <www.wto.org>

THINKING CRITICALLY ABOUT BUSINESS WRITING

Reading with an Eye for Writing in Business

Monitor your mail for a few days, saving everything that tries to sell a product, provide a service, or solicit information or money. Then go through these pieces of business writing, and choose the one you find most effective and best written. What about the writing appeals to you? gets and holds your attention? What in the piece of writing might lead you to buy the product, choose the service, or make a contribution? What might make the piece of writing even more effective? Bring the results of your investigation to class for discussion.

Thinking about Your Own Business Writing

Chances are, you have written a letter of application for a job, completed a résumé, or sent some business-related email or letters. Choose a piece of business-related writing that is important to you or that represents your best work, and then analyze it carefully. How clear is the writing? How well do you represent yourself in the writing? Do you follow the conventions for business letters, résumés, memos, and so on? Make notes on what you could do to improve this piece of writing.

▼ Writing Essay Examinations

68

In addition to the essay exams you will write in your college courses, you will probably need to write other "essay exams" at various times in your life. Some insurance companies ask for a personal statement to accompany applications, as do many loan applications, including those for student loans. One recent graduate found herself writing a very important "exam" as part of her efforts to adopt a child when she was asked for a lengthy biographical essay that included an analysis of personal strengths and goals.

While the purposes of essay exams can vary greatly, they all require the ability to recall information and present it effectively. This chapter discusses ways to prepare for essay exams, analyze essay questions, and write successful responses. ■

68a Preparing for essay examinations

In getting ready for an essay examination, nothing can take the place of knowing the subject well. You can, in other words, prepare for an essay examination throughout the term by taking careful notes on lectures, texts, and other assigned reading. You may want to outline a reading assignment, list its main points, list and define its key terms, or briefly summarize its argument. A particularly effective method is to divide your notes into two categories. In a notebook, label the left-hand pages "Summaries and Quotations." Label the right-hand pages "Questions and Comments." Then, as you read, use the left-hand page to record brief summaries of major points, the support offered for each point, and noteworthy quotations. On the right-hand page, record questions that your reading has not answered, ideas that are unclear or puzzling, and your own comments. This form of note-taking encourages active, critical reading and, combined with careful class notes, will do much to prepare you. Here are one student's notes on a chapter in a text on rhetoric:

For more on ⸱⸱⸱⸱⸱⸱⸱⸱●
summaries,
quotations, and
taking notes,
see 16e.

For help for mul- ⸱⸱⸱⸱●
tilingual writers
on preparing for
an essay exam,
see Chapter 58.

SUMMARIES AND QUOTATIONS	QUESTIONS AND COMMENTS
Rhetoric — "the art of discovering, in any particular case, all available means of persuasion." (Aristotle, on p. 3) All language *is* argumentative — purpose is to persuade	Maybe all language *is* persuasive, but if I greet people warmly, I don't *consciously* try to persuade them that I'm glad to see them. I just respond naturally.
To identify an *argument*, ask: 1. Does it try to persuade me? 2. Does it deal with a problem without a clear-cut answer? 3. Could I disagree with it?	Of all the statements that can be debated, I think the less absolute the possible answers, the more important the question and the harder to solve (otherwise the answer would be obvious).

In addition to taking careful, detailed notes, you can prepare for an essay examination by writing out essay answers to questions you think are likely to appear on the exam. Practicing ahead of time is much more effective than last-minute cramming. On the day of the exam, do ten to fifteen minutes of writing just before you go into the examination to "warm up" your thinking muscles.

● **EXERCISE 68.1**

Create a question you think you might be likely to encounter on an essay examination in a class you are currently taking. Then write a paragraph or two about what you would need to know in order to write an A+ answer.

68b Analyzing essay examination questions

Before you begin writing, read the question carefully several times, and *analyze* what it asks you to do. Most essay examination questions contain two kinds of terms, **strategy terms** that describe your task in writing the essay and **content terms** that define the scope and limits of the topic.

STRATEGY ┌───────── CONTENT ─────────┐
Analyze Jesus' Sermon on the Mount.

STRATEGY ┌───────── CONTENT ─────────┐
Describe the major effects of Reconstruction.

STRATEGY ┌─────────── CONTENT ───────────┐
Discuss the function of the river in *Huckleberry Finn.*

STRATEGY ┌────────── CONTENT ──────────┐
Explain the advantages of investing in government securities.

Words like *analyze, describe, discuss,* and *explain* tell what logical strategy to use and often set the form your answer takes. Since not all terms mean the same thing in every discipline, be sure you understand *exactly* what the term means in context of the material covered on the examination. In general, however, the most commonly used strategy terms have standard meanings, as shown on the following chart:

SOME COMMON STRATEGY TERMS

→ *Analyze:* Divide an event, idea, or theory into its component elements, and examine each one in turn.

   Analyze Milton Friedman's theory of permanent income.

→ *Compare and/or contrast:* Demonstrate similarities or dissimilarities between two or more events or topics.

   Compare the portrayal of women in *Beloved* with that in *Their Eyes Were Watching God.*

→ *Define:* Identify and state the essential traits or characteristics of something, differentiating it clearly from other things.

   Define *osmosis.*

→ *Describe:* Tell about an event, person, or process in detail, creating a clear and vivid image of it.

   Describe the dress of a medieval knight.

→ *Evaluate:* Assess the value or significance of the topic.

   Evaluate the contributions of Black musicians to the development of American music.

→ *Explain:* Make a topic as clear and understandable as possible by offering reasons, examples, and so on.

   Explain the functioning of the circulatory system.

→ *Summarize:* State the major points concisely and comprehensively.

   Summarize the major arguments against using animals in laboratory research.

Strategy terms give you important clues for the thesis of your answer. Sometimes, however, strategy terms are not explicitly stated in an essay question. In these cases, you need to infer a strategy from the content terms. For example, a question that mentions two groups working toward the same goal may imply comparison and contrast, and a question referring to events in a given time period may imply summary. Once you understand which strategy to follow, make sure you understand the meanings of all content terms. Particularly in technical or advanced courses, specialized language may need to be clarified. *Romanticism,* for instance, means one thing in the context of eighteenth-century literature and something else in modern art. Do not hesitate to ask your instructor to clarify terms you're unsure of.

68c Thinking through your answer and taking notes

You may be tempted to begin writing an essay examination at once. Time is precious — but so, too, are organizing and planning. You will profit, therefore, by spending some time — about 10 percent of the allotted time is a good rule of thumb — thinking through your answer.

Begin by deciding which major points you need to make and in what order to present them. Jot down support for each point. Craft a clear, succinct *thesis* that satisfies the strategy term of the exam question. While in most writing situations you start from a working thesis in outlining your topic, when writing under pressure you will probably find it more efficient to outline (or simply jot down) your ideas and craft your thesis from your outline. Suppose you were asked to define the three major components of personality according to Freud. This is a clear question, and you should be able to make a brief informal outline as a framework for your answer.

For more information on informal outlines, see 3e.

Id
basic definition — what it is and is not
major characteristics
functions

Ego
basic definition — what it is and is not
major characteristics
functions

Superego
basic definition — what it is and is not
major characteristics
functions

exam

68e 955

ACADEMIC WRITING

Revising and
Editing Your
Answer

From this outline, you can develop a thesis: *According to Freud, the human personality consists of three major and interlocking elements: the id, the ego, and the superego.*

FOR MULTILINGUAL WRITERS: Writing Notes in Your Native Language

Before writing an essay answer in English, consider making some notes in whatever language you are most comfortable writing in. Writing down your main points in your native language may help you organize your answer more quickly and ensure that you don't leave out something important.

68d Drafting your answer

Your goal in producing an essay examination answer is twofold: to demonstrate that you have mastered the course material and to communicate your ideas and information clearly, directly, and logically. During the drafting stage, follow your outline as closely as you can. Once you depart from it, you will lose time and perhaps have trouble returning to the main discussion. As a general rule, develop each major point into at least one paragraph. Be sure to make clear the connections among your main points by using transitions. *The last element of the human personality, according to Freud, is the superego.*

● For more on transitions, see 5d4.

Besides referring to your outline for guidance, pause and read what you have written before going on to a new point. This kind of rereading may remind you of other ideas while you still have time to include them; it should also help you establish a clear connection with whatever follows. If you are using an exam "blue book" or paper, write neatly, skip lines, and leave ample margins so that you have space for changes or additions when you revise. If you are writing your essay exam on a computer, use double spacing and paragraph indentations.

68e Revising and editing your answer

Leave enough time (at least five to ten minutes) to read through your essay answer carefully. Consider the following questions:

- Is the thesis clearly stated? Does it answer the question?
- Are all the major points covered?
- Are the major points adequately developed and supported?
- Is each sentence complete?
- Are spelling, punctuation, and syntax correct?
- Is the handwriting legible? If you are using a computer, take time to run your spell checker.

68f A student essay exam answer

See how one student handled an essay and short-answer examination in a first-year American history course. She had fifty-five minutes to answer two of three essay questions and three of five short-answer questions. She chose to answer the following question first.

> Between 1870 and 1920, African Americans and women both struggled to establish certain rights. What did each group want? Briefly analyze the strategies each group used, and indicate how successful they were.

This student began her exam with this question because she knew the most about this topic. With another essay and three short answers to write, she decided to devote *no more than twenty minutes* to this essay.

First, she analyzed what the question asked her to do, especially noting the strategy terms. She decided that the first sentence of the question strongly *implied* comparison and contrast of the two struggles. The second sentence asked for an explanation of the goals of each group, and in the third sentence, she took *analyze* and *indicate* to mean "explain what each group did and how well it succeeded." As it turned out, this was a very shrewd reading of the question. In a postexam discussion, the instructor remarked that those who had included a comparison and contrast produced better answers than those who did not. Note that, in this instance, the strategy the instructor expected is not stated explicitly in the question. Instead, class members were expected to read between the lines to infer the strategy.

The student then identified content terms around which to develop her answer: the groups—African Americans and women—and their actions, goals, strategies, and degrees of success. Using these terms, she spent about three minutes producing the following informal outline:

Introduction

goals, strategies, degree of success

African Americans

want equality
two opposing strategies: Du Bois and Washington
even with vote, great opposition

Women

many goals (economic, political, educational), but focus on vote
use male rhetoric against them
use vote to achieve other goals

Conclusion

educational and economic differences between groups

From this outline, the student crafted the following thesis: *In the years between 1870 and 1920, African Americans and women were both fighting for equal rights, but in significantly different ways.* She then wrote the following answer:

> The years between 1870 and 1920 saw   Thesis
> two major groups--African Americans and
> women--demanding more rights, but the two
> groups approached the problem of inequal-
> ity in different ways. Initially, women   Women
> wanted the vote, equality within the fam-
> ily, and equal job and education opportu-
> nities. Their attempts to achieve all
> these goals at once were unsuccessful, as   Goals
> men countered by accusing them of attack-
> ing the sanctity of the family institu-
> tion. (Demanding equality in the family
> meant confronting Christianity, which
> subordinated women to men.) With the lead
> of Carrie Chapman Catt, women narrowed
> their goal to a focus on the vote. They
> emphasized that they would vote to bene-   Strategy
> fit middle-class Americans (like them-
> selves), reduced the stridency of their
> rhetoric and said that they would clean

958

exam

68f

ACADEMIC WRITING

Writing Essay
Examinations

up an often corrupt government (they
turned the men's strategy against them
here by <u>emphasizing</u> their own purity and
virtue). They also invited Wilson to talk
at their conventions and won him to their
side. Because of their specific focus and Degree of success
reorganization, women did finally receive
the vote, which then gave them the power
to work toward their other reform goals.

Less well organized and less for- African Americans
mally educated than middle-class white
women, African Americans often were
unable to dedicate their full effort to Goal
the cause of equality because of severe
economic problems. In addition, their
leaders disagreed over strategy. Washing- Strategy (split)
ton told them to work hard and earn the
vote and equality, while Du Bois maintained that they, like all other Americans, deserved it already. African Americans also had to overcome fierce racial
prejudice. Even after they finally won
the vote, whites passed laws (literacy
tests and grandfather clauses) and used
force (particularly through the Ku Klux
Klan) to keep African Americans from vot-
ing. Therefore, even after the African Degree of success
Americans got the vote in name, they had
to fight to keep and use it.

Thus both women and African Ameri- Two groups con-
cans fought for (and are still fighting trasted
for) equal rights, but the women were
more successful in late nineteenth-
century America. Educated, organized,
and financially secure, they concentrated
their efforts on getting the vote as a
means to higher political objectives, and

exam

68g 959

ACADEMIC WRITING
Analyzing and
Evaluating Your
Answer

```
they got it. African Americans, on the
other hand, had to overcome great finan-
cial barriers that reduced access to
education and worked against strong
organization. Even after they received
the vote, these Americans were kept sub-
jugated by prejudicial laws and practices.
```

Although this essay answer is not perfect, as the analysis in 68g makes clear, it was accurate and complete enough to receive an A, and the instructor made only one criticism at the end: "No advances at all for African Americans?—e.g., education."

68g Analyzing and evaluating your answer

Although you will not have time to analyze your answers during an examination, you can improve your essay examination abilities by analyzing your answers later. When the student who wrote the answer in 68f did so, she went through her answer sentence by sentence to see how well she had answered the questions in 68e and what additional points she might have covered. Last, she analyzed her answer with her instructor's comments in mind.

- *Thesis.* I think my thesis worked, but it might have been clearer if I had named specific rights rather than just saying "more rights."
- *Major points.* I included all the points in my outline, but I should have developed the term *equality* more in discussing the African American struggle.
- *Spelling, punctuation, usage.* It would have been better to skim the essay over for spelling and punctuation errors (as in the sixth sentence).
- *Additional points.* I could have talked much more about individual women's contributions—no time.
- *Response to instructor's comments.* I should have listed African American advances, which I knew—my interpretation was too negative. I also know much more about Washington and Du Bois than I showed on the exam.

Analyzing her answer in this way allowed the student to see whether she tends to stray from the topic and whether she could improve certain elements—such as thesis and topic sentences—in future exams.

FOR COLLABORATION

Working with two classmates, go through your notes and files looking for every essay exam assignment you've been given. Pool your resources, and then spend some time working together to analyze these essay exam questions. What, if anything, do the questions have in common? In what ways are they distinct or different? What is each question asking students to do? Finally, choose one essay exam question, and brainstorm a list of everything you'd need to do to write an effective response to this question. Bring the results of your brainstorming to class for discussion.

THINKING CRITICALLY ABOUT ESSAY EXAMS

Read over an essay exam you've taken recently. Using the guidelines in 68b, analyze what the exam question asked you to do. Then reread your answer carefully. Did you do what the question asked — and if not, how should you have responded? Then, referring to 68c–68e, reconstruct how you went about answering the question. How could you improve the content and presentation of your answer? Note any new strategies you could use for improving your success in taking essay exams.

Assembling a Writing Portfolio

69

69a Considering the purpose and audience for a portfolio

What are the possible purposes for a writing portfolio: to fulfill course requirements? to show work at a job interview? to enter a competition? to keep a record of your college work? Each of these purposes will lead you to make different decisions about what to include and how to arrange a portfolio. If you are fulfilling an assignment, your instructor may specify exactly what you need to include.

Consider your audience. Is it your instructor? a prospective employer? a scholarship committee? Your audience will affect what you choose to include in your portfolio. If, for example, your audience is a writing instructor, you will need to demonstrate what you've learned; if it is a prospective employer, you may need to focus on what you can do.

EXERCISE 69.1

Make a list of the times you have organized some of your written work—to apply for a job, to create a record of your writing from middle through high school, or for some other reason. What spurred you on to carry out these tasks? Did you have an audience other than yourself in mind? What criteria did you use in choosing pieces of writing? Bring your list to class to compare with those of other students. If you have organized other kinds of work, such as photographs or drawings, for a specific reason, jot down notes on these tasks as well.

How many entries should you include in a portfolio? The answer depends on your purpose. If you are developing an electronic portfolio that will represent your accomplishments as a student, you may include a variety of materials — essays to problem sets to photos to Web texts to a résumé. In this case, it makes sense to include many *kinds* of materials because those reviewing your portfolio will click on only those items that interest them. If you are developing a portfolio for your writing class, however, you should probably limit yourself to five to seven examples of your writing. Here are some kinds of writing you might include in such a portfolio:

- an academic essay demonstrating your ability to argue a claim or position
- a personal essay that shows self-insight and demonstrates your ability to paint vivid pictures with words
- a Web text you have developed on a specific topic
- a brief report, prepared for any class or community project
- an essay or other writing project showing your ability to analyze and solve a problem
- your favorite piece of writing
- writing based on field and/or library research
- a piece of writing for a community group, club, or campus publication
- an example of a collaboratively written document, accompanied by a description of how the team worked and what you contributed
- an example of your best writing on an essay examination
- a multimedia presentation
- correspondence, such as a letter of inquiry, an email, or a job application
- a résumé

You should also include the assignments for this work, whenever applicable. If your portfolio is for a writing course, you may be expected to include examples of your notes and early drafts as well as any responses you got from other readers.

FOR COLLABORATION

Working with one or two members of your class, brainstorm about what each of you would most like your portfolio to accomplish — and which pieces of writing will best meet these goals. Take notes on your conversations with your team members, and bring your notes to class for discussion. Each team member should be prepared to explain the reasons behind the goals of and choices in his or her portfolio.

Once you have decided which items to include in your portfolio, several tasks still remain: preparing a written statement, organizing your material, and obtaining feedback from others.

■ *Preparing a written statement*

Regardless of how many and what kinds of writing examples you choose, you need to introduce a course-related portfolio with a written statement that explains and reflects on your work. This statement might be in the form of a memo, cover letter, personal essay, or homepage (for online portfolios). Whatever the form, your statement should include:

- *a description of what is in the portfolio:* what was the purpose for each work?
- *an explanation of your choices:* how did you decide these pieces of writing represented your best work?
- *a reflection on your strengths and abilities as a writer:* What have you learned about writing? What problems have you encountered, and how have you solved them?

■ *Organizing your portfolio*

Number all pages in consecutive order, and prepare a table of contents. Label and date each piece of writing if you haven't done so previously. Put a cover sheet on top with your name and the date; if the portfolio is for a class, include the course title and number (see sample cover in 8e). Assemble everything in a folder.

■ *Getting responses*

Once you have assembled your portfolio, seek responses to it from several classmates or friends and, if possible, from at least one instructor. To elicit the best responses, you may want to refer your reviewers to the guidelines on reviewing a draft in 4c. Revise accordingly.

If this portfolio is part of your work in a course, ask your instructor whether a few hand-done corrections are acceptable. If you intend to use it as part of a job search, however, you will want to print out clean copies. Either way, the time and effort you spend revising and editing the contents of your portfolio will be time well spent.

69d A student portfolio cover letter

Here is an excerpt from a letter that James Kung wrote to introduce his portfolio. Note that Kung does not simply describe the portfolio but analyzes both it and his development as a writer in some detail.

STUDENT WRITER

James Kung

December 6, 2002

Dear Professor Lunsford:

"Writing is difficult and takes a long time." This simple yet powerful statement has been uttered so many times in our class that it has essentially become our motto. In just ten weeks, my persuasive writing skills have improved dramatically, thanks to many hours spent writing, revising, polishing, and (when I wasn't writing) thinking about my topic. These improvements are clearly illustrated by the various drafts, revisions, and other materials included in my course portfolio.

[Here Kung lists all of the materials in his portfolio and mentions why he has included them—they point up his strengths and show how his writing has improved.]

I entered this first-quarter Writing and Rhetoric class with both strengths and weaknesses. I was strong in the fundamentals of writing: logic and grammar. I have always written fairly well-organized essays, and that held true for this class. However, despite this strength, I struggled throughout the term to narrow and define the various aspects of my research-based argument.

The first aspect of my essay that I had trouble narrowing and defining was my major claim, or my thesis statement. In my very first writing assignment for the class, the "Proposal for Research-Based Argument" (1A), I proposed to argue about the case of Wen Ho Lee, the Los Alamos scientist accused of copying restricted government documents, but most of the major claims I made were either too broad or too obvious. For example, in the second paragraph of the first page, I stated (without any evidence) that "the Wen Ho Lee incident deals with the persecution of not only one man, but of a whole ethnic [group]." You commented that the statement was a "sweeping claim" that would be "hard to support." In the first paragraph of 1A, I also claimed that the U.S. government and the media "acted unjustly and irrationally regarding this incident." Since many people who knew the Wen Ho Lee case agreed that the government and the media acted unjustly, this claim was somewhat obvious and thus not sufficiently arguable.

ACADEMIC WRITING

A Student Portfolio
Cover Letter

●⸺ For more on
conducting a
Toulmin analysis,
see Chapters 11
and 13.

After seeing the weaknesses in my claims, I spent weeks trying to rework and retool them to make them more specific and more debatable. I came up with so many claims that I almost lost interest in the Wen Ho Lee trial. Finally, as seen in my "Writer's Notebook on 10/16/02" (5A), I did a Toulmin analysis of my argument in order to find out exactly why I chose the Lee case as my topic in the first place. I decided that I had chosen this topic because of my belief that the political inactivity of Asian Americans contributed to the case against Wen Ho Lee. Therefore, I decided to focus on this issue in my thesis.

While my new major claim was more debatable than previous claims, it was still problematic because I had established a cause/effect claim, stating that the political inactivity of Asian Americans caused the Wen Ho Lee trial. As you pointed out, a cause/effect claim is one of if not the most difficult types of claim to argue. Therefore, I decided to once again revise my claim, stating that the political inactivity did not cause but rather contributed to racial profiling in the Wen Ho Lee case. This new claim can be seen in the full drafts of the paper (6C, 6D) and in the revised proposal (1B). In 6C, 6D, and the final draft, I tempered the claim to make it more feasible: "Although we can't possibly prove that the political inactivity of Asian Americans was the sole cause of the racial profiling of Wen Ho Lee, we can safely say that it contributed to the whole fiasco."

Since I had trouble narrowing and defining my major claim, I also had trouble defining my audience. When I first wrote my "Analysis of Audience and Sources," I barely even touched on issues of audience. On page 1, I briefly alluded to the fact that my audience was a "typical American reader," implying that my audience included anyone in the United States. However, after using Toulmin's analysis to restructure my claims, I decided to address my paper to an Asian American audience because, as stated in my "Revised Analysis of Audience and Sources," it would be advantageous in two ways. First, it would establish a greater ethos for myself, since I am an Asian American, specifically, a Chinese American. Second, it would enable me to target the people the Wen Ho Lee case most directly affects: Asian Americans. As a result, in my final research-based argument, I was much more sensitive to the needs and concerns of my audience, and my audience trusted me more.

Although working through my major claim and intended audience were critical to the success of my essay, the actual process of writing the essay was also important. For instance, when I wrote my first informal outline for the "Structure and Appeals" assignment, I had not yet put much of the research-based argument down on paper. Although the informal outline made perfect sense on paper, as I began actually to write my research paper, I found that many of the ideas that were stressed heavily in the informal outline had little relevance to my thesis and that issues I had not included in the informal outline suddenly seemed important.

[Kung goes on to discuss other aspects of his paper and his future writing plans.]

I hope to continue to improve my writing of research-based arguments. The topic that I am currently most interested in researching is the field of Eastern medicine. I am presently undergoing Chinese therapy for a back injury, so I would love to understand how it works. Eastern medicine is also a very controversial topic right now, one that interests a diverse audience, not just Asian Americans. When I have the time, I will probably apply for undergraduate research funds to work on this project, and I will be able to use all of the argumentative firepower that I have learned in this class.

Sincerely,

James Kung

James Kung

● **EXERCISE 69.2**

After reading James Kung's cover letter, write out some notes on its effectiveness. Try to consider how well he justifies his selections, reflects on what he's learned, and takes his audience into account.

69e Developing an electronic portfolio

Electronic portfolios provide new opportunities for students to demonstrate their full range of learning experiences to their teachers, advisor, parents, and potential employers. An electronic portfolio might be ideal for you if you want to share your work with others easily, either on a Web site or through email. If you choose or are required to develop an electronic portfolio, you will have many choices and will need to address several technological issues. Creating an electronic portfolio can be as simple as saving documents in a systematic way on your hard drive or as sophisticated as designing an interactive Web site (sometimes called a Web folio). Here are some questions to guide you as you develop an electronic portfolio:

- Taking into account the software available to you, the scope of your intended audience, and your course requirements (if the portfolio is for a class), would an online or offline electronic portfolio be most appropriate?
- Does your instructor, department, or university mandate the use of particular hardware and software? If they do not, what hardware and software will you use?
- Does your software allow all of your intended readers to access your portfolio? Does it enable you to integrate existing files (including multimedia) into your portfolio?
- If you're creating a Web folio, do you want your entire portfolio to be accessible to anyone on the Web, or do you want to password-protect part or all of your site?
- What kind of design do you want for your electronic portfolio? Is it user friendly and accessible to all?
- If some of the pieces in your Web folio contain references to material found on the Web, do you want to create links to those sources so that your readers can click on and go to them?

●---- For help with creating Web texts, see Chapter 9.

THINKING CRITICALLY ABOUT YOUR PORTFOLIOS

You can profit by analyzing your portfolio one last time before presenting it as finished. To do so, consider how your portfolio introduces your work to readers. How do the writing samples represent your strengths as a communicator? How well have you presented the portfolio physically? What could you change, add, or delete to make your portfolio more effective?

Glossary of Grammatical and Computer Terms

absolute phrase See *phrase*.

acronym a word, usually a noun, formed from the first letter(s) of several words, such as FAQ for *frequently asked questions*.

active voice See *voice*.

adjective a word that modifies, quantifies, identifies, or describes a noun or a word or words acting as a noun. Most adjectives precede the noun or other word(s) they modify (*a good book*), but a **predicate adjective** follows the noun or pronoun it modifies (*the book is good*). **Proper adjectives** are formed from or related to proper nouns (*Egyptian, Emersonian*) and are capitalized.

adjective clause See *clause*.

adjective forms changes in an adjective from the **positive degree** (*tall, good*) to the **comparative** (comparing two — *taller, better*) or the **superlative** (comparing more than two — *tallest, best*). Short regular adjectives (*tall*) add *-er* and *-est*, but most adjectives of two syllables or more form the comparative by adding *more* (*more beautiful*) and the superlative by adding *most* (*most beautiful*). A few adjectives have irregular forms (*good, better, best*), and some adjectives (*only, forty*) do not change form.

adverb a word that qualifies, modifies, limits, or defines a verb, an adjective, another adverb, or a clause, frequently answering the questions *where? when? how? why? to what extent?* or *under what conditions?* Adverbs derived from adjectives and nouns commonly end in the suffix *-ly*. *She will soon travel south and will probably visit her very favorite sister.* See also *conjunction*.

adverb clause See *clause*.

adverb forms changes in an adverb from the **positive degree** (*eagerly*) to the **comparative** (comparing two — *more eagerly*) or the **superlative** (comparing more than two — *most eagerly*). Most adverbs add *more* to form the comparative and *most* to form the superlative, but a few add *-er* and *-est* or have irregular forms (*fast, faster, fastest; little, less, least*).

agreement the correspondence of a pronoun with its antecedent in person, number, and gender or of a verb with its subject in person and number. See also *antecedent, gender, number, person*.

< > angle brackets sometimes called "right and left arrows," symbols that are used to enclose email addresses or Web site locations within other text. All characters within the brackets must be treated as a single unit, with no spaces between parts. Example: <http://www.mapquest.com>.

antecedent the specific noun that a pronoun replaces and to which it refers. A pronoun and its antecedent must agree in person, number, and gender. *Serena Williams often wins her matches.*

antithesis the use of parallel structures to highlight contrast or opposition, providing a pleasing rhythm.

appositive a noun or noun phrase that identifies or adds identifying information to a preceding noun. *Barry Bonds, the best homerun hitter, helped win the game. My sister Janet has twin boys.*

archive a collection of electronic files stored on a computer.

article *a, an,* or *the,* the most common adjectives. *A* and *an* are **indefinite;** they do not specifically identify the nouns they modify. *I bought an apple and a peach. The* is **definite** or specific. *The peach was not ripe.*

asynchronous communication online communication, such as email, involving a delay between the time a message is posted and the time it is received.

@ (the "at" sign) the part of every email address that occurs between the username and the domain name, indicating that someone is "at" a particular address. For example, <jrobinson@osu.edu> indicates that Jane Robinson gets email at OSU, an educational institution.

auxiliary verb a verb that combines with the base form or with the present or past participle of a main verb to form a verb phrase. The primary auxiliaries are forms of *do, have,* and *be. Did he arrive? We have eaten. She is writing.* **Modal** auxiliaries such as *can, may, shall, will, could, might, should, would,* and *ought* [*to*] have only one form

and show possibility, necessity, obligation, and so on. Also called **helping verb.**

\ (the backslash) the backward slash mark used mainly in DOS directory paths, as in <C:\windows\desktop\pcfile\survey>.

base form the form of a verb that is listed in dictionaries, such as *go* or *listen.* For all verbs except *be,* it is the same as the first-person singular form in the present tense.

bookmark a saved link to a Web site. Creating a list of favorites or bookmarks in a browser allows a user to save the addresses of Web sites so they can easily be revisited.

Boolean term a word like *and* or *or* that helps construct specific database or search-engine searches using multiple keywords. Example: *Mapplethorpe and censorship.*

browser a World Wide Web program for negotiating the Internet. Browsers display Web sites and allow users to click on hyperlinks to move among sites. Netscape Navigator and Internet Explorer are the two most commonly used. Some browsers such as Lynx display text but not graphics.

bulletin board service a local computer system that functions as an information clearinghouse for users, allowing people with common interests to post and receive messages.

case the form of a noun or pronoun that reflects its grammatical role in a sentence. Nouns and indefinite pronouns can be **subjective, possessive,** or **objective,** but they change form only in the possessive case. *The dog* (subjective) *barked. The dog's* (possessive) *tail wagged. The mail carrier called the dog* (objective). The personal pronouns *I, he, she, we,* and *they,* as well as the relative or interrogative pronoun *who,* have different forms for all three cases. *We* (subjective) *took the car to Chicago. My* (possessive) *friend drove. Maria met us* (objective) *downtown.* See also *person, pronoun.*

chat room See *IRC.*

clause a group of words containing a subject and a predicate. An **independent clause** can stand alone as a sentence. *The car hit the tree.* A **dependent clause,** as the name suggests, is grammatically subordinate to an independent clause, linked to it by a subordinating conjunction or a relative pronoun. A dependent clause can function as an adjective, an adverb, or a noun. *The car hit the tree that stood at the edge of the road* (**adjective clause**). *The car hit the tree when it went out of control* (**adverb clause**). *The car hit what grew at the side of the road* (**noun clause**). See also *nonrestrictive element, restrictive element.*

climactic order arranging ideas in order of increasing importance, power, or drama to build writing to a climax.

coined compound a combination of words linked by hyphens and used in an unexpected way, especially as an adjective: *an established Mommy-said-so fact.*

collective noun See *noun.*

comma splice an error resulting from joining two independent clauses with only a comma.

common noun See *noun.*

comparative degree See *adjective forms, adverb forms.*

complement a word or group of words completing the predicate in a sentence. A **subject complement** follows a linking verb and renames or describes the subject. It can be a **predicate noun** (*Anorexia is an illness*) or a **predicate adjective** (*Kim was anorexic*). An **object complement**

renames or describes a direct object (*We considered her a prodigy and her behavior extraordinary*).

complete predicate See *predicate.*

complete subject See *subject.*

complex sentence See *sentence.*

compound adjective a combination of words that functions as a single adjective (*get-tough policy, high school outing, north-by-northwest journey*). Most, but not all, compound adjectives need hyphens to separate their individual elements.

compound-complex sentence See *sentence.*

compound noun a combination of words that functions as a single noun (*go-getter, in-law, Johnny-on-the-spot, oil well, southeast*).

compound sentence See *sentence.*

compound subject See *subject.*

conciseness using the fewest possible words to make a point effectively.

conditional sentence a sentence that focuses on a question of truth or fact, introduced by *if* or its equivalent. *If we married, our parents would be happy.*

conjunction a word or words that join words, phrases, clauses, or sentences. **Coordinating conjunctions** (such as *and, but, or,* or *yet*) join grammatically equivalent elements (*Marx and Engels* [two nouns]; *Marx wrote one essay, but Engels wrote the other* [two independent clauses]). **Correlative conjunctions** (such as *both, and; either, or;* or *not only, but also*) are used in pairs to connect grammatically equivalent elements (*neither Marx nor Engels; Marx not only studied the world but also changed it*). A **subordinating conjunction** (such as *although, because, if, that,* or *when*) introduces a dependent clause and connects it to an independent clause. *Marx moved* *to London, where he did most of his work. Marx argued that religion was an "opiate."* A **conjunctive adverb** (such as *consequently, moreover,* or *nevertheless*) modifies an independent clause following another independent clause. A conjunctive adverb generally follows a semicolon and is followed by a comma. *Thoreau lived at Walden; however, he visited his aunt in Concord.*

coordinate adjective adjectives in a sequence that relate equally to the noun they modify and are separated by commas: the *long, twisting, muddy road.*

coordinating conjunction See *conjunction.*

coordination a way of relating separate but equal ideas or clauses in a sentence and clarifying the emphasis given to each, usually using a coordinating conjunction or semicolon. *The report was short, but it was persuasive.*

correlative conjunction See *conjunction.*

count noun See *noun.*

cumulative sentence a sentence that begins with an independent clause, followed by additional details in phrases and other clauses. *Sarah sat waiting, anxious and concerned that the class had been rescheduled.*

dangling modifier a word, phrase, or clause that does not logically modify any element in the sentence to which it is attached. *Studying Freud, the meaning of my dreams became clear* is incorrect because *the meaning* could not have been studying Freud. *Studying Freud, I began to understand the meaning of my dreams* is correct because now *I* was doing the studying.

database a collection of information, organized to facilitate searching for and retrieving information or data, often accessed via computer.

declarative sentence See *sentence.*

degree See *adjective forms, adverb forms.*

demonstrative pronoun See *pronoun.*

dependent clause See *clause.*

determiner in a noun phrase, a word used to identify or quantify the noun, including articles (*a, an, the*), possessive nouns (*Bob's*), numbers, and certain pronouns such as *my, our,* and *this.*

digital a term that has come to mean simply "electronic" or "wired."

direct address a construction that uses a noun or pronoun to name the person or thing being spoken to. *Hey, Jack. You, get moving.*

direct discourse a quotation that reproduces a speaker's exact words, marked with quotation marks.

direct object a noun or pronoun receiving the action of a transitive verb. *McKellan recited Shakespearean soliloquies.* See also *indirect object.*

directory a list or group of computer files that are somehow related; also called a folder. A directory can contain other directories, which are then called subdirectories.

directory path a listing of the order of directories and subdirectories a user must open to find a particular computer file. In DOS and Windows applications, directory paths are delineated by backslashes. For example, <C:\wp52\memos \walter.1> indicates that the file <walter.1> is in the directory <wp52>, subdirectory <memos>, on the drive designated <C:>.

domain name the characters and symbols identifying elements within a computer server on the Internet. Usually designating Web sites or email addresses, domain names have at least two parts, separated by dots. The first part designates the organization or server, and the final part identifies the type of organization operating the server, such as *.com* (commercial) or *.edu* (educational). Domains outside the United States often identify the country in which a server is located, such as *.uk* for Great Britain.

. (the dot) the period symbol called "dot" when used to separate parts of email or Internet addresses, as in <bgm2@umnvm1.umn.edu>.

download to move data or a file electronically, usually from one computer system to another.

elliptical construction a construction in which some words are left out but understood, often used in comparisons with *than* or *as. Josh is more aggressive than Jake* [*is*].

elliptical structure a compound structure with certain words omitted; appropriate when the omitted words are common to all parts of the compound. *The salad and entrée were good, but the dessert and coffee* [*were*] *only average.*

email (electronic mail) sending or receiving electronic messages by means of various programs that allow asynchronous communication over a network.

email address the string of characters identifying a location for sending or receiving email. An email address contains a username, the @ symbol, and the domain name, as in <gbowe @hopper.unh.edu>.

emoticon combination of characters used in online writing to indicate moods or facial expressions. Common emoticons include :-) (smile), :-((frown), and :-o (surprised).

emphasis the use of various devices to show which parts of a sentence (or piece of writing) are important.

exclamatory sentence See *sentence.*

expletive a construction that introduces a sentence with *there* or *it*, usually followed by a form of *be. There are four candidates for this job. It was a dark and stormy night.*

FAQ (frequently asked questions) a list of common questions, often about an online program or service (such as a listserv or newsgroup), and their answers.

faulty predication a mixed structure in which a subject and predicate do not fit together grammatically or logically, often resulting from using forms of *be* when another verb would be stronger.

file name the last part of a URL, indicating the specific computer file for which the URL is the address.

first person See *person.*

flaming personal attacks in email or other electronic communication; considered bad manners.

font the typeface (or style) and size of text characters.

forward slash See *slash.*

FTP (file transfer protocol) the electronic commands used to transfer files between computers on the Internet.

fused sentence a sentence in which two independent clauses are run together without a conjunction or punctuation between them. Also called **run-on sentence.**

future tense See *tense.*

gender the classification of a noun or pronoun as masculine (*god, he*), feminine (*goddess, she*), or neuter (*godliness, it*).

gerund a verbal form ending in *-ing* and functioning as a noun. *Swimming is good exercise.*

gopher a set of programs for accessing information on the Internet through a series of hierarchically arranged menus. Gopher underlies the search capabilities of Web browsers, but it is usually used to seek out text-based files.

hard copy a version of an electronic document or file that is printed out onto paper.

header the subject line of a listserv or newsgroup posting. By looking at the index of headers, users can determine the different threads of a discussion.

helping verb See *auxiliary verb.*

hit an electronic connection on the World Wide Web. A hit can be either a match with a keyword a user is searching for with a search engine (as in *Google's search for* firewalking *turned up thirty hits*) or the accessing of a Web site by a remote browser (as in *The Beanie Babies page received two thousand hits today*).

homepage the introductory page presented from a Web site; it offers access to links and other pages the site offers.

HTML (Hypertext Markup Language) an electronic coding system for creating World Wide Web pages that indicates how browsers should display text and graphic images onscreen.

hyperlink See *link.*

hypertext one or more documents coded in HTML that contain hyperlinks.

imperative mood the form of a verb used to express a command or a request. An imperative uses the base form of the verb and may or may not have a stated subject. *Leave. You be quiet. Let's go.* See also *mood.*

imperative sentence See *sentence.*

indefinite pronoun See *pronoun.*

independent clause See *clause.*

indicative mood the form of a verb used to state a fact or opinion or to ask a question. *Washington crossed the Delaware. Did he defeat the Hessians?* See also *mood.*

indirect discourse a paraphrased quotation that does not repeat another's exact words and hence is not enclosed in quotation marks. *Coolidge said that if nominated he would not run.*

indirect object a noun or pronoun identifying to whom or to what or for whom or for what a transitive verb's action is performed. The indirect object almost always precedes the direct object. *I handed the dean my application and told her that I needed financial aid.* See also *direct object.*

indirect question a sentence pattern in which a question is the basis of a subordinate clause. An indirect question should end with a period, not a question mark. *Everyone wonders why young people continue to take up smoking.* (The question, phrased directly, is "Why do young people continue to take up smoking?")

infinitive the base form of a verb preceded by *to* (*to go, to run, to hit*). An infinitive can serve as a noun, an adverb, or an adjective. *To go would be unthinkable* (noun). *We stopped to rest* (adverb). *The company needs space to grow* (adjective). An infinitive can be in either the active (*to hit*) or passive (*to be hit*) voice and in either the present (*to [be] hit*) or perfect (*to have [been] hit*) tense. An **infinitive phrase** consists of an infinitive together with its modifiers, objects, or complements. See *phrase.*

intensifier a modifier that emphasizes the word(s) it modifies. *I would very much like to go.* Despite their name, intensifiers are best avoided in academic writing.

intensive pronoun See *pronoun.*

interjection a grammatically independent word or group of words that is usually an exclamation of surprise, shock, or dismay. *Ouch! For heaven's sake, what do you think you're doing?*

Internet a worldwide network linking computers of all sizes and types and providing access to the World Wide Web, among other services.

interrogative pronoun See *pronoun.*

interrogative sentence See *sentence.*

intransitive verb a verb that does not need a direct object to complete its meaning. *The children laughed.*

inversion changing the usual word order of a sentence, such as putting a verb before a subject or an object before a subject and verb, to create surprise or emphasis. *Out of the store ran four grinning girls.*

IRC (Internet relay chat) an Internet service that allows synchronous online communication (like telephone conference calls) with others; the site storing chat messages is called a "chat room."

irregular verb a verb whose past tense and past participle are not formed by adding *-ed* or *-d* to the base form, such as *see, saw, seen.*

justify to square off the margins of a text so that the lines all align on one or both sides.

keyword a word or phrase used to search a computer database, typed into a search tool or engine's dialog box.

link a connection between two points on the World Wide Web that may be in the same or different sites. Links are indicated in text by the use of graphics or colored text and/or underlining. Also called **hyperlink** or "hotlink."

linking verb a verb that joins a subject with a subject complement or complements. Common linking verbs are *appear, be, become, feel,* and *seem. The argument appeared sound.* See also *verb.*

listserv the software that manages an email discussion group about a particular topic. Participants can send a "subscribe" command to add themselves to the mailing list.

main clause an independent clause. See *clause.*

main verb the verb that carries the central meaning in a verb phrase, such as *given* in the phrase *could be given.*

misplaced modifier a word, phrase, or clause positioned so that it appears to modify a word other than the one the writer intended. *With a credit card, Sam paid for the motel room and opened the door.* Unless the writer intended to indicate that Sam used the credit card to open the door, *with a credit card* should follow *room.*

mixed structure a sentence that contains an inconsistent grammatical construction, beginning with one grammatical pattern and then switching to another.

modal See *auxiliary verb.*

modem an electronic device connecting a computer to a telephone line or another line that allows it to communicate with other computers.

modifier a word, phrase, or clause that acts as an adjective or an adverb and qualifies the meaning of another word, phrase, or clause. See also *adjective, adverb, clause, phrase.*

MOO (multi-user domain, object-oriented) an online space where many people communicate synchronously at prearranged times, usually to discuss a particular topic.

mood the form of a verb that indicates the writer's or speaker's attitude toward the idea expressed by the verb. Different moods are used to state a fact or opinion or to ask a question (**indicative**); to give a command or request (**imperative**); and to express a wish, a suggestion, a request or requirement, or a condition that does not exist (**subjunctive**). *The sea is turbulent* (indicative). *Stay out of the water* (imperative). *I wish the water were calm* (subjunctive). See also *imperative mood, indicative mood, subjunctive mood.*

MUD (multi-user domain) an online space for synchronous communication, usually in the form of role-playing games.

netiquette a set of standards for behavior on a computer network or the Internet.

newsgroup an arrangement made by a group of people with a particular interest to maintain a space for postings about the topic on the Usenet network of news discussion groups.

noncount noun See *noun.*

nonrestrictive element a word, phrase, or clause that modifies but does not change the essential meaning of a sentence element. A nonrestrictive element is set off from the rest of the sentence with commas, dashes, or parentheses. *Quantum physics, a difficult subject, is fascinating.* See also *restrictive element.*

noun a word that names a person, place, object, concept, action, or the like. Nouns serve as subjects, objects, complements, and appositives. Most nouns form the plural with the addition of *-s* or *-es* and the possessive with the addition of *'s* (see *number, case*). **Common nouns** (*president, state, month*) name classes or general groups. **Proper nouns** (*Hillary Clinton, Florida, July*) name particular persons or things and are capitalized. **Collective nouns** (*family, committee, jury*) refer to a group of related elements. **Count nouns** (*woman, trees*) refer to things that can be directly counted. **Noncount nouns** (*sand, rain, violence*) refer to collections of things or to ideas that cannot be directly counted.

noun clause See *clause.*

noun marker See *determiner.*

noun phrase See *phrase.*

number the form of a noun or pronoun that indicates whether it is singular (*book, I, he, her, it*) or plural (*books, we, they, them, their*).

object a word or words, usually a noun or pronoun, influenced by a transitive verb, a verbal, or a preposition. See also *direct object, indirect object, object of a preposition.*

object complement See *complement.*

objective case See *case.*

object of a preposition a noun or pronoun connected to a sentence by a preposition. The preposition, the object, and any modifiers make up a **prepositional phrase.** *I went to the party without her.*

offlist sent to a member of a listserv or other online group but not to the entire group.

online connected to a network; on the Internet or the World Wide Web.

participial phrase See *phrase.*

participle a verbal with properties of both an adjective and a verb. Like an adjective, a participle can modify a noun or pronoun; like a verb, it has present and past forms and can take an object. The **present participle** of a verb always ends in *-ing* (*going, being*). The **past participle** usually ends in *-ed* (*ruined, injured*), but many verbs have irregular forms (*gone, been, brought*). Present participles are used with the auxiliary verb *be* to form the **progressive tenses** (*I am making, I will be making, I have been making*). Past participles are used with the auxiliary verb *have* to form the **perfect tenses** (*I have made, I had made, I will have made*) and with *be* to form the passive voice (*I am seen, I was seen*). These combinations of auxiliary verbs and participles are known as **verb phrases.** See also *adjective, phrase, tense, verbal, voice.*

particle a preposition or adverb that combines with a verb in a two-word verb: *the plane took off.*

parts of speech the eight grammatical categories into which words can be grouped depending on how they function in a sentence. Many words act as different parts of speech in different sentences. The parts of speech are *adjectives, adverbs, conjunctions, interjections, nouns, prepositions, pronouns,* and *verbs.*

passive voice See *voice.*

password a personal code used to access a computer account.

past participle See *participle.*

past perfect tense See *tense.*

past tense See *tense.*

perfect tenses See *participle, tense, verb.*

periodic sentence a sentence that builds toward a climactic ending by postponing the main idea until the very end, with modifiers preceding the independent clause. *Even though he walked home quickly during the rainstorm, Max was drenched.*

person the relation between a subject and its verb, indicating whether the subject is speaking about itself (**first person** — *I* or *we*), being spoken to (**second person** — *you*), or being spoken about (**third person** — *he, she, it,* or *they*). *Be* has several forms depending on the person (*am, is,* and *are* in the present tense and *was* and *were* in the past tense). Other verbs change form only in the present tense with a third-person singular subject (*I fall, you fall, she falls, we fall, they fall*).

personal pronoun See *pronoun.*

phrasal-prepositional verb a verb phrase made up of a verb, particle, and preposition: *put up with, get away with.*

phrasal verb a verb phrase made up of a verb and a particle that form a unit: *get over, pick the baby up.*

phrase a group of words that functions as a single unit but lacks a subject, verb, or both. An **absolute phrase** modifies an entire sentence. It usually includes a noun or pronoun followed by a participle (sometimes implied) or participial phrase. *The party (being) over, everyone left.* A **gerund phrase** includes a gerund and its objects, complements, and modifiers. It functions as a noun, acting as a subject, a complement, or an object. *Exercising regularly is a key to good health* (subject). An **infinitive phrase** includes an infinitive and its objects, complements, and modifiers. It functions as an adjective, an adverb, or a noun. *The seashore is the place to be* (adjective). *She went to pay her taxes* (adverb). *To be young again is all I want* (noun). A **noun phrase** includes a noun and its modifiers. *A long, rough road crossed the barren desert.* A **participial phrase** includes a present or past participle and its objects, complements, or modifiers. It functions as an adjective. *Absentmindedly climbing the stairs, he stumbled. They bought a house built in 1895.* A **prepositional phrase** is introduced by a preposition and ends with a noun or pronoun, called the object of the preposition. It functions as an adjective, an adverb, or a noun. *The gas in the laboratory was leaking* (adjective). *The firefighters went to the lab to check* (adverb). *The smell came from inside a wall* (noun). A **verb phrase** is composed of a main verb and one or more auxiliaries acting as a single verb in the sentence predicate. *I should have come to class.*

plural the form of a noun, pronoun, or adjective that refers to more than one person or thing, such as *books, we,* or *those.*

possessive case See *case.*

possessive pronoun See *pronoun.*

post to send a message, or posting, to a discussion group or site.

predicate the verb and related words in a clause or sentence. The predicate expresses what the subject does, experiences, or is. The **simple predicate** is the verb or verb phrase. *For years New York City has been a cultural center.* The **complete predicate** includes the simple predicate and any modifiers, objects, or complements. *John gave Sarah a diamond ring.* A **compound predicate** has more than one simple predicate. *The athletes swam in a relay and ran in a marathon.*

predicate adjective See *complement.*

predicate noun See *complement.*

prefix an addition to the beginning of a word to alter its meaning (*anti-French, undress*).

preposition a word or group of words that indicates the relationship of a noun or pronoun, called the **object of a preposition**, to another part of the sentence. *He was on top of the ladder before his sister climbed to the first rung.* See *phrase.*

present participle See *participle.*

present perfect See *participle, tense, verb, verbal.*

present progressive See *participle, tense, verb, verbal.*

present tense See *tense, verb.*

progressive tenses See *participle, tense, verb.*

pronoun a word used in place of a noun, usually called the **antecedent** of the pronoun. **Demonstrative pronouns** (*this, that, these, those*) identify or point to specific nouns. *These are Peter's books.* **Indefinite pronouns** do not refer to specific nouns and include *any, each, everybody, some,* and similar words. *Many are called, but few are chosen.* **Intensive pronouns** are used to emphasize their antecedents and have the same form as reflexive pronouns. *She wanted to cook dinner herself.* **Interrogative pronouns** (*who, which, what*) are used to ask questions. *Who can attend the meeting?* **Personal pronouns** (*I, you, he, she, it, we, you,* and *they*) refer to particular people or things. They have different forms (*I, me, my, mine*) depending on their case. (See also *case.*) **Possessive pronouns** (*my, our, your, his, hers, its, their, whose*) function as possessives in a sentence to show ownership. **Reciprocal pronouns** (*each other, one another*) refer to the individual parts of a plural antecedent. *The partners helped each other.* **Reflexive pronouns** (*myself, yourself, himself, herself, itself, ourselves, yourselves, themselves*) end in *-self* or *-selves* and refer to the subject of the sentence or clause in which they appear. *The students taught themselves to type.* **Relative pronouns** (*who, whom, whose, which, that, what, whoever, whomever, whichever,* and *whatever*) connect a dependent clause to a sentence. *I wonder who will win the prize.*

proper adjective See *adjective.*

proper noun See *noun.*

protocol the agreed command set used by many different kinds of computers to allow data exchange. Examples include FTP and telnet.

real-time communication See *synchronous communication.*

reciprocal pronoun See *pronoun.*

reflexive pronoun See *pronoun.*

regular verb a verb whose past tense and past participle are formed by adding *-d* or *-ed* to the base form (*care, cared, cared; look, looked, looked*). See also *irregular verb*.

relative pronoun See *pronoun*.

restrictive element a word, phrase, or clause that limits the essential meaning of the sentence element it modifies or provides necessary identifying information about it. A restrictive element is not set off from the rest of the sentence with commas, dashes, or parentheses. *The tree that I hit was an oak.* See also *nonrestrictive element*.

Rich Text Format (RTF) a file format that allows users with different word processors and operating systems to share text files.

root a word from which other words grow, usually through the addition of prefixes or suffixes. From the root *-dic-* or *-dict-* ("speak") grows *contradict, dictate, dictator, diction, predict*, and others.

run-on sentence See *comma splice, fused sentence*.

search engine one of a variety of programs on the World Wide Web that allows users to search for information by keyword. When a keyword is typed into a search engine, the program seeks out all Web sites containing that keyword and displays them in a list of hits. Examples: AltaVista, Google, Yahoo!

second person See *person*.

sentence a group of words containing a subject and a predicate and expressing a complete thought. In writing, a sentence begins with a capital letter and ends with a period, a question mark, or an exclamation point. A sentence may be **declarative** and make a statement (*The sun rose*), **interrogative** and ask a question (*Did the sun rise?*), **exclamatory** and indicate surprise or other strong emotion (*How beautiful the dawn is!*), or **imperative** and express a command (*Get up earlier tomorrow*). Besides having these functions, sentences are classified grammatically. A **simple sentence** is a single independent clause without dependent clauses. *I left the house.* Its subject, predicate, or both may be compound. *Sears and Roebuck founded a mail-order house and a chain of stores.* A **compound sentence** contains two or more independent clauses linked with a coordinating conjunction, a correlative conjunction, or a semicolon. *I did not wish to go, but she did.* A **complex sentence** contains an independent clause and one or more dependent clauses. *After he cleaned up the kitchen, Tom went to bed.* A **compound-complex sentence** contains at least two independent clauses and one or more dependent clauses. *We had hoped to go climbing, but the trip was postponed because she sprained her ankle.* See also *clause*.

sentence fragment a group of words that is not a grammatically complete sentence but is punctuated as one. Usually a fragment lacks a subject, verb, or both or is a dependent clause that is not attached to an independent clause. In academic and professional writing, fragments should usually be revised to be complete sentences.

sequence of tenses See *tense*.

serif refers to a font that has short lines extending from the strokes of a letter (*this is serif*). Sans serif refers to a font without these extending lines (this is sans serif).

server a computer that provides services, such as email or file transfer, in response to requests from other computers; often still called a mainframe.

.sig file identifying information that many writers attach to the end of their electronic messages, such as their name, title, addresses, and phone and fax numbers.

simple predicate See *predicate*.

simple sentence See *sentence*.

simple subject See *subject*.

singular the form of a noun, pronoun, or adjective that refers to one person or thing, such as *book*, *it*, or *this*.

/ (the slash) the forward slash mark, called just "slash" when used to separate parts of email addresses, URLs, and newsgroup names, as in <http://quinine.lists/quinine.html>.

split infinitive the often awkward intrusion of an adverb between *to* and the base form of the verb in an infinitive (*to better serve* rather than *to serve better*).

squinting modifier a misplaced word, phrase, or clause that could refer equally, but with different meanings, to words either preceding or following it. For example, in *Playing poker often is dangerous*, the position of *often* fails to indicate whether frequent poker playing is dangerous or whether poker playing is often dangerous.

subject the noun or pronoun and related words that indicate who or what a sentence is about. The **simple subject** is the noun or pronoun. The **complete subject** is the simple subject and its modifiers. In *The timid gray mouse fled from the owl*, *mouse* is the simple subject; *The timid gray mouse* is the complete subject. A **compound subject** includes two or more simple subjects. *The mouse and the owl heard the fox*.

subject complement See *complement*.

subject directory a hyperlinked list of sites, classified by subject, that results from a World Wide Web search.

subjective case See *case*.

subjunctive mood the form of a verb used to express a wish, a request or requirement, or a condition that does not exist. The present subjunc-

tive uses the base form of the verb. *I asked that he be present. Long live the Queen!* The past subjunctive uses the same verb form as the past tense except for the verb *be*, which uses *were* for all subjects. *If I were king, I would change things*. See also *mood*.

subordinate clause a dependent clause. See *clause*.

subordinating conjunction See *conjunction*.

subordination a way of distinguishing major points from minor ones. In dependent clauses, minor points are often specified by subordinating conjunctions such as *after, because*, or *so*.

suffix an addition to the end of a word that alters the word's meaning or part of speech, as in *migrate* (verb) and *migration* (noun).

superlative degree See *adjective forms, adverb forms*.

synchronous communication online communication in which messages are sent and received as they are being typed, with no delay, as in IRCs, MOOs, and MUDs. Also called **real-time communication.**

syntax the arrangement of words in a sentence in order to reveal the relation of each to the whole sentence and to one another.

telnet a program that allows use of one computer from another computer.

tense the form of a verb that indicates the time at which an action takes place or a condition exists. The times expressed by tense are basically **present, past,** and **future.** Each tense has **simple** (*I love*), **perfect** (*I have loved*), **progressive** (*I am loving*), and **perfect progressive** (*I have been loving*) forms. The relationship between the tense of the verb in the independent clause of a sentence and the tense of a verb in a dependent clause or verbal is called the **sequence of tenses.**

GLOSSARY OF GRAMMATICAL AND COMPUTER TERMS

third person See *person*.

thread a series of postings to a listserv or newsgroup about a particular topic.

~ (the tilde) a symbol often used to make URLs briefer, it stands in for a part of a longer directory path.

transitive verb a verb that takes a direct object, which receives the action expressed by the verb. A transitive verb may be in the active or passive voice. *The artist drew the sketch. The sketch was drawn by the artist.* See also *verb*.

underscore the line drawn under a word or between two words, often used to denote links in Web texts; also called *underlining*.

URL (uniform resource locator) a series of characters identifying the address of a homepage or Web page. The URL for *The St. Martin's Handbook* Web site is <www.bedfordstmartins.com/smhandbook>.

Usenet a network within the Internet that provides access to newsgroups. Most browsers provide support for and access to Usenet.

username the name—a series of characters—that identifies a computer user and, together with a password, provides access to programs, sites, or networks. Email addresses usually begin with a username.

verb a word or group of words, essential to a sentence, that expresses what action a subject takes or receives or what the subject's state of being is. *Edison invented the incandescent bulb. Gas lighting was becoming obsolete.* Verbs change form to show tense, number, voice, and mood. See also *auxiliary verb, intransitive verb, irregular verb, linking verb, mood, person, regular verb, tense, transitive verb, verbal, voice.*

verbal a verb form that functions as a noun, an adjective, or an adverb. The three kinds of verbals are gerunds, infinitives, and participles. See also *gerund, infinitive, participle.*

verbal phrase a phrase using a gerund, a participle, or an infinitive. See *phrase.*

verb phrase See *phrase.*

virtual existing only in electronic form; having no physical reality.

voice the form of a transitive verb that indicates whether the subject is acting or being acted on. When a verb is in the **active voice,** the subject performs the action. *Parker played the saxophone brilliantly.* When a verb is in the **passive voice,** the subject receives the action. *The saxophone was played by Parker.* The passive voice is formed with the appropriate tense of the verb *be* and the past participle of the transitive verb. See also *verb.*

Web See *World Wide Web.*

Web site any World Wide Web location.

wired electronic; online.

World Wide Web (WWW) a graphically based international service connecting hypertext data on the Internet.

▼ Glossary of Usage

Matters of usage, like other language choices you must make, depend on what your purpose is and on what is appropriate for a particular audience at a particular time. This glossary provides usage guidelines for some commonly confused words and phrases. For fuller discussion of these issues, you may want to consult one of the references listed in 28c.

a, an Use *a* with a word that begins with a consonant (*a book*), a consonant sound such as "y" or "w" (*a euphoric moment, a one-sided match*), or a sounded *h* (*a hemisphere*). Use *an* with a word that begins with a vowel (*an umbrella*), a vowel sound (*an X-ray*), or a silent *h* (*an honor*).

accept, except The verb *accept* means "receive" or "agree to." *Except* is usually a preposition that means "aside from" or "excluding." *All the plaintiffs except Mr. Kim decided to accept the settlement.*

advice, advise The noun *advice* means "opinion" or "suggestion"; the verb *advise* means "offer advice." *Charlotte's mother advised her to dress warmly, but Charlotte ignored the advice.*

affect, effect As a verb, *affect* means "influence" or "move the emotions of"; as a noun used by psychologists, it means "emotions." *Effect* is a noun meaning "result"; less commonly, it is a verb meaning "bring about." *The storm affected a* large area. Its *effects* included many power failures. The drug *effected* a change in the patient's *affect.*

aggravate The formal meaning is "make worse." *Having another mouth to feed aggravated their poverty.* In academic writing, avoid using *aggravate* to mean "irritate" or "annoy."

all ready, already *All ready* means "fully prepared." *Already* means "previously." *We were all ready for Lucy's party when we learned that she had already left.*

all right Avoid the spelling *alright.*

all together, altogether *All together* means "all in a group" or "gathered in one place." *Altogether* means "completely" or "everything considered." *When the board members were all together, their mutual distrust was altogether obvious.*

allude, elude *Allude* means "refer indirectly." *Elude* means "avoid" or "escape from." *The candidate did not even allude to her opponent. The suspect eluded the police for several days.*

allusion, illusion An *allusion* is an indirect reference, as when a writer hints at a well-known event, person, or quotation, assuming the reader will recognize it. An *illusion* is a false or misleading appearance. *The speaker's allusion to the Bible created an illusion of piety.*

a lot, lots, lots of *A lot* is spelled as two words. Avoid these informal expressions meaning "much" or "many" in academic or professional discourse.

already See *all ready, already.*

alright See *all right.*

altogether See *all together, altogether.*

among, between In referring to two things or people, use *between.* In referring to three or more, use *among. The relationship between the twins is different from that among the other three children.*

amount, number Use *amount* with quantities you cannot count; use *number* for quantities you can count. *A small number of volunteers cleared a large amount of brush.*

an See *a, an.*

and/or Avoid this term except in business or legal writing. Instead of *fat and/or protein,* write *fat, protein, or both.*

any body, anybody, any one, anyone *Anybody* and *anyone* are pronouns meaning "any person." *Anyone* [or *anybody*] *would enjoy this film. Any body* is an adjective (*any*) modifying a noun (*body*). *Any body of water has its own ecology. Any one* is two adjectives or a pronoun modified by an adjective. *Customers could buy only two sale items at any one time.*

anyplace In academic and professional discourse, use *anywhere* instead.

anyway, anyways In writing, use *anyway,* not *anyways.*

apt, liable, likely *Likely to* means "probably will," and *apt to* means "inclines or tends to." In many instances they are interchangeable. *Liable* often carries a more negative sense and is also a legal term meaning "obligated" or "responsible."

as *As* sometimes means "because" and sometimes means "when." Avoid using *as* if the meaning might be unclear. For example, does *Carl left town as his father was arriving* mean "at the same time as his father was arriving" or "because his father was arriving"?

as, as if, like Use *as* to identify equivalent terms in a description. *Gary served as moderator at the meeting.* Use *like* as a preposition to indicate similarity but not equivalency. *Hugo, like Jane, was a detailed observer.* In academic and professional writing, use *as* or *as if* instead of *like* to introduce a clause. *The dog howled as if* [not *like*] *it were in pain. She did as* [not *like*] *I suggested.*

assure, ensure, insure *Assure* means "convince" or "promise"; its direct object is usually a person or persons. *She assured voters she would not raise taxes. Ensure* and *insure* both mean "make certain," but *insure* usually refers to protection against financial loss. *When the city rationed water to ensure that the supply would last, the Browns could no longer afford to insure their car-wash business.*

as to Do not use *as to* as a substitute for *about. Karen was unsure about* [not *as to*] *Bruce's intentions.*

at, where See *where.*

awful, awfully *Awful* and *awfully* mean "awe-inspiring" and "in an awe-inspiring way." In academic and professional writing, avoid using *awful* to mean "bad" (*I had an awful day*) and *awfully* to mean "very" (*It was awfully cold*).

awhile, a while Always use *a while* after a preposition such as *for, in,* or *after. We drove awhile and then stopped for a while.*

bad, badly Use *bad* after a linking verb such as *be, feel,* or *seem.* Use *badly* to modify an action verb, an adjective, or another adverb. *The hostess felt bad because the dinner was badly prepared.*

because of, due to Use *due to* when the effect, stated as a noun, appears before the verb *be. His illness was due to malnutrition.* (*Illness,* a noun, is the effect.) Use *because of* when the effect is stated as a clause. *He was sick because of malnutrition.* (*He was sick,* a clause, is the effect.)

being as, being that In academic and professional writing, use *because* or *since* instead of these expressions. *Because* [not *being as*] *Romeo killed Tybalt, he was banished to Padua.*

beside, besides *Beside* is a preposition meaning "next to." *Besides* can be a preposition meaning "other than" or an adverb meaning "in addition." *No one besides Francesca would sit beside him.*

between See *among, between.*

breath, breathe *Breath* is a noun; *breathe,* a verb. *"Breathe,"* said the nurse, so June took a deep breath.*

bring, take Use *bring* when an object is moved from a farther to a nearer place; use *take* when the opposite is true. *Take this box to the post office; bring back my mail.*

but, yet Do not use these words together. *He is strong but* [not *but yet*] *gentle.*

but that, but what Avoid using these as substitutes for *that* in expressions of doubt. *She never doubted that* [not *but that*] *she would solve the case.*

can, may *Can* refers to ability and *may* to possibility or permission. *Since I can ski the slalom well, I may win the race.*

can't hardly *Hardly* has a negative meaning; therefore *can't hardly* is a double negative. This expression is commonly used in some varieties of English but is not used in standard academic English. *Tim can* [not *can't*] *hardly wait.*

can't help but This expression is redundant. Use the more formal *I cannot but go* or less formal *I can't help going* rather than *I can't help but go.*

censor, censure *Censor* means "remove that which is considered offensive." *Censure* means "formally reprimand." *The public censured the newspaper for censoring letters to the editor.*

compare to, compare with *Compare to* means "regard as similar." *Jamie compared the loss to a kick in the head. Compare with* means "to examine to find differences or similarities." *The article compares Tim Burton's films with David Lynch's.*

complement, compliment *Complement* means "go well with." *Compliment* means "praise." *Guests complimented her on how her earrings complemented her gown.*

comprise, compose *Comprise* means "contain" (the whole *comprises* the parts). *Compose* means "make up" (the parts *compose* the whole). *The class comprises twenty students. Twenty students compose the class.*

conscience, conscious *Conscience* means "a sense of right and wrong." *Conscious* means "awake" or "aware." *After lying, Lisa was conscious of a guilty conscience.*

consensus of opinion Use *consensus* instead of this redundant phrase. *The family consensus was to sell the old house.*

consequently, subsequently *Consequently* means "as a result"; *subsequently* means "then." *He quit, and subsequently his wife lost her job; consequently, they had to sell their house.*

continual, continuous *Continual* means "repeated at regular or frequent intervals." *Continuous* means "continuing or connected without a break." *The damage done by continuous erosion was increased by the continual storms.*

could of *Have,* not *of,* should follow *could, would, should,* or *might. We could have* [not *of*] *invited them.*

criteria, criterion *Criterion* means "standard of judgment" or "necessary qualification." *Criteria* is the plural form. *Image is the wrong criterion for choosing a president.*

data *Data* is the plural form of the Latin word *datum,* meaning "fact." Although *data* is used informally as either singular or plural, in academic writing, treat *data* as plural. *These data indicate that fewer people are smoking than years ago.*

different from, different than *Different from* is generally preferred in academic writing, although both phrases are used widely. *Her lab results were no different from* [not *than*] *his.*

discreet, discrete *Discreet* means "tactful" or "prudent." *Discrete* means "separate" or "distinct." *The leader's discreet efforts kept all the discrete factions unified.*

disinterested, uninterested *Disinterested* means "unbiased." *Uninterested* means "indifferent." *Finding disinterested jurors was difficult. She was uninterested in the verdict.*

distinct, distinctive *Distinct* means "separate" or "well defined." *Distinctive* means "characteristic." *Germany includes many distinct regions, each with a distinctive accent.*

doesn't, don't *Doesn't* is the contraction for *does not.* Use it with *he, she, it,* and singular nouns. *Don't* stands for *do not;* use it with *I, you, we, they,* and plural nouns.

due to See *because of, due to.*

each other, one another Use *each other* in sentences involving two subjects and *one another* in sentences involving more than two.

effect See *affect, effect.*

elicit, illicit The verb *elicit* means "draw out." The adjective *illicit* means "illegal." *The police elicited from the criminal the names of others involved in illicit activities.*

elude See *allude, elude.*

emigrate from, immigrate to *Emigrate from* means "move away from one's country." *Immigrate to* means "move to another country." *We emigrated from Norway in 1957. We immigrated to the United States.*

ensure See *assure, ensure, insure.*

enthused Use *enthusiastic* instead in academic and professional writing.

equally as good Replace this redundant phrase with *equally good* or *as good.*

every day, everyday *Everyday* is an adjective meaning "ordinary." *Every day* is an adjective (*every*) and a noun (*day*), meaning "each day." *I wore everyday clothes almost every day.*

every one, everyone *Everyone* is a pronoun. *Every one* is an adjective and a pronoun, referring to each member of a group. *Because he began after everyone else, David could not finish every one of the problems.*

except See *accept, except.*

explicit, implicit *Explicit* means "directly or openly expressed." *Implicit* means "indirectly expressed or implied." *The explicit message of the ad urged consumers to buy the product, while the implicit message promised popularity if they did so.*

farther, further *Farther* refers to physical distance. *How much farther is it to Munich? Further* refers to time or degree. *I avoided further delays.*

fewer, less Use *fewer* with nouns that can be counted. Use *less* with general amounts that you cannot count. *The world will be safer with fewer bombs and less hostility.*

finalize *Finalize* is a pretentious way of saying "end" or "make final." *We closed* [not *finalized*] *the deal.*

firstly, secondly, thirdly *First, second, third* are preferred in U.S. English.

flaunt, flout *Flaunt* means to "show off." *Flout* means to "mock" or "scorn." *The drug dealers flouted authority by flaunting their wealth.*

former, latter *Former* refers to the first and *latter* to the second of two items previously mentioned. *Rap and jazz remain popular; the former, which has been around for a few decades, sometimes shows the influence of the latter, which goes back much further.*

further See *farther, further.*

good, well *Good* is an adjective and should not be used as a substitute for the adverb *well. Gabriel is a good host who cooks well.*

good and *Good and* is colloquial for "very"; avoid it in academic and professional writing.

hanged, hung *Hanged* refers to executions; *hung* is used for all other meanings. *The murderer was hanged. The dog hung its head.*

hardly See *can't hardly.*

herself, himself, myself, yourself Do not use these reflexive pronouns as subjects or as objects unless they are necessary. Compare *Lisa cut her* and *Lisa cut herself. Jane and I* [not *myself*] *agree. They invited John and me* [not *myself*].

he/she, his/her Better solutions for avoiding sexist language are to write out *he or she,* to eliminate pronouns entirely, or to make the subject plural. Instead of writing *Everyone should carry his/her driver's license,* try *Drivers should carry their licenses* or *People should carry their driver's licenses.*

himself See *herself, himself, myself, yourself.*

hisself Use *himself* instead in academic writing.

hopefully *Hopefully* is often misused to mean "it is hoped," but its correct meaning is "with hope." *Sam watched the roulette wheel hopefully* [not *Hopefully, Sam will win*].

hung See *hanged, hung.*

if, whether Use *whether* or *whether or not* for alternatives. *She was considering whether or not to go.* Reserve *if* for the conditional. *If it rains tomorrow, we will meet inside.*

illicit See *elicit, illicit.*

illusion See *allusion, illusion.*

immigrate to See *emigrate from, immigrate to.*

impact Avoid the colloquial use of *impact* or *impact on* as a verb meaning "affect." *Population control may reduce* [not *impact*] *world hunger.*

implicit See *explicit, implicit.*

imply, infer To *imply* is to suggest indirectly. To *infer* is to guess or conclude on the basis of an indirect suggestion. *The note implied she was planning a party; we inferred we would not be invited.*

inside of, outside of Use *inside* and *outside* instead. *The class regularly met outside* [not *outside of*] *the building.*

insure See *assure, ensure, insure.*

interact with, interface with *Interact with* is a vague phrase meaning "do something that involves another person." *Interface with* is computer jargon for "communicate." Avoid both expressions in academic and professional writing.

irregardless, regardless *Irregardless* is a double negative. Use *regardless.*

is when, is where These vague expressions are often incorrectly used in definitions. *Schizophrenia is a psychological condition in which* [not *is when* or *is where*] *a person withdraws from reality.*

its, it's *Its* is the possessive form of *it. It's* is a contraction for *it is* or *it has. It's important to observe the rat before it eats its meal.*

kind, sort, type These singular nouns should be modified with *this* or *that,* not *these* or *those,* and followed by other singular nouns, not plural nouns. *Wear this kind of dress* [not *those kind of dresses*]. *Wear these kinds of hats.*

kind of, sort of Avoid these colloquialisms. *Amy was somewhat* [not *kind of*] *tired.*

later, latter *Later* means "after some time." *Latter* refers to the second of two items named. *Juan and Chad won all their early matches, but the latter was injured later in the season.*

latter See *former, latter* and *later, latter.*

lay, lie *Lay* means "place" or "put." Its main forms are *lay, laid, laid.* It generally has a direct object, specifying what has been placed. *She laid her books on the desk. Lie* means "recline" or "be positioned" and does not take a direct object. Its main forms are *lie, lay, lain. She lay awake until two.*

leave, let *Leave* means "go away." *Let* means "allow." *Leave alone* and *let alone* are interchangeable. *Let me leave now, and leave* [or *let*] *me alone from now on!*

lend, loan *Loan* is a noun, and *lend* is a verb. *Please lend me your pen so that I may fill out this application for a loan.*

less See *fewer, less.*

let See *leave, let.*

liable See *apt, liable, likely.*

lie See *lay, lie.*

like See *as, as if, like* and *like, such as.*

like, such as *Like* means "similar to"; use *like* when comparing a subject with examples. *A hurricane, like a flood or any other disaster, may strain emergency resources.* Use *such as* when examples represent a general category; *such as* is often an alternative to *for example. A destructive hurricane, such as Floyd in 1999, may drastically alter an area's economy.*

likely See *apt, liable, likely.*

literally *Literally* means "actually" or "exactly as stated." Use it to stress the truth of a statement that might otherwise be understood as figurative. Do not use *literally* as an intensifier in a figurative statement. *Mirna was literally on the edge of her seat* may be accurate, but *Mirna is so hungry that she could literally eat a horse* is not.

loan See *lend, loan.*

loose, lose *Lose* is a verb meaning "misplace." *Loose* is an adjective meaning "not securely attached." *Sew on that loose button before you lose it.*

lots, lots of See *a lot, lots, lots of.*

man, mankind To refer to human beings in general, use *people, humans, humankind, men and women,* or similar wording instead of *man* or *mankind.*

may See *can, may.*

may be, maybe *May be* is a verb phrase. *Maybe* is an adverb that means "perhaps." *He may be the president, but maybe he will lose the next election.*

media *Media* is the plural form of the noun *medium* and takes a plural verb. *The media are* [not *is*] *obsessed with celebrities.*

might of *Have,* not *of,* should follow *could, would, should,* or *might. We might have* [not *of*] *lost the game.*

moral, morale A *moral* is a succinct lesson. *The moral of the story is that generosity is rewarded. Morale* means "spirit" or "mood." *Office morale was low.*

myself See *herself, himself, myself, yourself.*

nor, or Use *either* with *or* and *neither* with *nor.*

number See *amount, number.*

off of Use *off* without *of. The spaghetti slipped off* [not *off of*] *the plate.*

OK, O.K., okay All are acceptable spellings, but avoid the term in academic discourse.

on account of Use this substitute for *because of* sparingly or not at all.

one another See *each other, one another*.

or See *nor, or*.

outside of See *inside of, outside of*.

owing to the fact that Avoid this and other wordy expressions for *because*.

per Use the Latin *per* only in standard technical phrases such as *miles per hour*. Otherwise, find English equivalents. *As mentioned in* [not *As per*] *the latest report, our town's average food expenses every week* [not *per week*] *are $40 per capita*.

percent, percentage Use *percent* with a specific number; use *percentage* with an adjective such as *large* or *small*. *Today, 80 percent of the members are male. A large percentage of the members are men*.

plenty *Plenty* means "enough" or "a great abundance." *They told us America was a land of plenty*. Colloquially, it is used to mean "very," a usage you should avoid in academic and professional writing. *He was very* [not *plenty*] *tired*.

plus *Plus* means "in addition to." *Your salary plus mine will cover our expenses*. Do not use *plus* to mean "besides" or "moreover." *That dress does not fit me. Besides* [not *Plus*], *it is the wrong color*.

precede, proceed *Precede* means "come before"; *proceed* means "go forward." *Despite the rain that preceded the game, it proceeded on time*.

pretty Avoid using *pretty* as a substitute for "rather," "somewhat," or "quite." *Bill was quite* [not *pretty*] *disorganized*.

principal, principle As a noun, *principal* refers to a head official or an amount of money; as an adjective, it means "most significant." *Principle* means "fundamental law or belief." *Albert went to the principal and defended himself with the principle of free speech*.

proceed See *precede, proceed*.

quotation, quote *Quote* is a verb, and *quotation* is a noun. *He quoted the president, and the quotation* [not *quote*] *was preserved in history books*.

raise, rise *Raise* means "lift" or "move upward." (Referring to children, it means "bring up.") It takes a direct object; someone raises something. *Ed raised his glass for a toast*. *Rise* means "go upward." It does not take a direct object; something rises by itself. *The fog rises slowly*.

rarely ever Use *rarely* by itself, or use *hardly ever*. *When we were poor, we rarely went to the movies*.

real, really *Real* is an adjective, and *really* is an adverb. Do not substitute *real* for *really*. In academic and professional writing, do not use *real* or *really* to mean "very." *The old man walked very* [not *real* or *really*] *slowly*.

reason . . . is because Use either *the reason . . . is that* or the word *because* — not both. *The reason the copier stopped is that* [not *is because*] *the paper jammed*.

reason why This expression is redundant. *The reason* [not *reason why*] *this book is short is market demand*.

regardless See *irregardless, regardless*.

respectfully, respectively *Respectfully* means "with respect." *Respectively* means "in the order given." *Aden and Anya are, respectively, a singer and a clown. Jaime treated his aunt respectfully*.

rise See *raise, rise*.

set, sit *Set* usually means "put" or "place" and takes a direct object. *Sit* refers to taking a seat and does not take an object. *Set your cup on the table, and sit down*.

should of *Have*, not *of*, should follow *could*, *would*, *should*, or *might*. *I should have dressed warmly*.

since *Since* has two uses: (1) to show passage of time, as in *I have been home since Tuesday;* (2) to mean "because," as in *Since you are in a bad mood, I will leave.* Be careful not to use *since* ambiguously. In *Since I broke my leg, I've stayed home, since* might be understood to mean either "because" or "ever since."

sit See *set, sit.*

so In academic and professional writing, avoid using *so* to mean "very." Follow *so* with *that* to show how the intensified condition leads to a result. *Aaron was so tired that he fell asleep at the wheel.*

someplace Use *somewhere* instead in academic and professional writing.

some time, sometime, sometimes *Some time* refers to a length of time. *Please leave me some time to dress. Sometime* means "at some indefinite later time." *Sometime I will take you to London. Sometimes* means "occasionally." *Sometimes I eat sushi.*

sort See *kind, sort, type.*

sort of See *kind of, sort of.*

stationary, stationery *Stationary* means "standing still"; *stationery* is writing paper. *When the bus was stationary, Pat wrote on her stationery.*

subsequently See *consequently, subsequently.*

such as See *like, such as.*

supposed to, used to Both expressions require the final *-d. He is supposed to attend.*

sure, surely Avoid using *sure* as an intensifier. Instead use *surely* (or *certainly* or *without a doubt*). *Surely the doctor will prescribe an antibiotic.*

take See *bring, take.*

than, then Use *than* in comparative statements. *The cat was bigger than the dog.* Use *then* when refer-

ring to a sequence of events. *I won, and then I cried.*

that, which A clause beginning with *that* singles out the item being described. *The book that is on the table is a good one* specifies the book on the table as opposed to some other book. A clause beginning with *which* may or may not single out the item, although some writers use *which* clauses only to add more information about an item being described. *The book, which is on the table, is a good one* contains a *which* clause between the commas. The clause simply adds extra, nonessential information about the book; it does not specify which book.

that, which, who Use *that* when referring to things or to a group of people. *A band that tours frequently will please its fans.* Use *which* only when referring to things. *The new album, which is the band's first in years, appeals to new listeners.* Use *who* to refer to people. *Alex is the band member who plays drums.* In conversation, *that* can be used to refer to an individual (*the man that plays drums*), but in academic and professional writing, use *who* (*the man who plays drums*).

theirselves Use *themselves* instead in academic and professional writing.

then See *than, then.*

to, too, two *To* generally shows direction. *Too* means "also." *Two* is the number. *We, too, are going to the meeting in two hours.* Avoid using *to* after *where. Where are you flying* [not *flying to*]?

to, where See *where.*

two See *to, too, two.*

type See *kind, sort, type.*

uninterested See *disinterested, uninterested.*

unique *Unique* means "the one and only." Do not use it with an adverb that suggests degree, such as *very* or *most*. *Adora's paintings are unique* [not *very unique*].

used to See *supposed to, used to*.

very Avoid using *very* to intensify a weak adjective or adverb; instead, replace the adjective or adverb with a more precise word. Instead of *very nice*, for example, use *kind, sensitive*, or *friendly*.

way, ways When referring to distance, use *way*. *Graduation was a long way* [not *ways*] *off*.

well See *good, well*.

when, where See *is when, is where*.

where Use *where* alone, not with words such as *at* and *to*. *Where are you going?* [not *Where are you going to?*].

whether See *if, whether*.

which See *that, which* and *that, which, who*.

who See *that, which, who* and *who, whom*.

who, whom In adjective clauses, use *who* if the following word is a verb. *Monica, who smokes incessantly, is my godmother*. (*Who* is followed by the verb *smokes*.) *Monica, who is my godmother, smokes incessantly*. (*Who* is followed by the verb *is*.) Use *whom* if the following word is a noun or pronoun. *I have heard that Monica, whom I have not seen for ten years, wears only purple*. (*Whom* is followed by the pronoun *I*.) Exception: When the expression *I think* comes before a verb, use *who*, not *whom*. *Monica, who* [*I think*] *wears nothing but purple, is my godmother*. (Ignore *I think;* use *who* because the next word is a verb, *wears*.)

who's, whose *Who's* is the contraction of *who is* or *who has*. *Who's the president of the club? Who's been using my computer? Whose* is a possessive form. *Whose coat is that on the chair?*

would of *Have*, not *of*, should follow *could, would, should*, or *might*. *Jason would have* [not *of*] *liked your old bike*.

yet See *but, yet*.

your, you're *Your* shows possession. *Bring your sleeping bag along. You're* is the contraction of *you* and *are. You're in the wrong sleeping bag*.

yourself See *herself, himself, myself, yourself*.

Acknowledgments *(continued from copyright page)*

Derek Bok. "Protecting Freedom of Expression on the Campus." From the *Boston Globe*, May 25, 1991. Courtesy of the author.

Gwendolyn Brooks. "We Real Cool." From *Blacks* by Gwendolyn Brooks. Reprinted by Consent of Brooks Permissions.

e.e. Cummings. "me up at does." From *Complete Poems 1904–1962* by e.e. Cummings. Edited by George J. Firmage. Copyright © 1923, 1925, 1926, 1931, 1935, 1939, 1940, 1944, 1945, 1946, 1947, 1948, 1949, 1950, 1951, 1952, 1953, 1954. © 1955, 1956, 1957, 1958, 1959, 1960, 1961, 1962, 1963, 1966, 1967, 1968, 1972, 1973, 1974, 1975, 1976, 1977, 1978, 1979, 1980, 1981, 1982, 1983, 1985, 1991 by George James Firmage. Reprinted by permission of Liveright Publishing Corporation.

Emily Dickinson. "Much madness is divinest sense" (#435) and "A litter madness in the spring" (#1333). From *The Poems of Emily Dickinson*, Thomas H. Johnson, editor, Cambridge, Mass: The Belknap Press of Harvard University Press. Copyright © 1951, 1955, 1979 by the President and Fellows of Harvard College. Reprinted by permission of the publishers and Trustees of Amherst College.

Joan Didion. Excerpt from "Georgia O'Keeffe." From *The White Album* by Joan Didion. Copyright © 1979 by Joan Didion. Reprinted by permission of Farrar, Straus & Giroux, LLC.

Robert Frost. "Fire and Ice." From *The Poetry of Robert Frost*, edited by Edward Connery Lathem. Copyright 1923, © 1969 by Henry Holt and Company. Copyright 1951 by Robert Frost. Reprinted by permission of Henry Holt and Company, LLC.

D. Letticia Galindo. "Bilingualism and Language Variation" (fig.4). From *Language Variation in North America*, p. 166, by A. Wayne Glowka and Donald M. Lance. © 1993 by Modern Language Association of America. Reprinted by permission of the Modern Language Association of America.

Nikki Giovanni. Excerpt from *Racism 101* by Nikki Giovanni. Copyright © 1994 by Nikki Giovanni. Reprinted by permission of HarperCollins Publishers, Inc.

Langston Hughes. "Harlem" ("Dream Deferred"). From *The Collected Poems of Langston Hughes* by Langston Hughes. Copyright © 1994 by The Estate of Langston Hughes. Used by permission of Alfred A. Knopf, a division of Random House, Inc., and Harold Ober Associates.

Steve Jones. "Lauryn Hill just shares the music." From *USA Today*, March 8, 2002. Copyright 2002, USA TODAY. Reprinted with permission.

June Jordan. "Aftermath" (6 lines). From *Naming Our Destiny* by June Jordan. Copyright © 1989 by June Jordan. Reprinted by permission of Thunder's Mouth Press.

Claudia Kalb. "Should You Have Your Baby Now?" Excerpt from article in *Newsweek*, August 13, 2001, p. 42. © 2001 Newsweek, Inc. All rights reserved. Reprinted by permission.

Jewel Kilcher. "Amen" (4 lines). © 1995 WB Music Corp. (ASCAP) & Wiggly Tooth Music (ASCAP). All rights adminis-

tered by WB Music Corp. All rights reserved. Used by permission. Warner Bros. Publications, U.S. Inc., Miami, FL 33014.

Martin Luther King Jr. Excerpts from "I Have a Dream," "Our God Is Marching On," and "Letter from Birmingham Jail." Copyright © 1963, 1964 by Martin Luther King Jr. Copyright renewed 1991 by Coretta Scott King. Reprinted by arrangement with The Heirs to the Estate of Martin Luther King Jr., c/o Writer's House, Inc., as agent for the proprietor.

Mary McCarthy. Excerpt from "A Tin Butterfly." From *Memories of a Catholic Girlhood* by Mary McCarthy. Copyright © 1951 and renewed 1979 by Mary McCarthy. Courtesy of the Mary McCarthy Literary Trust and Harcourt, Inc.

Modern Language Association of America. "Film Hero." From *Modern Language Association's International Bibliography* database. Reprinted by permission of the Modern Language Association of America.

Rodney Morales. Excerpt from "When the Shark Bites." © Rodney Morales. Reprinted by permission of the author.

George Orwell. Excerpt from *Shooting an Elephant and Other Essays* by George Orwell. Copyright © 1950 and renewed 1979 by Sonia Brownell Orwell. Reprinted by permission of Harcourt, Inc. Copyright © Mark Hamilton as the Literary Executor of the Estate of the late Sonia Brownell Orwell. By permission of Martin Secker & Warburg Ltd. and A.M. Heath & Company, Ltd.

Readers' Guide to Periodical Literature. "Heroes and Heroines in Motion Pictures." Copyright © the H.W. Wilson Company. Reprinted by permission of the publisher.

Peter Travers. "Movies: The Count of Monte Cristo." Review by Peter Travers. From *Rolling Stone*, February 14, 2002. © 2002 Rolling Stone LLC. All rights reserved. Reprinted by permission.

Tom Wicker. Excerpt from "About JFK's Assassination" from *The New York Times*, November 22, 1963. Copyright © 1963 by The New York Times Company, Inc. Reprinted by permission.

Richard Wright. Excerpt from *Black Boy* by Richard Wright. Copyright 1937, 1942, 1944, 1945 by Richard Wright. Copyright renewed 1973 by Ellen Wright. Reprinted by permission of HarperCollins Publishers Inc. and Johns Hawkins & Associates Inc.

Art

Arlo 'n Janis cartoon. By Jimmy Johnson, April 8, 2002. Reproduced by permission of Newspaper Enterprise Association, Inc.

Acterra Web Page. "Water Fluoridation" screen shot. © Acterra.org. Formerly Bay Area Action. Reprinted by permission.

"Boy Playing a Video Game." © Bill Varie/CORBIS. Reproduced by permission.

COLORS magazine screen grab. From www.BENETTON Web site. Courtesy COLORS and Benetton USA.

Corp flag spoof. From *Adbusters* Media Foundation. Image courtesy of www.adbusters.org.

FACE/OFF photo of Nicholas Cage and John Travolta. Reproduced by permission of Photofest, Inc.

Google Web page. "Hollywood movie heroes." © 2002 Google courtesy Google, Inc.

"How to Display the American Flag." Cartoon by Tom Meyer. From *The San Francisco Chronicle,* September 30, 2001. © San Francisco Chronicle. Reproduced by permission.

Lauryn Hill photo. Published in *USA Today,* March 8, 2002. © Scott Gries/ImageDirect. Reproduced by permission of ImageDirect.

"Linus traded in his security blanket . . ." Cartoon by Mike Luckovich. From the *Atlanta Journal Constitution,* September 18, 2001. Reproduced by permission of Mike Luckovich and Creators Syndicate, Inc.

Netsearch Web Page. Copyright © 2002 Netscape Communications Corp. Used with permission. All rights reserved.

NEWS from West Coast Environmental Law. Newsletter Web site. Courtesy of West Coast Environmental Law Research Foundation.

The New York Times **front page screen grab.** June 17, 2002. Copyright © 2002 by The New York Times Company, Inc. Reprinted by permission.

The Official Peanuts Website. www.snoopy.com. PEANUTS © United Feature Syndicate, Inc. Reproduced by permission of United Media.

Joseph C. Phillips photo. Leo Celano, photographer. Published in *Newsweek,* April 8, 2002.

Mary Pickford **movie still, circa 1915.** © 1978 Photographer/PMPTV.

Hidden painting on reverse side of "Portrait of a Man." From the Abby Aldrich Rockefeller Folk Art Center.

Stanford Writing Center **Web Page.** swcstanford.edu. Courtesy Stanford Writing Center.

SunSITE Web Page. "Catalog & Indexes" screen shot. © 1997 University of California Regents. All rights reserved. Reproduced by permission of U.C. Berkeley Library.

Yahoo! Web Page. Copyright © 2002 YAHOO! All rights reserved.

Index

ONLINE WRITING AND RESEARCH DIRECTORY

To find answers to questions about working online, look for computer icons in the margins of the *Handbook*. This advice appears on the pages noted below.

(Continued on p. I-41)

I-40

(Continued from p. I-40)

ADVICE FOR CONSIDERING DISABILITIES

Advice for making texts accessible to readers with disabilities and resources for writers with disabilities appear on the pages noted below.

FOR MULTILINGUAL WRITERS

Some instructors use these symbols as a kind of shorthand to guide you in revision. The numbers refer to a chapter number or a section of a chapter.

abb	abbreviation *55*
ad	adjective/adverb *36*
agr	agreement *34, 35*
awk	awkward
cap	capitalization *54*
case	case *32*
cliché	cliché *27d*
co	coordination *44a*
coh	coherence *5d, 43a*
com	incomplete comparison *36d*
concl	weak conclusion *4f, 5d, 19c*
cs	comma splice *39*
d	diction *27*
def	define *3d, 5e*
dev	development needed *5e*
dm	dangling modifier *41c*
doc	documentation *20, 21, 22, 23*
emph	emphasis unclear *43a*
ex	example needed *3d, 5e*
frag	sentence fragment *40*
fs	fused sentence *39*
hyph	hyphen *57*
inc	incomplete construction *42*
intro	weak introduction *4f, 5f, 19c*
it	italics (or underlining) *56*
jarg	jargon *27*
lc	lowercase letter *54e*
log	logic *11g, 13f*
lv	language variety *26*
mix	mixed construction *42a*
mm	misplaced modifier *41a*
ms	manuscript form *8*

no ,	no comma *48j*
num	number *55*
¶	paragraph *5*
//	faulty parallelism *5d, 45*
para	paraphrase *17a and c*
pass	inappropriate passive *33, 47b*
ref	unclear pronoun reference *37*
run-on	run-on (fused) sentence *39*
sexist	sexist language *25b, 35d*
shift	shift *38*
slang	slang *27a*
sp	spelling *30*
sub	subordination *44b*
sum	summarize *17a, d, and e*
t	tone *4g, 16c, 27a and d*
trans	transition *5d, f, and h, 46b*
u	unity *5c, 43a*
verb	verb form *33a, b, and c*
vs	verb sequence *33g*
vt	verb tense *33d, e, f, g, and h*
wrdy	wordy *43b*
wv	weak verb *47a*
ww	wrong word *4g, 27a and b*
,	comma *48*
;	semicolon *49*
. ? !	period, question mark, exclamation point *50*
'	apostrophe *51*
" "	quotation marks *52*
( ) [ ] —	parentheses, brackets, dash *53*
: / . . .	colon, slash, ellipses *53*
^	insert
~	transpose
○	close up
X	obvious error

Contents